INTERNATIONAL COURTS AND TRIBUNALS SERIES

General Editors: Philippe Sands,
Ruth Mackenzie, and Cesare Romano

INTERNATIONALIZED CRIMINAL COURTS

INTERNATIONAL COURTS AND
TRIBUNALS SERIES

A distinctive feature of modern international society is the increase
in the number of international judicial bodies and dispute settlement and implementation control bodies; in their case-loads; and in
the range and importance of the issues that they are called upon to
address. These factors reflect a new stage in the delivery of international justice. The International Courts and Tribunals series has
been established to encourage the publication of independent and
scholarly works which address, in critical and analytical fashion, the
legal and policy aspects of the functioning of international courts
and tribunals, including their institutional, substantive and procedural aspects.

INTERNATIONALIZED CRIMINAL COURTS AND TRIBUNALS

Sierra Leone, East Timor, Kosovo, and Cambodia

Edited by CESARE P. R. ROMANO,
ANDRÉ NOLLKAEMPER, AND JANN K. KLEFFNER

THE PROJECT ON INTERNATIONAL COURTS AND TRIBUNALS

This series has been developed in cooperation with the Project on
International Courts and Tribunals

OXFORD
UNIVERSITY PRESS

OXFORD

UNIVERSITY PRESS

Great Clarendon Street, Oxford OX2 6DP

Oxford University Press is a department of the University of Oxford.
It furthers the University's objective of excellence in research, scholarship,
and education by publishing worldwide in

Oxford New York

Auckland Cape Town Dar es Salaam Hong Kong Karachi Kuala Lumpur
Madrid Melbourne Mexico City Nairobi New Delhi Taipei Toronto
Shanghai

With offices in

Argentina Austria Brazil Chile Czech Republic France Greece
Guatemala Hungary Italy Japan South Korea Poland Portugal
Singapore Switzerland Thailand Turkey Ukraine Vietnam

Oxford is a registered trade mark of Oxford University Press
in the UK and in certain other countries

Published in the United States
by Oxford University Press Inc., New York

Library of Congress Cataloging-in-Publication Data

Internationalized criminal courts and tribunals: Sierra Leone, East Timor, Kosovo,
and Cambodia /edited by Casare P.R. Romano, André Nollkaemper, and Jann K. Kleffner.
    p. cm. – (International courts and tribunals series)
"The book is the direct result of a conference on this topic that was held in
Amsterdam on 25–26 January 2002."
Includes bibliographical references and index.
ISBN 0-19-927673-0 (hardcover: alk. paper) – ISBN 0-19-927674-9 (pbk. : alk. paper)
1. International criminal courts–Congresses. I. Romano, Cesare (Cesare P. R.)
II. Nollkaemper, André. III. Kleffner, Jann K. IV. Series.
KZ6310.I584 2004
345'.01–dc22
                                                                    2004021134

Crown copyright material is reproduced under Class Licence Number CO1P0000148
with the permission of HMSO and the Queen's Printer for Scotland

ISBN 0-19-927673-0 (hbk.)
ISBN 0-19-927674-9 (pbk.)

1 3 5 7 9 10 8 6 4 2

Typeset by Kolam Information Services Pvt. Ltd, Pondicherry, India
Printed in Great Britain on acid-free paper by
Biddles Ltd., King's Lynn

THIS BOOK IS A JOINT UNDERTAKING OF

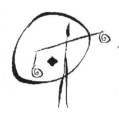

THE PROJECT ON P*i*CT
INTERNATIONAL COURTS AND TRIBUNALS

Amsterdam Center
for International
Law

No Peace Without
Justice

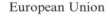

European Union

Open Society Institute

The Editors wish to acknowledge the generous financial assistance of the European Union and the Open Society Institute for the organization of the conference that led to this publication. The views expressed herein are those of the individual contributors and therefore in no way reflect any official position.

This book is dedicated to all those who suffered in Cambodia, East Timor, Kosovo, and Sierra Leone.

General Editors' Preface

This book is an edited and updated collection of papers emerging from a conference held in Amsterdam in January 2002. The conference was jointly convened by No Peace Without Justice, the Amsterdam Center on International Law and the Project on International Courts and Tribunals.

The book addresses a wide range of legal and policy issues arising out of the creation and operation of the so-called 'internationalized' criminal courts and tribunals—tribunals established and operated with a degree of participation of the international community—and analyses the place of such tribunals in the international criminal justice system. The context and experience of the establishment of internationalized criminal tribunals in Kosovo, East Timor, Sierra Leone, and Cambodia are considered in turn. Contributors include academics, officials and practitioners who have been closely involved in the evolution and operation of both internationalized and international criminal tribunals.

The contributors identify common challenges facing such tribunals. These include legal and policy issues, such as relations with other domestic and international courts, and with third states, and questions of applicable substantive and procedural law, as well as more practical operational issues, such as resource limitations and the complexities of integrating national and international elements into a functioning tribunal. However, the book also reveals and explores the heterogeneity among the existing and planned internationalized criminal tribunals, and the flexibility inherent in the broad concept of 'internationalized' tribunals.

As the international community continues to struggle with issues of post-conflict justice, the editors and the contributors to this book have provided a detailed and timely critical assessment of the concept of the internationalized criminal tribunals, and the potential role and limitations of such tribunals in contributing to justice and reconciliation. The book constitutes an important addition to the International Courts and Tribunal Series.

Ruth Mackenzie
Centre for International Courts and Tribunals
University College London
27 June 2004

Preface

Usually, prosecution of international crimes has been the task of national courts. This is so because, traditionally, only national authorities have at their disposal the coercive powers needed to ensure apprehension and prosecution of suspects, and enforcement of criminal sentences.

However, prosecution of crimes under international law by national courts presents two fundamental problems. First, national courts are often far from impartial, especially when they have to adjudicate on international crimes that were directed against or committed on behalf of their own state. Secondly, prosecuting international crimes can be a burdensome exercise, politically and materially. Only a few states have the capacity and willingness to carry out such prosecutions. These obstacles could lead to injustice against suspects or to impunity of perpetrators of international crimes.

These drawbacks of national courts led to efforts to try perpetrators of crimes against humanity by way of internationally established courts and tribunals

The Nuremberg and Tokyo military tribunals, established in the wake of the Second World War to prosecute German and Japanese crimes, broke new ground. It took several more decades, however, until the idea of international prosecution found broad acceptance, first in the creation by the UN Security Council of the International Criminal Tribunal for the Former Yugoslavia (ICTY) and the International Criminal Tribunal for Rwanda (ICTR) and finally in the establishment of the International Criminal Court (ICC).

While representing significant progress over the early patchy and timid attempts, ICTY, ICTR, and to a certain extent ICC, were and are still far from a 'silver bullet'. First, these tribunals are removed from the societies affected by the crimes they are supposed to prosecute. Proceedings take place hundreds of miles away from where they were committed. Having international criminal tribunals play a role in the reconciliation process seems considerably more difficult under these circumstances. Moreover, these courts are composed of judges who are not familiar with the realities 'on the ground' during the respective period in which the crimes were committed, or with the legal culture of the society concerned. Secondly, fully international criminal bodies tend to grow considerably in size, employing hundreds if not thousands of personnel, with significant costs, even when they can be shared by a large number of wealthy states. They are inclined to become organs with their own internal logic, momentum, and agenda, which can be influenced little by their creators, least of all by individual states. Thirdly, even in the case of ICC, they cannot address every possible situation, because of restrictions on their jurisdiction, either temporal, geographical, or otherwise.

Fourthly, although this does not apply to ICC, purely international tribunals are established without relying on the (remaining) existing judicial system in the state where the crimes occurred, but starting from a *tabula rasa*, a process which is time—and resource—intensive. Finally, the experience with international criminal tribunals with primacy over national courts suggests that even if there are remnants of a domestic judicial system in the state where the crimes occurred, international tribunals operate in significant isolation from such remnants, with only a limited contribution to efforts to rebuild that system.

Towards the end of the twentieth and the beginning of the twenty-first century, these considerations created room for the growth of a new generation of criminal justice bodies to prosecute international crimes and which could address the weaknesses of both international and domestic criminal courts. While this book was being prepared (2002–03), there were three active jurisdictions of this kind: the Serious Crimes Panels in the District Court of Dili (East Timor); the 'Regulation 64' Panels in the courts of Kosovo; and the Special Court for Sierra Leone. A fourth one, the so-called Extraordinary Chambers in the Courts of Cambodia, was about to be established. These four bodies are the subject of this book, and are grouped together here under the label 'internationalized criminal courts and tribunals'.

At times, these four bodies have also been dubbed 'hybrid' or 'mixed' courts and tribunals. However, it is the opinion of the editors of this book that the adjective 'internationalized' more adequately describes the nature of these bodies, while the other designations sometimes employed in literature fail to do so. It is the participation of the international community in the creation and management of these bodies that make them an intriguing object of study for the international legal scholar. The adjectives 'hybrid' or 'mixed' fail to highlight the role played by the international community.

Of course, labels are always generic. Using a common term to designate quite disparate bodies is not meant to suggest uniformity. 'Internationalization', indeed, can be a matter of degree. Sometimes it might be more correct to talk about the 'nationalization' of an international court (eg in Sierra Leone), rather than internationalization of a domestic forum.

The bodies considered in this book are not likely to remain the only ones of their kind. As this book went to press, talks for possible others to be created in Bosnia-Herzegovina, and Iraq, were under way. In the meantime, legal experts have been meeting under the auspices of the United Nations to draft legislation for use in post-conflict justice systems, basing themselves inter alia on the lessons learned from the experiences of the four internationalized court systems analyzed in this book. These developments suggest that the phenomenon of internationalized criminal courts will remain a recurrent theme in international criminal and transitional justice.

This book is the result of the intersection of No Peace Without Justice; the project on interactions between national and international law at the Amsterdam Center on International Law (ACIL), University of Amsterdam; and the Project on International Courts and Tribunals.

No Peace Without Justice (NPWJ) is an organization that works for the establishment of a fair and effective international criminal justice system for the prevention, deterrence, and prosecution of war crimes, crimes against humanity, and genocide, and in support of the rule of law and democracy. NPWJ's primary campaign is the establishment and effective functioning of the International Criminal Court. NPWJ has also conducted extensive field operations in Kosovo, East Timor, and Sierra Leone, including judicial assistance, documentation of wide-scale violations of the laws of war, conflict mapping, and outreach programmes. At the time of writing, NPWJ is beginning field operations in the Democratic Republic of Congo in support of the International Criminal Court. More information on NPWJ's campaigns in general can be found at www.npwj.org with more information on NPWJ's Sierra Leone Project (available at www.specialcourt.org).

The project on interactions between national and international law at the Amsterdam Center on International Law, University of Amsterdam, is a five-year research project, funded by the Netherlands Organisation for Scientific Research, which examines new forms of interactions between the international and the national legal orders and the emergence of what may best be described as a mixed legal order in which international law and national law are applied in a more or less integrated way. More information on this project can be found on its website (www.jur.uva.nl/aciluk/home.cfm).

The Project on International Courts and Tribunals (PICT), established in February 1997, is a joint undertaking of the Center on International Cooperation (CIC) at New York University and the Centre for International Courts and Tribunals at University College, London. PICT addresses the legal, institutional, and financial issues arising from the multiplication of international courts and tribunals and other dispute settlement bodies, as well as from the increased willingness of members of the international community to have recourse to them. PICT's website (www.pict-pcti.org) is a useful source of information on the project itself, and the activities of all international judicial bodies, including internationalized criminal ones.

Amsterdam /New York, January 2004
CR, AN, JK

Acknowledgements

This book has been made possible only by the enthusiastic and steady support of a large number of people whom we would like to acknowledge and sincerely thank.

Because the book is the direct result of a conference on this topic that was held in Amsterdam on 25–26 January 2002, first of all we need to extend our gratitude to all those who made the event possible, and have encouraged us to carry forward this project.

We are indebted to No Peace Without Justice (NPWJ), without whose support the conference would not have been possible. In particular, we need to extend our gratitude to the Honourable Gianfranco dell'Alba, Member of the European Parliament, Secretary General NPWJ; Senator Sergio Stanzani, President NPWJ; Niccoló Figà-Talamanca, Program Director; Antonella Dentamaro, Deputy ICC Project Director; and Claire Bisiaux, NPWJ legal expert seconded to the Sierra Leone Mission to the United Nations.

The conference, and as a result, this book, was made possible by funds granted to the three organizing partner institutions by the following: the European Commission; the Open Society Institute; the Netherlands Ministry of Foreign Affairs; the Netherlands Organization for Scientific Research (Pionier Programme); the Ford Foundation; the John D. and Catherine T. MacArthur Foundation; and the William and Flora Hewlett Foundation.

At the Faculty of Law of the University of Amsterdam, we received crucial help from Mary Footer, Deputy-Director of the Amsterdam Center for International Law, and Liesbeth Otte, of the Conference Office of the University of Amsterdam.

Nathan Miller, Furman Research Fellow of the NYU School of Law, carried out valuable background research and helped collect information about the work of the various internationalized criminal courts and tribunals.

We would also like to thank all the speakers at the conference who could not contribute to the book, but whose presentations or remarks were essential to the endeavour. These are: Sijbolt Noorda, President of the Board of the University of Amsterdam; Yi Kosal Vatanak, ADHOC Cambodia; Aderito de Jesus Soares, Ukun Rasik (a Legal Aid Foundation in East Timor); Theodor Meron, President and Judge at ICTY; Kenneth Fleming, former Head of Prosecutions at ICTR; Christer Karphammer, former Judge at the District Court of Mitrovica, Kosovo; Natasha Kandic, Humanitarian Law Centre, Belgrade; Horst Fischer, Professor at the Universities of Leiden and Bochum; Niccoló Figà-Talamanca, NPWJ Program Director; and Sharon Williams, Judge at ICTY.

Then we need to express our gratitude to all whose work has made this book possible. First, the authors of the various chapters: Antonio Cassese; Alain Pellet; Craig Etchenson; Mohamed Othman; Sylvia De Bertodano; Ernestine Meijer; Beth Lyons; Abdul Tejan Cole; Miatta Maria Samba; Giorgia Tortora; Phakiso Mochochoko; Alison Smith; William Schabas; John Cerone; Clive Baldwin; Jean-Christian Cady; Nicholas Booth; Daphna Shraga; Thordis Ingadottir; Bert Swart; Håkan Friman; Göran Sluiter; Morten Bergsmo; Markus Benzing; Mariacarmen Colitti; Luigi Condorelli; Théo Boutrouche.

Last but not least, we also gratefully acknowledge the help of Jake Kreilkamp, of the NYU School of Law, and Jessica Almqvist, Associate of PICT, who have provided help in regard to the background materials and the bibliographies, that of Elizabeth Davison who painstakingly copy-edited the original manuscript, and the constructive criticism offered by two anonymous reviewers. A special thank you goes to John Louth, OUP Commissioning Editor, for believing in this project and ensuring its publication, and Gwen Booth, OUP Assistant Commissioning Editor, for seeing it to the happy end.

Contents

Contents

List of Abbreviations

ACABQ	United Nations Advisory Committee on Administrative and Budgetary Questions
ACHPR	African Charter on Human and People's Rights
AFRC	Armed Forces Revolutionary Council
APC	All People's Congress
ASEAN	Association of Southeast Asian Nations
CAT	Convention Against Torture and Other Cruel, Inhumane or Degrading Treatment or Punishment
CAVR	Commission for Reception, Truth and Reconciliation in East Timor
CDF	Civil Defense Force
CEDAW	Convention on Elimination of All Forms of Discrimination Against Women
CERD	Convention on the Elimination of All Forms of Racial Discrimination
CIC	Centre for International Cooperation
CNRT	National Council of Timorese Resistance
CPP	Cambodian People's Party
CRA	Community Reconciliation Agreement
CRC	International Convention on the Rights of the Child
CRP	Community Reconciliation Process
DLU	Defence Lawyers' Unit
DNUM	Democratic National United Movement
DOJ	Department of Justice
DSRSG	Deputy Special Representative of the Secretary-General
ECHR	European Convention for the Protection of Human Rights and Fundamental Freedoms
ECOMOG	Economic Community of West African Monitoring Group
ECOWAS	Economic Community of West African States
FALINTIL	Armed Forces of National Liberation of East Timor
FRETILIN	Revolutionary Front of Independent East Timor
FRY	Federal Republic of Yugoslavia
FUNCINPEC	National United Front for a Cooperative, Independent, Neutral and Peaceful Cambodia
HPCC	Housing and Property Claims Commission
HPD	Housing and Property Directorate
ICC	International Criminal Court
ICCPR	International Covenant on Civil and Political Rights

ICESCR	International Covenant on Economic, Social and Cultural Rights
ICJ	International Court of Justice
ICRC	International Committee of the Red Cross
ICTR	International Criminal Tribunal for Rwanda
ICTY	International Criminal Tribunal for the former Yugoslavia
IJP	international judges and prosecutors
INTERFET	International Force for East Timor
IRI	International Republican Institute
JSMP	Judicial Systems Monitoring Programme
KFOR	Kosovo Peacekeeping Force
KJPC	Kosovo Judicial and Prosecutorial Council
KLA	Kosovo Liberation Army
KTA	Kosovo Trust Agency
KWECC	Kosovo War and Ethnic Crimes Court
LSM	Legal System Monitoring
LSMS	Legal System Monitoring Section (of the Human Rights Division of the OSCE Mission in Kosovo–Pillar three of UNMIK)
MOU	Memorandum of Understanding
NATO	North Atlantic Treaty Organization
NPWJ	No Peace Without Justice
NGO	non-governmental organization
OECD	Organization for Economic Cooperation and Development
OGP	Office of the General Prosecutor
OHR	Office of the High Representative
OHCHR	Office of the High Commissioner for Human Rights
OSCE	Organization for Security and Cooperation in Europe
PCA	Permanent Court of Arbitration
PNTL	East Timorese National Police
PRK	People's Republic of Kampuchea
RCG	Royal Cambodian Government
RUF	Revolutionary United Front
SCP	Serious Crimes Panel
SCU	United Nations Serious Crimes Unit
SECI	South-Eastern Europe Cooperation Initiative
SLA	Sierra Leone Army
SOC	State of Cambodia
SPDC	State Peace and Development Council
SRP	Sam Rainsy Party
SRSG	Special Representative of the Secretary-General
TNI	Tentara Nasional Indonesia. Indonesian National Armed Forces

TRC	Truth and Reconciliation Commission
UDHR	Universal Declaration on Human Rights
UNAMET	United Nations Mission in East Timor
UNAMSIL	United Nations Assistance Mission for Sierra Leone
UNDP	United Nations Development Program
UNESCO	United Nations Educational, Scientific and Cultural Organization
UNGA	United Nations General Assembly
UNHCR	United Nations High Commissioner for Refugees
UNMIK	United Nations Mission in Kosovo
UNMISET	United Nations Mission of Support in East Timor
UNPOL	United Nations Police
UNSC	United Nations Security Council
UNTAC	United Nations Transitional Authority for Cambodia
UNTAET	United Nations Transitional Administration in East Timor
UNTS	United Nations Treaty Series
USAID	United States Agency for International Development
USC	United States Code

Table of Cases

Table of Treaties

Table of International Instruments

Tables of Domestic Laws

Part I
Introduction

1

The Role of Internationalized Courts and Tribunals in the Fight Against International Criminality

*Antonio Cassese**

A. INTRODUCTION

Impunity for serious international crimes is still widespread. State officials engaging in criminal activity at home or abroad tend to protect one another, taking shelter behind the protection of traditional international rules safeguarding sovereign prerogatives of states. The new international law has already demolished one of the most powerful bulwarks of sovereign states, the doctrine of act of state or immunity of state officials from prosecution for international crimes perpetrated while in office. Another significant step forward has been made by many treaties imposing the principle of universal jurisdiction of state courts for large-scale offences such as grave breaches of the Geneva Conventions, torture, and serious acts of international terrorism.

These improvements, however, are not sufficient. One has to fight against the traditional reluctance of state courts to prosecute and bring to justice persons accused of international atrocities. In short one still has to strive to replace the Westphalian model of international society, geared to reciprocity and largely based on mutual respect among sovereign states, with the Kantian model, which hinges on a set of universal values transcending the immediate interests of each state, and which therefore gives pride of place to community interests.

In the struggle against impunity within this new model of the international community, there is no single panacea available. One has to rely skilfully upon a host of possible options, using each of them to suit best the historical, social, and legal conditions of each individual situation. One of these options, which is becoming increasingly significant, is the establishment of so-called mixed or internationalized courts or tribunals.

In this chapter I shall briefly address five main points. First, and by way of introduction, I shall outline a comparison between international criminal tribunals and courts and the so-called mixed or internationalized tribunals and courts. Secondly, I will deal with the reasons underlying the establish-

* Professor of International Law, Florence University; former President, ICTY.

ment of these particular mixed or internationalized courts. Then, I will move on to the main practical and legal problems that those courts are facing now. My fourth issue will be the areas where new internationalized courts could or might be established in the near future. Finally I will try to draw some general conclusions on the outlook for international criminal justice.

B. INTERNATIONAL OR INTERNATIONALIZED COURTS v. NATIONAL COURTS

Before I try to make a sketchy comparison between such international criminal courts as the two ad hoc international tribunals set up by the Security Council for the former Yugoslavia and for Rwanda and the so-called internationalized courts, I should take as a starting point a notion on which probably we all agree: that whenever we are faced with widespread, large-scale atrocities, the best response should be resort to *national* criminal courts.

Indeed, in principle national courts are the most appropriate forum for adjudicating international crimes. We all know that in the famous *Eichmann* judgment the Supreme Court of Israel stated that the territorial state, that is, the state where crimes have been committed, is the appropriate place for adjudication. Why? Because all the evidence normally is there, witnesses are there, and so on. However, this solution, which in principle should be by far the best, faces another problem. Why? Because normally atrocities or large-scale violations of human rights are carried out either by state agents, or by individuals acting in their private capacity but with the support or the sponsorship of the state authorities. It may also happen that state authorities condone or acquiesce in such atrocities. Therefore, national courts tend to be reluctant to render justice against people who may be part of the state's apparatus. Furthermore, as for crimes committed abroad by foreigners against other foreigners (for instance, crimes committed in Cambodia by Cambodians against other Cambodians) courts of other states tend to be reluctant to bring to justice the alleged perpetrators who may happen to be on their territory. This is because of the nationalistic and short-term ends often pursued by national courts. National courts tend to refrain from exercising universal jurisdiction. In this respect I find striking the US attitude. When they decided to implement the four Geneva Conventions of 1949, which, as we all know, proclaim in so many words the notion of universal jurisdiction, a statute was passed in the United States whereby grave breaches of the four Geneva Conventions shall be punished in the United States only when committed *by American* nationals or *against American* nationals. In this way, they thwarted the notion of universal jurisdiction, and fell back on the old notion of active or passive nationality.

C. INTERNATIONAL v. MIXED OR INTERNATIONALIZED COURTS

Faced with the situation where national courts are loath to bring to justice people accused of atrocities committed either on their own territory or abroad, we have to rely on other institutions. One of them is the international courts or internationalized courts.

When do states resort to those two categories of 'metanational' courts? When all the reasons I just set forth are compounded by the existence of exceptional circumstances, say, civil strife, international armed conflict, dictatorship in a particular country, or where there is a rift at the ethnic or religious level between groups in the country. Often these particular situations bring about the failure of national courts to bring to justice the people responsible for those crimes, or a collapse of the national judicial system, or the inability to prosecute people. One can therefore have resort to two options, either to international tribunals or to internationalized courts and tribunals.

Nobody would deny that resort to international tribunals may prove necessary whenever there is no possibility at all of relying upon national courts. Think of what happened in Yugoslavia. In 1993–94 it was unthinkable to rely on criminal courts in the various countries of the former Yugoslavia because trials would not have been fair. That is the first reason—not the collapse of the national judicial system but the inability of the national legal system to administer justice. The second reason is that there was the political will in the international community, for geopolitical reasons, to set up an international tribunal. And then, as the third reason, there was also the political will to find the money to finance those tribunals, because international tribunals are extremely expensive. This happened in the former Yugoslavia and Rwanda.

The other option, which is in principle available, is the creation of internationalized courts and tribunals. There, I think, there needs to be a set of factual or legal circumstances at hand so as to make this option viable. First of all, it is necessary for the national judiciary to be available, or partly available, so that to some extent one may rely on national courts. Secondly, I think, there is the need to assuage the nationalistic demands of the local population. This happens when national authorities regard the administration of justice as an essential attribute of state sovereignty.

On top of that you also need another set of circumstances, namely the lack in the international community, or in the United Nations, of the political will to deal with this matter at the international level by setting up an international tribunal proper. Or you may have the feeling in the international organization (which is normally the United Nations) that there is no hope of finding the necessary funding for an expensive international criminal tribunal.

These are to my mind the various considerations that may warrant in some particular cases the establishment of international tribunals proper while in other cases recourse to internationalized courts and tribunals.

D. MERITS OF MIXED OR INTERNATIONALIZED COURTS

What are the merits of internationalized courts and tribunals? There are quite a few. Some of them I have already listed. Others are as follows.

First of all, in rendering justice, persons, local prosecutors, or local judges are familiar with the territory, the language, the habits of the accused.

The second major merit is, to my mind, that trials are held in the territory where crimes have been perpetrated. These internationalized courts expose the local population to past atrocities with the two-fold advantage of making everybody cognizant of those atrocities, including those who sided with the perpetrators or alleged perpetrators, and bringing about a cathartic process for the victims or their relatives. How? Through public stigmatization of the culprits and, what also matters, just retribution. Vast exposure of past misdeeds contributes, I think, to the process of gradual reconciliation in the local community.

The third major advantage of internationalized courts is that they may produce a significant spill-over effect in that they may contribute to gradually promoting the democratic legal training of local members of the prosecution and the judiciary. In looking through the various documents available on East Timor, it is clear that this was a crucial point in East Timor. At the outset there were very few prosecutors and judges from East Timor. In one report of the UN Secretary-General to the Security Council, I read that there were about 20 to 26 prosecutors and about 10 to 20 judges. Therefore the problem which was raised was that of how to train judges and prosecutors from the local population so that they might be in a position to handle trials in a proper manner. The internationalized courts and tribunals may also serve this purpose.

Finally, I think that these internationalized courts and tribunals may expedite prosecutions and trials without compromising respect for international standards on human rights and international criminal law. This is crucial, I believe.

E. MAIN PRACTICAL PROBLEMS SUCH COURTS
MAY HAVE TO FACE

I will focus on some practical and legal difficulties, which seem to me to be the most conspicuous ones. First of all, there are two main practical problems.

One is to ensure that the international and the national components of these tribunals cooperate smoothly. Both the prosecution and the bench are of mixed composition and there you have this huge problem—to make sure that the local component, and the international component, do cooperate, do understand each other, do work effectively in their pursuit of the common and shared goal of rendering justice.

The second practical question is that of financial resources—finding the money to make those courts and tribunals work. I shall leave this problem aside, and concentrate on the other one that I have just outlined.

In this connection, let me just pick up the example of Cambodia. We know that there should be two prosecutors. One is a local prosecutor. The other one is an international prosecutor and the current law provides that if there are disagreements between these two prosecutors (there may also be disagreements between the two investigating judges as the inquisitorial approach has been adopted because of the French tradition) the matter is handed over to a Pre-trial Chamber of five judges which will have a say in settling the matter.

It is somewhat odd, to our sense of justice, to find that prosecutorial questions, even the question of whether or not to prosecute somebody or how to collect evidence, or what sort of evidence to gather against somebody, in short these typically prosecutorial matters, are submitted to a panel of five judges. That means that in Cambodia it will be a sore point to ensure cooperation between the two components.

The same applies to judges. Under the Cambodian Bill, still to be approved by Parliament, the Cambodian judges are in a majority (three to two), but a majority of four is required for any decision to be made. It follows that there can very easily be deadlock caused by dissensions on the bench when the judges do not reach agreement, with no apparent way out. This is then a major problem.

This problem is compounded by the need to amalgamate different legal philosophies. I wonder whether the international judges to be appointed, upon nomination by the UN Secretary-General, by the Cambodian authorities, will belong to the common law tradition. If so, there again will be a problem. For instance, in the International Criminal Tribunal for the former Yugoslavia we had to try to merge different views and approaches and philosophies of law, in the judicial process within the particular body.

In Cambodia the prevailing model will be the inquisitorial model. Although there have been attacks in the legal literature on the investigating judges, as well as suggestions that the institutional investigating judges should be abolished, by and large, I think that the inquisitorial model will be kept. One may wonder whether the international judges, if they have a common law background, would be in a position easily to reach this sort of amalgamation with the local component, when psychological, practical, and legal problems need to be addressed.

F. SOME LEGAL PROBLEMS WITH WHICH SUCH COURTS MAY HAVE TO COME TO GRIPS

Let me move on to what I perceive as some of the main *legal* problems that internationalized criminal courts and tribunals may face or are facing today. The first problem is the establishment of a body of law, that is a body of both substantive and procedural criminal law. This is not easy, although, of course, in Kosovo, in East Timor, and in Sierra Leone, there are a set of regulations or legal provisions which lay down the proper body of law to be applied by the relevant courts and tribunals.

In spite of this provision, which was helpfully made by the United Nations in particular in Kosovo and in East Timor, I have read in some reports of the UN Secretary-General to the Security Council, that problems still have indeed arisen both in East Timor and in Kosovo.

For example, in 1999 a regulation was adopted in East Timor stating that the laws applied there prior to 25 October 1999 shall apply in East Timor insofar as they do not conflict with the standards referred to in section 2 of the International Legal Standards and the fulfilment of the mandates given to the United Nations Transitional Administration in East Timor (UNTAET) by the UN Security Council Resolution. However, it would seem that the courts working in East Timor have faced serious problems in identifying parts of the applicable legislation that are consistent with international legal standards. In short, there is the question of reconciling the international legal standards to be applied with the local laws and regulations; it would seem that this is not an easy task.

The same applies to Kosovo. The UN Secretary-General, in his report of 15 December 2000, stated that significant outstanding issues include a lack of clarity among local judges as to whether international human rights standards were the supreme law in Kosovo. Again, that is a problem that must be faced.

An even more serious problem, as I can testify in light of the experience of the International Tribunal for the former Yugoslavia (ICTY), is the question of cooperation with national authorities of the local state or with foreign states.

Let me dwell on the case of Sierra Leone. The Special Court for Sierra Leone enjoys primacy over national courts. National courts and other authorities are duty bound, under an agreement signed recently between the United Nations and Sierra Leone, to cooperate with the Special Court and collect evidence, summon witnesses and bring witnesses to the Court and so on. However, what happens if national authorities fail to cooperate? What are the means available to the Special Court for inducing compliance with this basic obligation of cooperation? There is no mention of this problem in the relevant agreement, to the best of my knowledge. I wonder to what extent the skilful diplomats and lawyers who drafted the agreement and the Statute of the Sierra Leone Special Court took into account this particular problem.

The question of cooperation of states of the former Yugoslavia with ICTY was of enormous importance. Why? Because from the outset ICTY was faced with a clear refusal (sometimes overt, sometimes expressed in diplomatic language) of the national authorities to cooperate.

The problem becomes even more serious when you move on to the question of cooperation of countries other than that of *locus commissi delicti*. For instance, under the agreement and the Statute, the Special Court for Sierra Leone, as I said above, enjoys primacy over national courts. However, it has no primacy over courts or other authorities in the neighbouring countries. What happens if somebody who has been indicted for atrocities in Sierra Leone goes abroad and takes shelter in a neighbouring country, and this neighbouring country refuses to arrest him or to hand him over to the Special Court in Sierra Leone, or even to allow the prosecutor for the Special Court in Sierra Leone to question witnesses, or to send over witnesses living in neighbouring countries? The agreement is only binding upon the United Nations and Sierra Leone. It is not binding upon third countries, in particular neighbouring countries. One may well wonder whether the United Nations has any means available to force third countries to cooperate with the Special Court.

In looking through the various relevant documents, one can find some excellent reports made by the UN Secretary-General to the Security Council on East Timor. One really sore point mentioned there, which is always underlined by the Secretary-General, is that of the cooperation of Indonesia with the East Timor courts. On 6 April 2000 a Memorandum of Understanding was signed between Indonesia and UNTAET, the special administration for East Timor, regarding cooperation in legal, judicial, and human rights matters. However, although this agreement is binding upon Indonesia, it has never been implemented by Indonesia. There are some cases, reported by the UN Secretary-General, where a team from the Serious Crimes Investigation Unit in East Timor had sought to interview witnesses in Jakarta. When the Indonesian Attorney-General summoned those witnesses, they questioned the validity of the Memorandum of Understanding and did not appear.

This is a serious problem because most of the people accused of atrocities in East Timor have Indonesian nationality and live in Indonesia. Again, the cooperation of Indonesia is crucial if those people are to be brought to trial before the Special Panels in East Timor. So far Indonesia, on the one hand, has refused to cooperate with the Special Panels; but on the other hand, has decided to set up a special tribunal to try crimes committed in East Timor in 1999. It is a fact, however, at least according to the notes of the UN Secretary-General, that so far nothing significant has been achieved.

Probably this is the most serious problem that internationalized courts and tribunals have to face: when either suspects who are accused, or witnesses, are not in the country where such tribunals are rendering justice but have escaped abroad, and the foreign country is not prepared and ready to cooperate.

Another serious legal problem, which has already arisen, is the question of *legal aid*. These tribunals, to be credible, must be fair. They must respect all the basic principles of due process and, of course, the principle of equality of arms.

The accused must be put in a position to make his or her case before the tribunal. However, very often the accused (think of East Timor) are people who, besides being illiterate, have no financial means: they are indigents. They cannot afford to pay for defence counsel.

I think it is incumbent upon the international community to provide the accused with all the legal and financial resources necessary to make his or her case before the internationalized courts. To the best of my knowledge, so far only in East Timor has a regulation been passed providing for legal aid to those who have been accused of atrocities in East Timor.

G. SITUATIONS APPROPRIATE FOR ESTABLISHING MIXED OR INTERNATIONALIZED COURTS

I believe there are a number of situations in which it would be appropriate to set up such courts. I think in particular of countries where there is a total collapse of the judicial system, or where the judiciary is not in a position to render justice because civil commotion, civil strife, or hatred at the ethnic or religious level simply bring the national administration of justice to a stalemate.

Consider for example the case of Colombia, where I gather (from news reports and reports from reliable sources) that judges fear to take proceedings against terrorists or people suspected of appalling crimes because of security problems—they fear for their own lives. They would be happy, I think, if trials against people accused of atrocities or serious crimes could be heard before some sort of international or internationalized courts. This is therefore an area where such courts might play a role.

Another is a situation like that of Afghanistan. Crimes which have been committed in Afghanistan, according to the Americans and to news reports, in particular war crimes and crimes against humanity, could be tried by local judges, of course, on condition that such courts are strengthened by an international component. The international community should take upon itself the task of financing and establishing within the national judiciary courts that are of mixed composition, so that the local population can see the rendering of justice by their own people under the scrutiny, however, of an international component.

My view is that various crimes are suited for different solutions. For instance, terrorist crimes committed against Americans by people who have been arrested in the United States should probably be tried there—not, however, before the military commissions established by President Bush, but before civilian courts, with all the guarantees and safeguards of due process provided for in international law and the US Constitution.

Other people who have committed terrorist acts, or war crimes of terrorism or against humanity after the attack by the Americans on Afghanistan, should probably be tried before internationalized courts and tribunals so that the whole population can become involved in this judicial process. And then we may have trials against leaders, the most important people accused of alleged crimes of terrorism (say, Bin Laden, if he is arrested). They could be brought to trial before an international tribunal proper, which as I suggested some time ago in a few newspaper interviews, could be ICTY, if this tribunal received a broader mandate from the Security Council.

In this way, one could have a gradation of judicial responses to crimes committed in this particular area.

Another situation in which internationalized courts might prove appropriate is, for example, Palestine. I think it would perhaps be appropriate for the National Authority for Palestine to set up courts and tribunals in the occupied territories with an international component, to bring to trial those people who have been arrested and accused of terrorist acts against Israeli territory or Israeli nationals. Again, such a move would play a huge role psychologically and politically. The international component would, in a way, boost trials.

I am thinking of what happened to Hissein Habré, the Chadean dictator, who took refuge in Senegal and then under the 1984 Convention Against Torture was brought to trial there. The Supreme Court of Senegal held, on legal grounds (which may seem specious) that the Senegalese courts had no jurisdiction, not even under the Torture Convention. Afterwards, the President of Senegal decided that Hissein Habré should simply be expelled from Senegal. You have a case, here, where a former dictator, accused of serious cases of torture, is not being tried in his own country, but takes refuge abroad and the neighbouring countries or the countries of the area, on political grounds, refuse to do justice.

I read that Kofi Annan recently phoned the President of Senegal asking him not to expel Hissein Habré because there might be a chance of a trial being brought against him in Belgium. (I do not know whether this is correct, as it was a news report only.) If it is correct, then it is owing to this brave step by Kofi Annan (who again is proving to be a very good Secretary-General on human rights problems) that Hissein Habré has not yet been expelled from

Senegal. Recently Belgian investigating judges have initiated criminal proceedings against him, in the hope that Senegal will hand him over to them.

H. THE OUTLOOK FOR INTERNATIONAL CRIMINAL JUSTICE

I submit that today we should rule out the establishment of future ad hoc tribunals similar to those for the former Yugoslavia, or for Rwanda. I think this is no longer an option, as they are too expensive, trials are too lengthy, and they will be superfluous because of the setting up of the International Criminal Court.

We should, therefore, abandon the practice of the establishment of international criminal tribunals by the Security Council. We do not want the Security Council to be selective and decide to pick and choose and set up a tribunal only on political or geopolitical grounds. If we exclude that option, we are left with three options available: national courts, the ICC, and internationalized courts.

National courts, I think, may still play a huge role, of course, on condition that judges and prosecutors wake up, as it were, and become more sensitive to atrocities committed elsewhere in the world. My suggestion is that we should push national legislators to grant *universal jurisdiction* to national courts. I would not go so far as to suggest the Belgian and the Spanish models. I think that goes too far. It would be better to provide that universal jurisdiction may only be exercised whenever the accused is on the territory of the country wishing to prosecute that person. The custodian state, if it is vested with universal jurisdiction, may take precedence. Otherwise, we may be faced with the Belgian situation, where judges are flooded with complaints against dictators and generals from everywhere in the world. I would go for a moderate or not too broad notion of universal jurisdiction. But universal jurisdiction is a must and, of course, it will be important for states to implement international conventions, the Geneva Conventions of 1949, the Convention Against Torture, and indeed to implement those conventions in a proper manner. This is one approach.

The second way would be to have a distribution of tasks between national courts and the International Criminal Court (ICC). The ICC, because of the complementary principle, can step in only if national courts are unable or unwilling to prosecute. I think by and large this is a wise solution.

Could the setting up of internationalized courts constitute a valuable option or alternative to going before the ICC, when national courts are either unwilling or unable to render justice in a particular case, and there is no legal way to take the case to the ICC (for instance, because the ICC lacks jurisdiction)?

If a particular case cannot be heard by national courts nor be taken to the ICC, one could bolster the efficiency and the capability of national courts to do justice in a fair and proper manner by putting an *international component* within national courts.

This could be a good solution, subject, however, to a condition, namely, close scrutiny by the ICC, if it has jurisdiction, or by UN bodies, over the internationalized court. Otherwise the setting up of a mixed or internationalized court could, first of all, deprive the ICC of its role as a universal jurisdiction and, secondly, become a pretext for not doing justice in a proper manner.

I. CONCLUSION

Let me conclude by saying that international criminal law is a branch of law that more than any other is about human folly, human wickedness, and human aggressiveness. International criminal law deals with the darkest side of humanity. However, it also deals with the question of how society should attempt to limit violence and aggression as much as possible. I think that the magnitude of this task is such that there is no single response to the multifarious aspects of international criminality. Therefore, one must resort, I think, to a variety of responses, each best suited to a specific situation. I strongly believe that, in the long term, resorting to mixed or internationalized criminal courts and tribunals may prove to be one of the most effective societal and institutional devices of the many which are at present available to international law-makers.

2

The Second Generation UN-Based Tribunals: A Diversity of Mixed Jurisdictions

*Daphna Shraga**

A. INTRODUCTION

The establishment of the ad hoc international tribunals for the former Yugoslavia and Rwanda in 1993 and 1994 triggered a proliferation of international criminal jurisdictions. A precursor to the International Criminal Court—an international, truly universal criminal jurisdiction—they have become the model upon which the second generation, country-specific 'mixed tribunals', were conceived. In the decade that followed their establishment, a number of countries emerging from civil wars of extreme brutality, in which genocide, crimes against humanity, or war crimes were committed on a massive scale, called upon the United Nations to establish similar jurisdictions in their own territories. With their administration of justice systems devastated, biased, or otherwise lacking the necessary judicial and administrative capacity, these countries sought the technical and financial assistance of the United Nations in the conduct of complex prosecutions which they alone were unable or politically unwilling to undertake. In their desire to put an end to a historic cycle of impunity, they were also motivated by the interest to give the prosecution of the government's political enemies a stamp of international legitimacy.

The United Nations Security Council, as the parent organ of the ad hoc tribunals, has been reluctant to replicate the experience and establish additional judicial organs whose administrative structure and lengthy and costly proceedings would further increase the heavy financial burden on Member States of the Organization. In the face of the Security Council's reluctance, the focus of expectation shifted to the UN Secretariat to develop a model similar in form, substance, and international legitimacy to the ad hoc tribunals, but one which respects a nation's vision of justice, its choice of means of bringing it about, and its ownership, at least in part, of the judicial process. Thus, a model of a 'mixed tribunal' as a national court of mixed jurisdiction and composition was developed for Cambodia. It was soon followed by a *sui generis*, treaty-based court of similar jurisdiction and composition for Sierra Leone.

* Principal Legal Officer, Office of the Legal Counsel, Office of Legal Affairs, United Nations. The views expressed in this chapter are those of the author and do not necessarily reflect the opinion of the Office of Legal Affairs or of the United Nations.

Unlike the international criminal tribunals for the former Yugoslavia and Rwanda established as an enforcement measure under Chapter VII of the United Nations Charter, the legal basis for the establishment of the mixed tribunals for Sierra Leone and for Cambodia was consensual, and their legal status, applicable law, composition, and organizational structure had to be negotiated and agreed upon between the parties. It was in the nature of the negotiating process that political constraints imposed different legal choices on questions of jurisdiction, organizational structure, and composition of the mixed tribunals.

The mixed tribunals for Sierra Leone and for Cambodia inspired the creation of mixed jurisdictions in East Timor, Kosovo, and Bosnia and Herzegovina. In analysing the diversity of mixed jurisdictions from the vantage point of the United Nations, this chapter will focus on the Special Court for Sierra Leone and the Extraordinary Chambers for Cambodia, and conclude with a comparative analysis of the mixed composition panels of judges in the UN-administered territories of Kosovo and East Timor, and in the State Court of Bosnia and Herzegovina.

B. NEGOTIATING THE LEGAL FRAMEWORK FOR THE EXTRAORDINARY CHAMBERS AND THE SPECIAL COURT

1. The legislative process

The negotiating process for the establishment of the Extraordinary Chambers for Cambodia and the Special Court for Sierra Leone was conducted by the UN Secretariat for the most part in parallel and within the parameters determined by its political organs. It resulted, however, in the establishment of two very different mixed jurisdictions. A comparative analysis of the two legislative processes from the vantage point of the UN Secretariat is illustrative of the difficulties, both legal and political, of applying a single UN model of 'internationalized jurisdiction' in countries and circumstances as diverse as Sierra Leone and Cambodia.

More than two decades after the collapse of the Khmer Rouge regime, a request for assistance in the establishment of an international tribunal for Cambodia to prosecute Khmer Rouge leaders was put before the UN's political organs in 1997 by a letter addressed to the Secretary-General from the co-Prime Ministers of Cambodia.[1] A joint request for the establishment of a UN-based tribunal was possible in the political circumstances of Cambodia in June 1997 when a common position against Pol Pot would have secured, for a brief period of time, a delicate balance of power between the First and the

---

[1] Letter from the First and Second Prime Ministers of Cambodia addressed to the Secretary-General (21 June 1997) UN Doc A/51/930-S/1997/488, Annex.

Second Prime Ministers. It was soon, however, overtaken by events, both in Cambodia and in the United Nations.[2] With the July 1997 coup d'état which restored Hun Sen to power as the sole Prime Minister, the death of Pol Pot in April 1998, and the defection that year to the government's ranks of other Khmer Rouge leaders, notably Ke Pauk, Khieu Samphan, and Nuon Chea, Cambodia was disinclined to risk a seemingly peaceful demise of the Khmer Rouge with the prospects of international criminal prosecution.[3] In the United Nations, in the face of the Security Council's unwillingness to react to the request, the General Assembly took the lead.

In its resolution 52/135,[4] the General Assembly asked the Secretary-General to examine the Cambodian request for assistance, and if necessary, appoint a group of experts to evaluate the existing evidence and propose further measures as a means to bring about national reconciliation and address the question of individual accountability.[5] The Group of Experts appointed by the Secretary-General recommended the establishment of a UN-based international tribunal under Chapter VII or VI of the United Nations Charter to try Khmer Rouge officials for crimes against humanity and genocide committed in the period 1975 to 1979.[6] As neither the General Assembly nor the Security Council acted upon the recommendation, it was for the Secretary-General to take the initiative and offer his good offices in establishing a tribunal which, while 'international in character', would not necessarily be 'modelled after either of the existing ad hoc tribunals or be linked to them institutionally, administratively or financially'.[7]

Negotiations between the UN Secretariat and the government on a 'mixed jurisdiction' for Cambodia began in July 1999. They lasted for almost three years, until in February 2002 the Secretary-General decided to withdraw from the negotiations. In the course of the negotiations many legal and institutional issues were contentious. They included the question of whether the majority of judges should be Cambodian or international; whether the Prosecutor and the Registrar should be internationally appointed; the validity of the amnesty previously granted; and the primacy of the Agreement

[2] For the genesis of the Extraordinary Chambers, see also chapter 10 (Etchenson).

[3] SR Ratner and JS Abrams *Accountability for Human Rights Atrocities in International Law, Beyond the Nuremberg Legacy* (2nd edn Oxford University Press 2001); B Rajagopal 'The Pragmatics of Prosecuting the Khmer Rouge' (1998) 1 *Yearbook of International Humanitarian Law* 189; D Boyle 'Quelle Justice Pour les Khmer Rouges?' [1999] *Révue Trimestrielle des Droits de l'Homme* 773.

[4] UNGA Res 52/135 (12 December 1997) UN Doc A/RES/52/135 [16].

[5] Letter from the Secretary-General addressed to the President of the General Assembly (31 July 1998) UN Doc A/52/1007.

[6] 'Report of the Group of Experts for Cambodia established pursuant to General Assembly resolution 52/135' (16 March 1999) UN Doc A/53/850-S/1999/231, Annex; SR Ratner 'The United Nations Group of Experts for Cambodia' (1999) 93 *AJIL* 948.

[7] Identical letters from the Secretary-General to the President of the General Assembly and the President of the Security Council (15 March 1999) UN Doc A/53/850-S/1999/231, 3.

between the United Nations and the government over the Law on the Establishment of the Extraordinary Chambers.[8] A conflict over the status, composition, and organizational structure of the mixed tribunal, it was in fact a conflict of two visions of justice: an independent tribunal meeting international standards of justice, objectivity, fairness, and due process of law, and a politically controlled judicial process.

In announcing his decision to withdraw from the negotiations the Secretary-General explained that the Cambodian mixed tribunal did not measure up to international standards of justice, and that 'as currently envisaged ... [it] would not guarantee the independence, impartiality and objectivity that a court established with the support of the United Nations must have'.[9] The United Nations Secretariat also cited the lack of a clear mandate from either UN organ as an inhibiting factor. A mandate was soon to be given; though not the one the Secretariat had expected.

By Resolution 57/228, the General Assembly requested the Secretary-General to resume the negotiations with the government of Cambodia to conclude an agreement based on previous negotiations on the establishment of the Extraordinary Chambers, consistent with the provisions of the Resolution; consistent also with the subject matter and personal jurisdiction of the Chambers set forth in the Cambodian Law,[10] provided that international standards of justice are maintained, and that arrangements are made for an appellate Chamber.[11] In approving the Cambodian Law on the Extraordinary Chambers as the legal framework for a UN-operated court, the General Assembly gave implicit international legitimacy to the Cambodian justice system as a whole. The apparent contradiction between this and Resolution 57/225 adopted on the same day, by which the General Assembly noted with concern 'the functioning of the judiciary [in Cambodia] resulting from corruption and interference by the executive with the independence of the judiciary',[12] was completely disregarded.

---

[8] S Linton 'Cambodia, East Timor and Sierra Leone: Experiments in International Justice' (2001) 12 *Criminal Law Forum* 185, 187–202. While the question of the primacy of the Agreement over the Cambodian Law has never been conclusively determined, the Agreement between the United Nations and the Government of Cambodia of 17 March 2003 provides in Art 2(3) thereof, that: 'In case amendments to the Law on the Establishment of the Extraordinary Chambers are deemed necessary, such amendments shall always be preceded by consultations between the parties'.

[9] Statement by the UN Legal Counsel Hans Corell at the press briefing at UN Headquarters in New York (8 February 2002) available at www.un.org/News/dh/infocus/cambodia/corell-brief.htm.

[10] Law on the Establishment of Extraordinary Chambers in the Courts of Cambodia for the Prosecution of Crimes Committed During the Period of Democratic Kampuchea, promulgated on 10 August 2001. See www.ridi.org/boyle/kr_law_10-08-02.htm.

[11] UNGA Res 57/228 (18 December 2002) UN Doc A/RES/57/228.

[12] UNGA Res 57/225 (18 December 2002) on the Situation of Human Rights in Cambodia, UN Doc A/RES/57/225 [II,2].

In the negotiations that followed, the Secretary-General attempted unsuc-
cessfully to reverse the ratio between the national and international components, renegotiate the composition of the Chambers and their voting system,
as well as obtain the appointment of an international prosecutor and an
international investigating judge. They resulted in few modifications relating
mainly to the organizational structure of the Chambers and their reduction
from a three- to a two-tiered court. In concluding his report on Khmer Rouge
Trials, the Secretary-General remained unconvinced that the Agreement,
although improved upon its previous version, would ensure the credibility
of the Extraordinary Chambers given the precarious state of the Cambodian
judiciary.[13] The General Assembly, however, did not share his concerns, and
in its resolution 57/228B of 13 May 2003 approved the draft Agreement
between the United Nations and the Royal Government of Cambodia, and
urged the Secretary-General and the government to allow the draft Agreement to enter into force and implement it fully thereafter.

The negotiating process on the establishment of the Special Court for
Sierra Leone was initiated by the Security Council at the request of the
government.[14] Disinclined to establish a Chapter VII Special Court as its
own subsidiary organ, the Security Council, by Resolution 1315 (2000),
requested the Secretary-General to negotiate an agreement with the government of Sierra Leone to create an independent special court to prosecute
persons who bear the greatest responsibility for the commission of crimes
against humanity, war crimes, and other serious violations of international
humanitarian law. In the negotiations which ensued between the UN Secretariat and the government of Sierra Leone, there was little disagreement on
the principles of international jurisdiction, the status of the Court and its
constitutive instrument, its composition, including a majority of international judges and an international Prosecutor, organizational structure,
and the practical arrangements for its establishment.[15] They culminated two

---

[13] 'Report of the Secretary-General on Khmer Rouge Trials' (31 March 2003) UN Doc
A/57/769 [79].

[14] Letter from the Permanent Representative of Sierra Leone to the United Nations
addressed to the President of the Security Council (9 August 2000) UN Doc S/2000/786,
Annex. In his letter dated 12 June 2000, the President of Sierra Leone requested the Security
Council 'to initiate a process whereby the United Nations would resolve on the setting up of a
special court for Sierra Leone'. While not expressly requesting the establishment of a Chapter
VII court, it clearly envisaged a Security Council-created court. In language reminiscent of that
used in the Cambodian request, the President said: 'I am aware of similar efforts by the United
Nations to respond to similar crimes against humanity in Rwanda and the former Yugoslavia.
I ask that similar considerations be given to this request'. On the genesis and structure of the
Special Court, see also Chapter 7 (Smith).

[15] In his report to the Security Council on the Establishment of the Special Court for Sierra
Leone ('Report of the Secretary-General on the Establishment of a Special Court for
Sierra Leone' (4 October 2000) UN Doc S/2000/915), the Secretary-General submitted a draft
Agreement between the United Nations and the government of Sierra Leone with the Statute of
the Special Court annexed thereto. It was subsequently revised in communications exchanged

years later in the Agreement between the United Nations and the government of Sierra Leone on the Establishment of a Special Court for Sierra Leone, signed on 16 January 2002.[16]

2. *The role of 'third actors'*

The negotiating processes for the establishment of the Special Court for Sierra Leone and the Extraordinary Chambers for Cambodia were shaped by the political circumstances both in the countries concerned and at the United Nations, and their outcome was determined largely by the interaction between the various actors directly and indirectly involved.

In the case of Sierra Leone, Members of the Security Council acted jointly, unanimously, and as a coherent group in developing a common approach to the nature, jurisdiction, and organizational structure of the Special Court. The Security Council which in its Resolution 1315 (2000) initiated the negotiating process and determined its political and legal parameters, remained actively engaged in it until its successful completion. In this context also, a small group of interested states composed of Members of the Security Council and major donors was formed almost from the start to assist the Secretary-General in assessing the needs of the Special Court in funds and personnel. It would later be transformed into a Management Committee of the Special Court to oversee its efficient operation.[17]

The role of civil society representatives in Sierra Leone, a particularly vibrant group of local and international non-governmental organizations (NGOs), was unique. In its negotiations with the government, it was the Secretariat's policy to engage in a parallel dialogue with representatives of civil society to seek their views and address their concerns within the legal and

between the President of the Security Council and the Secretary-General (Letter from the President of the Security Council addressed to the Secretary-General (22 December 2000) UN Doc S/2000/1234; Letter from the Secretary-General addressed to the President of the Security Council (12 January 2001) UN Doc S/2001/40, and Letter from the President of the Security Council addressed to the Secretary-General (31 January 2001) UN Doc S/2001/95).

[16] The Agreement between the United Nations and the Government of Sierra Leone on the Establishment of a Special Court for Sierra Leone, and the Statute of the Special Court for Sierra Leone, were included in the 'Report of the Planning Mission on the Establishment of the Special Court for Sierra Leone transmitted by the Secretary-General to the President of the Security Council by Letter dated 6 March 2002' (8 March 2002) UN Doc S/2002/246, Annex, Appendix II and its Attachment. In March 2002, the Special Court Agreement (2000) (Ratification) Act 2002, was promulgated by the Sierra Leone Parliament, thus giving effect to the powers and competences of the Special Court in the national legal system of Sierra Leone. See generally, N Fritz and A Smith 'Current Apathy for Coming Anarchy: Building the Special Court for Sierra Leone' (2001) 25 *Fordham International Law Journal* 391; R Cryer 'A "Special Court" for Sierra Leone' (2001) 50 *ICLQ* 435; C Denis 'Le Tribunal Spécial pour la Sierra Leone' (2001) 34 *Révue Belge de droit international* 236.

[17] On the Management Committee of the Special Court, see Chapter 8 (Mochochoko/ Tortora).

political limitations imposed. The single most important contribution of the NGO community to shaping the Statute of the Special Court was in balancing the principle of judicial accountability of juveniles and the protection of existing child-care rehabilitation programmes.

The constructive attitude of the government of Sierra Leone, its genuine will to see that justice is done and be seen to be done, at the risk of political instability, if necessary, is perhaps the most important contributory factor to the successful outcome of the negotiations. In the establishment of the Special Court for Sierra Leone, the Security Council, Member States, the UN Secretariat, the government of Sierra Leone, and its civil society at large, formed a partnership. This was not to be the case in the negotiating process for the establishment of the Extraordinary Chambers for Cambodia.

An early attempt to engage the Security Council in the establishment of a Khmer Rouge tribunal failed for a number of reasons, and notably a threat by China to veto any Security Council resolution to that effect. In the negotiations between the UN Secretariat and the government of Cambodia, the Secretary-General acted within his general good offices mandate, but without a specific mandate from any of the UN organs. When in 2002, the General Assembly intervened to revive the moribund negotiating process, it mandated its resumption on conditions largely dictated by the government of Cambodia.

Interested Member States—and they were quite a few—did not act as a coherent group with a common approach. With very little in common, they were loosely united by the desire to entrust the Secretariat with the establishment and operation of the Extraordinary Chambers. In the negotiating process itself, however, they often intervened individually with the government of Cambodia to offer solutions which would then be imposed upon the Secretariat. In the political circumstances of Cambodia, the role played by civil society was marginal. While many in the NGO community questioned the credibility of a judicial process dominated by government-appointed judges, prosecutors, investigators, and support staff, they continued to believe that the UN engagement in the process was Cambodia's only hope to see justice done.

C. SUBJECT MATTER JURISDICTION

The similarities in the nature of the conflicts and the crimes committed in the former Yugoslavia, Rwanda, Sierra Leone, and Cambodia, imposed a similar choice of the applicable law in all jurisdictions whether national, international, or *sui generis*, in character. With few exceptions, therefore, they included the crime of genocide, crimes against humanity, and, depending on the nature of the conflict, war crimes and other serious violations of international humanitarian law.

The inclusion in the jurisdiction of the Cambodian Extraordinary Chambers of the crime of genocide within the restrictive definition of the Genocide Convention, presented legal and conceptual difficulties. More perhaps than any other mass killing in the second half of the twentieth century, the massive scale and systematic character of the killing by execution, starvation, malnutrition, and disease of an estimated 2 million Cambodians during the Khmer Rouge regime, resembled the crime of genocide. Perpetrated mostly, however, on political or social grounds by members of the same national, ethnic, religious, or racial group, the Cambodian so-called 'auto-genocide' did not amount technically to 'genocide' within the meaning of Article 2 of the Genocide Convention.[18] The Conventional crime of genocide was nevertheless retained in the Cambodian Law to the extent of its applicability to minority religious and ethnic groups, such as Muslim 'Cham' and ethnic Vietnamese, Chinese, and Thai minority groups.

In the Sierra Leone decade-long conflict which began in 1991, large-scale and systematic violations of international humanitarian law, abduction, mass rape, forced recruitment of children, and summary executions were committed by forces of the Revolutionary United Front (RUF). It was, however, the period following the joint invasion of Freetown by the RUF

---

[18] The crime of genocide is defined in Art 2 of the 1948 Convention on the Prevention and Punishment of the Crime of Genocide to mean any of the following: killing members of the group, causing bodily or mental harm, inflicting conditions of life likely to bring about the physical destruction of the group, imposing measures to prevent birth, or transferring children of the group, when 'committed with intent to destroy, in whole or in part, a national, ethnical, racial or religious group as such'. The Conventional definition of the crime of genocide was replicated in the Statute of the International Tribunal for the former Yugoslavia (3 May 1993) UN Doc S/25704, Annex, Art 4, and the Statute of the International Tribunal for Rwanda (UNSC Res 955 (1994), Annex, Art 2). In considering the Conventional limitations on the protected groups, ICTR in the *Akayesu* case, concluded that the crime of genocide was perceived 'as targeting only "stable" groups, constituted in a permanent fashion and membership of which is determined by birth, with the exclusion of the more "mobile" groups which one joins through individual voluntary commitment, such as political and economic groups' (*Prosecutor v Jean-Paul Akayesu* ICTR-96-4-T, Judgment [511]); SR Ratner 'The Genocide Convention after Fifty Years: Contemporary Strategies for Combating a Crime against Humanity' [1998] *ASIL Proceedings of the 92nd Annual Meeting* 1; WA Schabas *Genocide in International Law: The Crime of Crimes* (Cambridge University Press 2000) 118–19, 129; Ratner and Abrams (*supra* n 3) 26–45, 267–306; H Hannum 'International Law and Cambodian Genocide: The Sounds of Silence' (1989) 11 *Human Rights Quarterly* 82. At the Rome Conference, the definition of the crime of genocide engendered little controversy and was incorporated without change in Article 6 of the Statute of the International Criminal Court (ICC). In their reluctance to modify the definition and expand its scope 50 years after its adoption in the Genocide Convention and with the Cambodian killing fields present in their minds, Member States clearly, though implicitly, indicated their intention to maintain the definition of the 'ultimate crime' in its Conventional form and within the limitations established thereunder. E Fronza 'Genocide in the Rome Statute' in F Lattanzi and WA Schabas (eds) *Essays on the Rome Statute of the International Criminal Court* (Il Sirente 1999) vol I, 105.

and the Armed Forces Revolutionary Council (AFRC) on 6 January 1999, which marked the most intensified, systematic, and widespread violations of human rights and international humanitarian law against the population of the capital. For all of their brutality, however, the killings and mass executions were not committed on ethnic, religious, or racial grounds with an intent to annihilate the group distinguished on any of these grounds, as such. They were not characterized, therefore, legally as genocide.

While the crime of genocide was omitted from the Statute of the Special Court, two additional crimes were included to address the specificity of the Sierra Leone conflict: (1) attacks against peace-keeping personnel involved in a humanitarian assistance or peace-keeping mission as long as they are entitled to the protection given to civilians under the international law of armed conflict[19] (a reference to the hostage-taking of 500 peace-keepers in May 2000 by the RUF); and (2) conscripting or enlisting children under the age of 15 years into armed forces or groups, or using them to participate actively in hostilities, a practice prevalent among all armed groups involved in the conflict.[20]

As is warranted by the nature of the mixed jurisdiction, both the Cambodian Law on the Extraordinary Chambers and the Statute of the Special Court for Sierra Leone include common crimes which in the circumstances were judged complementary to the international crimes, and of particular relevance.[21]

D. PERSONAL JURISDICTION

Personal jurisdiction of a limited scope is another distinctive feature of both international and mixed tribunals. A definition of personal jurisdiction by reference to the hierarchical level of those presumed responsible or their relatively heavier responsibility for the crimes committed, was imperative, as it is inherent almost in the nature of any international criminal jurisdiction

---

[19] The crime of attacks against peace-keepers in Art 4(b) of the Statute of the Special Court replicates Art 8(2)(b)(iii) and (e)(iii) of the ICC Statute, and is based on the distinction between peace-keepers as 'civilians' in traditional UN Chapter VI operations, and peace-keepers as 'combatants' when pursuant to Chapter VII mandate, they are engaged in combat mission, or are otherwise acting in self-defence.

[20] Article 4(c) of the Statute of the Special Court. The prohibition on recruitment of children below 15 years of age is established in Art 4 (3)(c) of the 1977 Additional Protocol II to the Geneva Conventions, and Art 38(3) of the 1989 Convention on the Rights of the Child. It was for the first time criminalized and qualified a serious violation of the laws and customs of war in the ICC Statute (Art 8(2)(b)(xxvi) and (e)(vii)).

[21] The Cambodian Law on the Establishment of the Extraordinary Chambers includes the crimes of homicide, torture, and religious persecution under the 1956 Penal Code (Art 3), and the Statute of the Special Court includes offences relating to the abuse of girls under the 1926 Prevention of Cruelty to Children Act, and offences relating to wanton destruction of property (including arson) under the 1861 Malicious Damage Act (Art 5).

that it be so limited. Limitation to the political and military leadership alone, however, would not have satisfied the sense of justice and the principle of accountability of relatively low-level perpetrators. In the cases of Cambodia and Sierra Leone, it was the understanding of the parties that while restrictively defined, the personal jurisdiction of the Court should be interpreted to include the top military and political leadership, as well as others down the chain of command whose crimes were particularly singled out for their magnitude, brutality, or heinous nature.

A restrictive definition of the personal jurisdiction of the Extraordinary Chambers and the Special Court was for either government a politically imposed necessity. In the realities of Cambodia and Sierra Leone, where political stability was achieved through reintegration of ex-combatants into the regular armed forces and the society at large, political power-sharing and the grant of amnesties of various scope, it would have been the government's preference to spare from prosecution those among the most responsible who had defected to its ranks, or have since participated in a coalition government. A selective choice of the accused, however, presented for the United Nations a dilemma of reconciling peace and justice, and applying uncompromising international standards of justice in circumstances of fragile peace.

The personal jurisdiction of the Extraordinary Chambers in Cambodia extends to 'senior leaders and those most responsible for the crimes committed in Democratic Kampuchea'. At the time the definition was adopted two persons had already been detained in connection with the Khmer Rouge regime: Chhit Choeun, known as 'Ta Mok' or 'The Butcher', a Khmer Rouge army commander and a member of the Standing Committee, and Kaing Kek Ieu, more commonly known as 'Duch', the Director of the notorious Tuel Sleng prison. They have so far been the only two former Khmer Rouge members arrested in connection with the crimes falling within the jurisdiction of the Chambers. The most senior surviving members of the Khmer Rouge leadership, Nuon Chea, Pol Pot's former Deputy known as 'Brother No 2', Khieu Samphan, the Chairman of the Council of State of Democratic Kampuchea and the de facto Head of State since 1976, and Ieng Sary, the Deputy Prime Minister and Minister for Foreign Affairs of Democratic Kampuchea, are still living freely in the semi-autonomous region of Pailin and in the capital Phnom Penh.

The personal jurisdiction of the Special Court for Sierra Leone extends to 'persons who bear the greatest responsibility for serious violations of international humanitarian law ... , including those leaders who, in committing such crimes, have threatened the establishment of and implementation of the peace process in Sierra Leone'.[22] The latter limitation seemingly suggests that

---

[22] Statute of the Special Court (*supra* n 16) Art 1.

leaders of the RUF who reneged on their engagement to peace under the Lomé Peace Agreement, were to be prosecuted, or prosecuted first. The leaders of the AFRC, on the other hand, who may have committed no lesser crimes before the conclusion of the Lomé Peace Agreement, but who have since joined the government and are considered to have contributed to the establishment and implementation of the peace process, would be spared from prosecution, or be prosecuted last. It has been the understanding of the Secretary-General, however, that the reference to leaders who threatened the establishment and implementation of the peace process does not describe an element of the crime, but is a guidance for the Prosecutor in determining his prosecutorial strategy. The commission of any of the statutory crimes without necessarily 'threatening the peace' within the meaning of the Resolution, would not, in his view, detract from the international criminal responsibility otherwise entailed for the accused.[23] When on 10 March 2003 the first list of indictees was released, it included leaders of the RUF, AFRC, and the CDF, some of whom were instrumental in the peace process both at Lomé in 1999, and in Freetown in 2002.[24]

For all the limitations imposed on the personal jurisdiction of the Special Court for Sierra Leone, two additional categories of persons never before prosecuted in an international criminal jurisdiction were included in the personal jurisdiction of the Court: persons between 15 and 18 years of age, 'children' within the definition of the 1989 Convention on the Rights of the Child,[25] and members of UN peace-keeping or other UN-authorized operations.

1. Prosecution of 'juveniles' between 15 and 18 years of age

The acts of brutality and savagery committed by children on a large scale in the last phase of the conflict in Freetown in January 1999 required that this unique feature of the Sierra Leone civil war be addressed in all its horrific

---

[23] Letter from the Secretary-General addressed to the President of the Security Council (12 January 2001) UN Doc S/2001/40. The concurrence of the Council with that interpretation was expressed in the Letter from the President of the Security Council addressed to the Secretary-General (31 January 2001) UN Doc S/2001/95.

[24] On 10 March 2003, seven persons were indicted by the Special Court for war crimes, crimes against humanity, and serious violations of international humanitarian law, and in particular, murder, rape, extermination, acts of terror, sexual slavery, conscription of children into armed forces, and attacks on UN peace-keepers. They included: Foday Sankoh, the leader of the RUF (died of natural causes in detention), Johny Paul Koroma, leader of the 1997 coup d'état who ruled the country until ousted in 1998 and was later part of the coalition government (reportedly killed in Liberia), Sam Bockarie (Mosquito) (subsequently killed in Liberia), and Issa Sesay the RUF rebel commander, Alex Brima a member of the AFRC and Morris Kallon of the RUF, and Hinga Norman, the current Minister of Internal Affairs and the national coordinator of the CDF and the former leader of the Kamajors militia.

[25] Convention on the Rights of the Child, 1989 (1989) 28 ILM 1457.

aspects. Mindful of the moral dilemma of prosecuting child-victims who were transformed into perpetrators through abduction, drugs, physical and psychological abuse, and slavery of all kinds, the Secretary-General proposed that a process of judicial accountability be, in principle, provided for,[26] but that the Prosecutor be instructed that in exercising his discretionary power to prosecute juvenile offenders, he should 'ensure that the child-rehabilitation programme is not placed at risk and that, where appropriate, resort should be had to alternative truth and reconciliation mechanisms, to the extent of their availability'.[27]

In the course of the negotiations, few issues were as passionately debated as the prosecution of juveniles. For many, the very idea of prosecuting children—the traditional object of protection—in an international criminal jurisdiction, alongside mass killers and masterminds of genocide, crimes against humanity, and war crimes, was anathema. For representatives of civil society and childcare local and international NGOs, the prospects of prosecuting children posed a threat to the entire rehabilitation and reintegration programmes. For the Secretary-General and the government of Sierra Leone, it was a question of striking a balance between justice to victims, accountability of perpetrators, and the risks that a large-scale prosecution of juveniles might entail for the ongoing rehabilitation and childcare programmes. For the Security Council, it was ultimately a question of finding a political compromise between the principle of judicial accountability for all, including juveniles, and its impracticality in the circumstances. In the Letter of the President of the Security Council to the Secretary-General, Members of the Council opted for the Truth and Reconciliation Commission as the alternative non-judicial accountability mechanism to handle the plight of children, both as victims and perpetrators.[28]

While it was ultimately a prosecutorial choice not to indict children who committed crimes, but those who 'forced children to commit crimes', the statutory provision on prosecution of juveniles framed the issues of the debate on the role of children in the Sierra Leone conflict, and brought it to the fore of the Sierra Leone national consciousness.

---

[26] Under Art 7(1) of the Statute all necessary guarantees of juvenile justice were to be afforded. Juveniles before the Special Court were accordingly to be treated 'with dignity and a sense of worth, taking into account his or her young age and the desirability of promoting his or her rehabilitation, reintegration into and assumption of a constructive role in society, and in accordance with international human rights standards, in particular the rights of the child'.

[27] Statute of the Special Court (*supra* n 16) Art 15(5).

[28] 'Members of the Council continue to believe it is extremely unlikely that juvenile offenders will in fact come before the Special Court and that other institutions, such as the Truth and Reconciliation Commission, are better suited to address cases involving juveniles' (Letter from the President of the Security Council addressed to the Secretary-General (31 January 2001) UN Doc S/2001/95). On the Truth and Reconciliation Commission for Sierra Leone, see Chapter 9 (Schabas).

2. Peace-keepers

While in a number of peace-keeping operations, and notably in the Congo, Somalia, Bosnia and Herzegovina, and Mozambique, peace-keepers are known to have committed violations of international humanitarian law, no member of a UN peace-keeping operation has ever been prosecuted for any of these crimes before an international criminal jurisdiction. In the realities of the Sierra Leone conflict, however, where members of ECOMOG, the military wing of ECOWAS (Economic Community of West African States), allegedly committed summary executions, the possibility of prosecuting peace-keepers had to be addressed. In introducing, by analogy from the ICC Statute, the principle of 'complementarity', the Statute of the Special Court provides that peace-keepers who 'transgressed'—a code word for the commission of serious violations of international humanitarian law—will first be subject to the primary jurisdiction of their sending state, and may be subject to the jurisdiction of the Special Court only if the sending state is unwilling or unable to investigate or prosecute, and if the Court is authorized by the Security Council to exercise such jurisdiction on the proposal of any state.[29] The authorization in itself, however, would not guarantee the prosecution of those presumed responsible, if, in the absence of a surrender agreement between the Special Court and the sending state, or a Chapter VII Resolution, the 'unwilling or unable' state would refuse to surrender the accused to the jurisdiction of the Special Court.

E. TEMPORAL JURISDICTION

A determination of the temporal jurisdiction of any UN-based tribunal, whether international or mixed, is a time-frame put on the subject matter, personal, and territorial jurisdiction of the tribunal. For the United Nations, such a determination required a choice inclusive of the most notorious crimes in scale or heinous nature, the persons most responsible for their commission, and most distinctive geographical areas. Within the limitations imposed, the choice was to be balanced, objective, and impartial to avoid the perception

---

[29] Statute of the Special Court (*supra* n 16) Art 1(2) and (3). The Security Council proposed provision on the prosecution of peace-keepers before the Special Court for Sierra Leone is of particular interest in the light of the debate that took place in the summer of 2002 over the prospects of prosecuting members of peace-keeping operations before the International Criminal Court (ICC). By contrast to its position in the context of Sierra Leone, the Security Council, by UNSC Res 1422 (2002) (12 July 2002), directed the Court on the basis of Art 16 of the Statute of the ICC, to decline jurisdiction for a 12-month period in respect of any members of peace-keeping operations mandated or authorized by the Security Council, whose contributing states are not party to the Rome Statute and 'not commence or proceed with investigative or prosecution of any such case, unless the Security Council decide otherwise'.

that the exclusion of any groups of crimes, persons, or geographical areas was intended as a political statement.

For the relevant government, however, the determination of the temporal jurisdiction was a question, primarily, of historical truth. In the establishment of all UN-based tribunals, with the exception of ICTY, the governments concerned requested the extension of the temporal jurisdiction of the tribunal to put the events in historical perspective. For this reason, the government of Rwanda asked the Security Council that October 1990, rather than 1 January 1994, be determined as the commencement date of the temporal jurisdiction of ICTR to ensure that the massacres of 1991, 1992, and 1993 which preceded the 1994 genocide—their 'pilot projects' in the words of the then Rwandan Ambassador—be included in the temporal jurisdiction of the International Criminal Tribunal for Rwanda (ICTR). For this reason also, the government of Cambodia proposed that the temporal jurisdiction of the Extraordinary Chambers commence at 1971 to comprise the period of the US bombing campaign in Cambodia, and the government of Sierra Leone requested that the temporal jurisdiction of the Special Court be backdated to 1991, the beginning of the Sierra Leone conflict.

In both Cambodia and Sierra Leone, the demands of the governments were put forward at a relatively late stage of the negotiations, and in the case of Cambodia as a negotiating strategy. In both cases, the temporal jurisdiction remained as originally agreed: in Cambodia, from 17 April 1975 to 6 January 1979, the period of the Khmer Rouge regime, and in Sierra Leone, beginning at 30 November 1996, the date of the Abidjan Peace Agreement.[30]

F. THE ORGANIZATIONAL STRUCTURE OF THE MIXED TRIBUNALS

Just as in the case of the ad hoc international tribunals, the mixed tribunals for Sierra Leone and Cambodia are conceived as self-contained entities, with the Chambers, Prosecutor's Office, and the Registry forming part of one and the same structure. Unlike the former, however, they are distinguished by their mixed composition of national and international judges, prosecutors, and administrative support staff.[31]

---

[30] The choice of the commencement date was justified by the Secretary-General on the grounds that it would put the Sierra Leone conflict in perspective without unnecessarily extending the temporal jurisdiction of the Special Court and creating a heavy burden for the prosecution. It would also ensure that the most serious crimes committed by all parties and armed groups, in rural areas, the countryside and the capital Freetown, would be included in the jurisdiction of the Special Court ('Report of the Secretary-General' (*supra* n 15) [25]–[27]). For a fuller discussion of the temporal jurisdiction of the Special Court, see Chapter 7 (Smith).

[31] On the staffing of internationalized tribunals, see Chapter 12 (Romano).

The organizational structure of the Special Court for Sierra Leone is simple and minimalist in nature. It is composed of a Trial Chamber of three judges, of whom two are international, an Appeals Chamber of five judges, of whom three are international, and of an international Prosecutor and a Registrar. A Management Committee consisting of the major donors to the Special Court was formed, though not as part of the institutional structure of the Court, to 'assist the Secretary-General in obtaining adequate funding and provide advice and policy direction on all non-judicial aspects of the operation of the Court, including questions of efficiency'.[32]

The Extraordinary Chambers, as conceived under the Agreement, is a two-tiered court composed of a Trial Chamber and a Supreme Court Chamber, with an additional Pre-Trial Chamber constituted ad hoc to deal with eventual disagreements between the co-prosecutors and the co-investigating judges. Both the trial Chamber and the Pre-Trial Chamber are composed of five judges each, of whom two are international, and the Supreme Court Chamber is composed of seven judges, of whom three are international judges.[33] The investigations are directed by two co-investigating judges: one Cambodian and one international, and the prosecution, by two co-prosecutors similarly composed. The Registry, or the Office of the Administration is headed by a Cambodian Director and an international Deputy Director.

In comparison to the skeletal structure of the Special Court for Sierra Leone, the Extraordinary Chambers for Cambodia, though less convoluted and heavily staffed than originally conceived, are layered with deadlock-breaking mechanisms designed to achieve an artificial balance between the national and international components, while maintaining the numerical majority of the former. With a majority of Cambodian judges and prosecutors, however, drawn from a weak and politicized criminal justice system, the Extraordinary Chambers are likely to command little credibility.

---

[32] The Agreement between the United Nations and the Government of Sierra Leone (*supra* n 16) Art 7.

[33] The numerical majority of Cambodian judges in the two Chambers and the likelihood of a decision-making process along nationality lines, created the need for a qualified, so-called 'super-majority' vote, in which at least one foreign judge should have participated. An affirmative vote of a majority of judges-plus-one was, accordingly, required for any decision of the Trial Chamber and the Supreme Court Chamber, with the result that decisions which acquire a simple majority only would be non-conclusive. Decisions on conviction, in particular, adopted by a simple majority would be insufficient to convict, yet not enough to acquit, and in the circumstances would require the release of the accused. In the Pre-Trial Chamber, however, the situation is reversed, and on decisions to 'investigate or prosecute', a 'super majority vote' would be required to *block* an investigation or prosecution. Otherwise put, a decision by a simple majority would have the effect of allowing the investigation or prosecution to proceed.

G. THE RELATIONSHIP BETWEEN THE 'LAW OF THE MIXED TRIBUNALS' AND THE LAW OF THE SEAT—THE VALIDITY OF AMNESTIES

With the establishment of the mixed tribunals in the state of the seat and the concurrent operation of an international and national jurisdictions, questions of 'conflict of laws' were bound to arise. In Cambodia and Sierra Leone, the single most important question was the validity before the mixed tribunal of the amnesty granted under national law, and the extent of its applicability to the crime of genocide, crimes against humanity, and war crimes.[34]

1. Cambodia: the amnesty to Ieng Sary

By a 1996 Decree signed by King Sihanouk, Ieng Sary was granted amnesty in respect of his conviction in the 1979 trial on the charge of genocide, and for the crime of membership in the Khmer Rouge in violation of the 1994 Law on the Outlawing of the Democratic Kampuchea Group.[35] He was the only member of the Khmer Rouge leadership formally amnestied for crimes committed in connection with the Khmer Rouge regime.

Refusing to revoke the amnesty on grounds of its constitutionality,[36] the Cambodian government has undertaken in the Law on the Establishment of the Extraordinary Chambers not to request any further amnesty or pardon for persons falling within the jurisdiction of the Chambers.[37] It thus implicitly sanctioned the validity of the amnesty already granted. For its part, the United Nations maintained that while the grant of amnesty is a matter for the national authorities, its effect cannot extend to international crimes, such as, genocide, crimes against humanity, or war crimes. It proposed that in addition to the future-oriented undertaking, it be stipulated in the Law that amnesty granted in respect of any of the international crimes falling within the jurisdiction of the Extraordinary Chambers shall not be a bar to prosecution. The Law, as promulgated, contained no such provision. In reproducing

---

[34] In the case of Sierra Leone, the concurrent operation of both jurisdictions raised, in addition, the question of the relationship between the Special Court, an international law-created institution, and the Truth and Reconciliation Commission (TRC), a national law-created body. On the TRC, see in this book, Chapter 9 (Schabas).

[35] The amnesty Decree read, in part, as follows:'Amnesty is granted to Mr Ieng Sary, former Deputy Prime Minister responsible for Foreign Affairs in the Government of Democratic Kampuchea, who was sentenced to death and his property confiscated by order of the People's Revolutionary Court of Phnom Penh dated 19 August 1979 and with regard to penalties stipulated by the Law on the Outlawing of the Democratic Kampuchea Group which was promulgated by Royal Proclamation ... dated 15 July 1994'.

[36] Under Arts 27 and 90, respectively, of the 1993 Constitution of the Kingdom of Cambodia, the King has the right to grant amnesties and the Assembly, the power to approve amnesty laws: AP Blaustein and GH Flanz (eds) *Constitutions of the Countries of the World* (Oceana Publications 1994) Release 94–8.

[37] Law on the Establishment of the Extraordinary Chambers (*supra* n 10) Art 14.

Article 14 of the Law, Article 11 of the Agreement refers—though not by name—to the single amnesty granted to Ieng Sary, and provides that 'The United Nations and the Royal Government of Cambodia agree that the scope of this pardon is a matter to be decided by the Extraordinary Chambers'. Amnesty was thus recognized, in principle, subject to the court determination of its scope, validity, and applicability in the circumstances.

2. Sierra Leone: the amnesty to Foday Sankoh and the membership of the RUF

Under the Lomé Peace Agreement of 7 July 1999, concluded between the government of Sierra Leone and the RUF, 'absolute and free pardon' was granted to Foday Sankoh in person, and to the collectivity of combatants and collaborators 'in respect of anything done by them in pursuit of their objectives'. In that connection also, the government has undertaken not to take any legal action against any member of the rebel groups 'in respect of anything done by them in pursuit of their objectives' since March 1991 and until the signing of the Agreement.[38] The Special Representative of the Secretary-General who signed the Agreement as witness on behalf of the United Nations, appended a disclaimer to his signature which stated that the amnesty provision under the Agreement shall not apply to international crimes of genocide, crimes against humanity, war crimes, and other serious violations of international humanitarian law.[39] This position was later endorsed by the Security Council in its Resolution 1315 (2000).

With the incorporation of the Lomé Peace Agreement in the Sierra Leone Special Court (Ratification) Act 1999, the amnesty clause it contained became part of the law of the land. In the Statute of the Special Court, however, it was explicitly invalidated in respect of the international crimes falling within the jurisdiction of the Court.[40] A dual approach was thus adopted to the question of amnesty and its validity depending on the nature of the crimes, the time of their commission, and the jurisdiction before which they would be prosecutable. Accordingly, amnesty would bar the prosecution of all crimes, whether national or international, before the national courts of Sierra Leone; it would also bar the prosecution before the Special Court of common crimes committed before 1999. Amnesty, however, would not bar the prosecution before the Special Court of international crimes committed

---

[38] Peace Agreement between the Government of Sierra Leone and the Revolutionary United Front of Sierra Leone, Lomé, 1999, UN Doc S/1999/777, Art IX.

[39] Report of the Secretary-General (*supra* n 15) [23].

[40] Article 10 of the Statute provides in this respect: 'An amnesty granted to any person falling within the jurisdiction of the Special Court in respect of the crimes referred to in articles 2 to 4 of the present Statute shall not be a bar to prosecution'.

In determining the commencement date of the temporal jurisdiction of the Special Court at 30 November 1996, prior to the conclusion of the Lomé Agreement (7 July 1999), amnesty was also implicitly rejected.

at any time within its temporal jurisdiction, and of common crimes committed after 1999.[41]

In the negotiations on the establishment of the Special Court and the Extraordinary Chambers, the United Nations sought to define in retrospect the lawful contours of the amnesty granted and limit its effect to common crimes and crimes against the state (ie, insurrection and coup d'état). It sought above all to establish legal and moral standards for UN cooperation in the establishment of any UN-assisted mixed jurisdiction. Its success, or otherwise, in any given case, would be a test of the strength of its negotiating position.

H. THE UN-ADMINISTERED COURTS IN KOSOVO AND EAST TIMOR

At the time when the UN Secretariat was negotiating the establishment of the Special Court for Sierra Leone and the Extraordinary Chambers for Cambodia, the United Nations Transitional Administration in East Timor (UNTAET) established the 'Panels with Exclusive Jurisdiction over Serious Criminal Offences',[42] and the United Nations Interim Administration Mission in Kosovo (UNMIK) introduced throughout the courts of Kosovo a system of mixed composition of judges, prosecutors, and defence counsel.[43] Commonly associated with the mixed tribunals for Sierra Leone and for Cambodia because of the apparent similarities in their mixed jurisdiction and composition, the UN-administered courts in Kosovo and East Timor were fundamentally different in the circumstances of their establishment, and the legislative process by which they were established.

The UN Administrations for Kosovo and East Timor were established almost in parallel by Security Council Resolutions 1244 (1999) and 1272 (1999) to administer in circumstances of post-conflict societies, the territory of Kosovo pending a final determination of its status, and the territory of East Timor in transition to independence. The UN Administrations, entrusted with a comprehensive mandate for humanitarian, governance, economic reconstruction, and sustainable development, were endowed with all-embracing legislative and administrative powers, including the administration of justice. In the case of East Timor, in particular, UNTAET was also required by Resolution 1272 to bring to justice those responsible for serious

---

[41] DJ Macaluso 'Absolute and Free Pardon: The Effect of the Amnesty Provision in the Lomé Peace Agreement on the Jurisdiction of the Special Court for Sierra Leone' (2001) 27 *Brooklyn Journal of International Law* 347.

[42] On the Special Panels in East Timor, see Chapter 5 (De Bertodano).

[43] On the internationalized courts in Kosovo, see Chapter 4 (Cady/Booth), and Chapter 3 (Cerone/Baldwin).

violations of human rights and international humanitarian law committed in East Timor in the aftermath of the 30 August 1999 popular consultation. The UN Transitional Administrations inherited in both territories a virtually non-existent, devastated administration of justice, left practically decapitated with the massive flight of core members of the legal profession, judges, prosecutors, defence lawyers, and court administrators of Serb and Indonesian origin, respectively.

1. The Special Panels of Judges in East Timor

Faced with the challenge and inspired by the model of the mixed tribunals for Cambodia and Sierra Leone, UNTAET promulgated Regulation 2000/15 ('On the Establishment of Panels with Exclusive Jurisdiction Over Serious Criminal Offences)'. The Regulation establishes mixed panels of judges within the District Court and the Court of Appeals in Dili, with exclusive jurisdiction over the crime of genocide, war crimes, and crimes against humanity,[44] and a selected number of common crimes committed between 1 January and 25 October 1999. Each panel is composed of three judges, of whom two are international and one East Timorese, and a panel of five judges composed of three international and two East Timorese may be established in the Appeals Court in cases of special importance or gravity (section 22). The prosecution is conducted by the Serious Crimes Unit—a mixed composition unit operating as part of UNTAET and its successor mission UNMISET (United Nations Mission of Support in East Timor) under the authority of the General Prosecutor. No separate Registry was envisaged for the Special Panels, which like the District Court and the Court of Appeals are serviced by the existing court management.[45] Established by UNTAET Regulation, the 'Special Panels of Judges' were part of the existing court system of East Timor throughout the transitional period and post-independence.[46]

---

[44] Sections 4–6 of the Regulation. The definition of the crimes, with the exception of the crime of genocide, incorporates almost verbatim the definition of the crimes under the ICC Statute (Arts 7 and 8), not in force at the time of their alleged commission. It pays little regard to their relevance in the realities of East Timor, or their customary or conventional international law nature. The universal jurisdiction as defined in s 2 of the Regulation with respect to these crimes is likewise all-embracing. Accordingly, the Special Panels of Judges have jurisdiction irrespective of where, by whom, or against whom such crimes have been committed; irrespective also of the capabilities of the nascent, rudimentary East Timorese Administration of Justice and its powers to enforce such universal jurisdiction.

[45] For a critical note on the operation of the Special Panels, see Linton (*supra* n 8) 202–29.

[46] The continued operation of the Special Panels of Judges as mixed composition institutions through independence was guaranteed in the transitional provisions of the Constitution of the Democratic Republic of East Timor. Section 165 provides for the continued applicability of all Laws and Regulations in force in East Timor at the time of its adoption, to the extent of their consistency with the Constitution. More particularly, Art 163 of the Constitution provides for the continued operation of 'the collective judicial instance existing in East Timor, composed of

2. *Mixed composition of judges and prosecutors in the courts of Kosovo*

The attempt by UNMIK to establish a Kosovo War and Ethnic Crimes Court ('KWECC') as a special court of mixed composition and exclusive jurisdiction over serious violations of international humanitarian law and other ethnically motivated crimes, failed for a number of reasons.[47] However, the prospects of conducting complex prosecution of war crimes and crimes against humanity in a post-conflict Kosovan society before ethnic Albanian-dominated courts, in an atmosphere of fear and intimidation threatening the impartiality and independence of the judiciary, compelled the introduction into the existing court system of an international component of judges and prosecutors. It would be their task to train and monitor the local judges, enhance the existing standards of justice, and remedy a widely spread perception of a biased judicial process.

International judges and prosecutors were, accordingly, appointed or assigned on an as-needed basis or at the request of the prosecutor, the defence, or the accused to take part in a judicial or prosecutorial process of serious violations of human rights and international humanitarian law under the applicable Kosovo Criminal Code. A mixed composition of international judges and prosecutors was first introduced through UNMIK Regulation 2000/6[48] in the district court of Mitrovicë/Mitrovica as a response to the ethnic violence in the divided city. It was further extended throughout the courts of Kosovo by Regulation 2000/34 on the Appointment and Removal from Office of International Judges and International Prosecutors. Regulation 2000/64 on Assignment of International Judges and Prosecutors, empowers the Special Representative of the Secretary-General, upon a petition by a prosecutor, an accused, or defence counsel, to appoint an international prosecutor, an international judge, or a panel of three judges, of whom at least two are international (the so-called 'Regulation 64 Panels').

The success of the Kosovo 'mixed courts' was only partial. The limited number of international judges, their sporadic allocation to cases, and their marginal influence on decisions taken by a majority of local judges led in many cases to unequal treatment of defendants, and contributed little to the professional quality of the judicial process or its standards of justice. Their very presence in the courts of Kosovo, however, dispelled, in part at least, a perception of bias and judicial partiality.[49]

national and international judges with competencies to judge serious crimes committed between the 1st of January and the 25th of October 1999', for as long as it would deem necessary to conclude the cases under investigation.

[47] On these reasons, see further Chapter 3 (Cerone /Baldwin).

[48] UNMIK Regulation 2000/6 (On the Appointment and Removal from Office of International Judges and International Prosecutors).

[49] OSCE (Organization for Security and Cooperation in Europe) Mission in Kosovo, 'Report 9 On the Administration of Justice' (March 2002) 6–7; International Crisis Group,

3. The Special Chamber in the State Court of Bosnia and Herzegovina

By the end of 2002, a mixed court of a third kind was envisaged within the State Court of Bosnia and Herzegovina, as part of the overall completion strategy of ICTY. Constrained to wind down its Trial Chamber operation, at least by 2008, ICTY devised a two-pronged strategy whereby middle-level accused awaiting trial would be deferred to local courts in Bosnia and Herzegovina, thus allowing ICTY, in the words of the Security Council, to 'concentrate its work on the prosecution and trial of the civilian, military and paramilitary leaders suspected of being responsible for serious violations of international humanitarian law committed in the territory of the former Yugoslavia since 1991, rather than on minor actors'.[50]

In deferring to the local courts, however, ICTY had first to satisfy itself that the national jurisdictions are able to handle the cases deferred to them 'effectively and consistently with internationally recognized standards of human rights and due process'.[51] Realizing that members of the judiciary in Bosnia and Herzegovina still lack professional competence and the necessary experience for the conduct of complex prosecution of war crimes, and that both the judiciary and prosecution are ethnically biased, and politically and financially dependent on the executive and the legislature, and that corruption, intimidation, and acts of violence against members of the legal profession are widespread in many parts of the Federation, ICTY concluded that only a 'court within a court' in the form of a mixed composition Special Chamber constituted at a state-level court could guarantee prosecution in full respect for the integrity of the judicial process, impartiality, and due process of law.

In a report prepared jointly by the President, the Prosecutor, and the Registrar of ICTY on the *Judicial Status of the International Criminal Tribunal for the Former Yugoslavia and the Prospects for Referring Certain Cases to National Courts*,[52] ICTY recommended that a Chamber with the jurisdiction to try accused referred to it by ICTY be constituted within the State Court of Bosnia and Herzegovina, and include, initially, and until a domestic capacity is built, an international component alongside national, in its judiciary, prosecution, and court management.[53] It is envisaged that the Special Chamber would operate under the laws of Bosnia and Herzegovina, as reformed to

---

Finding the Balance: The Scales of Justice in Kosovo, ICG Balkans Report No 134 (Pristina/Brussels, 12 September 2002).

[50] Statement by the President of the Security Council UN Doc S/PRST/2002/21.

[51] Letter from the Secretary-General addressed to the President of the Security Council (17 June 2002) UN Doc S/2002/678.

[52] 'Report on the Judicial Status of the International Criminal Tribunal for the Former Yugoslavia and the Prospects for Referring Certain Cases to National Courts' (12 June 2002) UN Doc S/2002/678, Enclosure.

[53] ibid para 84.

incorporate violations of laws and customs of war and procedural guarantees of fair trial and due process of law. It would consist of two trial panels, each with three judges, of whom two will be international, and an appellate panel with three judges, of whom two are international. The Prosecutor's Office will include a War Crimes Department headed initially by an international Deputy Prosecutor.

The mixed composition panels in the Dili courts, in the courts of Kosovo, and the one proposed at the State Court in Bosnia and Herzegovina, were established to prosecute war crimes, crimes against humanity, and other serious violations of international humanitarian law in conditions where the local administration of justice is either non-existent, ethnically biased, inefficient, or otherwise inapt to conduct prosecution of such complexity and scope consistently with international standards of justice, impartiality, and due process of law. The Special Panels of Judges in East Timor were established virtually in a legal vacuum. In the absence of adequate criminal legislation, court infrastructure, trained judges, prosecutors, and court administrators, the need for a special panel of judges as a self-contained entity operating under a specific criminal legislation enacted for the purpose, was compelling. In the courts of Kosovo, by contrast, the appointment of international judges and prosecutors, including Regulation 64 Panels to serve in an already functioning court system (though ineffective, inefficient, and for the most part mono-ethnic) responded to the need to remedy a perception of bias, ethnic discrimination, and judicial partiality. The Special Chamber in the State Court of Bosnia and Herzegovina—yet another form of a mixed-composition 'court within a court'—is envisaged within the overall 'completion strategy' of ICTY as the only one court whose enhanced standards of justice would permit the deferral to it of pending prosecution.

I. THE DIVERSITY OF MIXED TRIBUNALS: IN SEARCH OF A MODEL JURISDICTION

For all the similarities between the mixed tribunals in their subject matter jurisdiction, their mixed international and national composition, and their linkage to the United Nations, no single model of internationalized jurisdiction has yet emerged. Different in the historical-political circumstances of their establishment, the mixed tribunals differ mainly in their legal nature and the nature of their founding instrument.

The Special Court for Sierra Leone, by far the preferred model of any UN-assisted mixed jurisdiction, was established by Agreement between the United Nations and the government of Sierra Leone, having the legal status of an international treaty-based organ. The Extraordinary Chambers were established by law, and although technically within the existing court system of

Cambodia, they are, in fact, a self-contained court with a separate organizational structure of judges, prosecutors, and court managers, whose operation is conditioned in its entirety on the implementation of the Agreement between the United Nations and the government. The mixed composition panels in the UN-administered territories are established by law or Regulation having the same effect. Operating under national law and as part of the existing court system, their legal status is that of national courts, their mixed composition and jurisdiction notwithstanding.

The choice of the founding instrument, in the case of the Special Court for Sierra Leone and the Extraordinary Chambers for Cambodia, was political. In the negotiating process on the establishment of the Special Court for Sierra Leone, the Council Members, the Management Committee, the UN Secretariat, and the government were united by a vision of an international-law created mixed tribunal, of substantial international component, operating in full respect for international standards of justice. In the case of Cambodia, a divided approach made it possible for the government to impose a national-law created tribunal composed predominantly of Cambodian nationals having a majority vote in all organs of the court, yet funded in its entirety by international funds. In the case of the UN-administered territories, the choice of the founding instrument was imposed by the nature of the UN Administration acting as the de facto government. No negotiating process preceded the establishment of the mixed composition panels for East Timor and Kosovo, and no political constraints inhibited the sole judicial discretionary power of the UN Transitional Administrator.

The diversity of mixed jurisdictions imposed by the specificities of each post-conflict situation has shifted the focus of the discussion from a search for a model jurisdiction to setting the benchmarks for UN cooperation in the establishment of a mixed jurisdiction. While the terms of the UN mandate and the choice of the constitutive instrument is ultimately a political choice, it remains the Secretariat's preference that a UN-assisted mixed jurisdiction be established as a treaty-based organ, whose applicable law and Rules of Procedure and Evidence are primarily international, whose organizational structure is a simple two-tiered court, and its international component is substantial with a majority of international judges, an international Prosecutor, and a Registrar. Should a national law containing the same international features be chosen as the mixed-tribunal founding instrument, it should be annexed to the Agreement and made an integral part thereof to ensure that it is not unilaterally amended by the government.

But whatever may have been the legal nature of its constitutive instrument, the success of any mixed tribunal will ultimately depend on the readiness of the government to comply with its orders and requests, and on the cooperation of third states and their willingness to sustain its operation through funds and personnel. For the community of donors, however, to be willing to contribute, it must be convinced that the mixed tribunal is independent, free from political interference, and affords guarantees of fairness, objectivity, and impartiality of the legal process. For the United Nations, the success of any mixed tribunal established in partnership with the national administration of justice will be measured also by its legacy of enhanced international standards of justice and a generation of skilled judges and prosecutors trained in the principles and procedures of international criminal justice.

Part II
Internationalized Criminal Courts and Tribunals

3

Explaining and Evaluating the UNMIK Court System

John Cerone and Clive Baldwin***

A. INTRODUCTION

The Kosovo courts[1] have been counted among the so-called 'hybrid' or 'internationalized' courts.[2] As with the Special Panels in East Timor ('Special Panels'), the Special Court for Sierra Leone ('Special Court'), and the envisioned Extraordinary Chambers in Cambodia ('Extraordinary Chambers'), the Kosovo court system is composed of both national and international judges and prosecutors, and is competent to apply laws with both a national and international character.

Yet, unlike the Special Court, which was established by treaty, and the Extraordinary Chambers, which would be created on the basis of domestic legislation, the Kosovo court system derives its competence from Regulations of the United Nations Interim Administration Mission in Kosovo (UNMIK), the authority of which is ultimately derived from a Chapter VII Resolution of the United Nations Security Council. While East Timor's Special Panels share a similar legal basis, they may be distinguished from the Kosovo court system on the grounds that international criminal law is expressly included within their subject matter jurisdiction and the fact that they are a discrete part of the East Timor judiciary. The Kosovo court system is unique in that there is no fixed internationalized court or panel.

* Professor John Cerone is Director of the Center for International Law & Policy at the New England School of Law. He previously served as Legal System Monitor and then Human Rights Legal Advisor with the OSCE-led Pillar of the United Nations Interim Administration Mission in Kosovo. The authors would like to thank Karen Corrie and Chante Lasco for research assistance. The information contained in this chapter is accurate as of summer 2002. The views expressed are solely those of the authors.

** Clive Baldwin is Head of International Advocacy at Minority Rights Group International. He previously served as Human Rights Legal Advisor with the OSCE-led Pillar of the United Nations Interim Administration Mission in Kosovo.

[1] The scope of this chapter is limited to the Kosovo court system established under the auspices of the United Nations Interim Administration Mission in Kosovo (UNMIK). It does not include any parallel court systems that may exist in Kosovo outside of UNMIK's authority.

[2] The classification of a court as 'internationalized' may rest on a variety of criteria, such as legal basis, function/mandate, location within or without the domestic court system, subject matter jurisdiction, oversight, and composition (personnel). Depending upon the criteria employed, an internationalized court may appear to have more of an international or more of a national character.

Rather, the international judges permeate the court system, sitting on panels throughout Kosovo on a case-by-case basis. The Kosovo court system is also distinguished by the fact that it is not mandated to apply directly international criminal law,[3] and the fact that its competence overlaps with an international criminal tribunal created by the Security Council (ie, the International Criminal Tribunal for the former Yugoslavia (ICTY)).

This chapter describes the nature and composition of the Kosovo court system, providing an overview of the legal framework within which it operates and highlighting the features that make it unique. It also evaluates the strengths and weaknesses of this form of internationalized court, both in design and execution, focusing primarily on the effectiveness of introducing international judges and prosecutors into the system.

B. LEGAL FRAMEWORK

1. UN Security Council Resolution 1244

According to UN Security Council Resolution 1244, UNMIK was mandated to 'provide an interim administration for Kosovo under which the people of Kosovo can enjoy substantial autonomy within the Federal Republic of Yugoslavia'.[4] It was made specifically responsible for, inter alia:

[p]romoting the establishment ... of substantial autonomy and self-government in Kosovo ... ; [p]erforming basic civilian administrative functions ... ; [o]rganizing and overseeing the development of provisional institutions for democratic and autonomous self-government ... ; [m]aintaining civil law and order; [p]rotecting and promoting human rights.[5]

'All legislative and executive powers, including the administration of the judiciary', were vested in UNMIK, to be exercised by UNMIK's chief administrator, the Special Representative of the Secretary-General (SRSG).[6]

The SRSG exercises his legislative powers primarily through the promulgation of UNMIK Regulations, which, together with Resolution 1244, are the supreme form of law in Kosovo.[7] As Resolution 1244 serves as the legal

---

[3] As explained below, the Kosovo courts apply international criminal law through the vehicle of pre-existing Yugoslav legislation.

[4] UNSC Res 1244 para 10.

[5] ibid para 11.

[6] 'Report of the Secretary-General on the United Nations Interim Administration Mission in Kosovo' ('Report of the Secretary-General') S/1999/779 (12 July 1999) para 39.

[7] ibid para 35 ff. Since mid-2000, in accordance with its mandate, UNMIK has gradually transferred the bulk of its authority to local bodies. However, even after the adoption in 2001 of the Constitutional Framework for Kosovo, UNMIK remains supreme with the SRSG retaining ultimate authority. In particular, the SRSG retains full control over the judiciary.

basis for the authority of UNMIK and the SRSG, the binding legal character of UNMIK Regulations is also derived from this source.

2. *The applicable law*

Following the withdrawal of the Serbian and Yugoslav forces, Kosovo was left in a law-and-order vacuum. Among the first acts of the SRSG in the summer of 1999 was the establishment of the law applicable in Kosovo.

While the extent to which the SRSG was mandated to fashion the applicable law was initially unclear,[8] he ultimately replaced the applicable law entirely. The law applicable in Kosovo, as established by the SRSG, was derived from four sources: Yugoslav law, Serbian law, Kosovan law, and international law.

The applicable law in Kosovo was laid down initially in UNMIK Regulation 1999/1 and later UNMIK Regulation 1999/24.[9] The latter Regulation took as its starting point[10] the national law in force on 22 March 1989—a date prior to the revocation of Kosovo's autonomy and a time when Kosovo was still largely regulated under Kosovan legislation.[11]

---

[8] It seemed from the initial Report of the Secretary-General that UNMIK would only be empowered to change the applicable law to the extent necessary to comply with human rights law or to otherwise carry out its mandate. See 'Report of the Secretary-General' (*supra* n 6) para 36 ('In implementing its mandate in the territory of Kosovo, UNMIK will respect the laws of the Federal Republic of Yugoslavia and of the Republic of Serbia insofar as they do not conflict with internationally recognized human rights standards or with regulations issued by the Special Representative in the fulfilment of the mandate given to the United Nations by the Security Council.'); ibid para 39 ('[The SRSG] will be empowered to regulate within the areas of his responsibilities laid down by the Security Council in its resolution 1244 (1999). In doing so, he may change, repeal or suspend existing laws *to the extent necessary* for the carrying out of his functions, or where existing laws are *incompatible with* the mandate, aims and purposes of the interim civil administration'); and ibid para 75 ('UNMIK will initiate a process to amend current legislation in Kosovo, *as necessary,* including criminal laws, the law on internal affairs and the law on public peace and order, in a way consistent with the objectives of Security Council resolution 1244 (1999) and internationally recognized human rights standards') (emphasis added).

[9] The adoption of Regulation 1999/1 resulted in widespread protest within the Kosovo Albanian Community because it retained as the applicable law the law in force in Kosovo in March 1999, a time at which the province was primarily governed by Serbian law. See also Chapter 4 (Cady/Booth).

[10] Regulation 1999/24 further provided: 'If a court of competent jurisdiction or a body or person required to implement a provision of the law, determines that a subject matter or situation is not covered by the laws set out in section 1.1 of the present regulation but is covered by another law in force in Kosovo after 22 March 1989 which is not discriminatory and which complies with section 1.3 of the present regulation, the court, body or person shall, as an exception, apply that law'. Thus, where a gap in the law was filled by a later-applicable provision of Yugoslav or Serbian law that complied with human rights standards, that later applicable provision would be applied. However, as the distinction between a gap-filler and an amendment is not always clear, the implementation of this provision has the potential to produce its own complications.

[11] Although the law in force on 22 March 1989 included Yugoslav and Serbian law, much of what in 1999 was regulated by Serbian law was in 1989 still regulated by Kosovan law. Thus, the new regulation replaced much of the previously applicable (under Reg 1999/1) Serbian law with Kosovan law.

While the bulk of the law applicable under UNMIK was derived from pre-existing domestic law, both international criminal and human rights law may be applied by the Kosovo courts. With regard to the former, international law is applied indirectly, through the vehicle of pre-existing domestic legislation. International human rights law, in contrast, has been rendered directly applicable by UNMIK Regulation.

I. International criminal law

Unlike East Timor, where the international law on genocide, war crimes, and crimes against humanity was incorporated by UN Regulation,[12] international criminal law is applicable in Kosovo through pre-existing domestic legislation.[13]

The Yugoslav Federal Criminal Code, which remained applicable through the promulgation of Regulation 1999/24, prescribes punishment for the crime of genocide, as well as various war crimes. However, crimes against humanity, as that category of crimes has come to be understood in international law, are not proscribed as such.[14]

The definition of genocide, set forth in Article 141 of the Federal Republic of Yugoslavia (FRY) Code, is modelled closely after the definition set forth in the 1948 Genocide Convention. However, the list of genocidal acts set forth in FRY law differs in that it includes 'forcible dislocation of the population'. This is particularly significant in light of the fact that this appears to have been the most widespread abuse perpetrated in Kosovo by Yugoslav and Serbian forces during the armed conflict.

The FRY Criminal Code also establishes individual criminal responsibility for the breach of a wide array of substantive norms of international humanitarian law—far more than is expressly required by the Geneva Conventions.[15] Articles 142 to 153 enumerate an extensive range of criminal

---

[12] See UNTAET Reg 2000/15.

[13] However, as noted above, such legislation was rendered applicable by UNMIK Regulation.

[14] However, as Yugoslavia has a monist legal system (see Art 16 of the FRY Constitution), it has been suggested that individuals could be prosecuted directly under international law for crimes against humanity. However, as no specific penalty is prescribed for crimes against humanity, strict application of the principle *nulla poena sine lege* might present an obstacle to this approach. To overcome this issue, ICTY looks to penalties for comparable crimes set forth in domestic law. While this approach may be acceptable for an international tribunal with a Chapter VII UN Charter-mandated jurisdiction, it is another matter for a forum acting essentially as an ordinary domestic court to adopt this approach. But see UNMIK Reg 2001/1 prohibiting trials *in absentia* for 'serious violations of international humanitarian law, as defined in Chapter XVI of the applicable Yugoslav Criminal Code or in the Rome Statute of the International Criminal Court'. The Regulation appears to contemplate the possibility of prosecutions for crimes under international law other than those expressly set forth in the FRY Criminal Code.

[15] Indeed, the FRY law on war crimes was cited in the International Committee of the Red Cross (ICRC) Commentaries for its expansive scope, not limiting itself to the mandatory

violations of the laws of war, including: war crimes against the wounded and sick,[16] civilians,[17] and prisoners of war;[18] denial of quarter;[19] marauding;[20] making use of prohibited means of warfare;[21] violating the protection granted to bearers of flags of truce;[22] impeding or preventing the wounded and sick or prisoners of war from exercising their rights under international law;[23] destroying cultural and historical monuments;[24] instigating an aggressive war;[25] and misusing international emblems (eg flags or emblems of the United Nations or Red Cross).[26]

In addition to the prohibition of ordering or committing these acts set forth in each article, Article 145 prescribes punishment for instigating or organizing a group to commit genocide or war crimes. Furthermore, the general part of the FRY Code makes broad provision for accomplice liability.[27] While the Code does not expressly provide for command responsibility, as that form of responsibility is understood in international law, it has been suggested that Yugoslavia's[28] ratification of Additional Protocol I to the Geneva Conventions of 1949 could serve as an adequate legal basis for prosecuting on the basis of command responsibility.[29]

While these provisions are set forth in domestic law, they retain their distinctively international character. This is particularly true for the law on war crimes, which refers back to international law for its application.[30]

criminalization of 'grave breaches' of the 1949 Geneva Conventions. See ICRC Commentary to the provisions of the Fourth Geneva Convention on repression of breaches.

[16] FRY Code art 143.

[17] ibid art 142.

[18] ibid art 144.

[19] ibid art 146. Article 146 prohibits killing or wounding an enemy who has laid down arms or unconditionally surrendered or has no means for defence (ie enemies placed *hors de combat*), and ordering that there be no survivors.

[20] ibid art 147.

[21] ibid art 148. 'Prohibited means of warfare' likely refers to the Hague law, which is the branch of humanitarian law that regulates the methods and means of warfare as set forth primarily in the Hague Conventions of 1899.

[22] FRY Code art 149.

[23] ibid art 150.

[24] ibid art 151.

[25] ibid art 152.

[26] ibid art 153.

[27] Criminal responsibility arises for anyone participating in one of the above acts in some way, including aiding, inciting, or organizing a group to perform the act: FRY Code arts 22–26. Note that attempt to commit the above acts is also punishable: ibid art 19.

[28] As of 4 February 2003, the name of the former Federal Republic of Yugoslavia was changed to Serbia and Montenegro.

[29] Report of the Legal Systems Monitoring System, OSCE Mission in Kosovo 'Kosovo's War Crimes Trials: A Review', (September 2002). This Report also notes that under art 239 of the Code, the fact that an act was carried out pursuant to superior orders is not a defence where 'the order has been directed toward committing a war crime or any other grave criminal offense, or if it was obvious that the carrying out of the order constitutes a criminal offense'.

[30] The relevant articles essentially make a *renvoi* to international law. For example, art 142 begins, 'Whoever *in violation of rules of international law effective at the time of war, armed*

II. International human rights law

The FRY Constitution provides that international law is an integral part of the domestic legal order. However, UNMIK went a step further and expressly incorporated international human rights law into the applicable law. The SRSG signed several regulations requiring the application of international human rights standards in Kosovo.[31] UNMIK Regulation 1999/24 stipulates that '[i]n exercising their functions, all persons undertaking public duties or holding public office in Kosovo shall observe internationally recognized human rights standards'.[32] It then provides an extensive list of major international human rights instruments from which these standards are to be drawn, including treaties to which the FRY was not a party.[33]

Initially there was serious disagreement within UNMIK as to whether human rights law was applicable in Kosovo and whether Regulation 1999/24 was sufficient to incorporate it.[34] Those supporting the interpretation that human rights law was rendered directly applicable cited UNMIK's mandate to 'protect . . . and promot[e] human rights',[35] suggesting that this could only be achieved through compliance with international human rights standards. This position was also supported by a statement of 4 July 1999 by then Acting SRSG Sergio Vieira de Mello,[36] as well as the Report of the UN Secretary General on the establishment of UNMIK.[37]

---

conflict or occupation' (emphasis added). Thus, it is essential to look to international humanitarian law to determine in what circumstances the subsequent enumerated acts are unlawful.

[31] See, eg, UNMIK Regs 1999/1, 1999/23, 1999/24.

[32] UNMIK Reg 1999/24, s 1.3.

[33] This list includes: Universal Declaration on Human Rights of 10 December 1948 (UDHR); European Convention for the Protection of Human Rights and Fundamental Freedoms of 4 November 1950 (ECHR) and the Protocols thereto; International Covenant on Civil and Political Rights of 16 December 1966 (ICCPR) and the Protocols thereto; International Covenant on Economic, Social and Cultural Rights of 16 December 1966 (ICESCR); Convention on the Elimination of All Forms of Racial Discrimination of 21 December 1965 (CERD); Convention on Elimination of All Forms of Discrimination Against Women of 17 December 1979 (CEDAW); Convention Against Torture and Other Cruel, Inhumane or Degrading Treatment or Punishment of 17 December 1984 (CAT); and International Convention on the Rights of the Child of 20 December 1989 (CRC).

[34] OSCE First Review of the Criminal Justice System (February–July 2000) s 3 (The Applicable Law). See also LSM Report no 2, 31 ('[I]nternational human rights laws were nonexistent in the local legal framework until the advent of the UN Interim Administration. Consequently, until this point, the local judiciary had no exposure to these laws nor other modern European laws and procedures. In October 2000, LSMS was informed by the president of the Mitrovica/Mitrovicë district court that such standards are not part of the applicable law and will not be applied by his judges').

[35] UNSC Res 1244 para 11.

[36] While recalling that KFOR was responsible for ensuring public safety and order until such time as UNMIK was capable of doing so, the Acting SRSG emphasized that KFOR would be bound by international human rights standards in the performance of these duties. Office of the Acting SRSG, UNMIK 'Statement on the Right of KFOR to Apprehend and Detain' (4 July 1999).

[37] See 'Report of the Secretary-General' (*supra* n 6) para 38 ('In exercising their functions, all persons undertaking public duties or holding public office in Kosovo will be required to

Eventually, the direct applicability of human rights law grew to be accepted.[38] Any remaining doubts were resolved with the promulgation of the Constitutional Framework, which incorporated most of the major international and European human rights treaties[39] and provided that '[t]he provisions on rights and freedoms set forth in these instruments shall be directly applicable in Kosovo as part of this Constitutional Framework'.[40]

Thus, Kosovo courts may apply international law in a number of ways. First, certain international norms were fully incorporated into pre-existing domestic legislation, rendered applicable by UNMIK Regulation. In such cases, what is applied is essentially domestic law, although the norms, as the domestic incorporation of international norms, retain an international character. Secondly, the Yugoslav law on war crimes refers back to international law for its application.[41] In such cases, what is applied is a combination of international and domestic law. Finally, the incorporation of human rights law into the applicable law by Regulation 1999/24 and Chapter 3 of the Constitutional Framework enables the direct application of this branch of international law by the Kosovo courts.

3. Structure and composition of the courts

I. The Kosovo court system

The Kosovo court system is based partly on Regulation 1999/24, which incorporated the FRY Law on the Courts, and partly on the Constitutional

observe internationally recognized human rights standards, and shall not discriminate against any person on any grounds, such as sex, race, colour, language, religion, political or other opinion, national, ethnic or social origin, association with a national community, property, birth or other status'). See also ibid para 42 ('In its resolution 1244 (1999), the Security Council requests UNMIK to protect and promote human rights in Kosovo. In assuming its responsibilities, UNMIK will be guided by internationally recognized standards of human rights *as the basis for the exercise of its authority* in Kosovo. UNMIK will embed a culture of human rights in all areas of activity, and will adopt human rights policies in respect of its administrative functions') (emphasis added).

[38] See, eg, *Belul Beqaj and Dita v Temporary Media Commissioner*, Office of the Media Appeals Board, Kosovo, FRY, www.osce.org/kosovo/media/ditavtmc (September 2000).

[39] Section 3.1 of the Framework states, 'All persons in Kosovo shall enjoy, without discrimination on any ground and in full equality, human rights and fundamental freedoms'. Section 3.2 then elaborates on the range of human rights norms that the Provisional Institutions of Self-Government must 'observe and ensure', including all those set forth in: the UDHR; the ECHR and its Protocols; the ICCPR and the Protocols thereto; CERD; CEDAW; the CRC; the European Charter for Regional or Minority Languages; and the Council of Europe's Framework Convention for the Protection of National Minorities. Noticeably absent from this list are the International Covenant on Economic, Social and Cultural Rights and the Convention Against Torture and Other Cruel, Inhumane or Degrading Treatment or Punishment, both of which had been included in Reg 1999/24.

[40] Constitutional Framework ch 3.3.

[41] See *infra* n 45.

Framework,[42] which was also promulgated as an UNMIK Regulation. As noted above, the authority of this legislation is derived from the authority of the SRSG provided for in Resolution 1244. From this perspective, an international instrument serves as the legal basis for the court system in Kosovo.

The Kosovo court system consists of 24 Minor Offence Courts, one Municipal Court for each of Kosovo's municipalities, five District Courts, and one Supreme Court.[43]

The Minor Offence Courts have jurisdiction over minor infractions, punishable by fine or up to 60 days' imprisonment. The Municipal Courts deal with most civil matters and criminal offences punishable with up to five years' imprisonment. The District Courts hear appeals from Municipal Courts and are courts of first instance for crimes punishable with more than five years' imprisonment and certain major civil matters.[44]

The Supreme Court is the highest judicial organ in Kosovo. The Constitutional Framework also provides for a Special Chamber of the Supreme Court on Constitutional Framework Matters, which will be responsible for deciding 'whether any law adopted by the Assembly is incompatible with this Constitutional Framework, including the international legal instruments specified in Chapter 3 on Human Rights'.[45]

II. The Kosovo War and Ethnic Crimes Court (KWECC) and 'Son of KWECC': the participation of international judges and prosecutors[46]

From early on, it was clear that due to the sensitive nature of many of the crimes committed during and after the conflict, the level of inter-ethnic hatred, and the chaotic and volatile climate in Kosovo following the end of the NATO bombing campaign, special measures would be required to ensure that criminal prosecutions would be conducted fairly and effectively.

However, unlike the approach adopted for the police service in Kosovo in which international police officers were given primary responsibility for law enforcement with the aim of gradually transferring expertise and responsibility to developing local authorities, UNMIK rejected the idea of creating an international judiciary for Kosovo. The Kosovan judges, many of whom had

---

[42] According to ch 1.4 of the Constitutional Framework, 'Kosovo shall be governed democratically through legislative, executive, and judicial bodies and institutions in accordance with this Constitutional Framework and UNSCR 1244(1999)'.

[43] See Constitutional Framework s 9.4.4 ('There shall be the Supreme Court of Kosovo, District Courts, Municipal Courts and Minor Offense Courts').

[44] There is also a Commercial District Court, which deals with economic and financial matters.

[45] Constitutional Framework s 9.4.11(a).

[46] See, for a full discussion of the role of international judges and prosecutors, Chapter 4 (Cady/Booth).

been practising judges in the 1980s, were seen as fully capable of handling the mounting caseload.

At the same time, a proposal had been circulating within UNMIK to create a Kosovo War and Ethnic Crimes Court (KWECC),[47] which would have provided for the participation of international judges, albeit limited to this one court. This proposal was similarly rejected. Various reasons have been cited for abandoning the concept of KWECC: the financial cost; the opposition of the Kosovo Albanian community, which claimed the Kosovo judiciary was capable of fairly and competently adjudicating these crimes; concerns about creating an additional jurisdictional layer between the Kosovo court system and ICTY; and the concerns of some NATO countries about the jurisdictional reach of such an institution.

By early 2000, the horrific violence in Mitrovica had made it clear that there were larger concerns about the fairness, competence, and human rights sensitivity of the judiciary. On 15 February 2000, days after the serious outbreak of violence in Mitrovica, a Regulation was hastily promulgated enabling the appointment of international judges and prosecutors[48] to the Mitrovica District Court and other courts within the territorial jurisdiction of the District Court (ie Municipal and Minor Offences Courts in Mitrovica).[49] However, UNMIK had great difficulty recruiting qualified individuals to serve as judges and prosecutors. Chief among the factors dissuading qualified personnel from taking such appointments was concern for personal security.[50]

Immediately after the Regulation was signed, an UNMIK Mission Member was persuaded to accept a position as an international judge and was appointed to the Mitrovica District Court. An international prosecutor was appointed soon after.[51] However, due to the ad hoc nature of these appointments, uncertainty about their role, and the conditions in which these personnel were deployed, little meaningful work was to be performed by them until months later.

---

[47] Initial proposals for KWECC envisioned granting the court subject matter jurisdiction over crimes under international law, as well as serious inter-ethnic offences under domestic law. The language of the proposed statute of the court was drawn largely from the ICTY Statute.

[48] International defence lawyers have not been formally introduced into the system. However, the OSCE has created an NGO, the Criminal Defence Resource Centre, which provides international assistance to local defence lawyers.

[49] UNMIK Reg 2000/6.

[50] Each international judge would be provided with four close protection officers and would be housed on the KFOR base in Mitrovica.

[51] According to the March 2000 Report of the Secretary-General on the progress of UNMIK, 'The first international judge and the first international prosecutor were appointed and sworn in on 15 and 17 February 2000 respectively'. 'Report of the Secretary-General on the United Nations Interim Administration Mission in Kosovo' S/2000/177 (3 March 2000).

Subsequently, through UNMIK Regulation 2000/34, the system of international judges and prosecutors was spread across Kosovo, including the appointment of international judges to the Supreme Court. The use of international judges and prosecutors is now governed by Regulation 2000/64, which allows 'the competent prosecutor, the accused or the defence counsel' to petition the Department of Justice for the assignment of an international prosecutor and the appointment of a panel consisting of a majority[52] of international judges on a case-by-case basis.[53] The SRSG holds the ultimate authority to approve or deny the petition.[54]

C. EVALUATION

Since 2000, the use of international judges and prosecutors in the Kosovo criminal justice system,[55] at both the trial and appellate levels, has been systematized. While the number of international judges and prosecutors has increased, assessing their success is difficult because it is not clear what their role was or is supposed to be.

---

[52] Under Reg 2000/64, the SRSG could appoint 'a panel composed only of three (3) judges, including at least two international judges, of which one shall be the presiding judge': Reg 2000/64 s 2.1(c). Previously, serious criminal cases were heard by a panel of three professional judges and two lay judges. Even when two international judges were appointed to such a panel, they still constituted a minority and could thus be out-voted.

[53] Regulation 2000/64 ('At any stage in the criminal proceedings, the Department of Judicial Affairs, on the basis of [a petition from the competent prosecutor, the accused or the defense counsel] or on its own motion, may submit a recommendation to the Special Representative of the Secretary-General for the assignment of international judges/prosecutors and/or a change of venue if it determines that this is necessary to ensure the independence and impartiality of the judiciary or the proper administration of justice'). Further, with the promulgation of Reg 2001/02, international prosecutors were empowered to intervene in cases already underway, to continue stalled prosecutions, and to appeal the dismissal of inquiries by judicial panels: Reg 2001/02 ss 1.4 and 1.5.

[54] The UN Secretary-General set forth the SRSG's power of appointment and removal of judges, as well as his responsibility to promote the independence of the judiciary, in his Report of 12 July 1999. 'Report of the Secretary-General' (*supra* n 6) para 40 ('The Special Representative will also have the authority to appoint any person to perform functions in the interim civil administration in Kosovo, including the judiciary, and to remove such persons if their service is found to be incompatible with the mandate and the purposes of the interim civil administration. Such authority shall be exercised in accordance with the existing laws, as specified previously, and any regulations issued by UNMIK. In exercising this function, the Special Representative will endeavour to have all elements of Kosovo society appropriately represented and to respect the requirements and procedures for appointments and nominations provided for under local law. He shall, furthermore, promote the independence of the judicial system as the guarantor of the rule of law').

[55] Under UNMIK Reg 2001/17 (On the Registration of Contracts for the Sale of Real Property in Specific Geographic Areas of Kosovo) a panel of international judges can review the decisions of the executive to restrict sales of property (normally because of inter-ethnic reasons). However, it appeared by mid-2002 that no such review had yet taken place, meaning that international judges had still been exclusively used in criminal cases.

Regulations 2000/6 and 2000/34 do not specify the purpose of infusing international personnel into the justice system, other than to 'assist . . . in the judicial process in Kosovo'. Nor does the 'Common Document'[56] between the SRSG and the Belgrade authorities of November 2001, which promised an increase in the numbers of international judges and prosecutors, explain why this was needed. The preamble of Regulation 2001/34 does make reference to the fact that:

the continued presence of security threats may undermine the independence and impartiality of the judiciary and impede the ability of the judiciary to properly prosecute crimes, which gravely undermine the peace process and the full establishment of the rule of law in Kosovo

but nowhere does it refer to the most glaring problems evidenced by the situation in Mitrovica that led to their appointment—discrimination before the courts and lack of human rights expertise.

The potential benefits of the introduction of international personnel into the justice system would appear to fall into two main areas: first, improving the degree and appearance of impartiality, and secondly, and more importantly, bringing international skills and knowledge, particularly in the fields of human rights and humanitarian law, into the justice system.

1. Impartiality

The main aim of grafting international judges and prosecutors into the existing system appears to have been to remove the appearance of bias in the most sensitive cases, notably war crimes trials. In early 2000, a number of Serbs in Kosovo were tried by Albanians with the memory of the crimes committed during 1998–99 still fresh. Not surprisingly, then, there were many allegations about partiality, and the appearance of bias in these cases. As noted above, these allegations came not only from Serbs but also from international observers such as the OSCE.[57] The main aim in bringing in international personnel, then, was to review these judgments as well as to ensure that new sensitive cases were heard without the possibility of serious allegations of bias.

From the perspective of appearance alone, this has been achieved. To date, most, if not all, of the war crimes judgments involving Kosovo Serbs have been reviewed by panels involving a majority of international judges,[58] and in

---

[56] UNMIK-FRY Common Document, signed in Belgrade by the UNMIK SRSG and a FRY representative, 5 November 2001.

[57] See OSCE Mission in Kosovo First Review of the Criminal Justice System in Kosovo (October 2000) www.osce.org/kosovo/documents/reports/justice.

[58] UNMIK Reg 2000/64.

many cases the judgments have been overturned.[59] For new cases, international prosecutors have begun investigations and international judges, presumably much more impervious to pressure than local judges, have both led investigations as investigating judges and comprised the majority on panels at trials. New cases involving both communities, such as investigations into former members of the KLA or the Serbian 'bridge watchers',[60] continue to give rise to serious controversy and are frequently accompanied by large public demonstrations.[61] In such an environment, a patently impartial judiciary is essential. Given that the international judges and prosecutors have been able to proceed with such cases, their presence has been a success. It is unfortunate, however, that the need was not recognized at the beginning of the UNMIK mission (in comparison to the immediate setting up of an international police force). An international judiciary in place at the time of the first trials would have avoided much controversy, and, perhaps, much conflict.

2. *Imparting knowledge and developing the law*

The presence of international judges and prosecutors has, therefore, improved the appearance of objectivity, which has allowed important cases to be reviewed and investigations launched. However, the presence of international personnel does not appear to have significantly improved the quality of the jurisprudence produced. The OSCE has noted, for example, that Supreme Court judgments in Kosovo are characterized by 'brevity [the average length of decisions is three to four pages], poor legal reasoning, absence of citations to legal authority, and lack of interpretation concerning the applicable law on war crimes and human rights issues'.[62] A significant factor contributing to this result is that the qualifications for becoming an international judge or prosecutor in Kosovo do not require any knowledge of Yugoslav law, or of international human rights or humanitarian law.[63]

---

[59] By September 2002, internationalized panels of Kosovo's Supreme Court had reversed 8 out of the 11 convictions they had reviewed in war crimes cases. The principal ground for reversal in these cases was the 'incomplete or insufficient' establishment of the factual basis of the verdict. 'Kosovo's War Crimes Trials: A Review' (September 2002) 48 http://www.osce.org/kosovo/documents/reports/human_rights/10_WarCrimesReport_eng.pdf.

[60] The phrase 'bridge watchers' refers to a group of Serbs in north Mitrovica who unofficially patrolled the bridge in order to control who passed into the north from the Albanian-controlled south.

[61] During the first half of 2002, thousands of Albanians in Kosovo demonstrated following the first arrests of former members of the KLA, charged with murdering Albanians during 1999. Similarly the arrests of leading members of the Serbian 'bridge watchers' in Mitrovica provoked mass demonstrations and riots in the Serb community.

[62] 'Kosovo's War Crimes Trials: A Review' *supra* n 60.

[63] Under Reg 2001/2, the 'criteria' for appointing international judges and prosecutors in Kosovo include: a university degree in law, five years of experience, high moral integrity, and a clean criminal record: Reg 2001/2 s 2.

The system for appointing international judges and prosecutors lacks transparency. The Kosovo Judicial and Prosecutorial Council has no authority in the appointment of international judges and prosecutors,[64] and the entire process is carried out behind closed doors. Further, there appears to be no quality control. Again, in contrast with the police service, there does not appear to have been any attempt to have UN Member States commit to supporting this programme with highly qualified personnel. Instead, UNMIK has had to rely on finding itself individuals who are willing to leave their positions in their home jurisdictions, possibly adversely affecting their careers, and move to Kosovo, and whose employers (usually Ministries of Justice) are willing to release them for at least six months.[65] Indeed the Common Document's reference to success being measured by an increase in the numbers of international judges and prosecutors overlooks any qualitative inquiry.

Given the defects in the appointment process, the mere presence of an international judge or prosecutor will not necessarily improve the quality of the legal decisions made. Indeed, when a judge is ignorant of the relevant domestic and international law, and has only been in Kosovo for a short period of time,[66] it is likely that serious errors will be made.[67]

Given that very few decisions of the Kosovo Supreme Court have been published, there are few examples of appeal judgments written by international judges being used to shape the application of the law, especially humanitarian law, to the circumstances in Kosovo.[68] One exception to this was the case of *Vuckovic*,[69] a Serb convicted of genocide. On appeal, the Supreme Court quashed the verdict and sent it back to the first instance court. The appeal judgment, written by an international judge, stated that no genocide took place in Kosovo in 1999. However, the OSCE criticized even this judgment as a wasted opportunity to 'thoroughly interpret the genocide statute FRY CC 141'.[70]

[64] See OSCE Mission in Kosovo Fourth Review of the Criminal Justice System in Kosovo (October 2000) www.osce.org/kosovo/documents/reports/justice ('OSCE, Fourth Review') 32.

[65] ibid 28 http://www.osce.org/kosovo/documents/reports/justice/criminal_justice4_eng. pdf.

[66] The first induction programme for international judges and prosecutors only began in June 2002. See OSCE Fourth Review (*supra* n 65) 22. According to a recent report of the Pearson Peacekeeping Centre, 'Even international judges and prosecutors emphasized that they are not well-versed in Kosovar or international war crimes and humanitarian law upon recruitment; that they were given no training at the outset of their missions; that they ... are given little opportunity to build their own capacity once appointed; and that they are appointed for too short a time [several months at a time instead of the one-year contract that is standard practice at ICTY] for them to work effectively': M Baskin, *Lessons Learned on UNMIK Judiciary* (Pearson Peacekeeping Centre 2002).

[67] The OSCE in its Review of Kosovo's War Crimes Trials cites a number of such errors: 'Kosovo's War Crimes Trials: A Review' (September 2002).

[68] ibid 48.

[69] ibid 15.

[70] ibid 50. The OSCE also noted that as this case was limited to acts committed by the accused in one particular locality, it was incorrect for the Supreme Court panel to assert that none of the acts committed by the Milosevic regime in 1999 constituted genocide: ibid.

International judges, then, do not appear to have been used to improve the legal decisions in key cases. Therefore, it is not surprising that there appears to have been no attempt to use international judges as a source of guidance and mentoring to the Kosovan judges, to teach them both law and judicial skills. Although this would appear to be an obvious use of such experts, such a mentoring role is not mentioned anywhere as an aim of the international judges in Kosovo. In fact, the international judges and prosecutors seem to have developed into a separate structure under the direct control of the UN Department of Justice, and have been kept largely isolated from the local judges and prosecutors.[71] As such, an opportunity is being lost to influence and internationalize the development of the Kosovo judiciary, one of the main potential gains of this hybrid system.

Another missed opportunity has come with the failure to use international judges to develop human rights law in Kosovo. As noted above, a key aim of UNMIK (and indeed the reason behind the international community's involvement in the province) is the protection of human rights. In the first place, this involves making human rights law directly applicable in Kosovo. However, although this has been done by law, specifically in the Constitutional Framework,[72] there is virtually no evidence of human rights law being directly applied by the judiciary in Kosovo in practice.[73] International judges, operating in a hybrid system, could have been used to start the process of educating Kosovan judges on how to apply human rights law on a day-to-day basis (assuming that international judges who understood and practised international human rights law had been hired). In particular, international experts sitting on the Supreme Court could have written judgments that would show how to apply human rights law to the facts of actual cases, and how to mesh human rights law with the existing law. This has not happened. Indeed, in all of its monitoring of the cases covered by international judges, the OSCE could only find one case in which an international judge attempted to apply human rights law, and that was when the judge was acting as an investigating judge.[74]

3. Independence

Not only did UNMIK miss an opportunity to educate the local judiciary, particularly in human rights law, it established a system in which the international judges and prosecutors are administered as a parallel structure, under the direct control of the UN executive power.[75] International judges

---

[71] See OSCE Fourth Review (*supra* n 65).   [72] See 46–47.
[73] OSCE Fourth Review (*supra* n 65) 15–16.   [74] ibid 16.
[75] For this section see in particular OSCE, Fourth Review (*supra* n 65) 27, and ABA/CEELI Judicial Reform Index for Kosovo (ABA/CEELI JRI) (April 2002) 40 (http://www.abanet.org/ceeli/publications/jri/jri_kosovo.pdf).

and prosecutors in Kosovo are appointed by the SRSG, their contracts are only for six months and they can be refused extensions. Even worse, they are treated as being subject to the direct supervision of the executive branch.[76] Under UNMIK Regulation 2000/64, the executive, in the form of the Department of Justice, decides which *individual* judges shall sit on which case.[77]

In sum, UNMIK has created a structure in which the international judges are under the control of the executive to the extent that the judges would not be considered independent under the European Convention on Human Rights, Article 6.[78] Far from improving and promoting the development of human rights in the judicial system in Kosovo, the hybrid system set up for international judges is actually promoting the opposite—it is encouraging a system where judges are seen as dependent on the executive. The nadir was reached with the passing of UNMIK Regulation 2001/18, which followed the heavy criticism of the UNMIK SRSG's use of his purported powers of 'executive detention' to detain persons in violation of orders for release issued by international judges. UNMIK attempted to remedy this, not by using the existing judicial system, including international judges, but by setting up a special chamber of judges from outside Kosovo, appointed by the SRSG specifically for the purpose of reviewing *in camera* his decision to detain persons in violation of court orders. In the end, only one such hearing was carried out, and the international judges, flown into Kosovo for one day, not surprisingly agreed with the SRSG.[79] Although the term of this panel has now lapsed, the example it has set, of the executive simply appointing its own pliant judges when it does not like a legal decision, is very unfortunate in a society attempting to create a modern, independent justice system.[80]

4. *Lessons to be learned*

The use of international judges and prosecutors in Kosovo has had both negative and positive effects. In general, the failure of the hybrid system to improve the quality of adjudication, to develop human rights law in Kosovo, or most notably to serve as a model for independent judicial decision-making, appears primarily attributable to the manner in which international

---

[76] See OSCE Fourth Review (*supra* n 65) 27, referring to the job description set out for international judges. In a recent report, the American Bar Association/Central and Eastern European Law Initiative has pointed out that the international judges in Kosovo were the only judges in Central and Eastern Europe who informed them that they were under instructions from the executive (ie the UNMIK Department of Justice) not to speak to outside actors: ABA/CEELI JRI (*supra* n 76).

[77] UNMIK Reg 2000/64 s 2.1.

[78] See inter alia Report of the European Commission on Human Rights *B Company v The Netherlands* (19 May 1994).

[79] See OSCE Fourth Review (*supra* n 65) in particular 37.

[80] ibid 37. See also Ombudsperson of Kosovo Special Report 4 (September 2001).

participation was conceived and employed. From the initial decision to introduce international personnel into the system, they were seen as an ad hoc solution to a particular problem, implemented not pursuant to the fundamental Mission objectives of consolidating the rule of law, securing justice, or promoting the development of human rights law, but in the more immediate interests of reducing tensions among the local populations. The experience does, however, provide several lessons for the future.

First, if international administrators, army, and police will be needed in post-conflict situations, so will international judges and prosecutors, and they should be involved at the very beginning of any international administration. This must be accompanied by the presence of independent legal system monitors who should be in place from the inception of law enforcement activity.

Secondly, the main purposes of introducing international actors into the justice system should be clearly considered and set out. In particular, the role to be fulfilled and the purpose to be served by international judges should be carefully delineated. Generally, this should be primarily to educate the local judges in the relevant law and to impart practical skills. It is essential to place in the highest courts international experts in international law, who understand the legal system in question and who are able to write judgments that can be disseminated.[81] The respective roles of international prosecutors and defence lawyers also need to be clarified.

Finally, and most importantly, international judges should set the highest example, particularly in their independence from the executive. Executive authorities should not have the degree of control that UNMIK has over international judges in Kosovo. Judges should be of the highest legal and personal quality, be able to stand up to pressure, and show, by example, how judges should practise their profession.

D. CONCLUSION

Assuming the relevant criteria are legal basis, personnel composition, subject matter jurisdiction, and function, the Kosovo courts in which international judges sit may properly be considered hybrid or internationalized courts. The legal basis of these courts may be found in UNMIK Regulations qua domestic legislation; however, the authority of these Regulations is derived from UN Security Council Resolution 1244, an international legal instrument. The

---

[81] While in many legal systems case precedent is not binding, it is almost always helpful as guidance. Translation of these judgments into local languages would of course be essential. The lack of translation services in Kosovo was a tremendous obstacle to effective law enforcement and undermined UNMIK's ability to comply with such fundamental democratic requirements as publication of the law. Most UNMIK Regulations entered into force long before they were translated into local languages or disseminated to the judges.

courts are staffed by a mix of Kosovan and international officials and apply both national and international law. While generally situated as domestic courts, they also perform a function peculiar to international courts—removing sensitive cases and those involving application of international norms from the exclusive province of domestic judges, who may lack the necessary objectivity and expertise.

Whether the system established in Kosovo can be deemed a success depends largely on the criteria used in conducting an evaluation. Although international human rights law was made directly applicable, the courts lack the resources and the capacity necessary to apply it. The international judges have failed to increase that capacity in any meaningful way. While their participation has lent an air of neutrality in relation to the tensions among Kosovo's different ethnic groups, the international judges have not achieved sufficient independence from the UNMIK executive.

4

Internationalized Courts in Kosovo: An UNMIK Perspective

Jean-Christian Cady* and Nicholas Booth**

A. THE BACKGROUND

The need for international judges and prosecutors in Kosovo became apparent within the first few months of the UN Mission in Kosovo (UNMIK), which was established pursuant to UN Security Council Resolution 1244 following the end of the NATO military action in June 1999.

During the armed conflict which preceded NATO's intervention, many human rights abuses and war crimes were committed against ethnic Albanian civilians, but Serb civilians too were victims of abductions, beatings, and executions at the hands of members of ethnic Albanian paramilitary forces such as the Kosovo Liberation Army (KLA), which also targeted ethnic Albanians suspected of collaboration with the Serbs. After the withdrawal of the Serbian forces, violence against Serbs and other minorities in Kosovo (in particular Roma), as well as ethnic Albanians suspected of collaboration with the Serbs, increased to an horrific level during the first months of the UN Mission.

UNMIK restarted the justice system in the first weeks of the new mission, staffing the courts with Kosovan judges and prosecutors. However, it quickly became clear that this new judicial system would not be capable of trying cases of war crimes and inter-ethnic crimes impartially. Reports came in that the courts, predominantly staffed with ethnic Albanians (who constitute 85 per cent of Kosovo's residents) were releasing ethnic Albanians charged with crimes against Serbs even where the evidence was strong. Conversely, Serbs were often placed in indefinite pre-trial detention without any apparent will to bring their cases to trial. Furthermore, attacks and threats were reported against judges, ensuring that even those members of the judiciary with the integrity to remain neutral in so charged an atmosphere were placed under intolerable pressure.

In this climate, the need for international judges and prosecutors to bring credible neutrality to criminal trials was recognized by UNMIK,

* Deputy Special Representative of the Secretary-General (DSRSG) for Police and Justice, United Nations Interim Administration Mission in Kosovo (UNMIK).
** Senior Adviser to the DSRSG for Police and Justice, UNMIK. The views expressed herein are those of the authors and do not necessarily reflect the views of the United Nations.

as by Amnesty International and other human rights monitors.[1] In December 1999, a special commission set up by the Special Representative of the Secretary-General (SRSG)[2] recommended the establishment of a new tribunal, the Kosovo War and Ethnic Crimes Court (KWECC), which would have both international and Kosovan judges, and would stand outside the existing court structure with special jurisdiction over war and inter-ethnic crime.

However, events were to take UNMIK along another course. In February 2000, a rocket attack against a UNHCR bus carrying Serbs, and the bombing of a local café, sparked a wave of violence in Mitrovica, in which many were killed and far more injured.[3] UNMIK quickly introduced a package of measures to restore law and order, including the appointment of international judges and prosecutors to the courts in Mitrovica.[4] UNMIK Regulation 2000/6[5] was passed in a matter of days, giving the SRSG power to make such appointments, and by 17 February 2000 the first international judge and prosecutor were in place,[6] with the power to take on any case pending before the Mitrovica courts.

Although it was thus born out of the crisis in Mitrovica, this reform came to be extended across the province. In April 2000, a number of Serb and Roma detainees began a hunger strike complaining at the length of their pre-trial detention, and shortly thereafter the SRSG promised the hunger strikers that international or Serb judges would preside over their cases. On 27 May 2000 Regulation 2000/6 was amended to enable the appointment of international judges and prosecutors to any court or prosecutor's office in Kosovo.[7] By the summer of 2000, six international judges and two prosecutors were appointed among the courts of Mitrovica, Pristina, Gnjilane, and Prizren. In September 2000, the idea of the KWECC was abandoned. The

[1] See, eg, 'Amnesty International's Recommendations to UNMIK on the Judicial System', AI Report EUR 70/006/2000 (February 2000), http://library.amnesty.it/isdocs/aidoc_everything.nsf/print/EUR700062000.
[2] The head of the UNMIK Mission (SRSG). The commission was set up by UNMIK Reg 1999/6 (On Recommendations for the Structure and Administration of the Judiciary and Prosecution Service). UNMIK Regulations are available at www.unmikonline.org.
[3] Mitrovica, a city in northern Kosovo divided into two halves by the river Ibar which runs east–west, has been a volatile city since the beginning of UNMIK's Mission in June 1999. Before the war it was ethnically mixed, with half of the population in the northern part of the city being Albanian, while some 300 Serb families lived south of the Ibar. As early as June 1999 Serbs in the southern part of Mitrovica began to move north of the Ibar, fearing revenge attacks from Albanians, since the part of Kosovo to the north of Mitrovica is predominantly inhabited by Serbs, while conversely Albanians in the northern part began to move in large numbers to the south.
[4] See UNMIK Press Releases UNMIK/PR/159 and UNMIK/PR/161. UNMIK Press Releases are available at at www.unmikonline.org.
[5] UNMIK Reg 2000/6 (On the Appointment and Removal from Office of International Judges and International Prosecutors).
[6] See UNMIK Press Release UNMIK/PR/163.
[7] See UNMIK Reg 2000/34, amending UNMIK Reg 2000/6.

objective of providing international involvement in trials of war and inter-ethnic crime had already been achieved, albeit by a route that no one had foreseen just a few months earlier.

One further legal reform was needed, however. Under the applicable law in Kosovo,[8] serious crimes are to be heard by panels of two professional and three lay judges. As the OSCE and other human rights observers pointed out, the assignment of even two international judges to hear such cases could not carry the majority and thus was insufficient to guarantee credible neutrality.[9] As a result, UNMIK Regulation 2000/64 was promulgated at the end of 2000.[10] This Regulation gave the prosecutor, accused, or defence counsel the right to ask UNMIK to intervene to assign international judges/prosecutors or a change in venue. Crucially, it gave UNMIK the right in such a case to designate a panel consisting of only three judges, including at least two international judges, of whom one would be the presiding judge. This inter-vention could take place at any stage in the proceedings, except where the trial session or (if appropriate) appeal had already commenced, since it was felt that this would be unduly disruptive to the conduct of proceedings, and that any bias emerging at this stage could be cured by the assignment of an international panel to hear an appeal or an extraordinary legal remedy against appeal.

Regulations 2000/6 and 2000/64 have remained as the legal framework for the deployment of international judges and prosecutors ('IJPs') ever since. It is worth underlining two cardinal features of this framework at the outset. First, international judges function as judges of the regular courts of Kosovo. Their powers and duties are those attributed to them by the Law on Regular Courts,[11] and they apply the same procedural and substantive laws as their local colleagues. But, secondly, unlike their local colleagues their assignment to cases does not depend on the president of the court in which they sit. The selection of cases on which IJPs sit is under international control. The IJPs themselves have the special power under Regulation 2000/6 to participate in any case in their court whenever they think an international judge or prosecutor should be present; and the SRSG can transfer any case to the jurisdiction of a special international panel under Regulation 2000/64.

---

[8] For the applicable law in Kosovo, see below.

[9] See, eg, OSCE Review of the Justice System in Kosovo (February 2000–July 2000) available at http://www.osce.org/kosovo/documents/reports/justice/.

[10] UNMIK Reg 2000/64 (On the Assignment of International Judges/Prosecutors and/or Change of Venue). The Regulation was initially enacted for a 12-month period, but was subsequently extended by UNMIK Reg 2001/34, UNMIK Reg 2002/20, and UNMIK Reg 2003/36. The Regulation will currently expire on 15 December 2004, but is likely to be further renewed at that stage, subject to review by the SRSG.

[11] Official Gazette of the Socialist Autonomous Province of Kosovo No. 21/78.

B. THE ADMINISTRATION OF THE IJP PROGRAMME

Executive power in Kosovo is shared between the SRSG and the Provisional Institutions of Self-Government which, in fulfilment of the mandate under UN Security Council Resolution 1244, were established by UNMIK Regulations 2001/9 (A Constitutional Framework for Provisional Self-Government in Kosovo) and 2001/19 (On the Executive Branch of the Provisional Institutions of Self-Government in Kosovo), and brought into being following the province-wide elections of November 2001.

Chapter 8 of the Constitutional Framework reserves to the SRSG the final authority over the appointment, removal from office and disciplining of judges and prosecutors, as well as the assignment of international judges and prosecutors, and authority over the police and prisons.[12] In May 2001, a new Police and Justice Pillar was established within UNMIK to coordinate the SRSG's reserved functions in the field of justice and home affairs.[13] Justice will remain under the ultimate responsibility of the international community until a functioning and independent justice system is established in Kosovo.

Although international judges sit side-by-side with their local colleagues in the same courts, they are not appointed the same way. IJPs are UN staff members, recruited like most Mission staff on renewable six-month contracts in response to open international vacancies. Independent in the exercise of their functions, administratively they report to the Director of the Department of Justice, and through him indirectly to the Deputy SRSG for Police and Justice and the SRSG.

They are supported by a special administrative unit within the Department of Justice which is operationally responsible for their assignments (and for the difficult task of ensuring the necessary coordination of their schedules, since the small pool of available judges and prosecutors requires them to travel often outside their 'home' court to sit on Regulation 2000/64 panels in other districts, so that in any one week a judge may have to be involved in a number of different cases in different courts). This unit also provides the special support that IJPs need. For instance, there is a large pool of specialized interpreters and translators for these proceedings which are always conducted in at least two and often three languages (Albanian, Serbian,

---

[12] See ch 8.1(g)–(j) of the Constitutional Framework. A number of operational responsibilities in the field of judicial affairs are transferred to the Provisional Institutions of Self-Government by ch 5.3 of the Constitutional Framework. These are performed by the Department of Judicial Administration within the Ministry of Public Services.

[13] The SRSG's powers and responsibilities in the field of justice and prisons are exercised through the Department of Justice. The UNMIK Police Commissioner controls the UNMIK police force, made up of international civilian police and a local police force, the Kosovo Police Service. Both the Director of the Department of Justice and the Police Commissioner report to the DSRSG for Police and Justice, who is the head of the Police and Justice Pillar.

and English). A Legal Unit coordinates the staff of legal officers who perform research and drafting for the judges and prosecutors.

Then there is the extremely important question of security for IJPs, who will often require some level of personal protection given the sensitivity of the cases they try. Until now, only IJPs have been assigned such security, because only they have tried cases sensitive enough to put them at risk. This is now changing. Some local judges and prosecutors have shown the courage and the integrity to begin to try organized crime cases, and unfortunately they have already shown themselves to be targets for violence.[14] As sensitive cases are gradually submitted to local or mixed international/local panels, the security assessment process must be extended also to the local judges and prosecutors.

Local judges and prosecutors are also formally appointed by the SRSG, but their selection procedure is very different. The Kosovo Judicial and Prosecutorial Council (KJPC), a body independent from the Provisional Institutions of Self-Government,[15] evaluates candidates for judicial and prosecutorial office and submits a recommended list to the SRSG for appointment (having given the Assembly of Kosovo the opportunity to present its advice on the recommended candidates).[16] While the SRSG remains technically free to disregard its advice, in practice the KJPC's recommendations are invariably followed. Unlike international judges and prosecutors, they are appointed on the longest tenure that UNMIK can grant—until the end of the Mission itself. The KJPC contains both international and local judges and prosecutors and other legal experts. The IJP programme does not in any way diminish UNMIK's responsibility to develop a competent and independent local judiciary, which is not only the future of the justice system in Kosovo, but also in large part its present, since, as will be seen below, local judges are responsible for the overwhelming majority of all cases.

1. Size of the programme

The importance of the IJP programme is disproportionate to the numbers of judges and prosecutors involved. From the initial two appointments of February 2000, the numbers grew gradually but modestly. The difficulty of recruiting suitable candidates presented a formidable barrier. Not only must they be excellent judges and prosecutors in their home jurisdictions—and therefore, by definition, personnel whom their home states are loath to lose—but they must also be able to work in English, the language of the Mission,[17]

---

[14] The attack in February 2003 on President Engjell Qeta of the Prizren District Court is a notable example.

[15] See ch 11.1(b) of the Constitutional Framework.

[16] See UNMIK Reg 2001/8 (On the Establishment of the Kosovo Judicial and Prosecutorial Council) and ch 9.4.8 of the Constitutional Framework.

[17] See UNMIK Reg 2000/46 (On the Use of Language in Court Proceedings in which an International Judge or Prosecutor Participates). Section 1.1 provides that 'If an international

and be prepared to live under the hardships which an assignment in Kosovo entails (not least, the need to live under close protection while trying sensitive cases).

By November 2001 there were 17 judges and prosecutors, and it was clear that this number was not adequate to deal with the number of inter-ethnic and war crimes cases alone. Kosovo Serbs accused of such crimes continued to protest that the lack of IJPs still resulted in unacceptably long periods to bring their cases to trial. In that month, it was agreed with the Yugoslav authorities that the number would be doubled to 34,[18] a target which, in fact, has still not been achieved because of the difficulties of recruitment.

It is important to bear in mind that the IJPs try only 3 to 4 per cent of the more serious criminal cases in Kosovo. Until the formation of the Special Chamber of the Supreme Court of Kosovo on Kosovo Trust Agency Related Matters (see below), no civil cases were tried by IJPs.

2. Criteria for assignment

Regulation 2000/6 places no conditions on the circumstances in which individual international judges and prosecutors may take cases,[19] just as Regulation 2000/64 places no conditions on the circumstances in which a special panel of international judges can be assigned to hear a case.[20] However, in

judge or an international prosecutor initiates or is participating in court proceedings, those proceedings shall be conducted in English, in addition to any other language or languages required by applicable law'. This means that court records and judgments are kept in English, and simultaneous interpretation is provided into the languages of the local judges, defence attorneys, parties, and witnesses.

[18] UNMIK–FRY Common Document of 5 November 2001.

[19] The relevant provisions of Reg 2000/6 (as amended) are as follows:

'1.2 International judges shall have the authority and responsibility to perform the functions of their office, including the authority to select and take responsibility for new and pending criminal cases within the jurisdiction of the court to which he or she is appointed;

1.3 International prosecutors shall have the authority and responsibility to perform the functions of their office, including the authority and responsibility to conduct criminal investigations and to select and take responsibility for new and pending criminal investigations or proceedings within the jurisdiction of the office of the prosecutor to which he or she is appointed'.

[20] The relevant provisions of Reg 2000/64 (as amended) are as follows:

1.1 At any stage in the criminal proceedings, the competent prosecutor, the accused or the defence counsel may submit to the Department of Judicial Affairs a petition for an assignment of international judges/prosecutors and/or a change of venue where this is considered necessary to ensure the independence and impartiality of the judiciary or the proper administration of justice;

1.2 At any stage in the criminal proceedings, the Department of Judicial Affairs, on the basis of the petition referred to in section 1.1 above or on its own motion, may submit a recommendation to the Special Representative of the Secretary-General for the assignment of international judges/prosecutors and/or a change of venue if it determines that this is necessary to ensure the independence and impartiality of the judiciary or the proper administration of justice.

keeping with the reason for which those Regulations were passed, the key factor which has always guided UNMIK in assigning IJPs to a case is the substantial risk of a miscarriage of justice. Usually this arises from the nature of the proceedings themselves. War crimes, cases of inter-ethnic violence or organized crime cases make up the majority. But the facts of individual cases can be taken into consideration too.

How are these criteria applied in practice? In answering that question it is important to remember the difference between Regulation 2000/6, which provides for the appointment of the international judge as a member of a regular court within the applicable law, and the powers of Regulation 2000/64 which enable cases to be tried by a special panel of three judges with an international majority. There are a number of different possibilities for intervention.

The most radical intervention is reserved for those cases whose sensitivity is so great that full international control is essential from the start. These cases include trials of those connected with leading political figures, those suspected of involvement in organized crime, and especially sensitive war crimes trials. In these cases, the local judges themselves sometimes inform the Department of Justice (confidentially) that they do not wish to take the case because of the danger to which this would subject them. These are the cases for which Regulation 2000/64 panels are used. Regulation 2000/64 is also used for appeal panels where there is a suspicion that the fairness of the original trial was marked by bias. While this form of intervention offers the greatest guarantee of neutrality, because international professional judges preside over the case and form the majority of the trial panel, the lack of involvement by local judges makes them less effective in building the capacity of local judges to tackle such cases in the future.

Conversely, where an international prosecutor or judge takes a case under Regulation 2000/6, local judges will always form the majority at the full trial—indeed, the prosecutor may be the only international involved in the case. This limited level of international involvement by itself should ensure that a fair procedure will be followed, while the greater involvement of local judges in the trial of such cases increases the opportunities for capacity-building. There remains, however, the risk that the local judges, through bias or pressure, will disregard the guidance of the international judge and

2.1 Upon approval of the Special Representative of the Secretary-General in accordance with section 1 above, the Department of Judicial Affairs shall expeditiously designate:
  (a) An international prosecutor;
  (b) An international investigating judge; and/or
  (c) A panel composed only of three (3) judges, including at least two international judges, of which one shall be the presiding judge, as required by the particular stage at which the criminal proceeding has reached in a case'.
Following the reorganization of the Department of Judicial Affairs in November 2001, its responsibilities in the field of IJPs were assumed by the new Department of Justice.

use their majority to return an unfair verdict. If this is felt to have occurred, it is always possible to ensure that the appeal is heard by a majority of international judges using Regulation 2000/64.

Striking the balance between these two instruments is at the heart of the Department of Justice's transition strategy. Since its inception, Regulation 2000/64 has continued to be regularly applied.[21] Justice for the most serious war and ethnic crimes lays the groundwork for the growth of a multi-ethnic and tolerant society, and that was one of the earliest priorities for the Mission. The majority of cases against Serb defendants have now been tried, and the remainder should be completed over the next year.

In 2002, the prosecution of war crimes committed by ethnic Albanians against other ethnic Albanians (largely those suspected of collaboration) started. This was a particularly sensitive issue since the defendants were leading members of the KLA, and since they have remained prominent in public life in Kosovo, either through their positions in the Kosovo Protection Corps (a civilian emergency preparedness corps which was formed upon the demilitarization of the KLA), and/or through their links to leading political figures. The first of these arrests gave rise to violent public disorder. Although inevitably each such arrest or conviction is met with further demonstrations organized by political factions supporting the accused, they are now peaceful and attract far fewer numbers than the several thousands who rioted at the time of the first arrests. So progress has been made towards establishing a culture in which everyone understands that no one is above the law.

C. THE FUTURE ROLE OF INTERNATIONAL JUDGES AND PROSECUTORS

It is sometimes thought that war and ethnic crimes are the only cases in which IJPs are deployed under Regulation 2000/64, and so some suppose that its main task has now largely been accomplished. This is far from true for two reasons.

First, the International Criminal Tribunal for the Former Yugoslavia (ICTY) has made it clear that it will refer many of the cases which come within the Tribunal's jurisdiction to be prosecuted in the courts of the place where the crime was committed. UNMIK works in close coordination with ICTY, which has its own offices in Kosovo.[22] Given the Tribunal's objective is to complete all first-instance proceedings by 2008,[23] a number of

---

[21] By way of illustration, the SRSG designated trial panels under Reg 2000/64 in 64 cases in 2002.

[22] On the question of the cooperation between the internationalized courts in Kosovo and ICTY, see also Chapter 3 (Cerone/Baldwin), and Chapter 17 (Sluiter).

[23] See, eg, 'Annual Report of the International Tribunal for the Prosecution of Persons Responsible for Serious Violations of International Humanitarian Law Committed in the

Kosovo-related cases are likely to be transferred for prosecution here in the near future.

Secondly, and perhaps even more importantly, the fight against organized crime has now become one of UNMIK's highest priorities. There is a direct relationship between political instability and organized crime. On the one hand, organized crime flourishes where the rule of law has been weakened by political instability. But the other side of the coin is just as important. Once it takes hold of a society, organized crime completes the vicious circle by keeping armed extremists and political leaders on its payroll to maintain that instability. Its illegal profits are sucked out of an already ailing economy.

So rooting out the organized crime that became endemic in Kosovo as a result of the conflict is not only a precondition to bringing stability to the region. It is also a precondition to establishing genuinely democratic institutions whose politicians are not in the pay of the Mob, courts which are free to decide without fear or favour, and a functioning economy.

In the first two years of the Mission, the IJPs served primarily to address war and ethnic crimes. It is only much more recently that organized crime has become another high priority. This is because UNMIK has had to build, from scratch, new institutions to detect and prosecute organized crime.

UNMIK has signed police cooperation agreements with neighbouring states and joined the Interpol system to ensure that investigators have the fullest intelligence about the activities of groups which operate on a multi-national basis.[24] UNMIK also operates telephone interception equipment which is an essential part of evidence-gathering for these crimes.[25]

A proper system of witness protection has been slowly built. This goes much further than simply taking measures for the anonymity of witnesses during court proceedings.[26] They must also be protected from retaliation outside the courtroom, since no system which provides adequate rights to the defendant can at the same time guarantee that the identity of witnesses will not be revealed. This is all the harder in a region as small and tightly-knit as

---

Territory of the Former Yugoslavia since 1991' (2002) (available at http://www.un.org/icty/pub.htm).

[24] At the time of writing, police cooperation agreements have been concluded with the former Federal Republic of Yugoslavia (now the Federation of Serbia and Montenegro), the Republic of Serbia, the Republic of Montenegro, the former Yugoslav Republic of Macedonia, and the Republic of Albania. Negotiations are pending with the Republics of Slovenia, Bosnia-Herzegovina, and Croatia. UNMIK entered into a Memorandum of Understanding with INTERPOL on 17 December 2002.

[25] The legal basis for covert surveillance is provided by UNMIK Reg 2002/6 (On Covert and Technical Measures of Surveillance and Investigation).

[26] This is provided for by UNMIK Reg 2001/20 (as amended) (On the Protection of Injured Parties and Witnesses in Criminal Proceedings).

Kosovo which affords no hiding place for those witnesses brave enough to give evidence against the criminal gangs. The problem is exacerbated by the existence of some highly irresponsible newspapers in Kosovo which have presented biased and inaccurate reports of high-profile criminal proceedings and have revealed the details of confidential witness evidence, thus placing the safety of witnesses in danger. In many cases UNMIK will have to find homes for these witnesses abroad, with a new identity and a new life. Some third countries have assisted with this witness resettlement programme, but much more assistance will be needed.

Trafficking in women and children is perhaps the ugliest of all the guises of organized crime. It is particularly prevalent in South-Eastern Europe, and Kosovo is a major destination for the victims of trafficking. UNMIK is actively participating in regional initiatives such as the South-Eastern Europe Cooperation Initiative (SECI) and the Stability Pact. It has set up a dedicated Trafficking and Prostitution Investigation Unit within the police which ensures the development of a specialized cadre of investigators, strategically focused on anti-trafficking operations but also specially trained to be able to deal sensitively with the victims of trafficking, vulnerable young women transported far from their homes and in fear both of law enforcement authorities and of retaliation from their pimps. It has passed Regulation 2001/4 (On the Prohibition of Trafficking in Persons in Kosovo), introducing stiff criminal penalties for the worst offences, while setting up a Victims Advocacy and Assistance Unit within the Department of Justice to ensure that the victims of trafficking are given necessary support and protection, both for their own welfare and in order that they may safely testify against their traffickers in court, in particular through the Interim Secure Facility for Victims of Trafficking which was opened in summer 2003 thanks to a generous donation from the United States.

The IJPs have a special role to play in the fight against trafficking. In this patriarchal society, local judges and prosecutors are still too inclined to regard victims of trafficking as prostitutes who are themselves criminals and do not merit the law's protection. Traffickers who come before local judges still receive disturbingly lenient sentences, and are let out on bail pending their appeal, enabling them to seek out and retaliate against the victims who gave evidence against them.

At this stage, UNMIK will therefore need to assign the majority of organized crime and trafficking cases to international panels under Regulation 2000/64. Nonetheless, at the same time UNMIK has begun to integrate the best local officers from the Kosovo Police Service into the police units that investigate organized crime. In the same way, it is important to begin to involve local judges and prosecutors in these cases wherever possible. UNMIK must leave Kosovo leaving behind a functioning, well-trained, and effective police and judiciary capable of continuing the fight against organized crime. UNMIK expect to make increasing use of the more limited intervention under Regulation 2000/6 even in organized crime cases. They are also for the first time assigning international judges to the Supreme Court so that the same transfer of skills and capacity-building work can be carried out at every level of the judicial system.

D. THE APPLICABLE LAW

Since international judges and prosecutors sit in the same courts as their local counterparts, it follows that they apply the same laws. The very first UNMIK Regulation which established the Mission's authority declared that the law in Kosovo, as it stood on 24 March 1999, just before NATO intervention, should remain in force, subject to international human rights norms and any Regulations to be passed by the SRSG.[27] This met with strong opposition from the local judiciary, who resented the application of any of the laws passed during Milosevic's regime. Consequently, UNMIK Regulation 1999/24 (On the Applicable Law in Kosovo) provided that the basis of the legal system should be the law as it stood on 22 March 1989, immediately before Milosevic's revocation of Kosovo's autonomy, and the ensuing decade of direct and discriminatory rule from Belgrade,[28] subject, once again, to overriding principles of international human rights,[29] and any subsequent Regulations passed by the SRSG.[30]

This change to the applicable law met with the acquiescence of the judiciary, but not with popular approval. There is still widespread dissatisfaction among certain politicians, judges, and prosecutors and sections of the public

[27] See UNMIK Reg 1999/1 (On the Authority of the Interim Administration in Kosovo), and in particular s 3, which originally provided that 'The laws applicable in the territory of Kosovo prior to 24 March 1999 shall continue to apply in Kosovo insofar as they do not conflict with standards referred to in section 2, the fulfillment of the mandate given to UNMIK under United Nations Security Council Resolution 1244 (1999), or the present or any other regulation issued by UNMIK'.

[28] See UNMIK Reg 1999/24s 1.1 which provides: 'The law applicable in Kosovo shall be:
  (a) The regulations promulgated by the Special Representative of the Secretary-General and subsidiary instruments issued thereunder; and
  (b) The law in force in Kosovo on 22 March 1989.
In case of a conflict, the regulations and subsidiary instruments issued thereunder shall take precedence'.

Note also however the provision in ibid s 1.2 that where a post-1989 law covers a previously unregulated situation or area, courts and other official bodies may apply that law provided that it is not discriminatory and complies with international human rights norms. Furthermore, criminal defendants are entitled to the benefit of any more favourable provisions in post-1989 laws: ibid s 1.4.

[29] Including the main UN human rights conventions and the European Convention for the Protection of Human Rights and Fundamental Freedoms.

[30] Including the Constitutional Framework (UNMIK Reg 2001/9), which has the same status as any other UNMIK Regulation.

with Kosovo's continued reliance on the law of the former Yugoslavia, which for Kosovo Albanians in particular is associated with a repressive socialist regime which is out of step with Kosovo's aspirations for its future. Despite this, criminal law in Kosovo was for the first four years of the Mission based on the former Yugoslav Criminal Procedure Code, and the former Yugoslav, Serbian, and Kosovan Criminal Codes as they all stood in 1989. Some essential changes were made: the death penalty was abolished,[31] the rights of arrested persons were brought up to international human rights standards by UNMIK Regulation 2001/28 (On the Rights of Persons Arrested by Law Enforcement Authorities), and the legal provisions on trafficking offences, terrorism, and sexual offences were strengthened in accordance with international norms.[32]

In addition to the political imperative for change, it was clear that the former Yugoslav criminal law needed to be modernized and brought into line with general trends in the region and in Europe. Slovenia, Croatia, and the Federation of Bosnia and Herzegovina have introduced fundamental reforms to their Criminal and Criminal Procedures Codes. Furthermore, substantial changes were required to ensure consistency with modern principles of international law and, in particular, with international human rights law. As a result, and following more than three years of intensive work, new criminal and criminal procedure codes were promulgated in July 2003.[33] The new Provisional Criminal Code introduces substantial reforms to the law on crimes against international law and sexual offences, and significantly modernizes the law on penal sanctions to broaden the regime of alternative punishments. The new Provisional Criminal Procedure Code introduces extensive reforms to strengthen prosecutorial capacity and increase the efficiency of proceedings as well as enhancing the protection of persons involved in the criminal justice system. The training of 370 judges and prosecutors, as well as police and practitioners, in the several hundred pages of new law took a number of months, and the new Codes entered into force in April 2004.

1. Introducing international judges and prosecutors to local law

The international judges and prosecutors come from every continent of the world and from many different civil and common law traditions. UNMIK relies greatly on Member States to recommend suitable candidates, but also

---

[31] Section 1.5 of UNMIK Reg 1999/ 24 (On the Law Applicable in Kosovo).

[32] See UNMIK Reg 2001/4 (On the Prohibition of Trafficking in Persons in Kosovo), UNMIK Reg 2000/12 (On the Prohibition of Terrorism and Related Offences), and UNMIK Reg 2003/1 (Amending the Applicable Law on Criminal Offences Involving Sexual Violence).

[33] See UNMIK Reg. 2003/25 of 6 July 2003 (On the Provisional Criminal Code of Kosovo) and UNMIK Reg. 2003/26 of 6 July 2003 (On the Provisional Criminal Procedure Code of Kosovo).

recruits candidates directly through open competitive advertisements (subject, of course, to the consent of the judiciary in their home countries). Candidates must have substantial experience as a professional judge dealing with criminal law cases in their home jurisdiction, as well as a knowledge of the civil law system and be familiar with international human rights standards and legal principles.

It is a great testament to their qualities that they have adapted with surprisingly little difficulty to Kosovo's criminal law and procedure. UNMIK has of course translated all the Codes and commentaries into English, and judges and prosecutors have helped compile reference works for the guidance of new IJPs. In most cases a short initial training course suffices to acquaint them with the local law and procedure. They work together with legal officers who help them with research on the applicable law as well as drafting.

They bring from their home jurisdictions a sensitivity to human rights norms, and an appreciation of the independence of the judiciary, which were not sufficiently embedded in the previous legal culture, and certainly when they work in collaboration with their local counterparts this undoubtedly helps spread a culture of human rights throughout the Kosovo justice system.

2. Civil cases

Civil cases, with two important exceptions, have remained the exclusive provision of the local justice system.[34]

The first exception was the creation in 1999 of the Housing and Property Directorate (HPD), with exclusive jurisdiction to determine sensitive residential property disputes which could not properly be left to the local justice system, such as claims from persons displaced from their property during or after the war (largely Kosovo Serbs), and from Kosovo Albanians claiming that their property rights were revoked or unrecognized as a result of the discriminatory laws of the Milosevic regime.[35] An international claims tribunal, the Housing and Property Claims Commission (HPCC), determines those disputes which cannot be resolved by mediation.

The difficulties of conflicts between this separate commission and the regular courts soon became apparent. Although the Regulation establishing the HPD made it clear that the HPCC's jurisdiction was exclusive and its decisions not subject to judicial review,[36] this still left open the possibility for conflict where a regular court decided that a claim fell outside the categories

---

[34] But note that, in common with many civil law systems, injured parties may participate in the criminal proceedings and claim an award of compensation against the defendant if convicted.

[35] See UNMIK Reg 1999/23 (On the Establishment of the Housing and Property Directorate and the Housing and Property Claims Commission).

[36] See ibid ss 2.5 and 2.7.

of exclusive jurisdiction in the HPD Regulation, but the HPD or HPCC took a different view. A circular was drafted to all the regular courts requiring them to suspend any proceedings concerning property which was the subject of an HPD claim until the HPD had resolved the claim or determined that it had no jurisdiction. However, unless one of the parties to a pending court claim was aware of a conflicting claim before the HPD and brought this to the court's attention, there was no way in which the court would know of the conflict.

Furthermore, a lack of resources caused the HPD to accumulate a large backlog of unprocessed cases, causing conflicting cases in the regular courts to be frozen for unreasonably long periods. Since the HPD fell outside the justice system, there was no method by which the Police and Justice Pillar could ensure a coordinated response to the problem.

The experience of the HPD Regulation highlighted some of the potential problems which may arise where a new, separate court with exclusive jurisdiction is created rather than (as with the IJP programme), 'internationalizing' the existing court system.

The second exception was established as part of the programme of privatization in 2003. Much of Kosovo's industry and commercial sector before the war was run by public and 'socially-owned' enterprises. Many of these enterprises are now in a near-bankrupt state, with their assets tied up in complex legal questions of ownership and unresolved creditor claims. In order to revitalize Kosovo's economy, UNMIK has set up a public agency, the Kosovo Trust Agency (KTA), to administer these enterprises and to spin off their assets to private enterprises.[37] The proceeds from these privatizations will be used to settle outstanding claims and then held in trust pending the resolution of Kosovo's final status. However, many of the creditors in question are Serbs, and Belgrade voiced strong opposition to the principle of privatization of assets belonging to the former Federal Republic of Yugoslavia, as well as to these claims being determined by the Kosovo regular courts, 90 per cent of whose judges are ethnically Albanian. Consequently, a new court has been established, called the Special Chamber of the Supreme Court ('the Special Chamber'),[38] with exclusive jurisdiction to determine these creditor claims, as well as any appeals against the KTA's decisions and related matters.

Despite its name, the Special Chamber is not in fact structurally part of the Supreme Court of Kosovo. The President of the Supreme Court has no jurisdiction over it or its judges, and it does not hear appeals from the regular courts. For the matters within its exclusive jurisdiction, it is the court of first and last instance (unless it chooses to exercise its power to refer claims back

---

[37] See UNMIK Reg 2002/12 (On the Establishment of the Kosovo Trust Agency).
[38] See UNMIK Reg 2002/13 (On the Establishment of a Special Chamber of the Supreme Court of Kosovo on Kosovo Trust Agency Related Matters).

to the regular courts for decision). It is composed of three international judges and two local judges. It works with a separate registry, separate staff, and under special rules of procedure. This was perhaps inevitable given the very special nature of the Special Chamber's work; and in any event, the Special Chamber is intended only to have a short life, because once the KTA has done its work there will be no more claims for it to decide.

The Special Chamber opened its doors to receive claims as recently as June 2003. UNMIK will apply the lessons learned from the experience of the HPD and will seek to ensure that questions of jurisdiction and conflicts with claims pending before regular courts can be resolved speedily; and at least the Special Chamber (unlike the HPD and HPCC) comes within the jurisdiction of the Police and Justice Pillar of UNMIK, which will help ensure optimum coordination between the jurisdictions.

E. CRITICISMS OF THE IJP PROGRAMME

1. *Too few judges and prosecutors*

The system UNMIK has established for international judges and prosecutors has not been without its critics. The most acute problem has undoubtedly been the need to tackle so many cases with so few judges and prosecutors. The assignment of Regulation 2000/64 panels, with two or three international judges hearing an entire case, places an especially heavy burden on resources, requiring an elaborate juggling act under which judges find themselves having to run a number of different trials side-by-side, often in different courts across the province. That in turn means that cases take longer to try than they should. The relatively short terms of office of international judges and prosecutors—many of whom stay for only six months or one year in the Mission—aggravates this problem.

While there is always room for improvement, we do not realistically believe that this problem can be avoided. International judges as we know them in Kosovo are something of a novelty in international peace-keeping. East Timor, Sierra Leone, and Bosnia provide the only other examples, all of them more recently established than in Kosovo. There is still only a very small international force of professional judges willing and able to leave their domestic jurisdictions for extended Mission service, compared to the large resource of professional international peace-keepers from whom missions are able to draw their staff. This is in stark contrast to the police. A long history of deployment of international peace-keeping forces means that many Member States of the United Nations have well-established procedures for recruiting and deploying large numbers of civilian police to missions such as UNMIK; whereas the channels for selecting and deploying suitable judges and prosecutors are much less well developed. The fact that the IJPs must be able to draft judgments and submissions and conduct proceedings in English places another real barrier to recruitment. UNMIK depends to a great extent on individual applications in response to vacancy announcements, and receives far fewer of these for judicial than for other Mission posts, and once they are recruited judges and prosecutors do not tend to stay as long as other Mission personnel.

2. *Capacity-building of local judges and prosecutors*

International judges are sometimes reproached for having done too little to build up the capacity of the local judiciary.[39] Indeed, sometimes it is supposed that the main justification for the appointment of international judges is their power to train the local judiciary in the application of international human rights norms.

The simple answer to this criticism is that capacity-building as such is not the primary function of the international judicial programme. International judges by and large do not have the necessary training to be educators, and they can only be involved in a small minority of the overall caseload.

This is not to say that capacity-building is not a vital objective for the justice system in Kosovo. Local judges throughout Kosovo still do not demonstrate adequate skills, and in particular an adequate understanding of human rights norms, but if any criticism is warranted then it should not be levelled at international judges, but at the Kosovo Judicial Institute, within the OSCE Institution Building Pillar—a training institute which has only ever provided a limited programme of voluntary courses for judges and prosecutors. What is needed is a thorough training programme which all judges and prosecutors must attend before they are appointed. The Kosovo Judicial Institute is now to be re-established to provide precisely this type of basic education.

However, we do accept that there is a role for IJPs to play in building the strength of the justice system in Kosovo. They do this, of course, in a limited way whenever they sit with local colleagues in Regulation 2000/6 cases, and it is very much part of the Department of Justice's transition strategy to rely more and more on this Regulation so that local judges have an increasing involvement, especially in organized crime cases. It is necessary to proceed step-by-step, though, as the primary objective of ensuring credible neutrality in sensitive cases cannot be compromised.

We also believe that the role of jurisprudence in the Kosovan justice system needs to be strengthened. The Supreme Court of Kosovo could play a much stronger role in giving guidance on the law to lower courts by the publication

---

[39] On this point, see Chapter 3 (Cerone/Baldwin), at pp. 52–4.

of its judgments. To this end, UNMIK has begun to appoint international judges to the Supreme Court who will work closely with their local colleagues to build up the Court's role in this area.

It is perhaps convenient to mention at this point the other major measures that UNMIK has undertaken in pursuit of its mandate to build a functioning, independent, and multi-ethnic justice system.

First, it is essential to have independent monitoring of cases to ensure that problems in the operation of the local justice system are brought to UNMIK's attention. This is OSCE's role, and its weekly reports on human rights and rule of law issues, together with six-monthly reviews of the criminal justice system, have proved invaluable in showing what reforms need to be undertaken. However, this is very costly on resources, and the great majority of civil cases in particular have not been adequately monitored.

Secondly, there must be an independent oversight mechanism to ensure that complaints of misconduct against judges and prosecutors are independently and fearlessly investigated. The Judicial Inspection Unit in the Department of Justice performs this role, presenting its reports to the KJPC which has the power to discipline local judges and prosecutors and, if necessary, recommend their removal from office.

Thirdly, building a multi-ethnic justice system (involving adequate representation of minorities amongst judges, prosecutors, and court staff, as well as adequate access to courts for all minorities) requires sustained and strategic effort under international control. The Judicial Integration Section of the Department of Justice was established for this purpose, following a commitment made in the UNMIK–Federal Republic of Yugoslavia Common Document of 5 November 2001,[40] and has achieved notable success in the first years of its existence, quadrupling the number of Serbian judges and prosecutors and substantially increasing the access of minority communities to courts.

Fourthly, adequate systems of criminal and civil legal aid must be established in compliance with international human rights norms. The criminal system is currently administered by the executive (Department of Judicial Administration within the Ministry of Public Services), while a civil legal aid pilot project is being jointly run by the European Agency for Reconstruction with the Kosovo Chamber of Advocates. UNMIK is now beginning to plan for the replacement of these two systems by an integrated and sustainable institution for the provision of legal aid.

Fifthly, those improperly detained by the police and courts must have adequate means of redress in accordance with the guarantees of Article 5 of the European Convention on Human Rights. Compensation for those

---

[40] The Common Document is available at http://www.serbia.sr.gov.yu/news/2001-11/14/320901.html.

wrongfully detained is determined by a special judicial commission which was re-established by UNMIK in accordance with the applicable law.

Finally, capacity-building is needed not only for judges and prosecutors, but for lawyers as well. In late 2001 the Bar Examination was re-introduced as the minimum qualification required to practise law in Kosovo, together with training administered in cooperation with the OSCE.

3. *Administrative and functional aspects of independence*

Criticism is often levelled at the separate rules that govern the recruitment and assignment of international judges and prosecutors, and in particular the fact that the executive (the SRSG acting in practice on the recommendations of the Department of Justice) has complete control over their appointment and assignment; furthermore, they are appointed on six-month contracts whose renewal is entirely at UNMIK's discretion. It is said that these very facts undermine their independence and are to be deplored.

These criticisms seem to us to be quite misconceived. Of course administrative independence and security of tenure are essential for the justice system which UNMIK must build for Kosovo's future, but the IJPs are not part of that future. They are a special force for intervention, to enable UNMIK to administer impartial justice at this early phase, when the local judiciary is too weak to be able to withstand the societal pressures on it in the aftermath of the conflict. Their appointment and deployment is therefore highly tactical, and must be under the United Nations' direct control (while remaining quite independent of the local judiciary, who play a major role in the administration of the Kosovo justice system). They are in Kosovo, like all UNMIK international staff, only for a short time, to help build a new society in Kosovo, and then to leave.

But it is important to distinguish between the appointment and deployment of judges and prosecutors, a strategic function which is quite properly under UNMIK control, from their independence in the exercise of their functions, which is sacrosanct. Once a judge has been assigned to a case, he or she will try it as he or she thinks fit, and UNMIK may not—and does not—interfere.

4. *Developing a human rights jurisprudence in Kosovo*

Another criticism levelled is that UNMIK's international judges and prosecutors have not helped develop the role of international human rights principles in Kosovan jurisprudence. This criticism is not well founded. Familiarity with international human rights standards is required of all IJPs, and UNMIK has been fortunate in attracting some candidates with particularly strong backgrounds in this area, notably a former judge of the

European Court of Human Rights, who sits on the Supreme Court of Kosovo. As a result, international human rights principles have been widely invoked in appellate decisions when ruling on the interpretation of the law and its application.[41]

However, this is an incidental benefit of the IJP programme, and not its primary rationale, which is the need to ensure impartial trials in sensitive cases, and to reverse biased trials on appeal. The 3 to 4 per cent of the more serious criminal cases which are tried with the involvement of international judges cannot on their own adequately impart a human rights culture into the judiciary at large. For that, as we have said, a proper system of training of judges needs to be introduced.

F. LESSONS LEARNED

In sum, what has the experience in establishing the internationalized judiciary in Kosovo taught UNMIK?

First, an international judicial presence is essential from the very start of a Mission in order to re-establish the rule of law in a society destabilized by ethnic violence or organized crime, working closely with an international civilian police force. Without this presence, UNMIK would have made no real progress in bringing the organized and war criminals to justice, and much of the work of the international police would have been frustrated. Indeed, exactly this was the experience of Bosnia, where an international judicial element has now been established within the new State Court to tackle the many serious crimes which the local judges and prosecutors have failed to address.

Secondly, the internationalization of the existing court system is a better solution than the creation of a separate jurisdiction. Although it developed more by force of circumstance than by design, as we have seen, the system of deploying judges side-by-side with local colleagues within the existing legal framework is more flexible, because it allows internationals to be deployed at different stages of a case and to differing degrees. Furthermore, it avoids problems of conflicts between jurisdictions; it is better accepted by the local judiciary itself; and it presents better opportunities for mentoring and institution-building of the local justice system. In short, it is a more sustainable solution. Ad hoc courts of extraordinary jurisdiction should be reserved for questions which arise only in the context of the Mission itself, so that there is no question of capacity-building or sustainability to be addressed, such as the Special Chamber of the Supreme Court whose functions are intimately linked with UNMIK's privatization agenda.

---

[41] Examples include *Bartetzko* (sentencing), *Idriz Seqiri* (effect of excessive pre-trial detention), *Gligorovski* (*in absentia* verdicts for humanitarian law violations), *Xhavit Hasani* (execution of foreign criminal sentences).

Thirdly, organized crime needs to be targeted as a priority from the start of any Mission. Inevitably, following inter-ethnic conflict, war and ethnic crimes have the highest profile and are addressed first. But organized crime is not only just as deadly to the establishment of the rule of law, democratic institutions, and a functioning economy, but its exponents are in fact closely linked with those who perpetrate ethnic violence and extremism.

Fourthly, international involvement is only one of the tools that are needed to fight these crimes effectively. A strong witness protection programme, adequate security measures, and the equipment to perform covert surveillance within a proper legal framework are equally important, and need to be put in place at the very start of any Mission.

Fifthly, the deployment of international judges and prosecutors is complementary, not alternative, to direct capacity-building of local judges and prosecutors. Internationals will inevitably be only a small minority of the total judiciary. Their primary focus is the trial of the cases assigned to them. The judicial training school which is now being established should have been one of the first priorities of the Mission.

5

East Timor: Trials and Tribulations

Sylvia de Bertodano*

One of the principal issues facing the United Nations Transitional Administration in East Timor (UNTAET) when it arrived in East Timor in October 1999 was the question of how those responsible for the violence of the preceding 10 months were to be brought to justice. In January 2000 an International Commission of Enquiry reported to the UN Security Council as follows:

> The United Nations should establish an international human rights tribunal consisting of judges appointed by the United Nations, preferably with the participation of members from East Timor and Indonesia. The tribunal would sit in Indonesia, East Timor, and any other relevant territory to receive the complaints and to try and sentence those accused ... of serious violations of fundamental human rights and international humanitarian law which took place in East Timor since January 1999.[1]

This recommendation was not acted on by the Security Council. Instead, reliance was placed on promises made by Indonesia that it would try its own suspects in Jakarta; and the Special Panels for Serious Crimes, composed of national and international judges, were established by UNTAET in East Timor's capital, Dili, to try suspects in East Timor.

The Special Panels for Serious Crimes in Dili are the first specially constructed internationalized courts which have tried serious crimes within a local justice system. However, due to a lack of commitment in terms of funding, personnel, and political will, the success of this experiment has been limited.

This chapter reviews the experiment in internationalized justice which is taking place in Dili. In an attempt to provide an overall assessment, it also reviews the progress of the ad hoc tribunal in Jakarta.

A. THE DILI TRIALS

The UN Serious Crimes Unit (SCU) in Dili, which is responsible for the investigation and prosecution of serious crimes committed during 1999,

* BA Hons Oxon (1990); barrister, 25 Bedford Row, London, specializing in international criminal law. Sponsored by No Peace Without Justice in 2001–2002 to work as a defence attorney before the Special Panels in East Timor, and to represent East Timor at the Preparatory Commission for the International Criminal Court.
[1] United Nations Office of the High Commissioner for Human Rights: 'Report of the International Commission of Enquiry on East Timor to the Secretary General (January 2000).

started its work in July 2000. Trials began before the Special Panels of the Dili District Court in early 2001. The statistics in August 2003 showed some degree of success: 301 alleged perpetrators had been indicted by the General Prosecutor in 65 indictments; 273 of those indicted were charged with crimes against humanity. There have been no cases in which war crimes or genocide have been charged (although the Court of Appeal has found a defendant, who was not so charged, guilty of genocide on appeal, see below).

By August 2003 judgment had been handed down against a total of 31 defendants. A further 35 cases were being tried or awaiting trial.

However, the system suffers from several serious flaws. The most significant are lack of cooperation with Indonesia; political considerations affecting prosecutions; financial and administrative problems; and uncertainty as to applicable law.

1. Lack of cooperation with Indonesia

A Memorandum of Understanding (MOU), signed on 6 April 2000 by the Indonesian government and UNTAET,[2] regulates among other matters the sharing of information between the two systems. This states:

The Parties shall, in accordance with the present Memorandum of Understanding, afford to each other the widest possible measure of mutual assistance in investigations or court proceedings in respect of offences the prosecution of which at the time of the request for assistance falls within the jurisdiction of the judicial authorities of the requested Party.[3]

It goes on to detail types of cooperation, and states:

The Parties undertake to transfer to each other all persons whom the competent authorities of the requesting Party are prosecuting for a criminal offence or whom these authorities want for the purposes of serving a sentence.[4]

In reality, however, there has been little cooperation offered by the Indonesian authorities. The Indonesian Parliament refused to recognize the validity of the MOU. All requests for transfer of suspects made by the Serious Crimes Unit in Dili have met with silence.[5] By August 2003 not one suspect had been transferred to East Timor by the Indonesian authorities. This means that suspects in most of the outstanding cases are still at large, and are unlikely ever to be brought to justice in East Timor.

---

[2] Memorandum of Understanding between the Republic of Indonesia and the United Nations Transitional Administration in East Timor regarding cooperation in Legal, Judicial and Human Rights Related Matters (MOU) (6 April 2000).
   [3] ibid s 1.1.
   [4] ibid s 9.1.
   [5] Interview with SCU Prosecutor, 15 November 2002.

Nor has any cooperation been given regarding other matters, such as the attendance of witnesses. Lists of potential witnesses have been given to the Indonesian authorities, with requests for their attendance. No formal reply has ever been received.[6] Thousands of Indonesian civilians who were living in East Timor in 1999 returned to Indonesia. When East Timor achieved independence on 20 May 2002, there were still an estimated 50,000 East Timorese refugees who had fled East Timor in 1999 living in West Timor and Indonesia. This means that a large volume of eyewitness testimony is simply unavailable to the courts in East Timor.

Inevitably, it is the principal suspects who remain in Indonesia under the protection of the Indonesian government, while those on trial in East Timor are far smaller fry. All defendants who are within the jurisdiction of the court are East Timorese citizens who are alleged to have been members of pro-autonomy (or, in one case, pro-independence) militia groups in 1999. Many are illiterate farmers who admit to the part they played in the crimes committed, and state simply that they were acting under the orders of their superiors, often under threat of force. Meanwhile, high-ranking militia commanders and members of the Indonesian military remain at large in Indonesia. In August 2003, these amounted to 221 of the 301 suspects indicted by the SCU.

This is comparable to the problem suffered by the International Criminal Tribunal for the former Yugoslavia (ICTY) in its early years. In that case, a changing political climate, and ultimately a change of government, meant that it was able to secure increasingly high-ranking defendants as the years passed, culminating in the arrest of President Milosevic in 2001. However, there is little likelihood that such a dramatic change in circumstances will take place in Indonesia. In the absence of the political will to conduct proper trials in Jakarta,[7] the most likely result is that the real leaders of the violence in East Timor in 1999 will never come to trial.

The feeling of injustice which this creates both among defendants who are on trial, and among victims of the violence, is understandably strong.

2. Political considerations affecting prosecutions

I. Conflict between prosecutions and refugee returns

After the result of the ballot was announced on 4 September 1999, an estimated 200,000 East Timorese fled, or were deported, to Indonesia. UNTAET was mandated by the Security Council to ensure their return and resettlement.[8] This part of the mandate created a potential conflict

---

[6] Interview with SCU Prosecutor, 15 November 2002.   [7] See below 91FF.
[8] UNSC Res 1272 (1999) para 10.

with another part, which was to ensure that the perpetrators of the 1999 atrocities are brought to justice. Many refugees were ex-militia who were afraid to return for fear of prosecution. Vigorous prosecution of the perpetrators could therefore discourage refugees from returning.

East Timorese militia leaders residing in West Timor have posed a particular problem, as they continue to have strong influence within their communities. These major suspects can be politically useful in the matter of refugee returns, and there is some concern that the aim of bringing them to justice has been compromised as a result. A report in May 2001 stated:

militia leaders and other prominent opponents of East Timor's independence ensconced in Indonesian West Timor are feted and treated like state visitors on UN sponsored 'look see' visits to East Timor, supposedly designed to encourage the return of refugees held captive by the militias in West Timor ... In the name of reconciliation the UNTAET Chief of Staff[9] spends much of his time courting militia leaders such as the Carvalho brothers whose militias razed Ainaro town to the ground.[10]

The Carvalho family cited in this report provides a good example of the danger of political objectives entering the legal process. It was not only the former Chief of Staff who was involved in negotiations with them: Xanana Gusmao, who became the first President of East Timor on 20 May 2002, had previously visited the Carvalhos in West Timor to negotiate returns.

But of most concern to those involved in the legal process is that members of the SCU were also involved in these negotiations, and there are fears that the will to prosecute the cases objectively was diminished as a result. Leading prosecutors visited West Timor during 2001, in the company of political leaders, to discuss terms with the Carvalho brothers. When Nemecio De Carvalho returned in October 2001 he was brought before the court as a suspect, released on bail, and was having dinner with the Chief of Staff and senior prosecutors at a restaurant in Dili the same evening.[11] His brother, Cancio, persuaded the United Nations to appoint and pay for a private defence attorney for him as a condition of his return. Having secured this unique privilege, he nonetheless failed to return in January 2002 as promised, citing unspecified 'technical reasons' for his decision to stay in West Timor.[12] In August 2003 he had still not returned.

---

[9] Malaysian diplomat N Parameswaran.

[10] Vanja Tanaja 'East Timor: UN Lets Indonesian Military Off the Hook' *Green Left Weekly* (9 May 2001, Issue 447), quoted in Suzannah Linton 'Cambodia, East Timor and Sierra Leone: Experiments in International Justice' (2001) 12 *Criminal Law Forum* 225.

[11] Pieter Smit 'Serious Crimes Unit in Third Major Crisis' *Timor Post* (13 November 2001).

[12] JSMP 'Return of Mahidi Militia Chief Canceled for 'Technical Reasons' (7 January 2002) www.jsmp.minihub.org/News/news8_1-3.htm.

In 2001 Suzannah Linton wrote:

The extent, if at all, to which UNTAET's cultivation of certain militia leaders has dictated investigation and prosecution strategy is unknown, but what is clear is that certain militia leaders involved in the reconciliation process are able to enter and leave East Timor without fear of arrest for serious crimes.[13]

II. Lack of coherent prosecution strategy

It is at best unfortunate that no proper prosecution strategy was developed by the SCU at the outset of its work. In the first two years of its operation, indictees were a haphazard mixture of various—but by no means all—political and military leaders; and of low-ranking militia members who just happened to be within the geographical jurisdiction of the court.

The mandate given to UNTAET by the Security Council included prosecuting 'those responsible' for the atrocities in 1999.[14] It is arguable that the SCU should have taken one of two courses: it should either have concentrated exclusively on the high command, prepared its cases, issued indictments and arrest warrants, and then reported back to the Security Council that it was unable to fulfil its mandate because Indonesia's failure to cooperate meant that it was unable to carry out arrests.

Alternatively, it could have acted like an ordinary domestic justice system, and investigated and prosecuted anyone within its jurisdiction against whom there was evidence, regardless of their role in the overall command structure.

In either case, it would have had a coherent strategy. The former course would have made it clear that Indonesia's lack of cooperation was making it impossible for it to fulfil its mandate. As it is, poor management led to a random and disorganized system. Many small-time militia members appear to have been indicted simply because they were in the wrong place at the wrong time, while higher ranking commanders are still at liberty. Whether a person is prosecuted or not appears to be the result of an accident of geography.

In January 2002 the leadership of the SCU changed when the post of Deputy Prosecutor for Serious Crimes was taken over by the experienced Norwegian prosecutor, Siri Frigaard. This led to a more coherent prosecution strategy, under which resources were concentrated on framing indictments against political and military leaders, whether or not they were in the jurisdiction of the court.

However, the early indictment policy and the impossibility of obtaining the attendance of those protected by the Indonesian government has meant that trials before the Special Panels are still exclusively of the small fry.

[13] Linton (*supra* n 10) 225.   [14] UNSC Res 1272 (1999) para 16.

There has therefore been no change to the feeling that the decision as to who will come before the courts has not been based on fair and objective criteria.

III. UN failure to support its prosecutors

Further difficulties have been caused by the fact that the strategy of issuing indictments of the high command failed to receive support from the United Nations. The credibility of the United Nations' resolve to provide justice with regard to the events of 1999 was thrown into doubt in February 2003 when an indictment was issued against seven high-ranking Indonesian officers, the most notable of whom was the former Minister of Defence and Commander of the armed forces, General Wiranto.[15] The former Governor of East Timor, Abilio Soares, was also charged.

General Wiranto had been named in the Indonesian Human Rights Commission Report published in January 2000[16] as bearing ultimate responsibility for the violence which occurred in East Timor in 1999. However, he was not among the 18 indicted by the Jakarta court.

The indictment issued by the SCU charges the eight men with crimes against humanity in the form of murder, deportation, and persecution. It charges the Indonesian military commanders with participating in the establishment of the armed militia groups, and participating in a policy of funding, training, arming, and directing the militia. Six of the officers are charged with both direct and superior responsibility; General Wiranto is charged solely on the basis of his superior responsibility.

The issuing of this indictment caused a political furore. Unlike previous indictees, Wiranto is still a leading figure in Indonesian politics; on 6 August 2003, after much speculation, he officially announced his intention to seek the nomination of Golkar, Indonesia's second largest political party, for the 2004 presidential election. It remains to be seen whether the fact that an application has been made to Interpol for an arrest warrant for him will hinder his political ambitions; certainly Wiranto himself seems undeterred by it.

While Wiranto responded to news of his indictment by making public protestations of his innocence, East Timor's political leaders were quick to distance themselves from the charges. The President of East Timor, Xanana Gusmao, issued a public statement in which he expressed regret that the Office of the General Prosecutor did not consult him before issuing the indictment, and stating that he considered that it was 'not in the national

---

[15] *Prosecutor v Wiranto and seven others* (24 February 2003) Indictment.
[16] KPP HAM 'Report on the Investigation of Human Rights Violations in East Timor' (31 January 2000).

interest to hold a legal process such as this one in East Timor'. He stressed the importance of the continued good relationship with Indonesia.[17]

It is notable that the President's statement referred to the indictment 'by the Deputy General Prosecutor', and referred to the fact that it was issued while the General Prosecutor was abroad. The Prosecution Office in East Timor is headed by a Timorese General Prosecutor; the Deputy General Prosecutor is a UN appointee who effectively heads the SCU. Therefore, the President was making it clear that he considered this indictment to be the responsibility of the United Nations, and not the Timorese authorities.

UNMISET[18] had other ideas: having been happy to accept the credit for all previous indictments, which had been issued under the UN stamp, it was quick to deny responsibility for this one. The day after the indictment was issued, the Special Representative of the Secretary General issued a press statement to clarify that 'while Indictments are prepared by international staff, they are issued under the legal authority of the Timorese Prosecutor-General. The United Nations does not have any legal authority to issue indictments'.[19]

At a Press Briefing in New York on the same day, UN spokesman Fred Eckhard told reporters: 'We hope that in future you'll say "East Timor indicts", and not "the United Nations indicts" '.[20]

While it is true that in independent East Timor, the United Nations is not the prosecuting authority, these statements are highly disingenuous. They belie the fact that the SCU, which is responsible for such prosecutions, is headed and staffed by international prosecutors who are UN employees; the Timorese prosecutors deal almost exclusively with ordinary crimes. The serious crimes process has been initiated, staffed and spearheaded by the United Nations. But it seems that for the United Nations, indicting the commander of the armed forces was a step too far: this was now a political rather than a legal matter.

It is, to say the least, distasteful, that the United Nations, which took credit for the serious crimes process when it was issuing indictments against the Timorese militia and the lower ranking Indonesian military, was so quick to disown it when it indicted those whom prosecutors perceived to be the real leaders of the atrocities. It is not a situation which gives hope for future UN-backed initiatives; the rule seems to be that trials of atrocities can only take place provided they do not rock the political boat. The fearless and impartial

[17] Statement by His Excellency Kay Rala Xanana Gusmao on the Indictment by the Deputy General Prosecutor for Serious Crimes of Indonesian Officers for Events in Timor-Leste during 1999.
[18] United Nations Mission in Support in East Timor—the follow-on mission, which succeeded UNTAET on 20 May 2003 when East Timor achieved independence.
[19] UNMISET *Serious Crimes Process in Timor-Leste* Press Release (25 February 1999).
[20] UN Daily Press Briefing by the Office of the Spokesman for the Secretary-General (25 February 2003).

pursuit of justice was dealt a severe blow by the United Nations' refusal to back its own prosecutors.

3. Financial and administrative problems

However, not all the problems suffered by the Special Panels can be blamed on political difficulties. In the view of many, the United Nations failed to commit the necessary support to the Panels to make the experiment viable even in its own limited terms.

The ambitiousness of the system established by the United Nations in East Timor should not be underestimated: the substantive provisions of an entirely new system of law, the Rome Statute for the International Criminal Court (ICC), were being used for the first time anywhere in the world. These provisions were to be implemented in a court system which had been decimated by the Indonesian withdrawal. There were almost no qualified lawyers in East Timor, no functioning courts or court system, and no one with any experience of how a court system should operate.

One of the first international lawyers to work within the Serious Crimes Unit in Dili, Suzannah Linton, writes:

it is not known why it was felt that the legal regime designed for the ICC could realistically be implemented in the district court of one of the world's poorest nations. ... It is no easy matter to investigate, prosecute, defend and try international crimes, particularly if this is to be carried out with due process, full respect for the rights of the accused and in a way which focuses on those most responsible. It is unknown if UNTAET seriously considered the costs that would arise out of having such an ambitious programme to prosecute atrocities at the District Court of Dili before it proceeded with the adoption of Regulation 2000/11.[21] In the time between the passing of that regulation and Regulation 2000/15,[22] no budget was prepared and approved to ensure the implementation of the Serious Crimes venture. Thus, the prosecution of Serious Crimes in East Timor has been crippled from the start by lack of resources.[23]

A number of human rights groups and international observers over the years have drawn attention to the problem of underfunding and inefficient use of resources. However, attempts to remedy the problem have been belated and inadequate. Sufficient appointments only began to be made in the summer of 2003, three years after the inception of the serious crimes process. By this time, many trials had already taken place with wholly inadequate resources which cast doubt on their fairness, and the political climate in East Timor was leaning towards amnesties in response to the inadequacy of the process. It is therefore arguably too late for the new appointments to have any real effect.

---

[21] UNTAET Reg 2000/11 (6 March 2000) (On the Organization of Courts in East Timor).
[22] UNTAET Reg 2000/15 (6 June 2000) (On the Establishment of Panels with Exclusive Jurisdiction over Serious Criminal Offences).
[23] Linton (*supra* n 10) 213–15.

These problems can be illustrated by looking at three principal areas.

I. Chambers

Each Panel is composed of three judges: two international judges and one East Timorese. In order for two trial Panels and one appeal Panel to operate, six international judges are needed. From June 2000 until July 2003 there was never a time when all these positions were filled. In October 2001 there were three international judges for the Special Panels, and two for the Court of Appeal. By January 2002 both of the Appeal Court judges had left the Mission. There were therefore no sittings of the Court of Appeal between November 2001 and July 2003, when new appointments allowed the Court of Appeal to restart its work. By that stage, there was a backlog of over 60 cases awaiting a hearing.

Until July 2003, there were never sufficient international judges for more than one trial panel to sit at once. From September 2002 there were only two international judges remaining in East Timor, sufficient for a single trial panel. In April 2003 this was reduced to one, and no panels could sit. New appointments were made in July 2003, so that for the first time since their inception, it was possible for two Special Panels to sit at once. However, it is regrettable that in August 2003 no Special Panels were sitting despite these recent appointments, due to judicial holidays. Court hearings were not scheduled to restart until September.

The result of these delays is that a backlog of cases has built up, and East Timor suffers from the same problem which has beset ICTR and ICTY: defendants are being kept in custody for unacceptably long periods awaiting trial. By August 2003 some defendants charged with serious crimes had been in custody for up to three-and-a-half years without a realistic trial date having been set.

In addition to the lack of judges there is an astonishing lack of judicial staff. There are no judges' clerks, researchers, or secretaries. The task of taking a note of the proceedings is left to the judges themselves. Any judgment has to be researched, written, and typed by the judges. More often than not these judges are not writing in their first language. The most substantial judgment to date was that in the *Los Palos* trial.[24] The judgment was written in English by judges from Brazil, Burundi, and East Timor. Grammatical and other corrections to the English version had to be made by the Australian translators before they could translate the document into Indonesian.

Most international judges who have been appointed to posts in East Timor have had no previous experience of international law. There is no library of texts for the judges to refer to. Until late in 2001 there was not even any

---

[24] *Prosecutor v Joni Marquez and nine others* 9/2000 (11 December 2001) Judgment.

Internet access. It is perhaps not entirely surprising that before the judgment in the *Los Palos* trial on 11 December 2001, no judgment contained any reference to any international criminal law. This was despite the fact that prosecution and defence had referred to such law in their closing submissions in several cases. Improvements can be noted towards the end of 2002 in the judgments of the Special Panels, which had begun to show a greater regard for international jurisprudence; however, it is notable that the judgment of the Court of Appeal in its most important and controversial case since it resumed work contained not a single reference to international law.[25]

II. Translation and interpretation

The Special Panels work in four official languages: Tetum, Indonesian, Portuguese, and English. Defendants tend to speak Indonesian and/or Tetum. National lawyers address the court in Indonesian. International lawyers speak predominantly English. Judges speak either English or Portuguese. Some defendants or witnesses speak none of these four languages but only a local dialect such as Fataluku or Bunak. Interpreting is therefore often done in relay across three or more languages.

This in itself causes a problem, which has been exacerbated by severe understaffing in the translation department. One person is often required to interpret in court for several hours without a break. Further, many of the interpreters have had no formal training, and no previous experience of legal interpretation. The accuracy of interpretation is therefore questionable.

In some cases the judges have attached substantial weight in their findings against an accused to inconsistencies in his statements. A report in November 2001 by the Judicial Systems Monitoring Programme (JSMP), whose observers have covered almost every trial hearing before the Special Panels, states that in one judgment:

the defendant's credibility was impugned because of apparent inconsistencies in his testimony as to whether or not he had a gun on the night of 25 September 1999. The possibility cannot be discounted that the alleged inconsistencies were simply the product of language difficulties between the participants in court.[26]

The interpretation problems therefore cast doubts over whether defendants are receiving fair trials.

III. Defence counsel

The Department of Justice has responsibility for the Defence Lawyers' Unit (DLU). Lack of capacity in defence is also an area of concern. By January

---

[25] *Prosecutor v Armando dos Santos* 16/2001 Court of Appeal Decision (15 July 2003).
[26] Judicial Systems Monitoring Programme *Justice in Practice: Human Rights in Court Administration* (November 2001) 31 www.jsmp.minihub.org/Reports/JSMP1.pdf.

2003 there were only 10 national lawyers to conduct all the ordinary crime cases in East Timor, as well as civil and family cases. They therefore had limited time to participate in long serious crimes trials. Furthermore, none of these lawyers had any court experience at all before the arrival of UNTAET in 1999. In practice, by 2003 they were taking no real part in the serious crimes process.

Serious crimes have been dealt with by a small number of international lawyers, usually about three at any one time, who have been assigned to the DLU. However, at least during the early stages of operation, they were often lawyers with no experience of court work, or of international or even criminal law. Therefore the assistance they were able to provide was often limited.

The *Los Palos* case, which took place during 2001, was the first crimes against humanity trial in East Timor—or indeed anywhere else—in which these crimes were tried under the substantive provisions of the Rome Statute. Ten defendants were represented by a total of three national and three international lawyers. One of the three international lawyers was present for only part of the case; another did not speak either of the languages (Indonesian and English) in which the prosecution witness statements were served. The only defence closing argument which referred to international legal authorities was that on behalf of the first defendant, who was represented by the only international lawyer in the case with any experience of criminal law.

The situation dramatically improved during the course of 2003. By August 2003 there were six international attorneys and three assistants working on trials, as well as some interpreters and administrative staff who are assigned to the DLU. While this is to be welcomed, it comes at a very late stage, after many of the trials have been completed.

Again, this puts a question mark over whether defendants have actually received fair trials.

IV. Conclusion

A report by the Judicial Systems Monitoring Programme (JSMP) in November 2001 called for:

an urgent review of the administrative structures that support the Special Panels for Serious Crimes, that the Special Panels be given the level of material and personnel support that they need to do their difficult job, and that significant improvements in the day to day running of the court are urgently needed. ... Although the transitional administration and the East Timorese political leadership have indicated a strong commitment to the protection of human rights, in practice the justice system is steering dangerously close to falling below international minimum standards.[27]

---

[27] Judicial Systems Monitoring Programme *Justice in Practice: Human Rights in Court Administration* (November 2001) 31 www.jsmp.minihub.org/Reports/JSMP1.pdf 33.

Despite such warnings, the situation in 2002 steadily deteriorated as already scarce resources were cut in the course of the overall downsizing of the UN Mission. Since achieving independence on 20 May 2002, East Timor has been governed by its own administration. However, international staffing matters and resources remain within the province of the United Nations. The increases in personnel during 2003 give some hope that the situation will improve. However, it may well be that the political responses to three years of failure mean that the impetus has gone out of serious crimes trials, and that these changes have come too late.

4. *Uncertainty as to applicable law*

On 15 July 2003 the newly restored Court of Appeal handed down a decision in the case of *Prosecutor v Armando Dos Santos*[28] that shook the foundations of the legal system in East Timor, and threatened to invalidate all decisions made by the Special Panels since their inception.

Armando Dos Santos was charged with three counts of murder as a crime against humanity. He was convicted by the Special Panel of murder as an ordinary crime under the Indonesian Penal Code.[29] This was in accordance with the previous interpretation of UNTAET Regulation 1999/1 (On the Applicable Law) (which continues to apply under section 165 of the Constitution of East Timor). UNTAET Regulation 1999/1 states that until replaced by subsequent legislation, 'the laws applied in East Timor prior to 25 October 1999 shall apply in East Timor'.[30]

The main points of the Court of Appeal decision can be summarized as follows:

(1) The Indonesian occupation of the Portuguese colony of East Timor was in violation of international law. Indonesian law was therefore never validly in force in East Timor. The laws applied in East Timor prior to October 1999 'could only be those which, in accordance with international law, were legitimately in force in that territory'.[31] UNTAET Regulation 1999/1 therefore refers to Portuguese, not Indonesian law.[32]

(2) UNTAET Regulation 2000/15, which defines Serious Criminal Offences in terms borrowed form the Rome Statute for the International Criminal Court,[33] cannot be applied to acts which occurred before the Regulation was enacted: this would be in violation of section 31 of the Constitution of East Timor, which states that '[n]o-one shall be tried and convicted for an act that does not qualify in law as a criminal offence at the time it was

---

[28] *Prosecutor v Armando dos Santos* (*supra* n 25).

[29] ibid (10 September 2002) Judgment.

[30] UNTAET Reg 1991/1 (27 November 1999) (On the Authority of the Transitional Administration in East Timor) s 3.1.

[31] *Prosecutor v Armando dos Santos* (*supra* n 25).

[32] The East Timorese judge on the Panel dissented from this part of the decision.

[33] UNTAET Reg 2000/15 (6 June 2000) (On the Establishment of Panels with Exclusive Jurisdiction over Serious Criminal Offences) ss 4–7.

committed';[34] and '[c]riminal law shall not be enforced retroactively, except if it is in favour of the accused'.[35] Therefore only Portuguese law can be applied to crimes committed before 6 June 2000.

(3) Under Portuguese law, the defendant is guilty of three crimes of murder and 'a crime against humanity in the form of genocide'.

(4) The sentence is increased from 20 to 22 years' imprisonment.

This decision is likely to have disastrous consequences for the future of serious crimes prosecutions in East Timor. There is no place for a detailed analysis of this decision here.[36] However, it is clear that the judgment, which is unsupported by reference to any international authorities, is seriously flawed in the following ways:

(1) There are vast numbers of factors which indicate conclusively that UNTAET intended to refer to Indonesian and not Portuguese law as the subsidiary legislation. This includes other parts of this and other regulations, which explicitly or implicitly refer to Indonesian law as the subsidiary legislation; and statements by the UNTAET officials in charge of framing the Regulations, which explicitly state that Indonesian law was intended as the subsidiary legislation, and give the reasons why.[37]

(2) The reasoning for the decision that the provisions of Regulation 2000/15 cannot be applied to the events of 1999, as criminal law cannot be enforced retroactively, gives no consideration to the existence of crimes against humanity, war crimes, and genocide as crimes under customary international law.

(3) The definition of genocide used by the court is incorrect under international law; it contains no mention of the special intent required for genocide, and fails to distinguish between genocide and crimes against humanity.

A subsequent judgment by one of the Special Panels declines to follow the Court of Appeal decision.[38] By August 2003, there was therefore serious uncertainty as to the application of law in East Timor over the whole period of UN involvement. With regard to serious crimes prosecutions, the validity of the previous three years' decisions of the Special Panels was thrown into doubt.

5. Summary

Indonesia's lack of cooperation in the work of the SCU has hampered its ability to fulfil the mandate given to UNTAET by the Security Council. But

---

[34] Constitution of the Democratic Republic of East Timor s 31(2).

[35] ibid s 31(5).

[36] For a detailed and critical analysis of this decision by the Judicial System Monitoring Programme, see *Report on the Court of Appeal Decision in the case of Armando Dos Santos* (22 August 2003) www.jsmp.minihub.org/Reports/jsmpreports/RepCofADosSantosEnglish.pdf.

[37] See eg Hansjoerg Strohmeyer 'Policing the Peace: Post-Conflict Judicial System Reconstruction in East Timor' (2001) 24(1) *University of New South Wales LJ* 171, 173–4.

[38] *Prosecutor v Domingos Mendonca* 18a/2001 (24 July 2003) Decision on Defence Motion for the Court to Order the Prosecutor to Amend the Indictment.

in addition, East Timor has been seriously let down by the United Nations. Despite the repeatedly stated commitment of the United Nations to prosecute the perpetrators of the atrocities of 1999, it has shown itself unwilling to provide a properly functioning system for the trials of those within its jurisdiction. Further, its refusal to back the independent decisions made by its own prosecutors to indict the Indonesian high command shows an even more damaging unwillingness to support the impartial distribution of justice.

Given the ambitious nature of the project which was being attempted, every effort should have been made to ensure that the Special Panels were properly supported. Caitlin Reiger of the JSMP writes:

> the experiment with an 'internationalised' justice system is struggling along. While I agree that such an approach should be seen as a useful alternative to the expense and other problems that have dogged the ICTR and ICTY, the East Timor experiment . . . should probably not have been attempted while simultaneously trying to build an entirely new justice system from virtually nothing, with inexperienced national personnel and often inappropriately recruited international staff.[39]

In terms of resources, there have been improvements during the course of 2003. However, it is likely that these have come too late to save the process from collapse. There are increasing calls among Timorese politicians for the granting of amnesties for the crimes of 1999. In an interview in June 2003, the Prime Minister Mari Alkatiri called for an amnesty for prisoners currently serving sentences in Timorese jails, stating that this was the only way to resolve the injustice resulting from the fact that the perpetrators of less serious crimes were being imprisoned, while those most responsible for the atrocities remained at large.[40] It has long been known that this is the course favoured by the President of East Timor. It is becoming increasingly likely that an amnesty or pardon of some kind will be granted to those within the jurisdiction of the court, which will put an end to the serious crimes process in East Timor.

B. THE JAKARTA TRIALS

In the light of the failures of the Special Panels in Dili, the only real hope of justice for those most responsible for the crimes committed in East Timor lay in the promises made by the Indonesians to try their own political and military leaders. Trials before an ad hoc tribunal in Jakarta started after repeated delays, and as a result of strong international pressure, in March

---

[39] Caitlin Reiger 'The East Timor Experiment with International Justice' paper presented at the conference 'Justice in the Balance: Military Commissions and International Tribunals in a Violent Age' Berkeley War Crimes Study Center, Human Rights Center, and Department of Rhetoric at the University of California, Berkeley 16 March 2002.
[40] 'PM Alkatiri Wants Amnesty for Crimes of 1999' *Lusa* Jakarta (12 June 2003).

2002. The law used is that of the Rome Statute for the ICC, which was incorporated into Indonesian law by the Indonesian Parliament in November 2000[41] (despite the fact that Indonesia has not signed or ratified the Statute). However, at the conclusion of the trials in August 2003 it was no longer possible to argue that they had brought any real measure of justice.

1. Limited jurisdiction

The ad hoc tribunal has jurisdiction over only two time periods (April and September 1999) and three districts (Dili, Liquica, and Suai). Essentially indictments are limited to the prosecution of five incidents of violence which occurred in 1999. Therefore there was no opportunity for the more general pattern of violence, and the role of state policy in orchestrating the violence, to be examined.

2. Omission of high-ranking suspects

There are indictments against 18 military and police officers, civilian officials, and militia members. There are no indications that any further indictments will be issued. There is no indictment against General Wiranto, the former Indonesian military commander, despite the fact that he was named in the original report of the Indonesian National Human Rights Commission of Enquiry in January 2000 as having overall responsibility for human rights offences. It is generally felt that those tried represented the 'second division', and not the top command.

3. Limited indictments

A report in May 2002 by the International Crisis Group observed that the indictments issued by the prosecution charge the commanders with little more than criminal negligence:

Both prosecution and defence portray the events of 1999 as resulting from a civil conflict involving two violent East Timorese factions in which Indonesian security forces were concerned and sometimes helpless bystanders. The evidence that this was not the case is overwhelming.

It concluded:

If the judges acquit the defendants, international outrage is a certainty. But even if they convict, the gravity of what occurred in East Timor will remain hidden, and the concept of crimes against humanity will be trivialized.[42]

---

[41] Law 2000/26.
[42] International Crisis Group *Indonesia: Implications of the Timor Trials* (Jakarta/Brussels 8 May 2002) 12 and 13.

By August 2003, trials had been completed against all of the 18 indictees: 12 were acquitted; those convicted received sentences of between 3 and 10 years. These sentences are extremely low compared with those imposed by the Special Panels in East Timor, who have sentenced low-ranking defendants convicted of crimes against humanity to periods of imprisonment up to 33 years and 4 months.

The popular view in Indonesia, reinforced by decades of government misinformation, is that the majority of East Timorese wanted integration with Indonesia, and that the UN ballot which produced a result in favour of independence was shamelessly rigged. The Indonesian military was unable to stop the violence which erupted in reaction to this.

The trials in Jakarta have served to reinforce that view. In one case, the court found that the violence occurred due to the fraudulent conduct of the popular consultation by the UN Mission which oversaw the ballot.[43] In most cases the verdicts appear to have reflected the allegations in the indictments that the violence was led by the East Timorese.

The overwhelming evidence from other sources is that the violence was instigated and controlled by the Indonesian military, acting in command of local militia groups. The Special Panels in Dili have found that it is established:

beyond reasonable doubt that there was an extensive attack by pro-autonomy armed groups supported by the Indonesian authorities targeting the civilian population in the area, namely those linked with political movements for the self-determination of East Timor.[44]

Given the limited extent of what the prosecution sought to prove in its indictments, evidence showing that this is the case never came before the Jakarta court.

4. Lack of commitment to justice

There have been strong indications that Indonesia is not committed to bringing justice, but simply to appeasing the international community.

One of the five cases originally designated for prosecution by the Indonesian Attorney-General was the killing of Dutch journalist Sander Thoenes in September 1999. There is evidence that he was gunned down by the retreating 745 Battalion on the outskirts of Dili, as part of a murderous rampage in which at least 10 people were killed. The Dutch government sponsored the Indonesian investigation into this incident, and a Dutch policeman joined

---

[43] 'Military Innocent: UN to Blame for Timor Atrocities' *Sydney Morning Herald* (17 August 2002).
[44] *Prosecutor v Joni Marquez and nine others* 9/2000 (11 December 2001) Judgment para 686.

Indonesian investigators on a visit to Dili to obtain evidence in March 2002.[45]

But, despite the conclusion of the Dutch investigator and senior prosecutors in the SCU in Dili that there is clear eyewitness evidence showing that Lieutenant Camilo Dos Santos of the 745 Battalion was responsible for the murder, the Indonesian investigators are understood to have reported that there is insufficient evidence to indict him.[46]

In a calculated snub to the UN authorities, Lieutenant Dos Santos, who is still a serving officer in the Indonesian military, was sent to a border opening ceremony in East Timor in early May 2002. He sat behind the Special Representative of the UN Secretary General, and was reported to seem 'in a relaxed mood'. By the time embarrassed UNTAET officials had discovered his identity it was too late to act.[47]

This lack of commitment to justice has also been observed in the sessions of the ad hoc tribunal. The public gallery of the court has been regularly packed with senior military commanders staging a show of support for the defendants. Demonstrations outside the court have at times been so loud that it has been difficult to hear the proceedings. Such measures can be expected to intimidate the specially appointed judges, most of whom have little experience of criminal trials.[48]

The farcical nature of the proceedings is well illustrated by the Damiri trial. General Damiri was the highest ranking officer indicted by prosecutors before the court. His trial was subject to constant delays when the General was unable to attend as he was fulfilling his military duties in other provinces of Indonesia. On 5 June 2003 the prosecutor demanded that the court acquit Damiri, saying that the case had not been proved against him. However, the prosecution did not drop the charges, and the court proceeded to find Damiri guilty. It then sentenced him to three years' imprisonment—a negligible sentence in light of the charges, and well below the 10-year minimum sentence required for crimes against humanity under Indonesian law. Despite this, the prosecution launched an appeal against Damiri's conviction.[49]

Like all other defendants, General Damiri has been released on bail pending his appeal. It is not anticipated that he will actually serve any time in prison. He has retained his army command; it is disquieting to learn that he is

[45] UNTAET 'Indonesian, Dutch Investigators Complete Thoenes Visit' Daily Press Briefing (8 March 2002) www.un.org/peace/etimor/DB/db080302.htm.
[46] 'Dutch Journalist Murder Case Likely to Close, Says Military' *Jakarta Post* (16 May 2002).
[47] 'Fury as Indonesian "Army Killer" Returns to East Timor' *The Telegraph* (12 May 2002).
[48] For reports on the progress of the trials in Jakarta see the Judicial Systems Monitoring Programme at www.jsmp.minihub.org.
[49] 'Indonesian Prosecutors Appeal General Damiri's Sentence, Seek Acquittal' *Lusa* (14 August 2003).

currently serving in Aceh, where there are widespread reports of violence by the Indonesian military in response to the independence movement, similar to that which occurred in East Timor in 1999.

5. Summary

The ad hoc tribunal in Jakarta is not bringing any real measure of justice for the atrocities in East Timor in 1999. As one Indonesian human rights lawyer put it:

From the beginning, the only purpose of these tribunals was to meet the pressure from both inside the country and from the international community. It is not to get justice for the victims, it's just lip service.[50]

In April 2003 a report by Amnesty International described the trials as not having been 'truthful, honest or fair'.[51] At the conclusion of the process, the Dili-based JSMP stated:

Throughout the trials the international community demanded that the Indonesian government strengthen the process in order to deliver credible outcomes and justice. This did not happen.[52]

C. CONCLUSION

A number of lessons can be derived from the experiment in justice for East Timor. First of all, no court system can operate without proper funding and management of resources: it should be recognized that a commitment to try crimes of this magnitude will always require a substantial financial commitment. This should be guaranteed in advance, before an inoperable system is put in place.

Secondly, no system can operate without proper prior assessment and planning. In the modern world there are many alternative ways in which justice in these types of situation can be achieved. There is no single way that will suit every situation. A system should not be set up until there has been a proper consideration of alternatives and potential difficulties.

Thirdly, it is impossible to achieve justice where the political will to ensure that justice is done does not exist. If a country, particularly a strong and strategically important one, chooses to protect its own people, there is little

---

[50] Lawyer Johnson Panjaitan, quoted in 'Hopes Fade for East Timor Justice' *BBC News* (13 May 2002) http://news.bbc.co.uk/go/em/fr/-/hi/english/world/asia-pacific/newsid_1984000/1984161.stm.

[51] Amnesty International *Indonesia and Timor-Leste: International Responsibility for Justice* (14 April 2003).

[52] JSMP *Court in Jakarta Completes Theatrical Performance* Press Release (6 August 2003).

that the international community can do to bring them to trial. In East Timor, this problem was exacerbated by an unwillingness on the part of the United Nations to endorse the necessity for fair and impartial trials of those alleged to hold the greatest responsibility.

There is still much talk in East Timor about the desirability of an international ad hoc tribunal. The glaring inadequacies of the trials in both Dili and Jakarta fuel hopes that the international community will declare that Indonesia has failed in its promise to bring justice for East Timor, and that an international tribunal will finally be put in place.

In practice that seems a highly unlikely outcome. Despite reports in August 2003 that an unnamed UN official in New York was still saying that an ad hoc tribunal for East Timor was a possibility,[53] it is no longer on the international agenda.[54] The crippling cost of the existing international tribunals, the embarrassing failures of ICTR, and the US desire not to antagonize the world's largest Muslim country while it is conducting a war against terrorism, means that no ad hoc tribunal is realistically going to be set up.

In any event, even the existence of an ad hoc tribunal would not ensure that those in Indonesia would ever be prosecuted. As ICTY discovered, arresting suspects who are protected by their state, even if the state is a relatively small one, is no easy task.

The real lesson, perhaps, is this: if a country defies the international community, flouts its commitments and obligations, and protects its criminals, the international community has a harsh choice between using force, and accepting that justice will never be done. As the ICC Statute has now come into effect, it is worth reflecting on this. In the future, it may be for the judges of ICC to decide under Article 17 of the Rome Statute whether a country has shown itself to be unwilling properly to prosecute its own offenders. Whether such a decision would make it any more likely that such offenders would be brought to justice appears still to be in doubt.

[53] 'UN Timor Tribunal "Possible"' *AFP* (8 August 2003).
[54] 'Annan Downplays International Tribunal for East Timor Suspects' Associated Press (16 May 2002).

6

Getting Untrapped, Struggling for Truths: The Commission for Reception, Truth and Reconciliation (CAVR) in East Timor

Beth S Lyons*

'People are trapped in history and history is trapped in them.'
James Baldwin**

A. INTRODUCTION

Truth commissions have become an almost ubiquitous policy option in the range of accountability mechanisms for human rights violations.[1] In East Timor, as in other countries labelled 'countries in transition' or 'countries in post-conflict situations', the Commission for Reception, Truth and Reconciliation in East Timor (Comissao de Acolhimento, Verdade e Reconciliacao de Timor Leste, or 'CAVR') is only one of multiple processes to deal with human rights violations of a past regime.[2] More specifically, it co-exists with criminal trials conducted by the Serious Crimes Panel,[3] and an Ad Hoc

* Beth S Lyons is a criminal defence attorney and an Alternate Delegate to the United Nations in New York for the International Association of Democratic Lawyers, a non-governmental organization, founded in 1946. The author is grateful to the editors, Jann Kleffner, Andre Nollkaemper, and Cesare Romano, and to Sylvia de Bertodano, Gloria Bletter, Federico Borello, Patrick Burgess, John M. Miller, Chidi Anselm Odinkalu, Dr. Fazel Randera, Caitlin Reiger, Anita Roberts, Charles Scheiner, Aderito de Jesus Soares, Cheryl Williams and Lynne Wilson, for their valuable assistance. She is especially appreciative to Kieran Dwyer for his essential comments. The views expressed are the author's, and she is responsible for any factual errors. Unfortunately, the author has not observed the CAVR process directly. Her comments are based on a review of the materials about the CAVR, and her experience with the Truth and Reconciliation Commission in South Africa.
** 'Stranger in the Village' in *Notes of a Native Son* (Beacon Press 1955).
[1] See Priscilla B Hayner *Unspeakable Truths: Confronting State Terror and Atrocity, How Truth Commissions Around the World are Challenging the Past and Shaping the Future* (Routledge New York and London 2001); Neil J Kritz (ed) *Transitional Justice: How Emerging Democracies Reckon with Former Regimes* (US Institute of Peace Press Washington 1995).
[2] In South Africa, the Truth and Reconciliation Commission functioned alongside the criminal justice system; if the TRC granted amnesty, the perpetrator was shielded from criminal and civil liability. In Sierra Leone, there is a Special Court and a Truth and Reconciliation Commission. In the case of Rwanda, there are criminal prosecutions in national courts, in the International Criminal Tribunal for Rwanda, and in the Gacaca Courts (for crimes excluding Category I crimes); there is also a National Unity and Reconciliation Commission.
[3] A Panel with Exclusive Jurisdiction Over Serious Criminal Offences was mandated by UNTAET Regulation 2000/15 (6 June 2000).

Human Rights Court, established by Indonesia.[4] Both of these have been dealt with in this book by de Bertodano.

The CAVR, established by a UN Transitional Administration in East Timor (UNTAET) Regulation,[5] is an independent state-sanctioned entity. Its objective is 'to promote national reconciliation and healing following the years of political conflict in East Timor, and in particular, following the atrocities committed in 1999'[6] through 'establishing the truth regarding the commission of human rights violations'.[7] It has three main functions: (a) to seek the truth about human rights violations, (b) to promote community reconciliation, and (c) to produce a report which documents the human rights violations and recommends how to protect human rights, and promote reconciliation. The CAVR is not a prosecutorial mechanism, although it has some 'quasi-judicial' aspects.

This chapter examines the CAVR, and identifies some of the potential areas of tension which it faces, particularly in its function as an accountability mechanism for human rights violations.[8] It is argued here that one fundamental area of tension may lie within the regulation's categorization of crimes, and its impact on the CAVR's two separate mandates for truth-seeking and for community reconciliation. In truth-seeking, the CAVR's investigation of human rights violations may include both 'less serious' and 'serious' crimes.[9] Similarly, in a community reconciliation process, testimony about a 'less serious' offence could also include a description of a more serious crime. This 'overlap' can present problems because there is no shared forum for the resolution of both types of crime: 'less serious' offences are resolved through the CAVR's Community Reconciliation Process, and 'serious crimes' are prosecuted by the Serious Crimes Panel.

This 'inconsistency' between inquiry and resolution is exacerbated by the difficulties of the criminal justice system in prosecuting alleged perpetrators of human rights violations, and the lack of affirmative political will of foreign entities to assist the CAVR's work. The cooperation of countries, especially Indonesia, who have supported and continue to harbour suspects identified as the alleged major perpetrators of human rights violations in East Timor, remains a major obstacle. Although the CAVR is an independent entity 'in its own right', and cannot be judged through a judicial lens, the fulfilment of the

---

[4] Indonesian Human Rights Court Act, Act 26/2000, House of Representatives of Indonesia.

[5] UNTAET Regulation 2001/10.

[6] ibid Preamble.

[7] ibid s 13.1.

[8] For the most recent information on the CAVR, see, CAVR website at www.easttimor-reconciliation.org; Judicial System Monitoring Programme at www.jsmp.minihub.org; and East Timor Action Network at www.etan.org. Additional resources/links are listed on these websites.

[9] The terms 'serious' and 'ordinary' are sometimes used to describe the two categories of crimes.

CAVR's objectives is related to the criminal justice system. The CAVR's significant achievements in respect to 'less serious' crimes are directly affected by how the Office of the General Prosecutor deals with 'serious crimes'.

At the time this chapter was written, the CAVR had completed less than half its tenure. Hence, it would be inappropriate, as well as impossible, to present conclusions about this ongoing process. The issues discussed here are being addressed by the CAVR, and assessments and evaluations are part of the day-to-day work of CAVR staff, and the communities which participate in its activities. The author's views are limited by her lack of direct experience with the CAVR's work, and especially with the survivors who testify in the CAVR hearings; as a result, the perspectives of the survivors are not specifically represented here.[10]

At the end of the day, the people of East Timor will make the determinant analysis and evaluation of the CAVR. For, human rights are about peoples' lives; and both the audible and the silent voices of survivors of human rights violations are pivotal in reaching any verdict on truth commissions, and on the struggles for accountability, justice, and the rule of law.

In this chapter, the following are discussed: the CAVR Regulation, the CAVR's practice, obstacles to finding truth, the relation between the CAVR and the formal justice system, and conclusions.

B. AN OVERVIEW OF THE CAVR REGULATION[11]

The CAVR is governed by UNTAET Regulation 2001/10 ('the Regulation'), which is divided into five parts, and includes the Establishment of the CAVR (Part II), Truth Seeking (Part III), and Community Reconciliation Procedures (Part IV) as its core.[12]

1. Origins of the CAVR

When East Timor held its first democratic elections in April 2002, it was a nation of survivors. There was virtually no one, among its 775,000 inhabitants, who had not endured human rights abuses during the quarter of a century of Indonesia's brutal, military occupation,[13] and the 'systematic

---

[10] The author is especially grateful to Kieran Dwyer, CAVR Advisor, and Patrick Burgess, Chief UN Legal Advisor to the CAVR, for their scrutiny on these points.

[11] A draft amendment to UNTAET Regulation 2001/10 has been proposed to replace references to the Transitional Administrator with the President of the Republic.

[12] Part I sets forth definitions of the terms employed in the Regulation while Part V contains other matters, including victim and witness protection and the principles which govern the treatment of both victims and perpetrators.

[13] According to estimates, the Indonesian invasion and occupation claimed the lives of 200,000 East Timorese: 'Background on East Timor and U.S. Policy' (October 1998) at

scorched-earth campaign' of the Indonesian military and militia forces in September 1999, which resulted in severe damage to an estimated 70 to 80 per cent of East Timor's infrastructure.[14]

The Commission for Reception, Truth and Reconciliation in East Timor ('CAVR') was established on 13 July 2001, with a broad mandate which included addressing these past abuses, and holding perpetrators accountable for human rights violations. The idea for a truth commission originated with Timorese human rights activists, whose proposal for a commission at the National Council of Timorese Resistance (CNRT) Workshop in June 2000 was subsequently endorsed by the CNRT Congress, held in August 2000. The Congress agreed that national consultations should be conducted, to ascertain whether the community wanted such a commission, and, if affirmative, what should be its mandate. A Steering Committee of East Timorese organizations,[15] supported by UNTAET's Human Rights Unit and UN High Commissioner for Refugees (UNHCR), conducted consultations over a several-month period with civil society in every district of East Timor. On 23 September 2002, the CAVR held its opening Community Reconciliation hearing in Maumeta, near Liquica.

2. Objectives, mandate, and composition

The CAVR's overall objective is to promote human rights, which includes:

(a) inquiring into the human rights violations which have occurred within the context of the political conflicts in East Timor;
(b) establishing the truth about these violations;
(c) reporting on the nature of these violations;
(d) identifying factors, including policies and practices by state and non-state actors, which may have led to them;
(e) where appropriate, recommending prosecution of perpetrators of human rights violations by the Office of the General Prosecutor; and
(f) assisting in restoring the human dignity of victims.[16]

---

www.etan.org. See also James Dunn, *East Timor, A Rough Passage to Independence* (Longueville Books Australia 2003) 278. The CAVR will be examining the number of deaths during this period, and their causes.

[14] 'East Timor Country Report on Human Rights Practices 2001' (US Department of State 4 March 2002).

[15] The Steering Committee included representatives of the CNRT (National Council of Timorese Resistance) Congress, representatives of various organizations, such as ET Wave, Association of Ex-Political Prisoners, Presidium Juventude, Fokupers, Yayasan HAK, the Catholic Church's Peace and Justice Commission, and representatives of UNTAET's Human Rights Unit and UNHCR, and was assisted by international experts in reconciliation.

[16] UNTAET Regulation 2001/10 s 3.1.

It is mandated to promote reconciliation; to support the reception and re-integration of individuals, who have committed minor criminal offences, into their communities; and to promote human rights.[17]

The CAVR is required to present its final report and recommendations to the President.[18] The report includes a summary of its findings, and recommendations for any reforms or other measures which should be taken to achieve the CAVR'S objectives, to prevent the repetition of human rights violations and to respond to the needs of the victims of these violations.[19]

The CAVR is empowered to operate as an independent authority, and its initial period of 24 months has been extended to October 2004.[20] The Commission is composed of seven National Commissioners, which includes five men and two women,[21] who were appointed by the Transitional Administrator, on the advice of a Selection Panel, consisting of representatives of political parties, the Transitional Administrator, civil society, and a religious entity.[22] Panel decisions are made by consensus, or, if this is not possible, by majority vote.[23]

The Panel also recommended 29 Regional Commissioners[24] to the Transitional Administrator. The Regulation specifies that special consideration be given to diverse experiences and views, including towards the past political conflicts, and regional and gender representation; and that a minimum of 30 per cent of Regional Commissioners are to be women.[25]

---

[17] ibid s 3.1(g), (h) and (i).

[18] See n 11 re replacement of original references to the Transitional Administrator.

[19] UNTAET Regulation 2001/10 s 21.

[20] ibid s 2. In May 2003, the Timorese National Parliament approved an amendment which extends the mandate of the CAVR to October 2004.

[21] Criteria for National Commissioners are listed in the UNTAET Regulation 2001/10 s 4.1. On 21 January 2002, seven National Commissioners were sworn in. They include Aniceto Guterres Lopes, Chairperson, a human rights practitioner and lawyer; Father Jovito Araujo, Vice Chairperson, a Catholic priest and youth advocate; Olandina Caeiro, a businesswoman and women's advocate; Jacinto Alves, a former political prisoner and independence activist; Jose Estevao Soares, a former pro-autonomy political activist and civil servant; Isabel Guterres, a nurse and humanitarian worker; and Reverend Agustinho de Vasconselos, a Protestant church minister and youth advocate.

[22] UNTAET Regulation 2001/10 s 4. In ibid s 4.3(a), the Regulation names the four political parties that existed prior to Indonesia's invasion (FRETILIN, the UDT, Kota, and Trabalhista), the NGO Forum, the Women's Network (Rede), the Catholic Church, the Political Prisoners' Association, the Association of the Families of the Disappeared, the UNTAET Office of Human Rights, and a representative of pro-autonomy groups.

[23] ibid s 4.3(f).

[24] See ibid ss 10 and 11 on regional commissioners and offices. Also, see CAVR website for a listing of Regional Commissioners.

[25] UNTAET Regulation 2001/10 s 11.1 and 11.4.

3. *CAVR functions and a two-tiered definition of crimes*

The CAVR Regulation identifies two separate functions: (a) truth seeking about human rights violations, and (b) community reconciliation. In turn, each function is informed by an explicit subject-matter distinction in the regulation between 'serious' crimes and 'less serious' crimes. The CAVR can investigate 'serious crimes' through its truth-seeking processes of hearings and inquiries, but it must refer these crimes to another forum, the Office of the General Prosecutor, for prosecution. However, the CAVR can investigate and resolve 'less serious' crimes through its Community Reconciliation Process (CRP), and is empowered to effectuate agreements of reconciliation.

Serious criminal offences include genocide, war crimes, crimes against humanity, murder, sexual offences, and torture.[26] For these serious crimes, the CAVR has broad investigatory powers but no power to prosecute or grant amnesty. The CAVR is tasked to determine whether the human rights violations were the 'result of deliberate planning, policy or authorisation on the part of a state or any of its organs, or any political organisation, militia group, liberation movement or other group or individual'.[27]

Less serious crimes, subject to the Community Reconciliation Process (see below), are found in Schedule I.[28] In determining whether a crime is eligible for the CRP process, the CAVR considers the following criteria: the total number of acts which the deponent has committed, his role in the crime, ie whether he 'organised, planned, instigated or ordered the crime' or was following orders.[29] The final criterion, which originally read, 'In no circumstances shall a *serious criminal offence* be dealt with in a Community Reconciliation Process' was amended on 18 May 2002 to read, 'In principle, *serious criminal offences,* in particular, murder, torture and sexual offences, shall not be dealt with in a Community Reconciliation Process'.[30] The amended language can be read to be more flexible, but is also more specific as to the crimes.

4. *Truth-seeking procedures*

Under Part III (Truth Seeking) of the Regulation, the CAVR is mandated to establish the truth about human rights violations,[31] defined as violations of

---

[26] UNTAET Regulation 2000/15 ss 1.3, 4, 5, 6, 7, 8, 9. Note: for purposes of prosecution by the Serious Crimes Panel, murder and sexual offences are defined by the East Timor Penal Code.

[27] UNTAET Regulation 2001/10 s 13.1(iv).

[28] These offences include 'theft, minor assault, arson (other than that resulting in death or injury), the killing of livestock or destruction of crops', where there has been no serious criminal offence: UNTAET Regulation 2001/10 Sch 1, 'Criteria for Determining Whether Offence Appropriately Dealt with in a Community Reconciliation Process'.

[29] ibid.

[30] ibid Sch I, s 4 amended by Directive on Serious Crimes 2002/09 On Amending the Criteria for Determining Whether Offence Appropriately Dealt with in a Community Reconciliation Process (18 May 2002).

[31] UNTAET Regulation 2001/10 s 13.

international human rights standards, international humanitarian law, and criminal acts,[32] which occurred between 25 April 1974 and 25 October 1999. The Regulation identifies two specific areas for particular consideration:

(a) the events before, during and after the popular consultation of 30 August 1999 which resulted in a loss of life, injury, destruction of property, the commission of sexual offences and the forcible deportations of persons; and

(b) the events and experiences of all parties immediately preceding, during and after the entry of Indonesia into East Timor on 7 December 1975, and the effect of the policies and practices of Indonesia and its forces present in East Timor between 7 December and 1975 and 25 October 1999.[33]

In carrying out its truth-seeking function, the CAVR is empowered to hold hearings,[34] which are generally to be public, and well-publicized,[35] inside and outside East Timor.[36] This jurisdictional breadth is coupled with broad investigatory powers to request information and witnesses,[37] to order witnesses to testify before the Commission,[38] and to order the production of documents and other evidence.[39] The CAVR also has search and seizure powers.[40] Witnesses enjoy the privilege of non-self incrimination,[41] and the right of legal representation.[42] A family privilege of non-self incrimination[43] also applies, and there are privileges for priests or monks, lawyers, and medical professionals.[44]

One of the CAVR's most significant strengths is its power to examine the role of international state and non-state actors in human rights violations.[45] The CAVR can request information from victims, witnesses and government officials in other countries,[46] and enter into cooperative agreements with official bodies of foreign countries.[47] The CAVR had planned to hold hearings in countries outside East Timor, but this project was cancelled in late 2003.

---

[32] ibid s 1(c).   [33] ibid s 13.2(a) and (b).   [34] ibid s 14.1(a).

[35] ibid s 16. Section 16.2 permits closed hearings only when it would be in the interests of justice or there is a likelihood that open proceedings would result in harm to any person. In these situations, any victim who has an interest in the proceedings may be present.

[36] ibid s 14.1(k).

[37] ibid s 14.1(b) and (g).

[38] ibid s 14.1(c) and (d).

[39] ibid s 14.1(e) and (f).

[40] ibid s 15.

[41] ibid s 17.1.

[42] ibid s 18.

[43] ibid s 17.2. This applies to the spouse or partner, parents, children, or relatives within the second degree of a witness.

[44] ibid s 17.

[45] ibid ss 3.1(d) and 14.1 (h).

[46] ibid s 14.1(h).

[47] ibid s 14.1(l).

These investigatory powers are similar to those of the Sierra Leone truth commission,[48] analysed in this book by Schabas,[49] but stand in contrast to a majority of predecessor truth commissions, where only some addressed the role of international state and non-state actors and their accountability for human rights violations.[50]

The results of the CAVR's investigatory efforts into the role of international actors in human rights violations are not limited to its truth-seeking function, and could impact also on the inquiries into the subject matter of the 'less serious' criminal offences in Schedule I. For example, this could apply in situations where the applicant in a CRP hearing is the member of a militia which was trained, armed and/or financed by other countries, such as Indonesia or the United States.[51]

5. The Community Reconciliation Process

A unique feature of the CAVR is its Community Reconciliation Process (CRP), whose objective is 'to assist the reception and reintegration of persons into their communities'.[52] The CRP is available to persons who have committed criminal or non-criminal acts in the context of the political conflicts in East Timor between 25 April 1974 and 25 October 1999.[53] However, a person who has committed a serious criminal offence is not eligible to participate in this process.[54]

An applicant ('deponent') must submit a written statement containing:

---

[48] Sierra Leone's Truth and Reconciliation Commission, established by the Truth and Reconciliation Commission Act 2000, empowers the Commission 'to request information from the relevant authorities of a foreign country and to gather information from victims, witnesses, government officials and others in foreign countries' (Pt III, s 8(1)).

The major difference between Sierra Leone and East Timor is that human rights violations in the former were the result of civil war, and, in East Timor, the result of an international conflict. However, in Sierra Leone, in the conflicts between 1991 and the signing of the Lomé Peace Agreement in 1999, there was a major foreign component, which included the mining companies and mercenary/security companies, such as Executive Outcomes. It is within the mandate of the truth commission to address the role of non-state international actors.

[49] See Chapter 9 (Schabas).

[50] The South Africa truth commission, for example, did not address this issue, but the reports of the truth commissions in Guatemala, Chad, and El Salvador discuss the role of international actors.

[51] The United States' role, and its relation to the Indonesian military has been well-documented. See www.etan.org for information, and additional source links.

[52] UNTAET Regulation 2001/10 s 22.1.

[53] ibid s 22.1.

[54] ibid s 31.1(d). Schedule I, point four states that 'In no circumstances shall a serious criminal offence be dealt with in a Community Reconciliation Process'. 'Serious criminal offences' are defined in s 1(m) as offences against the laws of East Timor, as defined in UNTAET Regulations 2000/11 (s 10.1) and 2000/15 (ss 1.3 and 4–9).

(a) a full description of the relevant acts;
(b) an admission of responsibility for such acts;
(c) an explanation of the association of such acts with the political conflicts in East Timor; and
(d) an identification of the specific community with which the deponent wishes to undertake a process of reconciliation and reintegration;
(e) a request to participate in a CRP;
(f) a renunciation of the use of violence to achieve political objectives; and
(g) the signature or other identifying mark of the deponent.[55]

The CAVR provides assistance to persons in making these statements (by writing down oral statements), and persons are permitted to submit revised statements if the initial ones are found to be deficient.[56] In facilitating the CRP, the CAVR is allowed to give priority to acts committed during 1999.[57]

The CRP Statement Committee assesses whether it can proceed with an application. Prior to accepting a statement, the Committee must inform the applicant that a copy of the written statement will be sent to the Office of the General Prosecutor, and that its contents may be used against the person in a court of law, should there be a decision to prosecute.[58] Where the Committee has determined that the acts are inappropriate for the CRP, the Committee notifies the applicant of its decision, and refers the statement, with the Committee's assessment, to the Office of the General Prosecutor.[59]

Responsibility for acting on applications is delegated to a Regional Commissioner, who convenes a CRP Panel, composed of three to five persons, including community representatives from the Community of Reception.[60] The CRP Panel then conducts a public hearing at which the applicant, the victims of the applicant's acts, and other community members with relevant information provide testimony.[61] If an applicant refuses to comply with the Panel's request for information, including responses to queries about the involvement of others in the acts, without valid justification, the CRP Panel can discontinue the hearing and refer the matter to the Office of the General Prosecutor.[62] The process can also be adjourned and referred to the Office of the General Prosecutor if 'credible evidence' is given that the applicant has committed a serious criminal offence.[63]

At the end of the hearing, the CRP Panel determines the appropriate act of reconciliation, including community service, reparation, public apology, and/or any other act of contrition.[64] The agreed upon act of reconciliation (Community Reconciliation Agreement or 'CRA') and the time limit for its performance is forwarded to the relevant District Court, and is registered as

---

[55] UNTAET Regulation 2001/10 s 23.1.   [56] ibid s 23.2 and 23.4.
[57] ibid s 22.3.   [58] ibid s 23.3.   [59] ibid s 24.4 and 24.5.
[60] ibid s 26.   [61] ibid s 27.1, 27.2, 27.3.   [62] ibid s 27.4
[63] ibid s 27.5.   [64] ibid s 27.7.

an Order of the Court.[65] The CRA must be 'reasonably proportionate' to the acts disclosed and cannot violate human rights principles.[66]

6. Amnesty

There is no provision for amnesty in the Regulation. In East Timor, as in most countries, the concept of amnesty is not a feature of local justice processes. Usually, perpetrators are held accountable for their crimes, accept responsibility, and make some form of compensation or reparation to the victim or victim's family.[67]

Within the Community Reconciliation Procedures, the Regulation contains a provision for immunity, which applies only to 'less serious' crimes. Successful completion of the CRA confers immunity from civil liability and criminal prosecution for the offences addressed in the Community Reconciliation Process.[68] However, the Regulation explicitly states that 'no immunity [for criminal liability] ... shall extend to *a serious criminal offence*'.[69] But, where there are ambiguities in categorizing 'serious' and 'less serious' crimes, there may also be the inherent danger that some serious crimes could 'slip through' the immunity net.

In a separate, yet related development, a draft Law of Amnesty and of the Pardon of Punishments was presented to East Timor's National Parliament on 25 May 2002.[70] After initial discussion, it was taken off the agenda and reintroduced in November 2003. The draft law was criticized by NGOs in East Timor and other human rights groups when it was first tabled.[71] It proposes the granting of amnesty for all 'crimes against the estate, committed until the day of 20th May 2002, that do not involve violence or threats';[72] for crimes committed until 30 September 1999, excluding those which are 'violent or sanguinary,' by the 'Timorese who were forced to integrate into the militias';[73] and for acts by 'members of any components of the Resistance who, in

---

[65] ibid ss 27.8 and 28.1.   [66] ibid s 28.2.

[67] Carolyn Bull 'Amnesty' (paper prepared for Interim Office, CAVR in East Timor, November 2001) available at www.easttimor-reconciliation.org.

[68] UNTAET Regulation 2001/10 s 32.

[69] ibid s 32.1. A strict reading of this section, in conjunction with the draft Amnesty Law, leaves open the possibility of civil liability for serious criminal offences. The draft Amnesty Law, in art 6, states that 'the present law does not include civil responsibility emerging from the crimes committed and outlines a time frame for actions of indemnity for losses and injury'.

[70] (Draft) Law 1/2002, 25 May 2002. Note: references are to the unofficial English translation; the original draft was in Portuguese, and there was much debate about the meaning and implication of Portuguese words.

[71] See the excellent critique, 'What Will be the Effect of the Draft Amnesty Law?' from the Judicial System Monitoring Programme (JSMP). Also, 'East Timor Amnesty Bill Flawed' (Human Rights Watch 18 July 2002). The CAVR Update (June–July 2002) includes a brief report on the amnesty issue.

[72] Draft Bill art 1.

[73] ibid art 2.

the past, integrated to criminal conduct, as long as they are not crimes of war, of genocide or against humanity as stated in Article 160 of East Timor Constitution'.[74] For crimes not covered by amnesty, but short of the violent, international crimes, pardons are proposed. For the least serious punishments of 10 years or less, pardons of two-thirds of the sentence mean that an offender serves one-third of the sentence. For punishments of 10 to 20 years, half the sentence is served; for more than 20 years, two-thirds is served.[75]

By excluding international crimes, and crimes of violence and threats from eligibility for amnesty, the drafters of the proposed Bill make it explicit that amnesties will not be used to shield perpetrators of these crimes from prosecution, as was the case of several instances in Latin America (Chile, Guatemala, El Salvador). However, the generality of the eligible crimes, combined with the absence of criteria for amnesty[76] or a process for applying for amnesty, makes it appear that the draft amnesty law basically grants blanket amnesty. The language is vague and general, and could be interpreted to grant amnesty for serious crimes, if they fall short of the most violent, internationally recognized crimes. For the Resistance, crimes under international law—war crimes, genocide, and crimes against humanity—are referenced as exclusions from amnesty; but for the militia, the excluded crimes are described as 'violent and sanguinary crimes.'[77]

In addition, as pointed out by the Judicial System Monitoring Programme, the failure of the draft Bill to distinguish between acts committed during political conflict and those committed during peacetime, as well as its granting of amnesty or pardons, could lead to an approbation of impunity. Since the United Nations' arrival, efforts have been underway to strengthen the judicial system, and to establish the rule of law. Amnesties or pardons for crimes which are committed during peacetime and are acts associated with political conflict could communicate the wrong message.

C. THE CAVR IN PRACTICE

The Community Reconciliation Process[78] provides a forum in which reconciliation for 'less serious' crimes can take place, and, through its preparations

---

[74] ibid art 3.   [75] ibid art 4.

[76] In South Africa, for example, for amnesty to be granted, an act, omission, or offence had to be associated with a political objective, and six criteria were examined: the motivation of the offender; the circumstances; the nature of the political objective; legal and factual nature of the offence; the objective of the offence (state v private entity) and the relationship between the offence and political objective, its directness or proximity or proportionality. See Promotion of National Unity and Reconciliation Act No. 34 ch 4 s 20.

[77] The distinction between these categories is unclear in the translation.

[78] See the CAVR Updates, as well as a recent report on Community Reconciliation in Timor-Leste, available at http://www.undp.org/bcpr/pubinfo/transitions/2003_04.

and hearings, gives a voice to both victims and perpetrators. The CRP hearing is conducted in the local language of the area. The first CRP hearing was held in Maumeta, near Liquica, on 23 August 2002. Between the first hearing and the end of November 2002, 143 perpetrators gave statements to the CAVR, and hearings involving 50 of these perpetrators had taken place.[79] By mid-October 2003, more than 1,100 perpetrators had requested CRPs; of these, 454 have participated in 82 hearings, 89 per cent; of which have resulted in Community Reconciliation Agreements.[80]

Preparation for each hearing is a three-month process, during which a CAVR team works in a sub-district of one of East Timor's 13 districts. After three months, the team moves on to another sub-district. During the first month, the CAVR team identifies a community, makes contact with community members who have been harmed by political conflicts, explains the CRP process, and asks community members if they want to participate. If the answer is affirmative, the team takes a statement from deponents. Since a deponent must apply to the CRP, this is a voluntary process whose success is determined by the willingness of a community and its organizations to assist the person. In the second month, the statements are sent to the Office of the General Prosecutor (OGP), which has to approve eligibility for a CRP, and the district team works with the community to prepare for hearings. In the third month, hearings take place. The hearings are public and involve both victims and perpetrators, as well as members of the community.[81]

To date, most perpetrators are low-level members of militia-type groups, which operated in 1999; they have committed relatively minor offences. The acts in the CRAs range from community work such as building a church or repairing a local school, to deponents giving symbolic gifts of *tais*[82] and traditional ornaments to 'symbolic' payment of livestock. For example, during the months of December 2002 and January 2003, 10 CAVR hearings were held, in the districts of Maliana, Aileu, Liquica, Ainaro, Ermera, and Oecussi. The grounds for an individual hearing included terrorizing/intimidation, assault, clarification of activities during the political conflict, pro-autonomy activities, threatening behaviour, involvement with the military, house burning, beatings, previous involvement with the militia/paramilitary groups, theft, and arson. All resolutions included apologizing and a commitment not to repeat the conduct. In addition, some individual CRAs required two months of compulsory attendance of a church group; contributing four

---

[79] CAVR Update (October–November 2002) www.easttimor-reconciliation.org.

[80] *La'o Hamutuk Bulletin*, Volume 4, Number 5, November 2003, 'Reviewing the East Timor Commission for Reception, Truth and Reconciliation' (CAVR).

[81] In South Africa, the Human Rights Violations Hearings and Amnesty Hearings were separate, and conducted by different committees of the Truth and Reconciliation Commission.

[82] Woven Timorese fabric.

days of labour to build a community hall; planting trees for 10 days on church land; and participating in a ceremony with community elders.[83]

In its truth-seeking function, the CAVR plans to collect up to 8000 statements about human rights violations which took place between 1974 and 1999. By mid-October 2003, approximately 5,900 statements had been taken in 51 of East Timor's 65 sub-districts.[84] In addition, there are also national thematic hearings which are conducted in Tetum, the national language of East Timor. National hearings have taken place on Political Prisoners (February 2003), on Women and Conflict (April 2003), and on Famine and Forced Displacement (July 2003). Other planned hearings include the civil war, massacres, and international actors. These national hearings, broadcast live across Dili on national television, have been viewed by a huge number of people.

The national hearing foci are based on the CAVR's research programme. Other key thematic areas targeted are the structure, policies, and practices of the Indonesian military and police; the structure, policies, and practices of FRETILIN and FALINTIL; children and youth; political party conflict and civil war; and the death toll. In January 2003, the CAVR established an Indonesia contact group in Jakarta to assist with research.

Community education and outreach efforts are central to the CAVR. In West Timor, the CAVR has assisted East Timorese refugees, and spearheaded a five-month outreach plan for small teams of West Timorese NGO workers and East Timorese living in West Timor. In March 2003, a CAVR delegation, led by its Chairperson, Aniceto Guterres Lopes, held discussions in West Timor with the East Timor Community Council (Makasti), a new organization established on 19 March 2003 by pro-autonomy political leaders, including Eurico Guterres. This organization has stated its commitment to a peaceful East Timor, free of hatred and revenge.

In December 2002, the CAVR commenced a weekly radio programme, 'Dalan ba Dame' (The Road to Peace), and Television Timor Leste has provided regular coverage of the Community Reconciliation Process.

Community groups meet to discuss and record the human rights history of their community, as part of the CAVR's Community Profiling Programme. In addition, the regular reports of 'Visits and Visitors' in the CAVR Updates reflect the importance of international consultation, support, and assistance to the CAVR, and the CAVR's international assistance to others who are considering establishing a truth commission.

1. The CAVR as a way to document history

For victims and survivors, the CAVR hearings offer public acknowledgement by an official, state-sanctioned entity of the human rights violations

---

[83] CAVR Update (December 2002–January 2003).   [84] See *supra* n 80.

that have been perpetrated, and demonstrate a commitment by the new government to eradicate the roots of these atrocities and build a culture based on human rights. But hearings to find out the truth are as much about the process as they are about substance. Often, those who have been victimized know what happened to them and their families and friends, but a truth commission can 'officially' document these experiences as part of the history of East Timor.

Many truths exist about the history of Indonesia's invasion and occupation, and the violence surrounding 1999, but access to venues for dissemination has never been an equal playing field. For example, clearly, Indonesia and the United States have not been barred from presenting their version of events. For the first time, however, the CAVR enables those who have survived to tell their stories, fill in the 'gaps' and write the missing history of what has happened. These processes are part of the restoration of human rights and dignity to the victims/survivors.

Victims of human rights violations do not easily 'forget' the voices, smells, clothing, or manner of those who violated them. The CAVR helps victims to exercise their right to know who violated them, and under whose orders. Through the inquiry, faces are given names. While it is likely that a victim may know the individuals in the local militia, the Indonesian forces, especially those in Jakarta, may be anonymous to their victims. The CAVR is mandated to determine the full context in which human rights violations occurred, and to fill in the missing information about who is responsible for the crimes, and who should be held accountable.

Moreover, the hearings of the CAVR refute any claims of the Indonesian government, the United States government and others in the world who will try to hide behind the excuse that 'they did not know' what happened for a quarter of a century in East Timor.

2. The CAVR as a means for dispute resolution

As noted by the Judicial System Monitoring Programme (JSMP), there is a proud tradition of community-based mediation and other forms of dispute resolution in local communities in East Timor. Some of these processes pre-date even the Portuguese colonial presence and are administered by local leaders such as the *lia nain* (traditional law person), and have been developed or adapted as alternatives to the corrupt and arbitrary nature of the Indonesian justice system.[85]

These dispute resolution mechanisms are not viewed as 'alternative' processes, but are accepted as the norm for the method of resolution of less-serious crimes; the external formal mechanisms are considered appropriate

---

[85] JSMP 'East Timor's New Judicial System' (2001) 2 (6, 7) *La'o Hamutuk Bulletin* (October) Pt 1. The JSMP website www.jsmp.minihub.org is an excellent source on the judicial system and related issues.

for serious crimes, such as murder (but not for rape or domestic violence).[86] The functioning of the CAVR as a dispute mechanism, then, falls within this customary framework. Difficulties can arise, however, when the matters in the CAVR do not fall squarely within its Schedule I. For example, as discussed earlier, individual criminal acts which are part of a pattern or policy could constitute a violation of human rights, and hence, be categorized as a serious crime.

There are also particular problems of resolving crimes against women and children outside the formal justice system, and in a community reconciliation process.[87] As Amnesty International has reported, prior to the establishment of the CAVR, several cases of violent crimes against women and children had been resolved outside the formal judicial process, for example, by payment of money and other means, sometimes against the victim's wishes.[88]

According to the UN High Commissioner for Human Rights' 2003 Report to the Commission on Human Rights, about 40 to 50 per cent of the cases reported to the PNTL (East Timor police) concern cases of domestic violence against women. Approximately 60 per cent of these domestic violence cases were resolved through mediation or traditional law, and there was inadequate prosecution of crimes against women. The report further concludes that:

> Prosecutors appear to have accepted local dispute resolution as the basis for closing or halting investigations, including those for the crime of rape. The possibility that cases might be resolved locally has also been used as justification for halting the formal investigation process.[89]

3. Reception and reconciliation

Why the need for reconciliation? We need to know the truth; We need to remember; We need to come to terms with and accept; We need to learn from; We need to forgive; We need to heal; and We need to move forward.[90]

As its name implies, a primary aim of the CAVR is reception and reconciliation for those persons who want to return to their communities. The term 'acolhimento' is translated into English as 'reception' or 'welcome',[91] but this

---

[86] Author's correspondence with Caitlin Reiger.

[87] For more information on the issues of women in East Timor, see the sources listed at www.etan.org/action/issues/women.htm and (2001) 2(5) *La'o Hamutuk Bulletin* (August) 'Issue Focus: Women and the Reconstruction in East Timor'. See also *infra* n 101 in reference to jurisdictional issues.

[88] See Amnesty International 'East Timor, Justice Past, Present and Future' (27 July 2001) s 7.1 available at www.amnesty.org. AI points out that truth commissions should not be seen as alternatives to justice, and should not interfere with a state's responsibility under international legal standards to prosecute perpetrators of human rights violations: ibid s 9.4.

[89] At paras 34–6.

[90] Address by President Xanana Gusmao (*infra* n 128).

[91] *Portuguese-English Dictionary* (compiled by Hygino Aliandro Pocket Books New York 1960).

does not represent the much fuller concept which the word embodies. Both terms, reception and reconciliation, together convey that the CAVR is part of the process of building a new society in East Timor, in which the respect for human rights is fundamental. This involves dealing with the past, for the purpose of creating new relationships among people in the present and in the future. This is similar to South Africa's Truth and Reconciliation Commission in South Africa, where its Chairperson, Archbishop Desmond Tutu, talked about *ubuntu*, 'the essence of being human', as its driving force, and (former) Minister of Justice Dullah Omar stressed the Commission's significance as part of the new government's commitment to building a human rights culture.[92]

Many of those people included in the reception committed no offences, but were forced to flee during the violence of 1999; for them, reconciliation does not apply. The CAVR offers an opportunity to return home safely to their communities, and a refuge from their horrible living conditions, many in militia-controlled camps in West Timor. As of November 2002, there were still more than 33,000 East Timorese refugees living outside East Timor, most of them in West Timor. In addition, nearly 1,500 East Timorese children who were separated from their parents in 1999 had been placed in orphanages and other institutions throughout Indonesia. Between April and August 2002, just over 24,500 East Timorese had repatriated.[93]

But for former militia members, the concepts of reception and reconciliation offer a way to re-integrate those who have committed crimes. For the new government of East Timor, the reception and reconciliation of former militia members is a way to reduce future conflict and avoid revenge, and create the groundwork on which to rebuild.

The reach of reconciliation extends broadly to everyone who was involved in the political conflict. As President Xanana Gusmao has pointed out, in addition to the crimes committed by the TNI or militias, the political parties in East Timor must recognize their crimes and mistakes.[94] However, given the refusal of Indonesia to cooperate with judicial requests, there is a possibility that reconciliation with Indonesian perpetrators will be one-sided, ie, 'victim-sided'.

The potential inequities of any reconciliation process are often exacerbated by the fact that the economic playing field is not level between victims and perpetrators. This is less likely to be the case in CRPs, where many of the

---

[92] Minister of Justice Dullah Omar, 'Introduction' to *Truth and Reconciliation Commission* (Justice in Transition on behalf of the Ministry of Justice 1994/95).

[93] For more information on the situation of refugees, see Chapter 5 (de Bertodano); Diane Farsetta 'Will the Refugees Be Forgotten?' (2002–03) 8(2) *East Timor Estafeta* (Winter); 'East Timor Issues Policy Paper on Refugee Returns' at www.easttimor-reconciliation.org; UNTAET 'Policy on Justice and Return Procedures in East Timor' and 'Refugees' (Fact Sheet 9 April 2002).

[94] See address by President Xanana Gusmao (*infra* n 128).

militia and low-level TNI perpetrators are very poor, as are the victims. However, economic inequity between victims and perpetrators can be a significant factor. Reconciliation with the government of Indonesia and its military leaders could possibly involve reparations from Indonesia, to both individual victims and to the new democratic state.

President Xanana Gusmao has emphasized that reconciliation must lead to economic and social justice:

Without a change of the current poor standard of life, the grief lived in the past will not be healed and reconciliation will be a lot harder to achieve ... All the sacrifices will only be honored when we reach an equitable level of development, based on steadfast determination to eradicate poverty in our country. It will be meaningless if we have all the perpetrators in jail, but the people continue to face infant mortality, endemic and epidemic diseases, without a decent house, without clean water and food.[95]

D. MEETING ITS OBJECTIVE: OBSTACLES TO FINDING THE TRUTH

Considering the Regulation establishing the CAVR, there appear to be two potential obstacles to seeking the truth about human rights violations in East Timor: (a) there is no mechanism to enforce the CAVR's broad investigatory powers, and (b) the CAVR offers no incentive, or 'carrot' to persuade perpetrators to come forward.

First, as human rights advocate Aderito de Jesus Soares, a jurist and former member of the Constitutional Assembly has pointed out, the main challenge facing the CAVR is how to obtain information and testimony from the major alleged perpetrators, now residing in Indonesia.[96] As an illustration of this problem, we refer to a two-day public hearing in April 2003 on Women and Conflict, during which witnesses, including women who were forced to be sex slaves, testified that rape, torture, and murder were part of an organized campaign by the Indonesian military to intimidate the East Timorese people.[97] Hypothetically, if Colonel X, who may have relevant information about these human rights violations or was named as an alleged perpetrator, had been invited or ordered to appear,[98] his attendance would

---

[95] ibid.

[96] Aderito de Jesus Soares 'The Untouched Truth Facing the Commission for Reception, Truth and Reconciliation in East Timor' (unpublished paper 2002).

[97] See CAVR Press Release, 22 April 2003; CAVR Update, April–May 2003; Guido Guilart 'Indonesia Military Accused of Sex Slavery' Associated Press 20 April 2003.

[98] Pursuant to UNTAET Regulation 2001/10 s 14: (CAVR's Inquiry Related Powers in Truth-Seeking). Note: the author has no knowledge as to whether similar requests or orders were made in reference to this hearing.

be a purely voluntary matter.[99] Most likely, Colonel X resides in Indonesia, and there is no obligation of Indonesia to transfer Colonel X to the CAVR.[100]

Secondly, the CAVR, within its truth-seeking function, does not offer any incentive for perpetrators to testify about their role in human rights violations, or 'serious crimes'. For example, no amnesty is offered as a shield for civil or criminal liability to those who give a full confession about their crimes in a truth-seeking hearing. Thus, participation by alleged perpetrators in CAVR investigations into human rights violations remains triggered by political will.

These obstacles impact on the CAVR's community reconciliation process, as well, in a situation where testimony at a CRP may also involve a serious crime. For example, a woman could testify about an assault (a Schedule I crime) by a militia member, but the assault could have led to, or resulted in, a rape or other sexual offence committed by his Indonesian commander.[101] Although the militia member, as an applicant for the CRP, has demonstrated that he is willing to accept responsibility for the assault, the Indonesian officer could still remain out of the CAVR's reach.

E. THE CAVR'S RELATION TO THE FORMAL JUSTICE SYSTEM

The CAVR, although a non-judicial mechanism with some 'quasi-judicial' powers, depends on the formal justice system in its day-to-day functions.

---

[99] Although there are penalties for non-compliance with orders of the CAVR, these are minimal for a military or government official, and would not, therefore, motivate cooperation.

[100] On the framework for cooperation with Indonesia, see Chapter 17 (Sluiter). Similarly, compliance with CAVR requests for foreign entities to provide additional information about the incidents in which perpetrators are alleged to have committed human rights violations is voluntary.

[101] As the hearing on Women and Conflict illustrates, the investigation of sexual crimes, including rape, as human rights violations falls within the CAVR's truth-seeking mandate (UNTAET Regulation 2001/10 s 13.2(a)). But, the resolution of these crimes is outside the CAVR's jurisdiction (although some of the acts involved in rape, such as assault, fall within Schedule I). How sexual crimes are categorized determines whether the Serious Crimes Panel can prosecute them. For example, the SCP has universal jurisdiction for genocide, war crimes, crimes against humanity and torture, but only limited jurisidiction for murder and sexual offences. See judgment in *P v Leonardus Kasa* Dili District Court, Special Panel for Serious Crimes 11/CG/2000 (9 May 2001) (held that Special Crimes Panel had no jurisdiction over an allegation of rape which occurred in West Timor in September 1999). The implications of the *Kasa* judgment for the prosecution of gender-based international crimes are addressed in an excellent paper by Susan Gail Harris 'Untold Numbers: East Timorese Women and Transitional Justice' (paper presented at 'New Challenges and New States: What Role for International Law' Proceedings of the 10th Annual Conference Australian and New Zealand Society of International Law 14–16 June 2002). The author appreciates the assistance of Caitlin Reiger on this point.

1. CRP and truth-seeking functions

The CAVR's key functions are legitimized by both the community and the formal justice system. At the community level, the presiding panel includes traditional leaders and other community members. In addition, the CRAs have a collective, contractual legitimacy: the perpetrator has a contract with the aggrieved person who is now being paid or compensated, and also with the community in which the person lives.

As to the criminal justice system, at the inception of the CRP process, the Office of the General Prosecutor is mandated to review deponents' statements, and to make decisions in cases where serious crimes are included. At the conclusion, the Community Reconciliation Agreements (CRAs) are reviewed and registered in the District Court,[102] which also is empowered to sanction deponents for non-compliance. Failure to agree to undertake the recommended act of reconciliation is a reason to refer the matter to the Office of the Prosecutor,[103] and failure to comply with the CRA obligations is punishable by a term of imprisonment not to exceed one year, or a fine not to exceed US$3,000, or both.[104] Similarly, within the CAVR's truth-seeking mandate, failure to comply with an order of the CAVR, or knowingly furnishing false and misleading information, are offences punishable by a term of imprisonment not to exceed one year, or a fine not to exceed US$3,000, or both.[105]

2. Statement sharing and confidentiality[106]

Mandatory statement-sharing provisions, as discussed above, obligate the CAVR to turn over statements to the Office of the General Prosecutor (OGP). According to the Regulation, the confidentiality of those matters which are confidential shall be preserved by commissioners and the staff, but the Commission can be compelled to release information at the request of the Office of the General Prosecutor.[107]

A Memorandum of Understanding on the sharing of information between the CAVR and the OGP specifies that:

With respect to the CAVR's truth seeking function [ie to establish the truth about human rights violations committed between April 1974 and October 1999] . . .

(a) The CAVR will release specific information it has gathered through its truth-seeking function to the OGP upon request and in circumstances where the confidentiality of witnesses or the victims is preserved to the greatest extent possible.

---

[102] UNTAET Regulation 2001/10 s 28.   [103] ibid s 27.9.
[104] ibid s 30.2.   [105] ibid s 20.
[106] ibid s 24.5. This analysis is based on a review of the Regulation. The practical relation between statement-sharing, confidentiality and self-incrimination and the CAVR and the OGP is not known to the author.
[107] ibid s 44.

(b) The OGP will request information only if it is deemed specifically relevant to an active criminal investigation or prosecution which has been initiated by the OGP independently of any information which has been requested from the Commission.

(c) The OGP is able to provide information to the CAVR that is relevant to its truth-seeking function only in circumstances where this does not prejudice ongoing investigation or prosecutions or the confidentiality of witnesses or victims and is consistent with the mandate of the OGP.[108]

The Memorandum applies only to 'serious crimes' information, and establishes two separate standards: for the CAVR, preservation of the confidentiality of witnesses or victims is 'to the greatest extent possible', and for the OGP, information is shared with the CAVR only in situations which do not *prejudice* the work of the OGP. Since the standard of prejudice is a higher one, this could be interpreted as assigning a higher priority to the prosecution of serious crimes, as opposed to seeking the truth about 'serious crimes'.

3. *Lack of reciprocity between the CAVR and the criminal justice system*

The criminal justice system is clearly integral to the day-to-day functioning of the CRP, from the OGP's vetting of statements for 'serious crimes', to the registration and enforcement of the Community Reconciliation Agreements by the courts, and the issuance of penalties for offences which obstruct the CAVR's work.[109] However, the corollary proposition, that the CRA is integral to the criminal justice system, does not appear to be true. First, a CAVR investigation of a matter does not bar any other competent authority from conducting its own investigation into the same matter.[110] This provision recognizes that the CAVR's objectives and inquiries, as a non-judicial entity, do not necessarily replicate those of judicial authorities.

Secondly, it is possible that the statement-sharing obligations between the CAVR and the OGP (and combined with the absence of any amnesty for 'serious crimes') could potentially affect both the CAVR Community Reconciliation Process and its truth-seeking function adversely. Significant considerations of due process protections for defendants could be presented, where the statements include admissions of 'serious crimes', which are subject to prosecution.

---

[108] Memorandum of Understanding Between the Office of the General Prosecutor (OGP) and the Commission for Reception, Truth and Reconciliation (CAVR) Regarding the Working Relationship and an Exchange of Information between the Two Institutions, 4 June 2002, para 9.

[109] These general offences include hindering the CAVR in its work; improperly influencing the CAVR; threatening or intimidating any person who is cooperating or intends to cooperate with the CAVR, including anyone involved in, or associated with, a Community Reconciliation Agreement; and the disclosure of confidential information: UNTAET Regulation 2001/10 s 39.

[110] ibid s 37.

For example, an applicant who is eligible for the CRP because he committed arson, could also have known about or been involved in another 'serious crime'; or, perhaps the single instance of arson was part of a larger systematic policy of destruction, perpetrated by the Indonesian military but carried out by individual militia members. Any 'serious crime' information in a statement could expose the applicant to potential criminal prosecution. The person could decide either not to come forward, or he could submit a statement to the CRP, but decide not to include information about the 'serious crime', or how the arson occurred. In either case, the CAVR objectives in its CRP, and its truth-seeking function to inquire about human rights violations could clearly be hindered.

In addition, statement sharing itself can contradict the CAVR's provisions which include the right to not incriminate oneself[111] and the confidentiality provision.[112]

While the CAVR clearly functions within a judicial context,[113] the traditional 'carrot/stick relationship' used to characterize the relation between a truth commission and the judicial system is not an accurate metaphor for the CAVR and its relation to the Office of the General Prosecutor. The CAVR offers no 'carrot', or a non-punitive alternative, in exchange for disclosures of truth about 'serious crimes' and refers these crimes to the OGP for prosecution, which could result in punishment, or 'the stick'. Therefore, the CAVR is not an alternative to prosecution, since its subject matter jurisdiction is 'less serious offences' and does not include 'serious crimes'.

But the effectiveness of the OGP and the Serious Crimes Panel in prosecuting 'serious' crimes influences the CAVR's community reconciliation function.[114] Any judicial weakness could signal to deponents in the CRP that if they fail to comply with their agreements, there would be no legal consequences. In addition, if the judicial system is not able to prosecute the serious crimes, this communicates a message to the alleged perpetrators that impunity will be tolerated. These consequences, together, could encourage a lack

---

[111] ibid s 17.1.

[112] ibid s 44. Similar potential problems exist in the case of Sierra Leone in respect to how information obtained by a truth commission is used by judicial bodies, and what safeguards exist against defendants' self-incrimination. See Chapter 9 (Schabas). In Sierra Leone's legislation, no provisions exist against self-incrimination or for mandatory statement sharing, although there are provisions which provide for confidentiality. See the Truth and Reconciliation Commission Act 2000, ss 7(3) and 14(3).

[113] For an excellent overview of the judicial landscape, including the roles of the United Nations, Indonesia, East Timor, and an International Tribunal, see the analyses in (2001) 2 (6, 7) *La'o Hamutuk Bulletin* (October) Pt 1, Issue focused on Justice, available at www.etan.org/lh/bulletins/bulletinv2n6.html.

[114] The weaknesses which have been identified in the OGP—a combination of the destruction of the judicial apparatus during the political conflicts, the lack of opportunities historically for the training of East Timorese jurists, and the general under-staffing and under-resourcing of the judiciary—have led to concerns and criticisms about the OGP's functioning. See further the JSMP's analyses about the judicial system.

of confidence in the judicial system at a crucial time, when a strong prosecutorial mechanism is a necessary foundation on which to establish the rule of law, and hold perpetrators of human rights violations accountable. To strengthen the judiciary, it has been suggested that rebuilding the judicial infrastructure should be a funding priority, with the establishment of a CAVR later in the context of a strong judicial system.[115]

The ability of the OGP to prosecute serious crimes referred by the CAVR was addressed in the Report of the UN High Commissioner for Human Rights, Mr Sergio Vieira de Mello.[116] He concluded that 'given the difficulties already faced by the Serious Crimes Unit and the Serious Crimes Panel, it is unclear, however, as to whether the serious crimes referred by CAVR to the Prosecutor could be taken up'.[117]

4. The problem with categorizing human rights violations[118]

Based on the Regulation, it appears that the two categories of crimes— 'serious' and 'less serious'—are quite distinct, and different powers to resolve each type of crime are assigned to the CAVR and OGP. This could be a potential area of tension, where there may be an overlap of 'serious' and 'less serious' crimes. The fundamental problem is the reality that human rights violations committed during political conflict defy discrete categories, and the experiences and testimony of witnesses are not easily compartmentalized.

First, it is difficult, if at all possible, to clearly demarcate the line between human rights violations and Schedule I crimes during political conflict.[119] The line is often blurred, if not impossible to define. Distinguishing instances of a 'common' crime of theft of livestock or property when acts of plundering are the military orders of the day is difficult. What might constitute a 'less serious' crime in one context can assume the character of a human rights violation in another context, depending on the perpetrator and the political context of the act. For example, crimes of arson or theft, committed under the direct orders of a militia leader, or with his unspoken sanction, could constitute human rights violations under international law.

---

[115] Conversation with Aderito de Jesus Soares (New York February 2003).

[116] 'Report of the United Nations High Commissioner for Human Rights: Situation of Human Rights in Timor-Leste' (4 March 2003) E/CN.4/2003/37.

[117] ibid para 32.

[118] The impact of the distinction between 'less serious' and 'serious' crimes is framed here from a theoretical perspective. As Kieran Dwyer and Charles Scheiner have pointed out to the author, the distinction between the crimes has not, in practice, proved to be significant, nor has it impacted negatively on the Community Reconciliation Process. But the distinction is relevant from the perspective of what crimes can fall in between the cracks.

[119] 'Political conflicts in East Timor' are defined as 'armed and non-armed struggles and discord related to the sovereignty and political status of East Timor, the organisation or governance of East Timor, the illegal Indonesian invasion and occupation of East Timor, or any combination of the foregoing': UNTAET Regulation 2001/10 s 1(j).

Secondly, the divisions beg the question of when a Schedule I crime rises to the level of a serious criminal offence or a human rights violation.[120] How much livestock must be killed or how many crops destroyed before an individual or a family is denied its livelihood, in contravention of the rights enshrined in international human rights and humanitarian law? A single act may constitute a 'less serious' crime, but when single crimes are repeated, they can be viewed, in the aggregate, as constituting a practice or policy. Thus, repeated single acts of arson by militia members can be qualitatively transformed into a pattern. In these situations, acts of omission (where a person had the opportunity, but did not try to stop the crime) could also constitute an offence.

In addition, the inclusion of socio-economic crimes which constitute human rights violations illustrates that the categorization is often not so distinct and clear-cut. Human rights violations are not restricted to the crimes of murder, torture, sexual assault, and the like, but include 'socio-economic crimes' as well. As applied to East Timor, this point is illustrated in the Dunn Report, which concludes:

The wave of violence [i.e. the militia violence, aided and abetted by the TNI during 1999] led to very serious Crimes Against Humanity. They included: killings, including mass murder, torture, abduction, sexual assault and assault against children, as well as mass deportation, and forced dislocation. The Crimes Against Humanity also include the massive destruction of shelter, and of services essential to the upholding of the basic rights of the East Timorese to healthcare and education. In addition there was a massive theft of the property of the people of East Timor.[121]

G. CONCLUSION

'If the truth is to be believed in this country, it must perhaps be written by those who bear the consequences of the past'.[122]

Certainly, the value of seeking the truth, the cornerstone of truth commissions, is indisputable. As Professor Jose Zalaquett, a former member of Chile's National Commission for Truth and Reconciliation, has pointed out, truth is one of the conditions of the legitimacy of a human rights policy—it must be known, complete, officially proclaimed, and publicly

---

[120] See *supra* n 71 for JMSP discussion of 'serious' and 'less serious' crimes.

[121] James Dunn 'Crimes Against Humanity in East Timor, January to October 1999: Their Nature and Causes' Executive Summary (14 February 2001) para 4. Dunn, a former Australian diplomat, served as an independent consultant to the Chief Prosecutor for UNTAET. This report on Indonesian military (TNI) crimes against humanity in East Timor was commissioned by the United Nations. It is available at www.etan.org.

[122] Antjie Krog *Country of My Skull: Guilt, Sorrow, and the Limits of Forgiveness in the New South Africa* (Times Books Random House 1998) 112.

exposed.[123] And, the legitimacy of the truth-finding mechanism must be established, in the first instance, by those who have suffered the human rights violations.

But whether a truth commission is an appropriate mechanism for a particular country is a determination which can only be made by its people. It is wrong to think of truth commissions as part of a 'pre-packaged formula' which should be uniformly implemented in every post-conflict situation to deal with atrocities of the past, and to hold perpetrators accountable for human rights violations. Especially within the last decade, there is a trend of truth commissions as the 'policy option of choice' for donor countries and agencies, and truth commissions have emerged as an expected transitional remedy in post-conflict situations. But whether and/or how to address human rights violations of the past, and to prevent their recurrence in the future, is part of a sovereign state's exercise of the right of self-determination. This means that the question, what is 'right' for country X, must be answered by country X.

Where a country decides to construct a truth commission, there will be no single, uniform answer as to whether and/or how it will help victims and survivors find justice. Any conclusions about truth commissions, including the CAVR, are interwoven with multiple notions of truth, justice, and accountability. A truth commission's investigation of human rights violations can play a key political role in the accountability of perpetrators. However, truth commissions are often judged by the one criterion which is outside of their mandates, and, hence, impossible to achieve: whether the commission can hold the major perpetrators—found at the highest levels of government and in the military—legally accountable for their acts, of commission and omission, which constitute state-sponsored crimes against human rights. Usually, the answer has to be 'no' because of the constraints on truth commissions. Truth commissions often have quasi-judicial powers to investigate the human rights violations of governmental and military leadership, but, as non-judicial entities, cannot prosecute alleged perpetrators. This inherent quandary—between broad powers to investigate human rights violations, but no mandate to hold perpetrators legally responsible— underscores the necessity for courts and tribunals to fill the prosecutorial gap in order to combat impunity.

Where judicial prosecutions are not effective, there is an even greater pressure on truth commissions to address their recurring dilemma: how to focus accountability on the leadership or 'big fish', when foot soldiers or 'little fish' may be the only perpetrators who, in reality, are within its reach.

---

[123] Jose Zalaquett 'Confronting Human Rights Violations Committed by Former Governments: Principles Applicable and Political Constraints' in Neil J Kritz (ed) *Transitional Justice: How Emerging Democracies Reckon with Former Regimes* (US Institute of Peace Press Washington DC 1995) vol I, 6–9.

In East Timor, the failure of the Indonesian courts to mete out justice, and the constraints on East Timor's judicial system, highlight that those at the highest levels of authority and leadership could gain a 'constructive immunity' from accountability and prosecution, while the foot-soldiers are held accountable by the CAVR through its Community Reconciliation Process.

One possible way to address this dilemma is to change the venue and orientation of truth commissions. The usual practice is to convene the commission in the country where the population has suffered human rights abuses, and has been victimized—in the Caribbean, Central America, Latin America, Africa, and Asia. For example, few state-sponsored commissions have been convened in Western Europe or North America, or in a major Asian country.[124] Rather than being *solely* convened at the crime scene where the victims are, truth commissions must also be convened where the alleged perpetrators (including the policy-makers) of those crimes live and work and are sheltered, and have received financing, training, and governmental support. Governments in some of these countries protect a disproportionate number of witnesses and alleged perpetrators, as well as documentary evidence.[125] Then, truth commissions may be better positioned to investigate the *missing, hidden, and covered-up truths* on the role of foreign governments in human rights violations.

In the case of East Timor, convening truth commissions in Indonesia and in the United States would significantly change the political equation and context.[126] The governments of Indonesia and the United States, based on their historic roles, are in pivotal positions to offer both documentary and testimonial evidence about human rights violations. However, to date, there has been a dearth of, if any, testimonies of high-ranking government and military leadership from these countries in the truth-seeking investigations of the CAVR.[127] Thus, it appears that the testimony of the major perpetrators has been missing from the truth-seeking hearings.

---

[124] The exceptions of which this author is aware are a truth commission in Germany in 1992 to examine the East German state, and a Presidential Truth Commission on Suspicious Deaths, established in South Korea in 2000. There also has been discussion about a truth commission to investigate the massacre related to the Jeju 3 April (Sasam) Uprising, on Jeju Island, South Korea, where the responsibility and role of the US military is a key issue.

[125] The issue of the destruction or removal of documentary evidence, such as state documents, can be important for truth commissions, and the international community, to address.

[126] East Timorese jurist and human rights advocate Aderito de Soares has proposed a truth commission in Indonesia. See *supra* n 96. For a US truth commission, see Joseph Nevins 'Time for a U.S. Truth Commission on East Timor' (17 May 2002) CommonDreams.org.

[127] Although information on the role of the United States and Indonesia in human rights violations has been documented by many sources, the issue is not simply obtaining or accessing the data. Both countries have a duty to uncover and investigate human rights violations, and to affirmatively demonstrate that the alleged perpetrators will be held accountable. In cases of torture, for example, there is a duty to prosecute. It is the author's opinion that the conduct of the United States and Indonesia, whether by acts of omission (the failure to take the initiative to

In addition, an International Criminal Tribunal for East Timor could be an appropriate forum to address the prosecutorial void. The struggle for self-determination in East Timor was an international struggle against Indonesia's occupation, and the crimes committed are appropriate to the jurisdiction of an international criminal tribunal. There have been numerous calls by East Timorese organizations, as well as the international community, for the establishment of an international ad hoc tribunal.

While it would seem logical that a truth commission would complement such a tribunal, the relationship between truth commissions and internationalized criminal bodies is neither inherently nor spontaneously complementary, and the procedures and objectives of each forum need to be evaluated in the particulars of a situation. Unlike judicial structures, truth commissions offer a transparency and accessibility through public hearings, and in public venues. The process of a truth commission—especially where it is predicated on active, intense community participation, as is the case in East Timor— permeates the national landscape and re-configures the agenda, and can contribute on many levels to truth, accountability, and reconciliation, and to a culture of human rights, as part of nation-building. But truth commissions cannot be a substitute for a strong judicial mechanism for the prosecution of human rights crimes.

However, the 'mixing' of judicial and non-judicial venues is often problematic, and can undermine the objectives of each forum. First, although commissions and courts or tribunals share the same subject matter— human rights violations—each forum has different goals. When a truth commission grants immunity from criminal or civil prosecution (through amnesty or another mechanism) to perpetrators in exchange for full disclosure of the truth, any possibility of punitive justice or damages for the victims evaporates. Secondly, the mixing of fora can compromise fundamental principles of due process and defendants' rights, where perpetrators' truths are revealed in a non-judicial setting of a truth commission and used as admissions in criminal proceedings.

Truth commissions, which evolve through a political process, illustrate that the political and judicial realms often overlap, but both can contribute to finding justice. No forum—truth commission, court or tribunal—has a 'monopoly' on holding perpetrators accountable for human rights violations. As President Xanana Gusmao has said, 'While we agree with the need for justice, this is also a political process and not merely a judicial one'.[128] But the contribution of each forum, alone or in combination, to the struggle for justice will, ultimately, be measured by the victims and survivors.

offer witnesses or documents to the CAVR) or commission (Indonesia's refusal to implement the judicial requests of the SCP) has been indicative of non-compliance with this duty.

[128] Address, 17 February 2003 at the Inauguration of former Balide Prison as the CAVR National Office, and the opening of National Public Hearing on Political Imprisonment.

7

Sierra Leone:
The Intersection of Law, Policy, and Practice

*Alison Smith**

A. INTRODUCTION

The Special Court for Sierra Leone was established in March 2002 to try those who bear the greatest responsibility for atrocities committed during the conflict in that country in the 1990s.[1] Yet, beyond the narrow letter of the Agreement establishing the Special Court, there are other broader aims, which include ending impunity, deterring would-be perpetrators, providing a measure of justice for the victims, helping to strengthen the rule of law in Sierra Leone, and contributing to capacity-building within the country, particularly for the legal profession. Thus, the Special Court has both backward- and forward-looking aims: to provide redress for what happened in Sierra Leone and to contribute to lasting peace, a strengthened rule of law, and the future protection of people involved with a conflict, both in Sierra Leone and elsewhere. Indeed, the Special Court has an important role to play in respect of the identification of customary international humanitarian law, and the advancement of the international rule of law.

* Alison Smith has been the chief legal adviser on the Special Court to the Office of the Attorney-General and Minister of Justice of Sierra Leone and the Country Director for No Peace Without Justice in Sierra Leone since August 2000. No Peace Without Justice also undertakes other activities in Sierra Leone, including sensitization on the Special Court throughout the country. Many of the arguments made in this chapter are based on developments observed in Sierra Leone and on the opinions given and knowledge offered by Sierra Leonean legal practitioners and members of civil society. I would like to thank all these people for their help and, importantly, H E Solomon E Berewa, Vice President of the Republic of Sierra Leone, Ambassador Alieu Kanu, Deputy Permanent Representative of the Republic of Sierra Leone to the United Nations, The Hon Eke A Halloway, Attorney-General and Minister of Justice of the Republic of Sierra Leone, and the members of the No Peace Without Justice team with whom I worked in Sierra Leone: Kizito Bangura, Claire Bisiaux, Niccolo' Figa'-Talamanca, Richard Bednarek, John Cerone, Catherine Gambette, Abdul Rahim Kamara, Tom Longley, Avril Rowe, John Stompor, Andrew Swindells, Giorgia Tortora, Pascal Turlan, and Aisha Wright.
[1] See Art 21 of the Agreement for the Special Court. The Agreement was signed on 16 January 2002 and the Ratification Bill passed through Parliament on 19 March 2002. The President assented to the Bill on 29 March 2002, whereupon Sierra Leone notified the United Nations that it had completed its internal ratification requirements.

All of these are noble aims and objectives, yet it has been suggested that there are other, ulterior motives for both Sierra Leone and the international community to create the Special Court. One theory was that the government was both seeking to increase its popularity prior to ending the state of emergency and holding national elections, as well as currying favour with the international community.[2] Cynically, it has been suggested that the primary motive for the international community to get involved was punishing the crimes committed against peace-keepers in May 2000. Had foreign peace-keepers not been put at risk, there would be no international interest in punishing atrocities committed in Sierra Leone. Suggestions have also been made that the Special Court is just another way for foreigners, particularly non-Africans, to create jobs for themselves and their friends without considering the broader implications of their actions or more appropriate ways in which funds could be utilized.[3]

While these suspicions, understandable as they may be, have little basis in fact, their mere existence could undermine the effective operations of the Special Court, since it requires the support of the people of Sierra Leone to be effective. Sierra Leoneans have the necessary information; their support is crucial if they are to cooperate with investigators and to give testimony at trial. Equally as important, if justice is to be done, the people of Sierra Leone will have to accept the judgments of the Special Court, which requires a belief in the credibility of the institution and its processes. None of these are possible unless Sierra Leoneans have a sense of ownership towards the Court and are involved in its work.

Be that as it may, the Special Court could easily dispel suspicion, win over cynics, and outweigh any perception that the motives for its establishment are primarily self-serving, through its work. Thus the critical question, and the test for the Court's ultimate success, is to what extent the Special Court might be able to fulfil the multiple objectives it has been designed to meet, a test that should be applied not just at the conclusion of its work but throughout its working life.

The success of the Special Court should by no means be considered certain, since the institutional design of the Court is marred by serious flaws, including the debatable temporal and subject matter jurisdictions, and the precarious financial mechanism for its funding. This chapter intends to focus on the first two of these shortcomings, examining what was done, what could have been done, and what should have been done while designing the Court, in the light of the Court's capacity to meet the lofty goals it has been given and fulfil the expectations of its ultimate beneficiaries.

---

[2] The state of emergency was lifted on 18 January 2002 and elections (which returned the ruling SLPP to power) were held across the country on 14 May 2002.

[3] These points have all been raised by participants at training seminars conducted by No Peace Without Justice in Sierra Leone and by others throughout 2001 to 2003.

B. WHO SHOULD BENEFIT FROM THE SPECIAL COURT AND HOW?

1. Beneficiaries inside Sierra Leone

The most obvious and direct beneficiaries of the work of the Special Court will be the people of Sierra Leone. Nearly everybody in Sierra Leone lost family members, lost limbs and/or had their homes and livelihoods destroyed, not only as an indirect consequence of legitimate fighting, but also as a direct result of methods of war that deliberately targeted the civilian population. In order for people to come to terms with these harms, there must not only be acknowledgement of their suffering, but also an accounting for the damage that has been done, by establishing who was responsible and—equally as important—who was not responsible. The Special Court, together with other accountability and post-conflict mechanisms and measures, can help accomplish these aims and help the people of Sierra Leone move towards a prosperous future.[4]

The Special Court has both the ability and the mandate to extract justice from those who were responsible at the highest levels of policy-making, namely those leaders who decided what methods of warfare were to be used. By targeting the leaders for prosecution, and increasing the disadvantages to leaders, the work of the Special Court has a greater chance of acting as a deterrent than if only rank and file soldiers were targeted for prosecution.

While responsibility will be attributed to individuals rather than on the basis of state or collective responsibility, the Court will eventually create an historical record of the truth, particularly when judgments are read alongside the report of the Truth and Reconciliation Commission and other information. The resulting consolidated record of what happened can be used not only to forestall denial of the atrocities, or individual responsibility, but also to avoid gratuitous and generic culpability. Avoiding blame being placed on an entire segment of society (eg 'children who fought for the RUF' or ex-SLA or AFRC forces) could facilitate the rehabilitation and reintegration of ex-combatants, particularly former child combatants.[5]

Finally, the Special Court could benefit directly the people of Sierra Leone by fostering training and education in Sierra Leone. Employing a significant number of Sierra Leoneans in all organs of the Court, both as administrative and professional staff, including investigators and prosecutors, has the advantage of exposing Sierra Leoneans, particularly legal and law enforcement

---

[4] Given that the Special Court will only be able to prosecute a limited number of people, and therefore hear testimony from a limited number of victims and witnesses, the bulk of the work in respect to acknowledgement will fall to other accountability mechanisms. The most notable of these is the Truth and Reconciliation Commission; see, Chapter 9 (Schabas).

[5] Hereinafter Revolutionary United Front (RUF); Sierra Leone Army (SLA) and Armed Forces Revolutionary Council (AFRC).

professionals, to an international criminal justice system, with higher technical and professional standards, allowing their familiarization with the adequate implementation of international human rights standards. These are lessons that Sierra Leoneans will be able to employ in their national justice system, including in the formulation of new laws and standards and the interpretation of existing laws.

In addition, the Statute provides that the Rules of Procedure and Evidence are those of the International Criminal Tribunal for Rwanda (ICTR), amended for the particular circumstances of the Special Court.[6] In amending the Rules, the judges may have recourse to relevant provisions of the Sierra Leone Criminal Procedure Act 1965. The judges have already taken an appreciable step in this direction, by actively participating in a seminar in Freetown at which members of the Sierra Leone Bar made submissions on their recommendations for amendments to the ICTR Rules.[7] By building on this and taking greater note of the Criminal Procedure Act in future amendments, the judgments of the Special Court will themselves have the ability to contribute to Sierra Leone's jurisprudence through the interpretation and application of those provisions, which would provide useful precedents for Sierra Leone courts and the lawyers practising in them.

However, as with all aspects of the Special Court, any impact it may have on the people of Sierra Leone will depend on how the Statute is implemented and how the Court operates. A crucial aspect of this is ensuring the people of Sierra Leone are kept involved and informed of its work, which the Special Court has been undertaking with increasing success through holding town meetings and undertaking public information and education activities in cooperation with civil society. The groundwork has been laid and it is now up to the officials of the Special Court to implement the provisions in a way beneficial not only for the work of the Special Court but in the broader context.

2. Beneficiaries outside Sierra Leone

Beneficiaries other than the people of Sierra Leone and its legal system are the international community at large and international law. While these beneficiaries could better be termed 'indirect' or 'secondary' beneficiaries, the ability of the Special Court to contribute to increased stability, both regionally and internationally, and to the development of international jurisprudence, is an important part of its potential legacy.

---

[6] Statute of the Special Court Art 14. The Rules of the Special Court were adopted by the Judges in plenary on 7 March 2003.

[7] The Seminar, organized by No Peace Without Justice in cooperation with the Sierra Leone Bar Association and the Special Court, was held in Freetown in December 2002.

Decisions of international judicial bodies can help clarify both treaty and customary international law. The impact of the International Criminal Tribunals for the former Yugoslavia and Rwanda on the development and clarification of international criminal law cannot be overestimated. Similarly, the Special Court will add its own contribution. Admittedly, a plurality of sources of interpretation and application of international criminal law could also entail fragmentation of the law and an increased risk of contradiction between the various judicial bodies. With this concern in mind, prior to the commencement of negotiations on the Special Court, the UN Security Council had requested the Secretary-General to consider whether the Special Court should share the Appeals Chamber of the International Criminal Tribunal for the former Yugoslavia (ICTY) and ICTR.[8] While this idea was eventually discarded for practical reasons, most notably the added time and financial burden on that Appeals Chamber, fragmentation can be avoided if the growing number of international criminal justice mechanisms turn to one another's jurisprudence for guidance in the application and interpretation of international humanitarian law.[9]

Strengthening international humanitarian law, particularly its enforcement, can help protect people involved in a conflict by deterring would-be perpetrators anywhere in the world. Crimes under international law are rarely the consequence of impulse, but are more often the result of deliberate choices made at the highest political and military levels by leaders weighing the pros and cons of waging war in certain ways. Among the factors that leaders consider in making these decisions is the likelihood of facing criminal prosecutions for the crimes committed during the conflict. The prosecution of leaders in the Sierra Leone conflict, coupled with the trial of President Milosevic at ICTY and the establishment of the International Criminal Court (ICC), will send a strong message to would-be perpetrators that the international community is becoming more active in the fight against impunity. The increased likelihood of facing criminal prosecution—both irrespective and because of their position as a leader—will act as a stronger deterrent when leaders are formulating their battle plans, provided that the Special Court and other international criminal justice mechanisms do their job effectively and efficiently.

---

[8] UNSC Res 1315 (2000) (14 August 2000) UN Doc S/RES/1315.

[9] It should be noted that Art 20 of the Statute expressly provides that 'judges of the Appeals Chamber of the Special Court shall be guided by the decisions of the Appeals Chamber of the International Tribunals for the former Yugoslavia and for Rwanda. In the interpretation and application of the laws of Sierra Leone, they shall be guided by the decisions of the Supreme Court of Sierra Leone'.

C. PARTICULAR ASPECTS OF THE SPECIAL COURT

1. Temporal jurisdiction

It is generally accepted that the conflict in Sierra Leone began on 23 March 1991, when forces of the RUF entered Sierra Leone from Liberia and launched a rebellion to overthrow the one-party government (ie the All People's Congress—(APC)), led by Joseph Saidu Momoh. This marked the start of protracted armed violence between organized armed groups that could not be said to have concluded at the time the negotiations for the Special Court commenced. Therefore, international humanitarian law applied across the territory of Sierra Leone from March 1991 until at least August 2000 and beyond, despite the various attempts at peaceful settlements.[10] Yet the Special Court will not have jurisdiction over acts committed since 1991; rather, its temporal jurisdiction begins on 30 November 1996, the date of the failed Abidjan Peace Agreement. This provision is the most obvious and striking example of policy and politics trumping the law, which has not gone unnoticed nor uncriticized in Sierra Leone and elsewhere.

The two most obvious dates for the commencement of the Court's jurisdiction would have been March 1991, the start of the conflict, or 7 July 1999, the date of the Lomé Peace Agreement, which granted combatants amnesties for acts committed in the furtherance of their objectives.[11] Yet, both dates were discarded.

While there were no political objections to the date of March 1991, it was rejected on the grounds that requiring the Prosecutor to investigate crimes committed since 1991 would have been too onerous a burden in terms of the time and cost of undertaking such investigations. Conversely, the date of the Lomé Peace Agreement was considered from the very start as being unacceptable, particularly to the United Nations, which had entered a disclaimer upon signing the Lomé Peace Agreement stating there could be no amnesty for crimes under international law.[12] For the United Nations to then negotiate a Court that would have given de facto recognition to the Lomé amnesty would have discredited its previous statements and stance on the granting of amnesties for these types of crimes.

---

[10] On 19 January 2002, Sierra Leone held a ceremony marking the end of disarmament and thus the end of the conflict, simultaneously lifting the state of emergency the country had been under since 1999. It could therefore be argued that the conflict ended on 19 January 2002 and would thus, in general, mark the end date for the temporal jurisdiction of the Court. However, it would not end the temporal jurisdiction for crimes against humanity (Art 2) or crimes under Sierra Leone law (Art 5), as these crimes do not require the nexus of an armed conflict to be prosecuted before the Special Court.

[11] See Art IX of the Lomé Peace Agreement.

[12] 'Report of the Secretary-General to the Security Council' (4 October 2000) UN Doc S/2000/915 para 23.

Given that neither of these dates was considered during initial negotiations as a starting point for the temporal jurisdiction of the Court, it was therefore necessary to select a third date from which the Court would have jurisdiction. In so doing, three considerations were borne in mind:

(a) the temporal jurisdiction should be reasonably limited in time so that the Prosecutor is not overburdened and the Court overloaded;
(b) the beginning date should correspond to an event or a new phase in the conflict without necessarily having any political connotations; and
(c) it should encompass the most serious crimes committed by persons of all political and military groups and in all geographical areas of the country.[13]

Three different dates were discussed in this context:

(a) 30 November 1996 (ie, the date of the failed Abidjan Peace Agreement);
(b) 25 May 1997 (ie, when the AFRC launched its coup d'état); and
(c) 6 January 1999 (ie, when the AFRC and RUF launched their attack on Freetown).

The date of 25 May 1997 was rejected as having too many political overtones, while 6 January 1999 was rejected as giving the impression of favouring Freetown over the provinces. The date of 30 November 1996 was therefore considered the most appropriate, as it represented the first time the fighting factions had attempted to reach a peaceful settlement of the conflict. Additionally, it was considered to encompass the most serious crimes committed in the provinces, thereby ensuring the Court would not be too 'Freetown-centred'. Sierra Leone and the United Nations therefore agreed that this would be a suitable starting date for the Court.

It has to be queried whether these reasons provide sufficient justification for setting a start date for the Court that is halfway through the conflict, a compromise criticized by Sierra Leoneans from all along the social, political, and professional spectrum.[14] The perception in Sierra Leone is that the Statute unjustly favours Freetown over the provinces, as the November 1996 date corresponds to the time when the capital first became a target of attack.[15] For the provinces, the conflict has generally been one long, continuous experience from the beginning of the 1990s, whereas Freetown witnessed intermittent episodes of violence only from the mid-1990s onwards.

Endowing the Special Court with temporal jurisdiction covering the whole period since the commencement of the conflict would have allowed for the creation of a much more credible institution and would have addressed the criticisms of many in Sierra Leone who view the limitation as arbitrary and

---

[13] ibid para 25.

[14] For example, this issue was criticized in every one of the 26 Special Court Training Seminars conducted by NPWJ, which were held in Freetown, Bo, Kenema, and Mile 91. These seminars attracted a total of over 600 participants, including civil society and human rights organizations, lawyers, Paramount Chiefs, police, teachers, combatants, and ex-combatants: not a single voice was raised in support of retaining the start-date at 1996.

[15] See n 12.

unjust. It would have kept faith with the tenets of international humanitarian law, which does not apply from some retrospectively set date, arbitrarily fixed mid-way through the conflict, but from the time the hostilities commence. It could also have fostered a more cooperative, complementary relationship with the Truth and Reconciliation Commission, which has a temporal jurisdiction dating from the beginning of the conflict until 7 July 1999.[16] In addition, it would have allowed the Prosecutor to focus more effectively on 'those who bear the greatest responsibility' for violations committed throughout the conflict, rather than only those which happened to occur during the last five years of the conflict. For all these reasons, having a temporal jurisdiction starting from 1991 would have facilitated greater public support for the Special Court, particularly within Sierra Leone, and increased the advantages for all beneficiaries both in and outside Sierra Leone.

For these reasons, on 20 August 2001, following consultations with the people of Sierra Leone, the government of Sierra Leone requested that the temporal jurisdiction of the Special Court be extended back to 1991.[17] However, the general feeling within the United Nations was that this issue should not be reopened, lest 'delicate' balances achieved during the negotiations be upset, thereby requiring re-opening of other aspects of the Statute or Agreement. In addition, the United Nations considered that an extension of the Court's temporal jurisdiction would increase the burden on the Prosecutor and the Court to an unacceptable level.[18] The United Nations further maintained that the Prosecutor would in any event also be relying on evidence relating to events before 1996 (provided it is relevant to cases before the Court), therefore crimes committed prior to 1996 would not necessarily be excluded from consideration by the Court.[19] In order to avoid further delay, the government therefore withdrew its request, while still maintaining the legitimacy of the reasons behind making it.[20]

While the validity of the UN responses can be debated, a valuable opportunity to increase the effectiveness of the Special Court, by providing accountability for the crimes committed in Sierra Leone, and, more broadly, to strengthen international humanitarian law by demonstrating its applicability throughout a conflict, has been lost.

---

[16] Truth and Reconciliation Commission Act 2002 s 6(1).

[17] '11th Report of the Secretary-General on the United Nations Mission in Sierra Leone' (7 September 2001) UN Doc S/2001/857.

[18] This is underscored by the fact that the proposed budget had already been reduced to below the bare minimum following consultations with UN Member States on likely availability of funds.

[19] Letter from the Office of Legal Affairs to the government of Sierra Leone (19 October 2001).

[20] Letter from the government of Sierra Leone to the Office of Legal Affairs (29 November 2001).

2. Subject matter jurisdiction

The subject matter jurisdiction of the Special Court includes selected crimes under both international law and Sierra Leone law. The crimes under international law consist of crimes against humanity; violations of common Article 3 of the Geneva Conventions and Additional Protocol II; and other serious violations of international humanitarian law, including crimes against peace-keepers and the recruitment of children.[21] These are crimes that were considered to have had the status of customary international law at the time they were allegedly committed. The crimes under Sierra Leonean law cover offences relating to the abuse of girls and wanton destruction of property, taken from Sierra Leone legislation from 1926 and 1861 respectively. This selection of subject matter jurisdiction was done to pre-empt any challenge to the Court's legality on the basis of the principle of *nullum crimen sine lege*,[22] since the acts these provisions are purporting to address had been criminalized at the time they were allegedly committed.

The subject matter jurisdiction of the Special Court was selected on the basis of directions in Security Council Resolution 1315 (2000), and, particularly with respect to crimes under international law, preconceived ideas about the nature of the conflict and the crimes committed during it. For example, the Special Court does not have jurisdiction over the crime of genocide, which is contained in the Statutes of ICTY, ICTR, and ICC,[23] because there had been no allegations that individuals had been targeted for intentional total or partial destruction on the basis of belonging to a national, ethnic, racial, or religious group.[24]

While it may be argued that the drafters of the Statute had little or no choice regarding the subject matter jurisdiction, the selection presented in the Statute contains significant overlaps in respect of the crimes that may be charged. More troubling, it limits the bases on which the Prosecutor may bring charges, removes the ability of the Court to determine the nature of the conflict on the basis of evidence presented to it, and reduces the Court's potential for contributing to the development of international criminal law.

The most notable example of overlap is crimes under Sierra Leone law in Article 5 of the Statute of the Special Court. In particular, certain offences relating to the abuse of girls may to be addressed by applying the Prevention of Cruelty to Children Act 1926 (ie abusing a girl under 13 years of age; between 13 and 14 years of age; and abducting a girl for 'immoral purposes');

---

[21] Crimes against humanity (Art 2); violations of Art 3 common to the Geneva Conventions and of Additional Protocol II (Art 3), and other serious violations of international humanitarian law (Art 4).

[22] 'No crime without law': also called the principle of non-retroactivity of criminal law.

[23] Statute of the ICTY Art 4; Statute of the ICTR Art 2; and Rome Statute of the ICC Art 6.

[24] Protected groups under the Convention on the Prevention and Punishment of the Crime of Genocide 78 UNTS 277.

and in case of wanton destruction of property (setting fire to buildings, private and public) the Malicious Damage Act 1861 is to be applied.[25] These were included at the request of the Security Council in the Resolution authorizing the Secretary-General to negotiate the Agreement and Statute for the Special Court.[26]

While the inclusion of these crimes highlights the nature of the Special Court as a hybrid institution, with an international legal basis, but mixed in jurisdiction and composition, one major problem is that they raise the de facto complication of a dual start-date for the temporal jurisdiction. The Statute of the Special Court provides for temporal jurisdiction that extends to acts committed before the Lomé Peace Agreement amnesty, providing that the amnesty will be no bar to prosecution in respect of crimes under international law. While questions can and should be raised about the constitutionality of the domestic implementation of this provision of the Lomé Agreement,[27] the Statute acknowledges that this amnesty will be valid in respect of those provisions of Sierra Leone law within the court's jurisdiction.[28] This leads to a situation in which the Special Court will be able to try violations of international humanitarian law committed since 30 November 1996 but can only try violations of the Sierra Leone provisions included in the Court's Statute committed from 7 July 1999. The resulting effect of creating a dual start-date for the Special Court's temporal jurisdiction is raising serious questions about the legitimacy of the Court in the eyes of the Sierra Leone public.

The rationale for the decision to create a Special Court that applies a mix of domestic and international substantive law is that certain crimes, or aspects of crimes, committed during the conflict are allegedly better regulated by Sierra Leonean law than by international law.[29] However, it can be argued

---

[25] It should, however, be noted that none of the indictments contain charges under these provisions.

[26] UNSC Res 1315 (2000) para 2.

[27] Those opposed to the amnesty may challenge the constitutionality of Art IX of the Lomé Peace Agreement, on the basis that no constitutional power exists by which to grant any individual immunity before a criminal trial has been concluded. The Constitution vests the prerogative of mercy in the President, who has the power 'to grant any person convicted of any offence against the laws of Sierra Leone a pardon, either free or subject to lawful conditions' (Sierra Leone Constitution 1991 s 63(1)(a)). It does not purport to endow the President with the ability either to grant a pardon before conviction or to guarantee anyone that criminal prosecutions will not be brought against them. Consequently, it might be argued that Lomé Art IX and any subsequent implementing legislation is unconstitutional and thus invalid, at least to the extent of its inconsistency with the Constitution.

[28] Article 10 of the Statute provides: 'An amnesty granted to any person falling within the jurisdiction of the Special Court in respect of the crimes referred to in articles 2 to 4 of the present Statute shall not be a bar to prosecution'. The omission of Art 5, which inscribes the provisions of Sierra Leone law, indicates that amnesties granted in respect of these crimes will be a bar to prosecution.

[29] 'Report of the Secretary-General on the Establishment of a Special Court for Sierra Leone' (2000) UN Doc S/2000/915 para 19.

that both the abuse of girls and malicious damage to property fall within the ambit of international crimes included in the Statute.[30] Again, it could be contended that the crimes under Sierra Leone law offer greater protection to a greater number of people, since they neither require proof of the existence of an armed conflict nor a widespread or systematic attack, which are respectively elements of war crimes and crimes against humanity.[31] Yet, the elements of the crimes under Sierra Leone law are more specific and arguably more difficult to prove,[32] and therefore their inclusion could create significant evidentiary difficulties. Finally, there is the further practical problem that prosecution of crimes on the basis of Sierra Leone law demands reliance on Sierra Leonean jurisprudence, which is largely unorganized or unavailable. Indeed, to ensure consistency in application of these laws, judges at the Special Court would need to have reference to court decisions issued by Sierra Leone domestic courts, but publication of Sierra Leone court decisions ceased in the 1970s.[33] Taking all of these considerations into account, it appears that any additional protection offered under Sierra Leone law creates more legal and practical problems than it solves.

More problematic, however, particularly from the perspective of how the conflict in Sierra Leone is viewed, recorded, and remembered, is the content of Article 3 of the Special Court Statute, which confers jurisdiction over violations of common Article 3 to the Geneva Conventions and Additional Protocol II (1977). By choosing these provisions (which apply during internal conflicts) instead of the grave breaches provision of the Geneva Convention[34] (which apply during international conflicts) the drafters of the Statute have determined a priori that the conflict in Sierra Leone has been internal and not international in nature.

---

[30] Article 2, concerning crimes against humanity, prohibits 'rape, sexual slavery, enforced prostitution, forced pregnancy and any other form of sexual violence'. It also prohibits 'persecution on political, racial, ethnic or religious grounds' and 'other inhumane acts'. Article 3, concerning violations of Art 3 common to the Geneva Conventions and of Additional Protocol II, prohibits 'acts of terrorism' and 'outrages upon personal dignity, in particular humiliating and degrading treatment, rape, enforced prostitution and any form of indecent assault'.

[31] However, the prosecutorial prescription that only 'persons who bear the greatest responsibility for serious violations of international humanitarian law and Sierra Leonean law' stand trial before the Special Court, makes it extremely unlikely that persons accused only of isolated crimes—acts which do not form part of a widespread and systematic attack—will be prosecuted before the Special Court.

[32] For example, the abuse of girls provisions would require proof of the child's age, be it 13 or 14. In a country where births are more often not registered or recorded than they are, this requirement of proof of age could pose problems that will be difficult to overcome.

[33] Verified by discussions with legal practitioners in Sierra Leone. Since the 1970s, Court decisions are only written in long-hand by the judges who decide the cases and are stored in loose piles in the basement of the courthouse. Many of these decisions were destroyed by fire and thus lost completely during the attacks on Freetown.

[34] See Geneva Convention IV Art 146.

At first sight this is understandable, since the conflict was consistently characterized in the media as a 'civil war' fought between government forces (the Sierra Leone Army) and domestic armed opposition groups (the Revolutionary United Front and the Armed Forces Revolutionary Council). However, characterizing the conflict as internal in nature was both disingenuous and potentially short-sighted. Even if it were accepted that the RUF entered Sierra Leone without the involvement of any other state—an assertion that can be questioned, particularly in the case of Liberia—it is a well known fact that the character of a conflict can change during its course from being internal in nature to being international in nature.

In the *Tadić* decision, the ICTY Appeals Chamber specifically addressed the question of when a conflict that is prima facie internal in nature may be regarded as involving forces acting on behalf of a foreign power, thereby transforming the conflict into one that is international in nature.[35] The Appeals Chamber identified three specific tests concerning the necessary degree of control by a foreign power to determine whether this had occurred, namely overall control of an armed group or individuals; specific instructions to an armed group or individuals; and actual behaviour of an armed group or individuals, irrespective of any specific instructions.

Thus the question of whether or not the conflict in Sierra Leone was an internal or international conflict at any point during the conflict essentially turns on a question of fact: were there armed forces involved in the conflict that were under the control of a state other than the one on whose territory the conflict was being fought? In this respect, it must be remembered that not only have there been allegations of Liberian involvement in the conflict in Sierra Leone, there have also been foreign troops—specifically the Economic Community of West African States (ECOWAS) Monitoring Group (ECOMOG), the United Nations Assistance Mission in Sierra Leone (UNAMSIL), and British forces[36]—operating on the ground at various points during the conflict. The question of whether this constitutes sufficient foreign involvement to transform the conflict from internal into international is a question of fact that was best left to be determined by the judges of the Special Court on the basis of relevant and available evidence.

Finally, irrespective of the appropriateness or otherwise of the crimes both included and omitted in the Statute, the adoption of a 'pick-and-choose' approach to the substantive law has forsaken a unique opportunity to reinforce the coherent development of international criminal law. It would have been much more insightful and serviceable to rely on the Elements of Crimes of the International Criminal Court, which were adopted by the Preparatory Commission for the Establishment of the International Court

[35] *Prosecutor v Tadić*, ICTY Appeals Chamber (15 July 1999) Judgment, point IV.B.3.

[36] The Statute gives the Court jurisdiction over peace-keepers, stating that any crimes allegedly committed by peace-keepers 'shall be within the primary jurisdiction of the sending State': art 1.

in June 2000 and approved by the Assembly of States Parties at their first meeting in September 2002.[37]

The Elements of Crimes flesh out the crimes contained in the Rome Statute for the ICC and were arrived at after many months of painstaking negotiations by the Preparatory Commission for the ICC. Delegations took great care to ensure that the substantive law to be applied by the ICC reflected customary international law. In fact, this was often reiterated in Rome during the negotiations on the Statute and at UN Headquarters, both in the context of the Elements of Crimes and the (still ongoing) discussions on the definition of the crime of aggression. The inclusion of the Elements of Crimes would have benefited both the Special Court and ICC. It would have given the Special Court greater direction in relation to the cases prosecuted before it, and it would have given the ICC a few years' head start, since the jurisprudential development of the Elements of Crimes would have been underway by the time the ICC commences operations.

D. CONCLUSION

The Special Court has been welcomed by many as a unique institution that can provide an alternative model to that provided by the current ad hoc tribunals for addressing conflicts not falling within the jurisdiction of the International Criminal Court.

However, it has to be questioned whether the Special Court will, or even could, be the role model some believe it should be. It is clear that politics, policy, and practical considerations have lessened the role the Special Court could have played, both in regard to the perception of the Court, and the impact it could have on the people and laws of Sierra Leone, and the international community. Extension of the temporal jurisdiction back to 1991 would have increased manifold the legitimacy of the Special Court in the eyes of the people of Sierra Leone and would have strengthened international humanitarian law, by reiterating that it applies throughout an armed conflict. Granting the Special Court jurisdiction over those crimes identified by the ICC Elements of Crimes as customary international law would have strengthened the application and development of international criminal law. Leaving the determination of the true nature of the conflict in Sierra Leone (internal or international) to the judges of the Special Court would also have increased the Special Court's legitimacy in the eyes of the people of Sierra Leone. Even more problematic is the question of the financial mechanism, together with the question of the budget and the amount of

---

[37] The Elements of Crimes were adopted by the Assembly of States Parties of ICC at its first meeting in September 2002.

money pledged for the work of the Special Court,[38] matters that have already attracted significant criticism in Sierra Leone and elsewhere.

One pertinent question consistently raised, particularly in Sierra Leone, is why there was so much delay in the establishment of the Court. The Prosecutor, Registrar, and other key officials began work in Freetown in June–August 2002. The first round of indictments was issued in March 2003, with subsequent indictments issued in the following months. As of September 2003, 13 indictments had been issued: nine indictees are in custody; two indictees (Foday Sankoh and Sam Bockarie) are dead with a third (Johnny Paul Koroma) thought to be dead; and the final indictee, Charles Taylor, has resigned as President of Liberia and is currently in Nigeria. Reasonable estimates suggest that trials could start as early as March 2004. While by UN standards this is relatively quick (a mere three years from the start of negotiations to the start of trials)[39] the people of Sierra Leone do not necessarily see it in such generous terms, particularly given that by the time trials start, many of the indictees will have been in pre-trial detention for up to 12 months. When this is compounded with the fact that the Court will not impose the death penalty,[40] which is largely favoured by much of the local population, and the date set for the temporal jurisdiction, many Sierra Leoneans wonder why the international community has made them wait for so long for a justice system they believe contains unjust and arbitrary limitations.

While the mere existence of the Special Court is already, in many ways, having a positive impact on the rule of law in Sierra Leone, the process by which it undertakes its work is equally important. The Court itself must adhere to the principles of the rule of law, in terms of following its own rules, abiding by the laws of Sierra Leone and abiding by international law and practice. The handling of Charles Taylor's indictment demonstrates this very clearly, as the Court—at the very least—appeared to violate its own orders relating to non-disclosure and to expect Ghana to violate its own domestic laws. On 4 June 2003, at a press conference in Freetown, the Prosecutor, David Crane, announced the indictment of Charles Taylor, which had previously been sealed by order of the Court and demanded that Ghana arrest President Taylor in Accra, where he was on an official visit, without having served the Ghanaian authorities sufficiently in advance. The public disclosure, which arguably had the effect of preventing the arrest, was

---

[38] For a detailed analysis, see, Chapter 8 (Mochochoko/Tortora). On the issue of financing of internationalized criminal tribunals in general, see also, Chapter 13 (Ingadottir).

[39] By comparison, one only needs to consider the situation in Cambodia, where negotiations between the United Nations and Cambodia began in 1997 and continued sporadically thereafter only to fall apart towards the end of 2001.

[40] Article 19 of the Statute for the Special Court limits the penalties that may be imposed to imprisonment for a specified number of years and forfeiture of property, proceeds, and any assets acquired unlawfully or by criminal conduct.

also in apparent violation of the non-disclosure order of Judge Bankole Thompson on 7 March 2003.[41]

Many of these issues are matters that can be addressed by carrying out a systematic and extensive public information and education campaign in Sierra Leone. The perception that Sierra Leoneans have of the accountability mechanisms working on their behalf is in itself paramount to their success. The Court must therefore ensure that it involves the general population at every step of the way, ensuring that people understand the processes and why certain things are done in certain ways. It is necessary not only to provide accountability for the people of Sierra Leone but also to ensure their cooperation with the Special Court by explaining the nature and work of the Special Court, and placing the drawbacks of the Special Court in the overall context of its positive aspects. While this is a gargantuan task, the support and participation of Sierra Leoneans is necessary if the Special Court is to operate most effectively and provide accountability and justice.

Ways must be devised to draw out positive implications of the choices that were made, in order to avoid charges that the Special Court is merely an effort to ease the conscience of the international community for failing to intervene sooner in Sierra Leone. It will only be through careful management, fail-safe witness protection, exemplary investigative, legal, and judicial work, and ensuring that the people of Sierra Leone are kept constantly informed, that the Special Court will be able to live up to its potential both for Sierra Leone and the rest of the world.

---

[41] The order for disclosure was made by Judge Pierre Boutet in Freetown on 12 June 2003.

8

The Management Committee for the Special Court for Sierra Leone

Phakiso Mochochoko* and Giorgia Tortora**

A. INTRODUCTION

Compared to the International Tribunals for the Former Yugoslavia (ICTY) and for Rwanda (ICTR) the creation of a Management Committee for the Special Court for Sierra Leone, comprising representatives of the UN Secretary-General and the government of Sierra Leone, as well as important political and financial sponsors of the Court, is a major innovation. It is the first attempt to establish and manage a tribunal with the direct involvement not only of the United Nations—as in the case of ICTY and ICTR—but also of the state on whose territory the crimes took place, and the donor community.

The aim of this chapter is to provide an overview of the process that led to the creation of the Management Committee, the role it plays and the future challenges it will face.

B. BACKGROUND

On 12 June 2002, the President of Sierra Leone addressed a letter to the United Nations requesting the assistance of the international community in investigating and prosecuting those responsible for the crimes committed during 10 years of conflict.[1] The Security Council responded to that request by adopting Resolution 1315 of 14 August 2000, which mandated the UN Secretary-General to negotiate with the government of Sierra Leone an agreement for the establishment of an independent Special Court to prosecute

---

* Phakiso Mochochoko is Legal Adviser to the International Criminal Court (ICC). He was part of the ICC advance team. Between 1994 and 2002 he served as Legal Adviser to the Mission of Lesotho to the United Nations and, in such capacity, he participated in the Group of Interested States and sat on the Management Committee for the Special Court.

** Giorgia Tortora was Liaison Officer at the Special Court for Sierra Leone between September 2002 and November 2003. She served between 2000 and 2002 as Adviser to the Mission of Sierra Leone following in particular the negotiations for the establishment of the Special Court between the government of Sierra Leone and the United Nations. She sat on the Management Committee as one of the Sierra Leone representatives.

[1] Letter from the Permanent Representative of Sierra Leone to the United Nations addressed to the President of the Security Council (9 August 2000) UN Doc S/2000/786.

those who bear the greatest responsibility for crimes against humanity, war crimes, and other serious violations of international law, as well as certain crimes under Sierra Leonean law.[2] The Security Council envisaged the Court to be financed through voluntary contributions of funds, equipment, and services including offers of expert personnel from states, intergovernmental organizations, and non-governmental organizations. To this end, the Secretary-General was requested to recommend the amount of contributions required for the operations of the Special Court.[3] The resolution was, however, silent on who would be responsible for raising and managing such funds.

The decision of the Security Council to fund the Special Court only through voluntary contributions raised several concerns and presented those involved in the negotiations with numerous challenges. Indeed, there are no precedents of international judicial bodies financed entirely out of voluntary contributions, and the sustainability of such a model has never been tested before.[4] Therefore, from the outset of negotiations, a major concern was ensuring that the Court will not be paralysed by lack of funding. The Secretary-General himself stressed this point, insisting with the Security Council on the need for 'a viable and sustainable financial mechanism for the Special Court'.[5] Considering the scope, costs, and long-term duration of the institutions in The Hague and Rwanda, the Secretary-General questioned the viability of voluntary contributions for the financing of the Court and strongly recommended that it be financed through assessed contributions.

The Secretary-General's arguments did not find sufficient support in the Security Council. While the Security Council reiterated its willingness to proceed with the establishment of the Special Court, it refused to reconsider the question of its financing.[6] Indeed, mounting concern about the ballooning cost of ICTY and ICTR, reports on their administrative inefficiencies, as well as the fact that some Member States on the Security Council would support the establishment of the Court only provided that they would not be obliged to pay for it, made voluntary contributions the only choice.

Nevertheless, the Security Council offered to support the efforts of the Secretary-General and the United Nations in establishing the new Court and securing funding, by suggesting that an oversight committee be formed whose responsibilities would include assisting in raising funds and providing advice on matters pertaining to the administration of the Court.

---

[2] UNSC Res 1315 (2000).   [3] ibid para 8.

[4] See further for the financing of internationalized courts, Chapter 13 (Ingadottir).

[5] 'Report of the Secretary-General on the establishment of a Special Court for Sierra Leone' UN Doc S/2000/915 para 70.

[6] Letter from the President of the Security Council addressed to the Secretary-General (22 December 2000) UN Doc S/2000/1234.

The roots of the Management Committee for the Special Court for Sierra Leone can thus be directly traced to the decision to finance the Court from voluntary contributions, the concerns expressed by the Secretary-General about the viability of such a scheme, and the firm intention of some Member States on the Council to sustain actively the whole process and to create to that effect a kind of 'friends of the Court' group.

C. NEGOTIATIONS ON THE MANAGEMENT COMMITTEE

The idea of a Management Committee was first canvassed in a letter from the President of the Security Council[7] in response to the Secretary-General's report. As it was explained, the Secretary-General recommended that the Court be financed through assessed contributions.[8] The Security Council, however, reiterated its support for the creation of a Court exclusively funded through voluntary contributions, and suggested the following:

In order to assist the court on questions of funding and administration, it is suggested that the arrangements between the Government of Sierra Leone and the United Nations provide for a management or oversight committee which could include representatives of Sierra Leone, the Secretary General of the United Nations, the Court and interested voluntary contributors. The management committee would assist the court in obtaining adequate funding, provide advice on matters of Court administration and be available as appropriate to consult on other non-judicial matters.[9]

No guidance, however, was given on the composition, specific mandate, and methods of operation of such a body.

In other words, while from the outset the Security Council insisted on a *sui generis* Court, financed by voluntary contributions, it seems it had not yet lucidly thought out how to secure such funding and manage it, nor does any deeper thinking seem to have gone into the consideration of the administrative and budgetary oversight of the Court. Conceptually, it was not evident if the Security Council's intention was to take the administration of the Court outside the UN system and the rules and UN financial regulations, or whether the Committee would merely be concerned with fund-raising for the Court. Additional guidance from the Council on these issues would have surely accelerated the negotiations and the actual commencement of the Court's operations.

Negotiations started immediately after the Secretary-General's appeal to all states to make contributions in funds, personnel, and services to the

---

[7] Letter from the President of the Security Council addressed to the Secretary-General (22 December 2000) UN Doc S/2000/1234.

[8] 'Report' (*supra* n 5) para 71.

[9] Letter from the President of the Security Council addressed to the Secretary-General (22 December 2000) UN Doc S/2000/1234.

Special Court.[10] On 27 March 2001, the Legal Counsel called the first informal meeting on the establishment of the Court and suggested the creation of the so-called Group of Interested States. The Group would meet regularly and discuss practical arrangements for the beginning of the Court's operation, including elements of the draft budget estimates, classification of posts and salaries for international and local personnel, and the creation of the Management Committee.

The Group would be made up of 'those States that would actually contribute in funds and in kind to the Special Court'. Member States that wished to be included amongst the group of interested states had to indicate their wish by submitting their names to the Secretariat within a week, that is to say, by 4 April 2001 at the latest.[11]

In his remarks to the meeting, the Legal Counsel expressed the hope that the Group would be as large as possible, hence the necessity to create a smaller sub-group, the Management Committee (the Committee), consisting of maybe 10 to 15 states and including representatives of the Secretary-General and the government of Sierra Leone.[12]

The Legal Counsel envisaged the Committee to act as an interlocutor for the Registrar, and its focus would be on administrative and budgetary matters. A determining factor for membership of the Committee would be 'the extent to which Member States contribute to the Special Court'. The Committee would draw up its own terms of reference, and states were invited to express their interest in sitting on the Committee.[13]

No one doubts the good intentions of the Legal Counsel in formulating proposals for the establishment of the Group of Interested States and Management Committee, suggesting criteria for membership, and providing indicative timelines for responses from states. After all, negotiations for the establishment of the Court had already been going on for too long, and the UN Secretariat was naturally anxious to see tangible progress towards the establishment of the Court, at a time when other issues such as the establishment of the Cambodia Extraordinary Chambers were on the agenda of the Office of Legal Affairs. This earnest attempt on the part of the Secretariat to speed up progress, however, may have been misunderstood by some

---

[10] The appeal was contained in the Secretary-General's letter (23 March 2001). It urged states to respond within 60 days by giving complete and definitive indications of what contributions they intended to make to the Court.

[11] This gave delegates only a week to seek instructions from their capitals on whether they could be part of the Group.

[12] Letter from the President of the Security Council addressed to the Secretary-General (December 2000) UN Doc S/2000/1234 Pt 2.

[13] It would appear from correspondence from the Office of Legal Affairs concerning the terms of reference for the Committee that the following states indicated an interest to serve on the committee: Canada; France; Germany; Jamaica; Lesotho; the Netherlands; Nigeria; Switzerland; United Kingdom; and United States.

delegations, eventually leading to diminished participation in the Group of Interested States.

To begin with, the idea that the Group should be restricted to 'states that actually contribute in funds and in kind' may have discouraged the participation of states that were not in a position to make contributions, but which were nevertheless interested in seeing justice done for the people of Sierra Leone. In addition, the concept of a *sui generis* tribunal, which was not just an effort of the international community, but also of the state where the crimes were committed, was new to many delegations, and they needed time to reflect and understand the idea. A one-week period to decide whether to join the Group may not have been adequate.[14] Moreover, in his letter of 23 March 2001, the Secretary-General had given states 60 days to indicate their contributions to the Special Court. Most countries have rigorous procedures for approval of expenditures, hence it must have been difficult for many states to indicate a willingness to be part of the Group while awaiting instructions from capitals. The result was that fewer states than expected were able to indicate their desire to be part of the Group within the specified time-frame.[15] The Court might have thus lost some of the potential contributors, and it will be for the Management Committee to bring them back.

The next few meetings of the Group were mainly devoted to the budget of the Court. The proposed budget covering the Court's activities for the first three years was US$30,155,677, US$42,550,367 and US$41,896,315 respectively, totalling US$114 m.[16] The Group's view was that the budget was unacceptable, especially considering that all funds would have to be collected exclusively through voluntary contributions. In addition, the budget seemed to be a carbon copy of the budgets of ICTY and ICTR, and failed to take into account the specific needs and conditions in which the Special Court was to operate. A review of the budget became necessary. The Group began meeting separately from the Secretariat to review the proposed budget and find a basis for agreement on a lesser total amount. Most capitals may have postponed decisions on their contributions pending the finalization of the revised budget. This may have further delayed progress on the establishment of the Court and on the establishment of the Management Committee.

---

[14] It should be recalled that, several months later, informal consultations held by the Mission of Sierra Leone to the United Nations with possible donors to the Court revealed that numerous Member States had not fully understood the total independence of the Court from the UN regular budget.

[15] Correspondence and invitations to subsequent meetings of the Group of Interested States between May and June 2001 indicate that membership varied between 15 to 17 countries: Canada; United States; United Kingdom; Finland; France; Germany; Sweden; Lesotho; Liechtenstein; Netherlands; Norway; Argentina; Japan; Malaysia; Nigeria; Switzerland; and Sierra Leone.

[16] Informal note of the Legal Counsel to Interested States (14 June 2001).

The Group was aware that administering the Court within the UN system, (ie applying all UN financial rules and regulations and staff regulations), with a drastically reduced budget would hamper the Court's work.[17] Loosening the ties with the UN system and devising a less expensive, but fairer and more efficient, managing scheme for the Court was seen as the only viable option. Amongst other things, this would entail finding alternatives to certain administrative and budgetary rules and regulations, in particular on personnel issues, in order to minimize costs. It was generally felt that a notional budget of US$15 to 18 million would suffice for the first year of operations, and there was general agreement to identify a proper structure to manage the Court.[18] To ensure a flexible and effective administration outside the United Nations the Management Committee was to be entrusted with the overall responsibility for the Court substantive administration over the non-judicial functions, endowed with budgetary oversight functions, as well as with the mandate to assist in ensuring a sufficient flow of funds.

Because it would have taken more time to finalize the budget, the Group could focus its attention on the Management Committee. It should be remarked that, from the beginning, consultations on the Court were attended by the Sixth Committee's legal experts and Secretariat staff from the Office of Legal Affairs, but not financial and/or administration experts from the Fifth Committee. While legal experts naturally focused on legal issues and policy decisions, they underestimated the complexity of many of the financial and administrative issues, which were later to haunt them and delay the establishment of the Court. For example, wrong assumptions were made concerning the Trust Fund for the Court and, in particular, the application or non-application of the UN financial rules and regulations, the involvement or non-involvement of the General Assembly and the Advisory Committee on Administrative and Budgetary Questions (ACABQ) in the review of the budget, and the need for administrative structures within the Office of Legal Affairs for operational aspects of the Court. In general, legal advisers acted on the assumption that the United

---

[17] Add to that that the United Nations has a 14 per cent overhead charge, ie for every US dollar given to the Court, 14 cents go to the United Nations to pay for administrative expenses.

[18] The revised draft budget set the financial requirements for the first three years of the Court's operations at respectively US$16,800,399, US$20,414,095, and US$19,585,696. That budget was presented on 14 June 2001, following lengthy informal consultations, which also involved the Security Council, and which showed the existence of a strong divergence of opinions. The United Nations was of the view that the draft budget it presented on 23 March 2001 was in conformity with the directions given by the Security Council, while several members on the Council stated that on no occasion did they imply that the Special Court should be administered entirely inside the UN system. The budget had to be reorganized to reflect the non-UN nature of the Court. It should be recalled that that was also the understanding of the government of Sierra Leone which, during the negotiations on the agreement and the Statute of the Court, requested that any reference to a UN Trust Fund and to a UN-administered Court be deleted, pending a thorough discussion of the matter with donor states.

Nations would have easily accepted their decisions on matters pertaining to the budgetary and administrative structure of the Court.

This has been one of the earlier weaknesses of the Committee. The later involvement of Secretariat staff from finance and human resources divisions, as well as states delegates from the Fifth Committee, facilitated the resolution of most of the administrative and financial management aspects of the Court.

D. NEGOTIATIONS ON THE TERMS OF REFERENCE OF THE MANAGEMENT COMMITTEE

Once an agreement was reached in principle on the Special Court's draft budget, negotiations started on the terms of reference for the Management Committee, revealing once again the existing tension between different organizational models for the Court and the difficulty of giving a precise content to the *sui generis* nature of the Court as far as the administrative structure was concerned.

The discussion on the terms of reference developed on the basis of two drafts: one prepared by the Secretariat and circulated on 17 April 2001,[19] and the other presented on 25 April 2001 by the United States.[20] While slightly different in their structure, both drafts focused the discussion on the following issues: (1) the legal basis of the Management Committee; (2) functions of the Management Committee vis-à-vis the UN system; and (3) membership of the Committee.

1. Legal basis of the Management Committee

In submitting their preliminary comments on the drafts, delegations expressed different views on whether the Committee should be a formal or informal arrangement. The issue was particularly relevant because it related to the determination of the functions that the Committee would be endowed with, and the legal status of the Committee's decisions vis-à-vis the Court, and the United Nations.

The Secretariat's draft envisaged the Committee as an informal arrangement, and as a consultative body with prime responsibility for ensuring adequate funds to the Court.

According to the Secretariat, the decision to establish a UN Trust Fund to collect contributions from donor states put the Court under the responsibility

---

[19] The draft was to be discussed at a meeting scheduled for 25 April 2001. The Legal Counsel's cover note to interested states ended as follows: 'If possible, the Terms of Reference should be finalized by 30 April 2001'. The Terms of Reference were adopted on 21 August 2001.

[20] The US version of the terms of reference of the Management Committee (24 April 2001, 15:00 hours).

of the UN system. Consequently, the Management Committee could not detract from the UN administrative 'chain of command'. According to the Secretariat's draft, the Committee would not be anything more than an informal forum where donors would consider the status of the Court's finances and discuss how to ensure that the Court receive adequate funds.

This approach, however, met with limited support. While states had widely different views, a majority progressively emerged in support of the creation of the Management Committee as an informal arrangement, but also as a body capable of having a real say on matters pertaining to the administration of the Court and taking decisions binding on the Court.

The Group considered precedents that could be of assistance in the discussion, and realized that several UN agencies exist which are largely funded through voluntary contributions and are overseen by a committee.[21] Nevertheless, as underlined by the Secretariat, in all previous cases the establishment of such committees followed the adoption of ad hoc resolutions by the General Assembly.

It was only because of the pressure exercised by the Group, and the determination of major donors to affirm the principle that the Court, as an institution independent from the United Nations, should not be obliged to adopt all UN rules and regulations, that the Secretariat agreed to establish the Management Committee as an informal arrangement, without precluding a priori a thorough discussion of its functions.

2. Functions of the Management Committee

While the Secretariat's and the US draft terms of reference list very similar functions and responsibilities for the Management Committee, they reflected different approaches to the issue. The Secretariat's draft stressed the role of the Committee in ensuring an adequate flow of funds to the Court. The US draft stressed the relevance of the Committee's oversight functions.

The Secretariat's draft, specifically, stated that:

the Management Committee shall undertake fundraising activities that will ensure that the United Nations Secretariat has obtained sufficient contributions in hand to finance the establishment of the Court and 12 months of its operations, as well as pledges equal to the anticipated expenses of the following 24 months.[22]

In addition, section III paragraph 4, reads:

---

[21] The UN High Commission for Refugees' (UNHCR's) Executive Committee (ExCom), for example, consists of 54 states interested in refugee issues. The ExCom works like a Board of Directors and it oversees both funding and policy issues for UNHCR. The arrangements within ExCom are very informal: the ExCom does not have terms of reference, meetings at the working level are informal and are convened on 'an as needed basis', and annual meetings are semi-formal.

[22] Secretariat's draft (17 April 2001) s III, para 3.

For the duration of the operation of the Special Court, the Management Committee shall make every effort to ensure the flow of adequate funds on a continuous basis to the Trust Fund, and shall continue to undertake fundraising activities to guarantee the continued operations of the Court.

The Secretariat's draft also stated, among other things, that the Committee 'shall assist' in securing the cooperation of third states with the Special Court. With regard to the non-judicial functions of the Court, the Secretariat's draft accorded to the Committee a purely consultative role.

Several members of the Group strongly opposed this approach. In their view, the Management Committee could not be considered exclusively responsible for ensuring the proper funding of the Court while having no say on the administration and management of the Court. That is to say, states would not accept that the Secretary-General and the United Nations be exempted from their responsibility to raise funds for the Court, while retaining full control over the spending of those funds. The US proposal, which more closely reflected the position of the majority of the interested states, became, on this point, the preferred option.

Also, no agreement could be found with regard to the suggestion that the Committee 'shall assist' in securing cooperation from third states. Indeed, several states and, first among them, Sierra Leone, were greatly dissatisfied with the decision of the Security Council not to make mention of Chapter VII in Resolution 1315. The porous borders of Sierra Leone and the regional nature of the conflict made it extremely likely that individuals under the jurisdiction of the Court would flee the country. Consequently, the decision of the Council to leave it to the Court to try to win the cooperation of third states on an ad hoc basis was quite disputable.[23] Sierra Leone, as well as others, opposed the inclusion of the Secretariat's suggestion, because it was misleading. Given the fact that the Committee will not have enforcement powers, imposing that obligation would have created the false impression that the problem of cooperation had been dealt with, thus weakening pressure on the Council to revise its position on the matter.

Four months after the Secretariat's draft was first presented, the Group reached an agreement on the Committee's functions. The Management Committee would: (i) assist, but not replace, the Secretary-General in ensuring that adequate funds are available for the operation of the Court; (ii) assist in the establishment of the Court, including in the identification of nominees for the positions of Registrar, Prosecutor and Judges for appointment by the Secretary-General; (iii) consider reports of the Special Court and provide advice and policy direction on all non-judicial aspects of the Court's operations; (iv) oversee the Court's annual budget and other financially related reports, and advise the Secretary-General on these matters; (v) encourage all

---

[23] For a further discussion, see Chapter 17 (Sluiter).

states to cooperate with the Court; and (vi) report on a regular basis to the Group.

The Management Committee was thus recognized as a key interlocutor of the Court, and the parties to the agreement, for all issues pertaining to the exercise of the non-judicial functions of the Court.[24]

3. Membership of the Committee

The Secretariat's draft suggested that the Committee comprise at least 10 and no more than 15 members, and that its composition be based on the tangible *interest* that members demonstrate in support of the Court. It was also envisaged that the parties to the agreement (ie the government of Sierra Leone and the Secretary-General) should be on the Committee.

The US proposal recommended that the Committee be composed of a minimum of six and no more than 15 members, and that consideration should be given to those states that demonstrated a tangible *support* for the Court. According to the US proposal, the Secretary-General and the government of Sierra Leone might have participated in the Committee, as appropriate.

In both drafts the only criterion for membership of the Committee was the tangible support of a state to the Court, that is, the level of its financial contribution. During the discussion on this matter, however, additional criteria were suggested: geographic representation; acknowledgement of the role of those states that had offered strong political support to the Court; and acknowledgement of those states that had devoted substantial resources to the resolution of Sierra Leone's conflict.[25] The final version of the terms of reference reads: 'the Committee ... will be open to important contributors willing to assume the functions'. In the practice of the Committee the notion of 'important contributors' has been interpreted so as to expand the membership of the Committee beyond the major financial contributors. Current states on the Committee are: Canada, Lesotho, the Netherlands, Nigeria, the United Kingdom, and the United States.[26]

With regard to the issue of the participation of the Secretary-General and the government of Sierra Leone on the Committee, the government of Sierra Leone actively campaigned to sit on the Committee on a regular basis. Continuing to participate in the process towards the establishment of the Court—created for the benefit of its own people—was considered crucial to

---

[24] Article 7 was added to the agreement to take into account the establishment of the Management Committee.

[25] Note that in any case members of the Management Committee had to have contributed financially to the Court.

[26] The Group of Interested States, following an expression of interest, selected the members of the Management Committee on November 2001.

keep a Sierra Leonean perspective in the negotiations, to provide all possible support to the Court, and to ensure proper coordination with regard to the practical arrangements needed for the actual commencement of the Court's operation. Eventually, despite some initial resistance and misunderstanding,[27] representatives of the government of Sierra Leone, as well as of the Secretary-General, were accepted as members of the Committee on a par level with donor states.

E. THE PLANNING MISSION

In his letter to the President of the Security Council dated 12 July 2001, the Secretary-General stated the intention to dispatch a planning mission to Sierra Leone:

to discuss with the Sierra Leonean authorities the practical implementation of the Agreement and the kind and scope of contributions expected in Sierra Leonean personnel and services, and to lay the ground work for the arrival of the advance elements of the Special Court, consisting of the nucleus administrative and prosecutorial staff.[28]

In the same letter, the Secretary-General also stated that the Planning Mission would be authorized after contributions pledged for the first year of the Court's operations had been made available to a UN Trust Fund.[29] The Planning Mission, originally envisaged for 15 October 2001,[30] left New York almost three months later, on 7 January 2002.

During those three months, the Group first, and the Management Committee later, faced a number of difficulties, mainly related to differences between donor states and the UN Controller, the officer responsible for the proper administration of UN finances. As mentioned above, the Secretary-General requested that all contributions pledged for the first year of the Court's operations be actually transferred to a UN Trust Fund before the Planning Mission could set off. However, some donors, having requested the inclusion of specific clauses in the agreements with the United Nations that usually precede transfers to any UN Trust Fund, were then prevented from making such transfers for several weeks.

[27] Representatives of Sierra Leone were not called to attend the first meeting of the Management Committee.

[28] See UN Doc S/2001/1693.

[29] It should be recalled that the Secretary-General accepted the view that the funds pledged for the first year would have been sufficient to commence the operations of the Court, only after repeated assurances by donor states of their support. On 12 July 2002, the Secretariat had received indications of contributions of funds for the first year of the Court's operations in the amount of US$15 million—a shortfall of about US$1.8 million.

[30] Legal Counsel proposed that date during the meeting of the Group of Interested States held on 24 September 2001.

Additional delays were also created by the refusal of the UN Controller to release funds to cover the expenses of the Planning Mission, unless all funds for the first three years of the Court's operations were actually paid or pledged, notwithstanding the fact that the Secretary-General had considered the level of resources already pledged sufficient to commence the establishment of the Court.[31] The resulting stand-off in the preparations for the Planning Mission eventually required the direct intervention of the ambassadors of the states sitting on the Committee and of the Secretary-General.[32]

Further, it should be recalled that on 20 August 2001, the government of Sierra Leone wrote to the Office of Legal Affairs with regard to the issue of the temporal jurisdiction of the Court, asking that the temporal jurisdiction be amended to commence not from 30 November 1996, as previously agreed, but from March 1991.[33]

While the government had wished that the matter could be discussed in Freetown, during the visit of the Planning Mission, the Legal Counsel made it clear that he would not recommend the departure of the Planning Mission until the matter was resolved.[34] The Management Committee maintained the same position. After several rounds of informal consultations which revealed the absence of support for the proposal, on 7 December 2001, the government of Sierra Leone, though unconvinced, communicated its intention not to pursue the issue any further to avoid additional delays.

On 26 December 2001, the Planning Mission was eventually authorized.[35] Having made its deployment possible, and having assisted in the finalization of its terms of references, the Members of the Management Committee participated in the Planning Mission[36] and were able to observe first-hand the difficulties that the Court would have to face, and to gain a deeper understanding of what structure the Court would need to have in order to succeed. The Committee later shared its experiences with the Group and contributed to the Planning Mission's report.[37]

---

[31] Letter from the Secretary-General to the President of the Security Council (12 July 2001) UN Doc S/2001/1693.

[32] It should be noted that despite the decision of the Secretary-General to proceed, in order to avoid further delays the Canadian government covered the United Nation's costs during the Planning Mission.

[33] On this point, see Chapter 7 (Smith).

[34] It was envisaged that the Planning Mission would also be the occasion for the formal signing of the agreement establishing the Special Court. That implied that the text of such agreement be finalized before the Planning Mission left New York.

[35] Letter from the Secretary-General to the President of the Security Council (26 December 2001) UN Doc S/2001/1320.

[36] This was the first time that states' representatives took part in a UN Mission.

[37] See letter from the Secretary-General to the President of the Security Council (6 March 2002) UN Doc S/2002/246 and Corr.1,2,3.

F. PRACTICAL ARRANGEMENTS FOR THE COURT'S START-UP PHASE

The presence of experts in administrative matters greatly assisted the members of the Management Committee to comprehend the requirements for the Court's appropriate functioning. In particular, it was clear that the Court could discharge its mandate only if allowed to apply the UN financial rules and regulations selectively.

Therefore, the Management Committee analysed, among other things, which UN rules and regulations the Court should be exempted from; how the Court should proceed with the classification of posts; which remuneration packages and which kind of contracts should be offered to the Court's staff. The experts, including the newly appointed Acting Registrar, were invited to New York and a number of documents were produced summarizing specific arrangements for the administration of the Court. All this work was carried out on the assumption that the United Nations would delegate a number of functions to the Registry, including recruitment, hiring and firing of personnel, and procurement, in order to take into account the particular nature of the Court and both its time and budget constraints.

However, preparations came to a halt when the UN Office of the Controller made it clear that the United Nations could not accept these arrangements, as no amendment of the UN rules and regulations would be possible without the involvement of the authority from which they emanated, that is to say, the General Assembly.[38]

It was at this point that the Management Committee called on states' representatives in the Fifth Committee to take part in its meetings and assist in finding a solution.

Several options were considered, including that of managing the Special Court as a UNDP project.[39] However, it took over three months before the administrative structure could be agreed upon and the Controller agreed to disburse to the Court its own funds. Again, the solution was the outcome of exhaustive discussions among the members of the Management Committee to find a common position, the involvement of all 26 donor states, and

---

[38] Referring the matter to the General Assembly was never considered a viable alternative by the Management Committee, because of the exceptional delays that would have created, but also because of the intention that the Court should be recognized as a *sui generis* institution in all aspects of its functions and should not be requested to undergo the 'ordinary' UN procedures.

[39] The suggestion made by the Office of the Controller was, however, totally unacceptable to the government of Sierra Leone. The government had negotiated the establishment of an impartial, independent *sui generis* Court, not a UNDP project, which would de facto bring the Special Court entirely under the UN system. In addition, the government also questioned the fact that a UN agency usually dealing with development would have the expertise necessary to administer an international tribunal.

negotiations to reconcile the different understandings of the Court's nature and functions within different UN departments.

On 1 July 2002, the Special Court officially started operations.

G. FUTURE CHALLENGES

From an early stage, the direct participation of UN Member States in the consultations for the establishment of the Special Court for Sierra Leone contributed to develop not only an innovative institution but also a radically innovative negotiating process. While the previous international tribunals were established with no input from the states of the former Yugoslavia and Rwanda, the Special Court for Sierra Leone is the outcome of an inclusive approach that greatly contributes to portraying the Court as a joint project between the United Nations and the government of Sierra Leone. The creation of the Management Committee is, on the other hand, the factor that has allowed the process to move forward and to overcome the innate diffidence of the UN bureaucracy to novelties.

The Management Committee has been the driving force in promoting innovative solutions and trying to prevent the Court from being re-absorbed by the UN administration, as well as to signal both to the government of Sierra Leone and the international community the seriousness of states' commitment to bringing justice back to the country.

In spite of the positive role that the Management Committee has been able to perform until now, major challenges still lie ahead. First, as the Court begins its operations, it is likely that the need for specific technical assistance will intensify. The Management Committee will not only require dedicated legal advisers, but also financial, personnel, and administrative experts to assess carefully the circumstances and provide sound and timely advice. As mentioned above, most of the meetings of the Management Committee are attended by legal advisers, and only recently experts of the Fifth Committee have been invited to participate. The Management Committee should be prepared to modify and adapt its composition more flexibly to the Court's needs.

Secondly, the Management Committee should make an additional effort to identify within the United Nations the officials who need to be involved in the discussion of particular issues. As demonstrated in the past, the internal exchange of information does not always work properly among departments of the UN Secretariat. The Management Committee should take upon itself the responsibility to prevent information bottlenecks hampering the Court's operations.

Thirdly, while the Court's performance will require constant monitoring to ensure that any problem is addressed as early as possible and that needed

reforms are implemented, the Management Committee should avoid imposing additional bureaucratic burdens on the Court's operations. The Management Committee was envisaged as a means to streamline the functioning of
the Court and to provide a quick-response system to its needs, rather than to
recreate the UN Advisory Committee on Administrative and Budgetary
Questions (ACABQ) or any similar body.

Fourthly, even though states are designated as members of the Management Committee, the role and commitment of individuals who represent
states in the Committee should not be underestimated. Much of the success
of the negotiations for the creation of the Special Court and the establishment of the Management Committee can be largely attributed to the consistent and tireless efforts, dedication, and collective responsibility of a core
group of individual diplomats and Secretariat personnel who passionately
believed in the hope of justice for Sierra Leone, and thus devoted their time
and energy to endless, and sometimes frustrating, meetings to find solutions
to many of the seemingly intractable problems.

However, as is well known, diplomats come and go, and as the baton is
passed from one diplomat to another within various Missions that are
members of the Management Committee, the institutional memory and the
much needed continuity might be broken. It remains to be seen whether the
new cadre of diplomats will serve the Management Committee with equal
zeal and dedication and have full appreciation of the heavy responsibility
that membership to the Committee entails. Active participation in the Committee's meetings will be crucial if the Committee is to provide the much
needed guidance to the Court.

Fifthly, while the direct involvement of donor states has provided the
Special Court with the political support needed to overcome a number of
difficulties, it is important that the Court is not, nor perceived as being,
unduly influenced by those states, so as to undermine its independence and
impartiality. It is thus essential that the Committee continues to discuss
thoroughly all matters relevant to the Court's administration, and that the
relationship with the Group is in no way loosened. The accurate circulation
of information among the members of the Committee and the Group will be
crucial for a sustained, transparent policy-making process.

Finally, the Management Committee should continue to assist the Secretary-General to ensure that the Special Court receives an adequate flow of
funds, and to mobilize states' support of the Court. While the Special Court
has demonstrated its capacity to operate within a limited budget,[40] the international community has so far failed to properly address the Court's financial
needs. As a consequence, on 26 February 2004, the Secretary-General reverted

---

[40] The Special Court closed its first financial year with a small surplus over the approved
budget of approximately US$19 million.

to the President of the Security Council to suggest bringing the financial crisis of the Court to the attention of the General Assembly.[41] In March 2004, following the submission of a Report[42] on the issue, the General Assembly authorized the Secretary-General to disburse US$40 million to the Special Court for the period from 1 July 2004 to 31 December 2005. The funds are to be charged to the Secretary-General's unearmarked balance of the provision for political missions and are a once-only, non-renewable contribution from the UN to the Court. The Management Committee should develop immediately an effective fundraising strategy to provide the Special Court with any additional resources required to complete the Court's legal proceedings and accomplish its exit plan.

H. CONCLUSION

The Management Committee is one of the most innovative aspects of the Special Court's functioning. The direct involvement of donor states has greatly benefited the negotiations for the Court's establishment, creating a strong incentive towards innovative solutions, and providing the political support for their practical implementation.

Also, because of the direct participation of representatives of the United Nations and of the government of Sierra Leone in the Management Committee, the parties to the agreement establishing the Court have been given the possibility to contribute to the whole process and to ensure that the letter and the spirit of the agreement and the Statute be preserved in the implementing phase.

The Court faces numerous difficulties: from the necessity of giving proper content to the notion of a *sui generis* institution to the limited resources available. The capacity of the Special Court to live up to expectations is uncertain, as is the capacity of the Management Committee to react properly to the Court's demands. However, it is indisputable that, should the Court be successful, it would become a ground-breaking model for the future establishment of similar institutions and reform of existing ones.

[41] UN S/2004/182.   [42] UN A/58/733.

9

Internationalized Courts and their Relationship with Alternative Accountability Mechanisms: The Case of Sierra Leone

*William A Schabas**

A. INTRODUCTION

Besides providing for a controversial amnesty,[1] the Lomé Peace Agreement pledged the establishment of a Truth and Reconciliation Commission (TRC), to be set up within 90 days. Efforts were soon directed to this task,[2] and legislation was adopted by Sierra Leone's Parliament on 22 February 2000.[3] Pursuant to section 6(1) of the Truth and Reconciliation Commission Act 2000, the Sierra Leone TRC was established to create an impartial historical record of violations and abuses of human rights and international humanitarian law related to the armed conflict in Sierra Leone, from the beginning of the conflict in 1991 to the signing of the Lomé Peace Agreement; to address impunity, to respond to the needs of the victims, to promote healing and reconciliation and to prevent a repetition of the violations and abuses suffered.

The renewal of fighting in May 2000 not only stalled the creation of the TRC, it also brought a reassessment of the legitimacy of the amnesty provided under Article IX of the Lomé Peace Agreement, which led to the request of the government of Sierra Leone that the United Nations establish a special tribunal. In January 2002 the United Nations and the government of Sierra Leone reached formal agreement on the project and in April 2002, the Special Court Agreement (Ratification) Act 2002 was adopted to enable the effective operation of the Court and to implement Sierra Leone's commitments under the agreement with the United Nations.[4]

* Professor of Human Rights Law, National University of Ireland, Galway, and Director, Irish Centre for Human Rights. The author is a member of the Sierra Leone Truth and Reconciliation Commission. This chapter is written in his private capacity and does not necessarily reflect the views of the other commissioners or of the Commission.
   [1] See Chapter 7 (Smith).
   [2] See Richard Bennett 'The Evolution of the Sierra Leone Truth and Reconciliation Commission' in UNAMSIL *Truth and Reconciliation in Sierra Leone* (Freetown 2001) 37–51.
   [3] 'Truth and Reconciliation Commission Act 2000' Supplement CXXXI (9) Sierra Leone Gazette.
   [4] Sierra Leone, like most common law countries based on English law, is dualist, and international agreements are not directly enforceable before its courts in the absence of such implementing legislation.

The two organizations—the TRC and the Special Court—began operations in mid-2002. Although they operated in parallel for more than eighteen months, the work of the TRC was essentially completed by the time actual trials of the Special Court began, in June 2004. After a somewhat erratic start-up period during which staff were recruited and premises obtained, the TRC began the formal phase of its activities in December 2002, with a four-month 'statement-taking' phase. More than 6,000 victims and perpetrators provided detailed and often quite gripping accounts of violations of human rights and humanitarian law during the conflict. This was followed by public hearings, held throughout the country between March and August 2003. The Commission was expected to present its final report in late 2004.

In March 2003, the Court issued eight indictments, the most celebrated being that of Liberian President Charles Taylor. A few more were released over the course of the months that followed, although the total number of accused is unlikely to exceed 15 or 20. The Court's investigative work was conducted throughout the operational period of the TRC. But by the end of 2003, when the TRC had wound down its work, the visible judicial activity of the Court consisted of hearings of preliminary motions, on matters such as jurisdiction, interim release and joinder of cases. As the second anniversary of the establishment of the Court approached, no dates had been set for the beginning of trials as such.

Both the Truth and Reconciliation Commission and the Special Court fit within the palette of transitional justice options being used to address impunity in post-conflict situations.[5] Bishop Joseph C Humper, Chair of the Truth Commission, has described the two institutions as 'going to the promised land, but by different roads'. In his letter of 12 January 2001 to the UN Security Council, the UN Secretary-General said that:

care must be taken to ensure that the Special Court for Sierra Leone and the Truth and Reconciliation Commission will operate in a complementary and mutually supportive manner, fully respectful of their distinct but related functions.[6]

The Planning Mission, sent by United Nations headquarters in early 2002 to make preparations for the work of the Special Court, recalled that the two institutions were to 'perform complementary roles' that are 'mutually supportive' and 'in full respect for each other's mandate'.[7]

---

[5] On the approaches taken in other countries, see Priscilla B Hayner *Unspeakable Truths, Facing the Challenge of Truth Commissions* (Routledge New York and London 2002) especially ch 7. On the compatibility and usefulness of both approaches, see Richard J Goldstone, 'Justice as a Tool for Peace-Making: Truth Commissions and International Criminal Tribunals' (1996) 28 *NYU J Int'l L and Pol* 485.

[6] Letter from the Secretary-General addressed to the President of the Security Council (12 January 2001) UN Doc S/2001/40 para 9.

[7] 'Report of the Planning Mission on the Establishing of the Special Court for Sierra Leone' UN Doc S/2002/246, annex, paras 49, 53.

Not all have been as even-handed in their assessment of the complementary roles of the two bodies. Amnesty International has written that the TRC's 'contribution to ending impunity is likely to be extremely weak or non-existent'. Furthermore, it has recommended that:

the government of Sierra Leone and the international community should acknowledge that, while the TRC may be able to make an important contribution to establishing the truth about human rights abuses and understanding the nature of the conflict in Sierra Leone, it should not be a substitute for prosecuting those responsible for serious crimes under international law.[8]

At the other end of the spectrum are those who view the Special Court as a provocative and troublesome initiative likely to interfere with and possibly compromise the peace process. Both extremes have had their part in the debate about the relationship between the Special Court and the TRC.

This chapter will compare the two organizations with respect to their legal status and functions, as well as their mandates and jurisdiction, before proceeding to consider some of the issues that may arise in the relationship between them.

B. LEGAL STATUS AND FUNCTIONS OF THE TWO INSTITUTIONS

The Truth and Reconciliation Commission is a creation of the Parliament of Sierra Leone, in pursuance of an undertaking found in Article XXVI of the Lomé Peace Agreement. Although it is a national institution, the TRC has an international dimension because of the participation of the Special Representative of the Secretary-General and the High Commissioner for Human Rights in its establishment. These two senior United Nations officials were responsible for recommending the appointment of the three members of the Commission who are not citizens of Sierra Leone.[9] The bulk of the financing for the Commission comes from international donors, with the Office of the High Commissioner assuming principal responsibility for fund-raising. Initially budgeted at US$10 million,[10] poor donor response resulted in a series of reductions. Ultimately, contributions to the TRC did not exceed US$4 million.[11] Throughout its operations the TRC was plagued with financial difficulties. It lacked adequate resources to ensure the necessary professional staff for research and investigation. This was a saga of missed opportunities,

---

[8] 'Sierra Leone: Renewed Commitment to End Impunity' AI Index, AFR 51/007/2001, 24 September 2001.
[9] Truth and Reconciliation Commission Act 2000 s 3.
[10] '14th Report of the Secretary-General on the United Nations Mission in Sierra Leone' UN Doc S/2002/679 para 27.
[11] '15th Report of the Secretary-General on the United Nations Mission in Sierra Leone' UN Doc S/2002/987 para 44.

due, in large part, to the failure of the international community to put its money where its mouth was.

The Commission's mandate has both fact-finding and therapeutic dimensions. As then-Attorney-General Solomon Berewa (currently Vice-President) put it:

> far from being fault-finding and punitive, it is to serve as the most legitimate and credible forum for victims to reclaim their human worth; and a channel for the perpetrators of atrocities to expiate their guilt, and chasten their consciences. The process has been likened to a national catharsis, involving truth telling, respectful listening and above all, compensation for victims in deserving cases.[12]

The 'Memorandum of Objects and Reasons', which is attached to the Truth and Reconciliation Commission (TRC) Act 2000, notes that the Peace Agreement 'envisaged the proceedings of the Commission as a catharsis for constructive interchange between the victims and perpetrators of human rights violations and abuses'. Although the TRC has no resources of its own to distribute to victims, it is authorized to make recommendations regarding the Special Fund for War Victims, whose establishment is provided for in Article XXIV of the Lomé Peace Agreement. More generally, the Commission may make recommendations with respect to the needs of victims. According to section 17 of the TRC Act, '[t]he Government shall faithfully and timeously implement the recommendations of the report that are directed to state bodies and encourage or facilitate the implementation of any recommendations that may be directed to others'. Although the TRC has no punitive mission, it overlaps with the Special Court to the extent that the latter is also envisaged to deliver 'truth-seeking', 'catharsis', 'expiation of guilt' and so on.

1. Temporal jurisdiction

The TRC's mandate, set out in section 6(1) of the TRC Act, is to prepare an historical record of the country from 1991, when the war began, until the Lomé Peace Agreement of 7 July 1999. The temporal overlap with the jurisdiction of the Special Court consequently covers the period between 30 November 1996 and 7 July 1999. However, the Act also requires the Commission to investigate and report on the 'antecedents' of the 'conflict'.[13] Moreover, the TRC is also charged with addressing impunity, responding to the needs of victims, promoting healing and reconciliation, and preventing a repetition of the violations and abuses suffered. This aspect of the mandate

---

[12] Solomon Berewa, 'Addressing Impunity using Divergent Approaches: The Truth and Reconciliation Commission and the Special Court', in *Truth and Reconciliation in Sierra Leone* (UNAMSIL Freetown 2001), 55–60, 59.

[13] Truth and Reconciliation Commission Act 2000 s 6(2)(a).

has no precise temporal framework. It would seem, therefore, that the TRC may inquire into events both prior to 1991 and subsequent to 7 July 1999, although the 'impartial historical record' that it prepares has a beginning and an end that are clearly defined by the statute. In any event, it only makes good sense for the TRC to take a broad view of its temporal framework, given the delay in its establishment and the clear relevance of events subsequent to signature of the Lomé Peace Agreement in the fulfilment of the TRC's mandate. In its practice, the Commission has been relatively unconcerned with the issue of 'temporal jurisdiction', looking at events even decades prior to the outbreak of the conflict, and taking evidence of violations that occurred well after the Lomé Peace Agreement.

The Special Court has a mandate that is defined as being 'since 30 November 1996'. There is no end-point to its temporal jurisdiction, although of course the Statute can always be amended by agreement of the two parties.[14] The reference in article 1 of the Statute to jurisdiction over those who have 'threatened the establishment of and implementation of the peace process in Sierra Leone' should be a warning that the Court may continue to exercise jurisdiction over events until the completion of the 'peace process'.[15]

To a large extent, the Special Court is a response to the amnesty granted by the Lomé Peace Agreement. Because of the amnesty, the national courts that would ordinarily have jurisdiction over offences committed in Sierra Leone are prevented from prosecuting offenders. Although the Special Court has primacy over national courts, and may require them to stay proceedings so as to enable the Special Court to proceed, it seems reasonable to expect that the Special Court will focus its relatively scarce resources on pre-Lomé offences. Since 1 July 2002, the International Criminal Court may also exercise jurisdiction over serious violations of international humanitarian law committed on the territory of Sierra Leone.

2. Territorial jurisdiction

The TRC's mandate refers to 'violations and abuses of human rights and international humanitarian law related to the armed conflict in Sierra Leone'. Nowhere does it specify that the violations and abuses must have occurred on the territory of Sierra Leone, as is the case with the Special Court.[16] Indeed, there are other signals in the Act that encourage the Commission to look abroad. Section 6(2)(a) indicates that the functions of the Commission

---

[14] Vienna Convention on the Law of Treaties (1979) 1155 UNTS 331 Art 39.

[15] In a recent report, the Secretary-General listed a number of benchmarks that need to be accomplished as part of the 'peace process': '15th Report' (*supra* n 11) para 13. The issue of the end-point for the Special Court is discussed by the Secretary-General in 'Report of the Secretary-General on the Establishment of a Special Court for Sierra Leone' UN Doc S/2000/915 para 28.

[16] On this point, see Chapter 7 (Smith).

include investigating 'the role of both internal and external factors in the conflict'. The TRC is to inquire into whether the conflict was 'the result of deliberate planning, policy or authorisation by *any* government'. Finally, it is empowered 'to request information from the relevant authorities of a foreign country and to gather information from victims, witnesses, government officials and others in foreign countries'.[17] The scope is broad indeed, with the only 'territorial' requirement being a relationship with the armed conflict in Sierra Leone. At the very least, the TRC is clearly mandated to consider the situation of war refugees in camps outside the country.[18]

Article 1(1) of the Statute of the Special Court refers to violations 'committed in the territory of Sierra Leone'. The judges will have to rule on the extent to which they are prepared to extend the territorial jurisdiction to cover acts and omissions that take place outside the country if they produce significant effects on the territory of Sierra Leone. The Statute allows prosecution of any person who planned, instigated, ordered, committed or otherwise aided and abetted in the planning, preparation or execution of a crime, even if this occurred outside Sierra Leone. The judges will be guided by comparative criminal law authorities on these complex matters. Because the Court is not created by the UN Security Council, it cannot threaten reluctant governments with enforcement measures in the same way that this has been done by the two ad hoc tribunals.[19]

3. Personal jurisdiction

The Truth and Reconciliation Commission is not engaged in prosecution, and so it is hardly appropriate to speak of 'personal jurisdiction'. The Act refers in several places to 'victims and perpetrators', suggesting that these two groups make up the Commission's principal constituency. Special attention is focused on children, including child perpetrators, as well as victims of sexual abuse.[20] But the Commission is also given a role in determining responsibilities, identifying the 'causes'[21] and the 'parties responsible',[22] and here its attention is directed to 'any government, group or individual'.[23] At the core of the Commission's mandate is the concept of 'human rights violations and abuses'. The Act seems to suggest that these may be

---

[17] Truth and Reconciliation Commission Act 2000 s 8(1)(f).

[18] On violations of the human rights of refugees from Sierra Leone committed in neighbouring states, see eg Human Rights Watch *Refugee Women in Guinea Raped* Press Release (13 September 2000).

[19] On this subject, see *Prosecutor v Blaskic* IT-95-14-AR108*bis* Judgment on the Request of the Republic of Croatia for Review of the Decision of Trial Chamber II (18 July 1997, 29 October 1997).

[20] Truth and Reconciliation Commission Act 2000 s 7(4).

[21] ibid s 6(2)(a).

[22] ibid s 7(1)(a).

[23] ibid s 6.

committed by individuals as well as governments, but the TRC will have to determine to what extent it is prepared to hold non-state actors responsible for human rights violations. Responsibilities might extend, for example, to transnational corporations or private security organizations.[24]

The Special Court's jurisdiction is defined in article 1 of the Statute as comprising 'persons who bear the greatest responsibility for serious violations of international humanitarian law and Sierra Leonean law committed in the territory of Sierra Leone since 30 November 1996'.[25]

Unlike the TRC, which can also examine the responsibility of 'groups', the Special Court's jurisdiction is confined to persons. There will be no determinations about the existence of 'criminal organizations',[26] although the Special Court may well get at them indirectly by prosecuting the leaders of such bodies. The reference to 'persons' in the Statute of the Special Court is not explicitly confined to physical persons, and the possibility of prosecution of transnational corporations cannot be ruled out.

There has been much interest in the question of child offenders.[27] The Statute of the Special Court gives it jurisdiction over persons who were at least 15 years old at the time of the crime.[28] The view was frequently expressed by both the Secretary-General and the Security Council that the Truth and Reconciliation Commission was probably a better venue for dealing with child or juvenile offenders. The Statute of the Special Court itself refers to 'alternative truth and reconciliation mechanisms'.[29] The Prosecutor of the Special Court, David Crane, has made several declarations indicating that he has no intention of pursuing juvenile offenders.

4. Subject matter jurisdiction

The Truth and Reconciliation Commission is charged with examining 'violations and abuses of human rights and international humanitarian law'. It is mandated to 'create an impartial historical record' of such violations and abuses[30] and to 'investigate and report on the causes, nature and extent' of the violations and abuses.[31] The Truth and Reconciliation Commission Act

---

[24] L Sanders 'Rich and Rare Are the Gems They Wear: Holding De Beers Accountable for Trading Conflict Diamonds' (2001) 24 *Fordham Int'l L J* 1402; William A Schabas 'Enforcing International Humanitarian Law: Catching the Accomplices' (2001) 83 *Int'l Rev Red Cross* 439.

[25] See Chapter 2 (Shraga).

[26] Unlike the situation at Nuremberg. On the usefulness of the concept of 'criminal organization' for contemporary prosecutions of serious violations of international humanitarian law, see Nina Jorgensen 'A Reappraisal of the Abandoned Nuremberg Concept of Criminal Organisations in the Context of Justice in Rwanda' (2001) 12 *Criminal Law Forum* 371.

[27] See Chapter 2 (Shraga).

[28] Statute of the Special Court for Sierra Leone art 7.

[29] ibid art 15(5).

[30] Truth and Reconciliation Commission Act 2000 s 6(1).

[31] ibid s 6(2).

2000 provides no further guidance on the scope of the terms 'human rights' and 'international humanitarian law'.

The prevailing contemporary view, confirmed by the 1993 Vienna Conference on Human Rights, is that the term 'human rights' refers to a broad range of norms, including civil, political, but also economic, social, and cultural rights. Such rights are said to be indivisible. The preamble to the African Charter on Human and Peoples' Rights appears to place even greater emphasis on economic, social, and cultural rights as they are seen as a guarantee for civil and political rights.[32] It should be noted, however, that the Lomé Peace Agreement proposes a rather narrower view of human rights confined essentially to civil and political rights. According to Article XXIV:

[t]he basic civil and political liberties recognised by the Sierra Leone legal system and contained in the declarations and principles of human rights adopted by the UN and OAU, especially the Universal Declaration of Human Rights and the African Charter on Human and Peoples' Rights, shall be fully protected and promoted within Sierra Leonean society. These include the right to life and liberty, freedom from torture, the right to a fair trial, freedom of conscience, expression and association, and the right to take part in the governance of one's country.[33]

Although international headlines were captured by reports of the most appalling attacks on the life and bodily integrity of innocent victims in Sierra Leone, the causes of the conflict may well be rooted in violations of economic and social rights. The TRC has already decided that for the purposes of its work it will adopt the broad view of 'human rights' found in the preamble to the African Charter.

The reference to 'international humanitarian law' is shared by the TRC Act and the Statute of the Special Court. In the case of the TRC, it is to examine 'violations and abuses' of international humanitarian law, while the Special Court is to prosecute 'serious violations' of international humanitarian law. The somewhat more limited subject matter jurisdiction of the Special Court is further restrained by the specific enumeration of crimes that it may prosecute.

The Special Court also has jurisdiction over crimes against humanity and certain specified violations of the laws of Sierra Leone, concerning sexual abuse of girls and destruction of property, that are not normally defined as serious violations of international humanitarian law. There is no direct

---

[32] African Charter on Human and People's Rights OAU Doc CAB/LEG/67/3 rev 5, 4 EHRR 417, 21 ILM 58. See especially the statement 'that it is henceforth essential to pay a particular attention to the right to development and that civil and political rights cannot be dissociated from economic, social and cultural rights in their conception as well as universality and that the satisfaction of economic, social and cultural rights is a guarantee for the enjoyment of civil and political rights'.

[33] For a similarly narrow view of the scope of the concept of human rights violations and abuses, as the term is used in the TRC Act, see Ilan Lax, 'Strategies and Methodologies for Finding the Truth' in *Truth and Reconciliation in Sierra Leone* (*supra* n 2) 61–87, at 65–6.

reference to these offences in the TRC Act although the underlying acts would likely fall within the rubric of violations and abuses of human rights.

C. THE 'RELATIONSHIP' BETWEEN THE TRC AND THE COURT

From the earliest discussions about the Special Court, attention has focused on the issue of the 'relationship' between the TRC and the Court. On 2 October 2000, subsequent to the Security Council Resolution but even prior to the Secretary-General's first draft, the US Institute of Peace, the International Human Rights Law Group and two experts, Priscilla Hayner and Paul van Zyl, held an expert round-table on how the two bodies would relate to each other.[34] The Secretary-General's Report of 4 October 2000, which first set out the draft statute and the reasoning behind it, said that:

relationship and cooperation arrangements would be required between the Prosecutor and the National Truth and Reconciliation Commission, including the use of the Commission as an alternative to prosecution, and the prosecution of juveniles, in particular.[35]

In November 2000, an international workshop organized by the Office of the High Commissioner for Human Rights (OHCHR) and the United Nations Assistance Mission for Sierra Leone (UNAMSIL) proposed establishing a consultative process 'to work out the relationship between the TRC and the special court'.[36]

Many believed that because the two bodies were directed to issues of accountability and impunity, it was only logical that their activities be associated. During 2001, in the context of discussions on the content of the draft statute of the Special Court, several of the relevant issues in the relationship between the two bodies were considered. There were frequent proposals for a 'relationship agreement' between the two institutions. In 2001, the Secretary-General reported that UNAMSIL and the OHCHR would be preparing 'general guidelines' for the relationship between the TRC and the Special Court.[37]

In December 2001, as part of its activities to prepare for the establishment of the TRC, the High Commissioner for Human Rights and the Office of Legal Affairs convened an expert meeting in New York. The meeting was described as follows in the report of the High Commissioner:

---

[34] Bennett (*supra* n 2) 43.

[35] 'Report of the Secretary-General on the Establishment of a Special Court for Sierra Leone' (*supra* n 15) para 8.

[36] 'Situation of Human Rights in Sierra Leone' UN Doc E/CN.4/2001/35, 13, para 41.

[37] '11th Report of the Secretary-General on the United Nations Mission in Sierra Leone' UN Doc S/2001/857 para 47.

The expert meeting on the relationship between the TRC and the Special Court was organised by OHCHR and the Office for Legal Affairs (OLA) of the United Nations in New York on 20 and 21 December 2001. The participants discussed the important issue of an amicable relationship between the two institutions that would reflect their roles, and the difficult issue of whether information could and should be shared between them. The pros and cons of a wide range of possibilities regarding cooperation between the Commission and the Court were examined. Based on those discussions, the participants agreed on a number of basic principles that should guide the TRC and the Special Court in determining modalities of cooperation. These principles include the following:

(i) The TRC and the Special Court were established at different times, under different legal bases and with different mandates. Yet they perform complementary roles in ensuring accountability, deterrence, a story-telling mechanism for both victims and perpetrators, national reconciliation, reparation and restorative justice for the people of Sierra Leone.

(ii) While the Special Court has primacy over the national courts of Sierra Leone, the TRC does not fall within this mould. In any event, the relationship between the two bodies should not be discussed on the basis of primacy or lack of it. The ultimate operational goal of the TRC and the Court should be guided by the request of the Security Council and the Secretary-General to 'operate in a complementary and mutually supportive manner fully respectful of their distinct but related functions' (S/2001/40, paragraph 9; see also S/2000/1234).

(iii) The modalities of cooperation should be institutionalised in an agreement between the TRC and the Special Court and, where appropriate, also in their respective rules of procedure. They should respect fully the independence of the two institutions and their respective mandates.[38]

In addition to the UN-sponsored meetings, some international NGOs developed some rather elaborate proposals on the type of provisions that might be governed by a relationship agreement. Although there was consideration of the possibility of joint or common efforts at witness protection, translation and public awareness, most of the reflection on how the two bodies might cooperate tended to dwell on what was called 'information sharing', something the December expert meeting had agreed was a 'difficult issue'. However, when the two bodies began work, neither showed any interest in a relationship agreement. The Prosecutor, David Crane, made several public declarations indicating he had no interest in obtaining information in the possession of the TRC, and he certainly did not ever offer to share information in his possession in the other direction. All of the talk, then, about a 'relationship agreement' was essentially ignored by the two bodies.

What may well be the most difficult issue in the relationship between the two bodies is the question of admissibility in a prosecution of

---

[38] UN Doc E/CN.4/2002/3 para 70.

self-incriminating evidence previously produced before the TRC. Astonishingly, this issue was hardly considered in the preliminary discussions within the United Nations and the NGO community. For example, the Human Rights Watch policy paper made no mention whatsoever of the issue of a right against self-incrimination, and instead proposed that self-incriminating testimony given to the TRC might, if given voluntarily, justify a 'reduced sentence' by the Special Court![39]

There was initially some evidence to indicate the importance of concerns by perpetrators inclined to testify before the TRC that such testimony could be used in prosecutions before the Special Court. For example, a 2001 Report by the Secretary-General indicated that the Revolutionary United Front (RUF) was 'receptive' to the TRC, but that it expressed 'concern over the independence of the Commission and the relationship between it and the Special Court'.[40] Many people, including NGOs associated with former combatants and participants in the abuses, indicated their willingness to cooperate with the TRC, but only on the condition that this material not be used for criminal prosecution. According to Human Rights Watch, doubt about the ability of the TRC to obtain information in confidence 'could potentially undermine the willingness of persons to come before the TRC to provide testimony'.[41]

It is difficult to assess how much these concerns affected the work of the TRC in practice. Some perpetrators did in fact come forward, but their numbers were never very important. Yet other truth commissions, where there was little or no threat to prosecution, were no more successful in convincing perpetrators to testify. Dramatically, in the final months of the TRC's work, some of the perpetrators who had been indicted and were in the custody of the Court actually requested the right to testify in public before the Commission, well aware of the fact that their testimony could be used against them in the subsequent trial. This suggests the relative insignificance of the threat of prosecution as a factor discouraging testimony before the Court.

The requests to testify, by Chief Hinga Norman and others, provoked the only public tension between the TRC and the Special Court during the existence of the two bodies. Although the Commission had concluded its hearings phase by the time Norman wrote from the Court's detention centre asking to testify in public, in late August 2003, the Commission agreed that

---

[39] Human Rights Watch *Policy Paper on the Interrelationship Between the Sierra Leone Special Court and the Truth and Reconciliation Commission* (18 April 2002). The issue is referred to, but only summarily, in the International Centre for Transitional Justice paper *Exploring the Relationship Between the Special Court and the Truth and Reconciliation Commission of Sierra Leone* (24 June 2002) 13.

[40] '11th Report' (*supra* n 37) para 44.

[41] Human Rights Watch *Policy Paper* (*supra* n 39) 2.

his testimony was important and that it was desirable, for the achievement of the TRC's mandate, that arrangements be made for this. To considerable surprise, however, when the Registrar was approached on this issue there was significant opposition, particularly from the Prosecutor. The Prosecutor contended that Norman might use his testimony to stir up social unrest within the country, and that he might also threaten potential witnesses.

The Registrar of the Court prepared a Practice Direction, outlining the conditions under which detained persons might testify.[42] Although the TRC felt that this went beyond his legitimate authority, and clashed with the objectives of the Commission, the net result of the Direction was to facilitate public testimony. Accordingly, the TRC prepared an application, which was argued before a single judge of the Court in October. The application was contested by the Office of the Prosecutor, who argued that public testimony by Norman would violate the *sub judice* rule, and that it might put 'in peril the fragile equilibrium which exists in Sierra Leone today'.[43] Judge Bankole Thompson, of the Trial Chamber, ruled against the application and denied Norman the possibility of testifying before the TRC. Judge Thompson based his reasoning on what he called the threat to Norman's presumption of innocence. Because the Commission, in its application, had stated that Norman was important to the narrative of the conflict, Judge Thompson said it had already judged him responsible.[44] The first real decision of the Court since it had begun work, the legal reasoning of Judge Thompson was frail in the extreme, and an embarrassment to the Court as a whole. In recognizing the importance of Norman in the conflict, the TRC had certainly done no more than the Prosecutor, who had chosen to indict him, and the judges of the Court, who had agreed there was enough evidence to confirm the indictment and to hold him in custody prior to trial. In any event, the presumption

---

[42] 'Practice Direction on the procedure following a request by a State, the Truth and Reconciliation Commission or other legitimate authority to take a statement from a person in the custody of the Special Court for Sierra Leone', adopted 9 September 2003, amended 4 October 2003. The Practice Direction is reproduced in *Prosecutor v Norman* (Case no SCSL-2003-08-PT), Decision on Appeal by the Truth and Reconciliation Commission of Sierra Leone ('TRC' or 'The Commission') and Chief Samuel Hinga Norman JP Against the Decision of His Lordship, Mr Justice Bankole Thompson Delivered on 30 October 2003 to Deny the TRC's Request to Hold a Public Hearing with Chief Samuel Hinga Norman JP, 28 November 2003, para 22.

[43] *Prosecutor v Norman* (Case no SCSL-2003-08-PT), Decision on the Request by the Truth and Reconciliation Commission of Sierra Leone to Conduct a Public Hearing with Samuel Hinga Norman, 29 October 2003, para 3. Also *Prosecutor v Norman* (Case no SCSL-2003-08-PT), Decision on Appeal by the Truth and Reconciliation Commission of Sierra Leone ('TRC' or 'The Commission') and Chief Samuel Hinga Norman JP Against the Decision of His Lordship, Mr Justice Bankole Thompson Delivered on 30 October 2003 to Deny the TRC's Request to Hold a Public Hearing with Chief Samuel Hinga Norman JP, 28 November 2003, para 26.

[44] ibid, especially para 13. See also: *Prosecutor v Gbao* (Case no SCSL-2003-09-PT), Decision on the Request by the Truth and Reconciliation Commission of Sierra Leone to Conduct a Public Hearing with Augustine Gbao, 3 November 2003.

of innocence belonged to Norman, and he was fully entitled to abandon it if he so chose.

The Commission appealed the decision to President Geoffrey Robertson, and a final decision was issued in late November.[45] Revising Judge Thompson's ruling, President Robertson warned that there were risks of self-incrimination which Chief Hinga Norman might run if he testified, but said that the decision on whether to do so must be his, as advised by his lawyers. 'The Court will not stop him from telling his full story to the Truth and Reconciliation Commission,' Judge Robertson said. But Judge Robertson did not allow for a public hearing, only an essentially private meeting between Norman and some of the Commissioners. But all along, Norman could always have transmitted testimony to the Commission and responded to its questions through his attorney, without ever needing to seek permission of the Court. In other words, President Robertson gave Norman and the TRC something that they already had. In the end, he never did testify before the TRC.

But Norman's eagerness to testify before the TRC confirmed my own doubts about the alleged negative influence the existence of the Court was said to have on perpetrators who were supposed to have been discouraged from testifying in front of the Commission. Norman's behaviour was the exact opposite of what so many had predicted would happen. Here was one of the most important alleged perpetrators, not only willing but eager to speak in public. In my view, based on intuitions gleaned from several months of TRC hearings, the real reasons why perpetrators agreed or refused to testify in hearings had little or nothing to do with prosecution and the Special Court. Some individuals—this was the case of the detainees who actually sought out the possibility—wish to give their version of the events, perhaps convinced that their activities and their motives will ultimately be understood. A similar phenomenon occurs daily in police stations around the world, where accused persons override conventional wisdom and the advice of defence counsel and insist upon speaking to investigators, despite the admonition that 'anything they say can and will be held against them'. On the other hand, there are those who are absolutely unable to speak in public about atrocities they have committed and for which they may bear responsibility. Their concerns are based not in fear of prosecution but shame over what they have done.

Certainly, there was never any legal guarantee preventing self-incriminating evidence adduced before the Commission being used against an accused in a prosecution before the Special Court or, for that matter, before the

---

[45] *Prosecutor v Norman* (Case no SCSL-2003-08-PT), Decision on Appeal by the Truth and Reconciliation Commission of Sierra Leone ('TRC' or 'The Commission') and Chief Samuel Hinga Norman JP Against the Decision of His Lordship, Mr Justice Bankole Thompson Delivered on 30 October 2003 to Deny the TRC's Request to Hold a Public Hearing with Chief Samuel Hinga Norman JP, 28 November 2003.

courts of Sierra Leone. It may well be that the Parliament of Sierra Leone did not include a provision dealing with self-incriminating testimony before the TRC when it enacted the enabling legislation because at the time no prosecutions were envisaged, a consequence of the amnesty in the Lomé Peace Agreement. The TRC was predicated on the concept that perpetrators as well as victims come forward to tell their story. Absent the threat of self-incrimination because of the amnesty, it was probably thought there was no need to deal with the point directly. In any case, the legislation does provide a mechanism to reassure perpetrators that self-incriminating evidence cannot be used against them for prosecution purposes, in enabling the TRC to take evidence on a confidential basis. The Act states:

At the discretion of the Commission, any person shall be permitted to provide information to the Commission on a confidential basis and the Commission shall not be compelled to disclose any information given to it in confidence.[46]

In practice, the TRC used this power quite regularly to reassure individuals that their statements would not be revealed to the Special Court.

The judges of the Special Court might have enacted a privilege for TRC testimony. Whatever its practical significance, it would have been a very valuable gesture of recognition of the complementary nature of the two bodies. The applicable instruments for the Special Court are certainly alive to the issue of self-incrimination. The Statute of the Special Court states that a person accused before the Court has the right '[n]ot to be compelled to testify against himself or herself or to confess guilt'.[47] Even witnesses are protected against self-incriminating testimony, by virtue of Rule 90(E) of the Rules of Procedure and Evidence of the International Criminal Tribunal for Rwanda which, pursuant to article 14(1) of the Statute of the Special Court, apply *mutatis mutandis*:

A witness may refuse to make any statement which might tend to incriminate him. The Chamber may, however, compel the witness to answer the question. Testimony compelled in this way shall not be used as evidence in a subsequent prosecution against the witness for any offence other than perjury.

It would seem reasonable for the Special Court to adopt a similar rule with respect to evidence given to the TRC. The existing Rule 90(E) is justified essentially by concerns of fairness to an accused, and there is no reason why the same logic should not apply in the case of TRC testimony. But when this solution was proposed, the judges of the Court showed no interest in addressing the problem.

Most of the 'relationship' discussion within the United Nations and the NGOs has been predicated on 'information sharing' between the Prosecutor

---

[46] Truth and Reconciliation Commission Act 2000 s 8(3).
[47] Statute of the Special Court for Sierra Leone art 17(4)(g).

and the TRC. It has had a fundamentally prosecutorial perspective, focusing on how the TRC might assist the Court in convicting perpetrators. But the investigative resources of the Prosecutor far exceed those of the TRC, and it would seem unlikely that the latter's materials can be of much real interest to the Prosecutor in preparing a case for trial. The Prosecutor has said as much in interviews with the media of Sierra Leone. Of course it can never be excluded that the TRC might obtain some unique information or evidence of great interest to the Prosecutor, but this is not really a major concern, and certainly does not justify elaborate arrangements for 'information sharing'. The real issue—and it must be a genuine concern of the Prosecutor—is that defence council will request materials in the possession of the TRC, including evidence given in confidence, in order to challenge the credibility of prosecution witnesses, especially victims. The defence will insist on having access to TRC testimony in order to verify that a witness is saying the same thing before the Special Court. If the TRC refuses to divulge such evidence, the defence will apply for a stay of proceedings, arguing a violation of fundamental rights. The reaction of the judges to such a scenario cannot be predicted, but the defence is sure to insist that the only appropriate remedy can be a stay of proceedings.[48]

One plausible solution would be to allow the judges alone to examine TRC testimony. If they were satisfied that the testimony was not relevant, because it was essentially the same as testimony given before the Special Court, then the testimony would not become public, and would not even be shown to either prosecution or defence. On the other hand, if the testimony was not the same, the judges would presumably have to admit it in evidence and allow the defence to proceed with its challenge to the credibility of the witness in question. Given such a prospect, the TRC might consider it impossible to breach, even in such a modest and limited way, any undertaking of confidentiality.

There can be no assumption that the defence would succeed in convincing the judges to order the TRC to produce evidence given in confidence. The Special Court is not, of course, subject to the legislation of Sierra Leone, which is the basis for classifying TRC evidence as confidential. But the judges of the Special Court might well decide that such testimony is in any case privileged, comparable to information given in confidence to a lawyer, a doctor, or a priest. The Rules of Procedure and Evidence applicable to the Special Court only address the issue of lawyer–client privilege,[49] but case law of the ad hoc tribunals has recognized that a broader set of norms applies to

---

[48] *Prosecutor v Tadić* IT-94-1-A judgment (15 July 1999) para 55; *Barayagwiza v Prosecutor* ICTR-97-19-AR72 decision (3 November 1999).

[49] Rules of Procedure and Evidence of the International Criminal Tribunal for Rwanda r 97.

other categories of privilege.[50] International criminal law on this issue continues to evolve.[51]

Thus, according to the most recent attempt to clarify the applicable principles, namely Rule 71 of the Rules of Procedure and Evidence of the International Criminal Court, three conditions must be satisfied for the Court to respect the claim to confidentiality. All three of them, listed in paragraphs (a), (b), and (c) of sub-rule 71(2), appear to apply to evidence given to the TRC in confidence. TRC testimony given on a promise of confidentiality is certainly given in the course of 'a confidential relationship producing a reasonable expectation of privacy and non-disclosure'.[52] Moreover, the very functions of the TRC require that perpetrators feel comfortable 'baring their chest' before the Commission, which answers the condition in paragraph (b). And finally, would the Court not conclude that recognition of the privilege furthers its objectives, given the complementarity between the TRC and Special Court, and their joint contribution to justice, accountability, and healing in Sierra Leone?[53]

But even if the judges are prepared to recognize that TRC testimony given in confidence is privileged, they may also conclude that respect for the privilege entails a breach of the right to a fair trial. And all concerned parties, including the Prosecutor and the TRC, have an interest in fair trials taking place. A truth and reconciliation commission will hardly want to contribute to a system of criminal justice where the rights of the accused are compromised. Nor will it want its zealous protection of confidential information to become the justification for a stalemate and ultimate failure of the Special Court, an initiative whose fundamental objective, which is to address impunity, is shared by both institutions. But there seems to be no obvious solution to the dilemma. It is, essentially, the same headache that arises with respect to all privileged information before all criminal courts.

---

[50] *Prosecutor v Simic and others* IT-95-9-PT Decision on the Prosecution Motion under Rule 73 for a Ruling Concerning the Testimony of a Witness (27 July 1999) (concerning information obtained by the International Committee of the Red Cross); *Prosecutor v Delalic and others* IT-96-21-A Decision on Motion to Preserve and Provide Evidence (22 April 1999) (concerning evidence of communications between the judges and their legal officers).

[51] cf eg r 71 of the Rules of Procedure and Evidence of the International Criminal Court: 'Report of the Preparatory Commission for the International Criminal Court, Addendum, Finalized draft text of the Rules of Procedure and Evidence' UN Doc PCNICC/2000/INF/3/Add.3. Although not bound by these Rules, the judges of the Special Court would be likely to view them as a helpful and persuasive attempt at codification.

[52] Rule 71(2)(a).

[53] Rule 71(2)(c). For a discussion of the interpretation of this provision, see Donald K Piragoff 'Evidence' in Roy S Lee (ed) *The International Criminal Court: Elements of Crimes and Rules of Procedure and Evidence* (Transnational Ardsley New York 2001) 349–402, at 361. Mr Piragoff says such objectives might include protection of the well-being, dignity, and privacy of victims, reparation for victims, rehabilitation, and respect for national legal systems, all of which are well within the remit of the Sierra Leone Truth and Reconciliation Commission.

Several provisions of the Truth and Reconciliation Act 2000 contemplate the question of confidential information. In addition to section 7(3) of the Act, cited above, which allows the Commission to declare certain evidence confidential, section 7(4) suggests that the Commission actually has a positive duty to prevent disclosure of certain information, in requiring it to 'take into account the interests of victims and witnesses when inviting them to give statements, including the security and other concerns of those who may wish to recount their stories in public'. The Commission is empowered to implement special procedures to address the needs of children or those who have suffered sexual abuses, matters that may also require some limitation of access to its proceedings. Members and staff of the Commission are prohibited from making private use of or profit from any confidential information gained as a result of their work, and a breach may result in dismissal.[54] At the conclusion of its work, and prior to its dissolution, the Commission is charged with organizing its archives and records, and determining which information may be made available to the public and when, and the measures 'necessary to protect confidential information'.[55]

The Special Court is of course empowered to make orders for the production of evidence. The prospect of an order from the Special Court directed to the TRC itself, or one of its members of staff, for the production of confidential information is certainly a plausible hypothesis. Human Rights Watch took the position that 'the Special Court should subpoena the TRC only as a last resort'.[56] But the question of both the legality of such an order and its enforceability arise.

The Statute of the Special Court indicates that it has 'primacy', and some NGOs, like the International Crisis Group, have mistakenly suggested that this subordinates the Commission to the Court. But the principle of primacy merely establishes a rule to govern conflicts between courts with concurrent jurisdiction.[57] It is totally irrelevant to the relationship between the Court and the TRC. Any suggestion of a hierarchy would be a great surprise, given the prior statements from a variety of United Nations sources to the effect that the two bodies were mutually supportive and complementary. Nevertheless, a January 2002 discussion paper prepared by the Office of the Attorney-General and Ministry of Justice of Sierra Leone, with the technical cooperation of the NGO No Peace Without Justice, insists that the TRC is subordinate to the Special Court:

The legal relationship between the Special Court and the Truth and Reconciliation Commission is clear. The Special Court is an international judicial body whose requests and orders require no less than full compliance by the Truth and Reconcilia-

---

[54] Truth and Reconciliation Commission Act 2000 s 14(3).   [55] ibid s 19(2).
[56] Human Rights Watch *Policy Paper* (*supra* n 39).
[57] Statute of the Special Court for Sierra Leone art 8(1).

tion Commission, as by all Sierra Leonean national institutions, in accordance to [sic] the international obligations agreed to by Sierra Leone.[58]

The basis of these obligations, according to the paper, is article 17 of the Agreement between Sierra Leone and the United Nations. Article 17 refers to obligations of the 'Government', requiring it to cooperate with the Court and to comply with its requests. It says nothing of the TRC, which is a body independent of the government of Sierra Leone.

Although it is created by international agreement between Sierra Leone and the United Nations, and not by the Security Council, the model for the Special Court is the International Criminal Tribunal for Rwanda (ICTR). Accordingly, both its Statute and its Rules of Procedure and Evidence are derived in large measure from those of ICTR. ICTR operates, for the purposes of arrest and transfer of suspects, gathering of evidence and similar functions, through requests to national governments for assistance. A broadly similar 'mutual legal assistance' approach exists for the Special Court, at least with respect to Sierra Leone itself.

On 25 April 2002, the national implementing legislation, the Special Court Agreement (Ratification) Act 2002, came into force.[59] Confirming the 'mutual assistance' model, the Act actually refers to 'Mutual Assistance between Sierra Leone and Special Court'.[60] It also contemplates the giving of 'Orders' by the Special Court. Any such 'Order' is to have the same effect as if it were issued by a judge, magistrate, or justice of the peace of a Sierra Leone court. The Act does not specify what matters may be properly included in an 'Order'. 'Orders' are governed by sections 20 to 22, and section 22 refers to a 'forfeiture order'. Given the general application of the 'mutual assistance' approach to relations between Sierra Leone and the Special Court, it would seem that the reference to 'Orders' in sections 20 to 22 ought to be interpreted rather narrowly.

The heart of the difficulty is a mysterious provision, section 21(2) of the Special Court Agreement (Ratification) Act 2002, which states:

Notwithstanding any other law, every natural person, corporation, or other body created by or under Sierra Leone law shall comply with any direction specified in an order of the Special Court.

This provision has been interpreted in several NGO studies as an authorization by the Special Court to order the TRC to divulge evidence obtained in confidence. For example, Human Rights Watch concludes summarily that:

---

[58] Office of the Attorney-General and Ministry of Justice Special Court Task Force 'Briefing Paper on Relationship between the Special Court and the Truth and Reconciliation Commission, Legal Analysis and Policy Considerations of the Government of Sierra Leone for the Special Court Planning Mission' available at www.specialcourt.org/SLMission/Planning Mission/BriefingPapers\TRC_SpCt.html.

[59] Supplement CXXXIII (22) *Sierra Leone Gazette*.

[60] Special Court Agreement (Ratification) Act 2002 Pt IV.

[b]ecause the TRC is a body created under Sierra Leone law, the Implementing Law creates a duty for the TRC to comply with orders of the Special Court. Because there are no exceptions stated in the Implementing Law, the implications are that the TRC would have to comply with all orders of the Special Court.[61]

It is argued that on a literal reading, the reference to any person or other body must necessarily include the TRC. Moreover, in a related argument it is suggested that section 21(2), as subsequent legislation, implicitly repeals the 'incompatible' confidentiality provisions in section 7 of the Truth and Reconciliation Commission Act 2000. These views are supported by use of the terms 'notwithstanding any other law', and by application of the maxim *leges posteriors priores contraries abrogant.* Such an interpretation seems far-fetched and manifestly incorrect, for a number of reasons.

The literal reading of section 21(2) that is being proposed leads to a patent absurdity. Under the 'golden rule' of statutory construction, courts should not follow a construction that gives an absurd or illogical result.[62] The provision in question surely cannot mean that an order from the Special Court would override any previous legislative provision or common law rule that might, in a literal sense, be incompatible with it. In this respect, it is helpful to consider whether the Special Court can also breach the confidentiality of other individuals or bodies in Sierra Leone who are entitled to protection. Several examples come to mind. Cabinet proceedings would be covered by confidentiality. Notes of deliberations of the Supreme Court and the Court of Appeal would also be protected. And what of immunities for diplomats and similar officials which, while subject to international law, depend for their implementation within Sierra Leone upon national legislation, just like the Special Court does? Under the extravagant literal interpretation that is proposed by some, section 21(2) would enable the Court to order the production of the files in the United States Embassy, or those of the Special Representative of the Secretary General.[63] These are all examples of confidentiality that is protected by prior legislation in Sierra Leone, be it statute law or common law, or customary international law. It is preposterous to argue that all of this is implicitly repealed by the Special Court Act, and that such a result was actually intended by Parliament.

The argument then retreats to the suggestion that section 21(2) targets the TRC, rather than all privileges and immunities. But that too is unsustainable, because the provision makes no reference whatsoever to the Truth and

[61] Human Rights Watch *Policy Paper* (*supra* n 39) 1–2. The position of the International Centre for Transitional Justice is only slightly less categorical: *Exploring the Relationship* (*supra* n 39) 5.

[62] *Grey v Pearson* (1857) 6 HLC 61, 106, 10 ER 1216, 1234.

[63] The United Nations very probably considers that the Special Representative of the Secretary-General and other Mission personnel are immune from process of the Special Court: *Prosecutor v Blaskic* IT-95-14-T Decision of Trial Chamber I on the Protective Measures for General Philippe Morillon, Witness of the Trial Chamber (12 May 1999).

Reconciliation Commission Act 2000, adopted by the same Parliament less than two years previously. Surely if Parliament had aimed section 21(2) at the TRC, it would have said so more explicitly.

The theory that section 21(2) gives the Court access to material considered confidential by the TRC leads to another absurdity. If it is indeed true that the Court can order production of such material, then potential sources and witnesses who have been properly informed of the state of the law will presumably refuse to cooperate with the TRC. To the extent that they agree with the legal observations of the various NGO papers, they will conclude that there is no assurance of confidentiality before the TRC and will simply refuse to testify or to assist the Commission. Indeed, many of them have already indicated this to be the case to the extent that there is any doubt about the TRC's undertakings of confidentiality. Moreover, in the case of confidentiality that is required to protect victims or witnesses, the TRC would itself be reckless to gather testimony and other evidence that might jeopardize their security if it could not be sure that confidentiality would never be breached.

In other words, if the literal interpretation of section 21(2) is indeed correct, it will be highly unlikely for the TRC to come into possession of confidential information at all. Perpetrators will refuse to provide it, and, in the case of vulnerable witnesses and victims, because of its duty of protection, the Commission will refuse to seek or accept it. The result, then, is obviously of no assistance to the Special Court. On such a reading of the Special Court Agreement (Ratification) Act 2002, all that the controversial provision does is to emasculate the TRC and to deny it a power previously deemed by Parliament to be necessary for its operations, while at the same time giving nothing whatsoever to the Court. But why would Parliament have used legislation governing the Special Court to withdraw a power from the TRC in return for no benefit to the Court? A scenario whereby poorly-informed perpetrators might be duped into giving information under a dishonest promise from the TRC that it could guarantee confidentiality, so as to make it subsequently available to the Special Court, could surely never have been entertained by the legislature. Where a literal reading generates absurd results, it must give way to other approaches to statutory construction.

Perhaps the most reliable approach is purposive interpretation. The Special Court was created not to marginalize or incapacitate the TRC, but rather to add a new dimension to the accountability process in Sierra Leone. This was recognized in UN Security Council Resolution 1370 (2000),[64] and in any number of United Nations documents. Nothing in the United Nations documentation on the Special Court, including reports and letters from the

---

[64] See para 17.

Secretary-General and resolutions of the Security Council, even hints at the idea of conflict, supremacy, paramountcy, or anything else that might necessitate some special provision for the relationship between Court and TRC. Both bodies involve partnerships with the United Nations and significant international participation. Both are expected to be independent and impartial, and they have provisions in the enabling instruments to ensure this is the case. They are said to be different approaches to the achievement of similar goals. The Special Court was never intended to compromise the efficacy of the TRC, but rather to complement its contribution to the search for justice and accountability, and the campaign against impunity. Thus, in the absence of an explicit statutory provision to the contrary, it must be assumed that the Special Court Agreement (Ratification) Act 2002 has no impact whatsoever upon the Truth and Reconciliation Commission Act 2000. Accordingly, the confidentiality provisions of the TRC Act have full force and effect. No order from the Special Court can breach such confidentiality.

On the assumption that all of this reasoning is incorrect, and that the alternative interpretation is valid, one would have expected the legislature to provide for the enforceability of an order to produce confidential information directed to the TRC, to its members, or to its staff. To put the question differently, what would be the consequence of a refusal by the TRC, or by its members or its staff, to divulge confidential information to the Special Court? The Truth and Reconciliation Commission Act 2000 protects Commissioners and the TRC staff from any liability for acts carried out within the scope of their duties.[65] Such duties include, inter alia, the protection of confidential information. Had the legislature truly meant to facilitate orders from the Special Court directed to Commissioners or to TRC staff, and to make one body prevail over another, it would have provided for some form of enforceability. The absence of such provision is only a further argument against the theory that the Special Court Act in effect 'trumps' the TRC Act.

It has been suggested that despite the TRC's decision not to make materials given to it in confidence available to the Special Court, an exception should nevertheless be made in the case of what is sometimes called 'decisive evidence of guilt or innocence'. Surely the TRC would not, it is argued, in the name of a rigorous policy of confidentiality, stand by passively while an innocent person was convicted or a guilty one discharged? The United Nations Planning Mission Report saw information 'essential for the conviction or acquittal of the accused' to be a justifiable exception to the general rule of confidentiality for the TRC.[66] One NGO has proposed a draft relationship agreement that would govern the determination of such matters.[67]

---

[65] Truth and Reconciliation Commission Act 2000 s 14(4).
[66] 'Report of the Planning Mission' (*supra* n 7) para 55.
[67] *Exploring the Relationship* (*supra* n 39).

What exactly such information might consist of is not always easy to determine. Few examples are given. One suggestion has been conflicting testimony: a prosecution witness says one thing before the Court and something else before the TRC. But evidence that somebody has lied can never be 'decisive evidence' of either guilt or innocence. The fact that a witness lied before the TRC does not mean he or she is not telling the truth before the Court, or vice versa. All that contradictory testimony proves is that the witness has lied at least once!

In reality, this problem is not at all peculiar to the relationship between the TRC and the Special Court. Indeed, the Special Court itself seems to allow for a situation where 'decisive evidence of guilt or innocence' cannot be used. Take the case of a confession of guilt by a witness which, in many legal systems would be deemed to be fairly 'decisive' inculpatory evidence. The Rules of Procedure and Evidence recognize that a person may, in testimony before the Court, be forced to admit guilt and to provide decisive evidence of it. Yet Rule 90(E) of the ICTR says that such decisive proof of guilt 'shall not be used as evidence in a subsequent prosecution'. Moreover, the Prosecutor may confront the same problem himself. In the course of his work, the Prosecutor, like many prosecutors in legal systems around the world, may find it necessary to make commitments of confidentiality so as to obtain evidence or otherwise facilitate investigation. Rule 70(B) of the ICTR Rules of Procedure and Evidence actually sanctify the ability of the Prosecutor to guarantee confidentiality, without exception, even in the case of 'decisive evidence of innocence or guilt'.[68] Yet no one is exercised about what he might do in such a situation. Even the defence may obtain information that decisively proves guilt or innocence, for example in the course of an interview with the accused. But the Rules say that such evidence is shrouded by lawyer–client privilege.

This concept of 'decisive evidence of guilt or innocence' does not appear to be particularly helpful to the discussion of the relationship between Special Court and TRC. If it were, one would expect to find judicial models for dealing with the issue in other legal systems because, after all, the problem is far from unique. Indeed, this probably explains why those concerned about the 'relationship' between the TRC and the Special Court have had to invent formulae in order to address this issue. To the extent that legal systems recognize the concept of privilege and protections against self-incrimination, they all have to live with the possibility that 'decisive evidence of guilt or innocence' will be occasionally unavailable.

This, by the way, does not in any way suggest indifference towards such difficulties. Should such a situation arise, the Truth and Reconciliation Commission, like all others in similar circumstances, who possess

---

[68] Rule 70(B).

information taken in confidence—lawyers, doctors, prosecutors, priests, and so on—would have to balance a number of conflicting concerns in an attempt to reach a solution consistent with fundamental principles of justice and human rights. Again, like all others in similar circumstances, it might be able to employ a variety of means and mechanisms in order to reach a fair result without compromising its commitment to confidentiality and its integrity.

There is considerable anecdotal evidence suggesting that many people in Sierra Leone seem confused about the distinctions between the two bodies. Interviews and discussions in the field report that Sierra Leoneans confuse the Commission and the Court and are unable to comprehend the differences in their roles and functions. Some have suggested that this may account for difficulties experienced by the TRC in soliciting testimony of perpetrators. Although some perpetrators have provided statements to the TRC, and a few have even testified publicly about their actions in the past, the response has not exactly been overwhelming. Among the explanations is the claim that perpetrators believe the TRC is in some way involved in criminal prosecution.

But there may be other ways to understand these issues. As for a generalized confusion about the nature of the two bodies, this should hardly be a surprise, especially in a country with such low levels of literacy and education. Even in modern, highly developed democracies, the general public is often unable to clarify relevant distinctions between, say, the Minister of Justice and the President of the Supreme Court, or make other somewhat sophisticated distinctions. To the extent that the general public in Sierra Leone confuses the TRC and the Special Court, this must indicate that people also comprehend the general purpose of both institutions, which is to provide accountability and address impunity. In other words, a degree of confusion should not necessarily be viewed in a negative light.

D. CONCLUSION

Although much intellectual and political energy has been expended by the United Nations and by international and national NGOs on the issue of the Sierra Leone Truth and Reconciliation Commission's 'relationship' with the Special Court ever since the proposal to create the latter was first mooted, most of the discussion and the ensuing proposals have not proven to be particularly helpful. In the case of the administrative or practical arrangements by which it was recommended that the two bodies share resources, once operational neither of the organizations has been able to see how this might actually work.

When the two bodies began work, there was great concern about overlap in their two mandates. These were not, by and large, shown to be of any significance. If there is an important lesson from the parallel existence of the two bodies, it is that they can work very comfortably together, without conflict or tension. They are partners in the struggle against impunity, but they have little common ground in terms of their day-to-day work. Given an appropriately benign and non-confrontational attitude of the personalities involved, there is no reason why this experience cannot be repeated in other contexts. In other words, although potential sources of tension and conflict exist, they can be managed and addressed.

The Truth and Reconciliation Commission and the Special Court have much in common in terms of their overall objectives. Together they will clarify the historical truth of the conflict in Sierra Leone, contributing to a better understanding of its causes and of the persons and factors responsible for it. The work of both bodies should undermine future efforts to distort and deform the truth. The two institutions will provide a forum for victims and, in some measure, offer them recognition, redress and a sense that justice has been done. Above all, to use the terms of the TRC mandate, both bodies will 'address impunity'. But this does not mean that they necessarily have much to share in terms of their methodologies and their resources. Perhaps the appropriate metaphor is that of building a house. The Truth and Reconciliation Commission is the plumber, and the Special Court is the electrician. The two trades work in different parts of the house, on different days, at different stages of the construction, and using different tools and materials. Nobody would want to live in a finished house that lacked either electricity or plumbing. In this sense, the 'relationship' is synergistic, but it probably involves little or no formal cooperation, as the practice of the two bodies in Sierra Leone appears to be demonstrating.

10

The Politics of Genocide Justice in Cambodia

Craig Etcheson*

A. INTRODUCTION

The single most sensitive issue facing Cambodia today concerns the question of accountability for the crimes of the Khmer Rouge regime. It is an issue which touches the hearts of each and every person in Cambodia. Everyone's lives are connected in some way, usually in many ways, to the Khmer Rouge. Every individual in the country had members of his or her family murdered by the Khmer Rouge. Thus it is a tremendously emotional matter for most citizens of Cambodia—and it is a tremendously intimate question for the entire political elite. Virtually every member of the elite class has been variously a subject of, a member of, allied to, and/or at war with the Khmer Rouge for more than three decades. Consequently, the matter of genocide justice in Cambodia is not merely a legal or political question—it is personal. Public opinion surveys suggest that the overwhelming majority of the Cambodian people want the Khmer Rouge leadership to be prosecuted for their crimes, but thus far the political elite has been very reluctant to grant this wish, in part because nobody has completely clean hands.

That crimes were committed during the Khmer Rouge regime between 1975 and 1979 is beyond debate. Research has demonstrated that some 2 to 2.2 million people perished—one-quarter to one-third of the entire population—during the three years, eight months and 20 days of Democratic Kampuchea, as the Khmer Rouge regime was officially known.[1] A nation-

* This chapter is based on presentations by the author at Harvard University's Kennedy School of Government and the US Foreign Service Institute. Craig Etcheson maintains a consulting practice in transitional justice and national reconciliation. He has been a member of the faculty at Johns Hopkins University's School of Advanced International Studies, Yale University's Center for International and Area Studies, and the University of Southern California's Institute for Transnational Studies. Dr Etcheson is the author of several books and book-length studies, including two forthcoming works, *After the killing fields: Lessons from the Cambodian Genocide*, and *The Extraordinary Chambers: The Establishment of the Khmer Rouge Tribunal*. Etcheson holds a PhD in International Relations from the University of Southern California (1985), and an MA in Politics and Economics (1978) as well as a BA in Politics and Psychology from the University of Illinois (1977).
[1] See 'Digging in the Killing Fields' in Craig Etcheson *After the killing Fields: Lessons from the Cambodian Genocide* (Praeger Publishers New York forthcoming). Recent demographic studies dovetail with the empirical data reported in the previous citation; see Patrick Heuveline ' "Between One and Three Million": Towards the Demographic Reconstruction of a Decade of Cambodian History (1970–79)' (1998) 52(1) Population Studies 49; and Marek Sliwinski *Le Génocide Khmer Rouge: un analyse démographique* (Editions L'Harmattan Paris 1995).

wide network of so-called 'security centres' was established by the Khmer Rouge, and an estimated 1.1 million people were executed within the maw of that bureaucracy.[2] Numerous legal studies have found a prima facie case that these killings constituted war crimes, genocide, and other crimes against humanity.[3] Measured by percentage of the national population killed, it was the worst mass murder of the twentieth century.

Yet, a quarter of a century after the regime that perpetrated these crimes was driven from power, no senior leader of that regime has yet faced justice before a court of law. Their impunity has not endured because of a lack of effort on the part of justice advocates; the struggle for genocide justice in Cambodia has been ongoing for more than 25 years.[4] Rather, the politics of achieving genocide justice in Cambodia have proven to be particularly intractable. The interests of both Cambodian domestic actors as well as actors in the many other nations that have chosen to involve themselves in Cambodia's affairs over the last three decades have intersected to create a terrible political tangle, one which has yet to be unravelled.

At a 1995 conference organized in Phnom Penh by Yale University's Cambodian Genocide Program in cooperation with the US Department of State, then-Second Prime Minister Hun Sen delivered a keynote address, and in reference to the notion of a tribunal for the Khmer Rouge, he declared, 'This is not about politics, this is about justice'.[5] In reality, of course, issues of transitional justice and accountability for serious violations of international humanitarian law are always intensely political. The politics behind the attempt to bring about justice in Cambodia is the topic of this chapter. The ensuing analysis addresses various political aspects associated with the proposed Cambodia tribunal, including domestic and international political dimensions of the dilemma that has thus far frustrated attempts to achieve justice for the crimes of the Khmer Rouge regime.

---

[2] Craig Etcheson ' "The Number": Quantifying Crimes Against Humanity in Cambodia' (Documentation Center of Cambodia Phnom Penh 2000); and Henri Locard 'The Khmer Rouge Gulag: 17 April 1975–7 January 1979' (unpublished paper Paris 1995).

[3] See, eg, Steven R Ratner and Jason S Abrams *Accountability for Human Rights Atrocities in International Law: Beyond the Nuremberg Legacy* (Oxford University Press Oxford 1997); UN General Assembly, UN Security Council (16 March 1999) UN Doc A/53/850, S/1999/231, Annex; 'Report of the Group of Experts for Cambodia Established Pursuant to General Assembly Resolution 52/135'; the full text of the Report of the Group of Experts is available at www.khmerinstitute.org/docs/UNKRreport.htm. See also Stephen Heder with Brian D Tittemore *Seven Candidates for Prosecution: Accountability for the Crimes of the Khmer Rouge* (American University War Crimes Research Office Washington DC June 2001).

[4] For a review of this long struggle for justice, see 'The Persistence of Impunity' in Etcheson (*supra* n 1).

[5] Author's notes on Second Prime Minister Hun Sen's address to the International Conference on Striving for Justice: International Law in the Cambodian Context, Phnom Penh, 22 August 1995.

B. DOMESTIC POLITICS

1. The ruling party: Cambodian People's Party

Currently, Cambodia's ruling party is the Cambodian People's Party, or CPP. The CPP traces its roots to the same conference in 1951 which the Khmer Rouge cite as their founding congress. Most of the CPP's senior cadres began their careers as low- or mid-level Khmer Rouge functionaries, fled to Vietnam to escape Khmer Rouge leader Pol Pot's vicious purges, and then formed a Marxist-Leninist front which took power after a Vietnamese invasion ousted the Khmer Rouge regime in 1979.[6] In 1989, as the Vietnamese occupation forces withdrew from Cambodia, the party publicly abandoned socialism along with command-and-control economic policies, and adopted the name CPP. The party did not, however, abandon its internal Leninist structure and procedures, which it retains to this day.

Within the ruling party, there is a complex mix of views on the tribunal. Some are strongly opposed to the idea, others are strongly supportive, and strict rules of party discipline make it difficult to discern where the balance of opinion lies. Even so, it is possible to identify various viewpoints within the party. A group we may designate as the 'Nativists' opposes any UN involvement in a tribunal, reflecting an abiding revulsion at external interference in Cambodia's internal affairs. For these people, the sovereignty issue is their lodestone. It is easy to dismiss claims of 'sovereignty' as mere posturing, but to do so is to underestimate the psychological importance and emotional potency of the question after nearly a century of French colonialism, the Japanese occupation in the 1940s, the US intervention in the early 1970s, the Vietnamese occupation of the 1980s, and the UN 'transitional authority' in the early 1990s. The Royal Government of Cambodia is now accepted as a legitimate state among the community of nations, and some Cambodian leaders are determined that their regime be treated with the deference traditionally accorded to sovereign entities.

Another group, the 'Rejectionists,' opposes the idea of any tribunal at all, on the grounds that it could be harmful to the process of national reconciliation. People holding this view see peace, security, and stability as the central issues. This is also an easy position for outsiders to dismiss out of hand, particularly in view of the total collapse of the Khmer Rouge political and military organizations in 1998. But after continual civil strife from 1968 to 1998, the public hunger for peace and stability in Cambodia in the wake of the 'Thirty Years War' is palpable. Moreover, the Royal Government's security officials know that there are still many trained and armed

---

[6] An excellent recent history of the formative days of Cambodia's ruling party is Evan R Gottesman *Cambodia After the Khmer Rouge: Inside the Politics of Nation Building* (Yale University Press New Haven 2002).

Khmer Rouge cadre in the hinterlands, some of whom are still fanatically loyal to the old hard-line Khmer Rouge leadership. They also know that, for example, a small unit commando attack on a tourist hotel at the Kampong Som beach resort would be easy to execute, and would have a devastating impact on the country's number one legitimate source of hard currency, tourism.

A third grouping is what may be termed the 'Protectionists'. They oppose any international involvement in the tribunal on the grounds that too many core CPP cadre have too many skeletons in their closets. For those of this persuasion, maintaining the unity and solidarity of the ruling party is the primary objective. There are a number of core members of the party (none of the most prominent names one tends to see in the press, but important figures within the party nonetheless) who would be potentially liable to indictment by a free and unfettered prosecutor. The party elders are supremely reluctant to sacrifice any core members over the Khmer Rouge accountability issue.

Counterpoised against these various threads of opposition to a tribunal (or at least to UN involvement in a tribunal) is another set of views within the ruling party that tends to be supportive of the idea of genocide justice in Cambodia. 'Internationalists' understand that cooperation with the United Nations on the tribunal can bring many side benefits in the international arena, from increased bilateral and multilateral aid, to greater political credibility in regional fora such as ASEAN and global fora such as the UN General Assembly. They view a fully legitimized tribunal as a way for Cambodia to become a fully accepted member of the international community. 'Modernizers' look to the domestic benefits of a well-conducted tribunal, including combating the culture of impunity, weeding out undesirable elements in the party, and providing a salutary example of the value of an independent judiciary. This last element is particularly salient for the Modernizers, as many of them see that the existing weak judiciary severely limits the possibilities for foreign investment and economic development. The 'Triumphalists' view a full-scale, fully internationally legitimized tribunal as the final act of revenge against those who destroyed Cambodia's revolution and wrought so much havoc, the final nail in the Khmer Rouge coffin. They would also see a tribunal as the final 'proof' that the party's perception of its own historical role is correct.

Where is the balance of opinion in the ruling party? This is difficult to determine, but many Cambodia watchers tend to believe that a solid majority of the rank and file members support a tribunal. Among the party leadership, however, views are decidedly more mixed, with several key members of the party's policy-making Politburo clearly uneasy at the prospect of real justice for the Khmer Rouge. Consequently, the consensus-driven 'democratic centralism' of the CPP's policy-making body has thus far yielded only tentative, halting steps toward the establishment of an accountability mechanism to bring the Khmer Rouge leadership to book. But there are other domestic actors who further complicate the political calculus of genocide justice in Cambodia, beginning with the CPP's junior coalition partner in the government, the royalist party.

2. The royalists

The royalist party, FUNCINPEC, was founded in the early 1980s by the former and now once-again King, Norodom Sihanouk.[7] The party has always functioned as little more than a vehicle to serve the personal interests of the royal family. Norodom Sihanouk established FUNCINPEC because he wanted to play a role in expelling the Vietnamese forces occupying Cambodia after the overthrow of the Khmer Rouge regime. Not incidentally, he also wanted to regain the throne. He achieved the first goal in 1989, and the second in 1993. In the eyes of many Cambodians, however, the royalists' legacy, as well as Sihanouk's personal legitimacy, were compromised by the fact that in the 1980s they joined an exile government dominated by the Khmer Rouge.

Since the royalists took the lead in forming a national government following the UN-sponsored election in 1993, FUNCINPEC has appeared to function primarily as a mechanism to buttress the prospects that Sihanouk's son, Norodom Ranariddh, will succeed his father on the throne. As an elite organization largely led by members of the royal family and their courtiers, FUNCINPEC has had difficulty building and maintaining a mass following. The party's electoral and political fortunes have steadily eroded since their victory in the 1993 elections. The royalist party was badly damaged when the CPP ousted Ranariddh from his role as First Prime Minister in a bloody 1997 coup, on accusations that the royalists were once again scheming with the Khmer Rouge.

After the 1998 national elections, FUNCINPEC again entered a ruling coalition with the CPP, this time officially relegated to the role of junior partner, with Ranariddh installed as President of the National Assembly. Premier Hun Sen evidently promised Ranariddh that he would one day become king if he ceased openly to oppose the ruling party's policies and personalities. As a result, ever since, Ranariddh has been a supremely compliant junior coalition partner, a stance that has further eroded the royalist party's popular standing. In the 2002 commune elections, for example, the royalists won control in only 10 of Cambodia's 1,621 communes.[8]

---

[7] FUNCINPEC is the French acronym for National United Front for a Cooperative, Independent, Neutral and Peaceful Cambodia.

[8] See, eg, 'Cambodia Ruling Party Wins Big in Local Voting,' *International Herald Tribune* (27 February 2002).

In terms of tribunal politics, all of this means that both Ranariddh and the FUNCINPEC party he leads have been Hun Sen's willing pawns in Parliament. However, at the same time, the royalist party in some ways has tried to distance itself from the tribunal, hoping for political gain in the event that the tribunal process goes poorly. For example, Ranariddh was absent for the final vote in the National Assembly on the tribunal law, even though he is the leader of that body, asserting that he had to attend a birthday party. He has also occasionally voiced his opinion that vigorous UN participation is necessary in any trials in order to ensure due process for Khmer Rouge suspects. 'I don't believe that the tribunal process will follow that required in a court of law and within the justice framework, even if there is participation of foreign judges', Ranariddh told reporters after the United Nations withdrew from negotiations. '[Without the participation of the United Nations] there will be no guarantees about transparency and justice'.[9]

3. *The opposition*

The Sam Rainsy Party (SRP) is the vehicle for the political aspirations of its namesake, Sam Rainsy, and it functions as Cambodia's opposition—though the SRP is not necessarily what one would term a 'loyal opposition'. Rainsy's party is a splinter group from the royalist party, from which he was expelled in 1995 for his outspoken criticism of corruption in the government in general and FUNCINPEC in particular. SRP has a small minority of members in both Houses of Parliament. The party campaigns on a platform of good government, and its founder is notable both for his exceptional personal courage and his seemingly irrepressible energy, as well as for his often shrill style and erratic approach. Rainsy has opposed the Royal Government's plans for a tribunal, arguing instead for an ICTY-style proceeding that would, not incidentally, also charge Hun Sen with war crimes and other international crimes. Rainsy enjoys strong backing from the Republican caucus in the US House of Representatives, which in 1998 adopted a Sense of the House resolution supporting his call for an international criminal tribunal to prosecute Cambodian Prime Minister Hun Sen.[10] Rainsy and his Republican partisans in the US Congress are unhappy with the Cambodia tribunal that emerged from the UN negotiations because, among other things, Hun Sen does not qualify under the personal jurisdiction criteria ('senior leaders of Democratic Kampuchea and those who were most responsible for the crimes and serious violations') embodied in that tribunal. Hun Sen was the equivalent of a county sheriff during the Khmer Rouge regime,

---

[9] Vong Sokheng 'Ranariddh Prefers UN Trial Role' *Phnom Penh Post* (12–25 April 2002).

[10] H Res 533 'Expressing Sense of House of Representatives Regarding Culpability of Hun Sen for War Crimes, Crimes Against Humanity, and Genocide in Cambodia' US Congress, House of Representatives (10 October 1998).

and no evidence has emerged suggesting that he is implicated in any crimes in that period.

4. The king

The position of His Majesty the King on the tribunal is most complex, and as with most other aspects of Cambodian politics, mostly opaque.[11] At one time or another, King Sihanouk has taken every conceivable position on the merits of a tribunal—pro, con, and ambiguous. He retains a visceral hatred of the Khmer Rouge for what they did to his kingdom, not to mention the fact that while they held him prisoner in his palace, 14 of his children and grandchildren were executed by the Khmer Rouge.[12] But there is a lingering sense that he suffers from some strain of the 'Stockholm Syndrome', retaining feelings of loyalty to former Khmer Rouge Deputy Prime Minister and Foreign Minister Ieng Sary, who was responsible for minding the deposed monarch during the civil war in the first half of the 1970s as well as during the Democratic Kampuchea regime in the second half of the 1970s. In 1996, Sihanouk was persuaded by the government to grant a Royal Pardon to Ieng Sary, washing away the death sentence imposed upon Sary's conviction for genocide at the 1979 People's Revolutionary Tribunal.[13]

Sihanouk's power as king today is tightly circumscribed by both the Constitution and the wiles of the ruling party, though he still wields a certain amount of symbolic power and has the experience to know when to show it for maximum effect.[14] The king's principal interest in a tribunal may ultimately be as a forum to declaim his innocence, as some still whisper that none of this would have happened in the first place were it not for Sihanouk's vain alliance with the Khmer Rouge, seeking revenge against Lon Nol and his associates for ousting him in 1970.[15] Then there is also the fact of the king's long-standing warm relations with the People's Republic of China; he still maintains a palace in Beijing. The PRC's opposition to an international

[11] A penetrating biography of Sihanouk, long banned in Cambodia, is Milton Osborne *Sihanouk: Prince of Light, Prince of Darkness* (Silkworm Books Chiang Mai 1994).

[12] Sihanouk's house arrest and other abuses suffered at the hands of the Khmer Rouge are recounted in his memoir, Norodom Sihanouk, *Prisonnier des Khmers Rouges* (Hachette Paris 1986).

[13] For more information on the 1979 genocide trial, see Howard J DeNike, John Quigley, and Kenneth J Robinson (eds) *Genocide in Cambodia: Documents from the Trial of Pol Pot and Ieng Sary* (University of Pennsylvania Press Philadelphia 2000). For a discussion of Ieng Sary's pardon, see 'Approaches to Reconciliation' in Craig Etcheson *Retribution and Reconciliation: Healing What Ails Cambodia* (Project Report to the US Institute of Peace Washington DC October 2002).

[14] Cambodia's present and past Constitutions can be found in Raoul Jennar *The Cambodian Constitutions 1953–1993* (White Lotus Bangkok 1995).

[15] eg, see 'King Says He's Willing to Stand Trial Alongside Khmer Rouge' Associated Press (4 January 1999).

tribunal may have some influence on him. Even so, Sihanouk has always been a master practitioner of telling people what they want to hear, and thus different people come away from an audience with Sihanouk bearing diametrically opposed versions of what the King really believes regarding the tribunal issue.

5. *Khmer Rouge*

The Khmer Rouge themselves have proven to be an unexpected 'wild-card' in Cambodian tribunal politics. The 'post-Khmer Rouge' political organ created in 1996 by former Khmer Rouge chieftain Ieng Sary, known as the Democratic National United Movement (DNUM), has sought to present a unified political line on the question of the tribunal on behalf of all former Khmer Rouge. DNUM has been lobbying the government with a mixture of threats of a return to violence, carefully targeted financial inducements, and good old-fashioned politicking, to ensure a minimum footprint for any judicial accountability on genocide.[16]

Over the course of the last several years, however, it appears that the Khmer Rouge leadership has been losing control over their own rank and file personnel and/or former personnel. With the fragmenting of the formerly monolithic Khmer Rouge into many isolated groups scattered mostly around the western and northern border areas, and the disintegration of the party's mechanisms of discipline, their erstwhile followers have begun to ask difficult questions. Many are coming to wonder why, when they devoted their entire life to the revolution, were so many members of their family executed as enemies of the people? Such questions have led an increasing number of rank and file Khmer Rouge to openly call for a tribunal for their former leadership, in hopes of finding answers to this question.[17]

An interesting illustration of this trend occurred several years ago, when a Cambodian NGO, the Center for Social Development, organized a 'national reconciliation forum', with public meetings in three Cambodian cities.[18] The first of these fora was held in Battambang City, near the heart of Khmer Rouge territory. Of the more than 100 people attending the forum, approximately 75 per cent were Khmer Rouge. Only one speaker at the meeting had

---

[16] eg, see former Khmer Rouge President Khieu Samphan's recent statement suggesting that there would be 'retaliation' for any attempt to bring him and his other surviving senior colleagues to justice in a court of law. 'Khmer Rouge Heads Want Truth Commission Instead of Trial' Agence France Presse (1 December 2002).

[17] For more detail on Khmer Rouge opinions regarding a tribunal, see Etcheson (*supra* n 13) especially chs 2 and 6.

[18] Chea Vannath 'Khmer Rouge and National Reconciliation' Stockholm International Forum on Truth, Justice and Reconciliation, 23–24 April 2002; and *The Khmer Rouge and National Reconciliation: Opinions from the Cambodians* (Center for Social Development Phnom Penh April 2001).

the courage to openly advocate a tribunal and call for accountability for the crimes of the Khmer Rouge. Most of the speakers at the forum were Khmer Rouge leaders, carefully selected to present a cohesive message, and that message was the value of stability, the danger of renewed war, and the importance of letting bygones be bygones. However, at the end of the forum, the organizers distributed an anonymous questionnaire: 75 per cent of the respondents endorsed the concept of a tribunal for the Khmer Rouge leadership, which meant that at least half of the former Khmer Rouge in the audience agreed with that view. Events like this strike fear into the hearts of the old guard, and suggest they have lost the hearts and minds of their own people.

6. The public

What about the Cambodian public in general? The data on this question is mostly anecdotal, but there have been several surveys in recent years attempting to plumb the depths of public opinion on the tribunal question. The results of these surveys have been quite consistent, with strong majorities of respondents, from 75 to 85 per cent, favouring a tribunal for the Khmer Rouge leadership.[19] This is a somewhat curious result in view of the fact that Cambodia has no real history of formal justice in the Western sense. In Cambodia, courts and legal proceedings have historically been the venue to punish offences against the sovereign or the state, with little concern for the rights of individual citizens. It is not for nothing that the Cambodian word which means 'prisoner' or 'suspect' translates literally as 'the guilty one'.

Of course, the Cambodian people have plenty of reason to believe that the government wishes to punish the Khmer Rouge, after two decades of government vilification of the Khmer Rouge and warfare against them. Every 20 May, the official annual 'Day of Hatred' against the Khmer Rouge is still observed, notwithstanding the imperatives of national reconciliation. When one probes beneath the surface of public attitudes in favour of a tribunal, however, what most often comes out is not a wish for retributive punishment, but rather a desire for answers, for an explanation to the elusive, existential question, 'Why?'. Why did Pol Pot do it? Why did we have to suffer so much? Why was our country destroyed by its own children? Under most circumstances, the adversarial or accusatorial format of criminal prosecution is not the best venue for finding answers to such questions, and therefore a tribunal may ultimately raise more questions among the general public than it answers. But the people want it anyway.

---

[19] One of the most methodologically competent of these surveys is reported in 'Doit-on poursuivre les chefs des Khmers Rouges?' (1999) 5 *IFRASSORC Revue Trimestrielle* (April).

Might a truth commission or some other species of truth-telling mechanism more adequately address the 'why' question? The report of the UN Group of Experts suggested a truth-telling mechanism as an adjunct to, but not a replacement for, an ad hoc international tribunal.[20] In early 1999, the Cambodian government briefly flirted with the idea of entirely abandoning retributive justice measures in favour of a truth commission, but subsequently showed no interest in pursuing any type of truth-telling mechanism.[21] A 1997 survey of political elites carried out under the auspices of the Documentation Center of Cambodia suggests a possible reason why that idea was never followed up. The study found that a 'large majority' of those surveyed believed 'a truth commission could not take place in Cambodia'.[22] As suggested above, there are elements of Cambodia's political leadership who believe there are some truths that may be better left unsaid.

In summary, then, the ruling party's lack of internal cohesion on the tribunal question is reinforced by broad divisions among other members of the country's political elite on the issue. Given the widespread popular demand for genocide justice in Cambodia, Cambodia's non-Khmer Rouge political elite is virtually unanimous in loudly proclaiming the necessity and inevitability of a tribunal, but at the same time, that elite seems to have encountered endless obstacles in actually bringing about an accountability process. With this domestic political setting as the background, the role of international political actors in the process of bringing about genocide justice in Cambodia has been crucial, though no less problematical.

C. INTERNATIONAL DIMENSIONS

1. *ASEAN states*

In addition to the domestic actors, a variety of regional, global, supranational, and transnational actors have also played an active role in discussions of the genocide justice issue in Cambodia. First, by virtue of their geographical proximity, one must consider Cambodia's neighbours in the Association of Southeast Asian Nations (ASEAN). Of these, Thailand and Vietnam are special cases due to their shared borders and intimate involvement with the Khmer Rouge issue. Thailand and Vietnam both have very

[20] Ninian Stephen, Rajsoomer Lallah, and Steven R Ratner 'Report of the Group of Experts for Cambodia Pursuant to General Assembly Resolution 52/135' (18 February 1999), reproduced in Identical Letters from the Secretary-General to the President of the General Assembly and the President of the Security Council (15 March 1999) UN Doc A/53/850, S/1999/231 Annex. A truth-telling mechanism is discussed in the Report at 60.
[21] Letter from Cambodian Prime Minister Hun Sen to United Nations Secretary-General Kofi Annan (3 March 1999) on file with author.
[22] Jaya Ramji and Christine Barton '*Accounting for the Crimes of the Khmer Rouge: Interviews with Cambodians*' (Documentation Center of Cambodia Phnom Penh Summer 1997) 13.

complicated histories in Cambodia in general and with the Khmer Rouge, in particular. The Vietnamese Communists were, in a sense, marriage partners of the Khmer Rouge during the Second Indo-China War, though they soon sued for divorce, engaging the Khmer Rouge in the first full-scale war between socialist nations in the Third Indo-China War. Thailand followed a converse trajectory, beginning as an enemy of the Khmer Rouge, and ending up serving as a life preserver for their apocalypse by providing sanctuary and military support when the Vietnamese overthrew the Khmer Rouge regime.

Though Vietnam views the Khmer Rouge as a mortal enemy, they have several problems that have induced them to take a low profile on the issue of the tribunal. One of the first and foremost is that after their recent military occupation of Cambodia for more than a decade, they do not wish to expose themselves to further accusations of interfering in Cambodia's internal affairs. Fortunately for them, it is easy to avoid any such perception because Vietnam has a close relationship with Cambodia's ruling party, and hence there are many channels through which they are able to make their views known on any matter of concern. Another issue for the Vietnamese is their own rapprochement with the People's Republic of China, and their sensitivity to China's opposition to the idea of a Cambodia tribunal. The ruling Vietnamese Communist Party sees no need to rub this issue in the face of their friends in the Chinese Communist Party.

To a certain extent, the Vietnamese may have the sense that they had their say in 1979, when they orchestrated the People's Revolutionary Tribunal, condemning Pol Pot and Ieng Sary to death. Ultimately, being hardcore realists, the Vietnamese know that the Khmer Rouge are, regardless of the tribunal question, finished as a political or military threat. As things stand, the Vietnamese seem relatively satisfied with their current relationship to the authorities in Phnom Penh. This is not to say, however, that the Vietnamese always see eye-to-eye with Cambodia's ruling party on the Khmer Rouge issue, because the question of genocide justice has caused bilateral strains from time to time. For example, after Prime Minister Hun Sen received surrendering Khmer Rouge leaders Nuon Chea and Khieu Samphan and suggested that the Cambodian people should 'dig a hole and bury the past', the Vietnam People's Army newspaper lashed out and demanded a tribunal, saying that Khmer Rouge 'crimes cannot be forgotten and must be punished'.[23]

Thailand, likewise, finds itself in a somewhat tricky situation. For centuries, the Siamese have not been shy about their willingness to host and sponsor Cambodians who are trying to seize state power. However, their most recent episode of such sponsorship, backing the Khmer Rouge for

---

[23] 'Vietnam Newspaper: Time Cannot Erase Genocidal Khmer Rouge Crimes' Associated Press (6 January 1999).

nearly two decades after they were driven from the seat of power, ended badly, with their clients on the losing end of the game. The Thais are now on something of a campaign to make amends with the winner of that struggle. This was first concretely seen in their cooperation with the surrender of the final elements of the Khmer Rouge political leadership late in 1998, and the capture of the last Khmer Rouge military leader, Ta Mok, early in 1999. With the election of Prime Minister Thaksin Shinawatra, this turn in Thai diplomacy accelerated rapidly. For example, Kraisak Choonhaven, the Chairman of the Thai Senate Foreign Relations Committee, visited Cambodia in March 2001 and publicly admitted past Thai support for the Khmer Rouge—something previously unheard of—declaring that this policy had been wrong and that Thailand owed Cambodia an apology.[24] In this emerging environment, it appears likely that Thailand will support Cambodia on the tribunal, whatever final form that tribunal takes.

The remainder of the 10 ASEAN states share no consensus on the tribunal issue, reflecting the general political incoherence that has emerged in ASEAN since the expansion of ASEAN's traditional six members to the present slate of 10 nations. Generally speaking, Singapore and the Philippines have been strongly supportive of the tribunal idea, while Myanmar, Indonesia, and Malaysia have tended more toward a negative perspective. Laos and Brunei have been relatively neutral, consumed with their own internal issues.

Singapore, despite the mildly authoritarian one-party rule by the People's Action Party, seeks to promote its image as the most cosmopolitan state in South-east Asia. One element of this image is that Singapore often sides with European countries on issues of international humanitarian law. Likewise, the Philippines tends to take a modernist approach to issues of international law, a tendency that has not changed with the recent rise to power of Gloria Arroyo. The Philippines has from time to time expressed an interest in helping to deal with the tribunal issue, at one point even provisionally agreeing to seat an international Cambodia tribunal in Manila, as suggested in the January 1999 Report of the UN Group of Experts.[25]

As the pariah state of South-east Asia, Myanmar's military junta, the State Peace and Development Council (SPDC), does not tend to figure prominently in most regional political calculations. During Cambodian Prime Minister Hun Sen's occasional outbursts of nationalistic rhetoric on the tribunal issue, nonetheless, SPDC spokesmen routinely respond with approving noises, insofar as they have developed a visceral dislike for any and all UN enforcement mechanisms. Indonesia has so many problems of its own that it, too, has maintained a fairly low profile on many regional issues in recent years. This tendency has become even more pronounced under President

---

[24] Tom Fawthrop 'Thai Senator Urges Apology' *Phnom Penh Post* (16–29 March 2001).
[25] 'Report of the Group of Experts for Cambodia' (*supra* n 20).

Megawati's troubled administration. But the tribunal issue has been an exception to this rule. Fearful of being held accountable for the carnage wrought in East Timor by the Indonesian military, Indonesia has been in a mood to oppose reflexively the application of any external accountability measures for violations of international humanitarian law.[26] Malaysia's former Prime Minister Mahathir, with his unique conception of 'Asian Values', similarly bridles against any attempt to defend international law when it could potentially threaten the interests of a regional ruling elite.

Thus, there is not a strong consensus on the tribunal issue within ASEAN. This fact, combined with ASEAN's slightly frayed principle of non-interference in the internal affairs of its members, means that neither ASEAN collectively nor any of its members individually are likely to exert a great deal of influence on the issue of the Cambodia tribunal. Thus it is all the more remarkable that at the 35th annual ASEAN Ministerial Summit meeting in Bandar Seri Begawan on 30 July 2002, Cambodia's South-east Asian partners acquiesced in that government's request to issue a call for renewed engagement by the United Nations in the tribunal negotiations, and pledged to support the Royal Government's 'continued efforts' to bring the Khmer Rouge to justice.[27] In line with that commitment, in the December 2002 UN General Assembly vote on a resolution requesting that the UN Secretary-General resume negotiations with the Royal Government on the establishment of a tribunal, all 10 ASEAN members supported the Resolution.

2. China

The great powers have had more influence on the tribunal negotiations than have regional actors. One of the most closely concerned countries has been China, and its position has been clear. The Chinese take a very dim view of international involvement in a Cambodia tribunal, for several obvious reasons. For one thing, they consider the concept of prosecuting the leaders of an Asian Communist revolution for the deaths of millions of people during the revolution to be a very bad precedent indeed. Moreover, as the principal ally and patron of the Khmer Rouge for some 30 years, they have no wish to hear unfortunate references to their state-to-state and party-to-party relations with the Khmer Rouge discussed in a genocide court. Finally, the Chinese know the value of long-term loyalty towards allies, and they are not about to betray their long-standing solidarity with the Khmer Rouge; that would send a most unfortunate signal to everyone who they are courting today.

---

[26] See also Chapter 5 (de Bertodano).
[27] Joint Communique of 35th ASEAN Ministerial Meeting, Bandar Seri Begawan (29–30 July 2002) para 45.

As a result, the PRC has pursued an aggressive lobbying strategy, attempting to kill the tribunal before it is born. Chinese officials have made clear that they would veto any attempt by the UN Security Council to create a Cambodia tribunal under the Council's Chapter VI or VII powers.[28] They have relentlessly opposed the efforts by the UN bureaucracy to persuade the Cambodians to adopt structures for the tribunal that meet what Kofi Annan calls 'international standards'.[29] Chinese officials have been omnipresent in Cambodia over the last several years, including visits by President Jiang Zemin and Premier Zhu Rongji, showering Cambodia with gifts and favours. They have repeatedly fêted Cambodian ruling party President Chea Sim in Beijing. They have funded the construction of a new building in the National Assembly compound and another in the Senate compound. China is funding military demobilization, military procurement, landmine removal, flood relief, energy development, agricultural irrigation, and many other projects in Cambodia. In November 2002, Chinese Premier Zhu Rongji visited Phnom Penh and forgave the Khmer Rouge state debt to China, reportedly amounting to as much as US$2 billion dollars.[30]

There are certainly other reasons for the intense Chinese interest in Cambodia, above and beyond opposing an international tribunal for the Khmer Rouge. Particularly important motivations for Chinese foreign policy behaviour in Cambodia include developing a strategic salient against ASEAN, and challenging US influence in the region at large. But even so, one of the principal facets of Chinese diplomacy toward Cambodia over the last several years has been to make sure that any Cambodia tribunal will not be harmful to their interests.

3. *United States*

The United States government has also been a consistent player on the Cambodia tribunal issue, at least since the US Congress forced a change of policy in the early 1990s. Since the passage of the 1994 Cambodian Genocide Justice Act, the US government has faithfully implemented that law, which made it the 'policy of the United States to support efforts to bring to justice those accused of crimes against humanity' in Cambodia.[31] In the early years of the Clinton administration, this support was mostly in the form of

---

[28] See, eg, the comments of Chinese Foreign Minister Tang Jiaxuan in Greg Torode, 'Beijing May Veto Genocide Tribunal' *South China Morning Post* (6 February 1999).

[29] 'Ex-UN Official: China Tried to Stymie Khmer Rouge Trial' Associated Press (12 November 2000).

[30] See, eg, Ek Madra 'China Forgives Cambodia Khmer Rouge-Era Debt' Reuters (3 November 2002).

[31] Cambodian Genocide Justice Act United States Congress PL 103–236, 30 April 1994, 108 Stat 486; 22 USC 2656". For more information on the origin and implications of the Cambodian Genocide Justice Act, see Etcheson (*supra* n 1).

financial assistance to the investigations being carried out by Yale University's Cambodian Genocide Program.[32] In subsequent years, under the leadership of Secretary of State Madeline Albright, with the ball being carried by Ambassador-at-Large for War Crimes David Scheffer, numerous initiatives were launched in an attempt to bring about accountability for the Khmer Rouge leadership. These included looking at the possibility of domestic US prosecutions for the murder of US citizens by the Khmer Rouge; an ill-fated draft Statute for an ad hoc tribunal tabled at the UN Security Council; efforts to persuade allies such as Canada and Australia to agree to prosecutions under the theory of universal jurisdiction; a covert attempt to purchase Khmer Rouge leader Pol Pot from his rebellious troops in barter for rice and medicine; and finally, attempting to serve as an 'honest broker' in the ongoing negotiations between the United Nations and the Cambodian government for the proposed mixed tribunal.[33]

Though they have not altered the long-standing Clinton policy, the Bush administration policy on the Cambodia tribunal has been less energetic than the Clinton team's efforts. There are fault lines among Republican activists that have resulted in an internal struggle over this issue. Some favour a proliferation of ad hoc international tribunals, courts with carefully circumscribed mandates, as a way to undermine the mandate of the International Criminal Court. The results of this policy tendency can be seen in continued US support of a Cambodian tribunal, along with other tribunals including those for Sierra Leone, Kosovo, and East Timor. There has also been renewed talk of an Iraq Tribunal from some circles within the Bush administration.[34] This perspective is often represented inside the State Department by Ambassador-at-Large for War Crimes Pierre Prosper.

On the other side of the policy divide, there is a very different current of thought animated by a neo-conservative political orientation. For activists of this school, such as Assistant Secretary of State Lorne Craner, there remains unfinished business from the Cold War, personified by post-Communist characters as diverse as Slobodan Milosevic of Yugoslavia, Jose Eduardo Dos Santos of Angola, and Hun Sen of Cambodia. From this perspective, the priority must be on purging the authoritarian rumps left behind in the collapse of world socialism, and attempting to reinforce such democratic trends as may emerge in these countries. In Cambodia, this means opposing Hun Sen and his Cambodian People's Party, along with opposing any distraction from the primary project. Such distractions include things like a

---

[32] For background on the Cambodian Genocide Program, see Craig Etcheson *A Brief History of the Cambodian Genocide Program and the Documentation Center of Cambodia* (Documentation Center of Cambodia Phnom Penh September 2000).

[33] These US policy initiatives are detailed in 'Negotiating Retribution' in Etcheson (*supra* n 13).

[34] eg, see Peter Slevin 'US Would Seek to Try Hussein for War Crimes' *Washington Post* (31 October 2002).

Cambodia tribunal. Thus do some Republican foreign policy activists and organizations, such as the International Republican Institute (IRI), view the Cambodia tribunal proposal so dimly. It is significant that both the former President of IRI, Lorne Craner, and IRI's former Asia Director, Paul Grove, are now in positions of policy influence at the US Department of State and in the US Senate, respectively.[35]

The US Congress is split. The House of Representatives is divided on the issue, with the initiative held there by anti-tribunal voices such as California's Dana Rohrabacher. In the Senate, until early 2001, there was a solid bipartisan majority in favour of continued support for the tribunal. Some creative legislation on the Cambodia tribunal issue was put forward by Republican Senator Mitch McConnell.[36] In 2001, however, McConnell announced his opposition to the tribunal as currently envisioned, and called on the Bush administration to reverse the US policy of support for genocide justice in Cambodia. It remains to be seen if the Bush administration's political appointees will exhibit enough energy, and are willing to expend enough political capital, to overcome the institutional momentum of the career bureaucracy on this issue. Thus it is presently unclear whether either of these two orientations among Republican foreign policy activists will eventually come to dominate Bush administration policy on the Cambodia tribunal, or whether we will continue to see a muddled and ongoing struggle between the two.

4. Other Western pro-tribunal nations and the European Union

Of European countries with a lively interest in the Cambodia tribunal issue, the British, Dutch, Danish, Norwegians, and Swedish have shown the most consistent level of interest in and support for UN involvement in a Cambodia tribunal. Along with two large English-speaking nations, Canada and Australia, this group has encouraged movement in the tribunal negotiations process not only by diplomatic means, but through other measures as well. For example, all seven have provided direct funding to the Documentation Center of Cambodia, an NGO in Phnom Penh that since 1995 has been gathering evidence of violations of international humanitarian law during the Khmer Rouge regime in preparation for an eventual tribunal. These countries have pressed hard in seeking to improve the quality of jurisprudence at a Cambodia tribunal. In this respect, it is notable that six of these seven (Australia was the sole exception) abstained in a UN General Assembly

[35] Lorne Craner is Assistant Secretary of State for Democracy, Human Rights, and Labor; Paul Grove is a foreign policy aide to Republican Senate Whip Mitch McConnell.

[36] At one point, McConnell inserted a provision into the annual Foreign Operations Act conditioning US foreign aid to Cambodia on the Royal Government's cooperation with the international community on bringing about a tribunal.

vote on 18 December 2002.[37] That vote resulted in the adoption of a resolution requesting that Secretary-General Kofi Annan resume negotiations
with the Royal Government on the establishment and implementation of the
tribunal. The abstainers felt that the effort was flawed by Cambodia's refusal
officially to co-sponsor the resolution, as well as by the flaccid negotiating
mandate given to the Secretary-General in the resolution.

The European Union, as distinct from its individual Member States, has
also been strongly supportive of the tribunal process, sometimes demonstrating a more flexible approach than the sum total of its members' views. For
example, throughout 2002, the European Union advocated a resumption of
negotiations between the United Nations and the Cambodian government on
the tribunal.[38] However, although the overwhelming majority of European
Union Member States individually expressed dissatisfaction with the December 2002 UN General Assembly resolution that restarted those negotiations,
the European Union itself hailed the outcome of the talks resulting from the
Resolution in terms distinctly more welcoming than those expressed by most
of its Members States.[39]

5. Japan

Japan has shown a strong and consistent interest in Cambodia for more than a
decade, beginning with the appointment of a Japanese diplomat as head of the
UN peace-keeping mission in Cambodia in the early 1990s, and the concurrent first-ever dispatch of Japanese armed forces to participate in a UN peace-
keeping operation. The Japanese also serve as co-chair of the Consultative
Group, which is the international aid donors' mechanism for Cambodia that
arose out of the 1991–93 UN intervention. In addition, Japan has been the
single largest bilateral provider of aid to Cambodia over the last decade,
focusing on large-scale infrastructure projects, including bridges, roads,
ports, hydro dams, water distribution, telecommunications, and power
plants. Japan's focused interest in developing close relations with Cambodia
has been reflected in their posture on the Cambodia tribunal, as well.

Japan has offered to provide a jurist to serve as one of the international
judges on a mixed national–international tribunal for Cambodia.[40] Moreover,
according to some in the diplomatic community, Japan at one time contemplated a contribution of as much as US$60 million dollars to the funding of the

[37] The vote on the Resolution (18 December 2002) is recorded at UN Doc A/57/556/Add.2.
[38] eg, see Molly Ball and Thet Sambath 'EU Meets Government on KR Trial' *Cambodia
Daily* (19 April 2002).
[39] 'Cambodian Cabinet Approves Khmer Rouge Trial Draft' Agence France Presse (28
March 2003).
[40] Naoko Aoki 'Hun Sen to Resume Talks with UN over Khmer Rouge Trial' *Kyodo* (11
January 2000).

tribunal.[41] As a measure of relative commitment, compare that amount to the mere US$2 million dollars that had been earmarked for purpose of Cambodia tribunal support in US legislation, prior to the November 2002 US election, at least. As recently as December 2002, Japan co-authored with France the successful UN General Assembly Resolution urging the UN Secretariat to re-engage with the Cambodia tribunal process.[42] Thus the Japanese remain very interested in the prospects for a Cambodia tribunal, and they have been showing that interest in concrete ways.

6. Russia, India, and France

Though they have obvious differences, Russia, India, and France can be grouped together for purposes of analysing Cambodia's tribunal politics. These countries have divergent interests in the region in general and Cambodia in particular, but all three share a somewhat equivocal view of UN involvement in a Cambodia tribunal. All three countries would be likely to support a decision by the Cambodian government to proceed with a tribunal absent the participation of the United Nations. Russian and Indian lawyers, along with French journalists, attended the 1979 People's Revolutionary Tribunal in Phnom Penh, which sentenced Pol Pot and Ieng Sary to death *in absentia*. Twenty years later, lawyers from all three countries were invited to Cambodia to consult with the government as it crafted the tribunal law in 1999 and 2000.[43] India has been the most aggressive in paving the way for an independent Cambodian tribunal, with Prime Minister Atal Behari Vajpayee publicly announcing in Phnom Penh on 9 April 2002, that his country would provide judges and other aid for a Cambodia tribunal if the United Nations declined to be involved.[44]

Though France has cooperated with the United Nations on the tribunal issue in various ways, the French have sent mixed signals on the tribunal from time to time. A French legal scholar was one of the principal architects of the first draft of the Cambodian tribunal law,[45] though that draft was rejected by UN legal experts as hopelessly incompatible with international legal standards.[46] Officials at the UN Secretariat have complained privately

---

[41] See Luke Hunt 'Tribunal Judges to Come from Eight Countries' Agence France Presse (22 August 2001). By 2004, Japan was considering a much more modest financial contribution to the tribunal.

[42] (18 October 2002) UN Doc A/57/556/Add.2.

[43] See, eg, 'Cambodia Seeks Suggestions on Law to Try Khmer Rouge' *Kyodo* (5 November 1999).

[44] 'Indian PM Says to Consider Providing Judge for Khmer Rouge Trials' BBC Monitoring Service (9 April 2002).

[45] See, eg, Anette Marcher 'National KR Tribunal Takes Shape' *Phnom Penh Post* (26 November–9 December 1999).

[46] The Cambodian first draft of a tribunal law is Loi relative à la répression des crimes de génocide et des crimes contre l'humanité (August 2000) (typescript copy on file with author). The United Nations's criticism of this draft is detailed in 'Comments on the Draft Law Concerning

on numerous occasions about the French role in the tribunal negotiations, and this long-standing aggravation may have been exacerbated by the December 2002 General Assembly Resolution, co-authored by France, which forced the Secretariat back into the negotiations it had abandoned 10 months previously.

7. *United Nations*

There is also one supranational actor deserving mention—the United Nations itself. Most often in matters of high politics, the United Nations acts as an agent for the Member States, but in the Cambodia tribunal saga, the UN role has been partially autonomous and highly complex. Action by UN officials was central in driving the whole tribunal process forward for more than five years. In June 1997, two officials of the UN Office for Human Rights in Phnom Penh, David Hawk and Brad Adams, worked with the Secretary-General's Special Representative for Human Rights in Cambodia, Ambassador Thomas Hammarberg, to get the signatures of Cambodia's then-Co-Prime Ministers on a letter requesting UN assistance in setting up a Cambodia tribunal. In turn, this led to the Secretary-General's appointment of the UN Group of Experts, who examined the situation in late 1998 and recommended in January 1999 that the International Criminal Tribunal for the former Yugoslavia should essentially be cloned for Cambodia.[47] The Cambodian government flatly rejected that proposal, leading to four years of on-again, off-again negotiations by the UN Secretariat, represented by the UN's Office of Legal Affairs, attempting to find a formula acceptable to the Cambodian government.[48] This process resulted in the tribunal law which was promulgated in Phnom Penh, but which the United Nations found to be unsatisfactory.[49]

Why has the United Nations pushed so hard? Part of it is the product of pressures from the five permanent members of the UN Security Council. The Chinese have resisted with all their might, but the United States has pushed back even harder, with support from Britain and France, while the Russians

the Punishment of the Crime of Genocide and Crimes Against Humanity' memorandum provided to the Cambodian government by UN Assistant Secretary for Legal Affairs Ralph Zacklin (27 August 2000) (copy on file with author).

[47] 'Report of the Group of Experts for Cambodia' (*supra* n 20).

[48] These negotiations are analysed in detail in 'Negotiating Retribution' in Etcheson (*supra* n 13).

[49] The tribunal law was promulgated with King Sihanouk's signature on 10 August 2001, and is formally titled the Law on the Establishment of Extraordinary Chambers in the Courts of Cambodia for the Prosecution of Crimes Committed During the Period of Democratic Kampuchea. An official English translation of the law is available at www.ridi.org/boyle/kr_law_10_08_02.htm. The United Nation's announcement that it would terminate the negotiations included criticism of the law; see United Nations *Daily Press Briefing by the Office of the Spokesman for the Secretary-General* Press Release (8 February 2002).

have been mostly passive, but in any case have never posed a serious obstacle. The result of this correlation of forces has been political support for the UN Secretariat's initiatives on the tribunal. But perhaps a more significant factor has been an idiosyncratic one, in the person of the Secretary-General himself. Over the resistance of his own legal advisers, Hans Corell and Ralph Zacklin, Kofi Annan personally kept this project alive long after his Office of Legal Affairs began advocating a UN withdrawal. One factor seems to be that Annan felt he and the United Nations had something to prove after the United Nations's debacles in Rwanda and the Balkans. The Secretary-General has publicly commented many times about the United Nations's failure to protect the people of Rwanda in 1994, and has vowed that the United Nations will improve its performance on issues pertaining to genocide for the remainder of his tenure. But whatever Annan's motivation, there is no question about the fact that he has led the United Nations to play a key role in seeking accountability for the crimes of the Khmer Rouge.

8. Non-governmental actors

There are also some transnational non-state actors that have had a notable impact on the course of tribunal negotiations, including Amnesty International and Human Rights Watch. Both of these venerable human rights organizations were generally supportive of the proposal put forward by the UN Group of Experts for a cloning of the ad hoc tribunals, but both have been fiercely critical of the tribunal law ultimately adopted by the Royal Government.[50] They argue that the Law on the Extraordinary Chambers constitutes 'second-class justice' for Cambodia, and that it sets an unfortunate precedent for the enforcement of international humanitarian law in view of the International Criminal Court. UN officials have been remarkably sensitive to criticism from these human rights groups, and have privately noted their pleasure at the support they received from both Human Rights Watch and Amnesty International for the decision to withdraw from the tribunal negotiations in February 2002.

Another important transnational actor is the Documentation Center of Cambodia. The Documentation Center has played and continues to play a significant advocacy role not only within Cambodia, but also on the international stage.[51] The Documentation Center is intended to serve as a permanent institute for the study of the Khmer Rouge regime, and to provide

---

[50] eg, see 'Cambodia: Tribunal Must Meet International Standards' *Human Rights Watch* (12 February 2002); and 'Cambodia: Cambodians Deserve International Standards of Justice' Amnesty International (19 November 2002).

[51] In the interests of full disclosure, the author would like to note that he has been personally involved with the Documentation Center from its inception in January 1995, when it was founded as the field office of Yale University's Cambodian Genocide Program.

resources for anyone who wishes to pursue legal action against Khmer Rouge perpetrators. Since it became an independent institute in January 1997, the Documentation Center has continued to pursue those goals. On the Cambodian domestic political scene, in some respects, the Documentation Center is a force to be reckoned with. Among Cambodian politicians, all of whom have had some sort of connection to the Khmer Rouge, no one knows exactly what is contained in the one million pages of primary documents held by the Center. This fact contributes materially to the high level of deference accorded to the Documentation Center in almost all quarters. It is certain, however, that among the enormous archive of documents and other materials gathered by the Documentation Center, there is plenty of evidence to trouble the defence attorneys of the surviving Khmer Rouge leadership, should they ever be brought to justice.

In general, then, it can be said that there is strong support across all categories of actors in the international community for the principle of genocide justice in Cambodia. Those few that have taken an opposing view, primarily the People's Republic of China, have been able to block certain potential mechanisms, such as a Security Council-mandated organ, but have not been able to stem the rising tide of international support for a tribunal. Even so, the interplay of overlapping interests among those members of the international community who do support the idea of a Khmer Rouge tribunal has ensured that the negotiating process would be long and Byzantine. When one combines this welter of contending international interests with the complexities of Cambodia's political views on the tribunal, the issue becomes almost impossibly complex. We will now turn to a brief consideration of the complexities in the interaction of these two levels of analysis.

D. INTERACTION OF DOMESTIC AND INTERNATIONAL POLITICAL DIMENSIONS

Cambodian Prime Minister Hun Sen faces the challenge of balancing these competing domestic and international viewpoints. It is difficult to assess how the Prime Minister intends to accomplish this balancing act by reference to his statements, because his recorded statements on the tribunal issue are contradictory. Looking at how the Prime Minister has managed the issue thus far in terms of concrete action, however, one can register slow—very slow—forward progress toward some sort of tribunal, but the pace of that progress is so glacial that one can legitimately doubt whether or not it will ever arrive at its destination.

That Cambodia may never achieve real genocide justice is one distinct possibility. At a CPP Central Committee meeting in February of 2000, Hun Sen addressed the gathered core members of the party, reassuring an anti-tribunal cadre that there was no need to worry about the tribunal, because he had successfully stalled progress on the negotiations for the previous three years, and he would continue to stall the international community until all of the key suspects had died natural deaths, thus rendering the entire question moot. Did Hun Sen say this simply as a tactic to cut off debate among Central Committee members opposed to a tribunal, or did it reflect his real intentions? The available evidence is consistent with either interpretation. In July 2001, however, CPP members who are in favour of a tribunal asserted that the party's Politburo had forged an internal consensus to go ahead with the tribunal. Exactly when and under exactly what circumstances such a tribunal would go ahead remained somewhat ambiguous. Again, then, the available evidence as to the real intentions of the ruling party leadership on the tribunal appears to be inconclusive. It may well be that this is precisely the impression the ruling party leadership wishes to give, because there are incentives for the CPP to leave the international community guessing about where this issue will finally come to rest.

The Royal Government often insists that it desires international assistance for a tribunal, and it continues to seek further negotiations with the United Nations for the establishment of such a tribunal. Some countries, such as the United States, say that Cambodian cooperation with the international community on establishing Khmer Rouge trials is a requirement for continued foreign aid. The Royal Government has consistently told these countries that it is doing its best to cooperate with the international community in general and the United Nations in particular on the Khmer Rouge trials. In part as a reward for this cooperative attitude on the tribunal issue, the international community has provided billions of dollars in aid to Cambodia over the last several years.

Other countries, the People's Republic of China in particular, have made clear that they oppose an international tribunal for the Khmer Rouge. The Royal Government always tells these countries that it is following the 'Two Victories Policy'. One of those 'victories' is to 'forget the past'. Avoiding a tribunal is one way to forget the past. To help encourage this friendly attitude from the Royal Government, China has provided huge amounts of financial assistance to Cambodia, by some estimates as much as billions of dollars in just the last few years.

In these circumstances, the Royal Government has a strong economic incentive to delay a Khmer Rouge trial indefinitely. As long as no trial has been convened, but a trial is still possible, China will continue to shower gifts on the government, hoping to influence that decision. And as long as the Royal Government continues to negotiate with the rest of the international community about a Khmer Rouge trial, Europe, Japan, United States, and other countries will provide foreign aid as an incentive to encourage Cambodia to 'continue to move in the right direction'.

Thus, the mere prospect of Khmer Rouge trials has produced a financial windfall for the Royal Government. The possibility that a tribunal might be established keeps billions of dollars of assistance flowing into Cambodia, both from those who oppose as well as those who support the idea of a trial for the Khmer Rouge. A final decision to convene such a tribunal, or to conclusively reject the idea of a genocide trial, would eliminate this ambiguity and result in the alienation of one or the other of two crucial international constituencies the Royal Government has been courting. For this reason, it is reasonable to suspect that the Royal Government may never come to a final decision about whether, or when, or how, to bring justice to the victims of the Khmer Rouge.

In this respect, Hun Sen's management of the tribunal issue illustrates an important technique of 'weak power diplomacy'. Hun Sen has a tendency to tell everyone what they want to hear, and then he 'wobbles' a bit to keep everyone off-balance and continuing to beat a path to his door with add-itional inducements. It is a technique he learned from his best teacher, Norodom Sihanouk. To Chinese audiences, Hun Sen repeats the same man-tra: Cambodia is following the 'Two Victories' policy, which is to forget the past and concentrate only on the future—forgetting the past being the key phrase the Chinese want to hear. To US audiences, Hun Sen demands that the tribunal be convened before the end of this year (no matter what year one might be talking about) arguing that the Cambodian people deserve justice for the crimes of the Khmer Rouge regime. To French, Russian, and Indian audiences, he complains about the bullying of the sole superpower and the dangers of UN interference in one's internal affairs, while lauding the import-ance of national sovereignty. To Australian, Canadian, and Dutch audiences, he speaks of the need for Cambodia to move beyond its Communist past and put to rest the ghosts of the Cambodian genocide. To Japanese audiences, he talks of the importance of developing Cambodia's economy, and the crucial role a prosperous, modern, leading Asian nation like Japan can play in the growth and strategic stability of the entire region. Hun Sen is a superb tactician, and is reputed to be a master-level chess player. It shows in the way he manages both his domestic and foreign policy challenges.

In January 2003, the Royal Government and the UN Secretariat resumed negotiations on the modalities for establishing a Khmer Rouge tribunal. The respective opening positions of the two sides could hardly have been further apart. The chief Cambodian negotiator, Minister of the Council of Ministers, Sok An, pointed to the 18 December General Assembly Resolution's request that 'the Secretary-General ... resume negotiations, without delay, to con-clude an agreement with the Government of Cambodia, based on previous negotiations, to establish Extraordinary Chambers' for a tribunal. Conse-quently, he argued, the discussions should pick up where they left off in February 2002, accepting the August 2001 Law on the Establishment of the

Extraordinary Chambers as a baseline for discussions, and proceeding to a negotiation of the Memorandum of Understanding between the Royal Government and the United Nations.

For his part, the chief UN negotiator, UN Legal Counsel Hans Corell, asserted that the Cambodian side held an entirely incorrect interpretation of the General Assembly Resolution. He pointed out that the Resolution 'emphasizes' that the 'Extraordinary Chambers [must] exercise their jurisdiction in accordance with international standards of justice, fairness and due process of law', and that it also stresses 'the importance of ensuring the impartiality, independence and credibility of the process, in particular with regard to the status and work of the judges and prosecutors'. Corell argued that because the existing Cambodian Law on the Extraordinary Chambers fails to meet these requirements, it was necessary to abandon the Law on the Extraordinary Chambers, and to begin the negotiations all over again with a clean slate, starting with the United Nations's original proposals tabled in August 1999. The two delegations met repeatedly during the second week of January 2003, though no progress was achieved in narrowing the yawning chasm between their respective positions. On the final day of the January talks, Cambodian negotiator Sok An met with Secretary-General Kofi Annan, who informed Sok An that there was no point in holding any further negotiations until Prime Minister Hun Sen agreed in writing to the new conditions the UN Secretariat was demanding.

But Annan and Corell had seriously misjudged the will of the international community on the tribunal issue, and they had also misjudged the political 'savvy' of the Cambodian government. One month after the end of the January talks, a delegation of diplomats called on Annan and Corell to express their collective unhappiness with Corell's interpretation of the December General Assembly Resolution. Representatives of the United States, France, India, Japan, the Philippines, and Australia informed the two international civil servants that the General Assembly had taken responsibility for the issue, that the task of the Secretariat was now simply to conclude an agreement on the tribunal, and that they should do so with dispatch.[52] Later that same day, Cambodia's permanent representative to the United Nations delivered a letter from Hun Sen to Kofi Annan, a letter that had been prepared two weeks previously, inviting Corell to Phnom Penh to continue the discussions.[53]

The die had been cast. One month later, Corell was in Phnom Penh, and agreement was quickly reached. On 17 March 2003, Corell and Sok An announced that they had initialled a document outlining the relationship

---

[52] Tom Fawthrop 'Khmer Rouge: "Last Chance" for Justice' *Asia Times Online* (19 February 2003).

[53] 'Report of the Secretary-General on Khmer Rouge Trials' (31 March 2003) UN Doc A/57/769.

between the United Nations and the Cambodian government for the conduct of the tribunals. The details later revealed that the agreement had been reached almost entirely on Cambodia's terms.[54] On 2 May, the Third Committee of the UN General Assembly approved the draft agreement,[55] and 11 days later, a plenary session of the full General Assembly adopted the Third Committee's report by consensus.[56] On 6 June 2002, UN Legal Counsel Hans Corell was back in Phnom Penh for the formal signing ceremony, raising the tribunal agreement to the status of an international treaty.[57]

All that remained before the United Nations and Cambodia could move to implementation of the tribunal was for Cambodia's Parliament to ratify the agreement, along with a few amendments to the 2001 tribunal law mandated in the new text. Ratification was not likely to happen until some time after the installation of Cambodia's new National Assembly, following national elections on 27 July 2003. At the United Nations, sources suggested that donor pledges were accumulating rapidly for the Trust Fund that would finance the tribunal, and a scramble was already on among interested Member States to nominate candidates for the international positions on the tribunal. But as Corell noted before the signing ceremony, 'It's far too early' to say when the tribunal will actually be convened and begin issuing indictments.[58] Despite the rapid pace of developments during 2003, then, it appeared that the Cambodia tribunal would not be in place before the end of 2004 at the earliest, and more likely, not until some time in 2005.

Meanwhile, there are reports that the health of several of the principal suspects, particularly Nuon Chea, Ieng Sary, and Ta Mok, continues to deteriorate. The long and Byzantine international political negotiations required to reach agreement on an accountability mechanism for the crimes of the Khmer Rouge regime had already allowed several key perpetrators, including Pol Pot, Son Sen, Yun Yat, and Ke Pauk, to evade their day in court through death. In Cambodia, time is on the side of impunity, not on the side of justice. So it is that an entire people's hopes to achieve accountability for one of the worst episodes of mass murder in modern history continue to be held hostage to the politics of genocide justice.

[54] 'Report of the Secretary-General on Khmer Rouge Trials' (31 March 2003) UN Doc A/57/769.
[55] 'Third Committee Approves Draft Resolution on Khmer Rouge Trials' (2 May 2003) UN Doc GA/SHC/3734.
[56] UNGA Res 57/228 on Khmer Rouge Trials (22 May 2003).
[57] Ker Munthit 'Cambodia, UN Sign Genocide Trial Pact' Associated Press (6 June 2003).
[58] Ker Munthit 'UN Chief Legal Counsel to Sign Genocide Tribunal Accord' Associated Press (5 June 2003).

11

The Extraordinary Chambers in the Courts of Cambodia for Prosecuting Crimes Committed by the Khmer Rouge: Jurisdiction, Organization, and Procedure of an Internationalized National Tribunal

*Ernestine E. Meijer**

A. INTRODUCTION

This chapter discusses certain aspects of the Extraordinary Chambers in the Courts of Cambodia (the 'Extraordinary Chambers'). It will focus in particular on the jurisdiction, organization and procedure of the Extraordinary Chambers. Elsewhere in this book a comprehensive overview of the historically relevant events[1] leading to the creation of the Extraordinary Chambers and a detailed description of the political background[2] is given. This chapter will only briefly go into the historical and political aspects, limiting it to the last phase of the negotiations between the United Nations and the Cambodian government which led to the adoption of the Agreement between the United Nations and the Royal Government of Cambodia concerning the Prosecution under Cambodian Law of Crimes Committed during the Period of Democratic Kampuchea ('the United Nations–Cambodia Agreement' or 'the Agreement').[3]

In 2001 the Cambodian government passed the Law on the Establishment of Extraordinary Chambers in the Courts of Cambodia for the Prosecution of Crimes Committed during the Period of Democratic Kampuchea ('the Law').[4] This law settled several of the legal and political controversies between the Secretary-General and the Cambodian government (unresolved

---

* Ernestine E Meijer was attorney-at-law with Van den Biesen advocaten in Amsterdam, and is currently a senior research fellow at New York University School of Law.

[1] See Chapter 12 (Romano).

[2] See Chapter 10 (Etcheson), and Chapter 2 (Shraga).

[3] For the official text, see UNGA Res 57/228B (22 May 2003).

[4] Law NS/RKM/0801/12, adopted in its final version by the National Assembly on 11 July 2001, approved by the Senate on 23 July 2001, pronounced as being fully in accordance with the Constitution by the Constitutional Council in its Decision 043/005/2001 KBTh Ch (7 August 2001) and signed by the Cambodian king on 10 August 2001 (translation in English: http://csf.colorado.edu/bcas/main-cas/camb-law.htm/ and www.derechos.org/human-rights/seasia/doc/krlaw.html).

in the previous negotiations) in favour of the Cambodian government. Confronted with this unsatisfactory *fait accompli* the Secretary-General decided on 8 February 2002 to leave the negotiations.[5]

In the spring of 2003, the Secretary-General, backed by General Assembly Resolution 57, 228,[6] resumed negotiations with the Cambodian government and in March 2003 it was announced that the United Nations and the Cambodian government had reached the Agreement. Both parties had agreed that the Agreement would have priority over the Law and that those provisions of the Law that did not correspond with the Agreement would be altered to fit the Agreement. In a report of 31 March 2003 to the General Assembly[7] the Secretary-General explained the course of the negotiations, how the General Assembly Resolution 57, 228 had been incorporated in the Agreement, the compromises that had been made by both parties, and the practical steps that would need to be taken to implement the Agreement. The Secretary-General expressed doubts about the Agreement, but pointed to the clause in the Agreement on the withdrawal of cooperation and assistance by the United Nations:

Should the Royal Government of Cambodia change the structure or organization of the Extraordinary Chambers or otherwise cause them to function in a manner that does not conform with the terms of the present Agreement, the United Nations reserves the right to cease to provide assistance, financial or otherwise, pursuant to the present Agreement.[8]

In the following, where necessary or elucidative, attention will be given to details of the history of the conflicting positions of the Cambodian government on the one hand and the Secretary-General on the other.

The General Assembly adopted the Agreement on 22 May 2003.[9] On 6 June 2003 the United Nations and the Cambodian government signed the Agreement. The text of the Agreement now awaits ratification by the newly elected Cambodian Parliament.[10] The text of the Law will need to be altered to fit the Agreement. At the time of writing of this chapter, the Agreement has not been ratified by the Cambodian Parliament and the provisions of the Law have not been changed, therefore all conclusions drawn in this chapter

---

[5] See statement and press briefing by UN Legal Counsel Hans Corell (8 February 2002) (www.un.org/News/dh/infocus/cambodia/corell-brief.htm and www.un.org/News/briefings/docs/2002/db020802.doc.htm).
 [6] UNGA Res 57/228 (27 February 2003).
 [7] UN Doc A/57/769.
 [8] Article 28 of the Agreement.
 [9] UNGA Res 57/228B.
 [10] Ratification by Cambodia is of the utmost importance. Article 30 of the Agreement prescribes that the Agreement will only be binding on the parties after it has been approved by the UN General Assembly (the UNGA has approved the agreement) *and after it has been ratified by Cambodia.*

regarding the structure and functioning of the Extraordinary Chambers are to be considered provisional.

B. RELATIONSHIP BETWEEN THE UNITED NATIONS–CAMBODIA AGREEMENT AND CAMBODIAN LAW

One of the most important reasons for the Secretary-General to break off negotiations with the Cambodian government in February 2002 was the position the Cambodian government had taken in respect of the relationship between the envisaged Agreement (at the time called the 'Memorandum of Understanding' or 'Articles of Cooperation') and the Law. An exchange of letters between the Cambodian government and the United Nations illustrates this. On 23 November 2001 the Cambodian Minister Sok An wrote to the UN Legal Counsel Hans Corell:

While the Articles of Cooperation may clarify certain nuances in the Law, and elaborate certain details, it is not possible for them to modify, let alone prevail over, a law that has just been promulgated.[11]

The UN Secretary-General's position was the complete opposite:

It has been the United Nations' consistent position that the Organization cannot be bound by a national law. Hence, the United Nations insisted throughout the negotiations, in accordance with the usual practice in concluding international agreements, that the United Nations and the Government should reach a controlling agreement. In addition, it has been the consistent position of the United Nations that the Law would have to conform to the contents of the agreement.[12]

The resumed negotiations in the spring of 2003 led the Secretary-General to conclude on this specific issue:

As it is now formulated, that text [of the Agreement], if it were to enter into force, would constitute an international agreement between the United Nations and Cambodia, which would fall to be implemented in accordance with the requirements of the law of treaties.... The draft agreement further specifies that it would apply as law within Cambodia. It follows from these provisions that Cambodia would be obligated to ensure that its national law conformed with the agreement and, to the extent that it did not do so, to amend its law in order to make it do so. Thereafter, Cambodia could not amend its national law except in a manner that was consistent with the provisions of the draft agreement.[13]

---

[11] See www.camnet.com.kh/ocm/government/government116.htm.
[12] Statement of 8 February 2002 (www.un.org/News/dh/infocus/cambodia/corell-brief.htm).
[13] See 'Report Secretary-General' (31 March 2003), UN Doc A/57/769, p 10.

All of this was laid down in Articles 2 and 31 of the United Nations–Cambodia Agreement which, in as far as relevant, read:

Article 2 The Law on the Establishment of Extraordinary Chambers

...

2. The present Agreement shall be implemented in Cambodia through the Law on the Establishment of the Extraordinary Chambers as adopted and amended. The Vienna Convention on the Law of Treaties, and in particular its Articles 26 and 27, applies to the Agreement.
3. In case amendments to the Law on the Establishment of the Extraordinary Chambers are deemed necessary, such amendments shall always be preceded by consultations between the parties.

Article 31 Application within Cambodia
The present Agreement shall apply as law within the Kingdom of Cambodia following its ratification in accordance with the relevant provisions of the internal law of the Kingdom of Cambodia regarding competence to conclude treaties.

The Agreement makes very clear that the United Nations–Cambodia Agreement prevails over the Law on the Extraordinary Chambers. However, the United Nations–Cambodia Agreement does not stipulate that the Law on the Establishment of Extraordinary Chambers should be *limited* to the implementation of the Agreement. This hierarchy between the Agreement and the Law is clear but the text of Articles 2 and 31 does generate confusion of a dogmatic nature. Article 2 provides for the Agreement to be implemented through the Law (implying that the Agreement itself has no direct effect in Cambodia, which can be characterized as a dualistic approach to the relationship between international and national law) whereas Article 31 of the Agreement provides that the Agreement applies *as law* (implying that the Agreement *does* have direct effect in Cambodia and does *not* need implementation in national law, which can be characterized as a monistic approach).

The choice for either dualism or monism is relevant only when in respect of a certain subject the national legal instrument (the Law) is less detailed than the international legal instrument (the Agreement) and the provisions of both instruments are not contradictory. In that situation the dualistic approach would require that the Law is amended and the Agreement's details are added to the Law, whereas in the monistic approach, the details would apply directly through the Agreement and no amendment of the Law would be necessary. The Cambodian Constitution does not shed any light on whether dualism (Article 2) or monism (Article 31) prevails in Cambodia.[14]

In all other situations there is no difference between monism and dualism:

---

[14] Constitution of the Kingdom of Cambodia, adopted by the Constitutional Council on 21 September 1993, amendments passed on 4 March 1999.

(a) when the provisions of the Law are less detailed than the Agreement and the Law is not in conformity with the Agreement, the Law needs to be adapted;
(b) when the provisions of the Law are more detailed than the Agreement and the Law is not in conformity with the Agreement, the Law needs to be adapted;
(c) when the provisions of the Law are more detailed than the Agreement and the Law and Agreement are not contradictory, the Law does not have to be adapted.

Based on the implicit content of the letter of 23 November 2001 of Minister Sok An[15] and on the Report of the Secretary-General of 31 March 2003,[16] we shall assume in this chapter that (moderate) dualism prevails within the Cambodian state structure, so if in respect of a certain subject the Law is less detailed than, but not contradictory to, the Agreement we shall assume that the Law needs to be amended and the Agreement's details added to the Law. However, it needs to be kept in mind that this is a mere assumption.

C. JURISDICTION

1. Temporal jurisdiction

Under the Agreement and the Law, the temporal jurisdiction of the Extraordinary Chambers extends from 17 April 1975 to 6 January 1979.[17] The period covered is the height of the reign of the Khmer Rouge.[18] It is not unusual for an internationalized judicial body to have jurisdiction only in respect of crimes committed during a specific period of time.[19] Yet it needs to be kept in mind that crimes such as the ones within the subject matter jurisdiction of the Extraordinary Chambers have been committed before *and* after this period. The Cambodian conflict, in reality, engulfed the country in violence from at least the end of the 1960s to the early 1990s and if a more expansive approach were to be taken to the conflict, similar events in Laos, Thailand, and Vietnam would also have to be considered.

[15] See *supra* n 11.

[16] At 10: 'It follows from these provisions that Cambodia would be obligated to ensure that its national law conformed with the agreement and, to the extent that it did not do so, to amend its law in order to make it do so'. International law such as the Agreement does not seem to apply directly within Cambodia, Cambodian law is used as a 'vehicle' for the provisions of the Agreement.

[17] First and third preambular paragraph, Arts 1, 5 and 6 of the Agreement; Arts 1 to 8 of the Law.

[18] 17 April 1975 being the date the Khmer Rouge overthrew Lon Nol and established Democratic Kampuchea and 6 January 1979 the date Pol Pot and the Khmer Rouge were overthrown by Vietnamese troops.

[19] The temporal jurisdiction of the special court for Sierra Leone is, eg, 'for serious violations of international humanitarian law and Sierra Leonean law committed in the territory of Sierra Leone since 30 November 1996'.

The choice to limit the temporal jurisdiction to the period from 17 April 1975 to 6 January 1979 was, at least in part, a pragmatic one, founded on the wish not to overburden the Extraordinary Chambers, the wish to enable the Extraordinary Chambers after their establishment to start their work promptly and the wish to limit the financial and human resources needed.

2. Subject matter jurisdiction

The Agreement repeatedly and in different levels of detail enumerates the crimes which are within the subject matter jurisdiction of the Extraordinary Chambers. In the third preambular paragraph it is stated in a general way that these are: 'crimes and serious violations of Cambodian penal law, international humanitarian law and custom, and international conventions recognized by Cambodia'. This is repeated in Article 1 of the Agreement, while Article 2, paragraph 1, provides that 'the Extraordinary Chambers have subject-matter jurisdiction consistent with that set forth in "the Law on the Establishment of the Extraordinary Chambers . . . " as adopted and amended by the Cambodian Legislature under the Constitution of Cambodia'.[20]

The reference to the Law in Article 2 notwithstanding, Article 9 of the Agreement gives a more detailed description of the crimes in question and lists:

the crime of genocide as defined in the 1948 Convention on the Prevention and Punishment of the Crime of Genocide, crimes against humanity as defined in the 1998 Rome Statute of the International Criminal Court and grave breaches of the 1949 Geneva Conventions and such other crimes as defined in Chapter II of the Law on the Establishment of the Extraordinary Chambers as promulgated on 10 August 2001.

The international crimes mentioned in the Agreement (genocide, crimes against humanity and grave breaches of the 1949 Geneva Conventions) can also be found in the Law. However, the definitions used in the Law are not identical to the definitions referred to in the Agreement.

The definition of genocide in the Law[21] duplicates the definition of Article 2 of the 1948 Genocide Convention. However, where the Law tries to duplicate Article 3 of the Genocide Convention, it is not identical. Contrary to Article 3 of the Genocide Convention, the Law does not allow for acts of 'direct and public incitement to commit genocide'[22] and 'complicity in genocide'[23] to fall under the subject matter jurisdiction of the Extraordinary Chambers. On the other hand 'participation in acts of genocide' is not

---

[20] This is in conformity with UNGA Res 57/228, under 2.
[21] Article 4 of the Law.   [22] Article 3(c) of the Genocide Convention.
[23] ibid Article 3(e).

mentioned in Article 3 of the Genocide Convention, but it does fall under the subject matter jurisdiction of the Extraordinary Chambers.[24]

As to crimes against humanity, the Law[25] is somewhat more limited than the Statute of the International Criminal Court, referred to in Article 9 of the Agreement.[26] More specifically, the Statute inter alia states as crimes against humanity:

— 'imprisonment or other severe deprivation of physical liberty in violation of fundamental rules of international law';[27]
— 'rape, sexual slavery, enforced prostitution, forced pregnancy, enforced sterilization, or any other form of sexual violence of comparable gravity';[28] and
— 'persecution against any identifiable group or collectivity on political, racial, national, ethnic, cultural, religious, gender..., or other grounds that are universally recognized as impermissible under international law, in connection with any act referred to in this paragraph or any crime within the jurisdiction of the Court'.[29]

The Law, on the other hand, refers only to, respectively:

— 'imprisonment';
— 'rape', and
— 'persecutions on political and religious grounds'.[30]

Moreover, the crime against humanity of 'enforced disappearance of persons'[31] is not in the Law at all. However, the use of the words 'crimes against humanity...*such as*'[32] in the text of the Law indicates that its enumeration of crimes is only indicative and not exhaustive.

When the more detailed description of the subject matter jurisdiction in Article 9 of the Agreement is compared with the subject matter jurisdiction as formulated in the Law (Chapter II), we can conclude that the two are not identical. In respect of two of the three categories of international crimes (genocide and crimes against humanity) the Law lacks clarity. The enumeration of the crimes in the Law does not match with the international legal instruments referred to in the Agreement.

In order to make the Law consistent with Article 9 of the Agreement, either the enumeration in the Law should be eliminated and replaced by a rule of reference, or the enumeration should be made fully consistent with the international legal instruments specified in Article 9 of the Agreement. The

---

[24] As to the practical and conceptual difficulties arising from the definition of genocide in the Genocide Convention, see Chapter 2 (Shraga).
[25] Article 5 of the Law.   [26] Statute of the International Criminal Court, Art 7.
[27] ibid Art 7(e).   [28] ibid Art 7(g).
[29] ibid Art 7(h).
[30] Article 5 of the Law.
[31] Statute of the International Criminal Court, Art 7(i).
[32] Article 5 of the Law, emphasis added.

former approach was adopted in the Law with regard to the other remaining crimes under international law, namely the destruction of cultural property[33] and crimes against internationally protected persons:[34] these are not defined separately in the Law, but the Law relies on the international definition of these crimes instead.[35]

3. Personal jurisdiction

The Agreement and the Law are identical as to which persons should be brought to justice, namely 'senior leaders of Democratic Kampuchea and those who were most responsible for the crimes and serious violations'.[36] This formulation of the Chambers' personal jurisdiction is open to different interpretations and shows the highly political and practical decisions that had to be made to get support within Cambodia for the Extraordinary Chambers.[37]

Questions that arise when reading this definition are how seniority is to be defined and how it can be established that a person is 'most responsible' (as opposed to, for example, 'more responsible' or 'substantially responsible'). These issues will have to be decided by the Extraordinary Chambers. Assuming that the Special Court for Sierra Leone, which has to decide on similar issues,[38] will rule on these matters before the Extraordinary Chambers start their work, guidance may be sought in the case law of the Special Court.

4. Amnesty

In 1979 a trial *in abstentia* was held in Cambodia in which Ieng Sary and Pol Pot were convicted of genocide.[39] In August 1996 the Cambodian king granted Ieng Sary amnesty, not only from his 1979 conviction for genocide but also from prosecution under a 1994 Cambodian Law which outlawed the Khmer Rouge.[40]

The United Nations at first held the position that an amnesty decreed on a national level could not apply to international crimes such as genocide. The Cambodian government, however, refused to repeal the amnesty for Ieng Sary. It had therefore included in the Law that it would not request any

---

[33] Pursuant to the 1954 Hague Convention for Protection of Cultural Property in the Event of Armed Conflict; Article 7 of the Law.

[34] Pursuant to the 1961 Vienna Convention on Diplomatic Relations; Art 8 of the Law.

[35] Articles 7 and 8 of the Law.

[36] Third preambular paragraph and Arts 1, 2, 5 and 6 of the Agreement; Arts 1 and 2 of the Law.

[37] See Chapter 10 (Etcheson).

[38] See Art 1 para 1 of the Statute of the Special Court for Sierra Leone.

[39] Judgment of the People's Revolutionary Court of Phnom Penh of 19 August 1979.

[40] Law on the Outlawing of the Democratic Kampuchea Group (15 July 1994).

further amnesty or pardon for persons investigated or convicted of one or more of the crimes under the jurisdiction of the Extraordinary Chambers.[41] This implied that the existing amnesty of Ieng Sary would be maintained. A compromise was found[42] for the text of the Agreement, with the effect that it is now a matter for the Extraordinary Chambers to decide to what extent Ieng Sary's amnesty will serve to bar his prosecution or conviction.[43] The Law will have to be amended accordingly.

D. GENERAL PRINCIPLES OF CRIMINAL LAW

1. Statute of limitations

The Agreement does not contain any provisions on a statute of limitations for the crimes within the jurisdiction of the Extraordinary Chambers, nor does it claim the non-applicability of a statute of limitations.[44] The drafters presumably took the position that for crimes against humanity, as well as the other international crimes, no statute of limitations applies. However, for the crimes under national criminal law of homicide, torture, and religious persecution,[45] the situation is different.[46] The 1956 Cambodian Criminal Code has a statute of limitations of 10 years and the Law on the Establishment of the Extraordinary Chambers has extended the limitation period for these crimes with 20 more years.[47]

This extension of the statute of limitations raises two questions, to which the available legal instruments do not provide an answer. First, can the Law have any effect on crimes for which the limitation period had already ended before the Law came into effect (under the 1956 Criminal Code the possibility to judge these crimes ended between 17 April 1985 and 6 January 1989)?[48] Has the possibility of trying these crimes simply revived by the entry into force of the Law? It is questionable whether affirmative answers to these questions are in conformity with the criminal law principle of non-retroactivity.

---

[41] Article 40 of the Law.

[42] See 'Report of the Secretary-General' (31 March 2003) UN Doc A/57/769, p 8.

[43] Article 11, para 2 of the Agreement.

[44] Like, eg, Art 29 of the Statute of the International Criminal Court.

[45] Crimes to which the Agreement refers in Art 2, para 1 by referring to the Law.

[46] For torture and religious persecution the situation is only different in as far as they are *not* committed as part of a widespread or systematic attack directed against any civilian population, with knowledge of the attack. If they *are* part of such an attack, they are considered crimes against humanity and the statute of limitations does not apply.

[47] Article 3 of the Law.

[48] The Law has no retroactive effect. It is in effect since it was signed by the Cambodian king on 10 August 2001. The Agreement also does not have retroactive effect. According to Art 32 of the Agreement, it shall enter into force on the day after both parties have notified each other in writing that the legal requirements for entry into force have been complied with. This will be after ratification of the Agreement by Cambodia.

Secondly, it appears to be the intention of the Law that the extension of the limitation period *only* applies in respect of the crimes of homicide, torture, and religious persecution when they are tried by the Extraordinary Chambers, since the Law extends the statute of limitations for the crimes of homicide, torture, and religious persecution 'which are within the jurisdiction of the Extraordinary Chambers'.[49] If this is true, it means that a person falling within the personal jurisdiction of the Extraordinary Chambers can be tried for homicide, torture, or religious persecution for 20 more years than any other person who committed homicide, torture, or religious persecution during the same period (who cannot be brought before the Extraordinary Chambers). One could argue that this is not consistent with the principle of equality before the law.

If the 20-year extension of the statute of limitations is upheld, the possibility to bring to trial those who committed the crimes of homicide, torture, and religious persecution during the height of the Khmer Rouge regime will expire between 17 April 2005 and 6 January 2009. Considering the speed of the establishment of the Extraordinary Chambers so far, it is not unlikely that some of the leaders and those most responsible will not be tried for these specific crimes due to preclusion of the right to prosecute by reason of lapse of time.[50]

2. Individual responsibility

The Agreement implies that acts within the jurisdiction of the Extraordinary Chambers engage the individual responsibility of the perpetrators but it does not detail the conditions and modalities of such responsibility. Article 29 of the Law *does* elaborate on the individual responsibility of those who fall under the jurisdiction of the Extraordinary Chambers.[51]

Those who plan, instigate, order, aid, abet or commit the crimes are individually responsible. This provision is comparable to Article 25 of the Statute of the International Criminal Court, but less elaborate. To name just two differences: the Law does not explicitly make punishable the act of providing the *means* for the commission of a crime[52] and the Law does not make punishable the *attempt* to commit a crime.[53]

Position or rank in the Khmer Rouge organization will not per se relieve a person of criminal responsibility and does not preclude that a relatively low-

---

[49] Article 3 of the Law.

[50] During a meeting in February 2000 of the Cambodian People's Party, Prime Minister Hun Sen told his party that he would stall the establishment of the Extraordinary Chambers long enough for all key suspects to have died a natural death. See Chapter 10 (Etcheson).

[51] The Agreement contains no provisions to this effect.

[52] Unlike Art 25, para 3(c) of the Statute of the International Criminal Court.

[53] Unlike ibid Art 25 para 3(f).

ranking officer can be 'most responsible'. The responsibility of a low-ranking officer does not dissolve because of the fact that he or she committed a crime while following an order, and a high-ranking officer has full criminal responsibility if a subordinate committed a crime under either his or her effective command and control or his or her authority and control, if the superior knew or had reason to know that the subordinate was about to commit such acts or had done so and the superior failed to take the necessary and reasonable measures to prevent or punish such acts.

The provision in the Law that the fact that a low-ranking officer was following an order does not take away his or her responsibility, introduces a standard that is more strict than, for example, the Statute of the International Criminal Court,[54] and somewhat more strict than, for example, the Regulation on the Special Panels in East Timor.[55]

E. ORGANIZATION OF THE EXTRAORDINARY CHAMBERS

A reoccurring source of conflict between the United Nations and the Cambodian government has been the organization of the Extraordinary Chambers.

1. Structure

From the outset, the Cambodian government opted for a three-tier structure: a trial court, an appeals court, and a supreme court.[56] The appeals court would decide on errors of fact and errors of law, either affirming, reversing, or modifying the decision of the trial court. The supreme court would make final decisions on facts and law (and not return the case to the appeals court). This is the structure laid down in the Law.[57]

In contrast, the United Nations was in favour of a (less extensive) two-tier structure, for several reasons. First of all, swift proceedings were considered important because some of the Khmer Rouge leaders eligible for prosecution are old and not in a good physical condition. If proceedings would be long and cumbersome, these leaders might be dead or physically unable to stand trial. Secondly, the prolonged Cambodian statute of limitations would make prosecution impossible by 6 January 2009 at the very latest. Thirdly,

---

[54] See ibid Art 25, para 3(a) and Art 28(b), which place responsibility for the crimes committed pursuant to an order with the superior giving the order.

[55] See UNTAET Reg 2000/15 (on the Establishment of Panels with Exclusive Jurisdiction over Serious Criminal Offences), s 21, which explicitly allows the fact that an accused person acted pursuant to an order of a government or of a superior to be considered in mitigation of punishment.

[56] The same structure as its 'regular' court system.

[57] Article 9 of the Law.

a two-tier structure would be less costly but it would still satisfy the minimal human rights requirement that there should be a possibility to appeal a criminal conviction.[58] The General Assembly in its Resolution of 27 February 2003 also requested that the structure of the Extraordinary Chambers be two-tiered.[59] In the negotiations following the Resolution, the Secretary-General objected to the more elaborate system laid down in the Law as it was considered 'highly complex' and 'afforded ample scope for obstruction and delay in the conduct of their proceedings'.[60] The Cambodian government finally agreed to the more simple two-tier structure and it was this structure that was laid down in the Agreement: a Trial Chamber and a Supreme Court Chamber, the latter serving as both appellate body and court of final instance.[61] The Law will have to be amended accordingly.

While generally speaking, a three-tier structure for a court system is preferable to a two-tier one, as it contains an additional safeguard that the relevant facts and law are being taken into account and justice is done (in fact, many national court systems have such a three-tier system), at the same time an additional instance can lengthen judicial procedures substantially and make them more costly for prosecution, defence, and the court system itself. In the case of Cambodia, where the aim was 'that the Extraordinary Chambers can be established *as early as possible*, begin to function *promptly* and thereafter operate on a sustained basis and in an *efficient* and *cost-effective* manner' because '[o]therwise, the opportunity of bringing to justice those responsible for serious violations of Cambodian and international law during the period of Democratic Kampuchea might soon be lost',[62] it was an understandable choice to create Extraordinary Chambers with a two-tier structure.

2. Composition of the Chambers

In respect of the composition of the Extraordinary Chambers, the United Nations had a strong preference for a majority of international (ie non-Cambodian) judges and a simple majority voting system.[63] The reason for this was the dubious reputation of the Cambodian judiciary, which is widely perceived as corrupt, lacking impartiality and independence.[64] The Cambo-

---

[58] See, eg, Art 14, para 5 of the 1966 International Covenant on Civil and Political Rights.
[59] At para 4(b).   [60] See 'Report of the Secretary-General' (*supra* n 42) 6.
[61] Article 3, para 2 of the Agreement.
[62] See 'Report of the Secretary-General' (*supra* n 42) 19, paraphrasing paras 1, 9 and 10 of UNGA Res 57/228 and the fourth preambular paragraph, emphasis added.
[63] It should be recalled that the initial proposal of the UN Group of Experts was for a tribunal consisting *only* of international judges ('Report of the Group of Experts for Cambodia pursuant to General Assembly Resolution 52/125' (18 February 1999)).
[64] In UNGA Res 57/225 (26 February 2003), the General Assembly 'note[d] with concern the continued problems related to the rule of law and the functioning of the judiciary [in Cambodia] resulting from, inter alia, corruption and interference by the executive with the independence of the judiciary' (s II, para 2).

dian government wanted the exact opposite: a majority of Cambodian judges and a simple majority voting system.

The United Nations and the Cambodian government had not formally reached agreement on this subject when the Law on the Extraordinary Chambers was passed. The Law provides for a majority of Cambodian judges in the Extraordinary Chambers.[65] In each of the Chambers a Cambodian judge is to be President[66] and the President appoints the clerks for his or her Chamber.[67] As a 'compromise'[68] it was included in the Law that a decision taken by the Extraordinary Chambers would have to have the support of a 'supermajority' of judges (a majority of the judges plus one).[69] The compromise was meant to take away some of the concerns of the United Nations as the 'supermajority' rule would provide a possibility for the international judges to block decisions considered political or otherwise dubious.

In the negotiations that took place in spring 2003 the United Nations again advocated that the Extraordinary Chambers should consist of a majority of international judges, deciding by simple majority (doing away with the 'supermajority' system).[70]

However, the Cambodian government refused to deviate from what was laid down in the Law regarding the composition of the Chambers and the decision-making system, so finally the Secretary-General acquiesced, but not without remarking that:

in view of the clear finding of the General Assembly in its resolution 57/225 that there are continued problems related to the rule of law and the functioning of the judiciary in Cambodia resulting from interference by the executive with the independence of the judiciary, I would very much have preferred that the draft agreement provide for both of the Extraordinary Chambers to be composed of a majority of international judges. I was, and continue to be, of the view that international judges, who would not be dependent in any way upon the executive authorities of Cambodia, would be much less likely to be influenced by, or yield to, any interference from that quarter. In addition, it would then not have been necessary to apply the problematic 'supermajority' formula, which was introduced into the negotiations by Member States, and not by the United Nations delegation.[71]

Article 3 of the Agreement embodies in essence the same provisions as the Law.[72] However, unlike the Law, the Agreement does not provide that the

---

[65] Article 9 of the Law.   [66] ibid art 11.   [67] ibid art 9.
[68] This compromise was introduced by US senator John Kerry in October 1999 in order to gain the support of the United Nations for Extraordinary Chambers with a majority of Cambodian judges.
[69] Article 14 of the Law.
[70] See 'Report of the Secretary-General' (*supra* n 42) 6 and 7. Both the Agreement and the Law also provide for reserve judges, reserve investigating judges and reserve prosecutors, to replace the sitting ones. This will not be discussed further in this chapter.
[71] See 'Report of the Secretary-General' (*supra* n 42) 11.
[72] The Trial Chamber would consist of three Cambodian judges and two international judges. The Supreme Court Chamber would consist of four Cambodian judges and three international judges.

President of each Chamber should be Cambodian. The provision that the defence, the prosecution *and the victims*[73] may appeal any decision of the Trial Chamber is not in the Agreement either.[74] As these provisions in the Law are not contrary to the Agreement, they do not have to be amended to be consistent with the Agreement.

3. Decision-making

Decision-making in each of the Chambers will start with an attempt to reach unanimity. If this is not possible, decisions will be taken following the 'supermajority' rule. When no unanimity can be reached, but there is a 'supermajority' decision, this decision will contain the views of both the majority and the minority of judges.[75]

By allowing for the composition of the Chambers and the 'supermajority' rule as described above to prevail in the Agreement, the United Nations may have agreed with a system leading to exactly what the United Nations feared most: obstruction of justice.[76]

A fictitious example of a 'worst case scenario' may clarify this. What if, after a complete trial in both instances, it were to become evident from the facts presented in the case that a Khmer Rouge leader was guilty of a crime against humanity? What if the three international judges in the Supreme Court Chamber were to vote 'guilty' but all four of the Cambodian judges voted 'not guilty', because of pressure by former Khmer Rouge officials who are not part of the government? In this situation there is neither the required unanimity nor a supermajority. The final decision of the Supreme Court Chamber would contain both the views 'guilty' and 'not guilty' and would not lead to a conviction. The Khmer Rouge leader would go free.

The example shows that the system as it has been laid down in the Agreement could lead to complete deadlock. Because this system has explicit UN approval and all of the rules of the Agreement have been followed exactly as it should, the criticism that it was a mock trial or a show trial would likely be countered with the argument that the United Nations legitimized such proceedings. In this scenario, a de facto mock trial would have taken place, but a mock trial based on an agreement to which the United Nations consented.

In such a situation the United Nations could not invoke Article 28 of the Agreement to withdraw its cooperation to the Extraordinary Chambers, as neither the structure nor the functioning of the Extraordinary Chambers would have been changed or impaired by the Cambodian government.

---

[73] It is remarkable that not only the suspect and the prosecutor, but also the victims can appeal a decision. See below for further discussion of this.

[74] Articles 17, 36 and 37 of the Law.

[75] See Art 4 of the Agreement and art 14 of the Law.

[76] See 'Report of the Secretary-General' (*supra* n 42) 6.

4. Nomination, appointment, and dismissal of international judges

International judges are appointed by the Cambodian Supreme Council of Magistracy upon nomination from a list of candidates prepared by the Secretary-General.[77] For the Cambodian judges the usual national procedure will be followed.

The procedure of nomination and appointment of the international judges laid down in the Agreement could potentially thwart the UN aim of keeping a certain level of control and ensuring a sufficient level of quality of the Extraordinary Chambers, because it leaves the decision on the appointment of an international judge entirely to the Cambodian Supreme Council of Magistracy. The Council has full power to refuse appointment of a judge nominated by the Secretary-General.

As to the dismissal of judges, neither the Agreement nor the Law contain provisions. Dismissal of both Cambodian and international judges is left entirely up to national legislation.

It is curious that the United Nations, having shown so little faith in the trustworthiness of the Cambodian government and the Cambodian judiciary, has not insisted on greater control in respect of the appointment and dismissal of international judges.

5. Investigating judges and prosecutors

I. Nationality

The nationality and number of investigating judges and prosecutors[78] was also a contentious issue between the United Nations and the Cambodian government. The United Nations argued for only one international (ie non-Cambodian) investigating judge and one international prosecutor.[79] The Cambodian government wished to have one international and one Cambodian investigating judge ('co-investigating judges') and a similar[80] system for prosecutors ('co-prosecutors') and laid down provisions to that effect in the Law.[81] In case of disagreement between the co-investigating judges or the co-prosecutors, the Law provided for a Pre-Trial Chamber to settle the disagreement (this dispute procedure will be discussed in more detail below).[82]

---

[77] Article 3 paras 1 and 5 of the Agreement; art 11 of the Law.

[78] Nomination and appointment of investigating judges (Art 5, para 5 of the Agreement; art 26 of the Law) and prosecutors (Art 6, para 5 of the Agreement, art 18 of the Law) is identical to the nomination and appointment of judges described above. The same goes for the absence of rules in respect of dismissal. The same critical remarks apply.

[79] See 'Report of the Secretary-General' (*supra* n 42) 7.

[80] The sole difference was that Art 18 of the Law initially provided explicitly for the appointment of only *one* international co-prosecutor with the competence to appear in all Chambers and provided for the appointment of *more than one* Cambodian co-prosecutor.

[81] Articles 16 and 23 of the Law.

[82] ibid art 20 of the Law.

During the resumed negotiations in spring 2003, the parties decided to follow the system laid down in the Law.[83] Accordingly, the Agreement now reflects the system of the Law: two co-investigating judges and two co-prosecutors who work in both Chambers (the Trial Chamber and the Appeals Chamber), and a Pre-Trial Chamber for the resolution of disagreements between the co-prosecutors and co-investigating judges.[84]

II. Decision-making and dispute resolution system of co-prosecutors and co-investigating judges

The basic assumption of the Law and the Agreement is that the two co-prosecutors agree on the prosecution. In case of disagreement about whether to continue a prosecution, the prosecution will proceed, unless one of the prosecutors requests the involvement of the Pre-Trial Chamber.[85]

This Pre-Trial Chamber, consisting of three Cambodian judges (one of them President) and two international judges,[86] decides on the matter placed before it by means of the written statements of the two prosecutors. The Pre-Trial Chamber decides by a 'negative supermajority' of four votes, that is: if no 'supermajority' can be reached, the prosecution proceeds.[87] Decisions of the Pre-Trial Chamber are not subject to appeal.

The same procedure applies in respect of a disagreement between the two investigating judges as to the investigation.[88]

The decision-making system developed for the co-prosecutors and the co-investigating judges is a practical one, which meets the requirement of the General Assembly that the Extraordinary Chambers function promptly and efficiently.[89] Unlike the voting system in the two Chambers there is no possibility of a deadlock.

A negative aspect of the pre-trial proceedings is the fact that judgments of the Pre-Trial Chamber cannot be appealed. Especially in the relatively indecisive situation where the Pre-Trial Chamber does not reach a unanimous or

---

[83] Before agreeing to this, the United Nations had suggested as an alternative to the Pre-Trial Chamber that 'in case of any disagreement between the Cambodian co-investigating judge and the international co-investigating judge regarding the conduct of judicial investigations, the views of the international co-investigating judge would be decisive', but the Cambodian government had refused to accept this alternative. The same happened to the analogous UN proposal with respect to the co-prosecutors. See 'Report of the Secretary-General' (*supra* n 42) 9 and 10.

[84] Article 5 para 1, art 6 para 1 and art 7 of the Agreement.

[85] Article 6 para 4 of the Agreement and art 20 of the Law.

[86] Nomination and appointment of the judges of the Pre-Trial Chamber (Art 7, para 2 of the Agreement, art 20 of the Law) is identical to the nomination and appointment of judges described above. The same goes for the total absence of rules in respect of dismissal. The same critical remarks apply.

[87] Article 7 of the Agreement and arts 20 and 23 of the Law.

[88] Article 5, para 4 and Art 7 of the Agreement and art 23 of the Law.

[89] See UNGA Res 57/228, para 1.

supermajority decision and investigation/prosecution proceeds, a suspect can wrongly become the subject of investigation/prosecution/proceedings, which may take a very long time and may have a significant impact on his or her life, without being able to prevent at an early stage that such investigation/prosecution/proceedings take place. Generally speaking, a suspect should have the possibility to take action at an early stage to prevent wrongful and unsubstantiated investigation or prosecution.[90]

The positive effect of the Pre-Trial Chamber decision not being appealable is that a potential instrument for the suspect to stall significantly the progress of proceedings, has been taken away. The 'obstruction and delay in the conduct of their proceedings', much feared by the United Nations,[91] is thus avoided.

6. Support services

The Law provided for support staff (eg law clerks, assistants, security personnel) to assist the two Chambers, the Pre-Trial Chamber, the prosecutors, and the investigating judges.[92] The number of Cambodian and international staff was to be in proportion to the number of Cambodian and international judges, prosecutors, and investigating judges.[93] This and some of the other requirements in the Law cannot be found in the Agreement. However, as the provisions on staffing in the Law are far more detailed than those in the Agreement and these provisions do not seem to be in disagreement with the Agreement, we should look at the Law in this respect.

All support staff will be supervised by the Office of Administration. The Office will have a Cambodian director and an international deputy director.[94] The Cambodian director will be responsible for the overall management of the Office, in as far as this does not concern international matters subject to UN rules. The director will also do the interviewing and hiring of Cambodian staff. The Cambodian staff will be selected from Cambodian civil servants or other qualified Cambodians and appointed and paid by the Cambodian government.

---

[90] Such a possibility could be deduced from the presumption of innocence of a suspect (see eg Art 66 of the Statute of the International Criminal Court).

[91] See 'Report of the Secretary-General' (*supra* n 42) 6.

[92] For a comprehensive study of the staffing of the Extraordinary Chambers, see also, Chapter 12 (Romano).

[93] Articles 9, 13 and 22 of the Law.

[94] Article 30 of the Law and Art 8 of the Agreement. In respect of appointment of the international Deputy Director of the Office of Administration, the Law provides for nomination by the Secretary-General and appointment by the Supreme Council of Magistracy (Art 31). The Agreement provides for appointment by the Secretary-General (Art 8, para 3). The Law will have to be adapted accordingly. There are no rules in respect of dismissal.

The deputy director will be responsible for the administration of the international components of the Extraordinary Chambers and will hire the international staff, paid by the United Nations.

7. *Assistance by Cambodian government*

The Agreement provides that the Cambodian government shall comply 'without undue delay' with 'any request' of the investigation, prosecution, and the Extraordinary Chambers.[95] The Law also provides for this assistance. It should, however, be noted that requests for assistance *by the Extraordinary Chambers* are not provided for in the Law.[96] The relevant articles of the Law spell out that the Cambodian government is under an unconditional duty to provide assistance[97] and the Agreement gives a non-exhaustive list of possible requests.[98]

An example of assistance provided pursuant to the Agreement and the Law is the obligation for the government to guarantee the security of the suspects.[99] To avoid the Cambodian government treating those former Khmer Rouge leaders who are currently cooperating with the government more leniently than others, it has been specifically provided in the Agreement that this security is guaranteed irrespective of whether a suspect has appeared voluntarily before the Extraordinary Chambers.[100]

Another example is the responsibility of the Cambodian government for the arrest (by Justice Police or other law enforcement elements, including the armed forces) of accused persons[101] and the obligation to bring them into custody immediately.[102]

F. PROCEDURAL LAW

1. *Relationship between national and international law*

In respect of procedural law, both the Law and the Agreement are relatively brief. The Agreement essentially leaves procedural matters to Cambodian law. It adds that:

---

[95] Article 25 of the Agreement.

[96] The Law has also limited the requests for assistance to those that are 'useful' to the prosecution or investigation (arts 20 and 23 of the Law). However, it is not likely that this limitation will have large practical consequences.

[97] Articles 20 and 23 of the Law.

[98] Articles 24 and 25 of the Agreement.

[99] Article 24 of the Agreement and art 33 of the Law.

[100] Article 24 of the Agreement.

[101] ibid Art 25(c).

[102] Article 33 of the Law.

[w]here Cambodian law does not deal with a particular matter, or where there is uncertainty regarding the interpretation or application of a relevant rule of Cambodian law, or where there is a question regarding the consistency of such a rule with international standards, guidance may also be sought in procedural rules established at the international level.[103]

The Law, like the Agreement, refers to national procedural law in the chapters on trial proceedings, prosecution, and investigation. The opening in the Law for the use of international procedural standards is drafted in a slightly more narrow way than the Agreement. Only '[i]f necessary, and if there are lacunae in these existing procedures', the Extraordinary Chambers, co-prosecutors, or co-investigating judges 'may seek guidance in procedural rules established at the international level'.[104] Inconsistency of Cambodian procedural law with international standards is not expressly mentioned as a ground for allowing the Extraordinary Chambers, co-prosecutors, or co-investigating judges to seek guidance in procedural rules established at the international level.

These provisions in the Agreement and the Law both leave room for uncertainty. It may not always be clear:

(a) that Cambodian law 'does not deal with a particular matter';
(b) that there is 'uncertainty regarding the interpretation or application' of Cambodian law;
(c) that there is an 'inconsistency with international standards';[105] or
(d) when it is 'necessary' to seek guidance at the international level.[106]

This lack of clarity could be a possible source of deadlock (resulting in delays) between the international judges, prosecutors, and investigating judges on the one hand (more likely to want to apply international rules to the procedure) and the Cambodian judges, prosecutors, and investigating judges on the other (more likely to want to apply Cambodian procedural law). It is therefore possible that procedural issues will be among the first 'conflicts' to be decided by the Pre-Trial Chamber.

2. Fair trial guarantees

The Law and the Agreement both have provisions on how a fair trial is to be guaranteed. The Agreement provides:

The Extraordinary Chambers shall exercise their jurisdiction in accordance with international standards of justice, fairness and due process of law, as set out in Articles 14 and 15 of the 1966 International Covenant on Civil and Political Rights to which Cambodia is a party.[107]

---

[103] Article 12 of the Agreement.   [104] Articles 20, 23, 33 and 36 of the Law.
[105] Article 12 of the Agreement.   [106] Articles 20, 23, 33 and 36 of the Law.
[107] ibid art 12.

In respect of trials behind closed doors,[108] and the rights of the defence,[109] the Agreement also refers to these Articles.

The Law provides that trials shall be fair and expeditious with full respect for the rights of the accused and for the protection of victims and witnesses,[110] lays down conditions to be met for a trial to be held behind closed doors,[111] and sums up the rights of the defence.[112] For all other procedural aspects the Law refers to the 'existing [Cambodian] procedures in force'.[113]

The Law is less elaborate than the Agreement on the fair trial guarantees. To state just one example, the Law provides for the possibility of a trial behind closed doors '[if] in exceptional circumstances the Extraordinary Chambers decide to close the proceedings for good cause in accordance with existing procedures in force', whereas the Agreement, in referring to Article 14 of the Covenant, provides that:

the press and the public may be excluded from all or part of a trial for reasons of morals, public order (ordre public) or national security in a democratic society, or when the interest of the private lives of the parties so requires, or to the extent strictly necessary in the opinion of the court in special circumstances where publicity would prejudice the interests of justice.

A study of the negotiations leading to the signing of the Agreement does not clarify why in the proceedings of the Extraordinary Chambers *only* the principles of Articles 14 and 15 of the International Covenant on Civil and Political Rights should be observed. The principles in, for example, Articles 9 and 10[114] of the Covenant are equally important. Also, there are

---

[108] Article 12, para 2 of the Agreement.   [109] Article 13 of the Agreement.
[110] Article 33 of the Law.   [111] ibid art 34.
[112] ibid art 35.   [113] ibid arts 33 and 34.   [114] Article 9:

'1. Everyone has the right to liberty and security of person. No one shall be subjected to arbitrary arrest or detention. No one shall be deprived of his liberty except on such grounds and in accordance with such procedure as are established by law.

2. Anyone who is arrested shall be informed, at the time of arrest, of the reasons for his arrest and shall be promptly informed of any charges against him.

3. Anyone arrested or detained on a criminal charge shall be brought promptly before a judge or other officer authorized by law to exercise judicial power and shall be entitled to trial within a reasonable time or to release. It shall not be the general rule that persons awaiting trial shall be detained in custody, but release may be subject to guarantees to appear for trial, at any other stage of the judicial proceedings, and, should occasion arise, for execution of the judgment.

4. Anyone who is deprived of his liberty by arrest or detention shall be entitled to take proceedings before a court, in order that that court may decide without delay on the lawfulness of his detention and order his release if the detention is not lawful.

5. Anyone who has been the victim of unlawful arrest or detention shall have an enforceable right to compensation.'

Article 10:

'1. All persons deprived of their liberty shall be treated with humanity and with respect for the inherent dignity of the human person.

2. (a) Accused persons shall, save in exceptional circumstances, be segregated from convicted persons and shall be subject to separate treatment appropriate to their status as unconvicted persons;

more up-to-date internationally accepted legal instruments with provisions on fair trial.[115]

In the interest of clarity and completeness it would be advisable that the Law, like the Agreement, explicitly refers to the provisions of the International Covenant on Civil and Political Rights.[116]

In respect of the right of the defence to counsel, some insufficiencies in the Law need to be highlighted. One of these relates to the right of defendants to choose counsel freely. Pursuant to Article 14, paragraph 3 of the International Covenant on Civil and Political Rights, referred to in the Agreement, the defendant is free to choose his or her counsel.[117] Assistance by a counsel, free of charge, is guaranteed if the defendant cannot afford counsel.[118] However, a provision on freedom to choose counsel is not in the Law and it should therefore be amended to include such a provision.

A second insufficiency relates to privileges and immunities of the defence counsel. Although it needs to be acknowledged that the Law and the Agreement provide that the counsel of the defence is not to be subjected by the Cambodian government to any measure that may affect the free and independent exercise of his or her functions[119] and both instruments also provide that the counsel has immunity from personal arrest or detention, and from seizure of personal baggage,[120] the Law is less strict than the Agreement on this point, adding that this immunity only relates to functions of the counsel *in the proceedings*.

Inviolability of all relevant documents and immunity from criminal or civil jurisdiction in respect of words spoken or written and acts performed as counsel are also part of the privileges.[121] Unlike the Law, the Agreement provides that immunity from criminal or civil jurisdiction shall continue to be accorded to the counsel after termination of his or her functions as a counsel.

An important feature missing from the privileges of the defence counsel in both the Law and the Agreement is the explicit right of the counsel to make telephone calls without the telephone conversation being recorded by, for example, the Cambodian government.

2. (b) Accused juvenile persons shall be separated from adults and brought as speedily as possible for adjudication.

3. The penitentiary system shall comprise treatment of prisoners the essential aim of which shall be their reformation and social rehabilitation. Juvenile offenders shall be segregated from adults and be accorded treatment appropriate to their age and legal status.'

[115] eg the Statute of the International Criminal Court.

[116] Especially since it could be inferred from the letter from Minister Sok An (23 November 2001) and the 'Report of the Secretary-General' (*supra* n 42) that international treaties (which would include the ICCPR) do not have direct effect within Cambodia.

[117] Article 13 of the Agreement.

[118] Article 24 of the Law and Art 13 of the Agreement.

[119] Article 42, para 3 of the Law, Art 21, para 1 of the Agreement.

[120] Article 42, para 3(a) of the Law; Art 21, para 2(a) of the Agreement.

[121] Article 42, para 3(b) and (c) of the Law; Art 21, para 2(b) and (c) of the Agreement.

A last remark with respect to the defence counsel concerns the provision in the Law and the Agreement that a lawyer can only be counsel if he or she is admitted by the Extraordinary Chambers. Neither the Law nor the Agreement provides for specific rules regarding this admittance. There is no reference to the 'existing procedures/law in force' either. One can therefore only guess how the Extraordinary Chambers will decide on admittance of a counsel. If the 'regular' decision-making procedure of the Extraordinary Chambers were to apply, the danger of deadlock in the Extraordinary Chambers, as discussed above,[122] cannot be excluded.

3. Victims and witnesses

When atrocities such as those committed by the Khmer Rouge are tried, victims and witnesses are a vital component in furnishing evidence of these atrocities and in particular of who committed and/or ordered them. Often—and especially in the case of Cambodia—there is a significant lapse of time between the period when the crimes were committed and the moment of bringing perpetrators to justice.

For victims and witnesses, giving testimony is an emotional task and a tremendous responsibility, as it involves remembering and reliving in detail what they have suffered or witnessed at the time and giving the most horrifying details of these events. In addition, they can be questioned (with a completely legitimate aim of challenging the truthfulness of their testimony) by the accused or his or her counsel. In actually facing the accused, witnesses and victims sometimes also run the serious risk of becoming the subject of acts of revenge and retaliatory measures by adherents of the accused. For these reasons, the Agreement and the Law contain special provisions regarding victims and witnesses.

The Agreement provides:

> The co-investigating judges, the co-prosecutors and the Extraordinary Chambers shall provide for the protection of victims and witnesses. Such protection measures shall include, but shall not be limited to, the conduct of in camera proceedings and the protection of the identity of a victim or witness.[123]

A similar provision can be found in Article 33 of the Law.

Although these provisions give some level of protection, it might nonetheless have been advisable to include more specific provisions in the Law and the Agreement in respect of the protection of victims and witnesses, eg the possibility of a programme providing for protective measures and security arrangements staying in effect as long as needed for the safety of the victim or witness, or of a counselling programme.[124]

---

[122] See above, section E. 3.   [123] Article 23 of the Agreement, emphasis in original.
[124] The Statute for the International Criminal Court contains such provisions, eg in Art 43.

As to the rights of the victims, the Law contains some provisions. A rather extraordinary one is the provision giving victims the right to appeal a decision of the Trial Chamber.[125] This right is not known to many criminal law systems.[126]

Furthermore, as in many civil law and common law systems, including the Cambodian legal system,[127] victims can take part in criminal proceedings as an 'injured party' and claim reparation.[128] The possibility of claiming reparation in criminal proceedings has the distinct advantage for the victim that he or she can take part in proceedings that have been initiated anyway by the prosecution, therewith not being under the obligation to initiate a separate civil trial and pay for the costs of such a trial.

The Law and the Agreement do not contain provisions in respect of reparation[129] of victims as a part of the criminal proceedings, but as has been explained above, the Cambodian Criminal Code provides for this.

4. Penalties

A first draft of the Law was rejected in 2001 by the Cambodian Constitutional Council for reasons of unconstitutionality, because it provided for the death penalty as the maximum penalty[130] for some of the crimes, while the death penalty had been abolished under the Cambodian Constitution.[131] On 19 June 2001, the draft Law was amended and the death penalty as the maximum penalty replaced by imprisonment for life.[132]

In the version of the Law[133] that was signed by the Cambodian king on 10 August 2001, the Trial Chamber may sentence the defendant to a penalty between five years and life imprisonment (with the possibility of combining this with seizure of 'personal property, money, and real property acquired unlawfully or by criminal conduct').[134] The maximum penalty of life imprisonment can also be found in Article 10 of the Agreement. Unlike the Law, the Agreement contains no minimum penalty.

---

[125] Articles 36 and 37 of the Law.
[126] The criminal law systems of the Netherlands and the United States, for example, do not have a right of appeal for victims.
[127] Cambodian Law on Criminal Procedure (8 February 1993), Art 9, Provisions of 10 September 1992 relating to the judiciary and criminal law and procedure applicable in Cambodia during the transitional period, Art 27.
[128] See in this respect Art 75 of the Statute for the International Criminal Court.
[129] Reparations could include restitution, compensation, and/or rehabilitation.
[130] Article 3 of the draft Law.
[131] Constitution of the Kingdom of Cambodia, Art 32.
[132] A specific paragraph to that effect has been added to Art 3 of the Law. Articles 38 and 39 of the Law have also been amended.
[133] ibid arts 38 and 39.
[134] ibid art 39. The property confiscated under this article is returned to the Cambodian state.

G. SETTLEMENT OF DISPUTES BETWEEN THE UNITED NATIONS AND CAMBODIA

The Agreement contains a provision on how to settle a dispute between the United Nations and the Cambodian government in respect of the functioning of the Extraordinary Chambers: this should be settled 'by negotiation, or by any other mutually agreed upon mode of settlement'.[135] Both instruments provide for the situation that a conflict cannot be settled and each instrument reflects the position that the United Nations and the Cambodian government have taken in the negotiations leading up to the creation of the Extraordinary Chambers and the level of distrust harboured between these parties.

The United Nations provided itself in the Agreement with the possibility to withdraw from the Agreement if the Cambodian government were to change the structure of the Extraordinary Chambers or otherwise cause the Extraordinary Chambers to function in violation of the Agreement.[136]

The Cambodian government had provided itself in the Law with the possibility to continue the Extraordinary Chambers on its own if the United Nations were to step out, either by appointing international judges that do not have the United Nations' approval or—as a last resort—by appointing Cambodian judges instead of the international judges, making the Extraordinary Chambers an entirely national tribunal.[137]

These provisions can be regarded as somewhat remarkable. Neither the legal instrument regarding the Special Panels in East Timor, nor the one regarding the Special Court in Sierra Leone (both internationalized tribunals) contains such provisions.

H. BEGINNING AND END

In order for the Extraordinary Chambers to start functioning as soon as possible and in the most effective manner, a so-called 'phased in' approach has been adopted for the establishment and functioning of the Extraordinary Chambers.[138]

This means that in the very first phase after establishment, both investigations and prosecutions will be initiated. For those already in custody,[139] the trial proceedings will proceed, while at the same time investigations are started in respect of other leaders and persons most responsible for the crimes within the jurisdiction of the Extraordinary Chambers, followed by their arrest by the Cambodian government.[140]

---

[135] Article 29 of the Agreement.   [136] ibid Art 28.
[137] Article 46 of the Law.   [138] Article 27 of the Agreement.
[139] Until now two persons have been held in custody: Ta Mok and Duch.
[140] The Cambodian government can of course only arrest those who are on Cambodian territory.

While negotiating the Agreement, parties worked with the assumption that all trials and appeals would be completed in a period of three years.[141]

Thus, the first year of operation would see a 'phased' establishment of the Trial Chamber and the co-investigating judges and full establishment of the Office of the Prosecution and the Office of Administration. These last two offices would function at full capacity throughout the estimated three years of operation.

The second year of operation would see full establishment of the Trial Chamber and the co-investigating judges. The Supreme Court Chamber would function for less than the full year.

The third year of operation would see a gradual winding down of the Trial Chamber and the co-investigating judges. The Supreme Court Chamber would operate throughout the year.[142] The Pre-Trial Chamber would not serve permanently, but only when their 'services' are needed.

The basic premiss of this schedule is that the Extraordinary Chambers are not meant to be permanent. The Law provides for the appointment of judges and prosecutors 'for the period of the proceedings'[143] and for the appointment of investigating judges 'for the period of the investigations'.[144]

Following the definitive conclusion of the proceedings, the Extraordinary Chambers will automatically dissolve.[145] No law of the Cambodian government or agreement between the Cambodian government and the United Nations is needed.

I. CONCLUSION

It was a gargantuan struggle to get to an Agreement on the establishment of the Extraordinary Chambers. The struggle, however, has not led to a very solid result. The initial disagreement between the two parties was fundamental: the Cambodian government wanted a national tribunal dominated by Cambodia, with assistance of the United Nations. The United Nations, represented by the Secretary-General, only wished to support and assist a predominantly international tribunal, because of the dubious reputation of the Cambodian judiciary.[146]

Confronted with this unbridgeable difference, the Member States of the United Nations chose to let their wish to bring to justice those responsible for one of the largest mass murders of the twentieth century prevail over the objections of the Secretary-General. An Agreement was concluded that is to a large extent a compromise and which on some important issues seems to

---

[141] This is the same time frame as provided for the Special Court in Sierra Leone.
[142] See 'Report of the Secretary-General' (*supra* n 42) 16 and 17.
[143] Articles 12 and 21 of the Law.   [144] ibid art 27.
[145] ibid art 47.   [146] A reputation recognized as such by the UN General Assembly.

follow the wishes of the Cambodian government more than it follows the wishes of the Secretary-General.

All the compromising and giving in by the United Nations to the demands of the Cambodian government has resulted in a structure of a dubious legal quality. This lack of quality is not so much in the substantive law that will be applied, but more in the procedural law and mostly in the structure of the court system. Although statements by the United Nations and the Cambodian government may suggest otherwise, the procedural law and the court structure have made the Extraordinary Chambers into a tribunal prone to very long procedures, obstruction, and delaying of justice.

Of course, whether the Extraordinary Chambers are able to do what they were established for will depend to a large extent on the willingness of the Cambodian government to cooperate with the Extraordinary Chambers, on the integrity of the judges, investigating judges, prosecutors, and support staff. If the government gives its full cooperation and all of the officials of the Extraordinary Chambers fulfil their tasks with the impartiality and integrity required, the Extraordinary Chambers may achieve the result aimed for: bringing to justice those responsible for the 'killing fields' of Cambodia.

However, it cannot be ruled out that, with the current legal instruments and with the Extraordinary Chambers functioning on the basis of those instruments, the willingness of the international community to compromise in order to bring justice to Cambodia may easily turn into the opposite: those responsible getting away with impunity for their complicity in one of the largest mass murders of the twentieth century.

Part III
Cross-Cutting Aspects

12

The Judges and Prosecutors of Internationalized Criminal Courts and Tribunals

Cesare P R Romano*

A. INTRODUCTION

In 1944, while the Allied troops were making gradual inroads towards Berlin and Tokyo, and the end of the Second World War was only a matter of time, the Brookings Institution and the Carnegie Endowment for International Peace gave the great US scholar and judge, Manley O Hudson, a grant to predict the future of international adjudication. The result of his study (which incidentally was facilitated by no less than Louis Sohn, then only a young research assistant) was published in an almost forgotten booklet entitled *International Tribunals: Past and Future*. In the section dedicated to the 'manning of international tribunals', he wrote:

The selection of the members of international tribunals frequently presents problems of great difficulty, and in some instances the structure of the tribunal is made to depend upon the solution given to these problems. No group of men exists which can be said to form a profession of international judges, and but few individuals are so outstanding as to be repeatedly called upon to serve as members of different tribunals. The number of men actually serving in such positions at any one time is quite limited, and their selection is usually determined by a variety of considerations, some of them more or less fortuitous. The role is not one offering a career for which men are, or can be, specially trained.[1]

The world in which Hudson practised was rather different from the one we are living in today. In his time there were very few permanent international judicial bodies, and ad hoc arbitration dominated the scene. International criminal tribunals would have appeared only within a few years. Nowadays, the sheer number of international judicial and quasi-judicial bodies makes it possible to argue that an 'international judicial operator' profession has emerged. Be that as it may, it is remarkable that about 60 years ago Hudson

---

* Associate of the Center on International Cooperation, New York University; Assistant Director of the Project on International Courts and Tribunals (PICT); Adjunct Professor of International Law, Fordham University, Visiting Professor, Duke University, School of Law.
[1] M Hudson *International Tribunals: Past and Future* (Carnegie Endowment Washington DC 1944) 32.

could pinpoint a serious of issues that were going to affect the development of the international judiciary, making his booklet transcend the epoch in which it was written.

This chapter will look at the question of staffing internationalized criminal courts and tribunals, and, specifically, it will analyse the judicial body's essential engine: judges and prosecutors. First, while all internationalized criminal courts and tribunals have the common feature of being staffed by a blend of international and local judges, prosecutors and staff, the mix can vary from case to case. This chapter will explain how and why. Secondly, we will look at what qualifications are required of judges and prosecutors, both local and international. Nationality, moral integrity, gender, and curriculum, meaning specific professional background and expertise, are factors that will be considered. Thirdly, the practical problem of identifying and recruiting outstanding individuals that match these criteria will be expounded. Finally, the question of the degree of independence of local and international judges and prosecutors serving in internationalized bodies will be tackled by concentrating on three particular aspects of this complex issue: procedures for appointment and dismissal of judges, length of service, and privileges and immunities.

However, before moving on to the analysis, it is necessary to introduce a few clarifications and some raw data. First, international judicial bodies other than criminal courts (eg the International Court of Justice, or the European Court of Justice) have two main components: judges and bureaucrats working in the Registry. International criminal tribunals differ from such 'ordinary' international judicial bodies in many regards, including the fact that they typically have a much larger staff, for, besides the two aforementioned components, there is also the personnel of the Office of the Prosecutor, and the ancillary services, such as the programmes for the protection of witnesses, detention facility, and security personnel.[2] Moreover, in the case of some internationalized criminal judicial bodies, besides adjudicating judges, there are also 'investigating judges'.[3] Thus, it should be

---

[2] This, incidentally, helps explain why the budget of international criminal courts and tribunals is much larger than that of 'ordinary' international judicial bodies. On the issue of the financing of internationalized criminal courts and tribunals, see, Chapter 13 (Ingadottir).

[3] The exact meaning of the term 'investigating judge' depends on the particular legal system. Thus, in civil law system traditions it indicates somebody who is half-magistrate and half-policeman. The Agreement of 6 June 2003 between the United Nations and the Royal Government of Cambodia concerning the Prosecution under Cambodian Law of Crimes Committed during the Period of Democratic Kampuchea (hereafter 'United Nations/Cambodia Agreement'), provides for investigating judges (Art 5), who are responsible for the actual conduct of investigation (a task which, ordinarily, in international criminal tribunals is left to the prosecutor). The text of the Agreement can be found at http://genocidewatch.org/CambodiaDraftAgreement17-03-03.htm. On this issue, see Chapter 11 (Meijer). Sometimes, it is instead a judge who is empowered to ensure that the rights of suspects under investigation, and those of victims of the suspected crime are respected, particularly in pre-trial matters. On the investigating judge, in particular in the case of East Timor, see Chapter 15 (Friman).

made clear that in this chapter, the term 'staff', or 'personnel', or 'man-power', of internationalized courts and tribunals is used in a restrictive sense, indicating first of all the judges, and then the Prosecutor and Deputy Prosecutor. All other individuals that contribute to the functioning of internationalized criminal judicial bodies, although essential, will be dealt with only marginally.

Admittedly, defence lawyers, who can be retained directly by the indictee, or, in the case of indigent ones, can be assigned, and paid for, by the tribunal, either by drawing from the private sector or, when available, from the tribunal's own defence unit, are equally essential to the delivery of international criminal justice. Judges and prosecutors may be the essential engine propelling criminal judicial bodies, but without defence counsel (and adept ones for that matter) the machinery will inevitably lead to injustice.

However, defence will not be addressed in this chapter for several reasons. First of all, proper treatment of defence in these bodies warrants a specific chapter, and not just a few paragraphs. This is beyond the scope of this already long piece. Secondly, this chapter is dedicated to the staff of internationalized courts and tribunals (with the above mentioned exclusion of the Registry staff), and defence counsel are (generally) not part of it. Thirdly, in this book Håkan Friman deals with the fair trial aspects of defence issues, and therefore the reader will find it convenient to refer to his contribution.

There is a second general note of caution that must be introduced before moving on to the core of this piece. Indeed, there are several substantial differences between the internationalized criminal bodies created in East Timor and Kosovo, on the one hand, and those in Sierra Leone, and the one planned for Cambodia, on the other, up to the point that it is possible to talk about two distinct genera in the family of internationalized criminal bodies.[4] One of such dissimilarities is the scope of the undertaking. As has been well detailed elsewhere in this book, in Sierra Leone and Cambodia the goal is ensuring actual prosecution of political and military leaders most responsible for international crimes.[5] It is a limited, albeit crucial, mission. Conversely, the task undertaken by the United Nations in Kosovo and East Timor is wide-ranging, encompassing the reconstruction of a viable, fair, and credible court system, including both criminal and civil jurisdictions; a task, admittedly, much larger in scope than just the prosecution of war crimes and crimes against humanity committed by the 'top brass'.

From this substantial difference in goal descends a difference in the number of individuals staffing the various internationalized bodies. Thus, it should be no surprise that while the internationalized judiciary in Kosovo

---

[4] On this distinction, see C Romano 'Mixed Jurisdictions for East Timor, Kosovo, Sierra Leone and Cambodia: The Coming of Age of Internationalized Criminal Bodies?' (2002) 2 *YB International Law and Jurisprudence* 97.

[5] See Chapter 7 (Smith), and Chapter 10 (Etcheson).

and East Timor involve dozens of international judges and prosecutors and, at least in the case of Kosovo, hundreds or local judges, the numbers of the Special Court for Sierra Leone (and possibly the internationalized body to be created for Cambodia) are more in line with those of traditional international criminal tribunals, with about a dozen judges and prosecutors, both local and international.

In particular, in November 2002, in Kosovo's 55 judicial institutions (from the Supreme Court to minor offences courts) there were 341 Kosovan judges and prosecutors,[6] supported by about 1,300 local staff.[7] At about the same time, there were 26 international judges and prosecutors deployed (16 judges and 10 prosecutors), with nearly 100 headquarters and support staff helping them.[8]

Judges and prosecutors in East Timor are fewer in number. In March 2003, there were around 13 East Timorese judges serving, including one on the Court of Appeal, two on the Serious Crimes Panels, and others in the Dili and Baucau District Courts. At about the same time (ie, beginning of June 2003), there were six international judges and eight prosecutors.[9] For what concerns support staff to international judges and prosecutors,[10] the Serious Crimes Unit, which carries out investigations, has a total staff of 124, of which 72 are international, including United Nations Volunteers, interpreters, UNPOL investigators, security, and others.[11] The Serious Crimes Panels are helped by 19 people.[12]

---

[6] Of those 341, 319 were ethnic Albanian, nine Bosnian, seven Turkish, four Serbian, and two Roma. UNMIK Presentation Paper (*infra* n 7) 14.

[7] UNMIK 'Pillar 1 (Police and Justice)' Presentation Paper (November 2002) 14. Available at www.unmikonline.org/justice/documents/PillarI_Presentation_Paper.pdf (site last visited 1 August 2003); UNMIK website (Judicial Development Division) www.unmikonline.org/justice/jdd.htm (site last visited 1 August 2003).

[8] Email from UNMIK, 'Pillar 1, Police and Justice', on file with the author.

[9] Four international judges were working at the Special Panels for Serious Crimes in Dili, while two international judges worked at the Court of Appeal. The eight international prosecutors were all working at the Serious Crimes Unit based in Dili. For the purpose of prosecution the districts of East Timor have been divided and assigned to four different teams. Each team covers four districts, except one team that covers three. In addition to the 13 districts existing in East Timor, the Gender Team and the National Team have been included. Thus, Team one covers the Districts of Bobonaro, Ainaro, Ermera, and Aileu; Team two: Baucau, Viqueque, Lautem, plus it includes the National Team; Team 3: Covalima, Manufahi, Manatutu, plus it includes the Gender Team; Team 4: District of Liquica, Dili, and Oecussi.

[10] Figures regarding support staff to the courts in East Timor where no international personnel serve are not available, but considering the number of courts active and the difficulty in recruiting skilled local human resources, it is likely to be very small.

[11] Email from Judge Sylver Ntukamazina, on file with the author.

[12] To be precise, four international and two East Timorese interpreters; two international legal researchers; three international transcribers; one international and three East Timorese court clerks; one international administrative coordinator; one international administrative assistant; one East Timorese Registrar and a driver. Email from Judge Sylver Ntukamazina, on file with the author.

Finally, as has been said, the Special Court for Sierra Leone involves a smaller number of judges and prosecutors as compared to East Timor and Kosovo. That is, there are three judges serving in the Trial Chamber,[13] and five in the Appellate Chamber,[14] plus two alternate judges.[15] There is a Prosecutor,[16] as well as a Deputy Prosecutor,[17] a Registrar,[18] and a Deputy Registrar.[19] Altogether the staff of the Special Court for Sierra Leone, including support and gratis personnel, and excluding judges, comprises 114 individuals, plus 24 more who, in April 2003, were under recruitment.[20]

B. MIXED STAFFING

A feature common to all internationalized criminal bodies, which sets them apart not only from international criminal bodies, but also from all other international judicial bodies *tout court*, is that they are manned both by national and foreign, or better, 'international' staff. Indeed, in ICTY or ICTR there are no citizens of the former Yugoslavia or Rwanda serving as judges or prosecutors. And yet the presence of foreign judges on national benches is not, by itself, enough to characterize a judicial body as 'internationalized'. It is, indeed, common practice amongst Commonwealth countries, especially those of the same region, to exchange judges. To illustrate with a particularly relevant case, Judge Isaac Aboagye, from Ghana, one of the alternate judges of the Sierra Leone Special Court, before being appointed had been serving since 1988 as Justice of the High Court of Botswana.

---

[13] Respectively Judge Pierre Boutet, Judge Benjamin Mutanga Itoe, and Judge Bankole Thompson.

[14] Respectively, Judge Emmanuel Ayoola, Judge Alhaji Hassan B Jallow, Judge Renate Winter, Judge Gelaga King, and Judge Geoffrey Robertson (President).

[15] Judge Isaac Aboagye, and Judge Elizabeth Muyovwe.

[16] Mr David Crane.

[17] Mr Desmond de Silva, QC.

[18] Mr Robin Vincent.

[19] Mr Robert Kirkwood. It should be noted that the constitutive instruments of the Special Court do not provide for a Sierra Leonean Deputy Registrar.

[20] The breakdown of the staff of the Special Court for Sierra Leone is as follows: Professional staff: 52 (16 United States, 10 Sierra Leone, seven United Kingdom, three Canada, three Australia, two Italy, two Gambia, one Zimbabwe, one Uganda, one Trinidad, one Panama, one Pakistan, one Ireland, one Ghana, one Finland, one Cameroon), of which 25 staff the office of the Prosecutor and 27 the Registry. It is interesting to note that a large majority of US nationals work in the Prosecutor's Office (12 out of 16) and that all of the staff of that office are solely from common law countries. Support staff: 58 people, of which 24 are international (four United Kingdom, three United States, two Canada, two India, two South Africa, two Tanzania, one Austria, one Eritrea, one Ghana, one Ireland, one Norway, one Senegal, one Syria, one Gambia, one Trinidad), and 34 Sierra Leoneans. Gratis personnel: two from Canada and two from Switzerland.

The reasons for mixing both international and national judges and court personnel are multiple.[21] For instance, local judges and court personnel are necessary to instill in the local population a sense of 'ownership' of the justice which is made in their name. This is what distinguishes internationalized criminal tribunals from classical international criminal tribunals, such as the International Criminal Court (ICC), the International Criminal Court for the Former Yugoslavia (ICTY), and the International Criminal Court for Rwanda (ICTR), which sit in countries other than those where the crimes have been committed. Again, international personnel are foremost there to ensure, sometimes by their very presence, actual or perceived fairness and impartiality in proceedings. By adding international judges and staff to local judges, the international community gives its blessing to what would otherwise be a purely domestic affair. Justice is no longer done only in the name of the people of the given country, but becomes an international concern.

However, there are other practical reasons for coupling international and local judges and court personnel. Internationalized criminal bodies are typically established in countries which have been ravaged by civil war, where the state judicial machinery is unable to deliver because either it has been dismantled, or it has been crippled by years of interference and hands-on control by political authorities. Thus, the presence of foreign judges and judicial staff is intended to make available particular expertise in the prosecution of serious international crimes. This is all the more needed, considering that international criminal law is a branch of international law which has undergone deep transformations and development over the course of the past few years, at a pace that outstrips the training capacities of most countries, including developed ones.

There are undoubtedly positive synergies between local and international judges. In some cases, capacity-building of local personnel might also be an important end. International judges and court staff could act as tutors of their national colleagues, training them in more efficient judicial practices and showing how to deliver justice which conforms to international standards. Local judges can provide international judges with understanding of the local habits, legal or social.

While all internationalized criminal bodies are manned by a mix of local and foreign personnel, the exact balance between the national and international components might vary from case to case. For instance, in most of the cases analysed in this book international judges are the majority of the bench, but that is not always the case. Similarly, the Prosecutor or the Registrar of the court are usually foreign while the Deputy is local, but, again, there are exceptions.

---

[21] On this point, see Chapter 1 (Cassese) and Chapter 20 (Condorelli/Boutruche).

To illustrate, Serious Crimes Panels in East Timor consist of two international and one local judge.[22] Panels take decision by majority vote, and each judge has equal weight in the decision.[23] The binary structure 'international/national' also characterizes the staff of other relevant judicial apparatuses (ie, Public Prosecution and Legal Aid Services). Then again, the Transitional Judicial Service Commission, which will be discussed below,[24] is unusual as it gives local judges the majority. It is composed of five individuals: three of East Timorese origin and two international, and the Chair is East Timorese.[25] This is probably so because the Transitional Judicial Service Commission regulates the career of East Timorese judges and not that of the international judges, and thus it is natural to give local personnel control.

In the case of Kosovo, the issue is more complex. International judges can be either the minority or the majority of the bench. As has been detailed elsewhere in this book, there are currently two types of international panels in the judicial system of Kosovo.[26] In one international panel judges are the minority, and in the other the majority. The former is provided for in UNMIK Regulation 2000/34,[27] and it permits international judges, each of whom is assigned to a specific court, to pick and choose the cases in which he or she will participate. A typical panel in a Kosovo district court is composed of two professional and three lay judges. Verdicts are by majority vote, and each judge (international or national) has an equal voice. In such a situation, the international judge is easily out-voted. The latter model, which has become the standard in high-profile cases, was created by UNMIK Regulation 2000/64.[28] It allows the prosecutor, defence counsel or defendant to request the appointment of an international judge or prosecutor to the case, a change of venue or, most importantly, the appointment of a three-judge panel with at least two international judges.

In the case of the Special Court for Sierra Leone, international judges are always the majority. In the Trial Chamber three judges serve, of whom one is appointed by the government of Sierra Leone, and two are appointed by the

---

[22] UNTAET Reg 2000/15 (On the Establishment of Panels with Exclusive Jurisdiction over Serious Criminal Offences) s 22.1. In cases of special importance or gravity a panel of five judges composed of three international and two East Timorese judges can be established: s 22.2. UNTAET Regulations are available at www.un.org/peace/etimor/UntaetN.htm.

[23] UNTAET Reg 2000/11 (On the Organization of Courts in East Timor) as amended by Regs 2001/14 and 2001/25, s 9.2.

[24] See pp 263–4.

[25] UNTAET Reg 1999/3 (On the Establishment of the Transitional Judicial Services Commission) as amended by Reg 2001/26, s 2.

[26] See Chapter 3 (Cerone/Baldwin), and Chapter 4 (Cady/Booth).

[27] UNMIK Reg 2000/34 amending UNMIK Reg 2000/6 (On the Appointment and Removal from Office of International Judges and International Prosecutors). UNMIK Regulations are available at www.unmikonline.org/regulations/index.htm.

[28] UNMIK Reg 2000/64 (On Assignment of International Judges/Prosecutors and/or Change of Venue).

UN Secretary General. Five judges serve in the Appeals Chamber, of whom two are appointed by the government of Sierra Leone, and three are appointed by the UN Secretary General.[29] Judgments are to be rendered by a majority of judges of the Trial Chamber or the Appeals Chamber.[30]

It should be noted that the Special Court Statute does not actually mandate a specific quota of Sierra Leonean or international judges. It regulates, instead, how and who is going to appoint them. Under the United Nations–Sierra Leone Agreement, the government of Sierra Leone and the Secretary General consult on the appointment of judges.[31] Once consultations have taken place, the Sierra Leone government is free to appoint foreign judges if it so wishes (which has actually happened),[32] or the UN Secretary General can appoint Sierra Leonean judges (which is, for obvious reasons, less likely to happen).

Finally, the Special Court Prosecutor and the Registrar are to be appointed by the Secretary General, but the Prosecutor is to be assisted by a Sierra Leonean Deputy Prosecutor. Unlike in the case of judges, the language of the Special Court Agreement and the Special Court Statute is very specific on this issue, saying that 'The Government of Sierra Leone … shall appoint a Sierra Leonean Deputy Prosecutor',[33] and that 'the Prosecutor shall be assisted by a Sierra Leonean Deputy'.[34] Yet, in reality, the Deputy Prosecutor eventually appointed is Desmond de Silva, QC, a Sri Lankan citizen by birth, naturalized UK citizen (but who is member of the Sierra Leonean Bar). To circumvent those specific provisions of the Special Court Agreement and Statute, those instruments were modified on 8 November 2002 by way of an amendment to Sierra Leone's Special Court Agreement Ratification Act 2002,[35] and a subsequent exchange of letters with the UN Office of Legal Affairs.[36]

As sketched at the time of writing, the Extraordinary Chambers in the Courts of Cambodia will not follow the same pattern which gives international judges and staff de facto control of the body. Indeed, in the

---

[29] Statute of the Special Court for Sierra Leone (hereafter 'Special Court Statute') Art 12. The text of the Special Court Statute can be found at www.sc-sl.org (site last visited 1 August 2003).

[30] Special Court Statute Art 18.

[31] Agreement between the United Nations and the Government of Sierra Leone on the Establishment of a Special Court for Sierra Leone (16 January 2002) (hereafter 'United Nations–Sierra Leone Agreement') Art 2.3. Text available at www.sc-sl.org (site last visited 1 August 2003).

[32] Sierra Leone appointed Mr Geoffrey Robertson, head of the Doughty Street Chambers, United Kingdom, who eventually became the President of the Court.

[33] Special Court Agreement Art 3.2.

[34] ibid Art 15.4.

[35] Special Court Agreement (Ratification) Act 2002 (2002) CXXX(II) *Sierra Leone Gazette* Supplement (7 March). The text is available at www.sc-sl.org (site last visited 1 August 2003).

[36] Email from Special Court Registry, on file with the author.

Cambodian case, international judges, instead of being the majority, are intended to be the minority.

The Cambodia–United Nations Agreement provides for a two-tier system, consisting of a Trial Chamber and a Supreme Court, acting both as appellate chamber and final instance.[37] The Trial Chambers are to be composed of five professional judges (three Cambodian, and two international); and the Supreme Court composed of seven judges (four Cambodian, and three international).[38] In both cases, the President of the Chamber is a Cambodian.

Yet, when it comes to taking decisions, Cambodian judges will still not be able to impose their will on international judges. According to the so-called 'Kerry compromise', first all decisions are to be approved by a super-majority vote (four out of five judges at the trial level; and five out of seven at the Supreme Court level).[39] The compromise gives international judges the possibility of blocking embarrassing decisions, provided that international judges could actually agree between themselves and team up against their Cambodian colleagues. Moreover, when there is no unanimity, decisions will contain both the views of the majority and minority.[40] Secondly, there will be two prosecutors: one Cambodian and one foreign. The co-prosecutors are supposed to work together to prepare indictments.[41] However, should disagreements arise between them, any of them can request to have the dispute settled by a Pre-Trial Chamber of five judges (three Cambodian and two international), again voting with a super-majority of four out of five votes.[42]

In sum, while all internationalized courts are by definition composed of a mix of national and international staff, the actual mix can vary to a large extent. The exact composition of the blend is ultimately dictated by the political and historical factors that influenced the establishment of the given body.

---

[37] United Nations/Cambodia Agreement Art 3.2

[38] Law on the Establishment of Extraordinary Chambers in the Courts of Cambodia (hereafter 'Extraordinary Chambers Law') Art 9. An English text of the Extraordinary Chambers Law can be found at www.derechos.org/human-rights/seasia/doc/krlaw.html (site last visited 1 August 2003), however, in the website there is no statement as to its exact source and under the Cambodian Constitution the only official language is Khmer. Moreover, after the conclusion of the United Nations/Cambodia Agreement, the Extraordinary Chambers Law will have to be modified accordingly (United Nations/Cambodia Agreement Art 2)

[39] ibid Art 4.1.

[40] ibid Art 4.2.

[41] ibid Art 6.

[42] ibid Art 7. The Pre-Trial Chamber decides disputes between the Co-Prosecutors according to an inverted super-majority, that is to say a majority plus one international judge is required to block prosecution proposed by one of the Co-Prosecutors. If there is no majority, the investigation or prosecution will proceed: ibid Art 7.4, last line. Decisions of the Pre-Trial Chamber on these matters cannot be appealed: ibid Art 7.4, first line.

C. QUALIFICATIONS

Hudson listed as 'factors to be considered in selecting members of international tribunals (in order of importance): nationality, moral integrity, profession, command of languages, age, and economic and social outlook [ie political ideas]'.[43] By and large the items listed, and the order in which he put them, are still valid nowadays. Incidentally, the fact that nationality still matters the most, *ceteris paribus*, is perhaps a sign of the chronic immaturity of the international system. General muttering aside, one could add that there is a tendency towards also requiring specific knowledge of criminal law and procedure, and that gender balance is beginning to emerge as an issue. We will address first the issues of nationality, moral integrity, gender, and professional background and expertise, while other relevant points will be made in the next section on the recruitment of personnel.

1. Nationality

Nationality, of course, matters. As has just been said, the distinction between local and foreign judges is at the very heart of the notion of an internationalized criminal body. Nationality also matters when it comes to the question of the selection of international judges. For instance, nominations for appointment to the Sierra Leone Special Court are made by Member States of the Economic Community of West African States and the Commonwealth, at the invitation of the UN Secretary-General.[44] Thus, the Special Court's judges are mainly from Commonwealth countries (Canada, Cameroon, Sierra Leone, Nigeria, Gambia, United Kingdom, and Zambia), and the Registrar is from the United Kingdom. The exceptions are Judge Renate Winter, who is Austrian,[45] and the Prosecutor, who is a US national.[46]

---

[43] Hudson (*supra* n 1) 33.

[44] United Nations–Sierra Leone Agreement Art 2.2.a and 2.2.c.

[45] It is interesting to note that Judge Winter before being appointed to the Special Court for Sierra Leone was serving as an international judge in the Kosovo Supreme Court. Previously, she was a judge in the Vienna Youth Court and had worked for the United Nations in Africa on projects relating to juveniles and child soldiers. This particular feature of her curriculum might have weighed decisively in her favour.

[46] Nationality, however, seems to be the decisive factor in selecting a US national for the role of Prosecutor, considering the important role the United States played in the establishment of the Special Court. However, unlike most, if not all, international judges and prosecutors, who have as a background a career in national courts or diplomacy, David Crane is a soldier by career. He has served in the Department of Defense for 30 years, where he held numerous key positions, including Director of the Office of Intelligence Review, Assistant General Counsel of the Defense Intelligence Agency, and Professor of International Law at the US Army Judge Advocate General's School. The particular choice of this individual undoubtedly appears to reflect the balance of power between the Pentagon and the Department of Justice on the one hand, and the State Department, on the other, under the George W Bush administration, more than any particular needs of the Sierra Leone Special Court.

In the Cambodian case, under the Cambodia–United Nations Agreement, nominations for international judges of the Extraordinary Chambers are to be made by the UN Secretary General, who is to prepare a list of no more than seven individuals, from which the Supreme Council of the Magistracy will appoint five to serve in the Chambers (Trial and Supreme).[47] Provided that the Cambodian project ever becomes a reality, and provided it does so on the basis of the Cambodia–United Nations Agreement, it is clear that the Secretary-General has no particular restriction to his discretion in nominating international candidates. It is likely, however, that he will try to include in the list judges from countries which have supported the establishment of the Chambers (eg, Japan, Australia, France, to name a few), or that will contribute significantly to the expenses of the endeavour, but be careful not to involve stakeholders in the judicial process (eg, China or Vietnam).

In the case of East Timor and Kosovo, where internationalized panels are part of UN missions, most judges and prosecutors have been provided by those countries that provide financial support for the endeavours. International judges and prosecutors in Kosovo come from quite a diversified number of countries, although OECD Member States provide the majority of them. Thus, in March 2003, of the 16 international judges, four were from the United States, two from Germany, and the remainder from the United Kingdom, Moldova, Poland, Cameroon, Italy, Hungary, Uganda, Philippines, Mauritius, and Canada.[48] Of the prosecutors, two were from Canada and Philippines, and one each from the United States, United Kingdom, Australia, Malawi, Germany, and Ireland.[49] Moreover, since the introduction of international judges and prosecutors in Kosovo, besides those currently serving, 17 judges and seven prosecutors have been deployed. Of the judges, four were from France, three from Germany, two from Denmark and Finland, and one each from Romania, Belgium Spain,

---

[47] United Nations/Cambodia Agreement Art 5.

[48] Leonard Assira (Cameroon) Pristina District Court; Paul Chevalier (Canada) Gnjilane District Court; Dierk Helmken (Germany) Prizren District Court; Feilitzsch von Freiherr (Germany) Gnjilane District Court; Hajnalka Karpati (Hungary) Prizren District Court; Annunciata Ciuravolo (Italy) Pristina District Court; Vinod Boolell (Mauritius) Gnjilane District Court; Tudor Pandtiru (Moldova) Kosovo Supreme Court; Lolita Dumlao (Philippines) Mitrovica District Court; M Klonowiecka (Poland) Pristina District Court; F Egonda-Ntende (Uganda) Pec/Peja District Court; Timothy Clayson (United Kingdom) Kosovo Supreme Court; Daniel Mabley (United States) Pristina District Court; Edward Wilson (United States) Prizren District Court; Marilyn Kaman (United States) Pec/Peja District Court; Robert Carolan (United States) Mitrovica District Court.

[49] Philip Alcock (United Kingdom) Mitrovica District Court; Paul Flynn (Ireland) Mitrovica District Court; Tom Hickman (United States) Prizren District Court; Christopher Maxwell (Australia) Office of the Public Prosecutor; Gary McCuaig (Canada) Pristina District Court; Kamudoni Nyasulu (Malawi) Pec/Peja District Court; Elizabeth Rennie (Canada) Gnjilane District Court; Jude Romano (Philippines) Prizren District Court; Raimund Sauter (Germany)-Pec/Peja District Court; Cecilia Tillada (Philippines) Gnjilane District Court.

Austria, Sweden, and Canada. Of the prosecutors, three were from the United Kingdom, two from the United States, and one each from Germany and Finland.

In East Timor, Portuguese-speaking countries (Portugal, Brazil, and Cape Verde) have provided a significant share of judges, that is to say four out of nine (the remainder are from Uganda, Burundi, Austria, Germany, and Italy), while prosecutors come from a widely diversified number of regions, such as Europe (Portugal, Norway, United Kingdom, Poland), Africa (Tanzania, Kenya, Gambia, Burundi), North America (Canada, United States), and South East Asia and the Pacific (Australia and Malaysia). It is interesting to note, and difficult to explain, that in East Timor, a substantial number of judges and prosecutors come from Africa, while Japan, which is a major donor, has provided none.

In sum, in the case of internationalized criminal courts nationality matters, but much less than in the case of elections of judges to other international judicial bodies, such as the International Court of Justice (ICJ) or ICC, where political considerations ultimately dictate the composition of the bench. In internationalized international criminal bodies, the principle of equitable geographic representation plays a substantially lesser role than in the case of traditional international judicial bodies. More than geopolitical considerations, the provenance of the political and financial backing of the operation carries much weight, and seems to play a tangible role in determining whether a given candidate has the 'right' nationality to be appointed.

2. Moral integrity

Despite the vagueness of the expression, 'moral integrity' is undoubtedly the first and minimum requirement for judicial office, either internationally or nationally.[50] To Hudson, it embraces:

more than ordinary fidelity and honesty, more than patent impartiality. It includes a measure of freedom from prepossessions, a willingness to face consequences of views which may not be shared, a devotion to judicial processes, a willingness to make the sacrifices which the performance of judicial duties may involve.[51]

---

[50] As Judge Elias, of the ICJ, once remarked, not without a certain wit, the requirement of moral integrity is 'probably the equivalent of an unimpeachable conduct as a public figure; in other words, the candidate need not to be an angel, though he must not be only a little better than a rascal'. TO Elias 'Does the International Court of Justice, as it is Presently Shaped, Correspond to the Requirements which Follow from its Functions as the Central Judicial Body of the International Community?' in Max-Planck-Institut für Ausländisches Öffentliches Recht und Völkerrecht (ed) *Judicial Settlement of International Disputes* (Springer Berlin 1974) 21–2. The passage is quoted in E Valencia-Ospina, 'Editorial Comment' in *The Law and Practice of International Courts and Tribunals* (2002) vol I No 1, 8–9.

[51] Hudson (*supra* n 1) 34.

Invariably statutes of international judicial bodies require judges to be persons of 'high moral character'.[52] The same is true also in the case of internationalized criminal courts and tribunals.[53] Yet, in certain cases, their basic instruments do elaborate upon the concept. Thus, the Statute of the Sierra Leone Special Court, as well as the Cambodia–United Nations Agreement, add that judges, both national and international, 'shall be independent in the performance of their functions, and shall not accept or seek instructions from any Government or any other source'.[54] Similarly, the East Timor Statute of Judicial Magistrates, which regulates the country's judiciary after the declaration of independence (19 May 2002),[55] provides that:

[j]udicial magistrates shall adjudicate in accordance with the Constitution, the law and their conscience and they shall not be subject to orders, instructions or directions, except for the duty of lower courts to obey decisions awarded by higher courts on cases appealed against.[56]

UNMIK Regulation 2000/57 (On the Appointment of Local Judges and Prosecutors) adds to these boilerplate provisions, that they must not have participated in discriminatory measures, or applied any repressive law or have implemented dictatorial policies, and not be registered with any political party or otherwise engage in political activity.[57] While these two provisos can be considered inherent in the requirement of impartiality that should characterize any judge, UNMIK Regulation 2000/57, and also for that matter UNMIK Regulation 2000/34, which applies to international judges, prescribe also that candidates must not have criminal records. Criminal records seem to be hardly compatible with the requirement of 'high moral character', but, while making them a disqualifying factor for international judges is only logical, in the case of local judges it might unnecessarily penalize

[52] Article 2 of the Statute of the International Court of Justice provides, eg: 'The Court shall be composed of a body of independent judges, elected ... from among persons of high moral character'. Other tribunals use language similar to that of the ICJ Statute, calling for the nomination and election of persons of high moral character (eg Rome Statute Art 36.3.a; European Convention on Human Rights Art 21.1; American Convention on Human Rights Arts 34, and 52; African Charter on Human and People's Rights Art 31; ICTY Statute Art 13), 'highest reputation for fairness and integrity' (ITLOS Statute Art 2). The Statute of the African Court on Human and People's Rights Art 31, requires 'personalities of the highest reputation' and recognized competence in the field or subject matter of the court.
[53] UNMIK Reg 2000/34 s 2.c; UNMIK Reg 2000/57 s 6.1; UNTAET Reg 2000/15 s 23.2; UNTAET Reg 1999/3 s 3.c (incidentally, this provision adds also that local candidates must have 'standing within the community'); Extraordinary Chambers Law Art 10; United Nations/Cambodia Agreement Art 3.3; Special Court Statute Art 13; United Nations–Sierre Leone Agreement Art 3.3.
[54] Special Court Statute Art 13; United Nations/Cambodia Agreement Art 3.3.
[55] 'Statute of Judicial Magistrates'. Available at www.jsmp.minihub.org/Legislation/LegEng/JudMagFinalEngfeb03.pdf (site last visited 1 August 2003).
[56] ibid s 4. The Statute of Judicial Magistrates applies, *mutatis mutandis*, and on a transitional basis, both to local and international judges. ibid s 111.
[57] UNMIK Reg 2000/57 s 6.1.

persons who actively resisted oppression. Then again, those who resisted oppression might not be the most dispassionate judges in cases involving their former persecutors.

3. Gender

It is only recently that equitable gender representation has begun to emerge as an issue for international courts and tribunals. Traditionally very few women, or none at all, have sat on the bench of international judicial bodies. Just as few have pleaded before them.[58] Currently, only the basic instruments of very few international judicial bodies contain provisions where specific reference is made to women's participation either as judges, or high-level court personnel. Besides, these few cases are in the field of human rights and international criminal law.

Thus, to illustrate, the International Criminal Court, and the African Court on Human and People's Rights, which has not yet become operational, have rules that make specific reference to women's participation as judges.[59] The European Court of Human Rights has a similar rule for internal appointments, (ie, the appointment of Presidents, Vice-Presidents, Registrars, and Deputy Registrars).[60] Finally, the Statute of the International Criminal Court requires the Prosecutor and Registrar in appointing staff to take into account fair representation of men and women.[61]

The provision of the Rome Statute on equitable gender representation has been the object of an intense campaign by certain progressive governments, and like-minded NGOs, to ensure they were actually implemented. Largely thanks to these efforts, the election of the first bench of ICC will likely go down in history not only for being the first, but also because it achieved the highest ratio of women to men ever for an international judicial body (ie, seven out of 18).

In internationalized criminal tribunals, women are present, both as judges and prosecutors, but are still rare sightings. Thus, in East Timor, of seven judges, including those currently serving and those who served in the past, all are male, while there have been five female prosecutors (out of a total of 18). The situation is only slightly better in Kosovo where, at the time of writing, of the 16 international judges, 11 were male and five female (Italy, Poland, Hungary, United States, Philippines); of the 10 prosecutors, eight

---

[58] On this issue see the background paper prepared by Jan Linehan for the seminar held by the Project on International Courts and Tribunals and Matrix Chambers, London (13 July 2001) available at www.pict-pcti.org//activities/meetings/London_07_01/Women1.pdf (site last visited 1 August 2003).

[59] Respectively, Rome Statute Art 36.8.a.iii and ACHPR Statute Arts 12.2 and 14.3.

[60] European Court of Human Rights, Rules of Court, as in force on 1 November 1998, Rule 14.

[61] Rome Statute Art 44.

were male and two female (Philippines, Canada). In the case of those who served in the past, of the 17 judges, five were female (France, Germany, Spain, Austria, and Sweden), and of the seven prosecutors, two were female (both from the United Kingdom).

Finally, in the Special Court for Sierra Leone there are just two women out of 10 judges, including the two alternate judges (Renate Winter and Elizabeth Muyovwe), while both the office of Prosecutor and Deputy Prosecutor are occupied by men.

4. Curriculum

I. Background

Judges of international courts and tribunals come, by and large, from three different walks of life: either they are academics, teaching international law in universities, and being specialized in the relevant area of law (ie criminal law, trade law, law of the sea, human rights law, etc); or they are professional judges, usually serving at fairly high ranks of the national judiciary; or they are civil servants, having served their state either as diplomats, or in any other position relevant for the given tribunal. The mix of these three main professional groups can vary from court to court, but will invariably be found in all of them (and in certain cases, some of the judges might have worn two or all of those hats during their career). Internationalized criminal courts and tribunals differ from classical international tribunals in the fact that they rely more on professional judges than on any of the other two traditional pools of appointees.

Again, it should be kept in mind that there is a difference between internationalized bodies like those established in East Timor and Kosovo and the cases of Sierra Leone and Cambodia. As has been explained, in the case of East Timor and Kosovo, the United Nations had to reconstruct the whole national judiciary, at all levels, and including both civil and criminal matters. International judges and prosecutors had been injected into the reconstituted national judiciary ad hoc to ensure that certain key investigations' trials would be carried out in an effective, impartial, and ultimately just manner. Hence, stress is put less on the highest qualifications, but rather on legal training, and, whenever possible, actual trial experience. Also, the number of judges needed to staff internationalized panels in Kosovo and East Timor is higher than that for ad hoc mixed bodies like those for Sierra Leone and Cambodia, where only a handful of international judges is needed.[62]

Thus, in Kosovo all judges and prosecutors must have a degree in law,[63] while this is not necessarily so in most international courts and tribunals.

---

[62] See pp 238–9.   [63] UNMIK Reg 2000/34 s 2.a; UNMIK Reg 2000/57 s 6.1.

Moreover, UNMIK Regulation 2000/34 requires that international judges and international prosecutors shall have been appointed and have served, for a minimum of five years, as a judge or prosecutor in their respective home country.[64] Local judges must have passed the examination for candidates for the judiciary, and have relevant work experience in the field of law, that is, three years for the position of a Municipal Court judge (or prosecutor) or of a judge of Minor Offences Appeals body, seven years for the position of a District Court judge (or prosecutor), and four years for the position of a Commercial Court judge.[65]

In East Timor, during the transitional phase, international judges merely needed to possess the qualifications required in their respective countries for appointment to judicial offices,[66] but no particular seniority was required. In the case of local judges, actual judicial experience was not required, as it is a fact that virtually no East Timorese could serve as a judge in East Timor during the long Indonesian occupation.[67] Candidates for judicial appointment simply needed to hold a university degree in law, from a recognized university, and have completed legal training. In addition to these minimal requirements, the Transitional Judicial Service Commission[68] could also take into account the following criteria: legal competence, taking into consideration academic qualifications, and relevant experience in a legal profession or as a civil servant.[69]

More than three years since the Indonesian withdrawal, the Statute of Judicial Magistrates has increased the threshold by requiring applicants, besides being nationals, and holding a university degree in law, to be older than 25 years of age; to be in full exercise of civil and political rights; to have completed a pre-entrance probationary period of two to three years, and have been rated 'good' on that; and to have taken and passed specific exams.[70]

In the case of Cambodia and Sierra Leone, the qualifications required from candidates to judicial and prosecutorial appointments are higher, and more akin to those required in classical international judicial bodies. Hence, judges of the Sierra Leone Special Court must 'possess the qualifications required in their respective countries for appointment to the *highest* judicial offices'.[71]

---

[64] UNMIK Reg 2000/34 s 2.b.

[65] UNMIK Reg 2000/57 s 6.1. In the case of applicants for the position of a judge in the Minor Offences Court, they must have passed the professional examination. For these judges, work experience is not required. ibid s 6.2.

[66] UNTAET Reg 2000/15 s 23.2.

[67] UNTAET Reg 1999/3 s 9.3.

[68] On the Transitional Judicial Service Commission, see pp 263–4.

[69] UNTAET Reg 1999/3 s 9.3.

[70] Statute of Judicial Magistrates s 25.

[71] Special Court Statute Art 13.1, emphasis added. Of the 10 judges appointed to the Sierra Leone Special Court, eight are Supreme or High Court judges (Judge Benjamin Mutanga Itoe, a Supreme Court justice from Cameroon; Judge Bankole Thompson, a former High Court justice from Sierra Leone; Judge Emmanuel Ayoola, a Supreme Court justice from Nigeria;

Similarly, 'The Prosecutor and the Deputy Prosecutor shall be of ... *extensive* experience in the conduct of investigations and prosecutions of criminal cases'.[72] The Law on Extraordinary Chambers as well as the Cambodia–United Nations Agreement do not explicitly require equally ponderous curricula from candidates (although they seem to be more demanding for the office of prosecutor than that of judge),[73] but, considering the high-profile cases that the judges and prosecutors of those Chambers might be called to handle, it is to be hoped that countries proposing candidates will put forward very experienced judicial operators.

II. Expertise

Among internationalized judicial bodies, particular expertise in a specialized area of law is generally considered a plus, but not a decisive requirement in selecting a particular candidate. That is surprising, considering the specialized nature of the cases they might eventually handle, involving intricate issues of criminal and international law. By comparison, the Rome Statute of the International Criminal Court requires that every candidate have established competence in *either* (i) criminal law and procedure, with relevant experience *or* (ii) relevant areas of international law such as international humanitarian law and the law of human rights, and extensive experience in a professional legal capacity relevant to the judicial work of the Court.[74]

In Kosovo, no particular knowledge of any area of law is required, either for local or international judges. Article 10 of the Law on Extraordinary Chambers simply asks judges to be 'experienced, particularly in criminal law or international law', while Article 3.4 of the Cambodia–United Nations Agreement mandates that 'in the overall composition of the Chambers due account shall be taken of the experience of the judges in criminal law,

Judge Alhaji Hassan B Jallow, a Supreme Court justice from the Gambia; Judge Gelaga King, a former Supreme Court justice from Sierra Leone; Judge Isaac Aboagye, a Ghanaian national serving as a High Court justice in Botswana; and Judge Elizabeth Muyovwe, a High Court judge from Zambia).

[72] United Nations–Sierra Leone Agreement Art 3.3. Emphasis added.

[73] 'The judges of the Extraordinary Chambers shall be appointed from among the existing judges or from judges who are additionally appointed, in accordance with the existing procedures for appointment of judges': Extraordinary Chambers Law Art 10; 'The judges shall be persons ... who possess the qualifications required in their respective countries for appointment to judicial offices': United Nations/Cambodia Agreement Art 3.3. 'The co-prosecutors shall possess a high level of professional competence and extensive experience in the conduct of investigations and prosecution of criminal cases': ibid Art 6.2.

[74] Rome Statute Art 36.b. An intricate election mechanism is to ensure that the bench as a whole is balanced between competence in criminal law and competence in international law. Out of the first 18 judges elected for ICC in February 2003, 10 were experts in criminal law, and eight experts in international law: www.iccnow.org/buildingthecourt/iccjudges.html (site last visited 1 August 2003).

international law, including international humanitarian law and human rights law'. Virtually the same provision is contained in UNTAET Regulation 2000/15.[75] Finally, Article 13.2 of the Sierra Leone Special Court mandates likewise, although particular mention is made of expertise in juvenile justice because of the nature of the conflict that ravaged that country, where children were widely employed as combatants.[76] Still, these provisions, which are rather hortatory, refer to the overall composition of the bench and do not mandate any minimum qualifications for any particular judge.

D. RECRUITING PERSONNEL

Almost 60 years ago, when the number of international courts could be counted on one hand, Hudson wrote: 'The selection of the members of international tribunals frequently presents problems of great difficulty'.[77] The proliferation of international courts and tribunals experienced since the end of the Cold War has further heightened the question. Recruiting staff, both local and international, for internationalized criminal bodies is not easily done.

Currently, around the world there are more than 200 individuals sitting on the bench of an international court or tribunal.[78] About one-third of these is appointed or elected every three to four years, which means that for the international judicial machinery to be able to continue running effectively, every four to five years between 30 to 40 highly skilled, trained, and motivated individuals must be found. Besides, in order to ensure representativeness of these judicial bodies, between half and two-thirds of the judges should be nationals of developing countries, which traditionally have few law schools with adequate international legal programmes.[79]

---

[75] UNTAET Reg 2000/15 s 23.2.
[76] United Nations/Cambodia Agreement Art 3.4   [77] See p 235.
[78] This figure is the result of the sum of the benches of: ICJ (15); ITLOS (21); ICC (18); ICTY (14 excluding *ad litem* judges); ICTR (nine excluding *ad litem* judges); WTO Appellate Body (10, being the sum of three panellists plus the seven members of the Appellate Body); ECHR (41); IACHR (7); ECJ (15, plus 15 of the Court of First Instance); European Free Trade Agreement Court (three); Court of Justice of the Andean Community (five); Central American Court of Justice (six); Court of Justice of the Common Market for Eastern and Southern Africa (seven): www.pict-pcti.org/matrix/Matrix-main.html (site last visited 1 August 2003).
[79] The 1994 UNESCO *World Directory of Research and Training Institutions in International Law* lists 578 institutions, of which 25 are labelled 'International and Regional' (eg, the European University Institute, or the International Development Law Institute) and 553 are national institutions. Of these, 396 were located in the 30 OECD countries (a ratio of 13.6 institutions per country), and the remaining 157 were in the rest of the world (less than one per country). UNESCO, *World Directory of Research and Training Institutions in International Law* (Blackwell Oxford 1994).

The world described by Hudson, where 'no group of men exists which can be said to form a profession of international judges, and ... [t]he number of men actually serving in such positions at any one time is quite limited', is long gone by.[80] Yet, in this age, international justice is an area of the job market where demand for professionals seems to exceed supply. The result of this situation is that more often than desirable, high-profile international judicial positions are filled by individuals who, while having most of the time extensive judicial experience domestically, are disturbingly rather oblivious to international law.

With regard to international judges, once again the cases of Cambodia and Sierra Leone, which are more akin to ad hoc international criminal tribunals, should be differentiated from those of East Timor and Kosovo. As was explained, in the latter cases the number of international judges to be selected, the requirements and the conditions in which recruitment takes place, are substantially different, and more arduous, than in the former cases.

First of all, suitable candidates usually must be identified and deployed quite rapidly. To illustrate, in the case of Kosovo, as was explained elsewhere in this book,[81] the appointment of international judges to the courts of Kosovo was by and large an afterthought spurred by the riots in Mitrovica in early January 2000. The Special Representative of the Secretary-General (SRSG) passed Regulation 2000/6 on 15 February 2000, and the first international judge was appointed the same day. The whole process for establishing and appointing international judges and prosecutors lasted less than 10 days. A few weeks after that, an international prosecutor was appointed. The second international judge was appointed in June 2000.

The United Nations does not keep lists of potential candidates for judicial positions in internationalized bodies. Recruitment is mainly ad hoc.[82] Whenever needs arise, job vacancies are posted on the UN website, and in some cases, but not systematically and only for high-level positions, notice is given to the various Member States' missions at the United Nations, who forward this to the competent ministries back home. Similarly, there is no judicial *Médicins Sans Frontières*-like NGO that could help call up international judges for rapid deployment.

---

[80] See p 235.   [81] See Chapter 3 (Cerone/Baldwin).

[82] Actually, the idea of keeping a list of potentially suitable candidates for appointment is as old as the international judiciary, as the Permanent Court of Arbitration (PCA), created in 1899, was in fact nothing more than a list of experts ready to be appointed to serve as ad hoc arbitrators. However, the list was not resorted to as often as envisaged. Until the end of the Second World War (ie the golden age of the PCA), some 500 individuals were included in the list, but only less than 30 were actually chosen. Of the 19 arbitrations held under the auspices of the PCA in the pre-1945 era, six were decided by arbitrators not chosen from the list. The PCA list still serves to elect judges of ICJ. National groups in the PCA (ie four individuals chosen by their country as members of the PCA) nominate candidates for ICJ. If a country is not a party to the Hague Conventions of 1899 or 1907 but party to the Statute of the ICJ, it will constitute a 'national group' ad hoc, along the lines of those at the PCA, to nominate candidates.

It goes without saying that this, combined with the need to ensure the swift beginning of operations of the judicial machinery, does neither invariably, nor necessarily, yield the most suitable appointees. As Hudson mildly put it: 'The ... selection [of people actually serving in international judicial bodies] is usually determined by a variety of considerations, some of them more or less fortuitous', such as stumbling upon a vacancy on the UN website, one might add today.

The ideal candidate for a position in an internationalized criminal court, either as judge or prosecutor, has extensive judicial and/or prosecutorial experience in criminal cases domestically, is well versed in international law, is able to work without problem in English and/or French, and, as far as possible, is familiar with the culture and traditions of the region where he or she will be posted, and is ready to endure the hardship of being posted in underdeveloped war-torn regions, and often having to live with substantial close protection, either for 24 hours per day and/or by living in the UN compound.

As remarked by Cady and Booth in this book, as contrasted to the large resources of professional peace-keepers from whom missions are able to draw their staff, there is only a very small international force of professional judges who match these requirements, and are willing and able to leave their domestic jurisdictions for extended mission service.[83] Besides, judges who can smoothly work in English, and at the same time are trained in civil law, are as rare as pandas.[84]

---

[83] See Chapter 4 (Cady/Booth).

[84] English is one of the languages used in internationalized courts in Kosovo, Sierra Leone, East Timor, and Cambodia. Of these, Kosovo, East Timor, and Cambodia have civil law legal systems, while only Sierra Leone is based on common law.

Despite the use of English as a modern *lingua franca*, internationalized courts rival the mythical Tower of Babel. The extreme case is that of East Timor, where the Serious Crimes Panels work in four official languages: Tetum and Portuguese (the two Timorese official languages), plus Indonesian and English. Defendants tend to speak Indonesian and/or Tetum. National lawyers address the court in Indonesian. International lawyers speak predominantly English. Judges speak either English or Portuguese. Some defendants or witnesses speak none of these four languages but only a local dialect such as Fataluku or Bunak. Interpreting is therefore often carried out in relay across three or more languages, in a situation of severe understaffing, casting doubts on the accuracy of interpretation.

Internationalized panels in the courts of Kosovo operate in three languages: Albanian, English, and Serbian, although the official language of 'Regulation 64' Panels is English (which helps international judges but creates problems for local ones). OSCE, Mission in Kosovo, Department of Human Rights and Rule of Law, Legal Systems Monitoring Section *Report 9: On the Administration of Justice* (March 2002) 18. OSCE Reports on Kosovo are available at www.osce.org/kosovo/documents/reports/justice. See also UNMIK Reg 2000/46 (On the Use of Language in Court Proceedings in which an International Judge or International Prosecutor Participates).

The difficulty in striking a logical balance between the need to use the local language and that to allow internationals to work is better illustrated by the puzzling compromise contained in the United Nations/Cambodia Agreement, whereby 'The *official language* of the Extraordinary Chambers and the Pre-Trial Chamber is Khmer' (Art 26.1), but 'The official *working* languages

Of course, given the extremely varied kind of situations in which international judges and prosecutors might be called to operate, it would be impossible to have a reserve army of volunteers with these skills to cover all of them.[85] Before deployment, appointees could undergo an intensive training course in local language, criminal laws, and procedure,[86] but often the unavailability of translations in English or French of those texts, and the difficulty in preparing reliable translations within the extremely short time required, severely hinders the work of international judges. When the country where international judges are to be deployed has a legal system based on the common law, problems might be even greater, because not only basic legal texts but also precedents need to be made available to international judges in a language they can understand. Besides, even when case law is actually in English, as in many Caribbean and African countries, it might very well be that judgments of local courts have not been duly collected, indexed, and systematized for years, as is the case, for instance, of Sierra Leone.

As contrasted to this bleak picture, recruiting judges for internationalized courts like those in Sierra Leone, or that planned for Cambodia, might seem a somewhat easier task. Yet there are different pitfalls. To illustrate, in Sierra Leone, in appointing Sierra Leone's judges, the Sierra Leone government contacted directly individuals that it thought had both a good curriculum and reputation. In the case of international judges, first the Under-Secretary-General for Legal Affairs, Hans Corell, convened an informal meeting of the UN Member States on the Special Court and asked states for candidates. Then, the Office of Legal Affairs shortlisted and interviewed seven of them. Five were eventually selected. The prosecutor was identified through a similar process. On the same date, Corell announced that consultations on possible candidates would take place with the Group of Interested States. Only two names were put forward, and one was eventually selected.[87]

---

of the Extraordinary Chambers and the Pre-Trial Chamber shall be Khmer, English and French' (Art 26.2). To complicate the matter further 'Translations of public documents and interpretation at public hearings into Russian may be provided by the Royal Government of Cambodia at its discretion and expense on condition that such services do not hinder the Proceedings before Extraordinary Chambers' (Art 26.3).

Finally, in Sierra Leone, English is the official language, but Krio, an English-based dialect, is widely used and will probably be spoken (sometimes solely) by several witnesses.

[85] On this point, see Chapter 4 (Cady/Booth).

[86] On this point, see Chapter 4 (Cady/Booth). Mark Baskin, in his paper on lessons to be learned on UNMIK judiciary, remarked that in Kosovo, at least during the early stages, 'the typical international legal officer had little training or knowledge about the specific circumstances of the Kosovo legal system, although a few had worked on legal reform of a similar system in Bosnia-Herzegovina': Mark Baskin *Lessons Learned on UNMIK Judiciary* (Pearson Peacekeeping Centre 2002) s 20.a.

[87] The second candidate, besides David Crane, was Kenneth Fleming, from Australia, Acting Head of Prosecutions of ICTR.

The extreme difficulty of identifying anybody close to the ideal candidate in a short time, the lack of a selected reserve roster, and the need for expediency has resulted in personnel staffing international courts and tribunals sometimes having curricula which hardly seem to fit the bill. But, probably it is the best that could be found in the circumstances.[88]

Even when there is actually a choice of suitable candidates, and time to select, often extra-legal considerations, and political interests, play a determinant role in picking a particular individual.[89] Indeed, the question of the selection and appointment of the international staff of internationalized criminal bodies, at least as regards judges and prosecutors, is also a matter in which the governments of the country from which appointees come do have a say, as the Sierra Leone case illustrates.

First of all, very often appointees are serving in the state administration in the home country. Unlike ordinary international courts and tribunals, where any active affiliation with national governments is considered incompatible with the principle of independence, in the case of internationalized criminal bodies, international judges and prosecutors very often do maintain their positions back home. Tenures are often not such as to make it possible for someone whose career has fairly advanced nationally to leave it all to retire, and become an international judge.[90] Nor do internationalized criminal bodies, which are, by definition, transient entities, offer anybody a reliable alternative to secure employment in the state administration back home. Hence, appointment and re-appointment of international judges and prosecutors is contingent upon consent by the national ministries of justice, or other relevant departments or institutions, from where they come. A government might not be willing to grant a judge or prosecutor leave to serve on an internationalized tribunal, or, if it cannot block it, it can actively hinder him/her by slowing his/her future career.

---

[88] Writing about UNMIK, Baskin noted that 'Some lawyers confessed that, before deployment, they had no experience on peacekeeping, knew little about Kosovo's political and legal circumstances, and generally required a good deal of time on the ground to acquaint themselves with the existing state of affairs. Others report that many lawyers (although far from all of them) who assumed great responsibilities were young and without experience in the type of work required by UNMIK': Baskin (*supra* n 86) s 20.a. Also, 'Kosovar jurists add that the international judges and prosecutors are not necessarily experts on war crimes and several said that the international judges are "not very good jurists"': Baskin (*supra* n 86) s 20. 'International personnel ... point out that it has been difficult to even find a sufficient number of well-qualified judges from civil law systems who speak English—and report that the second wave of recruitments was desperate in an effort to bring in any one who formally filled the bill and these are judges that often do not speak English well, have little prosecutorial experience, have little experience in criminal law or in war crimes. Even international judges and prosecutors emphasized that they are not well-versed in Kosovar or international war crimes and humanitarian law upon recruitment': Baskin (*supra* n 86) s 51.

[89] See *supra* n 46.

[90] See pp 265–7.

What if suitable international judges and prosecutors cannot be found at all, either because none is willing to take on the duty, or, more likely, because the respective governments do not want to cooperate with the internationalized judicial body? While this might sound a highly hypothetical question, seemingly in the Cambodian National Assembly's mind this was actually a distinct possibility, and, considering the travails of the creation of an internationalized criminal judicial body in that country to try Khmer Rouge leaders, something that should not be dismissed out of hand. Article 46 of the Law on the Establishment of Extraordinary Chambers provides that if any foreign judge or investigating judge or prosecutor fails or refuses to participate in the Extraordinary Chambers, the Supreme Council of the Magistracy shall replace that person by drawing from the lists from which the first list was drafted. If the lists are exhausted, vacancies are to be filled by the Supreme Council of the Magistracy from candidates recommended by the governments of Member States of the United Nations or from among other foreign legal personalities. If, following such procedures, there are still no foreign judges or foreign investigating judges or foreign prosecutors willing to go to Cambodia, then the Supreme Council of the Magistracy may choose Cambodian replacements.

Yet, in the negotiations culminating in the adoption of the Law on the Establishment of Extraordinary Chambers and leading to the Cambodia–United Nations Agreement, the United Nations strove in earnest to avoid the possibility that the Cambodian government might proceed to trials unilaterally, but still under the banner of the Extraordinary Chambers, by adding the provision whereby 'Appointment of international judges by the Supreme Council of the Magistracy shall be made only from the list submitted by the Secretary-General'.[91] It is thus likely that this provision will not make it into the revised Law on the Establishment of Extraordinary Chambers.

Recruiting personnel for internationalized courts is comparatively more complex than staffing international courts and tribunals because, besides the usual problems associated with finding suitable international personnel, competent local judges and prosecutors need to be found and enlisted. This is not an easy task. Often, the country where these courts are called to operate might have been wrecked by years of chaos and war. In other cases, minorities might have been long oppressed and persecuted, often denied an education, most of all in the legal profession. In this framework, when UN missions are deployed to rebuild the state administration and govern the territory, one of the most pressing problems is finding local personnel with adequate legal knowledge and experience.[92] The fact that UNTAET Regulation 2000/11 (On the

---

[91] United Nations/Cambodia Agreement Art 3.5.

[92] On the state of the local judiciary at the time of the deployment of UNTAET in East Timor, see, Chapter 3 (Cerone/Baldwin) and Chapter 4 (Cady/Booth). On the issues created by the ethnic divide between Kosovo-Albanian and Kosovo-Serb judges, see Chapter 3 (Cerone/Baldwin).

Organization of Courts in East Timor) needs to spell out the platitude that relatives cannot sit as judges on the same panel, is very telling as to how tiny the pool is of suitable local candidates for judicial positions.[93]

True, if few are to be found, more can be trained, but skilled judges are not created overnight, nor in one or two years if you have to teach somebody law in the first place. Besides, training is a lengthy and expensive process, and there is the risk that local people trained in law and judicial practice might later on join the ranks of the UN 'itinerant legal troops', thus bleeding the country of local legal talent.

Often training does not solve it all.[94] Local judges might lack the self-confidence which is the basis of independence and impartiality. Reliance on political authority is a bad habit that takes lengthy mental conditioning to be forgotten. For a local person, taking up office as a judge in a civil or criminal court is a politically-charged decision, one which might attract unwanted attention and serious threats. Finally, pay is often not such as to encourage suitable candidates to accept the position.[95] To that, one should add that local judges are usually prohibited by law from earning additional income besides the paltry salary.[96] While such a provision is reasonable per se, in the

---

[93]   UNTAET Reg 2000/11 ss 9.3 and 15.3.

[94]   In fact, sometimes it can create short-term problems. As the UN High Commissioner for Human Rights remarked in his report on East Timor 'compulsory training for Timor-Leste's judges, prosecutors and public defenders brought the court system to a virtual standstill between mid-September and mid-November 2002. No detention review hearings or other urgent matters were dealt with during this period, except on extremely ad hoc basis'. United Nations High Commissioner for Human Rights *Question of the Violation of Human Rights and Fundamental Freedoms in Any Part of the World, Situation of Human Rights in Timor-Leste* (4 March 2003) UN Doc E/CN.4/2003/37 para 4.

[95]   In Kosovo, in 2001, local judicial staff were paid a monthly salary of DM600 (judges) (about US$275 at conversion rates at that time), DM390 (staff—*(referenti)*) (about US$180), DM330 (beginners) (about US$150), and DM180 (secretaries) (about US$80): Baskin (*supra* n 86) s 66. In East Timor, judges and prosecutors are receiving a salary of US$360 per month. East Timorese judges of Special Panels are being paid US$650 per month: email from Judge Sylver Ntukamazina, on file with the author. International judges and prosecutors, in contrast, occupy UN positions ranging from P3 to P5, and are paid salaries and benefits corresponding to those of senior legal professionals in developed countries, which are many times higher than those of local judges. However, this is unavoidably so, as local judges could not be paid the salaries of international judges, making them extremely rich by local standards, while at the same time no one could ask international judges, who are already difficult to recruit, to work virtually pro bono. Lower salaries for local judges is not an issue in Sierra Leone, however, where both international and Sierra Leonean judges are paid the same salary, which is in line with that of high-level UN positions.

[96]   eg, UNTAET Reg 2000/11 s 2.4 provides: 'While in office, judges and prosecutors shall be barred from accepting political or any other public office, or from accepting any employment, including for teaching law, participating in the drafting of law, or carrying out legal research on a part-time basis, unless for honorary unpaid purposes'. The wording of UNMIK Reg 2000/57 is less detailed, but the results are similar (s 7.2). It provides that 'A judge or prosecutor shall not hold any other public or administrative office or engage in any occupation of a professional nature, whether remunerative or not, or otherwise engage in any activity incompatible with his or her functions'.

particular context in which internationalized criminal tribunals operate, it exposes local judges to dangerous temptations.

In sum, in internationalized criminal courts and tribunals, staff shortages are a concrete possibility. Needless to say, this can cripple even the best-planned operations. As a matter of fact, understaffing, due to a lack of suitable candidates as well as insufficient budgets, is one of the major problems affecting the internationalized judiciary in Kosovo and East Timor.

In the case of East Timor, the UN High Commissioner for Human Rights reported in March 2003 that:

a lack of personnel and training continue to result in delays in the administration of justice . . . Since December 2001, Timor-Leste has been without a functioning Court of Appeal, due to the lack of international judges . . . Prosecutions of serious crimes have suffered delays beyond the control of the Serious Crimes Unit and the Special Panel for Serious Crimes, attributable, inter alia, to the lack of sufficient number of international judges to allow two panels to function simultaneously.[97]

In Kosovo, in November 2002, UNMIK reported that:

The current number of international judges and prosecutors has increased to 26. While this is a large increase from the mid-August 2001 number of 11, it is significantly less than the goal of 34. It must be noted, however, that the addition of each judge and prosecutor necessitates an increase in support staff including interpreters, court recorders, and legal officers. Thus far, the number of posts provided for this has been far short of what is needed. The allocation of posts for these functions is critical in order to ensure that international judges and prosecutors function effectively in Kosovo and deal with an ever-increasing workload.[98]

Understaffing is also an issue for local judges. In March 2002, in Kosovo there were 80 vacancies for judicial positions.[99]

E. INDEPENDENCE OF THE JUDICIARY

The principle of the independence of the judiciary seems to enjoy universal recognition at the level of national legal system. Independence of the judiciary is generally held to mean, inter alia, that judicial functions must be exercised by office holders who enjoy extensive and well–defined guarantees concerning appointment to and removal from office; disciplinary accountability according to a well–defined code of ethics; clear procedures for the assignment of cases; and freedom from interference from undue influence.

---

[97] UNHCR Report (*supra* n 94) paras 4, 6, and 49.
[98] UNMIK Presentation Paper (*supra* n 7) 13. See also OSCE *Report* 9 (*supra* n 84) at 13.
[99] ibid at 8.

At the international level, however, it is only recently that the issue has begun emerging.[100] The area is fraught with difficulties and few navigational tools are available. Principles of independence in national legal systems cannot be imported lock, stock, and barrel into the international sphere, because the international and national context are fundamentally different. For one, at the international level there is no actual separation of powers, a concept which is the bedrock of independence of the judiciary at the national level. Thus, appointments to international courts and tribunals—a crucial facet, albeit only one of many, of the issue of independence—cannot be entirely insulated from political processes, whether national or international. Indeed, in most cases, states require a close involvement in the appointment process as a condition of their participation in certain international adjudications (a point which is most starkly demonstrated by the institution of the ad hoc judge in the International Court of Justice).

Again, some practical features of international adjudication raise different issues than in the national context. For instance, it is more common for international judges to be appointed for a limited period only. In many cases they are expected to be able to return to the active practice of international law after their term of office, particularly if they come from countries with a smaller pool of potential candidates. In some cases, the caseload generated by the tribunal does not justify full-time appointments, and the judges must therefore be able to have alternative and parallel careers.

Once appointed, international judges are sometimes claimed to be less accountable in their conduct and decision-making than national judges. At the same time, the very sensitivity of the matters that are submitted to them, which can often involve judging upon states, or high state officials, and their increasing authority, power, and visibility, requires careful preservation of independence.

If the dictates of international politics chip away at the principle of independence when it is to be applied to international judicial bodies *tout court*, in the case of *internationalized* criminal bodies the principle is warped to such an extent that it bears little resemblance to the original national template.

1. Appointment and dismissal of judges

With regard to judicial selection procedures, at the national level a wide array of methods are employed, ranging from direct election, parliamentary or governmental appointment, or competitive exams. Regardless of the procedure used, the principle of independence dictates that judges remain

---

[100] On the issue of the independence of the international judiciary, see the special symposium issue (2003) 2(1) *Law and Practice of International Courts and Tribunals*.

independent from the body or person electing them. This applies both to hiring and firing practices.

A feature that sets internationalized criminal tribunals aside from international criminal tribunals (ie, ICC, ICTY, and ICTR) is that while the judges of the latter group are chosen by way of a more or less transparent electoral process, those of the former are simply appointed. This is a distinction that has considerable bearing not only on the question of the actual, or even only perceived, independence of judges sitting on the bench of internationalized criminal bodies, but also on the problem of ensuring that only competent and able justices serve in those positions.

Once again, it is necessary to divide internationalized criminal bodies analysed in this book into two distinct genres, comprising, on the one hand, the cases of East Timor and Kosovo, and, on the other, those of Sierra Leone and Cambodia.[101]

In the case of East Timor and Kosovo the personnel of internationalized panels, including judges and prosecutors, are selected by the Special Representative of the Secretary General (SRSG) top-down, in a manner which is not substantially different from that used for any other branch of the administration of the given territory. The SRSG, whose powers derive from the Security Council and not from the Secretary-General, as the name might suggest, has ultimate hiring and firing powers over not only both national and international judges, the personnel of the Registry and Office of the Prosecutor, and the defence unit, but also policemen, prison guards, customs officers, and so on throughout the whole of the reconstructed state machinery.[102] In other words, when it comes to appointment of civilian personnel to the bureaucracy of the territory which he/she has been called to administer, the SRSG is accountable to the Security Council and no one else.

Still, considering the sensitivity of the issue, particularly as regards judges, both in the case of Kosovo and East Timor mechanisms have been put in place to ensure a modicum of transparency to the appointment process,

---

[101] On the issue of the independence of the appointment and dismissal of international judges and prosecutors, see also, Chapter 15 (Friman), at E.3.a.

[102] There are three categories of high-level appointments that the Secretary-General is allowed to make: (a) Special Representatives; (b) envoys; (c) other special high-level positions, including Special Advisors to the Secretary General: UNGA, Fifth Committee *Special Representatives, Envoys and Related Positions. Report of the Secretary General* (20 September 1996) UN Doc A/C/.5/50/72m 2. As a rule, Special Representatives have been authorized by the Security Council, and derive their powers from it. Since 1990, with the increased involvement of the United Nations in regional and local conflicts, Special Representatives have been given far-reaching mandates by the Security Council to oversee more than a dozen complex emergencies involving mixes of peace-keeping, peace enforcement, humanitarian, diplomatic, and other operations. On the Special Representative of the Secretary-General, see Cyrus R Vance and David A Hamburg *Pathfinders for Peace: A Report to the UN Secretary General on the Role of Special Representatives and Personal Envoys* (Carnegie Commission on Preventing Deadly Conflict 1997).

although this applies virtually only to local judges and prosecutors and not to international personnel. Indeed, both in Kosovo and East Timor, national and international judges and prosecutors are selected and appointed through fundamentally different procedures.

As described above, international judges and prosecutors are directly recruited and contracted by the United Nations, within the standard UN employment legal framework (ie, criteria, terms of contract, and procedures).[103] For the record, to date, no international judge or prosecutor has been dismissed from Kosovo's or East Timor's courts,[104] nor has anyone left before the end of their contract.[105]

Applying to judicial operators the same employment framework as for anyone else within an international organization (from typists at UN headquarters to humanitarian workers), by itself, is already hard to reconcile with the level of institutional independence that should be characteristic of any judiciary, be it national, international, or hybrid.

Conversely, local personnel are selected and appointed through special procedures, which nonetheless also fall short of minimum standards of independence. UNMIK Regulation 2001/8 established a nine-member Kosovo Judicial and Prosecutorial Council.[106] The Council is responsible, inter alia, for advising the SRSG on matters related to the appointment of judges, prosecutors, and lay judges, as required, and hearing complaints, if any, against any judge, prosecutor, or lay judge.[107] It invites, by public announcement, applications of legal professionals in Kosovo for service as judges and prosecutors, and makes recommendations to the SRSG about the hiring, sanctioning, and dismissal of judges, prosecutors, and lay judges. Moreover, 'Upon request of the Special Representative of the Secretary-General, the Council may render advice on other issues related to the judicial system'.[108] While the advice of the Council per se is not binding on the SRSG, in practice, the SRSG has invariably followed it.[109]

Another task of the Kosovo Judicial and Prosecutorial Council worth mentioning is the adoption (conditional upon the endorsement of the SRSG) of a code of ethics for judges, prosecutors, and lay judges.[110] The three codes were adopted on 31 July 2001, and endorsed by the SRSG in

---

[103] On recruiting at the United Nations, see pp 252–7.

[104] Email from Judge Sylver Ntukamazina, on file with the author; email from UNMIK, 'Pillar 1, Police and Justice', on file with the author.

[105] Considering how short contracts for international personnel are, this is hardly surprising. See p 266. Yet, short contracts also make it possible for international judges and prosecutors not to seek renewal and depart from the region in haste, leaving behind all outstanding cases unfinished, with dire consequences for the length of proceedings.

[106] UNMIK Reg 2001/8.

[107] ibid s 1.2.

[108] ibid s 1.2.

[109] See Chapter 4 (Cady/Booth).

[110] UNMIK Reg 2001/8, s 1.3.

November 2001.[111] These codes are essential because they establish the benchmark according to which the behaviour of local judges and prosecutors is evaluated.

These minimal guarantees notwithstanding, the SRSG retains king-like powers over the judiciary. Indeed, as much as judges, the members of the Council themselves are appointed by the SRSG.[112] Admittedly, Regulation 2001/8 lays down the criteria that the SRSG should follow in making up the Council,[113] and members of the Council swear before him 'to discharge the functions entrusted ... by UNMIK Regulation No. 2001/8, and administrative directions issued thereunder, and not to seek or accept instructions from any other source'.[114]

When it comes to dismissing the members of the Council for failure to comply with their obligations, the SRSG has also virtually unlimited powers. All he or she needs to do is to refer allegations to the Council, which submits a report to the SRSG within 30 days. The final decision is for the SRSG him- or herself, and, pending the report, he or she may suspend the member and 'in exceptional circumstances take such action as he may deem appropriate in the exercise of ... discretion'.[115]

Again, the Council procedure applies only to local judges. International judges are subject only to the control of UNMIK (Department of Justice— (DOJ)) and the SRSG. Thus, if a motion is introduced to disqualify panels of international judges ('Regulation 64' judges), the Director of the DOJ appoints another international judge to rule on the matter.[116]

In East Timor, UNTAET Regulation 1999/3 established the Transitional Judicial Service Commission. Like the Kosovo Judicial and Prosecutorial Council, the Transitional Judicial Service Commission's task is, *inter alia*, to draft a code of ethics and conduct for judges and prosecutors;[117] to recommend to the SRSG candidates for provisional judicial or prosecutorial office;

---

[111] Email from UNMIK 'Pillar 1, Police and Justice', on file with the author.

[112] UNMIK Reg 2001/8 s 2.2.

[113] ibid s 2.1: '[th]e composition of the Council shall be multi-ethnic and reflect varied legal expertise. The Council shall include both local and international members. Members of the Council shall be distinguished legal professionals, such as but not limited to serving or former members of the judicial and prosecutorial bodies, members of the bar, professors of law, meeting the highest standards of efficiency, competence and integrity. They shall be independent and impartial. They shall not hold any position incompatible with their functions as members of the Council'.

[114] ibid s 3.1. The term of office of the members of the Council is one year, but this term may be extended by the SRSG *ad libitum*: ibid s 3.3.

[115] ibid s 3.2.

[116] OSCE, Mission in Kosovo, Department of Human Rights and Rule of Law, Legal Systems Monitoring Section *Review of the Criminal Justice System (September 2001–February 2002)* 33. Actually, this procedure has not even been codified, but is merely a standing practice of the DOJ: ibid.

[117] To date, the code of ethics has not yet been adopted by the Transitional Judicial Service Commission.

and to provide advice on the promotion, re-assignment, or removal of judges or prosecutors.[118] Members of the Commission are appointed for six-month renewable terms by the SRSG 'after consultations with relevant East Timorese interlocutors and social groups'.[119]

It should be stressed that, as in the case of Kosovo, the Commission's work refers only to East Timorese judges, and it has no bearing on the selection, appointment, disciplining, and dismissal of international judges. Those are UN personnel, and, thus, remain subject only to UN regulations and practices.

As contrasted to UNMIK Regulation 2001/8, UNTAET Regulation 1999/3 is more elaborate, but the substance is the same, as ultimate authority about the hiring and firing of judges, and also of the members of the Commission, rests in the hands of the SRSG.

In sum, both in the case of Kosovo and East Timor, the SRSG has quasi-proconsular powers.[120] Challenging a decision of the SRSG concerning the appointment, sanctioning, or dismissal of judges and prosecutors would be extremely difficult, if not impossible, first because there is no forum competent to decide on the matter, and secondly, even if there was one, because it would raise the issue of the immunity of UNMIK and UNTAET and its structures and representatives.

In the case of Sierra Leone and Cambodia, conversely, decision-making powers on the selection, appointment, and dismissal of the bench, Prosecutor, and Registrar is not top-down, but partly horizontal, being equally split between the United Nations and the government of the country. In a way, it resembles the selection of judges of a classical arbitral tribunal. Of course, ultimately this significant difference between the East Timor/Kosovo case and the Sierra Leone/Cambodia case is the consequence of the fact that while in the case of the former group, the United Nations took over the administration of the territories, including the appointment of civil authorities, in the case of the latter the relevant internationalized criminal tribunal is constituted by agreement between the United Nations and the government in

---

[118] UNTAET Reg 1999/3 Art 1.   [119] ibid Art 2.5.

[120] Both in the case of Kosovo and East Timor grounds for dismissal of judges are spelled out. Namely, Art. 13.3 of UNTAET Reg 1999/3 provides that: 'Judges and prosecutors shall not be removed from office unless in case of: (a) Mental illness or physical incapacity which makes the performance of judicial or prosecutorial duties permanently impossible; (b) Serious violation of professional responsibilities, including the principles enshrined in the oath received by the Transitional Administrator [ie the SRSG]; (c) Acceptance of bribes or other emoluments beyond the granted remuneration, as determined by the Transitional Administrator; (d) Acceptance of political or any other public office; (e) A determination of false information having been provided in the application for professional service in judicial or prosecutorial office.'

Article 7.3 of UNMIK Reg 2000/57 provides that: 'no judge may be removed from office except on the ground of: (a) physical or mental incapacity which is likely to be permanent or prolonged; (b) serious misconduct; (c) failure in the due execution of office; or (d) having been placed, by personal conduct or otherwise, in a position incompatible with the due execution of office.'

power. Still, between the Sierra Leone and the Cambodian case there are significant differences due to the dissimilar roles played by the United Nations in the shaping of those judicial bodies.

As stated above, in the Special Court, Sierra Leone judges are appointed by the Sierra Leone government, and international judges by the UN Secretary-General.[121] The Special Court constitutive instruments are silent as to the question of the sanctioning and removal of judges who have violated their mandate. Supposedly, international judges will have their mandate terminated by the United Nations, and Sierra Leonean ones by the government. However, explicit rules on this should have been provided for, as discretion in these matters hardly accords with independence.

In the case of Cambodia, however, the local government seems to have, at least on paper, a stronger hand in the appointment and dismissal of judges and prosecutors. Indeed, as stated above, both local and foreign judges and prosecutors are to be appointed by the Supreme Council of the Magistracy.[122] The relevant documents available at the time of writing, however, are silent on whether the Supreme Council of the Magistracy can also remove them, and whether the UN Secretary-General will legally have a say in this.[123]

2. Length of service

When it comes to the independence of the judiciary, the length of the term of appointment of judges is generally considered a sensitive issue. Usually, there is a direct relationship between the degree of independence and the length of terms. Short terms of service, coupled with the decision about the renewal of the appointment being placed in the hands of a political organ, might make judicial operators over-responsive to the dictates of politics rather than justice. The same holds true, in general, for internationalized criminal bodies, but, again, a distinction should be made between the East Timor/Kosovo and the Sierra Leone/Cambodia cases, and between local and international judges.

In the case of Sierra Leone and Cambodia, no distinction is made between the term of appointment of local and international judges. In the case of

---

[121] See pp 241–2.   [122] See p 245.

[123] Yet, the United Nations/Cambodia Agreement provides that 'Should the Royal Government of Cambodia change the structure or organization of the Extraordinary Chambers or otherwise cause them to function in a manner that does not conform with the terms of the present Agreement [which arguably includes removing international judges and prosecutors against the will of the United Nations], the United Nations reserves the right to cease to provide assistance, financial or otherwise, pursuant to the present agreement' (Art 28). In case of dispute between the United Nations and Cambodia, settlement is to be sought by diplomatic means (negotiation), or any other means the parties may agree to. No unilateral resort to adjudication is provided (Art 29).

Cambodia it is simply said that judges and prosecutors, both local and international, will be appointed for the duration of the proceedings.[124] In Sierra Leone, judges, prosecutors, and the Registrar all have a three-year renewable tenure.[125] That is more or less in line with the term of appointment of judges at ICTY and ICTR (ie, four years),[126] which, like the Sierra Leone Special Court, are ad hoc international criminal tribunals, but shorter than those at ICC, which, however, is a permanent body (three, six, or nine years of tenure).[127]

Conversely, in East Timor and Kosovo, a distinction is actually made between local and international judges' tenures. In both cases, after an initial set up phase, local judges tend to be appointed for an indefinite term or for life, expressly in order to preserve their independence. In Kosovo, in the first years of operations local judges used to be appointed for one-year terms, but in December 2001 the Kosovo Department of Justice announced that local judges and prosecutors would begin to be nominated for an indefinite term that will terminate upon the completion of UNMIK's mission.[128]

In East Timor, there has been a similar move to appoint local judges for life. Section 28 of UNTAET Regulation 2000/11 provides that after an initial period of no less than two but no more than three years, judges shall be appointed for life. During the probation period the performance of judges is monitored by the Transitional Judicial Service Commission, and to preserve independence, the Commission's scrutiny is to be limited to the professional conduct of the judge (eg, the judge's integrity and dedication, regular attendance in court, ability to cope with the workload, impartiality shown in dealing with the cases) without touching upon the substantive decisions of the judge.

Conversely, in Kosovo and East Timor international judges serve an extremely short term (respectively six months and one year).[129] While this, combined with the fact that re-appointment is dependent on the decision of the SRSG, might cast some prima facie doubts as to the ultimate capacity of international judges of being really independent, it should also be considered that international judges in the end are part of a special international force of humanitarian assistance to enable the relevant UN mission to carry out its mandate (which is usually temporally limited). In many regards, they are not ultimately different from policemen, army personnel, humanitarian assistance specialists, and the like, who are deployed. As Cady and Booth in

---

[124] United Nations/Cambodia Agreement Arts 3.7, 5.7, 6.7.
[125] United Nations–Sierra Leone Agreement Arts 2.4, 3.1, 4.2; Special Court Statute Arts 13.3, 15.3, 16.3.
[126] ICTY Statute Art 13.4 and ICTR Statute Art 13.3*bis*.
[127] Rome Statute Art 36.
[128] OSCE *Review of the Criminal Justice System* (*supra* n 116) 26–7.
[129] Baskin reports that to date (end of 2001) no single international judge or prosecutor in the courts of Kosovo had been discontinued: Baskin (*supra* n 86) s 51.

this book aptly point out, while independence and security of tenure are essential for local judges and the eventual building of Kosovo's or East Timor's future, international judges are not part of that future.[130] The decision to deploy and withdraw international judges is a strategic function that should be in the hands of the United Nations (namely the SRSG), and free from restrictions.

3. Privileges and immunities

The issue of immunities of judges and prosecutors underscores the perhaps unavoidable disparity of treatment between local and international judges and prosecutors. Immunities of the latter are much wider in scope than those of the former.

Typically, in international courts and tribunals immunities are very detailed and substantial.[131] In the case of criminal bodies, such as ICTY, ICTR, or ICC, judges and prosecutors enjoy broad diplomatic privileges and immunities, similar to those of heads of diplomatic missions. In the case of internationalized criminal bodies, international judges and prosecutors largely benefit from similar standard immunities and privileges. Thus, for instance, in Cambodia, international judges and prosecutors, together with their families forming part of their household, will benefit from privileges and immunities, exemptions and facilities in accordance with the 1961 Vienna Convention of Diplomatic Relations, including immunity from arrest or detention; immunity from criminal, civil, or administrative jurisdiction; inviolability for all papers and documents; exemption from immigration restrictions and alien registration; immunities and facilities in respect of personal baggage; and exemption from taxation in Cambodia.[132]

Similar but less broad privileges and immunities are also granted to the rest of the court's international personnel[133] and counsel, whether Cambodian or foreign.[134] Cambodian judges and prosecutors and other Cambodian personnel are accorded immunity only from legal process in respect of words spoken or written and all acts performed in their official capacity, during and after the termination of employment.[135]

The same degree of protection is offered to international judicial operators in Kosovo and East Timor. Again, it should be recalled that internationals

---

[130] See Chapter 4 (Cady/Booth).

[131] On this point see D Shelton 'Legal Norms to Promote the Independence and Accountability of International Tribunals' in (2003) 2(1) *The Law and Practice of International Courts and Tribunals* 27–62.

[132] United Nations/Cambodia Agreement Art 19. Vienna Convention of Diplomatic Relations 1961 500 UNTS 95.

[133] United Nations/Cambodia Agreement Art 20.

[134] ibid Art 21.

[135] ibid Art 20.1.

are UN personnel, and as such they benefit from the usual privileges and immunities of the Organization.[136] Largely redundantly, UNMIK Regulation 2000/47 provides that the SRSG, the Principal Deputy, the other four Deputy SRSGs, the Police Commissioner, and other high-ranking officials designated by the SRSG 'from time to time' (hence arguably also judges and prosecutors) are immune from local jurisdiction in respect of any criminal or civil act committed in Kosovo,[137] as well as, of course, from local jurisdiction in respect of any civil or criminal act performed or committed by them in their official capacity in Kosovo.[138]

Local judges and prosecutors are not covered by these provisions. Thus, to illustrate, in East Timor they are subject to civil and criminal jurisdiction as regulated by the East Timor Constitution,[139] and, as regards disciplinary offences, to the Statute of Judicial Magistrates.[140]

However, the case of Sierra Leone is less straightforward. Part VIII of the Special Court Agreement Ratification Act 2002 regulates offences against administration of justice. Amongst these, the Act provides that:

(a) ... a judge or official of the Special Court, [who] corruptly accepts, obtains, agrees to accept or attempts to obtain for himself or any other person any money, valuable consideration, office, place or employment—(i) in respect of anything done or omitted or to be done in his official capacity; or (ii) with intent to interfere in any other way with the administration of justice of the Special Court ... commits an offence and shall be liable on conviction to a fine not exceeding thirty millions leones or to a term of imprisonment not exceeding ten years, or ... both ... [141]

At the same time, as in the case of Cambodia, Article 12 of the Special Court Agreement, entitled 'Privileges and Immunities of the Judges, the Prosecutor, and the Registrar', provides that judges, Prosecutor, and Registrar, together with their families forming part of their household, enjoy the same privileges and immunities, exemptions and facilities accorded to diplomatic agents which have just been listed above.[142] Similar but less broad privileges and immunities are also granted to 'international and Sierra Leonean personnel'[143] and counsel.[144]

---

[136] UN privileges and immunities are provided for in Art 105 of the UN Charter, and have been elaborated upon, inter alia, by the Convention on the Privileges and Immunities of the United Nations, adopted by UNGA Res 22A (I) (13 February 1946) UN Doc A/43.Ann.I, 1 UNTS 15 (corrigendum in 90 UNTS 327).

[137] UNMIK Reg 2000/47 s 3.2.

[138] ibid s 3.

[139] East Timor Constitution Title V. The English text of the East Timor Constitution can be found at www.jsmp.minihub.org/engconst.pdf (site last visited 1 August 2003).

[140] Statute of Judicial Magistrates chs VI and VII.

[141] Special Court Agreement Ratification Act 2002 s 39.

[142] United Nations–Sierra Leone Agreement Art 12.

[143] ibid Art 13.

[144] ibid Art 14.

Still, the Special Court Agreement does not specify whether Article 12 applies both to international and local judges, Prosecutor and Deputy Prosecutor, Registrar and Deputy Registrar, or only to the former group. On the one hand, logic dictates that it applies to both, perhaps with the exception of immunity from taxation for Sierra Leoneans, for two main reasons. First, the Special Court Agreement does specify that Article 13 refers to 'privileges and immunities of international and Sierra Leonean personnel', while the negotiators evidently did not feel the need to do so in the previous Article 12. Secondly, the last paragraph of Article 12 provides that:

the right and duty to waive immunity, in any case where it can be waived without prejudice to the purpose for which it is accorded, shall lie with the [UN] Secretary General, in consultation with the President [of Sierra Leone].[145]

On the other hand, if so, this would be a major departure form the principle that local judges are treated as their peers working in any other national court which has not been internationalized. Hopefully, this issue will be clarified in the United Nations–Sierra Leone Headquarters Agreement, which is still, at the time of writing, under negotiations.

F. CONCLUSION

The fate of institutions is determined by the people that work in them. Internationalized criminal courts and tribunals are no exception to this axiom. Whether they are here to stay or rather will pass down in history as a temporary measure pending the establishment of the International Criminal Court, and the expansion of its reach, ultimately depends on the qualities of those men and (few, alas) women.

Internationalized tribunals are a unique form of social experiment, where foreign and local judicial operators are put side by side, and pressed to work towards the achievement of a common goal. They are required to do so under rules that are fully familiar neither to the former nor to the latter, but a hurriedly concocted blend. To further complicate the exercise, they speak different languages. Often they work in highly precarious conditions, in tense environments, where they are united by common threats. Still, they have very different destinies, for the international personnel will eventually depart from the country leaving behind a legacy of trials and judgments, while local personnel remain to build upon those foundations laid together a hopefully peaceful and just future.

Foreign judges and prosecutors of internationalized courts are a new species in the international landscape: they are *homini novi*. They are partly

---

[145] ibid Art 13.3.

peace-keepers, as they are dispatched together with military troops, to the most unlikely places, to bring justice; partly diplomats, because they have to walk a very thin line between application of the law and reconciliation; partly pedagogues, because they have to instruct their national colleagues; partly scholars, because they are always aware that their decisions will be scrutinized with a magnifying glass in countless law schools for years to come; and, of course, judges and prosecutors, as they determine someone's freedom.

Unlike their counterparts back home, they do not have the luxury of time. They are asked to achieve a great deal with very little, and under political and administrative pressures that would be considered intolerable by their colleagues. Unlike judges and prosecutors of fully international courts, they are deeply embedded in the reality they are asked to judge. Pain, grief, and hatred is thrust before them daily. They do not sit in comfortable and fully equipped courtrooms in The Hague or Strasburg, but in hastily patched up buildings. To many they might seem ersatz and makeshift international judges, but their actions carry no less weight than those of their distinguished colleagues.

13

The Financing of Internationalized Criminal Courts and Tribunals

*Thordis Ingadottir**

A. INTRODUCTION

In recent years the financing of internationalized tribunals has gained increased attention. Towards the end of the 1990s, the rapidly ballooning budgets of the International Criminal Tribunal for former Yugoslavia (ICTY) and the International Criminal Tribunal for Rwanda (ICTR), brought to states' attention, and in particular to major donors, the issue of the costs of international criminal justice. Similar concerns did not prevent the adoption of the Rome Statute in 1998, which establishes a permanent international court—the International Criminal Court (ICC)—with mandate, structure, and procedures possibly requiring even more resources than those syphoned to ad hoc tribunals. But cost-related considerations did play a major role in the emergence of the hybrid or internationalized criminal tribunals.

Two examples illustrate this point. Commenting on the chosen form of the Special Court for Sierra Leone, then US Ambassador to the United Nations, stated: 'We wanted an international umbrella over the court but we didn't want to create a third tribunal because they are very expensive and very slow'.[1]

Similarly, financial concerns expressed by the UN Advisory Committee on Administrative and Budgetary Questions (ACABQ) played a considerable role in the abandonment of the proposed Kosovo War and Ethnics Crimes Court, and the preference for an intervention of international judges and prosecutors in the national system instead.[2]

One of the most important departures of the internationalized criminal tribunals from typical full international tribunals is the way in which they are funded. The full costs of ICTY and ICTR are incorporated in the budget of

* Thordis Ingadottir is an Associate at the Project on International Courts and Tribunals, at the Center on International Cooperation, New York University.

[1] 'U.N. to Establish a War Crimes Panel to Hear Sierra Leone' *New York Times* (15 August 2000) A6.

[2] See 'Report of the Advisory Committee on Administrative and Budgetary Questions' (13 November 2000) UN Doc A/55/624 para 32. Prior to ACABQ intervention, the UN Secretary-General had reported that local and international responses to the proposed court were favourable; see his Report (6 June 2000) UN Doc S/2000/538 paras 59–60. The concern of some UN officials appears to have been that the court would be an unnecessary and costly mini-ICTY; see Mark Baskin *Lesson Learned on UNMIK Judiciary* (Pearson Peacekeeping Centre 2002) para 41.

the United Nations, and therefore carried by the Organization's 191 Member States in accordance with a predefined scale of assessment. Similarly, the ICC is primarily funded by assessed contributions from states party to the Rome Statute. Conversely, while the bulk of the cost of the international panels in Kosovo and East Timor is incorporated in the budget respectively of UNMIK and UNTAET/UNMISET, important budgetary items were left to national authorities. These tribunals have also brazenly accepted voluntary contributions, whether in personnel or equipment. Significantly, the Special Court in Sierra Leone became the first internationalized tribunal to be funded solely by voluntary contributions.

Any evaluation of what amounts to expensive or cheap justice is fraught with difficulties. Judging only from the mandate of the internationalized criminal tribunals, their goal is certainly beyond price tags, making any findings impertinent.[3] However, the cost of the internationalized tribunals is markedly low, especially in comparison to ICTY, ICTR, and ICC. Judging from their low operational cost and number of indictments and judgments, one could assume they are extremely efficient organizations. Unfortunately, however, the tribunals have been subject to stark criticisms, and their lack of resources has raised serious questions about their status and defendants' rights to fair trial.

B. THE FINANCIAL FRAMEWORK OF INTERNATIONAL AND INTERNATIONALIZED CRIMINAL BODIES

1. International criminal tribunals (ICTY, ICTR, and ICC)

Being subsidiary organs of the Security Council of the United Nations, ICTY and ICTR are incorporated in the UN financial structure, and are subject to its financing, budgetary procedures, and administrative support and over-

---

[3] In calling for the establishment of the Special Court for Sierra Leone, the Security Council: 'Reaffirm[ed] the importance of compliance with international humanitarian law, and reaffirm[ed] further that persons who commit or authorize serious violations of international humanitarian law are individually responsible and accountable for those violations and that the international community will exert every effort to bring those responsible to justice in accordance with international standards of justice, fairness and due process of law ... [and] Recogniz[ed] that ... a credible system of justice and accountability for the very serious crimes committed there would end impunity and would contribute to the process of national reconciliation and to the restoration and maintenance of peace'. See UNSC Res 1315 (2000) (14 August 2000).

Recently, calling for international involvement in the establishment of the Extraordinary Chambers in Cambodia, the General Assembly recognized that: 'the accountability of individual perpetrators of grave human rights violations is one of the central elements of any effective remedy for victims of human rights violations and a key factor in ensuring a fair and equitable justice system, and ultimately, reconciliation and stability within a State'. See UNGA Res 57/228 on the Khmer Rouge trials (18 December 2002)

sight. The expenses of the tribunals are expenses of the United Nations in accordance with Article 17 of the UN Charter, having half of their appropriation assessed to UN Member States on the basis of the regular budget scale, and the other half on the basis of the peace-keeping budget scale. As responsible for the administration of the tribunals, the respective Registrars prepare the budget proposal of the tribunals, and submit it for approval to the UN General Assembly, which votes on it following scrutiny and recommendations of the UN Advisory Committee on Administrative and Budgetary Questions, and the Fifth Committee of the General Assembly.[4] The tribunals are subject to the UN financial regulations and rules, entailing oversight by organs such as the UN Committee on Contracts, and the UN Oversight Services. The tribunals enjoy the administrative assistance and support of the UN Secretariat, including its Office of Legal Affairs.

Unlike ICTY and ICTR, the International Criminal Court is not established within the sphere of the United Nations, and since it does not function within the wider scope of an international organization, the Court had to establish and operate its own financial system. This includes the financing and administration of its overseeing body, which is the Assembly of States Parties. The ICC and the Assembly of States Parties are financed from assessed contributions from states parties to the Rome Statute. The ICC scale of assessment is based on the scale adopted by the United Nations for its regular budget. Funds of the ICC can also be provided by the United Nations, subject to approval of the General Assembly, in particular in relation to the expenses incurred due to referrals by the Security Council (Article 115 of the Rome Statute). Voluntary contributions are allowed, as additional funds, in accordance with criteria on voluntary contributions adopted by the Assembly of States Parties. Following budget proposals from other organs of the Court, the Registrar elaborates a consolidated draft budget. This budget

---

[4] In December 2000, ICTY established a Coordination Council and Management Committee to ensure coordination between the different organs of the tribunal with respect to policy, budget, administration, and that the Registry would take this view into account; see 'Report of the International Tribunal for the Prosecution of Persons Responsible for Serious Violations of International Humanitarian Law Committed in the Territory of the former Yugoslavia since 1991' (17 September 2001) UN Doc A/56/352, S/2001/865 paras 40–47. Similarly, according to an ICTR Directive for the Registry of the ICTR, the Registrar shall regularly schedule meetings with the judges to work out means for enhanced cooperation and improved efficiency in the workings of the tribunal. This development follows events such as the dismissal of an ICTR Registrar, and conclusion by an Expert Group (appointed by request of the General Assembly) that the Registrar's authority over the budgetary process within the tribunals infringed on the independence of judges and the office of the Prosecutor; see 'Report of the Expert Group to Conduct a Review of the Effective Operation and Functioning of the International Tribunal for the Former Yugoslavia and the International Criminal Tribunal for Rwanda' (22 January 2000) UN Doc A/54/634.

is submitted to the Committee on Budget and Finance,[5] then following its recommendations, the Assembly of States Parties considers and decides the budget of the ICC. The Assembly of States Parties has adopted Financial Regulations and Rules governing the financial administration of the ICC, incorporating flexibility and scalability to take into account the unpredictable caseload of the Court.[6]

2. Internationalized criminal tribunals

The Serious Crimes Panels in East Timor operate in a multifaceted financial system. During the transitional period in East Timor, UNTAET was to provide the necessary financial and technical support to the courts in East Timor, included the Special Panels.[7] The cost of the panels and Serious Crimes Unit (SCU) has been included partly in the UNTAET budget and partly in the Consolidated Fund for East Timor. Since the independence of East Timor in May 2002, costs have similarly been shared by the East Timor government and UNTAET successor, the UN Mission of Support in East Timor (UNMISET). A judge, appointed by the President of the Court of Appeal, serves as a Judge Administrator in the District Court in Dili, and he or she is responsible to the President for all administrative matters of the Serious Crimes Panels. Similarly, the financing of the international panels and prosecution in Kosovo is disseminated between different budgets, the budget of UNMIK and the Kosovo Consolidated Budget. The International Judicial Support Division is located within the Department of Justice, which is headed by Office of the Deputy Special Representative of the Secretary-General. The division is subject to UN financial regulations and rules.

The Statute of the Special Court is almost silent on the financial system, only stipulating that the Registry shall be responsible for the administration and servicing of the Special Court (Article 16.1) and that the Registrar shall be appointed by the Secretary-General after consultation with the President

---

[5] Partly because of the experience of ICTY and ICTR, the ICC was given a different administrative hierarchy. The Presidency of the Court is responsibly for proper administration of the Court, with the exception of the Office of the Prosecutor (Art 38.3(a)). The Prosecutor shall have full authority over the management and administration of his/her office, including staff, facilities and other resources thereof (Statute of the ICC Art 42.2). The Registry is responsible for the non-judicial aspect of the administration and servicing the Court, without prejudice to the function and power of the Prosecutor (Art 43.1), and the Registrar exercises his function under the authority of the President of the Court (Art 43.2). See ICC Financial Regulations and Rules reg 3 and r 103.2. See also Establishment of the Committee on Budget and Finance, Resolution ICC-ASP/1/Res.4, Annex para 3.

[6] On the finances of the ICC, see Thordis Ingadottir and Cesare Romano 'The Financing of the International Criminal Court' in Thordis Ingadottir (ed) *The International Criminal Court: Recommendations on Policy and Practice—Financing, Victims, Judges, and Immunities* (Transnational Publisher 2003).

[7] See UNTAET Reg 2000/11 (On the Organization of Courts in East Timor) as amended by Reg 2001/25 (14 September 2001) s 34.

of the Special Court and shall be a staff member of the United Nations.[8] The Agreement between the United Nations and the Government of Sierra Leone on the Establishment of the Special Court stipulates that the expenses of the Special Court shall be borne by voluntary contributions from the international community (Article 6).[9] The agreement gives *interested states* the option ('may wish') to establish a management committee to assist the Special Court in obtaining adequate funding, provide advice on matters of court administration, and be available as appropriate to consult on other non-judicial matters (Article 7). A Management Committee, described in this book by Tortora and Mochochoko, was established in 2001.[10] According to the Sierra Leone Ratification Act 2002, the accounts of the Court shall be audited every six months by an auditor appointed by the Management Committee.[11] The administration and funds of the Special Court are not subject to UN financial regulation and rules.

Finally, the Extraordinary Chambers in Cambodia will be national courts, established by Cambodian national law, within the existing court structure of Cambodia, but established and operated with international assistance. The Chamber's administration will be split between a Cambodian Director and an international Deputy Director, the latter appointed by the UN Secretary-General. While the Cambodian Director will be responsible for the management of the office, the Deputy Director will be responsible for the administration of the international components of the operation, which will be subject to UN rules and procedures.[12]

C. FUNDING OF INTERNATIONAL AND INTERNATIONALIZED CRIMINAL BODIES

Adequate funding is a cornerstone for the independence of a judiciary. According to the United Nations Basic Principles on the Independence of the Judiciary:

---

[8] The Statute of the Special Court is available at www.sc-sl.org (site last visited April 2003). According to the Sierra Leone national legislation, its Ratification Act, the Registrar shall be responsible immediately to the President of the Special Court for the administration and financing of the court. See the Special Court Agreement, 2002, Ratification Act 2002, CXXX (II) *Sierra Leone Gazette* Supplement (7 March 2002).

[9] The Agreement between the United Nations and the Government of Sierra Leone on the Establishment of a Special Court for Sierra Leone, 16 January 2002, available at www.sc-sl.org (site last visited April 2003).

[10] The Management Committee currently comprises representatives of the Secretary-General and the government of Sierra Leone, Canada (the Chair), the Netherlands, Nigeria, Lesotho, United Kingdom and United States.

[11] The Special Court Agreement, 2002, Ratification Act 2002 (*supra* n 8) art 5.

[12] 'Report of the Secretary-General on Khmer Rouge Trials' (31 March 2003) UN Doc A/57/769 para 44.

It is the duty of each Member State to provide adequate resources to enable the judiciary to properly perform its functions ... The term of office of judges, their independence, security, adequate remuneration, condition of service, pensions and the age of retirement shall be adequately secured by law.[13]

Secure and reliable financing is also fundamental for the successful operation of an international court. This is even truer with respect to a criminal court, as it is largely responsible for its own litigation costs (ie, it is responsible for the cost of the prosecution and it will usually bear the cost, wholly or in part, of the defence). Insecure or insufficient funding can cause delayed investigations and interruptions in trials proceeding, thus resulting in the loss of essential evidence, delays in arrests, and the potential violation of a defendant's guaranteed right to a fair and speedy trial. Victim and witness protection could also be jeopardized. Finally, an underfunded court could force the prosecutor to make difficult choices between investigations, which could raise serious questions about his or her perceived independence and the integrity of the court itself.

1. Funding by assessed contributions

The international staff participating in the local courts of Kosovo are funded through UNMIK. Similarly, the bulk of the international staff of the Serious Crimes Unit and Panels in East Timor were funded through UNTAET, and now UNMISET (the SCU also has international gratis personnel). UN Member States are assessed with the cost of UNMIK, UNTAET, and UNMISET operations in accordance to the peace-keeping scale—meaning the permanent members of the Security Council are assessed at their rates on the regular budget scale, plus a surcharge, reflecting the permanent members' special responsibility under the UN Charter. Thus, the biggest contributors to the budget of the internationalized courts are the United States and Japan; the United States being assessed with approximately 27 per cent for the peace-keeping budget and Japan being assessed with close to 20 per cent.[14]

Regrettably, funding by assessed contributions is no guarantee for steady and reliable income. While payment of assessed contributions is

---

[13] The principles were adopted by the United Nations Congress on the Prevention of Crime and Treatment of Offenders, and endorsed by the UN General Assembly; see UNGA Res 40/32 (29 November 1985) and 40/146 (13 December 1985) principles 7 and 11. The principles were drafted for national courts, and in light of the structure of the internationalized tribunals in Kosovo and East Timor, they would be directly applicable to them.

[14] The scale for peace-keeping operations is based on a case-by-case basis and approved by the General Assembly. The methodology used was approved by UNGA Res 3101 (XXVIII) (11 December 1973). Under the method the assessment of the poorer countries is reduced in accordance with the regular budget scale, and the reduction is added to the assessment of the permanent members of the Security Council. When ICTY and ICTR were established, some states argued that the appropriation for the tribunals should be assessed solely on the basis of the peace-keeping budget scale, as the tribunals were sub-organs of the Security Council.

mandatory,[15] the history of the United Nations teaches that issues of non-payment are not moot. Both international and internationalized tribunals have, indeed, suffered through highly belated payments. As of December 2001, the unpaid assessment to ICTY and ICTR was US$43.8 million (US$14.7 million owed by the United States and US$14 million by the Russian Federation). The assessments for the first financial period of the ICC were due on 1 January 2003. In February the outstanding contributions totalled €21,771,633, a staggering 66 per cent of total assessments. Assessed contributions to the peace-keeping budget, which incorporates the cost of the international panels in Kosovo and Serious Crimes Panels in East Timor, are similarly overdue. As of June 2002, outstanding contributions to UNMIK were US$97.3 million, representing 8 per cent of the total assessed contributions (with only 72 Member States having paid in full), and at the same time, outstanding contributions to UNTAET and UNAMSIL were US$101 million, representing 8 per cent of the total assessed contributions (with only 25 members having paid in full).

Article 19 of the United Nations Charter and Article 112.8 of the Rome Statute of the ICC address the defaults on assessed contributions. Both articles make a Member State lose its voting right if the amount of its arrears equals or exceeds the amount of contributions due for two full years. In the light of the considerable arrears experienced by the tribunals, a more aggressive incentive for prompt payment should be considered. To facilitate sufficient cash flow to the tribunals, this penalty should be firmly enforced in case of non-payments. In addition, incentives and disincentives to promote prompt payments could be explored—such as interest payments, limiting the recruitment of staff from states in arrear, and restricted procurement opportunities.

2. Funding by voluntary contributions

Whether in the form of funds or equipment and staffing, the Special Court for Sierra Leone is funded solely by voluntary contributions. The parties to its founding treaty, the United Nations and government of Sierra Leone, do not shoulder any financial responsibility for the Court. This process of funding an international judicial body solely on the basis of voluntary contributions is quite extraordinary, and when the Security Council originally proposed the arrangement it caused quite a stir.[16] The Secretary General

---

[15] The International Court of Justice stressed in its Advisory Opinion on Certain Expenses of the United Nations (Article 17, paragraph 2, of the Charter), that the power to apportion expenses among parties also creates the obligation of each state to bear that part of the expenses apportioned to it: Certain Expenses of the United Nations (Article 17, paragraph 2, of the Charter), Advisory Opinion [1962] *ICJ Rep* 151.

[16] The Security Council, by UNSC Res 1315 (2000), requested the Secretary-General to negotiate an agreement with the government of Sierra Leone to create an independent special court. The resolution requested the Secretary-General to include recommendations on the

initially rejected the idea to fund the Special Court solely by voluntary contributions:

The risk associated with the establishment of an operation of this kind with insufficient funds, or without long-term assurances of continuous availability of funds, are very high, in terms of both moral responsibility and loss of credibility of the Organization, and its exposure to legal liability ... A special court based on voluntary contributions would be neither viable nor sustainable.[17]

Eventually, bowing to necessity, the Secretary-General accepted the proposed arrangement, provided that the process of establishing the Court would not commence until the United Nations had obtained sufficient contributions in hand to finance the establishment of the Court and 12 months of its operation, as well as pledges equal to the anticipated expenses of the following 24 months. Apparently, funding has primarily been provided by the United States, United Kingdom, and the Netherlands. The word 'apparently' is appropriate, because, regrettably, the Special Court Management Committee has adopted the policy of not making public the list of donors and the account remains confidential, even to contributors.

The funding of the proposed Extraordinary Chambers in the Courts of Cambodia has again given rise to the issue of voluntary contributions. According to the Law on the Establishment of Extraordinary Chambers in the Courts to Cambodia, the salaries of foreign judges and staff are to come from the countries that contribute them at the request of the UN Secretary-General, and their expenses borne by voluntary contributions. However, the Cambodian national budget is to bear the expenses and salaries of the Cambodian judges and staff.[18] The General Assembly, in its resolution requesting the Secretary-General to resume negotiation on the establishment of the Chamber, reiterated this funding mechanism by voluntary contributions.[19] As in the case of the Special Court for Sierra Leone, the

---

'amount of voluntary contributions, as appropriate, of funds, equipment and services to the special court, including through the offer of expert personnel that may be needed from States, intergovernmental organizations and non-governmental organizations': see UNSC Res 1315 (14 August 2000) (*supra* n 3) para 8(c).

[17] 'Report of the Secretary-General on the Establishment of a Special Court for Sierra Leone' (4 October 2000) UN Doc S/2000/916 para 70.

[18] Law on Establishment of Extraordinary Chambers in the Courts of Cambodia for the Prosecution of Crimes Committed During the Period of Democratic Kampuchea (10 August 2001) art 44. Notably, the initial international tribunal proposed to try Khmer Rouge officials was to be established and funded through the regular budget of the United Nations: see 'Report of the Group of Experts for Cambodia Established Pursuant to General Assembly Resolution 52/135' (16 March 1999) UN Doc A/53/850-S/1999/231, Annex para 177.

[19] In its resolution, the General Assembly requested the Secretary-General to include in his report recommendation on the 'amount of voluntary contributions of funds, equipment and services to the Extraordinary Chambers, inter alia, through the offer of expert personnel, that may be needed from States, intergovernmental organizations and non-governmental organizations': see UNGA Res 57/228 (27 February 2003) (*supra* n 3) para 9.

Secretary-General has once again voiced his concerns about this funding mechanism. In his report of March 2003, the Secretary-General rejected the General Assembly proposal of funding the Extraordinary Chambers by voluntary contributions. He later reached an agreement with the government of Cambodia that contained a new two-prong mechanism: While the salaries and cost of the Cambodian judges and Cambodian personnel are to be funded by the government of Cambodia, the salaries and cost of the international judges and staff are to be defrayed by the United Nations through assessed contributions. In his report the Secretary-General comments:

It is my view that an operation of this nature, mandated by Member States, would constitute an expense of the Organization under Article 17 of the Charter of the United Nations and should be financed from assessed contributions. A financial mechanism based on voluntary contributions would not provide the assured and continuous source of funding that would be needed to make it possible to appoint judges ... Nor would it provide a secure basis for the conduct of investigations, prosecutions and trials. The operation of a court should not be left to the vagaries of voluntary contributions. It could well be said that courts, as a matter of constitutional principle, should be financed by taxation or, at the international level, through the analogous mechanism of assessed contributions. Moreover, experience with the Special Court for Sierra Leone has proved that, if the assistance that the United Nations is to provide is to be funded by voluntary contributions, it would probably be more than a year before sufficient contributions were received to make that possible ... I am aware that a number of States have informally made statements to the effect that I would be able to depend on receiving the necessary voluntary contributions quickly and in full, to fund the United Nations contribution to the cost of the Extraordinary Chambers. However, I received similar informal assurances of support in the case of the Special Court for Sierra Leone.[20]

As pointed out by the Secretary-General, voluntary contributions are by their nature highly volatile and unreliable. They cannot provide long-term and secure funding, which is fundamental for the establishment and operation of any international tribunal. In the case of the Special Court of Sierra Leone, it started operation without sufficient pledges and it is having major difficulties in securing funds. Even the limited pledges made have not all materialized. This has had a dramatic effect on proposed budgets, which have had to be cut severely. As stressed by the President of the International Court of Justice in his address to the General Assembly, an international judicial body is not able to adjust its programmes to available resources—the process has to be the other way around.[21]

Funding by voluntary contributions is quite rare among other international courts and tribunals. Other international courts, such as the International

---

[20] 'Report of the Secretary-General on Khmer Rouge Trials' (*supra* n 12) paras 72–8.
[21] Address by the HE Judge Gilbert Guillaume, President of the International Court of Justice, to the UN General Assembly (26 October 2000).

Court of Justice and the International Tribunal for the Law of the Sea, only accept voluntary contributions to facilitate access to them, by way of trust funds to defray certain litigation costs, and not to finance general operations. ICTY and ICTR have accepted voluntary contributions, however these remain only a fraction of the regular budget of the tribunals, and are only used to cover extra-budgetary expenses. The Rome Statute of the International Criminal Court allows voluntary contributions as *additional* funds, and the Assembly of States Parties has adopted a strict criterion on their acceptance: the Registrar shall assure himself/herself that any offered contributions will not affect the independence of the court, and he/she shall report to the Assembly of States Parties all voluntary contributions offered, regardless of whether they were accepted or refused.[22] Voluntary contributions accepted for purposes specified by donors will be treated as trust funds or special accounts and kept separate from the General Fund of the Court, that is to say they will not credit the budget of the Court and thus reduce assessed contributions by states parties.[23]

Finally, reliance on gratis personnel by some of the internationalized criminal tribunals is also remarkable, since this is taboo at the standard international criminal tribunals. During the early years of ICTY and ICTR, gratis personnel were widely accepted.[24] Eventually, this practice was highly criticized, and many states raised concerns about the perceived independence of such personnel because they were most often employees of their governments. It was also argued that they negatively affected the

---

[22] See Assembly of States Parties to the Rome Statute of the International Criminal Court, Resolution ICC-ASP/1/Res11 (3 September 2002). The criteria for voluntary contributions to the Trust Fund for Victims differs. All contributions to the Trust Fund for Victims have to be approved by its Board of Directors. The Board must refuse voluntary contributions that are not consistent with the goals and activities of the Trust Fund. Furthermore, the Board must refuse voluntary contributions whose allocation, as requested by the donor, would result in a manifestly inequitable distribution of available funds and property among the different group of victims: see ASP Resolution ICC-ASP/1/Res.6 on the Establishment of a Fund for the Benefit of Victims of Crimes Within the Jurisdiction of the Court, and of the Families of Such Victims (9 September 2002) paras 8 and 9.

[23] The ICC has already received voluntary contributions and pledges thereof. For instance, the government of the host country, the Netherlands, will offer the interim premises for the Court free of rent for a period of 10 years starting from July 2002. This offer amounts to €33 million, including interior designs and a courtroom. Furthermore, they have offered 100 workstations, valued at €900,000. Finally, they offer to cover the cost of the provision of water, electricity, and natural gas to the premises during the first financial period, estimated at €165,000.

[24] ICTY had approximately 50 gratis personnel during 1995 to 1998. In 1995, this included 35 investigators/advisers assigned to the Office of the Prosecutor, including 21 contributed from the United States. In 1996 six out of nine trial attorneys at ICTY were gratis personnel: see Report of the Advisory Committee on Administrative and Budgetary Questions *Financing of the International Tribunal for the Prosecution of Persons Responsible for Serious Violations of International Humanitarian Law Committed in the Territory of the Former Yugoslavia* (10 April 1995) UN Doc A/50/925 and report issued by the Secretary-General *Gratis Personnel Provided by Governments and Other Entities* (21 November 1996) UN Doc A/51/688.

international character of the tribunals since gratis personnel were seconded primarily by developed countries (eg United States, Canada, etc). In response to this criticism, the General Assembly ended the practice and gratis personnel contracts were allowed to elapse in 1998.[25] This policy is reflected also in the Rome Statute, which specifies that the ICC can employ gratis personnel only in exceptional circumstances (Article 44.4 of the Rome Statute).

D. THE COST OF INTERNATIONAL AND INTERNATIONALIZED CRIMINAL TRIBUNALS

Prima facie, one would be justified in thinking that the budget of the internationalized criminal tribunals are of the same magnitude of full international courts. The Secretary-General of the United Nations relied on this very same assumption when he estimated that the Special Court for Sierra Leone would have a similar scope and duration as ICTY and ICTR.[26] As a matter of fact, the scope of the jurisdiction of the internationalized criminal bodies is equivalent, or close, to that of ICTY and ICTR: investigating and prosecuting crimes such as genocide, crimes against humanity, and war crimes. The Serious Crimes Panels in East Timor actually have an even broader mandate, as they have universal jurisdiction with respect to the crime of genocide, crimes against humanity, war crimes, and torture—a jurisdiction irrespective of where the crimes were committed, committed by whom, or against whom.[27] However, in reality, the cost of running internationalized tribunals has been moderate, and certainly far smaller than of ICTY, ICTR, and ICC.

1. International criminal tribunals (ICTY, ICTR, and ICC)

By any standard, the cost of ICTY and ICTR has been considerable. As of 2003, they have cost the UN Member States a total of US$1,309.8 million: US$728.8 million for ICTY and US$581 million for ICTR. With these financial resources, in the case of ICTY, 132 indictments against individuals have been issued (51 of these are currently in proceedings before the tribunal, 23 remain at large), and over 1,600 witnesses have testified at the tribunal. As of 31 December 2001, ICTY had issued close to 900 judgments and orders. As of April 2003, 85 accused have appeared before the tribunal: 31 are at

[25] See UNGA Res 51/243 on gratis personnel provided by governments and other entities (10 October 1997) UN Doc A/RES/51/243.

[26] See 'Report of the Secretary-General on the Establishment of a Special Court for Sierra Leone' (*supra* n 17) para 69.

[27] See UNTAET Reg 2000/15 (On the Establishment of Panels with Exclusive Jurisdiction over Serious Criminal Offences) (6 June 2000) ss 2.1 and 2.2.

pre-trial stage, eight are at trial stage, and 37 have been tried (of those two were recently sentenced, 10 are at appeal, 20 have received their final sentence, and five were found not guilty).[28] Currently ICTY has 16 permanent judges, and a pool of 27 *ad litem* judges (of which nine are being used), and as of April 2003 the tribunal had 1,248 staff members from 82 countries. The Prosecutor expects to finalize all investigations by 2004 (26 investigations remain, of which 17 have opened) and to complete first instance trials by 2008. When ICTY expects to finish all its work, in 2010, its total costs can be projected to have reached at least US$1.5 billion for 17 years of operation.

The figures for ICTR are similar. As of October 2002, ICTR had indicted 80 individuals, with 60 in custody and 20 at large. Eight individuals had been sentenced, one acquitted, 22 were involved in ongoing trials and 29 in custody were waiting for the commencement of their trials. Over 800 witnesses have testified before the tribunal. The tribunal has nine trial judges in Arusha, seven Appeals Chamber judges in The Hague (which it shares with ICTY), and 872 staff members. ICTR has considerable work ahead. Currently there are 17 persons on trial in seven cases, and 26 detainees are awaiting trial. Notably, the Prosecutor intends to prosecute 136 new suspects by 2005. To expedite the work of the tribunal, the Security Council recently agreed on the tribunal's request for a pool of *ad litem* judges, similar to the one at ICTY. Based on that development, the President estimates that the tribunal will be able to complete trials by 2011. The total expected cost of ICTR is therefore likely to top US$1 billion.

The budget for the first financial period of the ICC (September 2002 to December 2003) is €30,893,500; and it includes both the cost of the Court, as well as the Assembly of States Parties. Forty-three per cent of that is allocated to the Common Services Division, 22 per cent for the meeting of the Assembly of States Parties and its committees, 13 per cent to the Prosecutor, 9 per cent to the Chambers, and 9 per cent to the Registry. One million euro is kept for unforeseen expenses. A Working Capital Fund of €1,915,700 was established to cover the short-term liquidity requirements of the Court while it awaits assessed contributions. The budget for the first financial period includes 61 staffing posts for the period from September to December 2002 and 202 staffing posts in the year 2003. The budget for ICC for the year 2004 is expected to be close to €55 million.

2. *The internationalized criminal tribunals*

In contrast to fully international criminal courts and tribunals, internationalized bodies run on a shoestring. A few raw figures will illustrate the point.

---

[28] See information on ICTY website at www.un.org/icty/index.html (site last visited April 2003).

In East Timor, the first Serious Crimes Panel commenced its work in January 2001. The cost of the Serious Crimes Unit (SCU) and the Serious Crimes Panel was US$6.1 million in the year 2001, and US$6.3 million in the year 2002.[29] Itemized, in the year 2001 the cost of the prosecution—ie the budget of the SCU—was US$5.6 million or close to 90 per cent of the total costs, while the cost of the Serious Crimes Panel was US$427,332.[30] In 2001, approximately US$5.4 million was designated for salaries, US$200,000 for cost of the Special Panel (reconstruction needs, vehicle, computers, furniture, etc), and US$440,000 for capital costs/goods and services to the SCU. By October 2001, the SCU had filed 32 indictments, charging 62 individuals with crimes against humanity, 13 cases had been tried before the Serious Crimes Panel, and 11 judgments handed down, of which one was for crimes against humanity. As of February 2003, the SCU had filed 58 indictments, against 225 individuals, and 32 judgments had been handed down. It is expected that the Special Panel will be able to judge current indictments before mid-year 2004.

In Kosovo, the costs of the International Judicial Support Division are carried by the UNMIK budget. That includes salaries for the international judges and prosecutors, administrative and support staff, including legal officers, court recorders and interpreters. The UNMIK budget is not organized by total costs of each unit, but by total cost of personnel and total operational cost for the Mission. Consequently, there does not exist a costs figure for the division. However, for the sake of the exercise, by using average cost estimates for each international and national personnel, some extrapolations can be made. The division had 132 international personnel and 10 national personnel in the budget for July 2002 to June 2003, which total salary cost can be estimated at US$14.6 million. By pro-rating the operational cost of the Mission per personnel, the operational cost of the International Judicial Support Division can be estimated to be around US$653,000 for the same period. In total, the cost of the division can be estimated at US$15.2 million in the last year.

Currently, there are 15 international judges and 14 international prosecutors in Kosovo. That is a sharp rise from one international judge and one international prosecutor in February 2000, and 11 in August 2001. This jump coincides with their increased referrals and workload. In the year 2000, they participated in only 23 cases, 118 cases in 2001, and in the first nine months of 2002 they were participating in 177 cases. The UNMIK budget for July 2003 to June 2004 proposes increasing the number of judges and prosecutors for the division, and additional support staff, increasing the total number of

---

[29] These numbers were provided by officials of UNTAET; no combined official budget of the SCU and Panels exists.

[30] The cost of the repair of the SCU premises is not factored in this figure, nor the cost of eight UN vehicles and six donated vehicles from USAID.

personnel in the division from 142 to 150. That differs from other activities of the Mission, which will scale down next year by 550 people. The International Judicial Support Division is to phase out in the years 2005 to 2006, except for participation in the Supreme Court.

As of June 2002, the justice system in Kosovo had dealt with 17 cases in which acts of war crime and genocide have been charged and prosecuted.[31] Local prosecutors filed 13 of the 17 indictments and international trial panels have issued 10 judgments. While the work of the international staff has been considered essential for the Kosovo justice system, they have been criticized as being too expensive. For instance, while acknowledging their necessity, the International Crisis Group reports that 'international judges and prosecutors cannot remain in Kosovo forever—they are *extremely expensive* and currently do not contribute to the development of local capacity'.[32]

The original budget proposal for the Special Court for Sierra Leone, which was again prepared by the UN Secretary-General with ICTY and ICTR in mind, was US$114.6 million (US$30.2 for the first year, and US$84.4 for the following two). When it became clear that voluntary contributions would not even come close to this figure, the budget was scaled down to half of that, or US$56.2 million for the first three years of operation: US$16.6 million for the first year, US$20.2 million for the second year, and US$19.4 million for the third. Regrettably, these budget proposals were never made public so it is impossible to analyse them specifically. In the end, once the beginning of operations was nearing, the Special Court prepared adjusted budgets: US$19.2 million for the first year (July 2002 to June 2003), and US$24.8 million for the second year.

As with its trust fund account for voluntary contributions, the Special Court has adopted the policy of keeping its budgets confidential. According to a public summary, 40 per cent of the first year budget was for start-up cost (ie, costs related to construction, supplies, furniture, and infrastructure such as information, technology, and communications). Permanent staffing costs were 34 per cent of the first-year budget. The Special Court obtains substantial security, logistic, and technical support from UNAMSIL on a cost-reimbursable basis.

The Secretary-General appointed the Registrar of the Special Court in 2002, and the Prosecutor in April 2002. The Special Court started its operation in July 2002, with the Registry setting up temporary offices and the Office of the Prosecutor starting investigations. On 2 December 2002 the eight judges of the Court were sworn in. In January, the Registry

---

[31] For a comprehensive survey of these cases, see OSCE Mission in Kosovo/UNMIK 'Kosovo's War Crimes Trials: A Review' (September 2002) available at www.osce.org/kosovo/documents/reports/justice/(site last visited April 2003).

[32] International Crisis Group *Finding the Balance: The Scales of Justice in Kosovo*, ICG Balkans Report No 134 (12 September 2002) 9 (emphasis added).

moved to the permanent site of the Special Court. As of April 2003 the Office of the Prosecutor has indicted eight people for war crimes and crimes against humanity.

Finally, for what concerns Cambodia, only a preliminary estimate exists for the budget of the Extraordinary Chambers. It is estimated that an amount exceeding US$19 million is required for the establishment and operation of the Extraordinary Chambers, during its assumed three years of operation. Of this amount US$18.2 million would be personnel cost (US$4.2 for 80 posts in the first year, US$7.8 million for 91 posts in the second year, and US$6.2 million for 74 posts in the third year), US$372,300 for furniture and equipment, US$94,500 for travel, and US$324,900 for general operational expenses. The estimate does not include costs associated with improvement of premises and remuneration of defence counsel.[33]

E. CHEAP AND EFFICIENT TRIBUNALS?

Internationalized criminal courts and tribunals are certainly less expensive than ICTY, ICTR, and ICC. To summarize, the Serious Crimes Panels in East Timor are now running a yearly budget of around US$6 million, the international prosecution and panels in Kosovo about US$15 million, the Special Court in Sierra Leone about US$20 million, and the average yearly cost of the Extraordinary Chambers in Cambodia is expected to be between US$6 to 7 million. Altogether, these four bodies have an aggregate annual budget of about US$48 million, as contrasted to US$128 million for ICTY in 2003 alone.

The nature of their costs and distribution between organs is also far different. While in the case of internationalized tribunals (at least those fully operating), the bulk of the expenses come from the Office of the Prosecutor, the opposite is true at ICTY and ICTR, where the Registry is responsible for close to 70 per cent of the cost of the tribunals. The most expensive objects of expenditure for ICTY and ICTR Registries are translation costs, close to 13 per cent, and defence costs at the same percentage. To no surprise, these are exactly the same items which some of the internationalized criminal tribunals are desperately lacking.

In particular, the Serious Crimes Panel in East Timor has been faced with an extreme lack of sources. In November 2001, a report issued by an observer organization, the Judicial System Monitoring Program, revealed frightening details.[34] The three judges had to share an office and two computers (with no Internet access), there was no library (one book shelf with no books on

[33] See 'Report of the Secretary-General on Khmer Rouge Trials' (*supra* n 12) paras 56–71.
[34] See 'Justice in Practice: Human Rights in Court Administration' (November 2001) available at www.jsmp.minihub.org (site last visited April 2003).

criminal law or international humanitarian law), and there was no administrative support for the judges. Consequently, hearings were not announced, and judgments were not always published or translated. There was also an acute lack of defence lawyers. Similarly, the legal and administrative support for the international panels in Kosovo has frequently been criticized as inadequate, which has led to complications and delays in their work.[35] A recent report by UNMIK on the police and justice system has called attention to a shortage of support staff for international judges and prosecutors, and has called upon states to allocate the additional staff, stating that it 'is critical in order to ensure that international judges and prosecutors function effectively in Kosovo and deal with an ever-increasing workload'.[36] As in East Timor, the UNMIK budget does not cover costs related to defence counsel, this is left to the local budget. Noticeably, this may differ at the Extraordinary Chambers in Cambodia, as according to the Agreement between the Secretary-General and the government of Cambodia, the United Nations is to cover the costs related to remuneration of defence counsel.[37]

Other financial aspects of the internationalized tribunals are also problematic. The international judges of the internationalized tribunals are paid less than their colleagues serving at other international courts, which in part explains some of the difficulties in recruiting qualified judges to these tribunals. Short-term contracts and the financial instability of the institutions they serve make the recruitment even more difficult.[38] This has resulted in a lack of judges and high turnover leading to delayed proceedings, delayed justice, and ultimately higher cost.

It should be noted that national judges, sitting on the same panels as international judges do not necessarily enjoy equal treatment as their counterparts. For instance, the cost of a national judge on the Serious Crimes Panel in East Timor was US$4,332 in 2001, while the cost of the two international judges was US$213,000. The same policy was adopted in Kosovo, while the Special Court in Sierra Leone chose to pay all its judges the same salary. The low salaries of national judges serving on the internationalized tribunals can also jeopardize the integrity and independence of the institutions.[39] Similarly, their poor conditions have led to interference in

---

[35] See Baskin (*supra* n 2) para 52, and International Crisis Group Report (*supra* n 32) 8.
[36] See UNMIK *Pillar I, Police and Justice*, Presentation Paper (November 2002) 13.
[37] See 'Report of the Secretary-General on Khmer Rouge Trials' (*supra* n 12) Annex art 17.
[38] On this point, see Chapter 12 (Romano).
[39] On the poor condition of the national judges in Kosovo, and its effect on judicial independence and difficulties in recruitment, see International Crisis Group Report (*supra* n 32) 6–7, 11. The Group of Experts for Cambodia contemplated that financial support from international organizations and foreign governments could overcome some of its noted obstacles for national process, including 'by paying judges, prosecutors, and investigators enough to make bribery less likely': see 'Report of the Group of Experts for Cambodia' (*supra* n 18) para 136.

proceedings as national judges have refused to hear cases due to a dispute with national authorities about their contracts.[40]

The Serious Crimes Panels in East Timor and the international panels in Kosovo have been integrated into the national judicial system, which at the time did not exist or was in total disarray. This has had a severe impact on the funding and operating of these tribunals. Even when they have their own administrative system, as in the case of the Special Court of Sierra Leone, the lack of transparency in financial matters is troublesome. The Special Court's policy of keeping its budget and accounts of the voluntary trust fund confidential is regrettably counter-productive. As the Special Court is solely funded by voluntary contributions, transparency of its accounts is even more necessary, both to attract potential donors, and to preserve the independence of the Court. While no one should request publication of all the documentation required and produced by an organization such as the United Nations, an entirely opposite policy is even worse.

Markedly, internationalized tribunals do not address the issue of reparations to victims. In recent years, the mandate of international criminal tribunals has been expanded to provide restorative justice in addition to the traditional retributive justice. This is highlighted by the Rome Statute of the ICC, which gives the judges of the Court the mandate to decide on reparation to victims, including compensation (Article 75 of the Rome Statute). Similarly, a Trust Fund for Victims has been established, benefiting victims within the jurisdiction of the ICC and their families (Article 79 of the Rome Statute). A Board of Directors, to be elected later this year, has the mandate to set the activities of the fund and pledge for contributions. ICTY and ICTR have also been dealing with the issue. Late in 2000, in response to proposals from the prosecutors, the judges of both tribunals prepared reports on victims' compensation.[41] Both reports concluded that victims within their jurisdiction have a right in law to compensation for the injuries that they have suffered. While concluding that the statutes of the tribunals did not give them the mandate to decide on reparation to victims, they recommended that the matter should be brought to the attention of the Security Council to consider a possible mechanism for the payment of compensation to victims.

In contrast to these developments, none of the internationalized tribunals provide for reparation to victims. The Serious Crimes Panels in East Timor are to have a trust fund for victims, funded by forfeiture collected from the

---

[40] See Judicial System Monitoring Programme *Dispute over Judges' Contracts Stops Serious Crimes Cases* Press Release Dili (16 January 2001).

[41] See Letter from the Secretary-General addressed to the President of the Security Council (2 November 2000) UN Doc S/2001/1063; Letter from the Secretary-General addressed to the President of the Security Council (14 December 2000) UN Doc S/2000/1198.

convicted persons, but it has never been established.[42] Similarly, in the case of Sierra Leone, a special fund for war victims is contemplated in the Lomé Peace Accord, but that fund has similarly never been established.[43] Obviously, the internationalized tribunals will have to acknowledge the development and address the issue of reparation to its victims, and how it can be funded.

Finally, when looking at the cost of criminal tribunals it might also be useful to look at the bigger picture. Tribunals do not work in a vacuum, they are part of a much greater operation. While the cost of ICTY is now reaching US$800 million it should also be kept in mind that from 1992 to 1998 the international community spent between US$49 to 70 billion to end the conflict in Bosnia. As for the tribunals in Kosovo and East Timor, the cost of UNMIK for its four years of operation was US$1.5 billion, and the cost of UNTAET will reach US$1.6 billion by the middle of this year. Currently, UN Member States have been assessed with over US$2 billion for the cost of the UN Mission in Sierra Leone. In comparison, and in light of the significant role the tribunals are given with respect to restoration and maintenance of peace, and national reconciliation, their expenses seem reasonable.

F. CONCLUSION

While the idea of leaner and cheaper international criminal justice is attractive and justified in a period of general economic austerity, its practical translation is fraught with difficulties. The international panels in Kosovo and East Timor are partly relying on funding and administration of very weak national systems, with detrimental consequences. On top of that, the funding from the United Nations to these tribunals has been sparse. In fact, in some instances, the lack of resources has been so severe that it can be candidly stated that the United Nations, and the international community, have failed to meet established minimum standards of independent judiciary and fair trial. The attempt to fund the Special Court in Sierra Leone solely by voluntary contributions is running aground, and the Court has not been able to secure funding for its second year of operation. The Secretary-General

[42] See UNTAET Reg 2000/15 (On the Establishment of Panels with Exclusive Jurisdiction over Serious Criminal Offences) (6 June 2000) (*supra* n 27) s 25.

[43] According to Art XXIX of the Lomé Peace Accord the 'Government, with the support of the International Community, shall design and implement a programme for the rehabilitation of war victims. For this purpose, a special fund shall be set up'. According to the Sierra Leone Truth and Reconciliation Commission Act 2000, the Commission may provide information or recommendations to or regarding the Special Fund for War Victims provided for in Art XXIV of the Lomé Peace Agreement, or otherwise assist the Fund in any manner the Commission considers appropriate but the Commission shall not exercise any control over the operations or disbursements of that Fund.

should seriously consider bringing the matter to the attention of the Security Council and request that the funding of the Court be incorporated in the United Nations budget. At the same time, he should stay firm on his proposal that the cost of the international participation in the Extraordinary Chambers in Cambodia should be paid by the United Nations rather than by voluntary contributions as the General Assembly has proposed.

The proliferation of international and internationalized tribunals will only exacerbate the issue of their funding and how to raise adequate resources. At the present time, with the actual setting up of a new permanent International Criminal Court taking place, and the Court collecting the first assessments from its Member States, six international criminal tribunals are operating, each with its own budget, but all depending on the same funding resources. Despite the coming into being of the International Criminal Court, the establishment of new international and internationalized criminal courts is not precluded.[44] Parallel internationalized proceedings are likely to remain, as is currently being considered at ICTY.[45] The 11 September 2001 attacks have also reopened the discussion whether the international community should tackle the crime of terrorism through international prosecutions. The mechanisms for prosecuting international drug trafficking are still pending.[46] Inevitably, financial issues will play a significant role in future development. However, while the international community reiterates its commitment to international criminal justice, at the same time it will have to stand up fully to this pledge by providing the necessary material support. Delayed and hampered justice runs the risk of becoming poor justice or even justice denied.

[44] On this issue, see Chapters 19 (Colitti), 18 (Benzing/Bergsmo) and 20 (Condorelli/ Boutruche).

[45] See 'Report on the Judicial Status of the International Criminal Tribunal for the Former Yugoslavia and the Prospects for Referring Certain Cases to National Courts' (19 June 2002) UN Doc S/2002/678. ICTY recommends that a Chamber with the jurisdiction to try the accused referred by ICTY be established within the State Court of Bosnia and Herzegovina, and that international judges serve alongside the national judges at least for a set period: ibid para 85.

[46] Both these crimes were included in the Draft Statute for the International Criminal Court, but the proposal did not attract sufficient support. However, the Final Act of the Rome Conference '[r]ecommends that a Review Conference pursuant to article 111 of the Statute of the International Criminal Court consider the crimes within the jurisdiction of the Court': see Final Act of the United Nations Diplomatic Conference of Plenipotentiaries on the Establishment of an International Criminal Court, Annex I.E.

14

Internationalized Courts and Substantive Criminal Law

*Bert Swart**

A. INTRODUCTION

This chapter examines the substantive criminal law applicable in the internationalized courts created in East Timor and Sierra Leone as well as the internationalized court envisaged for Cambodia. Because the internationalized panels for Kosovo differ so much from the other three internationalized courts as far as purpose, jurisdiction, and applicable law are concerned, they will be treated less extensively.

After a brief discussion of the purpose of internationalized courts, this chapter will examine the jurisdiction and the applicable substantive law issues in these courts. Crimes under general international law, other international crimes, crimes under domestic law, and general principles of criminal law will be discussed subsequently.

B. THE PURPOSE OF INTERNATIONALIZED COURTS

International and internationalized criminal courts may be created for all kinds of purposes. The jurisdiction of these courts is not necessarily limited to international crimes in the strictest sense: aggression, genocide, crimes against humanity, and war crimes, which are crimes under customary international law and constitute crimes against the peace and security of mankind. It is, for instance, conceivable that the UN Security Council, acting under Chapter VII of the UN Charter, decides to create an international or internationalized court for the purpose of adjudicating terrorist crimes, drug crimes, crimes against internationally protected persons, or still other international crimes that have been created by treaties, if it is of the opinion that this would be necessary in order to maintain or restore international peace. Similarly, the Security Council could decide to create a court for the purpose of adjudicating international offences that the Council itself has created

* Former judge at the Amsterdam Court of Appeal and Professor of International Criminal Law at the University of Amsterdam; *ad litem* judge, ICTY.

under Chapter VII.[1] It is also conceivable that agreements between the United Nations and states, or between groups of states, are concluded not only for the purpose of adjudicating crimes under customary international law but also other international crimes.[2] Finally, internationalized criminal courts may, on occasion, also be created primarily for the purpose of adjudicating crimes under domestic law.

The internationalized panels for East Timor[3] and the Special Court for Sierra Leone[4] have been created primarily for the purpose of assisting a state in ending impunity for crimes against the peace and security of mankind and in bringing the perpetrators of these crimes to justice. That is also the purpose of the plans to create Extraordinary Chambers within the judicial system of Cambodia.[5] On the other hand, the situation is apparently rather different in Kosovo. Here, plans to set up a Kosovo War and Ethnic Crimes Court have been abandoned. Participation of international judges and prosecutors in the administration of criminal justice primarily serves the purpose of contributing to the building of a new national system of justice as a part of building more peaceful relations between different groups in a society.[6] Although international judges and prosecutors may, on occasion, be involved in the adjudication of international crimes, the emphasis is not on ending impunity for these crimes.[7] This may be due to the fact that there exists already an international tribunal with jurisdiction over international

---

[1] See, eg, Resolution 1373 (2001) (28 September 2001) with regard to the financing of terrorist acts as an offence created by the Security Council.

[2] Article 123 of the Statute of the International Criminal Court, for instance, provides for the possibility of amending the Statute for the purpose of including one or more international crimes that do not constitute crimes against the peace and security of mankind. Resolution E, attached to the Final Act of the 1988 Rome Diplomatic Conference, specifically mentions terrorist crimes and drug crimes as offences that could be included in the Statute.

[3] UNTAET Regulation 2000/15 (On the Establishment of Panels with Exclusive Jurisdiction over Serious Criminal Offences). See also Regulation 2000/11 (On the Organization of Courts in East Timor).

[4] The text of the Statute is included in 'Report of the Secretary-General on the Establishment of a Special Court for Sierra Leone' UN Doc S/2000/915. The Statute was later amended; see UN Doc S/2000/1234. See also the Special Court Agreement Ratification Act 2002, adopted in Sierra Leone in 2002.

[5] Law on the Establishment of Extraordinary Chambers in the Courts of Cambodia for the Prosecution of Crimes Committed During the Period of Democratic Kampuchea, promulgated on 10 August 2001. See www.yale.edu/cgp/KR_Law_trans. For the text of the draft Agreement between Cambodia and the United Nations see 'Report of the Third Committee of the UN General Assembly' UN Doc A/57/806. See also 'Report of the Secretary-General on Khmer Rouge Trials' UN Doc A/57/769.

[6] UNMIK Reg 2000/64 (On Assignment of International Judges/Prosecutors and/or Change of Venue).

[7] Moreover, their involvement in cases concerning international crimes seems to be rather rare. See Sylvia de Bertodano 'Current Developments in Internationalized Courts' (2003) 1 *J International Criminal Justice* 226, 239–40.

crimes committed in the territory of the former Yugoslavia, including Kosovo, since 1991 (ie ICTY).

C. JURISDICTION

The overall purpose for which an internationalized court is created will determine its jurisdiction *ratione materiae, personae, loci*, and *temporis*. With regard to any internationalized court the decision has to be made over to what categories of offences and offenders its jurisdiction extends, as well as where and when an offence must have been committed in order for the court to possess jurisdiction.

As far as the internationalized courts for East Timor, Sierra Leone, and Cambodia are concerned, their primary purpose is to contribute to ending impunity for crimes against the peace and security of mankind. In their constitutive instruments, these courts have, therefore, been given jurisdiction over war crimes, crimes against humanity, and, where East Timor and Cambodia are concerned, genocide. Apparently, there was no need to include the crime of aggression. In the case of Sierra Leone, the nature of the situation in which serious violations of international humanitarian law occurred was thought to make it superfluous to grant the Special Court jurisdiction over genocide and war crimes committed in an international armed conflict. Moreover, all three constitutive instruments grant the courts jurisdiction over limited categories of other offences. These may be international crimes, such as torture in time of peace or crimes against diplomats, or purely national ones, such as murder or sexual offences. While all three statutes make their own selection of offences in this respect, one must assume that the main reason for including them lies in the close connection between these crimes on the one hand and genocide, war crimes, and crimes against humanity on the other.

Conversely, the jurisdiction of the internationalized courts in Kosovo is very different. Here, no specific categories of offences have been singled out. Instead, a UN Mission in Kosovo (UNMIK) Regulation enables the Special Representative of the Secretary-General (SRSG) in Kosovo to appoint international judges and prosecutors in the various courts of Kosovo.[8] Another regulation empowers the SRSG to assign international judges and prosecutors to a specific case and/or to change venue 'where this is considered necessary to ensure the independence and impartiality of the judiciary or the proper administration of justice'.[9] It follows from these regulations that international judges and prosecutors may take part in the adjudication of any

---

[8] UNMIK Reg 2000/6 (On the Appointment and Removal from Office of International Judges and International Prosecutors), later amended by UNMIK Regs 2000/34 and 2001/2.
[9] UNMIK Reg 2000/64.

criminal offence where this would be conducive to the independence and impartiality of the judiciary or to the ability of the judiciary 'to properly prosecute crimes which gravely undermine the peace process and the full establishment of the rule of law in Kosovo'.[10]

There is a relation between the subject matter jurisdiction of the courts on the one hand and their jurisdiction *ratione temporis* on the other. The internationalized courts for East Timor and Sierra Leone have been created in order to adjudicate international crimes as well as some other categories of crimes committed during an international or internal armed conflict that came to an end before the courts were created. The same is true where plans for creating an internationalized court for Cambodia are concerned. The constitutive instruments of these judicial bodies contain specific provisions on the temporal jurisdiction. Apparently, the particular character of these historical conflicts has influenced the selection of international and other crimes over which these internationalized courts have, or will have, jurisdiction.[11] This is especially the case where the selection of purely 'domestic' offences is concerned. Here again, the situation in Kosovo is different. The jurisdiction of internationalized panels for Kosovo is not limited to events that occurred in a specific period of time before the panels were created. Their jurisdiction *ratione temporis* is not different from that of other courts in Kosovo.

Finally, for completeness' sake, a summary of the jurisdiction of the four internationalized courts *ratione personae* and *loci* should be given. As far as the Special Court for Sierra Leone is concerned, its personal jurisdiction is limited to 'persons who bear the greatest responsibility for serious violations of international humanitarian law and Sierra Leonean law'.[12] The Cambodian Law limits the jurisdiction of the Extraordinary Chambers to 'senior leaders of [the] Democratic Kampuchea and those who were most responsible for the crimes and serious violations of Cambodian penal law, international humanitarian law and custom, and international conventions recognized by Cambodia'.[13] On the other hand, there are no limitations with regard to specific categories of persons where the jurisdiction of the Panels for East Timor and the internationalized courts of Kosovo is concerned.

---

[10] ibid Preamble.

[11] Section 2 of UNTAET Reg 2000/15 confers jurisdiction over international crimes and some crimes under domestic law, but limits jurisdiction over the second category to crimes committed in the period between 1 January 1999 and 25 October 1999. Article 1 of the Statute of the Special Court for Sierra Leone confers jurisdiction over offences committed since 30 November 1996, Art 2 of the Cambodian Law over offences committed during the period from 17 April 1975 to 6 January 1979.

[12] Article 1 of the Statute. This Article also provides for (subsidiary) jurisdiction over peace-keepers and related personnel with regard to 'any transgressions' committed during peace-keeping operations undertaken with the consent of the government of Sierra Leone.

[13] Article 1 of the Cambodian Law.

Neither the Cambodian Law nor the regulations in force in Kosovo contain explicit provisions with regard to the geographical jurisdiction of the internationalized courts. Section 2 of UNTAET Regulation 2000/15 establishing Special Panels for East Timor vests them with 'universal jurisdiction' over international crimes. This contrasts with Article 1 of the Statute of the Special Court for Sierra Leone, which limits the jurisdiction of the Court to crimes committed on Sierra Leonean territory.

D. APPLICABLE LAW

The constitutive instruments of the internationalized courts for East Timor and Sierra Leone not only determine the extent of their jurisdiction but equally determine the substantive law that they have to apply. In both cases, the specific crimes under general international law over which the courts have jurisdiction are specified. Moreover, one can also find provisions on general principles of criminal law applicable to these crimes, as well as on penalties that may be imposed in the case of conviction. The same is true for the Cambodian Law on the Establishment of Extraordinary Chambers. Finally, the constitutive instruments of these three bodies define, either autonomously or by reference to national law, other offences over which the jurisdiction of an internationalized court extends.

Again, the situation is rather different in the case of Kosovo. There, internationalized Panels have to apply the criminal law of Kosovo, which includes provisions in the Criminal Code on international crimes. Moreover, they may have to adjudicate crimes created by the SRSG pursuant to the legislative powers conferred upon him. On several occasions, the SRSG has made use of his power to do so.[14]

Where the adjudication of international crimes is concerned, all four internationalized courts are confronted with a mixture of international and national law, and each of them in its own way. This raises the general issue of the relationship between international law and national law.

It is self-evident and imperative that an internationalized court should apply the body of customary international law and treaty law that is applicable to crimes under general international law. This is not only true for the definition of those crimes but also for general principles of criminal law and

---

[14] See, eg, UNMIK Reg 2000/4 (On the Prohibition Against Inciting to National, Racial, Religious or Ethnic Hatred, Discord or Intolerance), Reg 2000/52 (On the Import, Manufacture, Sale and Distribution of Pharmaceutical Products, Including Narcotic Drugs and Psychotropic Substances), Reg 2001/4 (On the Prohibition of Trafficking in Persons in Kosovo), Reg 2001/12 (On Terrorism and Related Offences), and Reg 2001/22 (On Measures Against Organized Crime). The SRSG may, where necessary, amend the Criminal Code in force in Kosovo. An example is provided by UNMIK Reg 2003/1 (Amending the Applicable Law on Criminal Offences Involving Sexual Violence).

for other matters, to the extent that rules of international law are available. In this respect, the situation of an internationalized court is not different from that of a truly international court. On the other hand, to the extent an internationalized court has jurisdiction over purely domestic offences, it will, as a matter of course, have to apply domestic law.[15]

There is a third scenario. An internationalized court might have jurisdiction over international crimes not amounting to crimes under general international law. In this case, it will have to apply international treaties creating these crimes, provided that the state in which the internationalized court operates is a party to these treaties, and to the extent the applicable treaties have, in the field of substantive law, more to offer than a mere definition of the offence or the offences. For the rest, it will have to apply national law. In this respect, the interesting questions are whether some international crimes by treaty have already evolved into crimes under customary international law at the time they were committed, and, if so, when did this occur. These questions arise with regard to the crime of torture in section 7 of UNTAET Regulation 2000/15, and to destruction of cultural property during an internal armed conflict and crimes against internationally protected persons, included in Articles 7 and 8 of the Cambodian Law.

It is a basic principle of international law that a state may not invoke the provisions of its internal law as a justification for its failure to comply with rules of customary international law or treaty law.[16] However, this is not to say that national courts are always in a position to apply international law and to disregard domestic law whenever it conflicts with international law. Whether, and to what extent, they will be able to do so basically depends on national constitutional principles governing the implementation of international law in the domestic legal order. Since internationalized criminal courts (with the notable exception of the Special Court for Sierra Leone) are part of the national legal system, when applying international law in criminal cases they might well be faced with the same problems and difficulties as ordinary national criminal courts. It is, therefore, important to look more closely at the constitutional position of these courts.

As far as the internationalized courts for Kosovo and East Timor are concerned, they have been created by SRSGs, deriving their mandate from

---

[15] In the same sense, see the 'Report of the Secretary-General' (*supra* n 4) 5. It should be noted, however, that the question of what exactly constitutes domestic law may not be easily determined. In both East Timor and Kosovo, this has given rise to controversy. As to the former, see the decision of the Court of Appeal in *Prosecutor v Armando dos Santos* (15 July 2003) available at www.jsmp.minihub.org/judgmentspdf/courtofappeal/Ct_of_App-dos_Santos_English22703.pdf, in which the court held that 'the laws in force in East Timor prior to 25 October 1999' were those of Portugal rather than Indonesia, the latter having been regarded as applicable law thus far. For Kosovo, see Chapter 3 (Cerone/Baldwin).

[16] cf Art 27 of the Vienna Convention on the Law of Treaties.

UN Security Council Resolutions adopted under Chapter VII.[17] These Resolutions have vested the SRSG with all legislative and executive authority with respect to Kosovo and East Timor. In the case of East Timor, the SRSG has promulgated UNTAET Regulation 1999/1, declaring in section 3 that the laws in force in East Timor at the date of the relevant Security Council Resolution 'shall apply in East Timor insofar as they do not conflict with … the fulfilment of the mandate given to UNTAET …, or the present or any other regulation and directive issued by the Transitional Administrator'. Section 3 of UNTAET Regulation 2000/15, establishing Panels with exclusive jurisdiction over serious criminal offences, refers to Regulation 1999/1. In addition, it provides that the panels shall 'apply …, where appropriate, applicable treaties and recognized principles and norms of international law, including the established principles of the international law of armed conflict'. It would seem that, pursuant to both Regulations, the Special Panels will have no difficulties in applying international law and disregarding conflicting domestic criminal law.

The SRSG for Kosovo has also promulgated a regulation with regard to applicable law. Section 3 of UNMIK Regulation 1999/1 on the authority of the interim administration in Kosovo is almost identical to section 3 of the UNTAET Regulation 1999/1. However, this SRSG, in creating internationalized Panels, has not addressed in general terms the constitutional relationship between international law and domestic criminal law. It would, therefore, seem that these Panels will have to solve problems that might arise as to conformity with the existing legal rules in Kosovo with regard to the implementation of international law in the domestic legal order of Kosovo.

As far as the Special Court for Sierra Leone is concerned, its Statute is based on an agreement between the United Nations and Sierra Leone. Although there is no provision in the Statute comparable to section 3 of UNTAET Regulation 2000/15, the other provisions of the Statute clearly suppose that the Court, in adjudicating international crimes, will have to disregard Sierra Leonean law where it would conflict with international law.

Finally, in the case of Cambodia the Extraordinary Chambers will apparently have to solve conflicts between international and domestic law in conformity with Cambodian constitutional law. Article 2(2) of the Draft Agreement between Cambodia and the United Nations, however, provides that:

The present Agreement shall be implemented in Cambodia through the Law on the Establishment of the Extraordinary Chambers as adopted and amended. The Vienna Convention on the Law of Treaties, and in particular its Articles 26 and 27, applies to the Agreement.[18]

---

[17] UNSC Res 1244 (1999) (10 June 1999) and 1272 (1999) (25 October 1999).
[18] For the text of the draft Agreement see *supra* n 5.

A lesson to be learned from this overview could be that, in future efforts to establish internationalized courts, the United Nations might insist on the inclusion in the constitutive instruments of similar bodies of a provision explicitly authorizing, or requiring the court to apply international law where national law would conflict with international law.[19]

In moving on to the analysis of the applicable law, since the internationalized Panels for Kosovo differ so much from the other three internationalized courts where purpose, jurisdiction, and applicable law are concerned, they will not be discussed in more detail in this chapter.

1. Crimes under general international law

In selecting and defining the crimes under general international law over which the internationalized courts have jurisdiction the constitutive instruments of the courts for East Timor and Sierra Leone and the Cambodian Law make choices. These choices are not always the same and give rise to a number of questions.

I. Genocide

UNTAET Regulation 2000/15 and the Cambodian Law closely follow the text of Article 2 of the 1948 Genocide Convention as regards the general definition of the crime of genocide.[20] Yet, the same is not true for the specific acts amounting to genocide, enumerated in Article III of the 1948 Convention. Article 4 of the Cambodian Law contains an enumeration of its own, which does not mention direct and public incitement to commit genocide as a separate form of genocide and, therefore, seems to be more restrictive. On the other hand, in section 4 of UNTAET Regulation 2000/15 there is no reference at all to Article 3 of the 1948 Convention. Instead, section 14 dealing with the matter of individual criminal responsibility determines the question of what persons may be held responsible for having committed genocide. In this, the Regulation follows the example of Articles 7 and 25 of the Rome Statute of the International Criminal Court. As a result, the Regulation

---

[19] Article 21 of the Rome Statute of the ICC could serve as an example.

[20] Daryl Mundis's critique that the definition of genocide in the Cambodian Law deviates from that in the Convention may have been based on an erroneous translation. See Daryl A Mundis 'New Mechanisms for the Enforcement of International Humanitarian Law' (2001) 95 *American J Int'l Law* 934, 941. Apart from that, one may wonder whether the events in Cambodia in the 1970s amounted to genocide where the Cambodian population at large is concerned. However, according to the Group of Experts for Cambodia, a number of minority groups had, at any rate, been singled out as special targets. See 'Report of the Group of Experts for Cambodia Established Pursuant to General Assembly Resolution 52/135' UN Doc A/53/850 paras 62–5.

covers all acts enumerated in the Genocide Convention with, possibly, a partial exception for conspiracy to commit genocide.[21]

It should be noted that genocide has not been included in the Statute of the Special Court for Sierra Leone, the Security Council being of the opinion that there was no need to do so.[22]

II. Crimes against humanity

Crimes against humanity are included in the constitutive instruments of the internationalized courts for East Timor and Sierra Leone as well as in the Cambodian Law. In defining crimes against humanity, Article 2 of the Statute of the Special Court for Sierra Leone, and Article 5 of the Cambodian Law, follow the definition in Article 3 of the Statute of the ICTR; partly in the case of the Statute, wholly in that of the Law. Section 5 of UNTAET Regulation 2000/15, on the other hand, draws its inspiration from the far more elaborate and detailed definition of Article 7 of the Rome Statute. As a result, there are some material differences between the concepts of crimes against humanity in the three constitutive instruments.

It is not clear why the negotiators of the Statute of the Special Court for Sierra Leone and the Cambodian Law have decided to follow the definition of crimes against humanity of the Statute of the ICTR, rather than that of ICTY. Selecting the ICTR instead of the ICTY Statute provides the advantage that, in order to constitute crimes against humanity, the crimes must have been committed in armed conflict, whether international or internal in character. The nexus between crimes against humanity and war crimes can no longer be considered to be part of customary international law.[23] On the other hand, selecting the ICTR instead of the ICTY Statute has its own drawbacks, since the ICTR Statute requires that to be crimes against humanity crimes must have been committed as part of a widespread or systematic attack against any civilian population 'on national, political, ethnic, racial or religious grounds'. The quoted words seem to imply that all relevant acts must have been committed with discriminatory intent on the part of their author. However, as has been held by the Appeals Chamber of ICTY, like the war crimes nexus, discriminatory intent is not required by customary international law, with an exception for persecution.[24] The negotiators of the

---

[21] See William A Schabas 'Article 6 Genocide' in Otto Triffterer (ed) *Commentary on the Rome Statute of the International Criminal Court* (Nomos Verlagsgesellschaft Baden-Baden 1999) 11516.

[22] See UNSC Res 1315 (2000).

[23] *Prosecutor v Duško Tadić* IT-94-1-AR72 Decision on the Defence Motion for Interlocutory Appeal on Jurisdiction (2 October 1995) 138–42. According to the Group of Experts for Cambodia, the nexus had already ceased to exist in 1975; (*supra* n 20) para 71. Apparently, this is also the point of view adopted in the Cambodian Law.

[24] *Prosecutor v Duško Tadić* IT-94-1-A Judgment (15 July 1999) 273–305.

Statute for the Special Court were, therefore, on solid ground when they decided to depart from the ICTR Statute in this respect.[25] A second difference with the ICTR Statute is the explicit mention of 'sexual slavery, enforced prostitution, forced pregnancy and any other form of sexual violence' alongside rape as crimes against humanity. Here, the influence of the Rome Statute is discernible.[26]

Section 5 of UNTAET Regulation 2000/15 copies Article 7 of the Rome Statute almost verbatim. Thus, it avoids the problems that could have arisen by following the Statute of the ICTY or that of ICTR. Be that as it may, there are a number of differences between UNTAET Regulation 2000/15 and the Rome Statute. I will not discuss all of them, but only mention the most important and striking one.[27] Unlike Article 7(2)(a) of the Rome Statute, the Statute for East Timor does not define what amounts to an attack directed against any civilian population. The omission seems to be deliberate and to find its origin in the fear that the rather controversial definition of the term 'attack' contained in the Rome Statute unduly restricts that concept with regard to situations in which an attack against a civilian population is characterized by its widespread, rather than its systematic, nature.[28]

III. War crimes

East Timor relevant Regulations, the Statute of the Special Court for Sierra Leone, and the Cambodian Law all include war crimes among the prosecutable crimes. However, they do so in rather different ways, which reflect the different historical and political events that led to their creation.

As far as East Timor is concerned, section 6 of UNTAET Regulation 2000/15 is, on the whole, a faithful reproduction of Article 8 of the Rome Statute.[29] Hence any critique of section 6 of that Regulation is tantamount to a critique

---

[25] Meanwhile, in *Prosecutor v Jean-Paul Akayesu* Judgment (1 June 2001), the Appeals Chamber of ICTR has softened the impact of the requirement considerably by holding that it does not relate to the intent of the individual person but only restricts the jurisdiction of the tribunal to widespread or systematic attacks against a civilian population that are based on discriminatory grounds.

[26] See Micaela Frulli 'The Special Court for Sierra Leone: Some Preliminary Comments' (2000) 11 *European J International Law* 857, 863–64; Suzannah Linton 'Cambodia, East Timor and Sierra Leone: Experiments in International Justice' (2001) 12 *Criminal Law Forum* 185, 234.

[27] For an exhaustive analysis of all differences see Kai Ambos and Steffen Wirth 'The Current Law of Crimes Against Humanity: An Analysis of UNTAET Regulation 15/2000' (2002) 13 *Criminal Law Forum* 1. See also Linton (*supra* n 26) 207–8.

[28] See Ambos and Wirth (*supra* n 27) 3, 30–4.

[29] There are two differences of minor importance. Understandably, s 6(1) of the Regulation avoids the emphasis placed in Art 8.1 of the Rome Statute, on 'war crimes committed as part of a plan or policy or as part of a large-scale commission of such crimes', since this jurisdictional element in the Rome Statute may have no relevance for the situation in East Timor. Secondly, it omits the proviso in Art 8.2.(b)(XX) on means and methods of warfare where the existence of a 'comprehensive prohibition' is concerned.

of the Rome Statute. This chapter, however, is not the place for an analysis in depth of Article 8 of the Rome Statute.

Since the events in Sierra Leone were not considered to amount to an international armed conflict, the Statute of the Special Court for that country has regard solely to war crimes committed in an internal conflict. Articles 3 and 4 of the Statute borrow from the Statute of the ICTR as well as the Rome Statute. Article 3 of the Statute reproduces Article 4 of the ICTR Statute almost verbatim.[30] In addition, Article 4 defines three more crimes in language copied from Article 8.2(e) of the Rome Statute.[31] It is not clear why other crimes defined in that particular part of the Rome Statute have not been included in the Statute for Sierra Leone.[32]

The most interesting case is that of Cambodia. Article 6 of the Cambodian Law confers jurisdiction on the Extraordinary Chambers with regard to grave breaches of the 1949 Geneva Conventions.[33] There is no provision in the Law with regard to war crimes committed in an internal armed conflict, although conduct which nowadays would be considered to amount to such crimes surely must have been far more widespread in Cambodia at the time of the Khmer Rouge than violations of international humanitarian law committed in an international armed conflict. The explanation lies in the fact that Cambodia had not become a party to the Additional Protocols before 1980 and that the criminal nature of violations of international humanitarian law committed in an internal armed conflict was held to be not yet part of customary international law in the 1970s.[34]

2. *Other international crimes*

The Cambodian Law covers some international crimes other than crimes against the peace and security of mankind discussed above. Article 7 of the Law confers jurisdiction on the Extraordinary Chambers over breaches of the 1954 Hague Convention for the Protection of Cultural Property in the Event of Armed Conflict, partially also covered as a war crime by Article 6. Moreover, Article 8 grants jurisdiction over crimes against internationally protected persons 'pursuant to the Vienna Convention of 1961 on Diplomatic Relations'.[35] These two crimes have been included in the Law because

[30] While the Statute for Sierra Leone omits the words 'shall not be limited to' this does not seem to have particular consequences.

[31] Attacks against the civilian population, attacks against peace-keeping personnel, and conscription or enlistment of children under the age of 15 years.

[32] See Linton (*supra* n 26) 235.

[33] Surprisingly, Art 6 speaks about 'the Geneva Convention', without specifying which of the four Conventions. Presumably, this is a typing error. There are some minor differences in language between the list of breaches in the Law and those in the Conventions.

[34] See 'Report of the Group of Experts' (*supra* n 20) paras 72–5; Linton (*supra* n 26) 195.

[35] The Vienna Convention itself contains no penal provisions. Suggestions to include the crimes defined in the 1973 Convention on the Prevention and Punishment of Crimes Against

they occurred during the period with regard to which the Extraordinary Chambers have temporal jurisdiction. For roughly the same reason, the Special Group of Experts for Cambodia suggested in its Report that forced labour and torture should also be brought under the jurisdiction of a special court as international crimes.[36] That suggestion was only followed to the extent that torture is a crime under Cambodian Law, and thus it is within the jurisdiction of the Chambers.

There is a remarkable provision in UNTAET Regulation 2000/15 with regard to torture. Section 7 contains a definition of torture, inspired by the definitions in the well known Declaration of the UN General Assembly of 9 December 1975[37] and the 1984 Torture Convention,[38] although it differs from both in some respects. A study of the structure of the Regulation reveals that sections 1 and 7 of the Regulation aim at criminalizing the act of torture as a singular crime, to be distinguished from torture as a crime against humanity and torture as a war crime.[39] Under sections 1 and 7, for conduct to amount to torture it is not necessary that it be committed as part of a widespread or systematic attack against a civilian population nor that it occurred during an international or internal armed conflict. At first sight, it looks as if section 7 intends to characterize torture as a distinctive crime under customary and treaty international law. However, there is a fundamental difference between the definition of torture in section 7 on the one hand and those of the 1975 Declaration and the 1984 Convention on the other. Unlike those, section 7 does not require that severe pain or suffering is inflicted 'by or at the instigation of a public official' (the formula of the Declaration) or 'by or at the instigation of or with the consent or acquiescence of a public official or other person acting in an official capacity' (the formula of the Convention). Under section 7, torture, therefore, can be committed by any person in any personal circumstances. This might well widen the concept of torture beyond customary international law and treaty law.[40] One gets the impression, however, that the main, or additional, intention of the framers of the Regulation has been to

---

Internationally Protected Persons, Including Diplomatic Agents, were not followed, apparently for the reason that Cambodia is not a party to the Convention. See Linton (*supra* n 26) 196–7.

[36] 'Report of the Group of Experts' (*supra* n 20) paras 77–8.

[37] UNGA Res 3452 (XXX).

[38] 1465 UNTS 85.

[39] Given the fact that torture is listed in s 1(3) as a separate crime in addition to war crimes and crimes against humanity, s 7 is not meant to offer guidance solely for the interpretation of the term 'torture' in the provisions on crimes against humanity and war crimes, as Ambos and Wirth (*supra* n 27) 66, suppose. See also Linton (*supra* n 26) 210.

[40] Involvement of a state agent in the act of torture is not a requirement for torture as a war crime or crime against humanity; see especially the Trial Chamber of ICTY in *Prosecutor v Dragoljub Kunarać and others* IT-96-23-T and IT-96-23/1-T Judgment paras 488–97, and the Appeals Chamber in the same case, paras 142–8. There may be sound arguments for arguing that this should not be an element of torture as a distinctive crime under customary international law. On the other hand, arguments for maintaining the requirement are given by Antonio

define, or redefine, torture as a common crime under domestic law.[41] Thus, sections 1 and 7 of the Regulation would achieve the criminalization of two different forms of torture: torture as a crime under international law and torture as a crime under domestic law not satisfying all requirements of torture as an international crime.

3. Crimes under domestic law

A remarkable feature of UNTAET Regulation 2000/15, the Statute of the Special Court for Sierra Leone, and the Cambodian Law is that they all grant jurisdiction over a number of offences under domestic law. Murder, sexual offences, and, possibly, torture in the case of East Timor;[42] sexual offences against young girls, destruction of property, and arson in the case of Sierra Leone; and homicide, torture, and religious persecution in that of Cambodia. The main reason for granting concurrent jurisdiction over these offences lies in the fact that the crimes listed were likely to have been frequently committed by persons over which the Panels, Court, and Extraordinary Chambers have personal jurisdiction in the period of time over which their temporal jurisdiction extends. In the case of Sierra Leone, an additional consideration has been that some types of conduct criminalized in Sierra Leonean law were considered to be 'either unregulated or inadequately regulated under international law'.[43]

A number of arguments, most of them sound, have been advanced in favour of this policy, which, for obvious reasons, could not be adopted in the statutes of the two ad hoc tribunals, and in that of the International Criminal Court.

First, by charging an accused with international crimes as well as domestic crimes, special rules with regard to sentencing for concurrent offences may become applicable, limiting the maximum punishment that may be imposed. Secondly, if the accused is acquitted of having committed an international crime, the internationalized court is able to decide whether or not the same conduct amounts to a crime under domestic law, thus making it unnecessary to expose the accused to a new trial for the same conduct in a different court.[44] Thirdly, and more pragmatically, crimes under domestic law are

---

Cassese *International Criminal Law* (Oxford University Press Oxford 2003) 118. For a detailed analysis of the concept of torture in UNTAET Reg 2000/15 and in other texts see Ambos and Wirth (*supra* n 27) 65–70.

[41] Section 1(3) mentions torture as a distinct crime after murder and sexual offences, two (other) categories of crimes under domestic law.

[42] The Group of Experts suggested that a number of other crimes under Cambodian law should also be included. See 'Report of the Group of Experts' (*supra* n 20) paras 86–8.

[43] 'Report of the Secretary-General' (*supra* n 4) para 19.

[44] The provisions on *ne bis in idem* in UNTAET Reg 2000/15 and in the Statute of the Special Court for Sierra Leone do not prohibit the trial of an accused who has been acquitted of

often easier to prove since proof of an international crime usually also requires proof of additional elements.[45] Evidence of this is offered by the case of East Timor, where, for some time, because of lack of sufficient resources available to investigate the international aspects of a crime, a number of accused have been charged solely with crimes under domestic law.[46] It is difficult to condone this practice because it does insufficient justice to international crimes, and it could only be accepted as a form of *force majeure*. Finally, if, as is true for East Timor and Sierra Leone, the temporal jurisdiction of an internationalized court includes crimes that may have occurred in a relatively distant past, the option of prosecuting a person for crimes under domestic law might become especially important if that person is suspected of conduct that did not yet constitute a crime under general international law at the time of his conduct, or when it seems uncertain whether this was the case.

4. *General principles of criminal law*

'General Principles of Criminal Law' is a term used by the Rome Statute of the International Criminal Court as a heading to Part 3 of the Statute. Together, the 12 Articles of this Part of the Statute cover a wide variety of issues that, assuming that the Court has jurisdiction, determine whether or not a person allegedly having committed an international crime may be prosecuted before the Court and can be held criminally responsible for his or her conduct. The provisions of Part 3 have regard to the nature and content of individual criminal responsibility,[47] to the availability of justifications and excuses,[48] and to other obstacles that may or may not bar prosecution or punishment.[49] With some limited exceptions, the provisions mentioned here aim to reflect customary international law.

What are the general principles of criminal law that are applied by the internationalized courts and what do their constitutive instruments say about them? In this regard, one has to keep in mind that there is one major difference between the internationalized criminal courts and the international

---

having committed an international crime by another court on the grounds that the conduct may also amount to a crime under domestic law.

[45] 'Report of the Group of Experts' (*supra* n 20) para 88. See also Linton (*supra* n 26) 241, supposing that this may be more conducive to an expeditious trial.

[46] Guy Cumes 'Murder as a Crime Against Humanity in International law: Choice of Law and Prosecution of Murder in East Timor' (2003) 11 *European Journal of Crime, Criminal Law and Criminal Justice* 40, 62–64. See also Linton (*supra* n 26) 217–18.

[47] Article 25 on individual criminal responsibility generally; Art 27 on the irrelevance of official capacity; Art 28 on the responsibility of superiors; Art 30 on the mental element; Art 33 on superior orders.

[48] Article 31 on grounds for excluding criminal responsibility; Art 32 on mistake of fact and mistake of law.

[49] Articles 22 to 24 on the legality principle; Art 26 on persons under the age of 18; Art 29 on statutes of limitation.

criminal courts. Unlike international courts, internationalized courts do not only possess jurisdiction over crimes against the peace and security of mankind but also over a number of crimes under domestic law. As has been discussed,[50] in the cases of East Timor and Cambodia there is also jurisdiction over a third category: international crimes usually not regarded as being crimes against the peace and security of mankind.

As stated earlier,[51] one cannot but assume that internationalized courts will have to apply customary international law relating to general principles of international law when adjudicating genocide, crimes against humanity, and war crimes. On the other hand, it stands to reason that they apply domestic law where the adjudication of crimes under domestic law is concerned. In the case of international crimes other than crimes against the peace and security the answer is less clear. There seems to be no compelling logical reason to apply 'general principles of criminal law', that have been developed in customary international law with regard to crimes against the peace and security of mankind, to other international crimes when the criminal nature of an act is not based on customary international law but solely on treaties that require implementation in domestic legislation in order for that act to constitute a crime. But even when they are crimes under customary international law, which is the case for torture and may well be the case, too, for destruction of cultural property during an international or internal armed conflict and crimes against internationally protected persons, there is no compelling logical reason to apply to them general principles that have been developed with regard to crimes against the peace and security of mankind, although this would probably be the simplest and the best solution from a systematic and practical point of view.

The Statute of the Special Court for Sierra Leone and the Cambodian Law recognize the importance of the distinction between international and domestic crimes. In both cases, the negotiators appear to have been aware that different regimes should be applied to different crimes: general principles of international criminal law to crimes against the peace and security of mankind, and principles of national criminal law to crimes under domestic law.

Article 6(5) of the Statute for the Special Court for Sierra Leone explicitly refers to this distinction. This is less so in UNTAET Regulation 2000/15, which approaches the matter in a quite different manner. General principles of criminal law, as codified in either the Rome Statute or the statutes of the ad hoc international tribunals, have been generally declared applicable to all crimes, including crimes under domestic law. To this there are two exceptions only: the first concerns command responsibility; the second statutes of limitation. It is not clear to me what considerations are at the basis of this

---

[50] See 296–8.   [51] See 290

choice, which, on occasion, might have negative consequences for the accused as far as individual responsibility for domestic crimes is concerned.

As far as destruction of cultural property and crimes against internationally protected persons are concerned, the Cambodian Law declares the rules with regard to individual criminal responsibility laid down in the Statutes of the two ad hoc tribunals applicable to them.

There is a considerable difference in the manner in which the Statute of the Special Court for Sierra Leone and the Cambodian Law, on the one hand, and UNTAET Regulation 2000/15, on the other, lay down the general principles of criminal law to be applied to international crimes. The Statute of the Special Court and the Cambodian Law both reproduce the Articles in the Statutes of the ICTY and ICTR on individual criminal responsibility, which, among other things, deal with official position, responsibility of superiors, and superior orders. The Statute of the Special Court also incorporates the Articles in the Statutes of the two ad hoc tribunals on concurrent jurisdiction and *ne bis in idem*. Both the Statute and the Law have a special provision on amnesties and pardons. Moreover, the Cambodian Law declares that no statute of limitations applies to genocide and crimes against humanity, while the Statute of the Special Court for Sierra Leone contains a separate provision on minors.

Conversely, UNTAET Regulation 2000/15 is far more elaborate and detailed. Its provisions on general principles of criminal law are reproductions of those of the Rome Statute of the International Criminal Court. However, to this there are some striking exceptions. The provisions in the Regulation on command responsibility and superior order do not copy those of the Rome Statute but have been borrowed from the Statutes of the ad hoc tribunals. Moreover, unlike the Rome Statute, Regulation 2000/15 has no provision on jurisdiction over minors.

Compared to Regulation 2000/15, the provisions on individual criminal responsibility in the Statute of the Special Court and the Cambodian Law are rather rudimentary. In particular, they do not cover a variety of personal defences which might relieve a person of individual criminal responsibility. Obviously, the rudimentary nature of the two texts is due to the fact that the Statutes of the ad hoc tribunals are also silent on these matters. The silence of the Statutes of the ICTY and ICTR rests on the consideration that it should be left to the two tribunals themselves to determine the limits of individual criminal responsibility on the basis of customary international law as well as general principles of law recognized by civilized nations.[52] One may hope and expect that the internationalized courts for Sierra Leone and Cambodia will do the same and will, in particular, draw inspiration and guidance from the

---

[52] 'Report of the Secretary-General Pursuant to Paragraph 2 of Security Council Resolution 808 (1993)' UN Doc S/257/04 para 58.

case law of the tribunals. As detailed above, the main problem here, especially in the case of Cambodia, might be that principles of national constitutional law prevent the internationalized courts from applying international law.[53]

In the case of East Timor, this problem certainly does not exist. There is, however, the question of why Regulation 2000/15 follows the Rome Statute in almost all respects but refuses to do so where command responsibility, superior orders, and minor age are concerned.[54] Since, to my knowledge, there is no official document explaining the intentions and choices of the framers of the Regulation, one can only speculate about the reasons. The most likely explanation is probably that, in the opinion of the framers, the Rome Statute less accurately reflects international customary law than do the Statutes of the ad hoc international tribunals and the case law of the tribunals. In the case of command responsibility, they may, for instance have had objections against the causality requirement laid down in Article 28 of the Rome Statute, or may have thought that the responsibility of superiors other than military commanders has been too narrowly defined. In the case of superior orders, they may have been of the opinion that Article 33 of the Rome Statute gives too much room to the defence of superior orders where war crimes are concerned. In the case of minors, they may have thought that, notwithstanding Article 26 of the Rome Statute, there is no reason to exempt categorically persons under the age of 18 from being prosecuted for international crimes. Whatever the explanations might be, it is obvious that the choices made favour the more strict and exacting approach over the more lenient and liberal one.

It is not necessary to discuss all general principles of criminal law enshrined in one or more of the constitutive instruments of the three internationalized courts. I will, therefore, limit myself to a discussion of matters that have a special significance for East Timor, Sierra Leone, or Cambodia: *nullum crimen*, the position of juveniles, and statutes of limitation. There is also good reason to discuss briefly provisions on amnesties and pardons in two of the three cases.

I. *Nullum crimen sine lege*

The Panels for East Timor, the Special Court for Sierra Leone, and the Cambodian Extraordinary Chambers all have jurisdiction over events that

[53] See Linton (*supra* n 26) 197, supposes that, in the absence of a special provision in the Cambodian Law on defences, the Extraordinary Chambers will have to apply the provisions of the Cambodian Penal Code to defences advanced with regard to international crimes.

[54] The fourth difference with the Rome Statute is that Art 24 of the Rome Statute, dealing with non-retroactivity *ratione personae*, has not been repeated in the Regulation. Meanwhile, the first paragraph of Art 24 is not directly relevant to the situation in East Timor. The subject matter of the second paragraph, dealing with issues of transitory law, is covered by ss 2 and 3 of the Regulation.

occurred before they were created. UNTAET Regulation 2000/15 defines no specific starting date for the temporal jurisdiction of the Panels over international crimes, but it may be assumed that their jurisdiction extends over these crimes committed since the invasion of East Timor by Indonesia, an event that occurred on 7 December 1975. The Special Court for Sierra Leone has jurisdiction over offences committed since 30 November 1996, the Cambodian Extraordinary Chambers over offences committed in the period from 17 April 1975 to 6 January 1979. In itself, conferring retroactive jurisdiction on newly created criminal courts does not violate international human rights standards provided that these courts 'genuinely afford the accused the full guarantees of fair trial'.[55] However, since the constitutive instruments of the three internationalized courts also define the international crimes over which the courts have jurisdiction, as well as a number of general principles of criminal law applicable to these crimes, the issue of retroactive application of criminal statutes inevitably arises.

Of the constitutive instruments of the three bodies considered here, UNTAET Regulation 2000/15 is the only one to include provisions on the principle of *nullum crimen, nulla poena sine lege*. Section 12 of that Regulation basically follows the text of Article 22 of the Rome Statute, while section 13 follows the text of Article 23. Moreover, Section 2.4, provides that the Panels 'shall have jurisdiction ... only insofar as the law on which the serious criminal offence is based is consistent with Section 3.1 of UNTAET Regulation No. 1999/1'. Regulation 1999/1, in its turn, requires all persons undertaking public duties or holding public office in East Timor to observe, inter alia, the International Covenant on Civil and Political Rights. This includes Article 15 of the Covenant. In addition, section 3 of Regulation requires the Panels to apply, 'where appropriate, applicable treaties and recognized principles and norms of international law'. The legality principle may be said to belong to these principles. On the other hand, the Statute of the Special Court for Sierra Leone and the Cambodian Law are entirely silent on the issue of retroactivity. They share this characteristic with the Statutes of the ICTY and ICTR. However, the incriminations in the Statutes of the ad hoc tribunals are based on the premiss that the tribunals should only apply 'rules of international humanitarian law which are beyond any doubt part of customary law',[56] and the same premiss will, therefore, apply in the case of Sierra Leone and Cambodia.[57] Finally, both states are parties to the International Covenant.

The *nullum crimen* principle requires that the criminal nature of conduct which violates rules of customary international law has been recognized as

---

[55] *Prosecutor v Duško Tadić* IT-94-1-AR72 Appeals Chamber ICTY Decision on the Defence Motion for Interlocutory Appeal on Jurisdiction (2 October 1995) para 45.

[56] 'Report of the Secretary-General' (*supra* n 52) para 34, with an explicit reference to the *nullum crimen* principle.

[57] See also 'Report of the Secretary-General' (*supra* n 4) para 12.

such in international law at the time of the conduct. This should not be confused with the case of conduct that has been defined as criminal in international conventions, but which has not yet become the object of a norm of customary international law. In similar situations, it is only reasonable to require that the relevant conduct has been made a criminal offence before the conduct occurred pursuant to the laws of the state party wanting to exercise jurisdiction.[58] In the former case, individual criminal responsibility is solely determined by international law, in the latter it is not.

It would seem that the constitutive instruments of the three internationalized courts are based on the same premises. As has already been mentioned, the reason why the Cambodian Law does not include war crimes committed in an internal armed conflict is that, on the one hand, violations of international humanitarian law had not yet become crimes under customary international law in the 1970s and, on the other hand, that in that period, Cambodia had not yet become a party to the 1977 Additional Protocols.[59] As far as Sierra Leone is concerned, a discussion between the Secretary-General of the United Nations and the Security Council is revealing. The original proposal of the Secretary-General did not contain a wholesale prohibition on the conscription or enlisting of children under the age of 15 years as a war crime, but solely their abduction and forced recruitment for the purpose of using them to participate actively in hostilities. In his Report, the Secretary-General doubted whether the wider prohibition of Article 8.2(e)(vii) of the Rome Statute had already become part of customary law in every respect.[60] Having apparently no such doubts, the Security Council amended the proposal and ensured its conformity with the Rome Statute.[61]

There seems to be one major difference between international criminal courts and national criminal courts in the respect they have to pay to the *nullum crimen* principle with regard to international crimes. Since individual responsibility for crimes under general international law directly derives from international law itself, international courts only have to take international law into account. In each individual case, they have to assess whether a given conduct amounted to a crime under international law at the time of that conduct, and whether the accused can be held accountable pursuant to general principles of international criminal law existing at that time. It is not their responsibility to assess whether or not the same would be true under the domestic laws of the state on whose territory the conduct occurred, although there are examples in which they have performed that check, without being

---

[58] In the same sense Art 39 of the International Law Commission's Draft Statute for an International Criminal Court UN Doc GAOR A/49/10, 112–14. See also Bruce Broomhall 'Article 22' in Otto Triffterer (ed), (*supra* n 21) 461–2.

[59] See 296

[60] 'Report of the Secretary-General' (*supra* n 4) para 18.

[61] UN Doc S/2000/1234.

obliged to do so, with a view to making sure that the accused could without any doubt know that his conduct was criminal.[62]

However, for national courts the matter is more complicated. They may not ignore domestic law unless there is a clear legal basis in domestic law for so doing. Presumably, domestic law will require them to assess whether the conduct constituted an international crime pursuant to domestic law at the time the conduct occurred. They may, therefore, have to perform a double check: the one involving international law, the other domestic law. As a consequence, cases may present themselves in which the accused is charged with conduct for which he can be held responsible pursuant to domestic law, but not yet pursuant to international law. Domestic law with regard to command responsibility could, for instance, impose more exacting standards on individual persons than international law did at the time of the conduct. It would then violate the *nullum crimen* principle to convict the accused for having committed an international crime. Provided that the internationalized courts are, under domestic law, permitted to apply Article 15 of the International Covenant on Civil and Political Rights directly, this will be the inevitable and proper decision for them to take.[63] On the other hand, there may be cases in which the accused can be held responsible pursuant to international law but not pursuant to domestic law. The most likely example of such a situation probably is the one in which, at the time of the conduct, domestic law did not yet have adequate criminal legislation with regard to crimes under general international law. Domestic principles with regard to *nullum crimen* might then make it inevitable for an internationalized court to acquit the accused, even though Article 15(2) of the International Covenant would perhaps not forbid the retroactive application of domestic legislation incriminating 'any act or omission which, at the time when it was committed, was criminal according to the general principles of law recognized by the community of nations'.[64]

Internationalized criminal courts are, as it were, to a greater or lesser degree 'embedded' in a national legal system.[65] The question, therefore, is what law they should apply in tackling issues of retroactivity. The answer is very clear for East Timor. Pursuant to section 12 of UNTAET Regulation

---

[62] See, eg, *Prosecutor v Duško Tadić* (*supra* n 55) paras 135–6 (violations of international humanitarian law in internal armed conflicts); *Prosecutor v Anto Furundija* IT-95-17/1-T Judgment para 167 (rape).

[63] Cambodia and Sierra Leone are parties to the Covenant, while UNTAET Reg 1999/1 has made it part of the law of East Timor.

[64] For an example see the recent decision of the Dutch Supreme Court of 18 September 2001 (2002) *Nederlandse Jurisprudentie* 559 (*Bouterse*). Meanwhile, there seems to be no consensus on the question of whether Art 15 of the International Covenant has regard only to events that have occurred during the Second World War or has a wider scope. See Machteld Boot *Nullum Crimen Sine Lege and the Subject Matter Jurisdiction of the International Criminal Court* (Intersentia Antwerp/Oxford/New York 2002) 137–41, 158–70.

[65] For further discussion, see Chapter 16 (Kleffner/Nollkaemper).

2000/15, a person may not be held criminally responsible unless the conduct in question constituted, at the time it took place, a crime under international law or the laws of East Timor. This clearly means that for a person to be convicted of an international crime it suffices that the conduct was criminal pursuant to international law at the time it occurred. It does not matter whether or not, at that time, his conduct was also an international crime pursuant to domestic law.[66] The Statute of the Special Court for Sierra Leone and the Cambodian Law are entirely silent on the matter. Presumably, however, the solution is not different from the one chosen for East Timor: only international law at the time of the conduct matters. Otherwise, the definitions of international crimes in the Statute and the Law as well as the setting up of the two internationalized courts might perhaps make limited sense.

II. Juveniles

The Statute of the Special Court for Sierra Leone is unique in including provisions on jurisdiction over juveniles. The Cambodian Law and UNTAET Regulation 2000/15 do not contain a similar provision. In the case of Cambodia, the small group of persons who might have to stand trial does not include persons who were juveniles at the time they allegedly committed crimes over which the jurisdiction of the Extraordinary Chambers extends. However, more surprising, at first sight, is the absence of a provision in UNTAET Regulation 2000/15, since a provision on that matter can be found in the Rome Statute. Article 26 of the Rome Statute provides that ICC shall have no jurisdiction over any person who was under the age of 18 at the time of the alleged commission of a crime. However, Article 26 is a provision of a purely jurisdictional character. It does not provide that persons under the age of 18 may under no circumstances be held criminally responsible for their acts, but leaves that matter entirely to national jurisdictions. In this sense, Article 26 does not really express a 'general principle of criminal law'. It is, therefore, not surprising that UNTAET Regulation 2000/15 has refrained from including a similar provision in its text. As a consequence, the matter is entirely governed by the law of East Timor.

Juveniles played a major role in the Sierra Leonean conflict. Massive resort to child soldiers was a characteristic of this conflict, which gave it a badge of shame. In his Report on the establishment of a Special Court for Sierra Leone, the Secretary-General of the United Nations spoke of a 'difficult moral dilemma' and a 'terrible dilemma' in explaining the various options

---

[66] On the other hand, the text implies that a person could be convicted if the conduct did not constitute a crime under general international law but amounted to a crime pursuant to domestic law. This is, however, only possible for crimes over which the Panels have jurisdiction.

for dealing with international crimes committed by children, most of them former child soldiers and themselves victims of abduction, forced recruitment, sexual abuse, or other war crimes.[67] The proposals by the Secretary-General, as amended by the Security Council, struck a compromise between highly diverging opinions on what to do with juveniles and attempt to strike a balance between the various interests involved. Hence, under Article 7 of its Statute, the Special Court has no jurisdiction over persons under the age of 15 at the time of the alleged commission of the crime. Yet, this does not exclude their trial by other courts in Sierra Leone. Moreover, Article 7 applies a special regime to persons who were between 15 and 18 years old when they allegedly committed a crime, in which a strong emphasis is placed on a rehabilitative approach. Imprisonment is excluded as a penalty in Article 19 of the Statute, while Article 15 urges the Prosecutor carefully to consider in each individual case whether alternatives to prosecution should be preferred. Since, pursuant to Article 1 of the Statute, the Special Court has jurisdiction solely over 'persons who bear the greatest responsibility for serious violations of international humanitarian law', very few juveniles are expected to be tried by it.[68] The practice that will develop in Sierra Leone with regard to juvenile offenders might well set a precedent for other states struggling with the terrible problem of child soldiers.

III. Statutes of limitation

There are no statutes of limitation in the Statute of the Special Court for Sierra Leone. This is probably due to the fact that the temporal jurisdiction of the Court is limited to international crimes and crimes under Sierra Leonean law committed since 30 November 1996. On the other hand, the temporal jurisdiction of the Panels in East Timor and the Extraordinary Chambers in Cambodia being far wider, the question whether or not statutory limitations apply to crimes committed in a rather distant past becomes an important one.

On this matter, UNTAET Regulation 2000/15 again follows the Rome Statute. Like Article 29 of the Rome Statute, section 17 of the Regulation provides that genocide, war crimes, and crimes against humanity shall not be subject to any statute of limitations. The same is true for torture, defined in section 7 as a discrete crime not amounting to a crime against humanity or a war crime. As has been discussed, section 7 of Regulation 2000/15 has not only regard to torture as an international crime, defined in the Torture Declaration and the Torture Convention. It also covers torture not committed by, or at the instigation of a public official, and makes that a crime under domestic law. It is not self-evident that this crime under domestic law

---

[67] 'Report of the Secretary-General' (*supra* n 4) paras 32–3.   [68] Linton (*supra* n 26) 237.

should not be subject to any statute of limitations and that the normal rules with regard to statutory limitations in the law of East Timor should not apply.

The Cambodian Law is more timid in eliminating statutes of limitation. Pursuant to Articles 4 and 5 of the Law, no statute of limitations applies to genocide and crimes against humanity. However, there is no similar provision with regard to the grave breaches of the Geneva Conventions. The same is true for destruction of cultural property in violation of the 1954 Hague Convention and for crimes against internationally protected persons. As far as crimes under Cambodian law are concerned, Article 3 of the Law extends the statute of limitations set forth in the Cambodian Penal Code for an additional 20 years. Admittedly, it is difficult to discover the logic behind this system. Why should statutes of limitation continue to apply to war crimes without any exception while they have been eliminated for genocide and crimes against humanity? Why should more lenient rules apply to war crimes, destruction of cultural property, and crimes against diplomats than to the crimes under domestic law over which the Extraordinary Chambers have jurisdiction?

UNTAET Regulation 2000/15 and the Cambodian Law apply to events that have occurred before the Regulation and the Law entered into force. It is not wholly impossible that, as a result, persons could be tried for crimes with regard to which limitation periods have already elapsed. In the past, this has always been the most controversial aspect of eliminating statutory limitations retrospectively. It is, therefore, important to note that, in abolishing statutes of limitation for specific categories of international crimes, neither the Regulation nor the Law make an exception for cases in which limitation periods had already run out.

IV. Amnesties and pardons

Like statutes of limitation, amnesties and pardons are also sensitive issues in international criminal law. The problem of what to do with them has arisen in the case of Sierra Leone as well as that of Cambodia. As far as Sierra Leone is concerned, Article IX of the 1999 Lomé Peace Agreement granted 'absolute and free pardon' to the parties in the conflict that raged in Sierra Leone in the 1990s. However, the SRSG appended a disclaimer to his signature of the Agreement to the effect that the amnesty provisions 'shall not apply to international crimes of genocide, crimes against humanity and other serious violations of international humanitarian law'.[69] On 14 September 1996, the Cambodian king granted pardon to Khmer Rouge leader Ieng Sary who, in 1979, had been tried and convicted *in absentia* on a charge of

---

[69] 'Report of the Secretary-General' (*supra* n 4) para 23.

genocide by a special court established by the People's Republic of Kampuchea after the invasion of Cambodia by Vietnamese troops, and had been sentenced to death. One may have doubts about the fairness of that trial.

Article 10 of the Statute of the Special Court for Sierra Leone provides that amnesties granted in the past in respect of crimes against humanity and war crimes shall not be a bar to prosecution before the Special Court. This provision does not cover future amnesties or pardons after conviction by the Special Court, but one may suppose that they would, to say the least, violate the spirit of the Statute. On the other hand, Article 40 of the Cambodian Law provides that the Cambodian government shall not submit to the Cambodian king requests for the granting of amnesties or pardons to persons 'who may be investigated for or convicted of' crimes over which the Extraordinary Chambers have jurisdiction, regardless of whether an investigation or conviction concerns international crimes or crimes under domestic law. This leaves open the question of what to do with the pardon granted in the past to Ieng Sary. For a long time, this issue has been a major bone of contention between the United Nations and Cambodia and one of the reasons why, in 2001, they were unable to reach an agreement on the establishment of an internationalized court for Cambodia.[70] A compromise has apparently been reached in 2003 to the effect that 'the scope' of the pardon granted to Ieng Sary 'is a matter to be decided by the Extraordinary Chambers'.[71]

The question of whether amnesties and pardons granted in respect of crimes against the peace and security of mankind violate customary international law, and whether exceptions to this rule are permitted, does not seem to be entirely settled yet.[72] However, the Statute of the Special Court for Sierra Leone and, to a lesser extent, the Cambodian Law certainly contribute to the emergence or strengthening of such a rule.

E. GENERAL OBSERVATIONS AND CONCLUSIONS

At the end of this chapter, a number of general observations can be made and conclusions drawn. The first and perhaps the most important one is that, in creating internationalized criminal courts for the purpose of adjudicating international crimes, one should be aware that their integration in a national legal system might make it difficult for them to apply international law to the fullest extent. Measures should, therefore, be taken where necessary to ensure

---

[70] For the relevant documents see Ben Kiernan 'Cambodia and the United Nations: Legal Documents' (2002) 34 *Critical Asian Studies* 611.

[71] See 'Report of the Third Committee' (*supra* n 5) 8.

[72] For a recent overview see Andreas O'Shea *Amnesty for Crime in International Law and Practice* (Kluwer Law International The Hague/London/New York 2002).

that these courts are able to apply international law where domestic law conflicts with it.

The Regulation for East Timor, the Statute of the Special Court for Sierra Leone, and the Cambodian Law all show some measure of eclecticism in defining the crimes under customary international law over which the Panels, the Court, and the Chambers have jurisdiction. The Statutes of the ICTY and ICTR and that of the permanent International Criminal Court are their main sources of inspiration. However, each of the three charters for an internationalized criminal court makes its own choices in this respect and these choices are by no means always identical. It is not always clear why one template has been preferred over another. The main justification for deviating from the Statutes of the ad hoc international tribunals or that of the permanent ICC seems to be that these Statutes do not always accurately reflect customary international law. Examples are the elimination of the requirement of discriminatory intent in the definition of crimes against humanity in the Sierra Leonean Statute, and the omission of a definition of the term 'attack' in the Regulation for East Timor. In both cases, the decision not to follow the example of a Statute of an international tribunal or court was well founded. Conversely, one may note that, in some cases, a decision not to deviate from the chosen template carries the risk that insufficient justice is done to customary international law.[73] More generally, the constitutive instruments of the three internationalized courts show that opinions on what constitutes customary international law may evolve or change in a short time, as may well be true, too, for customary law itself. As far as jurisdiction over crimes under domestic law is concerned, concurrent jurisdiction over international crimes and crimes under domestic law has many advantages and could be pursued in a more methodical way by future internationalized courts.

The constitutive instruments of the three internationalized courts show again variation and eclecticism in defining general principles of criminal law applicable to crimes under general international law. Generally, incorporation of the provisions of the Rome Statute should be preferred since they are far more complete and detailed than the provisions in the Statutes and the case law of the ad hoc tribunals and offer, therefore, more guidance to an internationalized court. However, in this respect UNTAET Regulation 2000/15 is 'over-inclusive' in that it declares most of these principles to be applicable to crimes under domestic law too. This raises issues of fairness and legal certainty.

As far as the principle of *nullum crimen sine lege* is concerned, the question of how and to what extent it should be applied by an internationalized court

---

[73] The requirement of discriminatory intent in Art 5 of the Cambodian Law, for instance, or the incomplete list of violations of the laws and customs in armed conflicts not of an international character in s 8.1(e) of UNTAET Reg 2000/15.

seems, to some extent, to depend on one's view on the relationship between an internationalized court and the legal system of the state on whose territory that court operates. The more one sees an internationalized court as an integral part of the national court system, the more reason there is to pay full respect to the embodiment of this principle in domestic law.[74] Constitutive instruments of future internationalized courts should, therefore, clarify to what extent domestic law with regard to the principle of *nullum crimen* remains relevant for an internationalized court.

Retroactive application of the elimination of statutes of limitation to limitation periods that have already expired, and the retroactive nullification of amnesties or pardons granted in the past, may well come into conflict with basic principles of domestic constitutional law or domestic criminal law. Retroactivity is, therefore, acceptable only to the extent that such measures have a firm and unequivocal basis in customary international law. At the same time, adoption of such measures may well help to develop or fortify rules of customary international law in the matter, a paradox of some sort.

---

[74] The same is true for the principle of *ne bis in idem*.

15

Procedural Law of Internationalized Criminal Courts

Håkan Friman*

A. INTRODUCTION

This chapter will discuss the criminal procedures applied (or to be applied) by internationalized courts in Kosovo, East Timor,[1] Sierra Leone, and Cambodia.[2] Developments for the period up to August 2003 have been incorporated.

One expected result of the introduction of internationalized courts is positive spillover effects for the domestic legal system. It is hoped that their establishment will help in restoring the country's legal system as well as strengthening local capacity-building and respect for the rule of law. Additionally, these efforts are meant to guarantee the impartial and neutral conduct of the criminal proceedings and, hopefully, to inject fair trial standards into ordinary domestic court proceedings. Hence, the procedural standards for these courts are important for achieving these sought-after effects.

It needs to be noted at the outset, however, that a minimalist approach is chosen for an assessment of the procedural regimes of the internationalized criminal courts, as its main focus is on a comparison between certain procedural features and fundamental international human rights standards for a fair criminal process, as set forth primarily in the 1966 International Covenant on Civil and Political Rights (ICCPR), as well as standards relating to juveniles and to victims and witnesses.

A number of necessary caveats follow from this approach. An assessment as to whether the procedural regimes are indeed fair and provide justice in actual practice goes beyond the scope of the present chapter. Nor does the latter seek to provide answers to the question whether and to what extent the proceedings are *conceived* as fair by the general public because they take due

---

* Former Associate Judge of Appeals, Sweden; Deputy Director, the Swedish Ministry of Justice; EO Professor of Procedural Law, University of Pretoria, South Africa; Visiting Professor, University College London, United Kingdom.
[1] Although East Timor has, on 27 September 2002, been admitted as the 191st Member State of the United Nations as 'Timor-Leste', the old name is used in this chapter.
[2] The chapter will not address the interesting recent development of an internationalized court in Bosnia and Herzegovina (B&H), which is presently being established in cooperation between ICTY and the Office of the High Representative (OHR): press releases issued by ICTY (www.un.org/icty/pressreal/2003) and OHR (www.ohr.int) on 21 February 2003.

account of the legal tradition of the national system in question.[3] Finally, the following analysis is based on the assumption that international standards for the proper administration of justice can and should apply to rich and poor states alike, regardless of whether a given State's national judicial system has been affected by armed conflict or other periods of large-scale turmoil. This assumption entails that one accepts that the introduction of modern criminal procedures is an expensive exercise and that training and infrastructure will be required.

Hence, the present exercise is mainly conducted with the eyes of a human rights lawyer and focused on statutory law, which in turn entails limitations concerning the conclusions that one may draw.

Following a brief presentation of the procedural law that is applicable to each of the internationalized courts (Part B), different criteria for the assessment of procedural regimes will be explored (Part C). In the subsequent section (Part D), particular procedural features of the different regimes will be assessed against international standards for fair and expeditious proceedings in accordance with the International Covenant for Civil and Political Rights (ICCPR) and some other international instruments. The concluding remarks, finally, include a summing up of the presentation and a discussion of possible preparatory steps that might be taken in order to overcome some identified shortcomings in the criminal procedures of internationalized courts, such as the ones established in Kosovo and East Timor.

B. APPLICABLE PROCEDURAL LAW

1. Kosovo and East Timor

Not only did the judicial system as such have to be constructed or reconstructed in Kosovo and East Timor, legal reform was also called for. After the initially chosen approach led to considerable legal and political difficulties, UNMIK eventually made the old Kosovo Criminal Code—ie the laws in force before 22 March 1989—applicable.[4] The defendant in criminal proceedings will, however, have the benefit of the most favourable provision in the criminal laws which were in force in Kosovo between that date and the adoption of the Resolution. This thereby applicable criminal law was no more democratic than the other—it was a political and not substantive call for change—and the amendment did not resolve the problem of identifying

---

[3] These are predominantly civil law traditions in the case of Kosovo and Cambodia and the common law tradition in the case of Sierra Leone. In East Timor, an initial civil law system has become increasingly intertwined with common law features.

[4] UNMIK Reg 1999/24 (12 December 1999) amending Reg 1999/1 (and later amended by UNMIK Reg 2000/59 (27 October 2000)). For a discussion of how such a change in approach came about, see Chapter 4 (Cady/Booth).

the applicable law since there were several types of law in force on 22 March 1989, including laws of the Federal Republic of Yugoslavia (eg the Code of Criminal Procedure).[5] The move also counteracted the intention to have Serbian judges serving in the Kosovo courts.

Besides the Code of Criminal Procedure of the Federal Republic of Yugoslavia, a large number of UNMIK regulations relate to procedural law. Such regulations range from the use of language in proceedings with international participation,[6] to prohibition of trials *in absentia* for serious violations of international humanitarian law,[7] the admissibility of certain witness statements,[8] 'co-operative witnesses',[9] protection of victims and witnesses,[10] covert and technical measures of surveillance and investigation,[11] and written records of interviews as evidence.[12] Other regulations relate to matters of pre-trial detention,[13] or detention pending extradition.[14] Here too, there is much confusion in practice about the applicable law, which affects the practical implementation by the courts and undermines the entrenchment of democratic practices.[15]

In East Timor, the establishment of the Serious Crimes Panels was accompanied by new legislation in the field of criminal procedure.[16] The Panels are required to apply the law of East Timor as promulgated by UNTAET and any subsequent UNTAET regulations and directives as well as, where appropriate, applicable treaties and recognized principles and norms of international law.[17]

In practice, this mixed system of applicable laws in East Timor means that judges and other lawyers must apply three sources of law: the transitional administration's regulations, domestic law, and international human rights

---

[5] eg Hansjörg Strohmeyer 'Making Multilateral Interventions Work: The U.N. and the Creation of Transitional Justice Systems in Kosovo and East Timor' (2001) 25 *Fletcher Forum of World Affairs* 107, 111–12; Independent International Commission on Kosovo *Kosovo Report* (Oxford University Press Oxford 2000) 113; Simon Chesterman *Justice Under International Administration: Kosovo, East Timor and Afghanistan* (International Peace Academy September 2002) 5 (available at www.ipacademy.org; last visited 31 August 2003).
[6] UNMIK Reg 2000/46 (15 August 2000).
[7] UNMIK Reg 2001/1 (12 January 2001).
[8] UNMIK Reg 2000/17 (23 March 2000).
[9] UNMIK Reg 2001/21 (19 September 2001).
[10] UNMIK Reg 2001/20 (19 September 2001).
[11] UNMIK Reg 2002/6 (18 March 2002).
[12] UNMIK Reg 2002/7 (28 March 2002).
[13] UNMIK Reg 1999/26 (22 December 1999) (extension of periods of pre-trial detention) and UNMIK Reg 2001/28 (11 October 2001) (rights of person arrested).
[14] UNMIK Reg 2000/14 (18 March 2000).
[15] eg Marcus Brand 'Institution-Building and Human Rights Protection in Kosovo in the Light of UNMIK Legislation' (2001) 70(4) *Nordic J of Int L* 461, 470.
[16] See most notably UNTAET Regulation 2000/15, containing certain procedural provisions.
[17] UNTAET Reg 2000/15 (6 June 2000) s 3 (referring to the law promulgated by ss 2 and 3 of UNTAET Reg 1999/1).

law. This is not an easy task, particularly in respect of criminal procedures. In order to streamline and modernize the criminal procedures, UNTAET by regulation introduced a Code of Criminal Procedure.[18] Earlier drafts of the Code were criticized for being vague and inconsistent, and the final Code contained elements from different legal traditions and was to be applied alongside the Indonesian Criminal Code, which led to further criticism from some quarters.[19]

Upon the transfer of power from UNTAET to East Timorese institutions, the new East Timor Constitution provides that laws and regulations in force in East Timor shall continue to apply to all matters insofar as they are not inconsistent with the Constitution and the principles laid down therein.[20] Consequently, the criminal procedures to be applied in accordance with UNTAET's regulations are still applicable and will be analysed here.

2. Sierra Leone and Cambodia

The Special Court for Sierra Leone is explicitly an ad hoc arrangement that does not form part of Sierra Leone's ordinary legal system and crimes are not prosecuted in the name of the Republic of Sierra Leone.[21] Thus, the Court needs its own criminal procedures. Apart from setting forth some fundamental due process rights of the accused, the Statute for the Special Court directs that the Rules of Procedure and Evidence of the ICTR ('the ICTR Rules') shall apply.[22] Thereby comprehensive and tested, but not necessarily (and not in all parts) non-controversial, criminal proceedings are provided for. Due to structural differences between ICTR and the Special Court, however, particularly in relation to powers vis-à-vis other states, the Special Court cannot apply all of the ICTR Rules *sic et simpliciter*.[23]

The ICTR Rules are to apply as they were at the time of the establishment of the Special Court. Hence, later amendments by ICTR to its Rules do not apply, *ipso facto*, which would otherwise have been very problematic for the Special Court since such amendments are entirely outside the control of the Court. It would also have meant a dual system of amending the Rules of

---

[18] UNTAET Reg 2000/30 (25 September 2000), later amended by UNTAET Reg 2001/25 (14 September 2001).

[19] eg Colin McDonald 'Out of the Ashes: A New Criminal Justice System for East Timor' Conference Paper presented to the International Society for the Reform of Criminal Law, 30 August 2001, available at www.isrcl.org/papers/McDonald.pdf (last visited 31 August 2003) 13.

[20] The new Constitution of East Timor (s 165), adopted on 22 March 2002 and entered into force on 20 May 2002; a translation into English is available at www.jsmp.minihub.org (last visited 31 August 2003).

[21] Special Court Agreement (Ratification) Act 2002 s 11.2 and 13; CXXX No II *Sierra Leone Gazette* Supplement (7 March 2002), available at www.specialcourt.org/documents/ImplLegn.html (last visited 31 August 2003).

[22] Article 14.1 of the Statute for the Special Court for Sierra Leone.

[23] See also p 346.

Procedure and Evidence since the judges of the Special Court are empowered, in respect of this Court, to amend the ICTR Rules or adopt additional rules. This may be done if the applicable rules 'do not, or do not adequately, provide for a specific situation'.[24] In so doing, the judges are to be guided by the Sierra Leonean Criminal Procedures Act 1965.

The Statute of the Special Court also provides, somewhat oddly, that the Appeals Chamber, but not a Trial Chamber, shall be guided by the decisions of the Appeals Chamber of ICTY and ICTR (and in respect of Sierra Leonean law, by the decisions of the Supreme Court of Sierra Leone).[25] This was introduced after the idea that the Special Court should share the Appeals Chamber with ICTY and ICTR had been raised but rejected.[26] The provision is framed in general terms and would therefore also cover case law on procedural matters.

A process for proposing amendments to the ICTR Rules in respect of the Special Court was commenced soon after the agreement on the Statute was concluded, and proposals were submitted by, inter alia, the Sierra Leone Bar Association and the Office of the Attorney-General and Minister of Justice of Sierra Leone.[27] These contain proposed amendments for the adaptation of the ICTR Rules to the Special Court (ie in light of its Statute and the Agreement between the United Nations and Sierra Leone). The Rules of Procedure and Evidence of the Special Court ('the Special Court Rules'), which entered into force on 12 April 2002, were amended by the judges on 7 March 2003.[28] The amended Rules depart from the ICTR Rules on a number of points, in particular in bringing procedures more in line with the laws and traditions of Sierra Leone as recommended by the Sierra Leone Bar Association.[29] Proposals for further amendments may be made by a judge, the Prosecutor, the Registrar, or the Defence Office (established by the

---

[24] Article 14.2 of the Statute for the Special Court for Sierra Leone.

[25] ibid Article 20.3. The Trial Chamber shall, however, 'have recourse to' ICTR practice (and practice of the Sierra Leonean courts) regarding sentencing, as appropriate: Article 19.1.

[26] 'Report of the Secretary-General on the Establishment of a Special Court for Sierra Leone' (4 October 2000) UN Doc S/2000/915; Robert Cryer 'A Special Court for Sierra Leone?' (2001) 50 *ICLQ* 435, 437; Avril McDonald 'Sierra Leone's Shoestring Special Court' (2002) 84(845) *IRRC* 121, 137–8.

[27] Sierra Leone Bar Association 'Report on the Special Court: Rules of Procedure and Evidence' (seminar on 3 December 2002) and 'Considerations of the Office of the Attorney-General and Minister of Justice on the Proposed Rules of Procedure and Evidence for the Special Court' (circulated at the same seminar), both documents on file with the author.

[28] Rules of Procedure and Evidence of the Special Court for Sierra Leone, as amended (Middle Temple, London) on 7 March 2003; available at www.pict-pcti.org/news_archive/03/03Mar/Si (last visited 31 August 2003) and at the Special Court's home page www.sc-sl.org (last visited 31 August 2003). The Rules have subsequently been amended.

[29] These amendments relate to matters such as defence disclosure, evidentiary matters, and the power of judges to order additional evidence. See further 355 ff. For similar ideas, eg Micaela Frulli 'The Special Court for Sierra Leone: Some Preliminary Comments' (2000) 11 *EJIL* 857, 860; Celina Schocken 'The Special Court for Sierra Leone: Overview and Recommendations' (2002) 20 *Berkeley J of Intl L* 436, 444.

Rules), as well as by the Sierra Leone Bar Association or any other entity invited to make proposals.[30]

In contrast to the Special Court for Sierra Leone, the Extraordinary Chambers in Cambodia are intended to form part of the domestic justice system.[31] As a consequence thereof, trials are to be conducted 'in accordance with existing procedures in force', which means Cambodian procedural law.[32] In addition, the Act on the Establishment of Extraordinary Chambers provides for guidance in procedural rules established at the international level only if necessary and if there are lacunae in the existing procedures.[33] This would not be an effective safeguard against application of any domestic procedural rules that do not meet international standards of fairness. However, the Draft Agreement of 17 March 2003 expands the possibility to resort to international procedural rules by providing that this may be done '[w]here Cambodian law does not deal with a particular matter, or where there is uncertainty regarding the interpretation or application of a relevant rule of Cambodian law, or where there is a question regarding the consistency of such a rule with international standards'.[34]

The Law on the Establishment of Extraordinary Chambers, in addition to defining the jurisdiction and principles of substantive criminal law, also includes some provisions regarding the criminal proceedings, relating to the conduct of investigations, protection of victims and witnesses, public trials (with exceptions), and certain fundamental rights of the accused, appeals, and the working language of the Chambers.[35] Besides, the Draft Agreement seeks to remedy some potential shortcomings and provide certain guarantees for the criminal proceedings being conducted in accordance with international standards of justice, fairness, and due process of law.[36]

---

[30] Rule 6.1 of the Rules of Procedure and Evidence of the Special Court for Sierra Leone.
[31] Article 2 of the Law on the Establishment of Extraordinary Chambers in the Courts of Cambodia. That the Extraordinary Chambers are to be national courts, within the existing court structure of Cambodia, is also upheld by the Draft Agreement of 17 March 2003; attached to UNGA Res 57/228B; see also 'Report of the Third Committee' (6 May 2003) UN Doc A/57/806.
[32] Law on the Establishment of Extraordinary Chambers in the Courts of Cambodia, art 33; Art 12.1 of the Draft Agreement (*supra* n 31). The applicable law is Law (Kram) on Criminal Procedure (8 February 1993), adopted by the State Assembly on 28 January 1993. A translation into English by the Council of Jurists is available at www.bigpond.com.kh/Council_of_Jurists/ Penal/pen002g. htm (last visited 31 August 2003).
[33] ibid; during the earlier rounds of negotiations, the United Nations had suggested a similar provision on guidance in procedural rules established at the international level, but eventually, due to resistance of the Cambodian government, this was watered down; eg Daryl Mundis 'New Mechanisms for the Enforcement of International Humanitarian Law' (2001) 95(4) *AJIL* 934, 941.
[34] Article 12.1 of the Draft Agreement (*supra* n 31).
[35] Articles 23–4, 33–7, and 45 of the Law on Criminal Procedure (*supra* n 32); see eg Suzannah Linton 'Comments of the Draft Agreement between the United Nations and the Royal Government of Cambodia Concerning the Prosecution under Cambodian Law of Crimes Committed during the Period of Democratic Kampuchea' (April 2003) 40 *Searching for the truth*, available at www.dccam.org (last visited 1 June 2003).
[36] Articles 12.2 and 13 of the Draft Agreement (*supra* n 31).

C. CRITERIA FOR ASSESSMENT OF THE PROCEDURAL REGIMES

When identifying those human rights which are capable of providing guidelines and being a yardstick for fair criminal procedures, the initial question to be answered relates to the reasons for establishing procedures that are in conformity with international standards. The adherence to internationally recognized human rights standards has been held out as necessary for ICTY and ICTR as a consequence of the fact that they represent an intrusion into the domestic affairs of states in an area at the very heart of state sovereignty—the prosecution of crimes.[37] To make this intrusion acceptable, the tribunals must apply fundamental human rights standards applicable to criminal trials when prosecuting states' nationals. Although there are substantive differences regarding the relationship vis-à-vis states, and thus the intrusiveness, the same argument can be made in respect of the International Criminal Court. Consequently, adherence to international fundamental human rights standards is an essential element for the legitimacy of these courts. But to what extent can this argument be made also for the internationalized courts?

In seeking an answer to this question, the mode of establishment of the internationalized courts considered here is important. While the Special Court for Sierra Leone and the Extraordinary Chambers in Cambodia are established by agreement between the international community and the state in question, the internationalized courts in East Timor and Kosovo are the invention of the respective international administration. It is clear that the latter courts could more easily be considered imposed. In the latter cases, however, as in Cambodia, the courts are not international institutions separate from the national judicial system but they are instead made a part of it. Hence, neither of these courts represents an imposed super-structure that substitutes national prosecutions, and the above-mentioned argument for applying international human rights standards cannot be used here.

Quite apart from this, however, it is often emphasized that the international community, represented by the United Nations, has a responsibility to ensure that the criminal procedures for the international and internationalized courts, which it has been instrumental in establishing, meet the highest international standards for criminal procedure. This is not the least important when the criminal proceedings are predominantly directed against leaders and others 'most responsible' for atrocities and, thus, likely to be attacked on political grounds. It would be contradictory indeed if judicial institutions created by, or with the assistance of, the United Nations would transgress international human rights standards achieved with great travail over the years. One of the aims of the United Nations, according to the UN

---

[37] eg Antonio Cassese 'Opinion: The International Criminal Tribunal for the Former Yugoslavia and Human Rights' (1997) 4 *European Human Rights L Rev* 329, 332.

Charter (Article 1), is exactly to promote and encourage respect for human rights and fundamental freedoms for all. Consequently, the assumption is that criminal procedures that the United Nations promotes should be human rights-centred.

1. Standards derived from international human rights treaties

Following the general preambular principles of fundamental and equal human rights and the dignity and worth of the human person of the UN Charter, the 1948 Universal Declaration of Human Rights[38] and, thereafter, the 1966 International Covenant on Civil and Political Rights (ICCPR)[39] enumerate some fundamental procedural rights in criminal proceedings. With 149 ratifications (as of 9 December 2002), the ICCPR enshrines very widely shared expectations of fairness regarding the rights of the accused in a criminal trial. Although there may be disagreement regarding aspects of the detailed procedural guarantees, many of which also require a well-developed and resourced legal system, the fair trial standards set forth in the ICCPR could be used to gauge national and international legal systems.

The fair trial standards thus derived from treaty law may not, however, be binding vis-à-vis non-party states and international organizations such as the United Nations. Such effect would instead require that the norms belong to the corpus of international law, be considered customary international law or 'general principles of law recognized by civilized nations'.[40] However, beyond the question whether the fair trial rights of the ICCPR (and other international human rights instruments), in full or in part, have acquired the status of customary international law or general principles of law, it is not the formal binding effect of a certain right for the respective court that is in focus for the limited purpose of the review in question here, but instead an assessment whether the procedural regime contains provisions that protect the rights in question. It is generally the core right as such, not the preferred way of implementing it into a national system, which is used for reference.

2. Standards derived from the international criminal courts

A comparison with treaty standards is not the only available option. Another approach would be to examine the procedures of the internationalized courts

---

[38] UNGA Res 217A (3rd Session) (10 December 1948).

[39] International Covenant on Civil and Political Rights of 16 December 1966, 999 UNTS 171.

[40] Article 38.1 of the Statute of the International Court of Justice. In support of human rights as 'principles of international law', see eg Philipp Alston and Bruno Simma 'Sources of Human Rights' (1992) 12 *Austrian Yearbook of Int'l L* 82; see also Christoph Safferling *Towards an International Criminal Procedure* (Oxford University Press Oxford 2001) 26–7.

against the procedures of ICTY, ICTR, and ICC, which are indeed sometimes mentioned as possible exemplary standards for future international criminal trials.[41]

At the time of the International Military Tribunal in Nuremberg, criminal procedures with both accusatorial and inquisitorial features were established and applied.[42] Although the procedures were predominantly accusatorial, the application of them in practice problematic, and the fair trial protection poor by today's standards, the Nuremberg trials showed that elements of different legal traditions could be combined. This has been further reinforced by the criminal procedures of ICTY and ICTR, which, to an even higher degree, protect rights of the accused and encompass procedural features from various legal models. Also, the procedures of ICC, which are the result of negotiations among a very large number of states, follow this path and, in addition, rights of victims of crimes have been further developed. The criminal procedures and experiences of the ad hoc tribunals and ICC, which are generally considered in keeping with the highest international standards, could also assist internationalized courts and even in the development of national proceedings.[43]

Hence, the international courts provide examples of *sui generis* procedural regimes with elements of the different legal traditions while at the same time they meet high human rights standards. However, these procedural regimes are also informed by international standards as set forth in international treaties, particularly the ICCPR, and would not carry an analysis of the limited nature as provided here much further than an assessment vis-à-vis the ICCPR itself,[44] with one exception. The balancing of the rights of the person suspected or accused of a crime against the rights of others, particularly the victims of crimes, has been further refined by rules for the tribunals and ICC and this development will be taken into account when assessing the procedures of the internationalized courts.

---

[41] eg Cassese (*supra* n 37) 330.

[42] Agreement for the Prosecution and Punishment of the Major War Criminals of the European Axis Powers and Charter of the International Military Tribunal ('the London Charter') (8 August 1945) 82 UNTS 279.

[43] eg Marieke Wierda 'What Lessons Can be Learned from the Ad Hoc Criminal Tribunals' (2002) 9 *UC Davis J of Intl L & Policy* 13.

[44] It could be argued that the standards set forth for the tribunals and ICC, which are of course underpinned by concrete procedures, provide examples of commonly shared procedural rules of greater specificity against which the procedures of the internationalized courts could also be assessed. However, it is questionable to what extent the development of these procedures with elements from different legal traditions really indicates an ideological acceptance or whether they are rather the result of pragmatism, ie the wish actually to achieve international adjudication; eg Mark Findlay 'Synthesis in Trial Procedures? The Experience of International Criminal Tribunals' (2001) 50 *ICLQ* 26, 52–3.

3. Standards derived from national law

Alternatively, certain common standards for fair criminal procedures could be deduced from an examination of national law, in particular national constitutions.[45] Common standards derived in this way would support a claim that they represent general principles of law and, thus, be binding for all. However, this method would again come down to rights of a general nature, much like the ICCPR and other treaties. In respect of the more concrete scheme for guaranteeing rights, the varying ideals of the different legal traditions would again come to the fore and conclusive standards are difficult to derive from national law. Moreover, this approach would often require comparison being made with international instruments, such as the ICCPR.

D. PROCEDURAL STANDARDS FOR FAIR AND EXPEDITIOUS PROCEEDINGS

1. Applied or proposed international procedural standards

Both UNTAET and UNMIK made the application of national laws subject to their conformity to 'internationally recognised human rights standards'.[46] Thereafter, UNMIK took a step further in specifying international instruments reflecting such standards that shall be 'observed'.[47] But even without specification, the same global instruments will also be taken into account in East Timor. The instruments specified by UNMIK are the 1948 Universal Declaration of Human Rights, the 1950 European Convention for the Protection of Human Rights and Fundamental Freedoms (ECHR) and the Protocols thereto, the ICCPR and the Protocols thereto, the 1965 International Covenant on Economic, Social and Cultural Rights, the 1979 Convention on the Elimination of All Forms of Discrimination Against Women, the 1984 Convention Against Torture and Other Cruel, Inhumane or Degrading Treatment or Punishment, and the 1989 International Convention on the Rights of the Child. It was not clear, however, whether these conventions are directly applicable law in Kosovo and the use of the term 'observed' suggested rather a declaratory political commitment.[48] Kosovo

---

[45] A large study where 139 national constitutions and 10 international instruments were examined with a view to extract common due process rights is presented in M Cherif Bassiouni 'Human Rights in the Context of Criminal Justice: Identifying International Procedural Protections and Equivalent Protections in National Constitutions' (1993) 3 *Duke J of Comparative & Intl L* 235.

[46] See p 323.

[47] UNMIK Reg 1999/24 (12 December 1999) s 1 (later amended by UNMIK Reg 2000/59 (27 October 2000)).

[48] eg Brand (*supra* n 15) 475–6.

still forms part of the Federal Republic of Yugoslavia and, arguably, is still bound by international treaties entered into by that state. But the future status of Kosovo is unclear and it is highly questionable whether Kosovo, represented by the UN interim administration, could adhere to the conventions in its own right. Nevertheless, the UNMIK Regulation also obliged those holding or taking public office in Kosovo to uphold internationally recognized human rights standards, and more recently the direct applicability of such standards have been clarified in the constitutional framework for provisional self-government adopted by UNMIK.[49]

In East Timor, the comprehensive legal regime introduced by UNTAET enshrines international human rights standards for criminal proceedings. Hence, at least the statutory framework offers a good protection of human rights. Importantly, the suspect or accused is protected if the applicable law is amended insofar as the law more favourable to that person will apply.[50] In respect of substantive criminal law, this forms part of the internationally acclaimed principle of legality (eg Article 15 ICCPR), but the protection is of course also useful as regards the application of criminal procedural law. Some guarantees in criminal proceedings are also set forth in the new Constitution.[51]

The Statute for the Special Court for Sierra Leone contains a customary list of basic due process rights for the accused, which includes a fair and public hearing (subject to measures for victims and witness protection), the presumption of innocence, and rights against self-incrimination, to representation, to be present throughout the proceedings, and to examine and present evidence.[52] Also the more specific procedural rules as set forth in the applicable Rules of Procedure and Evidence provide a high standard of procedural protection in line with international human rights instruments.

Regarding Cambodia, the Law on Extraordinary Chambers includes a provision (Article 35) which essentially repeats Article 14.3 of the ICCPR and it does allow, but only under limited circumstances, that guidance is sought in 'procedural rules established at the international level' (Article 33). In this case, procedural standards have been one stumbling block in reaching an agreement with the United Nations.[53] Both the procedures of the Cambodian Criminal Procedure Code and the procedural provisions laid down in the Law on Extraordinary Chambers have been widely criticized for offering insufficient protection and not meeting international standards. Concerning

---

[49] UNMIK Reg 2001/9 (15 May 2001) ch 3 s 3.3.

[50] UNTAET Reg 2000/15 (6 June 2000) s 3.2.

[51] The new Constitution of East Timor (*supra* n 20) s 34.

[52] Article 17 of the Statute for the Special Court for Sierra Leone, supplemented by rights of the suspect in Rule 42 of the Rules of Procedure and Evidence.

[53] eg Mundis (*supra* n 33) 939–42; Jelena Pejic 'Accountability for International Crimes: From Conjecture to Reality' (2002) 84 *IRRC* 13, 18.

the Criminal Procedure Code, issues such as access to evidence and court files, access to counsel, the right to confront the accusers, and the right to cross-examine witnesses have been held out.[54] Moreover, the special regulation for the Extraordinary Chambers is said to fail in ensuring the independence of judges and prosecutors, adequate protection of witnesses, and the right to (international) counsel.[55]

However, the Draft Agreement of 17 Match 2003 between the United Nations and the Cambodian government seeks to enhance the fair trial guarantees. The Chambers are to exercise their jurisdiction in accordance with 'international standards of justice, fairness and due process of law, as set out in Articles 14 and 15 of the [ICCPR]',[56] and the explicit reference to the Vienna Convention on the Law of Treaties[57] affirms that invocation of national law to escape international treaty obligations is prohibited. Additionally, certain rights relating to fair and public hearings and to the accused and his or her defence are further elaborated in the Agreement.[58]

2. Some fundamental procedural standards

I. Fair and public hearing by a competent, independent, and impartial tribunal

The right to a 'fair and public hearing by a competent, independent and impartial tribunal' is anchored in Article 14.1 of the ICCPR, and is a cornerstone for upholding the procedural standards and checking compliance with them. Furthermore, the tribunal must be established by law.

Whether hearings are considered fair depends upon an evaluation of the entire procedural set-up. The more specific rights following in Articles 14 and 15 ICCPR serve as a yardstick. But the right to a fair trial is considered broader than these rights taken together and the concept of 'equality of arms' is central for the assessment.[59] To complicate the matter further, very different views exist as to how 'equality of arms' is best upheld. These views often reflect differences in legal traditions with a dividing line between the (adversarial) common law and the (inquisitorial) civil law tradition. This division and the factual differences in modern legal systems cannot be explored and

---

[54] eg Human Rights Watch *Core Issues in Khmer Tribunal Law Unresolved* Press Release (21 January 2000).

[55] eg Mike Jendrzejczyk 'Cambodians, Too, Deserve Justice' *Int Herald Tribune* (27 December 2002); Human Rights Watch *Cambodia: Khmer Rouge Tribunal Must Meet International Standards* HRW Documents on Cambodia (19 December 2002).

[56] Article 12.2 of the Draft Agreement (*supra* n 31).

[57] ibid Art 2.2; see p 322.

[58] See further below.

[59] Manfred Nowak *U.N. Covenant on Civil and Political Rights: CCPR Commentary* (NP Engel Kehl 1993) 246–7.

qualified here. Yet, to make it very simple, an adversarial approach would focus more on the parties and their freedom and opportunities of action or inaction, while an inquisitorial approach would also take into account the safeguards provided by a more impartial prosecutor and more active judges. The minimum rights provided, however, stem from the common law notion of 'due process of law', which have shifted the focus to the parties and more specifically to the defendant. This, in turn, may lead observers to focus on the particular minimum rights, and sometimes to ignore the broader assessment of the protection offered by the system examined.

One example would highlight the issue. A question that has proven highly controversial in various contexts is whether trials in the absence of the accused should be allowed.[60] Both before ICTY and ICTR, as well as before ICC, trials *in absentia* are prohibited. Yet, such trials are known in some domestic systems, including in domestic law to be applied by internationalized courts. This is the case in Kosovo, where the domestic Criminal Procedure Code permits trials *in absentia*, which was also applicable for the 'Regulation 64 Chambers' until UNMIK prohibited such trials in early 2001.[61] Trials *in absentia* are not allowed in East Timor.[62] But in Sierra Leone, the judges have gone in the opposite direction and amended the ICTR Rules, which prohibit trials *in absentia*, so that such trials are permissible under certain circumstances, one basic condition being that the accused has made his or her initial appearance before the Court.[63] The new scheme established coincides with recent case law in the United Kingdom.[64] Finally, trials *in absentia* are allowed in Cambodian criminal proceedings, and have not been ruled out for the Extraordinary Chambers.[65] Either solution is, however, open for criticism.

Other examples relate to disclosure and presentation of evidence and the scope of intervention of judges in the investigation and at trial, ie in areas where different legal traditions offer different solutions.

The right to public hearings is guaranteed by all internationalized courts examined in this book. It is not, however, an absolute right under international standards, and Article 14.1 of the ICCPR, as well as the rules for the internationalized courts, provide for exceptions. Most of these are

---

[60] Regarding the debate on this issue in relation to ICC, see Håkan Friman 'Rights of Persons Suspected or Accused of a Crime' in Roy S Lee (ed) *The International Criminal Court: The Making of the Rome Statute* (Kluwer Law International The Hague 1999).

[61] UNMIK Reg 2001/1 (12 January 2001).

[62] UNTAET Reg 2000/30 (25 September 2000), as amended by Reg 2001/25 (14 September 2001) s 5.

[63] Rule 60 of the Rules of Procedure and Evidence of the Special Court; cf Rule 61 of the ICTR Rules which does not provide for a trial *in absentia* that may result in a verdict.

[64] For a review of recent British case law regarding a trial in the absence of the accused, P W Ferguson 'Trial in Absence and Waiver of Human Rights' (2002) *Criminal L Rev* (July) 554.

[65] Articles 114–17 of the Law on Criminal Procedure (*supra* n 32).

straightforward and reflect exceptions also provided for in most national systems. An elaborated provision applies in East Timor which makes exceptions for qualified information in respect of national security, the privacy of persons, and 'the interests of justice'.[66] The Statute of the Special Court for Sierra Leone only mentions measures ordered for the protection of victims and witnesses, while further exceptions follow from the Rules of Procedure and Evidence.[67] The Cambodian Law on Extraordinary Chambers uses the very loose formula that trials shall be public unless the Chamber, in exceptional circumstances, decides to close the proceedings 'for good cause in accordance with existing procedures in force'.[68] The ordinary criminal procedure is equally vague and provides for *in camera* hearings when proceedings in open court are deemed to be dangerous to the public order and good tradition.[69] However, the Draft Agreement between the United Nations and Cambodia provides for access to the proceedings by representatives of UN Member States, the Secretary-General, media, as well as national and international NGOs, and prescribes that '[a]ny exclusion from such proceedings in accordance with the provisions of Article 14 [of the ICCPR] shall only be to the extent strictly necessary in the opinion of the Chamber concerned and where publicity would prejudice the interests of justice'.[70]

The institutional guarantee of a competent, independent, and impartial tribunal established by law is also crucial for fairness. Competence is here meant as a specification of the requirement that the tribunal is established by law. Both in Sierra Leone and in Cambodia, the internationalized courts are based on national law. The situation is somewhat more precarious in respect of Kosovo and East Timor where the legislative body (ie the UN Missions) derive their powers from Security Council Resolutions and ultimately from Chapter VII of the UN Charter. The idea that the establishment of criminal courts may be created under Chapter VII—ie as a means contributing to the restoration of international peace and security—was controversial when ICTY and ICTR were established and challenged in the very first case before ICTY.[71] However, the Appeals Chamber upheld the constitutionality of the tribunal and its legality is no longer seriously questioned.

The question of independence relates to the executive and legislative branches of the state and focuses on the selection and appointment of judges

---

[66] UNTAET Reg 2000/30 (25 September 2000), as amended by Reg 2001/25 (14 September 2001) s 28.

[67] Article 17.2 of the Statute for the Special Court for Sierra Leone and Rules 78–9 of the Rules of Procedure and Evidence.

[68] Article 34 of the Law on Extraordinary Chambers in the Courts of Cambodia.

[69] Article 129 of the Law on Criminal Procedure (*supra* n 32).

[70] Article 12.2 of the Draft Agreement (*supra* n 31).

[71] *Prosecutor v Tadić* IT-94-1 Decision on the Defence Motion for Interlocutory Appeal on Jurisdiction (2 October 1995) (1996) 35 ILM 32.

(and prosecutors) as well as their roles and functions in the exercise of their office, ie both institutional and functional independence.[72] Also the issue of impeachment of officials is of importance here. The risk of undue pressure is of course increased in cases as potentially sensitive as the ones handled by the internationalized courts. Hence, it has been viewed as crucial to operate them with international judges and prosecutors in a decisive position. The most telling examples are the internationalized courts for Sierra Leone and in Cambodia where the international influence both in institutional and in functional terms differ fundamentally.[73] While in Sierra Leone the prosecutor and the majority of judges will be international and appointed by the UN Secretary-General, the opposite is envisaged for Cambodia and two co-prosecutors, one international and one Cambodian, will operate side-by-side with a complicated procedure developed for settlement of disputes between them. Moreover, all appointments are to be made by a Cambodian body, the Supreme Council of the Magistracy, and nominations of replacements for international officials are to be made by Cambodian authorities. The practical impact of international judges does also depend upon the court's decision-making process, ie whether unanimity is required or majority decisions allowed. As part of a compromise for Cambodia, brokered by US Senator John Kerry, majority decisions requiring a qualified majority ('super-majority') are prescribed so that a decision will always depend upon the affirmative vote of at least one international judge.[74]

The Cambodian approach, which has been at the centre of the controversy between Cambodia and the United Nations, has prompted serious concerns. This is particularly troublesome since strong political interests are involved and, as noted by the Group of Experts,[75] a prevalence of corruption and political influence over the judiciary exist in general. Under such circum-

---

[72] On this issue, see Chapter 12 (Romano).

[73] Some concerns regarding independence have also been advanced regarding the internationalized courts of Kosovo and East Timor. Regarding Kosovo: OMIK/LSMS *Review of the Criminal Justice System, September 2001–February 2002* (2002) 25–44. Reports published by OMIK/LSMS (the Legal Systems Monitoring Systems of the Organization for Security and Cooperation in Europe [OSCE] Mission of Kosovo) are available at www.osce.org/kosovo/documents/reports/justice (last visited 31 August 2003). In East Timor, UNTAET Reg 2000/11 (6 July 2000) (On the Organization of Courts in East Timor) contains provisions aimed at ensuring the independence of the judiciary, including provisions on rights and duties of judges (ss 2 and 28–32). More recently, however, concerns have been expressed regarding the future impartiality of judges and prosecutors because of provisions in the Judicial Magistrates Statutes adopted by the national Parliament on 3 September 2002: 'Report of the Secretary-General on the United Nations Mission of Support in East Timor' (6 November 2002) UN Doc S/2002/1223.

[74] Article 14 of the Law on Extraordinary Chambers in the Courts of Cambodia.

[75] Report of the Group of Experts established by UNGA Res 52/135 (12 December 1997); see Identical Letters from the Secretary-General to the President of the General Assembly and the President of the Security Council (15 March 1999) UN Doc A/53/850, S/1999/231; Steven R Ratner 'The United Nations Group of Experts for Cambodia' (1999) 93 *AJIL* 948; Mann Bunyanunda 'The Khmer Rouge on Trial: Whither the Defence?' (2001) 74 *Southern California L Rev* 1581, 1619.

stances, the risk is that a formal provision that judges shall be independent in the performance of their functions will be of little help in practice.[76] In fact, on the same day as the General Assembly adopted Resolution 57/228 on resumed negotiations with Cambodia, the Assembly also adopted Resolution 57/225 on the situation of human rights in Cambodia where it expressed concerns regarding the continued problems related to the rule of law and the functioning of the judiciary resulting from, inter alia, corruption and interference by the executive. In his report on the subsequent Draft Agreement, the Secretary-General took note of this finding and other worrying reports and expressed his concerns that established international standards of justice, fairness, and due process might not be ensured.[77] Hence, the public trial guarantees are particularly important for scrutiny of the proceedings.

The functional independence is linked to the prerequisite that the tribunal must be impartial in its administration of justice in individual cases. From a formal point of view, this requires regulation of the disqualification of judges in a particular case. Such rules apply, albeit with varying scope and content, for the internationalized courts. But even so bias may occur in practice. It may be particularly difficult for local judges and prosecutors with personal experiences from atrocities where ethnicity played a major role. Also, public pressure can be very strong. In Kosovo's 'Regulation 64 Chambers', local judges were initially in the majority and there was a clear tendency that the local Kosovo-Albanian judges would outvote the international judge and generally regard Serbs as automatically guilty of war crimes and other offences while Albanians were only rarely condemned.[78] The Regulation had to be amended so that international judges and prosecutors were given a stronger role. In addition, ethnic diversity and minority participation were given priority in the appointment of judges and prosecutors. Hence, the impartiality of the courts (and prosecutors) was necessary for providing equality before the courts, another basic right set forth in Article 14.1 ICCPR. For the 'Regulation 64 Chambers', these measures have essentially solved the problem, but for the judicial system in general much of it still remains.[79]

II. Presumption of innocence and burden of proof

The presumption of innocence is an essential principle of a fair trial (Article 14.2 ICCPR) and must be applicable throughout the proceedings until a final verdict is reached. It applies for all internationalized courts in question. The

---

[76] Article 10 of the Law on Extraordinary Chambers in the Courts of Cambodia.

[77] 'Report of the Secretary-General on Khmer Rouge Trials' (31 March 2003) UN Doc A/57/769 para 28.

[78] According to UNMIK lawyer Michael Hartmann; John Lloyd 'We Came Here to Build a State That's All' *Financial Times* (31 December 2002).

[79] eg OMIK/LSMS *Report 9: On the Administration of Justice* (March 2002) 4–7 (see *supra* n 73).

principle has a number of important procedural consequences. Most important is that the prosecutor must prove the guilt of the accused—ie the prosecutor has the burden of proof—and that in case of doubt the accused must be acquitted (*in dubio pro reo*).

However, the standard of proof for establishing guilt has been very difficult to establish in international instruments and a proposal for setting out the standard 'beyond reasonable doubt' in ICCPR was defeated.[80] Nevertheless, an international or internationalized criminal court cannot operate without a settled standard, and in spite of the lack of a specified standard set forth in their respective Statutes, both ICTY and ICTR have prescribed the standard of 'guilt beyond reasonable doubt'.[81] For ICC, this standard is mandated by the (state-negotiated) Statute.[82] By application of the (amended) ICTR Rules, the same standard will be explicitly provided for the Special Court for Sierra Leone. For the other three courts, which operate in countries influenced by the civil law tradition, the standard of proof to apply is not laid down in statutory law (not even in the new Rules of Criminal Procedures adopted by UNTAET). Nonetheless, this is also the case in many national jurisdictions and will most likely not lead to a different standard in practice since the formula 'guilt beyond reasonable doubt' is considered to be a generally recognized principle of law.[83]

Also, the right of an accused not to be compelled to testify against him- or herself or to confess guilt (Article 14.3(g) ICCPR) follows from the presumption of innocence and is applicable in the proceedings before the internationalized courts as a matter of right. But in order to be meaningful, the presumption must be backed up by more specific provisions actually enforcing and safeguarding the principle. Both more substantive rules, such as the application of presumptions for establishing a crime, and more clear-cut procedural rules, for example regarding self-incrimination, are of importance. This is another area where the views may differ in different legal traditions. Thus, different assessments may be made regarding the compatibility of the legal regimes of the various internationalized courts depending on the preferences of the observer. When the procedures are mixed and include elements from different legal traditions, as in the case of the Rules of the Special Court for Sierra Leone and in the UNTAET Rules of Criminal Procedure, the evaluation is even more difficult to make.

III. Deprivation of liberty

Deprivation or restriction of a person's liberty are of course very serious measures which go to the core of human rights and require strict statutory

---

[80] Nowak (*supra* n 59) 254.
[81] Rule 87 of the ICTY and ICTR Rules of Procedure and Evidence, respectively.
[82] Article 66 of the Rome Statute of the International Criminal Court.
[83] Nowak (*supra* n 59) 254.

safeguards. Globally recognized rights and standards are provided in Article 9 ICCPR. The procedural safeguards include a right to be brought promptly upon arrest before a judge (or a similar judicial officer), and be tried within a reasonable time or be released.

Indeed, the question of deprivation of liberty and the procedural safeguards to be applied seems to be one of the main reasons for the establishment of judicial structures by the UN transitional administrations in Kosovo and East Timor.[84] Typically, internationalized courts are established and begin their operations when suspects have already been arrested. This was the case in Kosovo and East Timor where the international military forces KFOR and INTERFET carried out large-scale arrests in order to restore peace and security in the respective territories. In Sierra Leone, too, many of those most likely to face the Special Court are already in custody (apprehended by national authorities).

The legal basis for the arrests is normally weak, eg a general peace-keeping mandate or extraordinary constitutional emergency powers, and so are the procedural safeguards for those arrested or detained. Realizing this, both UNMIK in Kosovo and UNTAET in East Timor introduced interim mechanisms. Creating such a system ad hoc and in the midst of events is of course very difficult. Delays and mistakes risk affecting the general public's confidence in the Mission's activities. Hence, it has been suggested that UN Missions should develop a 'quick-start package' of law enforcement-related legislation and a judicial structure for speedy interim use.[85]

In East Timor, a suspect may only be held for 48 hours before being brought before a judge or released, and the pre-trial detention of a suspect, which may only be ordered for crimes that carry more than one year of imprisonment under the law, must be reviewed by an investigating judge every 30 days.[86] For pre-trial detention longer than six months from the arrest, special requirements apply. However, during the initial period after the first judges and prosecutors had been appointed, but before the courts of East Timor had actually been established, some suspects were apprehended and detained. The validity of warrants for detention issued by prosecutors or investigative judges before the courts were established was in serious doubt, and as a remedy UNTAET adopted a controversial provision on retroactive validation of such premature warrants.[87] This initial practice

---

[84] eg Hansjörg Strohmeyer 'Collapse and Reconstruction of a Judicial System: The United Nations Missions in Kosovo and East Timor' (2001) 95 *AJIL* 46, 49, 51.

[85] ibid 61–2; Strohmeyer (*supra* n 5) 122; Wendy S Betts et al 'Special Feature: The Post-Conflict Transitional Administration of Kosovo and the Lessons Learned in Efforts to Establish a Judiciary and Rule of Law' (2001) 22 *Michigan J of Int'l L* 371, 383–4; Frederick Rawski 'To Waive or Not to Waive: Immunity and Accountability in U.N. Peacekeeping Operations' (2002) 18 *Connecticut J of Int'l L* 103, 132. See further pp 356–7.

[86] UNTAET Reg 2000/14 (10 May 2000) (amending UNTAET Reg 2000/11) s 12a.

[87] ibid s 12a.10; Suzannah Linton 'Rising from the Ashes: The Creation of a Viable Justice System in East Timor' (2001) 25 *Melbourne U L Rev* 122, 134.

was, to say the least, questionable in light of the international standard that no person 'shall be subjected to arbitrary arrest or detention' or 'be deprived of his liberty except on such grounds and in accordance with such procedures as are established by law' (Article 9 ICCPR).

In spite of good rules on deprivation of liberty, a proper operation of the rules may be hampered by practical problems. Particularly problematic is when the problems result in long periods of detention without trial. Furthermore, inexperience or disregard for the rules may lead to detainees being held without a valid warrant of arrest. All this has occurred in East Timor where it has been reported that almost one-third of the detention population was illegally detained.[88] Initial confusion as to the division of jurisdiction and responsibilities between the ordinary and the Serious Crimes Panels, also led to cases where detention orders lapsed and were remedied by the Serious Crimes Panel in the form of a blanket extension for all detainees, something later quashed on appeal.[89] An additional problem is the absence of an effective mechanism for monitoring the implementation of standards and investigation of complaints. As a result, East Timorese prisons have suffered from unrest and mass escapes. These experiences also show that it is essential to bridge any immediate measures for arrest and detention with the more permanent subsequent legal order.

Problems regarding deprivation of liberty have also been experienced in Kosovo, some of them related to practical difficulties in observing time limits. The applicable Code of Criminal Procedure includes a six-month maximum period for pre-trial detention, which was considered too short, and UNMIK adopted a Regulation allowing extension of the time to a maximum of one year (after special judicial review).[90] This measure, which only applies to crimes that may lead to a five-year prison sentence, was criticized and even denounced as unlawful by OSCE's Mission in Kosovo, which itself forms part of UNMIK.[91] Generally welcomed, however, was a Regulation on the treatment of and certain procedural rights (eg to assistance of defence counsel) for persons arrested by law enforcement authorities.[92]

---

[88] 'Report of the Secretary-General on the United Nations Mission of Support in East Timor' (*supra* n 73) para 16. Some difficulties seem to be of a continuing nature and the Judicial System Monitoring Programme (JSMP) has reported that as late as in January 2003, 31 persons were illegally detained but subsequently released by the court: JSMP Press Release (20 January 2003). JSMP reports, press releases, etc. are available at www.jsmp.minihub.org (last visited 31 August 2003).

[89] *Julio Fernandez and 19 others v Prosecutor General* Criminal Appeal No 2 of 2001 (14 February 2001), with a separate opinion by one of the judges; Suzannah Linton 'Prosecuting Atrocities at the District Court of Dili' (2001) 2 *Melbourne J of Int'l L* 414, 426–30.

[90] UNMIK Reg 1999/26 (22 December 1999).

[91] OMIK/LSMS *Report 6: Extension of Time Limits and the Rights of Detainees: The Unlawfulness of Regulation 1999/26* (26 April 2000) (see n 73).

[92] UNMIK Reg 2001/28 (11 October 2001). See also Art 10 ICCPR.

But the difficulties in establishing law enforcement authorities has led to another problem, which is extra-judicial detention by 'executive order' of the Special Representative of the Secretary-General or by 'special holds' of KFOR. These measures have been criticized for a lack of a clear legal basis (ie the general mandates given by the Security Council), and non-compliance with human rights guarantees against arbitrary arrests.[93] The use of extra-judicial detention has decreased substantively and certain measures have been taken to improve the rights of the detainees, such as the adoption of a KFOR Directive[94] setting out some policies and procedures and a temporary Detention Review Commission for extra-judicial detentions by executive orders.[95] While derogation from the safeguards on deprivation of liberty is possible under ICCPR (Article 4), the conditions are very strict and the practice, which seems to be motivated primarily by the lack of able and willing civilian authorities, is highly questionable from a human rights perspective.

In respect of arrest and detention, the Special Court for Sierra Leone has amended the ICTR Rules of Procedure and Evidence. In so doing, the Special Court has done away with the controversial requirement that release may only take place 'in exceptional circumstances', something that has been criticized as making deprivation of liberty the rule and freedom the exception.[96] Unlike ICTR, the Special Court sits in the country where the atrocities were committed and where many of the perpetrators are present. Sierra Leonean law prescribes that an arrest warrant issued by the Court shall, for the purposes of execution, have the same force and effect as a domestic arrest warrant, which has been taken into account in the Court's rules on execution of arrest warrants.[97] Additionally, the Special Court is facing a problem similar to that of East Timor since most of the leaders of the Revolutionary United Front (RUF), widely held as mainly responsible for most of the atrocities, are already deprived of liberty under emergency provisions of the Sierra Leonean Constitution.[98] How such prolonged and somewhat irregular

---

[93] OMIK/LSMS (*supra* n 73) 45.

[94] COMKFOR Detention Directive 42 (9 October 2001).

[95] UNMIK Reg 2001/18 (25 August 2001) (remaining in force for three months).

[96] Rule 65 of the Rules of Procedure and Evidence of the Special Court for Sierra Leone. This criticism was mainly raised against the requirement of 'extraordinary circumstances' in the ICTY Rules, which has remained in the ICTR Rules until an amendment on 2 June 2003 (Rule 65); eg Anne-Marie La Rosa 'A Tremendous Challenge for the International Criminal Tribunals: Reconciling the Requirements of International Humanitarian Law with Those of Trial' (1997) 37(321) *IRRC* 635; Matthew DeFrank 'Provisional Release: Current Practice, A Dissenting Voice, and the Case for a Rule Change' (2002) 80 *Texas L Rev* 1429.

[97] The Special Court Agreement, 2002, (Ratification) Act s 23; Rule 55 of the Rules of Procedure and Evidence.

[98] Abdul Tejan-Cole 'The Special Court for Sierra Leone: Conceptual Concerns and Alternatives' (2001) 1 *African Human Rights LJ* 107, 120–1; Stuart Beresford and A S Muller 'The Special Court for Sierra Leone: An Initial Comment' (2001) 14(3) *Leiden J Int'l L* 635, 650–1; Suzannah Linton 'Cambodia, East Timor and Sierra Leone: Experiments in International Justice' (2001) 12(2) *Criminal L Forum* 185, 241.

detention without charge could be converted into a valid pre-trial detention ordered by the Special Court is yet to be clarified. The first indictments of the Special Court were directed against, inter alia, five persons already held in custody.[99]

Finally, the Cambodian Code of Criminal Procedure provides that a person arrested shall be brought to court within 48 hours and there is also a time limit within which an appeal of a detention order must be dealt with.[100]

Like ICTY and ICTR, but with the exception of East Timor,[101] internationalized criminal courts do not have provisions on compensation to persons who were illegally detained, prosecuted, or convicted. Such a right to compensation, which is provided for in other international instruments (eg Articles 9.5 and 14.6 ICCPR) and for ICC (Article 85 of the Rome Statute), appears to be particularly pertinent to provide for where unlawful or at least very doubtful arrests have been commonplace, and good arguments could be made in favour of the international community providing for a scheme of this kind when it engages in judicial activities.[102] It may be noted, however, that compensation schemes can be more or less far-reaching and that the rights to compensation set forth in the ICCPR and other instruments are rather narrow in scope.

IV. A trial without undue delay

Everyone under criminal charges must have the right to be tried without undue delay (Article 14.3(c) ICCPR). Anyone arrested shall be tried within a reasonable time or released (Article 9.3 ICCPR). What this means in practice is debatable, however, and highly complex cases such as international crimes of the kind under the jurisdiction of internationalized courts will inevitably

---

[99] These five persons (Sankoh, SCSL-2003-2; Sesay, SCSL-2003-5; Brima, SCSL-2003-6; Kallon, SCSL-2003-7; and Norman, SCSL-2003-8) were indicted and arrested by the Special Court on 10 March 2003 and appeared before a judge on 15 March. Thereafter, other individuals have been indicted and detained or provisionally detained awaiting indictment. As of 29 May 2003, the Court has indicted nine individuals, seven of whom are in custody. See the Court's official home page at www.sc-sl.org (last visited on 31 August 2003). Two of the accused, including Sankoh, have since died and the indictments against them have been withdrawn.

[100] Law on Criminal Procedure (*supra* n 32) Arts 38 and 79. Except for one senior member, Sam Bith, who was convicted and jailed for life in December 2002, the leadership of Khmer Rouge are reported to live as free men in Cambodia: 'Leader of Khmer Rouge Gets Life in Jail' *The Times* (24 December 2002).

[101] UNTAET Reg 2000/30 (25 September 2000) as amended by Reg 2001/25 (14 September 2001) s 52.

[102] eg Gilbert Bitti 'Compensation to an Arrested or Convicted Person' in Roy S Lee et al (eds) *The International Criminal Court: Elements of Crimes and Rules of Procedure and Evidence* (Transnational Publishers Ardsley New York 2001) 623; Stuart Beresford 'Redressing the Wrongs of the International Justice System: Compensation for Persons Erroneously Detained, Prosecuted, or Convicted by the Ad Hoc Tribunals' (2002) 96 *AJIL* 628.

take longer than ordinary crimes. The length of preparations and trials before ICTR and ICTY is not encouraging in this regard.[103]

In comparison, the criminal proceedings before the Serious Crimes Panels of East Timor have been completed much faster than the cases before ICTY and ICTR and to date some 30 accused have been tried. Most of them, however, have resulted only in convictions for 'ordinary crimes' like murder. Regarding more complex international crimes, such as crimes against humanity, especially cases with multiple defendants, the proceedings have, as with ICTY and ICTR, been very complex and slow. Additionally, all cases, irrespective of whether they include ordinary or international crimes, have been unnecessarily delayed due to practical problems, eg the lack of proper court administration and keeping of a court calendar, transport of detained defendants, scarcity of judges, etc, which have resulted in postponements.[104] The experiences are similar in Kosovo, although the judicial process there has also been described as snail-like.[105]

In Sierra Leone, at the time of writing, proceedings have yet to begin. However, it should be noted that certain amendments to the ICTR Rules have been made in the interest of speeding up the proceedings, for example by reducing the maximum time periods for certain measures.

Appropriate and modern procedures should enhance the manner of investigating and adjudicating on crimes in a speedy and yet fair manner. Applicable law in the state in question may be antiquated, and this will then affect an internationalized court simply adhering to the existing law. This has been the case in Kosovo and East Timor where the interim administrations have introduced, by regulation, legal mechanisms filling gaps in the existing laws. On the other hand, highly sophisticated procedures also require well-trained professionals dealing with them and the effectiveness and appropriateness of the 'state-of-the-art' system introduced in East Timor has sometimes been questioned.[106]

---

[103] At ICTR, eg, the cases against one accused who was arrested in June 1995 and transferred to the tribunal in November 1996 (Ndayambaje, ICTR-96-8) and four accused who were arrested in March 1996 and transferred in January 1997 (Bagasora, ICTR-96-7; Ntagerura, ICTR-96-10A; Nsengiyumva; ICTR-96-12; and Nahimana, ICTR-96-11) are not yet finally disposed of. At ICTY, eg, the cases against one accused surrendering voluntarily in April 1996 (Blaskic, IT-95-14), two accused surrendering voluntarily in October 1997 (Kordic & Cerkez, IT-95-14/2), and four accused arrested in April or May 1998 and transferred shortly thereafter (Kvocka et al, IT-98-30/1), are at the appeals stage. In an address to the Security Council on 29 October 2002, Claude Jorda, then President of ICTY, declared that the trials at ICTY lasted an average of 17 months: ICTY Press Release JDH/P.I.S./708-e, available at www.un.org/pressreal/p708-e.htm.

[104] eg, the JSMP (*supra* n 88) has established that more than half the scheduled hearings between the beginning of September and mid-October 2002 (17 of 29) were postponed because judges were not available or the parties required more time for preparations; JSMP Press Release (11 October 2002), available at www.jsmp.minihub.org/News/12N_10_02.htm (last visited 31 August 2002).

[105] *Kosovo Report* (*supra* n 5) 112–14.

[106] eg Linton (*supra* n 98) 213–14; William Burke-White 'A Community of Courts: Towards a System of International Criminal Law Enforcement' (2002) 24(1) *Michigan J of Int'l L* 1, 69.

V. Right to defence and free legal assistance

The right to defence according to Article 14.3(d) ICCPR consists of a number of individual rights such as the right to be present[107] and defend oneself in person, to choose one's own counsel, to be informed of the right to counsel, and to receive free legal assistance. In addition, the accused must have adequate time and facilities to prepare the defence, including communications with counsel, and a right to call and examine witnesses (Article 14.3(b) and (e) ICCPR). The right to conduct one's own defence without legal representation is treated differently nationally, and at least before the European Court of Human Rights, the assignment of defence counsel against the will of the accused is considered permissible in the interests of justice. But such assignment is unthinkable in many national systems, and ICTY has instead opted for the assignment of so-called *amicus curiae* counsel to assist the court in safeguarding the rights of the accused, but not to impose representation.[108]

The following survey will focus on the right to free legal assistance of the accused person's own choosing. To be sure this is an essential component for 'equality of arms' in the proceedings, particularly when both the crimes and the law are very complex, and thus for fairness.

A party to any proceeding before a court in East Timor has the right to a legal representative of his own choosing.[109] The right to select and be assisted by a lawyer at all stages of criminal proceedings is also guaranteed by the Constitution.[110] In order to ensure, inter alia, that persons involved in criminal investigations or criminal proceedings will indeed have access to the legal advice, assistance, and representation that he or she is entitled to, UNTAET has established a Legal Aid Service.[111] It operates through a system of public defenders. Upon arrest, the police or investigating judge shall inquire whether the suspect wishes to have legal counsel and, if so, contact the Legal Aid Office for designation of a public defender. Additionally, a court may request that a public defender is assigned. A 'means-test' is applied. Public defenders operate under a code of conduct which includes duties to protect the interests of clients and confidentiality, to the court and to act with independence.[112]

---

[107] See p 329.

[108] *Prosecutor v Milosevic* (IT-02-54). This approach was confirmed by the Trial Chamber in its oral ruling on 18 December 2002, rejecting a motion by the Office of the Prosecutor that defence counsel should be imposed on the accused; see Reasons for Decision on the Prosecution Motion Concerning Assignment of Counsel (4 April 2003).

[109] UNTAET Reg 2000/11 (6 July 2000) s 27 and Reg 2000/30 (25 September 2000) s 6, both as amended by Reg 2001/25 (14 September 2001).

[110] The new Constitution of East Timor (*supra* n 20) s 34.

[111] UNTAET Reg 2001/24 (5 September 2001), which also repealed all Indonesian laws applicable to East Timor in relation to the provision of legal aid (s 29).

[112] ibid Schedule.

In Kosovo, domestic law on criminal procedure provides that the accused has the right to present his own defence or defend himself with the assistance of defence counsel of his own choice, a right that applies throughout the entire course of the criminal proceedings.[113] Domestic law was criticized, however, for not sufficiently providing for a right to legal representation in respect of detained suspects, and UNMIK subsequently adopted a Regulation with provisions to remedy these shortcomings.[114] The same Regulation also addressed other problematic issues in national law, such as confidential communications between an arrested person and the defence counsel and interviews with the suspect in the presence of counsel.[115]

Legal assistance is of limited use in practice, however, if the defence counsel are inexperienced, which has often been the case in East Timor and also in Kosovo. In an attempt to remedy this, prosecutors have deviated from adversarial trial principles and tried to help defence counsel by coaching them in different ways and even in making motions and objections. While inexpert defence counsel is a serious problem, criticism of this prosecutorial practice is not very well founded since the legal tradition of East Timor is rather one of civil law where the prosecutor plays the role of an 'officer of justice' rather than a partisan advocate.[116] Other measures have also been taken in order to improve the quality of representation provided to the accused, although problems still remain. One initiative is the OSCE-funded Criminal Defence Resource Centre in Kosovo which focus on improving the capacity of defence counsel by case-related assistance, research, and training. Another measure is international public defenders.

The Statute of the Special Court for Sierra Leone (Article 17.4(d)) repeats the language of the ICCPR. In enforcing this right, an effective public defender scheme has been identified as a priority also for this Court and the amended Rules of Procedure and Evidence also make provision for a Defence Office.[117] The formal requirements for counsel to be assigned by the Defence Office, which will be the case when the suspect lacks sufficient means to pay for counsel, are slightly higher than for defence counsel in general

---

[113] Articles 11 and 67 of the FRY Law of Criminal Procedure.

[114] UNMIK Reg 2001/28 (11 October 2001) ss 2, 3; OMIK/LSMS *Report No 7: Access to Effective Counsel. Stage 1: Arrest to the First Detention Hearing* (23 May 2000) (see n 73).

[115] The FRY Law of Criminal Procedure Article 74 provides for access and communications, but with far-reaching limitations. A further problem has been the lack of access to court documents, something that is also provided for in the Law of Criminal Procedure Article 73: OMIK/LSMS *Report No 8: Access to Effective Counsel. Stage 2: The Investigative Hearings to Indictment* (20 July 2000) (see n 73).

[116] For a critical view: David Cohen 'Seeking Justice on the Cheap: Is the East Timor Tribunal Really a Model for the Future?' (2002) 61 *Asia Pacific Issues: Analysis from the East-West Centre* (August) 5–6.

[117] Rule 45 of the Rules of Procedure and Evidence of the Special Court for Sierra Leone; interview with the Court's then President Geoffrey Robertson QC on 'Hard Talk' BBC News 24 (27 January 2003).

before the Court.[118] Foreign counsel are also allowed to represent a suspect or accused.

The recourse to foreign defence counsel, or rather that lack of such an option, was one major point of controversy regarding the Extraordinary Chambers in Cambodia. The provisions of the Law on Extraordinary Chambers on the right to counsel, as compared to the provision of the Memorandum of Understanding with the United Nations, have been interpreted to prohibit foreign defence counsel from representing the accused and it is also unclear whether free legal assistance applies only during the investigation or also at trial.[119] However, the Draft Agreement specifically addresses the issue and prescribes that the right to defence counsel in the Law on Extraordinary Chambers shall mean 'that the accused has the right to engage counsel of his or her own choosing as guaranteed by the [ICCPR]'.[120] It is also envisaged that the accused might engage, or be assigned, counsel who are not Cambodian nationals.[121]

VI. Language issues

The question of language is a great difficulty in criminal proceedings in many parts of the world. Within a national jurisdiction there may be a large number of languages and dialects that prevents all participants to the proceedings from using one common language. This calls for extensive interpretation and translation of documents. Additional problems occur when the level of literacy and education is low.

The accused has an internationally recognized right to free assistance of an interpreter if he or she cannot speak the language of the court (eg Article 14.3(f) ICCPR). In order to function, the court will also have to provide witnesses and others who are required to appear with interpretation when necessary. Additionally, the accused is entitled to be informed in detail of the nature and charge against him or her and translation of documents is often required in order to uphold the accused person's right to prepare his or her defence.

Languages are, and will be, a major obstacle in all the internationalized courts. The working languages of the courts in East Timor during the

---

[118] ibid Rule 45 compared with Rule 42 (seven and five years' professional experience and fluency in the English language).

[119] eg Mundis (*supra* n 33) 941; Arts 24 and 35 of the Law on Extraordinary Chambers in the Courts of Cambodia; art 76 of Law on Criminal Procedure (*supra* n 32); Human Rights Watch 'Cambodia: Tribunal Must Meet International Standards' *HRW World Report 2002* (12 February 2002) available at www.hrw.org/press/2002/02/cambodiatribunal.htm (last visited 31 August 2003).

[120] Article 13.2 of the Draft Agreement (*supra* n 31).

[121] ibid. Art 21.3; see also 'Report of the Secretary-General on Khmer Rouge Trials' (*supra* n 77) para 49.

transitional period are Tetum, Portuguese, Bahasa Indonesia, and English.[122] In Kosovo, the 'Regulation 64 Panels' are working in three languages, Albanian, English, and Serbian.[123] The Extraordinary Chambers in Cambodia will have Khmer as the official working language, but with translations into English and French.[124] The Special Court for Sierra Leone will operate in English,[125] but the accused or suspect will have the right to use his own language and so also, with permission, may other persons appearing before the court.[126] This is a pertinent move since local languages, such as Krio, are more widely spoken than English. Operating in more than one language means that the court will always need interpretation and extensive translations of documents.

The right to free interpretation if the accused cannot understand or speak the language used in the court[127] applies in all the internationalized courts. However, the quality of this assistance may vary. Development of interpretation and language skills, including language training for the judges, have been held out as priority areas in East Timor[128] and in Kosovo,[129] but serious problems and shortage of qualified interpreters and translators still remain. The same will most likely be experienced in Sierra Leone and Cambodia.

In addition to the risk of rendering criminal proceedings unfair, linguistic problems may also result in an incorrect outcome of the case. Some judges and prosecutors are unfamiliar with the local language or languages and others are required to work in a language that is not their native tongue. The uncertainty stemming from the fact that all communications, oral as well as written, must go through an intermediary applies to all of them.[130] Additionally, both ICTY and ICTR have experienced long delays due to translations of long and numerous documents and the same may also occur in the internationalized courts.

---

[122]   UNTAET Reg 2000/11 (6 July 2000) s 36.

[123]   UNMIK Reg 2000/46 (15 August 2000).

[124]   Article 45 of the Law on Extraordinary Chambers in the Courts of Cambodia. The Draft Agreement (*supra* n 31) Art 26 also introduces an option for the government of Cambodia to provide translations and interpretations at public hearings into Russian.

[125]   Article 24 of the Statute for the Special Court for Sierra Leone.

[126]   Rule 3 of the Rules of Procedure and Evidence of the Special Court for Sierra Leone. On the need for interpretation, see eg Schocken (*supra* n 29) 460.

[127]   ie the formula of the ICCPR; cf the more far-reaching statutory right before ICC which refers to 'a language that the person fully understands and speaks', also covers necessary translations, and is extended to anyone who is questioned in the investigation: Arts 55.1c and 67.1f of the Rome Statute.

[128]   'Report of the Secretary-General on the United Nations Mission of Support in East Timor' (*supra* n 73) para 15.

[129]   OMIC/LSMS *Kosovo's War Crimes Trials: A Review* (September 2002) (see n 73).

[130]   These problems are illustrated by the *Los Palos* case (*Prosecutor v Marques* Case 9/2001 Judgment by Dili Special Panel (11 December 2001)); see eg Burke-White (*supra* n 106) 71 (with further references).

Language is not the only problem, though. Cultural differences may also lead to misunderstanding and misinterpretation. ICTR has experienced severe problems relating to linguistic particularities and cultural differences, for example in relation to terms such as 'rape'.[131] Other examples, which may also apply in other parts of the world, could be different concepts of time, methods of referring to events and people in narratives, unawareness of the date of birth or exact age, or an oral story-telling tradition which means that the originator of the story (ie the actual eye-witness) may not be known. This may hamper the prosecutor's decision on prosecution, the accused person's success with their defence, and ultimately the court's ability to assess correctly the evidence of a case. In particular, the judges must be cognizant of the high risk of misunderstanding and misjudgement and only carefully attach weight to observations such as inconsistencies in different statements and the unwillingness or inability to describe an incident of a very sensitive nature. Conclusions that derive from experiences in one cultural context are not necessarily accurate in a different context.

VII. Right of appeal

The International Military Tribunals at Nuremberg and Tokyo did not have any appellate jurisdiction or appellate bodies. However, since then international law has developed into a right for everyone who is convicted of a crime to have the conviction or sentence reviewed by a higher tribunal according to law (eg Article 14.5 ICCPR). Consequently, a right to appeal and an Appeals Chamber is provided for in the Statutes of ICTY and ICTR as well as in the Rome Statute of the ICC. Unlike some national jurisdictions, these international courts also accord the prosecutor a right to appeal an acquittal and, in respect of ICC, also convictions and sentences on behalf of the convicted person.[132]

All internationalized courts provide a right to appeal. Both in Kosovo and in East Timor, the transitional administration established new Appeals Courts.[133] The Court of Final Appeal in Kosovo, which is an ad hoc institution, has the powers of the Supreme Court which exercised jurisdiction in Kosovo, but is limited to appeals in criminal matters (including detention terms) against decisions of District Courts. The East Timorese Court of Appeal, located in Dili, has jurisdiction to hear appeals of final judgments

---

[131] eg *Prosecutor v Akayesu* (ICTR-96-4) Judgment (2 September 1998) paras 145–56, where the Trial Chamber stated the linguistic and cultural factors that it had taken into account in assessing the evidence; (1998) 37 ILM 1399.

[132] Article 25 of the ICTY Statute, Art 24 of the ICTR Statute, and Art 81 of the Rome Statute of the ICC.

[133] UNMIK Reg 1999/5 (4 September 1999) s 1 and UNTAET Reg 2000/11 (6 March 2000) ss 14–15 with later amendments.

rendered by any District Court. In both systems, any party may appeal a final decision by a District Court and the Appeals Court can confirm, reverse, or modify the decision and may also send the case back for retrial. An appeal may be made on factual, legal, or procedural grounds.

The Special Court for Sierra Leone has been influenced by ICTY, ICTR, and ICC and the Statute provides for an Appeals Chamber, and a right for both convicted persons and the prosecutor to appeal the Trial Chamber's judgments on factual, legal, or procedural grounds.[134] It is expressly provided that the Appeals Chamber shall seek guidance in the decisions of the ICTY and ICTR Appeals Chamber.[135] Nothing is said about the Trial Chamber in this regard and this may prove problematic in practice, particularly in light of the fact that the status of the Appeals Chamber's decisions as precedents for the Trial Chamber is not a settled issue. An appeal may also be lodged on the ground of a procedural error and the Appeals Chamber may affirm, reverse, or revise the appealed decision, but not send proceedings back to the Trial Chamber.[136]

In Cambodia, it was long envisaged that the existing three-tier court system should operate with Extraordinary Chambers of the trials court, the appeals court, and the Supreme Court.[137] With the Draft Agreement, however, a simplified two-tier system was proposed where the Supreme Court functions as both appellate chamber and final instance.[138] Appeals may be lodged by the accused (or convicted) person and prosecutor, but also by victims, and the higher court may affirm, reverse, or modify the impugned decision.[139] Both issues of fact and of law may be argued and adjudicated.

It is self-evident that the right to appeal requires that a genuine review take place. In practice, however, appeals in East Timor are surrounded by serious practical and other problems. A fundamental obstacle is that the Court of Appeal in East Timor has not had enough judges to hear appeals and this cannot be resolved until the new body for appointment of judges, the Superior Council of the Judiciary, is functioning.[140] In effect, the right to an effective appeal has not been upheld.[141] Moreover, once appeals are being

---

[134] Article 20 of the Statute for the Special Court for Sierra Leone.
[135] ibid Art 20.3.
[136] ibid Art 20.1-2. For additional comments, see Beresford and Muller (*supra* n 98) 648.
[137] Article 2 of the Law on Extraordinary Chambers in the Courts of Cambodia.
[138] Article 3.2b of the Draft Agreement (*supra* n 31). Whether the Law on Extraordinary Chambers will be amended to allow the Supreme Court to order a retrial before the lower court remains to be seen.
[139] Articles 36–7 of the Law on Extraordinary Chambers in the Courts of Cambodia.
[140] 'Report of the Secretary-General on the United Nations Mission of Support in East Timor' (*supra* n 73) para 14; JSMP *The Right to Appeal in East Timor: JSMP Thematic Report 2* (October 2002) (see n 88).
[141] However, new judges for the Court of Appeal, both national and international, have been sworn in in May 2003 and, hence, the Court is now functioning for the first time since November 2001. The JSMP reports a backlog of some 60 civil and criminal cases and its

heard, certain inadequacies in the practice of the lower courts, such as a lack of transcripts of the trials and imperfect presentation of the reasoning in judgments, will most likely complicate the work of the Appeals Chamber.[142] In some cases, this may have the result that an effective review is impossible and that a retrial will have to be ordered.

In Kosovo, various problems have been experienced, too. According to the Legal Systems Monitoring Section of the OSCE Mission in Kosovo,[143] the judgments of the Supreme Court, many of them very brief, have suffered from poor legal reasoning, absence of citations to legal authority, and lack of interpretation concerning the applicable law on war crimes and human rights issues. This is even more noticeable since the Supreme Court has reversed a large number of decisions without providing clear guidance to the lower courts.

VIII. *Ne bis in idem* and concurrent jurisdictions

It is an internationally recognized principle that no one shall be tried or punished again for an offence for which he or she has already been finally convicted or acquitted (eg Article 14.7 ICCPR). However, the operation of this principle is not exactly the same in different legal traditions (ie the principle of *ne bis in idem* in civil law jurisdictions, and double jeopardy in common law jurisdictions). Moreover, the international standard only applies to criminal proceedings in one and the same country, but not in relation to final judgments handed down by an international or foreign court. It is nevertheless possible to introduce this principle or other forms of coordination in agreements between states,[144] or in treaties establishing an international criminal jurisdiction, such as ICC.[145]

Hence, in the case of internationalized courts in East Timor, Kosovo, and Cambodia, which are all intended as domestic judicial institutions, the principle will apply. In the case of Cambodia, the special Law on Extraordinary Chambers does not explicitly regulate the principle of *ne bis in idem* and, thus, the Chambers will have to rely on the ordinary law of criminal procedure. It is therefore very unlikely that an Extraordinary Chamber could again try someone who has already been tried, albeit under circumstances that could

---

account of cases contains at least 12 cases where appeals have been filed against judgments handed down in April–October 2001 and where a date for appeals proceedings has yet to be fixed (see n 88).

[142] eg Cohen (*supra* n 116) 5; Linton (*supra* n 89) 456.

[143] OMIK/LSMS (*supra* n 129) 38, 48. Also the judgments of the trial courts have been criticized for similar reasons.

[144] eg in international agreements on enforcement of foreign criminal judgments such as the Council of Europe European Convention on the International Validity of Criminal Judgments (28 May 1970) 70 ETS Art 55.

[145] cf Art 20 of the Rome Statute.

be considered a sham. A second trial in such a case would require an exception from the principle of *ne bis in idem*, as can be found in the ICC Statute, and also in the applicable criminal procedure for East Timor.[146]

In the case of the Special Court for Sierra Leone, on the other hand, it had to be established if and how such a principle should be applied. Hence, the Statute provides for the principle to apply in the relationship between the Special Court and national courts of Sierra Leone, with some exceptions when a national decision shall not bar a trial before the Special Court and, in such case, a previously imposed and served sentence shall be taken into account by the Special Court.[147] However, no similar provision has been implemented in the Special Court Agreement (Ratification) Act 2002 and it is not clear whether a principle of *ne bis in idem* is to be applied by Sierra Leonean courts in respect of the Special Court's decisions. Moreover, the *ne bis in idem* provision of the Statute only regulates the relationship between the Special Court and the courts of Sierra Leone and it does not apply to courts of third states, which is understandable considering the legal construction for the establishment of the Special Court.[148] In addition to this principle, however, the Statute also authorizes the Special Court to request a national court to defer to the competence of the Special Court, a provision that is underpinned both in national law and in the Court's Rules of Procedure and Evidence, and that may lead to the permanent discontinuance of domestic proceedings.[149] It may be noted that the authorization to request discontinuation of proceedings, according to the Rules, is not limited to apply vis-à-vis the courts of Sierra Leone but refers to 'a court of a State', which of course does not in itself oblige a third state to adhere to such a request.[150]

Furthermore, in some of the cases criminal trials have had to be coordinated with other proceedings, such as truth and reconciliation processes in which perpetrators of crimes under the jurisdiction of the court may also take part. Here, issues such as the use of information gathered in one process as evidence in the other will have to be addressed.[151] A further problem occurs if such a process also involves amnesty. Thus, the controversial amnesties granted in the Lomé Accords, which were 'absolute and free' and covering

---

[146] UNTAET Reg 2000/30 (25 September 2000) as amended by Reg 2001/25 (14 September 2001) s 4.2; see eg Linton (*supra* n 98) 198.

[147] Article 9 of the Statute for the Special Court for Sierra Leone.

[148] cf McDonald (*supra* n 26) 131.

[149] Article 8.2 of the Statute for the Special Court for Sierra Leone; Rules 9–13 of the Rules of Procedure and Evidence of the Special Court for Sierra Leone; the Special Court Agreement, 2002, (Ratification) Act s 14.

[150] Rule 9 of the Rules of Procedure and Evidence. On the relationship between internationalized courts and national jurisdictions, see Chapter 16 (Kleffner/Nollkaemper).

[151] For a discussion of these aspects in relation to the Truth Commissions in Sierra Leone and East Timor, see Chapters 9 (Schabas) and 6 (Lyons).

also crimes against international humanitarian law[152] will need to be addressed, notwithstanding that it was agreed in the Statute for the Special Court that amnesties granted in an earlier peace agreement should not be a bar to prosecution of the *international* crimes under the Special Court's jurisdiction. This formulation appears to suggest that the amnesties do apply to crimes under Sierra Leonean law.[153]

Amnesty (and royal pardon) is also an issue in respect of the Extraordinary Chambers in Cambodia where one top Khmer Rouge commander and potential defendant, Ieng Saray, was granted amnesty.[154] The Cambodian law that was adopted deleted an explicit provision that amnesties should not bar prosecution which was included in the earlier draft statute as agreed with the United Nations.[155] The question was brought back to light in the Draft Agreement, however, whereby the Cambodian government undertakes not to request new amnesties or pardons for the relevant crimes and the scope of the pardon granted Ieng Sary is left to the Extraordinary Chambers to decide.[156]

There might also be the case where an international criminal court or a foreign court, exercises jurisdiction over the same crimes, for instance ICTY with respect to Kosovo[157] and the Indonesian Special Human Rights Court with respect to East Timor. This may call for some kind of coordination. It should be restated, however, that only in the second situation, ie the application of the principle when the internationalized court forms part of a domestic legal system, is there an internationally recognized standard to be applied. Consequently, the determination of the issue in the other cases depends on other circumstances. In the case of ICTY, the primacy accorded to that tribunal by the Security Council (ie in its Statute) means that domestic proceedings must yield to international proceedings. Consequently, the *ne bis in idem* principle would have to apply for 'Regulation 64 Panels' in respect of judgments by ICTY. As for East Timor, in 2000 UNTAET and Indonesia have concluded a Memorandum of Understanding on judicial cooperation,

---

[152] Article IX of the Peace Agreement Between the Government of Sierra Leone and the Revolutionary United Front of Sierra Leone, 7 July 1999, available at www.sierra-leone.org/lomeaccord.html (last visited 31 August 2003).

[153] Article 10 of the Statute for the Special Court for Sierra Leone; Daniel J Macaluso 'Absolute and Free Pardon: The Effect of the Amnesty Provision in the Lomé Peace Agreement on the Jurisdiction of the Special Court' (2001) 27 *Brooklyn J of Intl L* 347.

[154] eg Stephen Herder with Brian D Tittemore *Seven Candidates for Prosecution: Accountability for the Crimes of the Khmer Rouge* (War Crimes Research Office Washington College of Law American University and Coalition for International Justice June 2001) available at www.wcl.american.edu/warcrimes/khmerrouge.cfm (last visited 31 August 2003); Burke-White (*supra* n 106) 38.

[155] eg Mundis (*supra* n 33) 941.

[156] Article 11 of the Draft Agreement (*supra* n 31).

[157] There are presently ongoing proceedings before ICTY relating to crimes committed in Kosovo, eg *Prosecutor v Milutinovic and others* (IT-99-37), *Prosecutor v Milosevic* (IT-02-54), and *Prosecutor v Limaj and others* (IT-03-66).

but it does not include any provision on *ne bis in idem* or coordination of the exercise of concurrent jurisdiction.[158]

An additional complication in Kosovo is that there is a parallel structure of courts where courts in Serb-dominated parts of northern Kosovo remain answerable to Belgrade and not to UNMIK, a situation that has not yet been resolved.[159] This has given rise to *ne bis in idem* issues in concrete cases where persons being tried by one court have later been indicted for the same crimes by another court.[160]

3. *Standards relating to juveniles and to victims and witnesses*

I. Juvenile offenders

It has long been recognized that juvenile offenders should be treated differently and be accorded additional protection. Protection of child rights is provided in the ICCPR, including that criminal procedures shall be framed in a way that takes their age into account and the desirability of rehabilitation is highlighted (Article 14.4).[161] A cornerstone for the protection of juveniles is the 1989 Convention on the Rights of the Child, where the rights contained in the ICCPR were compiled and further developed (Article 40). How these procedural safeguards should be respected in practice has been elaborated in a number of so-called 'soft law' instruments.[162] Nonetheless, there is no fixed minimum age of criminal responsibility in international law and this has created difficulties when establishing international criminal jurisdictions, such as in the case of ICC.[163] In that particular instance, the stratagem adopted was not to elaborate on the age for criminal responsibility and instead to focus on the Court's exercise of jurisdiction, which was finally decided applied to those aged 18 at the time

---

[158] Memorandum of Understanding regarding Cooperation in Legal, Judicial and Human Rights Related Matters concluded by the Republic of Indonesia and UNTAET (6 April 2000) available at www.jsmp.minihub.org (last visited on 31 August 2003).

[159] OMIK/LSMS (*supra* n 79) 7–8.

[160] ibid where one case, which did not violate Art 14.7 ICCPR since the first judgment was not final when the second indictment was filed, is reported.

[161] Other procedural provisions to protect juveniles in the ICCPR are: Art 6.5 on prohibition of death penalty, Art 10.2-3 on separation from adults in pre-trial detention and prisons, and Art 14.1 on exception from the principle that judgments be made public.

[162] United Nations Standard Minimum Rules for the Administration of Juvenile Justice ('Beijing Rules') adopted by UNGA Res 40/33 (29 November 1985) and 45/112 (14 December 1990); United Nations Guidelines for the Prevention of Juvenile Delinquency ('Riyadh Guidelines') adopted and proclaimed by UNGA Res 45/112 (14 December 1990); United Nations Rules for the Protection of Juveniles Deprived of their Liberty adopted by UNGA Res 45/113 (14 December 1990).

[163] Per Saland 'International Criminal Law Principles' in Roy S Lee (ed) (*supra* n 60) 200–2; Human Rights Watch *Justice in the Balance: Recommendations for an Independent and Effective International Criminal Court* (Human Rights Watch New York 1998) 55–7.

of the offence, all with the understanding that this should not prejudice any position in international law.[164]

The issue of juvenile offenders has been a particularly burning question in relation to the atrocities of the Sierra Leone conflict, where child soldiers were often involved, and almost every account of the Special Court deals with the issue. In an earlier draft of the Statute, the Secretary-General proposed that the tribunal should have jurisdiction over persons who were 15 or older at the time of the alleged commission of the crime and that a special Juvenile Chamber should be established,[165] but the proposal was later amended. There is still a theoretical possibility that young offenders will be brought before the Special Court, but the Statute sets forth a preference for child-rehabilitation programmes and alternative truth and reconciliation mechanisms, and prohibits prison sentences upon a conviction.[166] Additionally, young offenders are entitled to special treatment and protection in accordance with international standards should they come before the Court.[167] For example, protection of privacy in cases involving children may explicitly motivate closed trial sessions.[168]

The Transitional Rules of Criminal Procedure for East Timor contain advanced provisions regarding juvenile offenders, including a minimum age of criminal responsibility set at 12 years of age (when the crime was allegedly committed), and prosecution of minors between 12 and 16 years is restricted to certain serious crimes.[169] The Rules also provide procedural safeguards for measures such as restriction on deprivation of liberty, investigative measures, and participation of parents, guardians, or the closest relatives. On 2 December 2002, the Serious Crimes Panel of Dili District Court sentenced the first minor to be tried by that Panel.[170] The minor, whose name has been protected, was convicted of three counts of murder and sentenced to 12 months' imprisonment (out of which almost the full time had been served in pre-trial detention).

---

[164] Article 26 of the Rome Statute for the International Criminal Court; Roger S Clark and Otto Triffterer 'Article 26' in Otto Triffterer (ed) *Commentary on the International Criminal Court: Observers Notes, Article by Article* (Nomos Verlagsgesellschaft Baden-Baden 1999) 499.

[165] 'Report of the Secretary-General on the Establishment of a Special Court for Sierra Leone' (*supra* n 26) para 7.

[166] Articles 15.5 and 19.1 of the Statute for the Special Court for Sierra Leone.

[167] ibid Art 7 provides: 'Should any person who was at the time of the alleged commission of the crime below 18 years of age come before the Court, he or she shall be treated with dignity and a sense of worth, taking into account his or her young age and the desirability of promoting his or her rehabilitation, reintegration into and assumption of a constructive role in society, and in accordance with international human rights standards, in particular the rights of the child'.

[168] Rule 79A of the Rules of Procedure and Evidence of the Special Court for Sierra Leone.

[169] UNTAET Reg 2001/25 (14 September 2001) (amending earlier Regulations) ss 45–46.

[170] *Prosecutor v X* Case 4/2002, where the defendant claimed to have been 14 at the time of the crimes (September 1999): JSMP Press Release (3 December 2002) (see n 88).

In Kosovo, the applicable domestic law prescribes that a trial shall be scheduled within a short time (eight days) from the issuance of the indictment in juvenile cases,[171] and there are also other safeguards for juvenile offenders. At least one juvenile has been charged with genocide, later amended to other crimes, and sentenced to a juvenile correctional facility (in a trial with an international prosecutor and an all-local panel). UNMIK rules also impose special protection for persons under the age of 18 who have been arrested.[172]

Finally, the Cambodian Law on Criminal Procedure also contains some special provisions on juvenile offenders, including an automatic right for an undefended minor accused of a crime to have a defence counsel appointed.[173]

II. Victims and witnesses

In recent years, the victims of violations of human rights and humanitarian law have gained increasing international attention. This trend, with a first concrete point of departure created by the 1985 Declaration of Basic Principles for Victims of Crimes and Abuse of Power,[174] has also put an emphasis on the participation of victims in criminal proceedings and on remedies for reparations. Traditionally, victims have been accorded a limited and auxiliary role in such proceedings, mainly as a means of evidence, but a broader role has been advanced, not least by the establishment of international criminal tribunals, and the ICC.[175] In fact, an important objective behind their creation has been considerations relating to the interests of victims. It is too early, however, to conclude that consistent international standards for the role of victims in criminal proceedings have been established. Still, national laws in this respect contain considerable differences, both in substance and in form.

---

[171] Article 484 of the FRY Criminal Procedure Code.

[172] UNMIK Reg 2001/28 (11 October 2001) ss 3–4.

[173] Law on Criminal Procedure (*supra* n 32) art 76.

[174] UNGA Res 40/34 (29 November 1985); Roger S Clark *The United Nations Crime Prevention and Criminal Justice Program* (Univ of Pennsylvania Press Philadelphia 1994) 180–98.

[175] eg Theo van Boven 'The Position of the Victim in the Statute of the International Criminal Court' in Herman von Hebel et al (eds) *Reflections on the International Criminal Court* (TMC Asser Press The Hague 1999) 77–89; Michael Bachrach 'The Protection and Rights of Victims under International Criminal Law' (2000) 34(1) *Int'l Lawyer* 7; Gilbert Bitti and Håkan Friman 'Participation of Victims in the Proceedings' in Roy S Lee et al (eds) (*supra* n 102) 456–74; Luc Walleyn 'Victimes et témoins de crimes internationaux: du droit à une protection au droit à la parole' (2002) 84(845) *Int'l Rev of the Red Cross* 51. It is also argued that states plagued with impunity should grant victims greater standing in the prosecution process, see eg Raquel Aldana-Pindell 'In Vindication of Justiciable Victims' Rights to Truth and Justice for State-Sponsored Crimes' (2002) 35 *Vanderbilt J of Transnational L* 1399. For a more critical view of the ICC regime for victims, see José E Alvarez 'Post International Criminal Court Challenges' *International Legal Challenges for the Twenty-first Century: Proceedings of a Joint Meeting of the Australian & New Zealand Society of International Law and the American Society of International Law* (26–9 June 2000) 131, available at http://law.anu.edu.au/anzsil/Conferences/2000ASILProceedings.pdf (last visited 31 August 2003).

Nevertheless, both the rationales behind the internationalized criminal courts and their links to international humanitarian intervention in the wake of violent conflicts have created expectations of criminal proceedings where victims' interests are also recognized. Sometimes it has even been argued that international tribunals, as opposed to national trials, may better fulfil victims' expectations for achieving justice.[176] Thus, it is interesting to compare how these issues have been dealt with by internationalized criminal courts.

The Serious Crimes Panels in East Timor apply a sophisticated scheme in respect of victims.[177] They are obliged to take appropriate measures to protect the safety, physical, and psychological well-being, dignity, and privacy of victims (and witnesses). The provisions, which are very similar to those of ICC, also highlight factors that shall be taken into account, such as age, gender, health, and the nature of the crime. Moreover, victims are entitled, inter alia, to request the prosecutor to conduct specific investigations or measures and to be heard in the court proceedings, which are all measures clearly inspired by the ICC procedures.[178] A victim may also request a review of a prosecutor's decision to dismiss a case.[179] Further, a Trust Fund is to be established for the benefit of victims of crimes within the jurisdiction of the Panels and of their families, into which the money and other property collected through fines, forfeiture, foreign donors, or other means may be transferred.

Similarly, the Special Court for Sierra Leone has retained the advanced provisions on protection of victims and witnesses of the ICTR Rules.[180] A Victims and Witnesses Unit is to be established to advise the Court and provide assistance to victims and witnesses.[181] These Rules do not, however, provide for the participation of victims in the criminal proceedings in their own right. Furthermore, the judges of the Special Court have decided to leave issues of victims' compensation to domestic courts and national legislation, in just the same way as the ICTR Rules do.[182] This was done in spite of a proposal to bring the provisions in line with Sierra Leonean law which grants the convicting court the power to make compensation orders on the application of the prosecutor (on behalf of the victim).[183] Hence, an opportunity to

---

[176] eg Richard Goldstone 'The United Nations' War Crimes Tribunals: An Assessment' (1997) 12 *Connecticut J Int'l L* 227.

[177] UNTAET Reg 2000/15 (6 June 2000) ss 24–5; Mohamed Othman 'Peacekeeping Operations in Asia: Justice and UNTAET' (2001) 3(2) *Int L Forum* 114, 122.

[178] UNTAET Reg 2001/25 (14 September 2001) s 12.

[179] ibid s 25.

[180] Rules 69 and 75 of the Rules of Procedure and Evidence of the Special Court for Sierra Leone.

[181] ibid Rule 34.

[182] ibid Rule 105.

[183] Criminal Procedure Act 1965 s 54; Proposal by Glenna Thompson for the Sierra Leone Bar Association; 'Report on the Special Court Rules of Procedure and Evidence Seminar' (*supra* n 27) 12.

advance the rights of victims by applying existing national law was lost. The Court has a temporal mandate which is limited, however, and is obviously very cautious to meet the deadline and thus not inclined to take the risk of potentially protracted proceedings.

UNMIK has issued Regulations for the protection of victims (injured parties) and witnesses in Kosovo. These are far-reaching and include provisions on so-called 'anonymous witnesses', that is to say witnesses whose identity is not disclosed to the accused.[184] Even if such a practice has not been ruled out completely, inter alia by the European Court of Human Rights, and the UNMIK Regulation adheres to the conditions set forth by that Court, the use of anonymous witnesses has been very controversial when practised by ICTY, or discussed in respect of ICC.[185] Moreover, UNMIK has introduced a scheme for so-called 'co-operative witnesses' who may be granted immunity from prosecution and punishment in return for testifying against someone else, and reduction or relief from punishment for a perpetrator who otherwise is cooperating voluntarily, which to be sure are also controversial measures.[186]

The Extraordinary Chambers in Cambodia will be under a general obligation to provide for the protection of victims and witnesses, which may include *in camera* proceedings and protection of identity.[187] The Draft Agreement explicitly obliges the judges and prosecutors to provide for protection, and mentions *in camera* proceedings and identity protection as examples, but how these measures will actually be dealt with in practice is uncertain and there has been criticism that the protection will not meet sufficient standards.[188] Cambodian criminal procedures do, however, provide for some victim participation in the proceedings and for compensation claims to be lodged and adjudicated in the criminal proceedings.[189]

III. Child victims and witnesses

It is being increasingly acknowledged that children who are victims of crime or witnesses in criminal proceedings should be treated with particular care

---

[184] UNMIK Reg 2001/20 (19 September 2001) ss 4–5.

[185] eg Silvia Fernández de Gurmendi and Håkan Friman 'The Rules of Procedure and Evidence of the International Criminal Court' (2000) 3 *YB of Int'l Humanitarian L* 289, 322–3; Claus Kreß 'Witnesses in Proceedings Before the International Criminal Court: An Analysis in Light of Comparative Criminal Procedure' in Horst Fischer et al (eds) *International and National Prosecution of Crimes Under International Law: Current Developments* (Berlin Verlag Berlin 2001).

[186] UNMIK Reg 2001/21 (19 September 2001).

[187] Article 33 of the Law on Extraordinary Chambers in the Courts of Cambodia.

[188] Article 23 of the Draft Agreement (*supra* n 31); for a critical view, see Linton (*supra* n 35).

[189] eg arts 9, 10, 17, 19, and 131 of the Law on Criminal Procedure (*supra* n 32).

and be given additional support and protection. The experience of children, who have to face the criminal justice system and, more specifically, have to testify in court, can be traumatic due to inadequate and non-child-adapted procedures or practices. Thus, the rights of the child and even the rights of the accused to a fair trial may be affected. No international standards in this regard have yet been developed, but certain efforts are being made,[190] and the issue has been brought up in respect of, for example, the ICC.[191] However, neither the international criminal courts, nor the internationalized ones provide a full scheme for dealing with child victims and witnesses of crime.

The Transitional Rules of Criminal Procedure for East Timor provide that age is one factor to take into account when taking measures to protect the safety, physical and psychological well-being, dignity, and privacy of victims and witnesses, as is the circumstance that the crime involves violence against children.[192] Further, the Rules contain safeguards for the questioning of a minor in the investigation, which do not seem to be limited to offenders.[193]

Similarly, the Special Court for Sierra Leone is to provide appropriate measures to facilitate the testimony of vulnerable victims and witnesses, which should include children, and the Victims and Witnesses Unit is also to have experts in trauma relating to violence against children.[194] The Special Court has not adopted the same approach to the question of competency of child witnesses as ICTR.[195] A child may not be compelled to testify under a solemn declaration (oath) before the Court and the testimony is permitted only if the child has sufficient maturity and is not subject to undue influence. The Court does not, however, explicitly provide that such testimony requires corroboration.

E. CONCLUSION

1. Adherence to fundamental human rights standards

The most fundamental human rights standard in respect of criminal proceedings is that of 'fair trial'. This concept has more than one meaning, however,

---

[190] One contribution is the Guidelines on Child Victims and Witnesses of Crime developed by the international NGO the International Bureau for Children's Rights (IBCR); a draft version is available at www.ibcr.org/vicwit/final_Guidelines.htm (last visited 31 August 2003).
[191] eg Silvia Fernández de Gurmendi 'Definition of Victims and General Principle' in Roy S Lee et al (eds) (*supra* n 102) 433–4.
[192] UNTAET Reg 2001/25 (14 September 2001) s 36.8.
[193] ibid s 46.2.
[194] Rules 34, 75, and 79A of the Rules of Procedure and Evidence of the Special Court for Sierra Leone.
[195] ibid Rule 90C; cf Rule 90C of the ICTR Rules.

and comprises institutional guarantees (eg independence and impartiality), moral principles (eg the presumption of innocence), and various procedural rights (eg the right to counsel or not to be arbitrarily detained).[196] This survey has mainly focused on the last aspect and, additionally, only to a limited extent.

In general, the internationalized criminal courts are statutorily well equipped for adherence to fundamental international human rights standards, the Extraordinary Chambers in Cambodia being the exception in respect of certain rights. In East Timor and Kosovo this is the result of a development of the applicable law. Moreover, in these two cases, where internationalized courts have been tested in practice, numerous practical problems have been experienced and led to serious questions about the quality of justice. Nevertheless, the problems have mainly been due to capacity constraints, lack of experience, and misunderstandings, but hardly to any wilful violations of fundamental standards or of the applicable law. Consequently, some observers have concluded that most of these problems, if not all, could be alleviated by additional resources, careful staff recruitment, and other practical arrangements.[197] A question mark in this regard, however, is raised by the problems of coordination between arrest and detention conducted by international military forces in order to secure peace and security and the re-established judicial system. Particularly in Kosovo, international standards have not been observed regarding similar extra-judicial deprivation of liberty and it is questionable whether this falls within the ambit of an acceptable derogation of the internationally recognized rights.

2. Applicable law

I. Agreement between a state and the international community

In the case of international courts being established pursuant to agreements between a state and the international community (ie the United Nations), there is much leeway for the parties to chose what criminal procedures to apply. In Sierra Leone, the choice was an already established international regime that meets the highest international standards.

In Cambodia, on the other hand, domestic law is designated to apply and in spite of the introduction of certain safeguards to meet fundamental standards of fairness and due process, serious concerns remain as to whether acceptable procedural standards will be upheld in the future criminal proceedings. In addition, the domestic law which will apply is said to be contradictory in part and may not be easily accessible even for local lawyers, not to mention international ones. Thus, even if due process standards are

---

[196] eg Safferling (*supra* n 40) 30–1.　　　[197] eg Burke-White (*supra* n 106) 74.

enshrined in the constituting agreement, these standards will have to be underpinned by procedures that actually implement them.

II. Transitional administration of a territory

In Kosovo and East Timor, UNMIK and UNTAET had the difficult but important task of creating a legal system ad hoc, on the fly, and in the midst of events. The initial approach to use a formula whereby the existing law was applied with a general exception for provisions incompatible with international human rights law has, in hindsight, proved to be inadequate and created serious problems of interpretation and application in practice.[198] Moreover, the legitimacy of existing laws may be questioned. While the continuation of the already existing procedural law was probably the only practicable solution for the Missions at the time, the obstacles stemming from the application of multiple laws and standards, some domestic, some international, could and should be remedied.

Lacking an internationally developed interim criminal code,[199] the options for a transitional administration include: (1) to accept that existing domestic laws continue to apply (or possibly the revival of laws from an earlier period of independence), (2) to accept that no national laws apply in an interim period, or (3) to take an even more active role as law-maker and impose a brand new legal system. Experience shows, however, that the domestic law would have to be thoroughly analysed from the outset, a process that requires substantive resources and could be plagued by practical difficulties. To accept a legal vacuum is certainly not a good option either. Thus, extensive new legislation appears to be an attractive alternative. However, the subsequent method chosen by UNTAET, ie the development of new comprehensive legislation on criminal procedures, has also been criticized and its 'enthusiasm for law-making' described as misplaced in the light of the Mission's transitional nature and the subsequently independent state's right of choice.[200] In sum, none of the alternatives is without complications.

III. Legal traditions and the procedural law of international criminal courts

For legitimacy, (re-)establishment of the rule of law, positive spillover effects for the domestic legal system, and for practical reasons, the basic features of the criminal procedures should not be completely unfamiliar to local lawyers and the general public. Preferably, the applicable procedural law of an internationalized court should not deviate radically from the legal tradition of the country in question. A brand new procedural system would also lead to

---

[198] See also Strohmeyer (*supra* n 5) 112.   [199] On this point see pp 334 and 356–7.
[200] Linton (*supra* n 87) 137.

uncertainty, due, for instance, to a lack of legal precedents. Consequently, the *sui generis* criminal procedures of the international criminal courts, with components from both the common law and the civil law tradition, may not be ideal to apply, even when they are readily available for implementation and, in the case of ICTY and ICTR, generally well-tested in practice. Not surprisingly, the Special Court, for which the ICTR Rules were designated as applicable law, has amended the procedural law in a direction that more resembles domestic law.

The merger of elements of different criminal procedures is not an easy proposition. Judges, prosecutors, and defence counsel from different countries will necessarily need time to get accustomed to and develop such procedures. The criminal proceedings in East Timor, set forth in the new comprehensive Code, represent a hybrid system which mainly draws from the civil law tradition, but also includes elements from common law jurisdictions and provisions from the procedures of ICTY and ICTR as well as ICC. Regarding the difficulties, one of the international judges in East Timor, Judge Luca Ferrero, from Italy, has been quoted as saying:[201]

> It means that a common law adversarial system of the prosecutor is working with a 90 per cent civil law inquisitorial system panel using laws from different sources. It sounds like a weird experiment.

Also in respect of the 'Regulation 64 Panels' of Kosovo, the mixed and complex system of criminal procedures seems to have created problems in respect of, inter alia, indictments and presentation and assessment of evidence.[202] Nonetheless, and quite apart from the problem of departing from the legal tradition of the country in question, ICTY and ICTR are examples that mixed procedures can work but it requires adequate resources and well-trained lawyers.

3. A 'start-up kit' and standard law of criminal procedures

In order to remedy some of the initial problems and need for immediately applicable criminal procedures, it has been suggested that UN Missions should develop a 'quick-start package' of law-enforcement related legislation, and a judicial structure for speedy interim use.[203] The idea has been embraced by the UN Panel on Human Rights Operations (in the so-called Brahimi Report),[204] and work has begun on the elaboration of the practical aspects of criminal procedures (as opposed to substantive elements of the law

---

[201] Reproduced in McDonald (*supra* n 19) 18–19.   [202] eg OMIK/LSMS (*supra* n 129).
[203] See references in n 85.
[204] (21 August 2000) UN Doc A/55/305, S/2000/809, 55.

itself, which was not considered practicable).[205] In this context, the UN Secretary-General has stressed that such rules should take fully into account various international human rights instruments, such as the ICCPR. So far, however, only an inventory of existing guidelines has been made.[206]

A 'quick start package' would be intended only as a first step so that immediate action can be taken in observance of international human rights standards. An interim solution of this kind would alleviate, inter alia, problems of the kind experienced in Kosovo and East Timor regarding deprivation of liberty by international military forces. It could also counteract a problem such as that experienced in East Timor where judges were appointed and began their work before the courts from which their authority derived were actually established. But the rights of an arrested person also include the right to trial within a reasonable time (or release) which means that a more permanent system and criminal procedures must be in place for the investigation, prosecution, and adjudication of criminal cases. Hence, a 'quick start package' is not enough. It would, however, give some extra time for reconstruction of the judicial system and development of laws. This is not the least important in respect of such complex cases as those concerning genocide, crimes against humanity, and war crimes. Arguably, it would be a worthwhile effort to develop a standard 'quick start package' for immediate use, including ideas as to how this regime could be linked to a subsequent and more permanent procedural code. A more comprehensive and sustainable criminal procedure legislation would, in turn, preferably be developed with due regard to the existing legal tradition (or traditions) and in cooperation with local stakeholders.

A 'quick start package' would not, however, address the need for establishing criminal procedures for internationalized courts in cases such as Sierra Leone and Cambodia, ie where the court is independent from the national system or a sovereign and functioning state wishes to apply its existing procedures. In such cases, the international community supporting the project (ie the United Nations) and the state would have to agree what criminal procedures should be applied. While in the former case a standard code would be helpful, at least as a starting point, it appears unrealistic to expect such a code to be acceptable in the latter case. Thus, amending the existing legal order is a more feasible alternative. In any case, the existing legal tradition should be taken into account so that the outcome is somewhat familiar to lawyers and the broader public in the country in question.

---

[205] 'Report of the Secretary-General on the Implementation of the Report of the Panel on United Nations Peace Operations' (20 October 2000) UN Doc A/55/502, 32–4.

[206] UN Executive Committee on Peace and Security (ECPS) Task Force for Development of Comprehensive Rule of Law Strategies for Peace Operations 'Final Report' (15 August 2002) 11–12.

Finally, in spite of the establishment of the permanent International Criminal Court, internationalized courts are not an endangered species and development of ever more refined methods for ensuring fair trials by such institutions will be necessary.[207]

---

[207] Efforts are currently being undertaken, however, and a series of draft model codes—including a Transitional Criminal Code, Transitional Code of Criminal Procedure, and a Transitional Detention Act—have been drafted by an international expert team in a project by the Irish Centre for Human Rights ('Applicable Law in Complex Situations'), which is a component of the US Institute of Peace's 'Project on Peacekeeping and the Administration of Justice'.

16

The Relationship Between Internationalized Courts and National Courts

Jann K Kleffner* and André Nollkaemper**

A. INTRODUCTION

Each of the four internationalized courts that are discussed in this book is embedded into, or grafted onto, the national legal order of one particular state: Yugoslavia/Kosovo, East Timor, Sierra Leone, and Cambodia. It is that connection that makes the courts 'internationalized' rather than 'international'.

The linkage to a particular state raises the question how the internationalized courts are related to the national courts of that state.[1] Some of the suspects who are or may be prosecuted before internationalized courts, might also have been or could be prosecuted before national courts. Does the establishment of the internationalized court mean that national courts can no longer exercise jurisdiction over these suspects? Or can the national courts still exercise jurisdiction, but subject to review of the internationalized court? These types of questions are to some extent comparable to the relationship between national courts and international courts. However, there is reason for a separate treatment of the relationship between internationalized and national courts, for internationalized courts have a much closer relationship with national courts and the legal questions therefore are different than for a truly international court.

In this chapter, we will examine six questions that have arisen or that may arise pertaining to the relationship between internationalized courts and national courts: (1) whether national courts have jurisdiction over acts that are within the jurisdiction of an internationalized court; (2) if so, what rules govern concurrent jurisdiction between national and internationalized

* PhD Research Associate and Lecturer in International Humanitarian Law, Amsterdam Center for International Law, Faculty of Law, University of Amsterdam.

** Professor of Public International Law and Director of the Amsterdam Center for International Law, Faculty of Law, University of Amsterdam.

The authors wish to thank Sylvia de Bertodano, Jean-Christian Cady, Craig Etcheson, Mohamed Othman, Caitlin Reiger, and the members of the Pionier team at the Amsterdam Center for International Law for their helpful comments and suggestions.

[1] We understand the term 'national courts' broadly and use it to refer both to 'regular courts' that existed prior to the establishment of the internationalized court (Sierra Leone, Cambodia), and to non-internationalized courts that have been installed by an interim administration (Kosovo and East Timor).

courts; (3) whether individuals can resort to a national court to challenge the legality of establishment of an internationalized court; (4) whether national courts can review judgments of an internationalized court; (5) whether suspects that have been tried in an internationalized court could later also be tried in a national court or vice versa; and (6) the authority of judgments of internationalized courts for national courts.

It will appear from our analysis that the interaction between internationalized and national courts cannot easily be captured in general principles that are equally valid for all internationalized courts. The differences in the procedures by which these courts are established, as well as in their jurisdiction and authority, resist generalization. Nonetheless, a few patterns can be found. The dominant theme that emerges from this chapter is that internationalized courts have largely been separated and isolated from the national courts. It is only in rare and narrowly defined circumstances that national courts can act with regard to matters within the jurisdiction of an internationalized court.

Three qualifications are necessary. First, we will confine ourselves to the jurisdiction of national and internationalized courts over serious crimes,[2] as it is for those crimes in particular that the internationalized courts were set up.[3] Secondly, in principle we confine ourselves to national courts of the state to which the internationalized court has been connected and do not examine the relationship with courts of third states.[4] Thirdly, the chapter does not cover the relationship between internationalized courts and non-judicial national arrangements, in particular truth and reconciliation commissions.[5]

B. OVERLAPPING JURISDICTION OF INTERNATIONALIZED AND NATIONAL COURTS

A first question to be examined is whether the jurisdiction of the internationalized courts is an exclusive one. Can serious crimes only be tried by the internationalized courts, or do they also fall within the jurisdiction of a national court? This question is particularly relevant since, due to the operation of the *ne bis in idem* principle (see section F), a trial of a suspect in a national court could preclude a subsequent trial by an internationalized court.

---

[2] We understand the term 'serious crimes' to cover international crimes and serious crimes under national law.

[3] In any case in Sierra Leone, Cambodia, and East Timor.

[4] Other aspects of the relationship with (the courts of) other countries are dealt with in Chapter 17 (Sluiter).

[5] On the truth and reconciliation institutions in Sierra Leone and East Timor, see Chapters 9 (Schabas) and 6 (Lyons).

1. Kosovo

In Kosovo, competence in respect of serious crimes has not been limited to one particular internationalized court.[6] Serious crimes can be prosecuted throughout Kosovo, by all courts that have territorial jurisdiction under local law (the Law on Courts of Serbia and Montenegro).[7]

In terms of their composition, only some of the Kosovo courts have actually been internationalized. As of 14 April 2003, 17 international judges were placed at the District and Supreme Courts of Kosovo.[8] Courts with international composition thus exist next to courts, which, in terms of their composition, are still national courts, even though the applicable law of all courts has been internationalized.[9]

Whether or not a 'non-internationalized' court could assume jurisdiction over serious crimes is governed by the Law on Courts of Serbia and Montenegro. However, in practice the possibility of a national court exercising jurisdiction is only speculative, since, at the moment, should a non-internationalized court assume jurisdiction, that court would probably be internationalized *de imperio* by the Special Representative of the Secretary-General (SRSG). The SRSG can, upon recommendation of the Department of Judicial Affairs, assign international judges/prosecutors where this is considered necessary to ensure the independence and impartiality of the judiciary or the proper administration of justice.[10] In practice, crimes connected to the 1998–99 conflict have been dealt with exclusively by district courts that have been internationalized by the SRSG.[11]

A separate question is whether the courts of Serbia and Montenegro[12] could exercise jurisdiction over crimes within the jurisdiction of the internationalized Kosovo courts. UN Security Council Resolution 1244 (1999) does not invalidate any jurisdiction that Serbian courts may have under national law.[13] The authority of the Special Representative of the

---

[6] See Chapters 3 (Cerone/Baldwin), and 2 (Shraga).

[7] See Chapter 3 (Cerone/Baldwin).

[8] 'Report of the Secretary-General on the United Nations Interim Administration Mission in Kosovo' (2003) UN Doc S/2003/421 para 15.

[9] See Chapter 14 (Swart).

[10] UNMIK Regulation 2000/64, Article 1.3.

[11] OSCE *Kosovo's War Crimes Trials: A Review* (September 2002) 11.

[12] Following the adoption and the promulgation of the Constitutional Charter of Serbia and Montenegro by the Assembly of the Federal Republic of Yugoslavia on 4 February 2003, the name of the State of the Federal Republic of Yugoslavia was changed to Serbia and Montenegro. When reference is made to the current state of affairs, this chapter will refer to Serbia and Montenegro. When reference is made to the legal situation before the change of names, reference is made to Federal Republic of Yugoslavia.

[13] On 8 July 2002, this year, the District Court in Prokuplje found Nikolic, a former Yugoslav Army reservist, guilty of killing two Kosovo Albanian civilians near Penduh village in Kosovo on 24 May 1999 and sentenced him to eight years in prison (www.hlc.org.yu/english/wct/wct14.htm). On 11 October 2002, the Military Court in Nic, central Serbia, handed down the

Secretary-General is limited to Kosovo. In this respect a shared jurisdiction may exist.

Not every jurisdiction that Serbia and Montenegro may exercise with respect to Kosovo is lawful, however. Article 1.1 of UNMIK Regulation 1999/1 provides: 'All legislative and executive authority *with respect to* Kosovo, including the administration of the judiciary, is vested in UNMIK and is exercised by the Special Representative of the Secretary-General.' This provision seems to render illegal the re-establishment of 'Kosovo' District Courts within Serbia proper after the war by Serbia. Serbian authorities have transferred many of the court files from Kosovo to those courts. In his report to the Security Council of 14 April 2003, the Secretary-General noted that 'Belgrade-supported parallel structures now exist in virtually all municipalities that have a sizeable Kosovo Serb population'.[14] It appears that suspects arrested by authorities in northern Mitrovica have been brought to trial before the court in Kraljevo, in Serbia proper, where they have been tried under Serbian law.[15] This form of concurrent jurisdiction between regular (Serbian) courts and internationalized courts seems to violate Article 1.1 of UNMIK Regulation 1999/1. This view is shared by UNMIK, which has attempted to dismantle the parallel structures.[16]

2. East Timor

According to UNTAET Regulation 2000/11, judicial authority in East Timor 'shall be exclusively vested in courts that are ... composed of both East Timorese and international judges'.[17] This suggests that the entire court system of East Timor, composed of four District Courts and one Court of Appeal,[18] is internationalized. However, a full internationalization of the

---

first ruling in a case of a war crime committed during the armed conflict in Kosovo. Two former soldiers of the Yugoslav Army were convicted for killing two Kosovo Albanian civilians and burning their bodies. The suspects were sentenced to five years and three years in prison. A senior military security officer who ordered the crime was sentenced to seven years. See www.hlc. org.yu/english/wct/wct17.htm.

[14] 'Report of the Secretary-General on the United Nations Interim Administration Mission in Kosovo' (14 April 2003) UN Doc S/2003/421 para 46.

[15] OSCE *Report 9: On the Administration of Justice* (March 2002) 8.

[16] UN Doc S/2003/421 para 19: 'UNMIK attempted to dismantle the parallel courts supported by Belgrade and worked to establish a unified justice system under UNMIK. Seven Kosovo Serb judges were appointed in the northern part of Kosovo and the Minor Offences and Municipal Courts in both Leposavic and Zubin Potok were officially opened under UNMIK administration on 13 January'.

[17] Section 1 (judicial authority) of UNTAET Reg 2000/11 (On the Organization of Courts in East Timor) as amended by Reg 2001/25 (14 September 2001).

[18] Cf ibid ss 7 and 14. The structure of the judiciary is in the course of being modified by Title V of the Constitution of the Republic of East Timor of 20 May 2002 (available at www.etan.org/etanpdf/pdf2/constfnen.pdf). However, the transitional provisions relating to the judiciary (ss 163 and 164) provide that '[t]he collective judicial instance existing in East

East Timorese judiciary was never seriously contemplated by UNTAET, and not implemented in practice.[19] Internationalization has only occurred with regard to the District Court in Dili.[20]

Such Panels have *exclusive* jurisdiction over serious criminal offences. These are, on the one hand, the international crimes of genocide, crimes against humanity, war crimes, and torture, and, on the other hand, the domestic offences of murder and sexual offences, insofar as they were committed in the period between 1 January and 25 October 1999 in the territory of East Timor.[21] In respect of these crimes, there is thus no role for non-internationalized courts.

The jurisdiction of the Special Panels over murder and sexual offences committed in East Timor prior to 1 January 1999, appears to be not of an exclusive nature and is shared with other 'non-internationalized' District Courts,[22] subject to the clause which requires that the law on which the serious criminal offence is based is consistent with internationally recognized human rights standards,[23] to the possibility that a Special Panel requests a deferral,[24] and to the exceptions to the principle of *ne bis in idem*.[25] So far, no proceedings have been conducted with respect to serious offences committed outside the period that is reserved for the District Court in Dili and conse-

Timor, composed of national and international judges with competencies to judge serious crimes committed between the 1st of January and the 25th of October 1999, shall remain operational for the time deemed strictly necessary to conclude the cases under investigation' (s 163(1)) and that '[t]he judicial Organization existing in East Timor on the day the present Constitution enters into force shall remain operational until such a time as the new judicial system is established and starts its functions' (s 163(2)). Also see s 164, providing, inter alia, that the highest judicial instance of the judicial organization existing in East Timor (i.e. currently the Court of Appeal) shall exercise the functions and powers of the Supreme Court of Justice until such a time as the latter is established (s 164(2)).

[19] Amongst other factors, the lack of international judges, even in the Special Panels, has hampered the application of the Regulation in Practice. On the latter aspect, see de Bertodano 'Current Developments in Internationalised Courts' (2003) 1 *J Int'l Criminal Justice* 231.

[20] More specifically, its Special Panels established in accordance with section 9.3 of UNTAET Regulations 2000/11 and 2000/15 (On the Establishment of Panels with Exclusive Jurisdiction over Serious Criminal Offences)—UNTAET Reg 2000/15 (5 July 2000). For a discussion of the operation of these Special Panels, see Chapter 5 (de Bertodano). According to the Former General Prosecutor of UNTAET, Mohamed Othman, the only exception to the rule that no other courts have been internationalized is that UNTAET once sent a Bangladeshi investigating judge to the Baucau Court: Mohamed Othman, e-mail to the authors (28 May 2003).

[21] UNTAET Reg 2000/15 (5 July 2000) s 2. Note that s 9.4 of UNTAET Reg 2000/11 clarifies that the establishment of Special Panels 'shall not preclude the jurisdiction of an international tribunal for East Timor over the offences, once such a tribunal is established'. However, as the establishment of such a tribunal seems highly unlikely (see Chapter 5 (de Bertodano)), the Special Panels have exclusive jurisdiction over serious crimes.

[22] Section 2.3 of Regulation 2000/15 expressly limits *exclusive* jurisdiction over murder and sexual offences only to the period between 1 January 1999 and 25 October 1999.

[23] cf s 5 of UNTAET Reg 2000/11.

[24] Section 1.4 of UNTAET Reg 2000/15, see also p 366.

[25] These are specified in section 11.3 of Regulation 2000/15. See p 373.

quently, the question whether and to what extent 'non-internationalized' District Courts share the jurisdiction with the Serious Crimes Panels has not arisen in practice.[26]

3. Cambodia

According to the Agreement between the United Nations and Cambodia, as approved by the General Assembly on 13 May 2003, the Extraordinary Chambers will be established in the existing court structure of Cambodia.[27] One thus cannot speak of 'internationalized courts' (the Extraordinary Chambers) and 'national courts': the Extraordinary Chambers are regular Cambodian courts, be it with some special features, in particular in terms of their composition and the applicable law.[28]

The question whether the jurisdiction of the Extraordinary Chambers is shared with the non-internationalized parts of the judicial system seems, to a large extent, a theoretical one. There has been little inclination to prosecute the suspects with greatest responsibility for the genocide in the regular Cambodian courts; indeed that has precisely been the reason for the establishment of the Extraordinary Chambers. The possibility of any court wishing to step in seems remote. Nonetheless, a few observations on the jurisdiction of the regular courts can be made.

The jurisdiction of the Extraordinary Chambers appears to be exclusive in so far as they will have jurisdiction over suspects of genocide, crimes against humanity, suspects responsible for the destruction of cultural property during armed conflict pursuant to the 1954 Hague Convention for Protection of Cultural Property in the Event of Armed Conflict, and suspects responsible for crimes against internationally protected persons pursuant to the 1961 Vienna Convention on Diplomatic Relations, and which were committed during the period from 17 April 1975 to 6 January 1979. To the extent that these are not defined in the other provisions of Cambodian criminal law, including the 1956 Penal Code, the normal courts would appear to have no jurisdiction over these crimes.

The subject-matter jurisdiction of the Extraordinary Chambers also covers homicide, torture, and religious persecution. These crimes are defined under national Cambodian law and would in principle also fall within the jurisdiction of regular Cambodian courts. However, also in respect of these crimes

---

[26] For an overview, see Judicial System Monitoring Programme www.jsmp.minihub.org/Trialsnew.htm.
[27] Article 2 of the Law on the Establishment of Extraordinary Chambers in the Courts of Cambodia for the Prosecution of Crimes Committed During the Period of Democratic Kampuchea; Art. 2 of the Agreement of 17 March 2003 between the United Nations and the Royal Government of Cambodia concerning the Prosecution under Cambodian Law of Crimes committed during the Period of Democratic Kampuchea.
[28] See Chapter 14 (Swart).

the jurisdiction of the Extraordinary Chambers appears to be exclusive if one considers the temporal jurisdiction of the Extraordinary Chambers. The Law on the Extraordinary Chambers extends the statute of limitations set forth in the 1956 Penal Code for an additional 20 years for the crimes within the jurisdiction of the Extraordinary Chambers. Presumably, prosecution of these crimes under the other provisions of the national criminal code would be barred because the statute of limitations would be in effect.[29] For this reason, no overlap in jurisdiction between the Extraordinary Chambers and the regular courts in respect of homicide, torture, and religious persecution appears to exist.

4. Sierra Leone

The Special Court for Sierra Leone does not form part of the judiciary of Sierra Leone.[30] Its jurisdiction over 'those persons who bear the greatest responsibility for serious violations of international humanitarian law and Sierra Leonean law committed in the territory of Sierra Leone since 30 November 1996'[31] in principle is concurrent with that of national courts of Sierra Leone.[32] No provision of the Special Court Agreement of the Ratification Act precludes jurisdiction of the ordinary courts. Thus, national courts of Sierra Leone may, to the extent that national law allows for prosecution of the crimes within the jurisdiction of the Special Court, exercise jurisdiction over these crimes.

5. Summary

From the above, it emerges that the jurisdiction of each of the four internationalized courts is delineated from that of regular courts in a different way. Only in Cambodia the jurisdiction of the internationalized courts appears to

---

[29] The contents of the applicable national penal law of Cambodia is difficult to ascertain. Cambodia has six legal codes that could in theory be applied in various ways to the crimes in question here. In addition to the French-inspired 1956 Penal Code and the Law on the Extraordinary Chambers, there exists a body of socialist decree law created in the early 1980s under the People's Republic of Kampuchea (PRK); a criminal code written in haste by the State of Cambodia (SOC) just before the arrival of the UN Transitional Authority for Cambodia (UNTAC) forces in the early 1990s; a criminal code written by the United Nations in 1992–93; and an emerging body of criminal procedure and law promulgated since the formation of the Royal Cambodian Government (RCG) in 1993. Although formally any new law promulgated since 1993 supersedes previous law, in practice this is routinely ignored and prosecutors and courts may use elements from among each of these different codes in the course of proceedings. Information provided by Craig Etcheson.

[30] cf s 11(2) of the Special Court Agreement (Ratification) Act 2002.

[31] Article 1 of the Agreement between the United Nations and the Government of Sierra Leone on the Establishment of a Special Court for Sierra Leone and Art 1 of the Statute of the Special Court for Sierra Leone.

[32] Article 8(1) of the Statute.

be an exclusive one. In the three other cases a certain concurrent jurisdiction may exist. The internationalized courts in Kosovo have not been given an exclusive jurisdiction, but in practice the possibility that 'non-internationalized' Kosovo courts try suspects of serious crimes is negated by the likelihood that the SRSG would internationalize that court. Concurrent jurisdiction may exist, however, with the courts of Serbia and Montenegro. In East Timor, internationalized courts have been given exclusive jurisdiction over most serious crimes, but jurisdiction over murder and sexual offences committed in East Timor prior to 25 October 1999 is shared with 'non-internationalized' District Courts. In the case of Sierra Leone jurisdiction is shared.

C. REGULATION OF CONCURRENT JURISDICTION BETWEEN INTERNATIONALIZED AND NATIONAL COURTS

For the three situations in respect of which concurrent jurisdiction may exist, the question arises how the exercise of concurrent jurisdiction has been regulated. In each of these cases, the chosen solution, even though formulated in different ways, is that the national courts may have to defer to the internationalized courts.

In respect of Kosovo, the concurrence with the jurisdiction of the ordinary courts of Serbia and Montenegro is subject to Resolution 1244 (1999) and the relevant UNMIK Regulations. The allocation in Article 1.1 of UNMIK Regulation 1999/1 of 'all legislative and executive authority *with respect to* Kosovo', to UNMIK, to be exercised by the Special Representative of the Secretary-General, would appear to give him the power to intervene in cases in Serbian courts '*with respect to* Kosovo' and, possibly, to have those cases transferred to Kosovo. UNSC Resolution 1244 (1999) demands full cooperation in the implementation of the Resolution.

As to the situation in East Timor, if East Timorese courts would assume jurisdiction, a Special Panel may have deferred to itself a case which is pending before another panel or court in East Timor 'at any stage of the proceedings, in relation to cases of serious criminal offences listed under section 10 (a) to (f) of UNTAET Regulation No. 2000/11, as specified in Sections 4 to 9 of [Regulation 2000/15]'.[33] Neither section 10(a) to (f) of UNTAET Regulation 2000/11,[34] nor sections 4 to 9 of Regulation 2000/15, are limited *ratione temporis*, which suggests that the capacity of the Special Panels to request a deferral applies irrespective of the time when the serious offences were committed, thus equally covering those which fall into the jurisdiction of other 'non-internationalized' District Courts.

---

[33] Section 1.4 of UNTAET Reg 2000/15.
[34] After having been amended by UNTAET Reg 2001/25 (14 September 2001), it became s 9.

The situation for the Special Court for Sierra Leone is comparable. The Special Court for Sierra Leone may formally request a national court to defer to its competence at any stage of the procedure.[35] The relationship between the Special Court and national courts of Sierra Leone thus resembles the one between ICTY and ICTR and national courts.[36]

The Rules of Procedure and Evidence[37] implement the primacy of the Special Court and specify the legal framework for deferrals. Rule 9 provides that the Trial Chamber of the Special Court may issue an order or request that courts of a state defer to the competence of the Special Court under one of four conditions, namely where: (i) crimes which are the subject of investigations or proceedings instituted in the courts of a state are the subject of an investigation by the Prosecutor; (ii) such crimes should be the subject of an investigation by the Prosecutor considering, amongst other things, the seriousness of the offences; the status of the accused at the time of the alleged offences; the general importance of the legal questions involved in the case; or (iii) such crimes are the subject of an indictment in the Special Court; or (iv) fall within Rule 72(B).[38] According to Rule 10, an order for deferral shall be issued by the Trial Chamber if it appears to it that any of the first *three* conditions mentioned in Rule 9(i) to (iii) are satisfied. It is not immediately obvious how an order for deferral under the fourth condition (cases falling within Rule 72(B))[39] is to be issued. It would seem from the wording of Rule 10 that the Trial Chamber is not obliged to issue an order for deferral in such a case.[40] In case of non-compliance by the government of Sierra Leone with

---

[35] Article 8(2) of the Statute.

[36] The comparison to the two ad hoc tribunals is, however, subject to the important qualification that, due to their different legal bases, the primacy of the Special Court is confined to national courts *of Sierra Leone*. The two ad hoc tribunals being established by Security Council Resolutions under Chapter VII are competent to issue orders binding on all UN Member States in accordance with Art 25 of the UN Charter, while the Special Court is established by an Agreement between the government of Sierra Leone and the United Nations, thus not possessing binding force beyond the parties to the Agreement. Cf 'Report of the Secretary General on the Establishment of a Special Court for Sierra Leone' UN Doc S/2000/915 (4 October 2000) para 10.

[37] Rules of Procedure and Evidence, adopted on 1 August 2003.

[38] Rule 72(B) deals with preliminary motions by the accused, which are (i) objections based on lack of jurisdiction; (ii) objections based on defects in the form of the indictment; (iii) applications for severance of crimes joined in one indictment under Rule 49, or for separate trials under Rule 82(B); (iv) objections based on the denial of request for assignment of counsel; or (v) objections based on abuse of process. Thus, if such objections or applications were made in the courts of a State, the Prosecutor would be entitled to apply for an order or request for deferral.

[39] ibid.

[40] Presumably, cases falling within Rule 72(B) were not included because Rule 72(D) provides for the possibility that some of the preliminary motions envisaged in Rule 72(B) are decided by the Appeals Chamber, namely, if such motions raise, in the opinion of the Trial Chamber, 'a substantial issue relating to jurisdiction; or an issue that would significantly affect the fair and expeditious conduct of the proceedings or the outcome of a trial, and for which an immediate resolution by the Appeals Chamber may materially advance the proceedings', cf Rule

an order for deferral, the Trial Chamber may refer the matter to the President of the Special Court 'to take appropriate action'.[41] At the time of writing (January 2004), no orders or requests for deferral have been issued by the Special Court.

The concurrent jurisdiction between the Kosovo court, the East Timorese Serious Crimes Panels and the Special Court for Sierra Leone, on the one hand, and the national courts of Serbia and Montenegro, the national courts of East Timor and the national courts of Sierra Leone, on the other, thus is regulated along similar lines. While only the legal framework of the Special Court for Sierra Leone expressly refers to 'primacy', each of those internationalized courts has the competence to request deferrals from the respective national courts at any stage of the proceedings.

D. CHALLENGING THE LEGALITY OF ESTABLISHMENT OF INTERNATIONALIZED COURTS IN NATIONAL COURTS

As the experiences with the ICTY and the ICTR have shown, indictees can try to challenge the legality of the establishment of international tribunals, not only before the tribunals themselves[42] but also in national courts.[43] Such challenges may also be directed against internationalized courts. For instance, in particular circumstances it might be claimed that an internationalized court lacks a proper legal basis and therefore a trial before an internationalized court would violate Article 14 of the ICCPR, which provides that in the determination of any criminal charges, 'everyone shall be entitled to a fair and public hearing by a competent, independent and impartial tribunal *established by law'*. This is a difficult area. On the one hand, national courts may play an important role in the overall systems of checks and balances in regard of international or internationalized institutions. On the other hand, national courts may show bias or nationalism that was precisely the reason why internationalized rather than national courts were used.[44]

In considering the possibility of a challenge to the legality of the establishment of internationalized courts, the case of the Kosovo and East Timor

---

72(D)(i) and (ii), thus requiring a ruling by the Appeals Chamber before an order for deferral can be issued.

[41] Rule 11.

[42] International Criminal Tribunal for the former Yugoslavia (ICTY) in *Prosecutor v Tadić* IT-94-1-AR72 Decision on the Defence Motion for Interlocutory Appeal and Jurisdiction, Appeals Chamber, Judgment (2 October 1995) para 38, available at www.un.org/icty.

[43] *Milosevic v The Netherlands* Judgment (29 June 2001) (2001) 48 *Netherlands Int'l L Rev* 357.

[44] For a fuller discussion, see Erika De Wet and André Nollkaemper 'Review of Security Council Decisions by National Courts' (2002) 45 *German YB Int'l L* 166–202; Erika De Wet and André Nollkaemper (eds) *Review of the Security Council by Member States* (Intersentia, 2003).

courts on the one hand, and that of the Sierra Leone Court and the Cambodian Extraordinary Chambers, on the other, must be differentiated. As the former courts are established under the authority of the UN Security Council, and the Security Council has vested its power in the SRSG, a challenge to the establishment of the Kosovo and East Timor courts is in fact a challenge to a decision emanating from the Security Council acting under Chapter VII of the UN Charter. International law can allow for a challenge to Security Council decisions in a national court only under restrictive conditions. A review by national courts of the legality of Security Council resolutions, or their application, may undermine the efficiency of the Charter system, as it would open the door for states to evade their Charter obligations.[45] This problem was raised when Slobodan Milosevic challenged the jurisdiction of ICTY before the District Court of The Hague.[46] While the Dutch court rejected the claim, its reasoning did rely on the Appeals Chamber of ICTY's decision on the defence motion for interlocutory appeal on jurisdiction in the *Tadić* case.[47] By accepting the conclusion of the Appeals Chamber that the Security Council does have the power to establish ICTY as a measure for maintaining or restoring international peace and security, the Dutch court did not take the position that a national court would, as a matter of principle, lack the jurisdiction to review a Security Council decision establishing an international tribunal.[48] This scenario might be relevant for challenges to the legality of the establishment of internationalized courts under the authority of the Security Council.

The situation is different in the case of the Cambodia Extraordinary Chambers. The question here is whether national courts could review the legality of the Law on the Establishment of Extraordinary Chambers. Under Cambodian constitutional law,[49] such a review would appear to be possible before the Constitutional Council, in accordance with the relevant provisions that apply to an assessment of the constitutionality of laws after their

---

[45] Jost Delbrück 'Article 24' in Bruno Simma (ed) *The Charter of the United Nations: A Commentary* (Oxford University Press Oxford 1995) 414; Christian Walter 'Constitutionalizing (Inter)national Governance: Possibilities for and Limits of the Development of International Constitutional Law' (2001) 44 *German YB Int'l L* 170, 197.

[46] After his arrival in the Netherlands, where he was detained in the detention facilities of ICTY, Mr Milosevic requested the Dutch Court in summary proceedings to order the State of the Netherlands to release him. One of the grounds invoked by Mr Milosevic was that ICTY lacked a legal basis, as Chapter VII of the UN Charter does not give the Security Council competence to establish a criminal tribunal. *See* for a discussion Johan G Lammers, 'Challenging the Establishment of the ICTY before the Dutch Courts: The Case of *Slobocan Milosevic v The Netherlands*, in Erika De Wet and André Nollkaemper (eds) *Review of the Security Council by Member States* (Intersentia, 2003), 107–11.

[47] See n 42.

[48] *Milosevic v The Netherlands* Judgment (29 June 2001) (2001) 48 *Netherlands Int'l L Rev* 357.

[49] Constitution of Cambodia of 21 September 1993, available at: www.constitution.org/cons/cambodia.htm.

promulgation. Article 122 of the current Constitution provides that 'the King, the prime Minister, the President of the Assembly, one-tenth of the assembly members or the courts, may ask the Constitutional Council to examine the Constitutionality of [laws]' and grants citizens 'the right to appeal against the Constitutionality of the laws as through their representatives or the President of the Assembly'.

A challenge in the national courts of Sierra Leone to the legality of the establishment of the Special Court would in effect be a challenge to the treaty that established the Special Court, or to the procedure that led to the adoption of the approval of the Treaty. In at least three cases before the Special Court the argument has been made that the conclusion of the Special Court Agreement violated the constitution of Sierra Leone.[50] Conceivably, the same argument could be made before the Sierra Leone Supreme Court in accordance with section 127(1) of the Sierra Leone Constitution.[51] This argument was considered by Judge Mutanga Itoe of the Trial Chamber of the Special Court for Sierra Leone in his ruling on *habeas corpus* in *Prosecutor v Tamba Alex Brima*.[52] The Applicant argued the Special Court is part of the judicial hierarchy of the courts of Sierra Leone as provided for under the Constitution of Sierra Leone and that it thus falls under the supervisory powers of the Supreme Court. The Trial Chamber rejected the argument. It stated that the Special Court owed its existence not to the Constitution of Sierra Leone, but solely to Security Council Resolution 1315 (2000) and the Agreement between the United Nations and Sierra Leone. It also considered that the Sovereign People and Sovereign Parliament of Sierra Leone, in enacting the 1991 Constitution in a time of peace, 'never could have enacted or even envisaged constitutional structures which were supposed to regulate a post civil war stabilizing institution' such as the Special Court. It therefore concluded that application of the Constitution was limited to Courts created by that Constitution. It remains to be seen whether it will be attempted to pursue the argument in the courts of Sierra Leone.

It can be concluded that the legality of the establishment of internationalized courts can be challenged in national courts only under very limited

---

[50] Special Court for Sierra Leone, *Prosecutor v Tamba Alex Brima* SCSL-03-06-PT, Ruling on the Application for the Issue of a Writ of Habeas Corpus (22 July 2003); *Prosecutor v Morris Kallon* SCSL-03-07-PT, Preliminary Motion Based on Lack of Jurisdiction: Establishment of Special Court violates Constitutions of Sierra Leone (filed on 16 June 2003); *Prosecutor v Sam Hinga Norman* SCSL-03-08-PT, Preliminary Motion Based on Lack of Jurisdiction: Lawfulness of the Court's Establishment (filed on 26 June 2003). At the time of writing, no ruling had been given on the last two motions.

[51] The section provides: 'A person who alleges that an enactment or anything contained in or done under the authority of that or any other enactment is inconsistent with, or is in contravention of a provision of this Constitution, may at any time bring an action in the Supreme Court for a declaration to that effect'.

[52] Special Court for Sierra Leone, *Prosecutor v Tamba Alex Brima* (*supra* n 50).

circumstances as far as those internationalized courts which emanate from binding Security Council resolutions are concerned. With regard to those internationalized courts that are established by treaty or national law, the possibilities for challenges generally will be wider. In all cases, the prospects for such challenges will largely be determined by national law.

E. REVIEW OF DECISIONS OF INTERNATIONALIZED COURTS BY NATIONAL COURTS

Another possible interaction between national and internationalized courts is that it may be attempted to resort to national courts in order to challenge a decision, order or judgment of an internationalized court. In terms of legal policy, similar considerations apply as those noted with respect to challenges to the legality of the establishment of internationalized courts. While it may be said that national courts have a role to play in the overall systems of checks and balances,[53] assuming such a role brings a distinct danger of undermining the efficacy of internationalized courts.

In Kosovo, no cases are known to the authors in which judgments of internationalized courts were reviewed by 'non-internationalized' courts. It has been reported, however, that appeals would be filed in Serbian courts against judgments of the parallel court system (which, as noted above, in itself is illegal).[54] Appeals in the Serbian courts against decisions of internationalized courts certainly would be precluded by Resolution 1244 (1999), and the ensuing obligation of Serbia and Montenegro to cooperate with UNMIK.

The same result is warranted when considering judgments emanating from the internationalized courts in East Timor, Cambodia, and Sierra Leone. In these cases, the relevant instruments suggest that there is no room for reviews by national courts, because an internationalized appellate structure has been established for that purpose. In East Timor, judgments of the panels with exclusive jurisdiction over serious criminal offences are appealable to the—equally internationalized—Special Panel of the Court of Appeal.[55] In Cambodia, appeals and resort to the Supreme Court are within the Extraordinary Chambers structure[56] and similarly, the Agreement on the Establishment as

---

[53] Christoph H Schreuer, 'The Implementation of International Judicial Decisions by Domestic Courts', (1975) 24 *ICLQ* 182 (noting that implementation of international judicial decisions need not be 'slavish and mechanical').

[54] See www.hlc.org.yu/english/toka/toka45.htm (stating that 'Four Kosovo Albanians from the so-called "Urosevac Group" received the judgment handed down against them by the Pristina District Court two and a half years after the event. The Court thus denied these four men, who have been illegally held since June 1998, the right to defend themselves. Their defense counsel, including Humanitarian Law Center attorneys, can only now lodge an appeal with the Serbian Supreme Court').

[55] cf s 15.4 of UNTAET Reg 2000/11 and s 22.2 of UNTAET Reg 2000/15.

[56] cf Arts 36 and 37 of the Law on the Establishment of Extraordinary Chambers, (*supra* n 27).

well as the Statute of the Special Court for Sierra Leone provide for an Appeals Chamber as integral part of the Special Court,[57] competent to conduct appellate and review proceedings.[58]

The conclusion that national courts could not review judgments of internationalized courts, would equally seem to apply to other decisions of internationalized courts, because such review takes also place within the internationalized structures.[59] As a rule, national courts can thus not review such decisions.

However, an additional aspect arises in this regard in relation to the Special Court for Sierra Leone. Article 16 of the Agreement between the government of Sierra Leone and the United Nations provides that the government 'shall cooperate with all organs of the Special Court at all stages of the proceedings'[60] and 'shall comply without undue delay with any request for assistance by the Special Court or an order issued by the Chambers'.[61] If one were to understand the duty to cooperate to extend not only to the 'government' in the narrow sense but more broadly also to other branches of the state of Sierra Leone with functions other than executive ones, a review by the judicial branch appears to be excluded. This view also finds support in the Sierra Leone implementing legislation. Section 21(2) of the Special Court Agreement (Ratification) Act 2002 states that '[n]otwithstanding any other law, every natural person, corporation, or other body created by or under Sierra Leone law shall comply with any direction specified in an order of the Special Court'. However, if one considers certain other provisions with a bearing on the relationship between the national courts of Sierra Leone and the Special Court, the situation is less clear. Section 14 of the Special Court Agreement (Ratification) Act 2002, for instance, provides that the Attorney-General shall grant any request for deferral or discontinuance in respect of any proceedings pursuant to Article 8 of the Statute of the Special Court 'if in his opinion there are sufficient grounds for him to do so'. The latter qualification of the duty to grant such requests suggests that there is room for review, albeit by the Attorney-General, rather than a national court.[62]

---

[57] cf Art 2 of the Agreement and Arts 11, 12 of the Statute.

[58] cf Arts 20, 21 of the Statute.

[59] For East Timor, see ss 23, 27 of UNTAET Reg 2000/30 (On the Transitional Rules of Criminal Procedure) as amended by Reg 2001/25 (September 2001) in conjunction with s 15.4 of UNTAET Reg 2000/11 and s 22.2 of UNTAET Reg 2000/15; for Cambodia, Art 12 in conjunction with Art 3(2)(b) of the Agreement between the United Nations and Cambodia, and Arts 36, 37 of the Law on the Establishment of Extraordinary Chambers.

[60] Article 16(1) of the Agreement.

[61] Article 16(2) of the Agreement.

[62] The Act also provides room for review by national courts with respect to the execution of requests for assistance, cf s 16 of the Act, which provides: '(1) Subject to subsection (2), if the Special Court makes a request for assistance, it shall be dealt with in accordance with the relevant procedure. (2) If the request for assistance specifies that it should be executed in a particular manner or by using a particular procedure that is not prohibited by Sierra Leone law,

The foregoing suggests that, as a rule, national courts of the state to which the different internationalized courts are connected do not seem to have any possibility to review judgments or decisions of the latter. With regard to certain decisions of the Special Court for Sierra Leone other than judgments, however, this rule is arguably subject to exceptions.

F. *NE BIS IN IDEM*

A further question that needs to be addressed is whether the judgments of internationalized courts trigger the principle of *ne bis in idem* as a bar to subsequent trials by national courts. The same question arises in the reverse situation where the prior trial took place in a national court. While it seems that the first question has to be answered in the negative with respect to all four internationalized courts, the latter question raises a number of interesting issues.

In East Timor, Judgments of the Panels with exclusive jurisdiction over serious criminal offences in principle are final.[63] UNTAET Regulation 2000/15 on the principle of *ne bis in idem* bars a subsequent trial before a Special Panel,[64] and before another East Timorese court.[65]

In the reverse situation, the principle of *ne bis in idem* allows for exceptions. A person may be tried again before a Special Panel if the proceedings in the other court 'were for the purpose of shielding the person concerned from criminal responsibility for crimes within the jurisdiction of the panel' or 'otherwise were not conducted independently or impartially in accordance with the norms of due process recognized by international law and were conducted in a manner which, in the circumstances, was inconsistent with an intent to bring the person concerned to justice'.[66] These exceptions reproduce verbatim the corresponding provision of the ICC Statute.[67]

In Sierra Leone, national courts of Sierra Leone are barred from trying a person for acts for which he or she has already been tried by the Special Court.[68] Comparable to the situation in East Timor, exceptions apply in the

the Attorney-General shall use his best endeavours to ensure that the request is executed in that manner or using that procedure'. Whether such a request for assistance has indeed been dealt with in accordance with the relevant procedure (s 16(1)) and whether a particular procedure is not prohibited by Sierra Leone law (s 16(2)) could presumably be reviewed by national courts. Also note that s 18(2) of the Act envisages the possibility of the Attorney-General's refusing or postponing the execution of a request for assistance in whole or in part, in case of which 'he shall notify the Special Court accordingly and shall set out the reasons for that decision'.

[63] Assuming that they are not appealed, see p 371
[64] UNTAET Reg 2000/15 s 11.1.
[65] ibid s 11.2.
[66] ibid s 11.3. This is reiterated in s 4.2 of UNTAET Reg 2000/30 .
[67] Article 20(3) of the Rome Statute.
[68] Article 9(1) of the Statute. Similarly, s 23(9) of the Sierra Leone Constitution, provides that '[n]o person who shows that he has been tried by *any competent court* for a criminal offence

reverse situation of a prior trial in a national Sierra Leonean court. The Statute bars a subsequent trial by the Special Court, except if the act for which the person concerned was tried was characterized as an ordinary crime, or if the proceedings in the national court 'were not impartial or independent, were designed to shield the accused from international criminal responsibility or the case was not diligently prosecuted'.[69] The second exception creates a limited competence of the Special Court to review proceedings in national courts.

In Kosovo the matter is not as expressly regulated. However, under UNMIK Regulation 1999/24, as amended, both the European Convention for the Protection of Human Rights and Fundamental Freedoms and the Protocols thereto, as well as the International Covenant on Civil and Political Rights are part of the law applicable in Kosovo. Both documents recognize the *ne bis in idem* principle.[70] Neither of them expressly provides for its application in the relation between courts of different states.[71] The question is whether the relationship between Serbia and Montenegro, on the one hand, and Kosovo, on the other, should be considered as an international relationship for purposes of the application of the *ne bis in idem* principle. It would seem that, in view of the fact that formally Serbia and Montenegro is still a sovereign state that includes Kosovo,[72] as well as the fact that, in the relationship between national courts and international courts the *ne bis in idem* principle applies, the better position is that the *ne bis in idem* principle does apply. This would mean both that a final judgment of an internationalized

and either convicted or acquitted shall again be tried for that offence or for any other offence of which he could have been convicted at the trial for that offence save upon the order of a superior court made in the court of appeal proceedings relating to the conviction or acquittal;' (emphasis added), which would appear to cover judgments of courts other than Sierra Leonean ones for the purpose of *ne bis in idem* to the extent that such courts are considered 'competent'.

[69] Article 9(2) of the Statute. Article 9(3) provides that '[I]n considering the penalty to be imposed on a person convicted for a crime under the present Statute, the Special Court shall take into account the extent to which any penalty imposed by a national court on the same person for the same act has already been served'.

[70] Article 14(7) of the International Covenant on Civil and Political Rights; Art 4 of Protocol No 7 to the European Convention on Human Rights.

[71] As a rule, states do not apply the principle of *ne bis in idem* in their mutual horizontal relationship, thus allowing the prosecution of a person again at a later stage for the same offence for which he or she has been convicted or acquitted by the courts of another state. This practice has also been held to be compatible with international human rights requirements, such as Art 14 (7) of the 1966 International Covenant on Civil and Political Rights, see eg Human Rights Committee, *AP v Italy*, Communication 204/1986 (1987) UN Doc CCPR/C/OP/1, 67. See also C van den Wyngaert and G Stessens, 'The International *Non Bis In Idem* Principle: Resolving Some of the Unanswered Questions' (1999) 48 *ICLQ* 779, 781–82. However, in its judgment of 11 February 2003 in Joined Cases C-187/01 and C-385/01, the European Court of Justice held in a case governed by the Schengen Convention that a person may not be prosecuted in one Member State for the same facts which, in another Member State, have been finally disposed of without recourse to a court.

[72] UNSC Res 1244 (1999) reaffirms the 'commitment of all Member States to the sovereignty and territorial integrity of the Federal Republic of Yugoslavia'.

court would preclude a subsequent trial in a national court, and that a final judgment in Serbia and Montenegro would preclude a trial for the same act in Kosovo.[73]

After what has been said previously about the exclusive jurisdiction of the Cambodian Extraordinary Chambers,[74] there is no doubt that judgments of the Extraordinary Chambers necessarily will be final for other Cambodian courts and that suspects cannot afterwards be tried by 'non-internationalized' parts of the judicial system. The reverse situation, in which Cambodian courts have conducted trials with regard to crimes that fall into the jurisdiction of the Extraordinary Chambers prior to the coming into operation of the latter, however, is more complex. This question remains to be solved with regard to the trials conducted by the 1979 People's Revolutionary Tribunal in Phnom Penh, which sentenced Pol Pot and Ieng Sary to death *in absentia*.[75] Pol Pot has died in the meantime, but Ieng Sary, although pardoned in 1996, remains one of the potential suspects to be tried by the Extraordinary Chambers. Whether and to what extent the conviction and subsequent pardon affects a new trial will have to be decided by the Extraordinary Chambers.[76]

In conclusion, both in the case of East Timor and Sierra Leone, the *ne bis in idem* principle is subject to certain exceptions in the case in which an indictee has been tried first before a national court and then before an internationalized one, provided that the first trial was conducted for the purpose of shielding the person concerned, or was otherwise inconsistent with the intent to bring that person to justice. Such an approach confirms a trend with respect to *international* criminal courts and tribunals,[77] and accentuates the 'international courts' traits of internationalized courts in East Timor and Sierra Leone. Absent specific regulation, ie in the internationalized courts of Kosovo and Cambodia, a prior trial in a national court of Kosovo, Serbia and Montenegro, and Cambodia would seem to bar a subsequent trial in the internationalized courts. It is less clear, whether the aforementioned exceptions to the *ne bis in idem* principle where the first trial was conducted for the

---

[73] This latter situation arose when a Kosovo Serb had been acquitted by a Serbian court but was later indicted for the same offence by an internationalized court in Kosovo. In this instance, a Kosovo Serb, residing in a village within the Zubin Potok municipality, was indicted and tried for an alleged murder by the District Court of Kraljevo (Serbia proper) that assumed the territorial competence of the Mitrovicë/Mitrovica District Court. After being tried and acquitted by the former court, the defendant was indicted for the same offence by the Mitrovicë/Mitrovica District Court on 23 August 2001, and later detained by order of the same court on 30 August 2001; see OSCE *Report 9: On the Administration of Justice* (March 2002) 8. This case arose in implementation of the parallel system discussed above, but the same scenario may happen when a suspect is actually within the jurisdiction of the courts of Serbia.

[74] See pp 358–65.

[75] See Chapter 10 (Etcheson).

[76] Art 11(2) of the Agreement of 17 March 2003 (*supra* n 27).

[77] cf Arts 10 ICTY, 9 ICTR, 20 ICC.

purpose of shielding the person concerned, or otherwise inconsistently with the intent to bring that person to justice, apply also to the internationalized courts of Kosovo and Cambodia. Support for an affirmative answer is provided by the fact that the latter are internationalized and thus presumably less susceptible to bias. They could be said to exercise legitimate control functions with regard to national courts, which operate in an environment characterized by serious challenges to an effective, independent, and impartial judiciary.[78] On the other hand, as has been shown in this book,[79] the independence and impartiality of internationalized courts is not an axiom, and any possible exception to the *ne bis in idem* principle, on the ground that a judgment was adopted for the purpose of shielding a person, raises the question whether it should not equally apply to judgments of internationalized courts.

G. AUTHORITY OF JUDGMENTS OF INTERNATIONALIZED COURTS

A final issue to be considered is the legal weight, or more specifically the precedential value, of decisions of internationalized courts for subsequent decisions of the courts of the national legal order in which the internationalized court is embeddded. One of the justifications for the establishment of international courts and tribunals is to make available expertise in the prosecution of serious international humanitarian law violations, and to allow for capacity-building in the national systems, in particular as concerns the interpretation and reception of international (human rights, criminal, and humanitarian) law.[80] Potentially, the interpretation and application of international law by internationalized courts may help build a case law that supports national courts in determining, interpreting and applying international law. This is particularly relevant as in the three cases where internationalized courts are integrated in the national system (Kosovo, East Timor, and Cambodia), the applicable law has been internationalized.[81] In each of these cases, international law, to some extent, had domestic

---

[78] In addition, Canada has adopted the mentioned exceptions in the context of proceedings with regard to genocide, crimes against humanity, and war crimes, while otherwise recognizing the principle of *ne bis in idem* vis-à-vis foreign courts, cf s 12 of the Crimes Against Humanity and War Crimes Act. While this is not enough evidence for identifying a trend that these exceptions emerge in the relation between courts of different states, it is nevertheless noteworthy that s 12 did not meet any challenges by other states, although its application would clearly involve an assessment of the adequacy of proceedings conducted in a foreign state.

[79] cf eg, Chapter 3 (Cerone/Baldwin) on the independence of internationalized courts in Kosovo.

[80] See C R Romano and T Boutruche 'Tribunaux pénaux internationalisés: état des lieux d'une justice «hybride»' (2003) *Revue Générale de Droit International Public* 109, 114.

[81] On applicable law in internationalized criminal courts, see Chapter 14 (Swart).

validity before the arrival of the internationalized courts, and the judgments of internationalized courts may have an impact on the practice of national courts in regard to the application of international law.

As a general matter, judgments and decisions of internationalized courts can be relevant for the determination of rules of law. Article 38(1)(d) of the Statute of the International Court of Justice provides that judicial decisions are subsidiary means for the determination of rules of law. 'Judicial decisions' include decisions of national courts.[82] This certainly would hold for internationalized courts, which have the added authority of international judges. Arguments that are usually put forward to qualify the relevance of judgments of national courts in the determination and development of the law (eg, national courts generally will be tied to the national legal system,[83] have an at least partly national rather than international outlook,[84] and generally lack expertise in applying international law[85]) have less weight in the case of internationalized courts. Conceivably their decisions and judgments may carry weight for subsequent decisions of national courts. The extent to which this actually will be the case may in part depend on the quality of the judgments.[86]

H. CONCLUSION

It is difficult to draw some general conclusions on the relationship between internationalized and national courts. The relationship between national courts and internationalized courts differs from case to case. Moreover, there is only scant practice that could validate generalizations on the basis of the constitutive documents.

One general conclusion that can safely be drawn is that for most of the questions considered in this chapter the internationalized courts have largely been separated and isolated from the national courts. The jurisdiction of internationalized courts either de jure or de facto is mostly of an exclusive nature. To the extent that jurisdiction is concurrent (East Timor and Sierra Leone), the internationalized court has primacy and can request the deferral of a case. The powers of national courts to review the legality of the

---

[82] Rosalyn Higgins *Problems and Process* (Clarendon Press Oxford 1994) 218; Jennings and Watts (eds) *Oppenheim's International Law* (9th edn Longman London 1992) 41–2; Robert Y Jennings 'What is International Law and How Do We Tell It when We See It?' (1981) 38 *Schweizerisches Jahrbuch für Internationales Recht* 77; Menzel and Ipsen *Völkerrecht: ein Studienbuch* (2nd edn Beck Munich 1979) 87–8.

[83] *Oppenheim's International Law* (*supra* n 82) 42; Georg Schwarzenberger, *A Manual of International Law* (6th edn Professional Books Ltd Milton 1976) 30.

[84] Antonio Cassese 'Remarks on Scelle's Theory of "Role Splitting" (dédoublement fonctionnnel) in International Law' (1990) 1 *EJIL* 210.

[85] Higgins (*supra* n 82) 218; Schwarzenberger (*supra* n 83) 30.

[86] As noted elsewhere in this book, that is not to be taken for granted.

establishment of the internationalized courts or to review decisions of national courts is limited at best. The judgment of an internationalized court in principle bars a subsequent trial by the respective national courts.

However, the separation between internationalized and national courts is not complete. It appears that under narrowly circumscribed conditions, national courts may be able to review the legality of the establishment of internationalized courts. These functions of national courts may be considered as checks and balances vis-à-vis the internationalized courts, though they must be treated with much caution as they may have the potential to undermine the purposes for which the internationalized court was set up.

In the long term, the most important aspect of the interaction between internationalized and national court may be the influence that the decisions of the internationalized courts have on the practice of national courts. The relationship between national courts and internationalized courts must be assessed in the light of the aims that underlie the establishment of internationalized courts. Central amongst these is the contribution of internationalized courts to the rebuilding of the national judicial system.

17

Legal Assistance to Internationalized Criminal Courts and Tribunals

*Göran Sluiter**

A. INTRODUCTION

In order to carry out their mandates, internationalized criminal courts and tribunals require effective legal assistance, not only by the authorities of the states where these institutions operate, but also by third states and international organizations. Since internationalized tribunals and courts lack enforcement powers of their own, they need external cooperation to carry out several vital activities, in particular the collection of evidence and the arrest of accused persons.

The central question is how internationalized criminal tribunals can obtain the necessary assistance and to what extent states are under a duty to cooperate with them. The answer to this question may give us an idea as to whether the internationalized criminal tribunals can actually fulfil their mandates or are predestined to administer a weakened form of international justice. This question will be analysed separately for the prosecutions under the authority of the United Nations (Kosovo and East Timor), on the one hand, and for the Sierra Leone and Cambodia prosecutions, on the other.[1] Indeed, because the former have been created under a legal framework

* Lecturer in International Law, Utrecht University and Judge at the Utrecht District Court.
[1] The negotiations between Cambodia and the United Nations on the establishment of Extraordinary Chambers were for a considerable period of time unsuccessful. On 8 February 2002 the United Nations announced its withdrawal from the negotiations. At the end of 2002, however, the UN General Assembly requested the UN Secretary-General 'to resume negotiations, without delay, to conclude an agreement with the Government of Cambodia, based on previous negotiations': Resolution 57/228 (2002) on Khmer Rouge Trials (18 December 2002) UN Doc A/RES/57/228). A Draft Agreement between the United Nations and the Royal Government of Cambodia Concerning the Prosecution under Cambodian Law of Crimes Committed during the Period of Democratic Kampuchea was then recommended to the General Assembly for adoption by the Third Committee on 6 May 2003: 'Report of the Third Committee' (6 May 2003) UN Doc A/57/806. The General Assembly approved the draft Agreement by consensus on 13 May 2003 (Press Release GA/10135).

The operation of the Cambodia internationalized criminal court will be governed by this draft Agreement adopted by the General Assembly and the domestic Law on the Establishment of Extraordinary Chambers in the Courts of Cambodia for the Prosecution of Crimes Committed During the Period of Democratic Kampuchea, promulgated into Cambodian law on 10 August 2001, and the object of Art 2 of the draft Agreement. (Hereinafter 'draft Agreement between the United Nations and Cambodia' and 'Cambodian Law on Extraordinary Chambers'.)

substantially different from that of the latter, which are the result of bilateral agreements between the states concerned and the United Nations, separate treatment is warranted.

However, before focusing on the legal assistance regimes of the four internationalized criminal tribunals, there are two preliminary topics to be discussed. First a distinction will be made between the different forms of assistance the internationalized tribunals will need. Secondly, the two distinct models of legal assistance with which the international community is now familiar will be introduced. One model is characteristic of the provision of legal assistance between sovereign states and the other is typical of the provision of assistance to international criminal tribunals. Analysis of these two models will help characterize and evaluate the 'legal assistance models' of the internationalized criminal tribunals.

B. VARIOUS FORMS OF COOPERATION

Cooperation in a legal sense with the internationalized criminal tribunals can be divided into three main categories: arrest and transfer of the accused, cooperation related to investigations and the production of evidence, and cooperation with respect to the enforcement of sentences. All these three forms of legal assistance are essential for the effective functioning of tribunals.

First, it is self-evident that tribunals, in order to function effectively, should be able to count on the assistance of states in the arrest and transfer of accused persons. It must be mentioned that the legal frameworks of the UNTAET Serious Crimes Panels in East Timor and UNMIK courts in Kosovo explicitly exclude the possibility of trials *in absentia*.[2] The legal framework of the Sierra Leone Special Court and the legal framework of the Cambodia Extraordinary Chambers are not as explicit on this point, but one may expect that in light of the right attributed to the accused to be tried in his presence[3] and in light of the reduced authority of *in absentia* verdicts, these bodies will avoid conducting trials *in absentia*, in particular when an individual is accused of the most serious international crimes. Thus, the arrest of accused persons will in the first place require the assistance of states

---

[2] See s 5 of UNTAET Reg 2000/30 (On the Transitional Rules of Criminal Procedure) as amended by Reg 2001/25 (14 September 2001); see also UNMIK Reg 2001/1 (On the Prohibition of Trials in Absentia for Serious Violations of International Humanitarian Law).
[3] See Art 17(4)(d) of the Statute of the Special Court for Sierra Leone; Art 13 of the draft Agreement between the United Nations and Cambodia declares Art 14 of the International Covenant on Civil and Political Rights (1966), which includes the right to be tried in one's presence, applicable. Furthermore, Art 33 of the Cambodian Law on Extraordinary Chambers seems clearly directed at trials in the presence of the accused only.

where the internationalized tribunals are established, but also other states' assistance may be needed, especially that of neighbouring states.

Cooperation with respect to the production of evidence takes a variety of forms. It may consist in the taking of testimony or the provision of information by a state at the request of the trial forum. Certain forms of assistance may also involve the use of coercive measures, such as the forcible delivery of a witness before the court.

For the collection of evidence and the arrest of accused persons, internationalized courts need first of all the assistance of those states in whose territory the accused is to be found. Usually, these are the states where the crimes have been committed. Yet, the experience of ICTY and ICTR demonstrates that the collection of evidence may not always be left to the states in whose territory evidence can be found, but is increasingly undertaken by the tribunals themselves by means of so-called onsite investigations. Be that as it may, even this 'self-help' requires at a minimum passive assistance in the sense that the state concerned condones the investigations, without interference. Moreover, it cannot be excluded that evidence, especially in the form of witnesses, may also be located in the territory of other states, especially neighbouring states. In order for the investigations and prosecutions to be fruitful it is indispensable that the internationalized tribunals can dispose of all the necessary (incriminating and exculpatory) evidence. Thus, provision of legal assistance to that end by *all* states may be required.

Unlike the two above-mentioned forms of legal assistance, cooperation with respect to the enforcement of sentences is generally not confined to a particular state. In principle, a sentence, such as a sentence of imprisonment, can be executed in any state which is willing to do so. This may be different when the penalty includes the forfeiture of (unlawfully acquired) property or the proceeds of crime.[4] For the execution of similar penalties, assistance of one state in particular may be required. Again, in many cases this will be the state where the crimes have been committed, but that could extend to other states, especially neighbouring states.

This chapter focuses on the first two dimensions of legal assistance (ie the arrest and transfer of accused persons and assistance with respect to the collection of evidence). The enforcement of sentences will not be analysed here, because it may be expected in practice not to be as problematic as the other forms of assistance. As was already mentioned, the most important sentence to be imposed imprisonment can be executed in every state—and the states where the internationalized criminal courts operate, or will operate, can be expected to execute sentences of imprisonment in good faith.

---

[4] See Art 19(3) of the Statute of the Special Court for Sierra Leone, which provides for this penalty, just like s 10(1)(c) of UNTAET Reg 2000/15 (6 June 2000) (On the Establishment of Panels with Exclusive Jurisdiction over Serious Criminal Offences).

C. MODELS OF LEGAL ASSISTANCE:
HORIZONTAL AND VERTICAL

At present, there exist two ways of legally organizing the provision of legal assistance. One is typical of the provision of legal assistance to national courts and the other is typical of the provision of assistance to international criminal courts. The legal assistance relationship between states and international criminal courts can be described as 'vertical'. The concept of vertical legal assistance was introduced by the ICTY Appeals Chamber in the *Blaskic subpoena* case, with a view to indicate the hierarchy between the jurisdiction of the ad hoc tribunals and national criminal jurisdictions, and in order to indicate the consequences thereof for the provision of legal assistance by states.[5] The 'vertical' model is, from the perspective of the trial forum, a highly effective legal assistance regime. Its distinctive features are: far-reaching duties on states to cooperate;[6] the absence of a reciprocal cooperation relationship (the existing international criminal tribunals, ICTY, ICTR, and ICC, have no duty to provide assistance to states); and most importantly that disputes between the requesting international court and the state as regards the request for cooperation are to be settled unilaterally by the requesting side, be that ICTY, ICTR, or ICC.[7]

The 'vertical' legal assistance model differs considerably from the traditional 'horizontal' model of cooperation in criminal matters between sovereign states. First, cooperation between states is based on reciprocity. The principle of reciprocity is laid down in the various legal assistance treaties. These treaties themselves already guarantee the provision of assistance on a reciprocal basis, but sometimes contain the explicit obligation that the contracting parties provide *each other* with the widest possible assistance.[8] Secondly, in various inter-state legal assistance treaties there are a considerable number of grounds on which assistance may be refused.[9] Finally, if, in the horizontal legal assistance relationship, a dispute occurs regarding the extent of the duty to cooperate, the dispute is expected to be settled through usual means of dispute settlement (diplomatic means or third party adjudication). Although a considerable number of legal assistance treaties do not

---

[5] See *Prosecutor v Blaskic* IT-95-14-AR108*bis* A Ch. (29 October 1997) Judgment on the Request of the Republic of Croatia for Review of the Decision of Trial Chamber II of 18 July 1997 in Klip/Sluiter ALC-I-245 para 47.

[6] The existence of far-reaching duties to cooperate with international criminal tribunals appears from the absence of grounds for refusal in the Statutes of the ICTY and ICTR and only very few such grounds in the ICC Statute.

[7] See G Sluiter *International Criminal Adjudication and the Collection of Evidence: Obligations of States* (Intersentia Antwerp 2002) 81–9.

[8] cf, eg, Art 1 of the European Convention on Mutual Assistance in Criminal Matters (20 April 1959) 30 ETS.

[9] See, eg, ibid Art 2, and Art 4 of the UN Model Treaty on Mutual Assistance in Criminal Matters (UNGA Res 45/117 (1990)).

provide for compulsory settlement of disputes through arbitration or adjudication, states may still agree to accept the ICJ's jurisdiction over a dispute.[10] In the horizontal cooperation relationship it is unthinkable that either the requesting or requested side will decide unilaterally over disputes regarding the duty to provide legal assistance.

The 'vertical' model of legal assistance undoubtedly provides international judicial bodies with great advantages. It would therefore be tempting to extend this model to the internationalized criminal courts. However, it should be noted that the vertical model is the result of certain special features of the existing international criminal tribunals which the new internationalized courts do not necessarily share.

First, the subject matter jurisdiction of ICTY, ICTR, and ICC can be said to justify the adoption of a vertical legal assistance model. Because international crimes can be said to affect the interest of every member of the international community, states are prepared to engage in a vertical cooperation relationship. The nature of genocide, crimes against humanity and war crimes is such that even in the cooperation relationship between sovereign states one can already witness the gradual disappearance of traditional obstacles to effective assistance. That is the case, for example, of the political offence exception which appears more and more difficult to apply as a ground to refuse assistance to prosecutions of the most serious international crimes.[11] Likewise, one has difficulty in applying the double criminality requirement to crimes under international law, for which an international

---

[10] A distinction should be made between on the one hand Conventions of which legal assistance is only one element and on the other hand Conventions of which legal assistance is the exclusive object. The first category includes the 'specialized' UN Conventions combating organized crime and drug trafficking. These Conventions provide for compulsory dispute settlement mechanisms, being the ICJ, but it should be noted that states may make and have made reservations to the relevant provisions (see Art 32(2) of the United Nations Convention Against Illicit Traffic in Narcotic Drugs and Psychotropic Substances, Vienna (19 December 1988) 27627 UNTS and Art 35(2) of the United Nations Convention Against Transnational Organised Crime (December 2000) (2001) 40 ILM 335. The second category includes the European Convention on Mutual Assistance in Criminal Matters (20 April 1959) 30 ETS, the Inter-American Convention on Mutual Assistance in Criminal Matters (1992) and the UN Model Treaty (UNGA Res 45/117 on Model Treaty on Mutual Assistance in Criminal Matters (14 December 1990) UN Doc. A/RES/45/117). These Conventions do not contain provisions related to the settlement of disputes.

[11] See eg, Art 7 of the Genocide Convention (1948) which provides that genocide shall not be considered a political offence for the purposes of extradition; Art 1(a) of the Additional Protocol to the European Convention on Extradition (1975) provides that crimes against humanity, as provided by the Genocide Convention, shall not be considered as political crimes for the purpose of extradition.

ICTY decisions have furthermore excluded war crimes and torture from the 'political offence' realm; see *Prosecutor v Tadić* IT-94-1-AR72 A Ch (2 October 1995) Decision on the Defence Motion for Interlocutory Appeal on Jurisdiction (Tadić (1995) I ICTY JR 353) in Klip/Sluiter ALC-I-33 para 57, and *Prosecutor v Furundzija* IT-95-17/1-T T Ch II (10 December 1998) Judgment para 57.

obligation may exist to incorporate them into domestic law and to establish jurisdiction over them.

It is true that, like ICTY, ICTR, and ICC, internationalized criminal courts have been established, also, to prosecute individuals for the most serious international crimes and this may be advanced as an argument in favour of a more vertical legal assistance model. However, it should be noted that all four instances of internationalized prosecutions are not exclusively concerned with international crimes. The Special Court for Sierra Leone has the power to prosecute a number of crimes under Sierra Leonean law.[12] Similarly, the Cambodian Law on Extraordinary Chambers provides for the prosecution of crimes under the Cambodian Penal Code.[13] In East Timor, UNTAET has established Panels with exclusive jurisdiction over serious criminal offences. The latter also include 'ordinary crimes', namely murder and sexual offences.[14] The situation in Kosovo is that 'internationalized Panels' can deal with 'sensitive cases'.[15] Such cases include prosecutions for war crimes, genocide, but also the 'ordinary crimes' of murder, illegal possession of weapons, and drug trafficking.[16]

Although the 'ordinary crimes' included within the subject matter jurisdiction of the internationalized criminal tribunals might be heinous, still they are not international crimes. This may indeed affect the cooperation relationship between states. States could argue that legal assistance, expressing international solidarity, should not go as far as regards the prosecution of ordinary crimes as with respect to prosecutions for international crimes. One can imagine that a state may be more prepared to assist the Kosovo internationalized Panels in the prosecution of a case of genocide than in, for example, the prosecution of a case of human trafficking.

The ad hoc tribunals for the former Yugoslavia and Rwanda derive their authority from the widespread support of the international community. The same can in my view also be said for the International Criminal Court, since the number of ratifying states rapidly increases. Some have gone so far as to argue that because of this these international tribunals should not be

[12] See Art 5 of the Statute of the Special Court for Sierra Leone. The 'national crimes' consist of offences relating to the abuse of girls and offences relating to the wanton destruction of property.

[13] See Art 3 of that Law. The crimes under Cambodian law are homicide, torture, and religious persecution. Of course, torture is also an international crime.

[14] See s 1.3 of UNTAET Reg 2000/15 (6 June 2000) (On the Establishment of Panels with Exclusive Jurisdiction over Serious Criminal Offences).

[15] Section 2 of UNMIK Reg 2000/64 (15 December 2000) (On Assignment of International Judges/Prosecutors and/or Change of Venue) allows for these establishments; see also 'Report of the Secretary-General on the United Nations Interim Administration Mission in Kosovo', UN Doc S/2001/926, 2 October 2001, para 49.

[16] See 'Report of the Secretary-General on the United Nations Interim Administration Mission in Kosovo' (2 October 2001) UN Doc S/2001/926 para 49.

considered as foreign courts, but rather an 'extension of domestic courts'.[17] The support for international criminal justice is to a considerable degree based on the view that prosecution of international crimes will contribute to international peace and security. The ad hoc tribunals for the former Yugoslavia and Rwanda have been established by the UN Security Council for this sole purpose. The preamble to the ICC Statute also recognizes that the commission of international crimes threatens international peace and security.

It is the perception of international criminal tribunals by the international community as important human rights supervisory mechanisms and instruments to restore and maintain international peace and security that fully justifies a vertical cooperation relationship. The endeavours of internationalized prosecutions also receive international support and have international participation. The United Nations participates in and supports all four internationalized criminal tribunals, albeit in different ways. Does this warrant a more vertical cooperation relationship with states?

A distinction should be made between the East Timor and Kosovo Panels on the one hand, and the Sierra Leone and Cambodia tribunals, on the other. The prosecutions in Kosovo and East Timor are the result of the transitional administration of these regions by the United Nations. The administration of justice, in particular the prosecution of the most serious crimes, is an important part thereof. Since it is the view of the UN Security Council that in both situations the civil administration is necessary in order to restore international peace and security, one would expect that UN Member States have an obligation to ensure that UNMIK and UNTAET can fulfil their mandates.[18] However, the Security Council has not imposed such an obligation on UN Member States in explicit terms. This could mean one of two things. It is possible that the Security Council considers the duty to provide legal assistance an integral part of the duty incumbent on UN Member States to give effect to the relevant Security Council resolutions, based on Chapter VII of the UN Charter, establishing the transitional administrations. In other words, there would be no need to mention explicitly the obligation to provide legal assistance. However, it could also be that the Security Council considered the administration of justice, in particular the prosecution of international offences, as only a part of the mandates of UNTAET and UNMIK, which is in itself not so important as to result in the imposition of obligations on UN Member States similar to that towards ICTY and

---

[17] G Strijards 'De weergalm van een Romeins applaus—De totstandkoming van een internationaal strafhof' (1999) 17 *Nederlands Juristenblad* (30 April) 768; in more detail, from the same author, *Een Permanent Strafhof in Nederland* (WLP The Hague 2001) 46–51. See my critical remarks on that view; Sluiter (*supra* n 7) 80–1.

[18] See UNSC Res 1272 (1999), operative para 7: 'Stresses the importance of cooperation between Indonesia, Portugal and UNTAET in the implementation of this resolution'.

ICTR.[19] It is also possible that the Security Council deemed the imposition of a duty to provide legal assistance not indispensable for the execution of the mandates of UNTAET and UNMIK. Should the administration of justice in East Timor and Kosovo in practice be unable to proceed without the provision of assistance, a duty to provide assistance could be the subject of a future Security Council resolution.

The Sierra Leone Special Court and Cambodia 'courts' (will) receive the support of the United Nations on different legal grounds, as they have been created by international agreements and not Security Council resolutions. There are, however, also crucial differences between the Special Court for Sierra Leone and the proposed Cambodian Extraordinary Chambers. The Sierra Leone Court Agreement was concluded at the explicit request of the UN Security Council.[20] In subsequent resolutions, the Security Council has also stressed the importance of the Court's work and has called upon and urged states to cooperate.[21] The Sierra Leone Court is furthermore a new organ which has international legal personality and is formally not embedded in the UN system or the Sierra Leonean national legal order.[22] This legal personality and the important role of the Security Council in its establishment can be used as arguments in favour of adopting a vertical legal assistance relationship.[23]

As to the Cambodian case, the Extraordinary Chambers are not 'created' at the request of the UN Security Council, but at the initiative of the Cambodian government. Unlike the Sierra Leone Court, the Extraordinary Chambers will be part of the existing court structure in Cambodia.[24] The involvement of the United Nations in the Extraordinary Chambers consists essentially in enhancing the authority of the *national* court system and in providing practical assistance by the provision of 'international judges'. The 'Cambodian solution' for these reasons does not display the same degree of support and participation of the international community, which can be advanced as an argument in favour of a more horizontal cooperation model.

The engagement in a close legal assistance relationship depends to a considerable degree on the trust in the quality of the criminal procedure of the requesting side. States tend not to conclude legal assistance treaties with states that do not have strong guarantees for due process and do not respect

[19] cf UNSC Res 827 (1993), operative para 4, and 955 (1994), operative para 2.

[20] See UNSC Res 1315 (2000).

[21] See UNSC Res 1470 (2003), especially operative para 11 and 1478 (2003), especially preambular para 10.

[22] 'Report of the Secretary-General on the Establishment of a Special Court for Sierra Leone' (4 October 2000) UN Doc S/2000/915 para 9.

[23] As will be further examined below, urging all states to cooperate in UNSC Res 1470 could already be considered as a step towards a more vertical legal assistance regime. Future resolutions could further strengthen that development.

[24] See Art 2 of the Cambodian Law on Extraordinary Chambers.

the rule of law. It should be mentioned that human rights treaties play an increasingly important role in the provision of legal assistance.[25] For example, a state party to the European Convention on Human Rights may incur responsibility under that Convention when it exposes an individual to serious human rights violations in another state.[26]

I believe it is no exaggeration to say that ICTY, ICTR, and ICC have been endowed with a vertical cooperation regime in the expectation, even conviction, that they would observe the highest standards of criminal justice, from the investigational phase up to and including the execution of sentences.[27] Internationally protected human rights are therefore part of the legal frameworks of all the international criminal tribunals.

With respect to the internationalized criminal tribunals it is also of vital importance that they observe the highest standards of criminal justice with a view to close cooperation relationships with states. It is therefore not a surprise that all four internationalized criminal tribunals in one way or another reserve a prominent, even superior, place to international human rights in the 'applicable law'.[28] This is certainly beneficial to the provision of legal assistance, but much will depend on the actual operation in practice of these internationalized tribunals.[29] The participation of national judges in

---

[25] See Ch Van den Wyngaert 'Rethinking the Law of International Criminal Cooperation: The Restrictive Function of International Human Rights Through Individual-Oriented Bars' in Albin Eser and Otto Lagodny (eds) *Principles and Procedures for a New Transnational Criminal Law: Documentation of an International Workshop in Freiburg, May 1991* (Max-Planck-Institut für Ausländisches und Internationales Strafrecht Freiburg im Breisgau 1992) 489–503.

[26] Landmark decision is the *Soering* case, in which the European Court of Human Rights ruled that extradition of an individual by the United Kingdom to the United States, where the individual risks a death sentence, would violate the United Kingdom's obligations under Art 3 of the European Convention on Human Rights; see *Soering v United Kingdom* Series A, vol 161 Judgment (7 July 1989).

[27] I believe that, in spite of very few regrettable decisions, which occur (unfortunately) from time to time in every criminal jurisdiction, ICTY and ICTR operate in full respect of internationally recognized human rights; see in more detail G Sluiter (*supra* n 7) 36–9. See also the decision of the European Court of Human Rights in the *Naletilic* case, when it found that '[ICTY] offers all the necessary guarantees including those of impartiality and independence'. See *Naletilic v Croatia* Application 51891/99 Decision on Admissibility (18 October 1999).
As to ICC, the importance attached to internationally protected human rights appears from the hierarchically superior place attributed to that body of law; see Art 21(3) of the ICC Statute.

[28] See s 1.3 of UNMIK Reg 1999/24 (On the Law Applicable in Kosovo) as amended by Reg 2000/59 (27 October 2000); see the entire UNTAET Reg 2000/30 (On the Transitional Rules of Criminal Procedure) as amended by Reg 2001/25 (14 September 2000), which contains in various provisions rights of the accused; Art 17 of the Statute of the Special Court for Sierra Leone contains the rights of the accused; furthermore the Court's Rules of Procedure and Evidence, which entered into force on 12 April 2002 and were amended on 7 March 2003, add to the legal protection of the accused; finally, Art 13 of the draft Agreement between the United Nations and Cambodia ensures that the accused receives the protection of Arts 14 and 15 of the ICCPR.

[29] In this respect, one has to look with concern at the decision of 12 January 2001 of the East Timor Special Panel in which individuals for whom the orders of detention had expired were ordered to be held in detention; in more detail, see S Linton 'Cambodia, East Timor and Sierra Leone: Experiments in International Justice' (2001) 12 *Criminal Law Forum* 226–7.

a sometimes very delicate political environment may give rise to doubts regarding the tribunals' independence and impartiality. It is therefore with good reason that the international community has insisted on a vital role for the 'international judges' in the decision-making process. There are some other aspects of the internationalized criminal tribunals which may raise concerns and may constitute an obstacle to the provision of legal assistance. For example, unlike ICC, the Special Court for Sierra Leone has jurisdiction over persons who were 15 years of age at the time of the alleged commission of the crime.[30] Exercise of criminal jurisdiction over juvenile offenders may be unacceptable in the eyes of certain states and impede provision of assistance by these states.

One could conclude from the above general observations that the mandates, nature, and legal frameworks of the internationalized criminal tribunals warrant the adoption of a legal assistance model which can be positioned somewhere between the horizontal and vertical legal assistance models. In the next two paragraphs, focusing on the tools to request legal assistance and the corresponding duties of states, it will be examined whether this is in fact the case.

D. LEGAL ASSISTANCE TO THE KOSOVO AND EAST TIMOR PANELS

In this section it will be examined how the Panels of Kosovo and East Timor can obtain the necessary legal assistance. A distinction will be made between the positions and duties of the temporary administrations, the states most concerned, Indonesia and the Federal Republic of Yugoslavia, and other states.

1. East Timor and Kosovo: UNTAET/UNMISET and UNMIK

It is self-evident that the Special Panels in East Timor and Kosovo should receive the widest assistance of their creators: UNTAET and UNMIK. The latter have been endowed with extensive powers by the UN Security Council to fulfil their mandates.[31] As a result, at the request of the Special Panels UNTAET and UNMIK should be expected to arrest suspects and secure evidence located on the territory covered by their mandates. These tasks are

---

[30] See Art 7(1) of the Statute of the Special Court for Sierra Leone.

[31] Concerning UNTAET, see UNSC Res 1272 (1999), in particular operative para 4: '[a]uthorises UNTAET to take all necessary measures to fulfil its mandate'; as to the powers of UNMIK, see UNSC Res 1244 (1999), in particular operative para 7: '[a]uthorizes Member States and relevant international organizations to establish the international security presence in Kosovo as set out in point 4 of annex 2 with all necessary means to fulfil its responsibilities under paragraph 9 below'.

not necessarily performed by the multinational military forces assisting UNMIK and UNTAET, but can also be performed by, for example, international police personnel recruited.[32] As to the existing—or if they have collapsed entirely, rather future—court structures in Kosovo and East Timor, including the national police forces operating under their authority, it is important that they cooperate fully with the Special Panels. UNTAET has regulated the relationship between the courts in East Timor. Section 10 of UNTAET Regulation 2000/11 (On the Organization of Courts in East Timor) obliges any District Court to cooperate with requests for various acts of assistance issued by another District Court.

Thus, one can safely conclude that the Special Panels prosecuting international crimes committed in East Timor and Kosovo should be able without much difficulty to obtain the accused and evidence located in East Timor and Kosovo, provided of course that UNMIK and UNTAET offer the widest possible assistance. In this respect, there appears not to be considerable difference between these Panels and any other domestic court embedded within an existing court structure in a state. The Kosovo and East Timor Panels have the considerable advantage over the existing international criminal tribunals in that they do preside over a 'police force' capable of using coercive measures, within a geographically limited area.

2. Federal Republic of Yugoslavia, and Indonesia

The above-mentioned advantage, however, cannot negate the fact that additional assistance may be required. This may potentially concern all states, but there is good reason to concentrate first on the provision of legal assistance by two particular states, the Federal Republic of Yugoslavia and Indonesia. As to the Kosovo situation, a considerable portion of 'war crime cases' may involve accused and witnesses who were part of the Yugoslav forces and are now again residing in the Federal Republic of Yugoslavia. Likewise, the vast majority of perpetrators of the serious crimes committed in East Timor are said to remain in Indonesia.[33] How can the cooperation of these important two states be obtained?

An important basis for a duty to provide assistance may be found in the relevant Security Council resolutions. The Security Council, acting under Chapter VII of the UN Charter, has installed UNTAET and UNMIK with a view to restoration and maintenance of international peace and security.

---

[32] As to the role of international police personnel, it is explicitly provided for in UNSC Res 1244 (1999) establishing UNMIK, operative para 11(i): '[d]ecides that the main responsibilities of the international civil presence will include: ... (i) Maintaining civil law and order, including establishing local police forces and meanwhile through the deployment of international police personnel to serve in Kosovo'.

[33] Linton (*supra* n 29) 223.

It appears self-evident that it would impose a duty on the states most concerned, Indonesia and the Federal Republic of Yugoslavia, to cooperate in the implementation of the resolutions establishing UNMIK and UNTAET.

When establishing UNMIK, the Security Council 'demanded' that all states in the region cooperate fully in the implementation of all aspects of the resolution concerned.[34] The language used, in particular the words 'demands' and 'cooperate fully', can legitimately be interpreted as imposing a clear and even unconditional duty on the Federal Republic of Yugoslavia to assist UNMIK in the fulfilment of its mandate, which includes the administration of justice. What are the consequences thereof for the provision of legal assistance? Whenever the Special Panels in Kosovo are in need of accused persons or evidence located in the Federal Republic of Yugoslavia, the Yugoslav authorities should in my view provide the assistance as if the request were coming from, for example, a Belgrade District Court. It should be noted that Kosovo is not a sovereign state, but still part of the Federal Republic of Yugoslavia.[35] As a result, requests for assistance coming from Kosovo courts, including the Special Panels which can be considered part of the Kosovo court structure, cannot in my view be seen as requests for assistance coming from another jurisdiction. This may be of vital practical importance for the legal assistance process, because the Federal Republic of Yugoslavia categorically has refused the surrender of nationals to *other* jurisdictions, including that of ICTY, over a long period of time. Whereas the UNMIK Panels may enjoy the advantages of being part of the Yugoslav court structure, they should not suffer from the restrictions thereof. Because of the 'internationalized' status of the UNMIK Panels, various obstacles to Yugoslav national courts, such as, for example, the immunity under national law for politicians or military figures, should not apply to the Panels.

UN Security Council Resolution 1272 (1999) establishing UNTAET does not contain similar language with respect to Indonesia. The reference to cooperation in this resolution reads as follows: 'Stresses the importance of cooperation between Indonesia, Portugal and UNTAET in the implementation of this resolution'.[36] It would amount to a too-extensive interpretation to infer from this wording the imposition of a duty to cooperate on Indonesia. This is apparently also the view of the two entities most concerned, UNTAET and Indonesia. The Memorandum of Understanding (MOU) they have concluded, regulating various aspects of cooperation between the two and which will be further discussed below, is not based on the

---

[34] See operative para 18 of UNSC Res 1244 (1999).
[35] Note part of the preamble to UNSC Res 1244 (1999): 'Reaffirming the commitment of all Member States to the sovereign and territorial integrity of the Federal Republic of Yugoslavia'.
[36] Operative para 7 of UNSC Res 1272 (1999).

assumption of a full and unconditional obligation incumbent upon Indonesia to provide UNTAET with all necessary assistance.[37]

Thus, unlike the Kosovo Panels, the UNTAET Panels cannot use relevant Security Council resolutions as the legal basis for a duty incumbent upon Indonesia to provide legal assistance. Compared to the Kosovo Panels, the East Timor Panels are in a weaker position. In order to secure the necessary assistance, in legal and other matters, they had to negotiate a memorandum of understanding with the government of Indonesia, because there were no other agreements in place that could serve as a legal basis for a fruitful cooperation relationship. Since Indonesia had no express obligation under UN Security Council Resolution 1272 (1999) to cooperate with UNTAET, but was nevertheless expected to do so given operative paragraph 7 of that Resolution, the result was that Indonesia could not blatantly refuse the conclusion of a cooperation agreement,[38] but it succeeded in avoiding the imposition of extensive duties. Thus, the agreement contains rather far-reaching grounds for refusal, is based on reciprocity, and does not contain a compulsory dispute settlement mechanism.

Regarding the transfer of accused persons, which will in practice be the most needed and also the most sensitive form of assistance, the MOU contains two important grounds for refusal. Section 9.2 of the MOU contains the double criminality requirement. Section 9.3 contains furthermore the following ground for refusal:

Each Party shall have the right to refuse a request for such transfer if the carrying out of legal proceedings by authorities of the requesting Party would not be in the interest of justice.

Given its vague terms, this ground is highly susceptible to abuse. According to section 9.4 of the MOU a state party must submit the case for which transfer is requested to its own competent authorities for prosecution, when the state party decides to refuse the transfer. However, under this provision there is only an *aut dedere aut iudicare* duty when the transfer is refused because the conduct is not criminal under the laws of the requested state. Section 9.4, read in conjunction with section 9.2, still, however, allows for refusal of a request for transfer 'in the interest of justice', a ground which is susceptible to various interpretations. In case of refusal on this vague ground there exists no duty to prosecute for domestic authorities, hereby allowing the accused person to evade criminal prosecution in both East Timor and Indonesia.

---

[37] This has of course much to do with the difference in events leading to the establishment of UNMIK and UNTAET. The former was clearly the result of the defeat of the Federal Republic of Yugoslavia following the widespread NATO bombardments against various targets on its territory. A similar armed attack has never been launched against Indonesia.

[38] See Memorandum of Understanding between the Republic of Indonesia and the United Nations Transitional Administration in East Timor Regarding Cooperation in Legal, Judicial and Human Rights Related Matters, Jakarta (5 April 2000).

In addition to the limited duty to provide assistance, reciprocity characterizes the cooperation agreement between UNTAET and Indonesia. Pursuant to section 1.1 of the MOU the parties shall afford to each other the
widest possible measure of mutual assistance in investigations or court
proceedings. Also other provisions in the MOU, containing more detailed
obligations, are based on a reciprocal cooperation.[39] The positive aspect of
reciprocity is that it could be seen as Indonesia seriously preparing for the
prosecution of the accused of Indonesian nationality. Indonesia has established a special ad hoc court for East Timor, although its jurisdiction *ratione
temporis* is limited to events after the 1999 referendum.[40]

The horizontal character of the cooperation relationship between
UNTAET and Indonesia is probably best reflected by the absence of a
compulsory dispute settlement mechanism. According to section 15.2, any
dispute as to the interpretation or implementation of the MOU shall be
settled amicably through consultation or negotiation.

What does the adoption of a horizontal legal assistance model mean for the
provision of assistance in practice? It is not true that every horizontal cooperation relationship results in ineffective legal assistance. However, a relationship as sensitive as that between East Timor and Indonesia requires a more
solid legal assistance model. The implementation of the MOU by Indonesia
has been reported to be far from satisfactory. Indonesia has refused to
provide the requested assistance on a number of occasions.[41] Although one
could probably accuse Indonesia of not implementing the MOU in good
faith, one should also recognize that the terms of the latter have not really
been established with a view to the most effective assistance.[42]

The cooperation relationships between UNMIK and UNTAET on the one
hand, and the Federal Republic of Yugoslavia and Indonesia on the other
hand, have been discussed above. It should be noted that UNMIK and
UNTAET are only temporary administrations, which has consequences for
the legal assistance relationships.

This is the case in particular for the East Timor Special Panels. As of 20
May 2002, East Timor is an independent and sovereign state. This does not
put an end to the involvement of the United Nations. There is a successor to
UNTAET, namely the UN Mission of Support in East Timor (UNMISET),
that takes over a considerable part of the mandate of UNTAET, including
assistance in the conduct of serious crimes investigations and proceedings.[43]

---

[39] See ibid s 9.1. [40] Linton (*supra* n 29) 222.
[41] For a more detailed account, see ibid 223.
[42] Note that Linton mentions that Indonesia has refused to transfer suspects to East Timor
'despite the terms of a Memorandum of Understanding' (see ibid). In my view Indonesia could
refuse this transfer *because of* the terms of the MOU.
[43] UNMISET has been established by UNSC Res 1410 (2002) (17 May 2002). Regarding
the role to be played by the United Nations after independence of East Timor, see 'Report of the

What does this mean for cooperation in criminal matters between East Timor and Indonesia? The MOU in force formally only governs the legal assistance relationship between UNTAET and Indonesia. Although one may expect the MOU to continue to apply between Indonesia and UNMISET, as the successor of UNTAET,[44] the succession offers an opportunity for Indonesia to limit the provision of legal assistance on the basis of the formal argument that there is no applicable source of international law obliging it to cooperate. It is not an attractive alternative to negotiate a new MOU between UNMISET and Indonesia, because Indonesia may use this negotiation process to reduce or pull out of certain obligations set out in the 'UNTAET MOU'. It is for these reasons to be regretted that the Security Council, when establishing UNMISET, has not anticipated this problem of legal succession.

The birth of East Timor as a sovereign state may have consequences for the legal assistance relationship with Indonesia. Now having international legal personality, East Timor may enter into legal assistance agreements with other states, including Indonesia. With a view to effective prosecutions in East Timor of international crimes, it is to be recommended that East Timor conclude such legal assistance treaties as soon as possible. Regarding the relationship with Indonesia, it is to be hoped that East Timor will also be allowed to make use of the MOU or, even better, supplement the MOU with a (more effective) bilateral legal assistance treaty.

When the UN administration in Kosovo will end is uncertain, just as it is uncertain what will be the status of Kosovo thereafter. Given the commitment to the sovereignty and territorial integrity of the Federal Republic of Yugoslavia in the preamble to Security Council Resolution 1244 (1999) it appears at this moment that Kosovo will remain part of the Federal Republic of Yugoslavia. Whether or not in that situation international crimes will be prosecuted in Kosovo courts, and whether or not the authorities of the Federal Republic of Yugoslavia will assist these courts in that respect, will depend on the internal political situation and is principally an internal matter. It should be mentioned in this respect, however, that the Federal Republic of Yugoslavia has a duty under a number of treaties, and possibly also under customary international law, to either extradite or prosecute persons accused of serious international crimes. As a result, when federal authorities attempt to halt or hamper prosecutions of international crimes by Kosovo courts this may entail the violation of the international *aut dedere aut iudicare* obligation incumbent on the Federal Republic of Yugoslavia.

Secretary-General on the United Nations Transitional Administration in East Timor' (17 April 2002) UN Doc S/2002/432 paras 62–98.

[44] This appears at least to be the assumption of the UN Secretary-General, who states that UNMISET 'would continue to cooperate with Indonesian investigators in their efforts to make inquiries into the past crimes'; ibid para 78.

3. Other states

When we look at the possibilities to obtain the legal assistance of other states, a distinction should be made between the situation in which assistance is sought by UNTAET/UNMISET or UNMIK and the situation in which the assistance is sought by East Timor or the Federal Republic of Yugoslavia.

The Special Panels in East Timor have the advantage that both East Timor, now an independent state, and UNMISET may seek legal assistance for their benefit. Given the importance they both attach to the Special Panels one may expect that they will actively seek the assistance of other states, when needed. The efforts of UNMISET can be expected to be more successful. Requests for assistance from the United Nations will probably carry more weight, using the argument that the mandate of the Special Panels flows from Chapter VII-based UN Security Council resolutions and that effective prosecution contributes to the restoration of international peace and security. What is more, the UN Charter can serve as an important treaty basis for some forms of assistance, such as extradition.[45] East Timor, as a new sovereign state, not succeeding any state, cannot make use of existing legal assistance treaties and thus will initially have to obtain important forms of legal assistance on an ad hoc basis.

Unlike the East Timor Panels, the Kosovo Panels can at present exclusively rely on UNMIK seeking the assistance of states, when required. Requests coming from UNMIK enjoy the same advantages as described above with respect to requests for assistance issued by UNMISET. Yet, with respect to both situations, there is no clear-cut obligation for states to comply with them. If in the future the Federal Republic of Yugoslavia wishes to seek the assistance for the benefit of the prosecution of international crimes by courts in Kosovo, it has probably more legal assistance relationships at its disposal than East Timor.[46] Yet, it should be noted that the

---

[45] It should be noted that numerous national extradition acts require a treaty basis for the extradition of persons.

[46] The former Yugoslavia has concluded a number of bilateral extradition and legal assistance treaties, with, inter alia, Poland, the Soviet Union, France, Federal Republic of Germany, Belgium, and the United States (see Treaty Concerning Legal Relations in Civil and Criminal Cases with Poland (with exchange of letters) (6 February 1960) 521 UNTS 37; Treaty Concerning Legal Assistance in Civil, Family and Criminal Cases with the USSR (24 February 1962) 471 UNTS 195; Convention Concerning Reciprocal Legal Assistance in Criminal Matters with France (29 October 1969) 760 UNTS 386; Extradition Treaty with Germany (26 November 1970) 994 UNTS 95; Convention Concerning Extradition and Judicial Assistance with Belgium (4 June 1971) 872 UNTS 3; Treaty Concerning Judicial Assistance in Criminal Matters with Germany (1 October 1971) 966 UNTS 153; Bilateral Extradition Treaty with the United States (25 October 1901), in M Cherif Bassiouni, *International Extradition: United States Law and Practice* (Oceana Publications Dobbs Ferry New York 2002) App II, 925.

It is an interesting question, which is beyond the scope of this chapter, whether with respect to all these treaties the Federal Republic of Yugoslavia can be seen as the legal successor of the former Socialist Federal Republic of Yugoslavia. Concerning membership of the United Nations this question was answered in the negative and the Federal Republic of Yugoslavia

Federal Republic of Yugoslavia is not a party to important multilateral European instruments, such as the European Convention on Extradition and the European Convention on Mutual Assistance in Criminal Matters.

4. *Relationship between the Kosovo Panels and ICTY*

A unique feature of the internationalized Panels in Kosovo is that they have concurrent jurisdiction with ICTY. Pursuant to its Statute, ICTY has jurisdiction over war crimes, crimes against humanity, and genocide committed after 1 January 1991 on the territory of the former Yugoslavia. Article 9(2) of the ICTY Statute gives the tribunal primacy over national courts. One could argue that the internationalized Panels (partly) derive their authority from UNMIK, and ultimately the UN Security Council, and for that reason cannot be equated with a 'national court'. Since both ICTY and the internationalized Panels ultimately derive their authority from the Security Council, their relationship should also be determined by the Council. In this respect, one should mention operative paragraph 14 of UN Security Council Resolution 1244: 'Demands full cooperation by all concerned, including the international security presence, with the International Tribunal for the Former Yugoslavia'. It is fair to infer from this paragraph that ICTY also enjoys primacy over the internationalized Panels, even if the latter cannot be regarded as part of the international security presence. This paragraph also implies that the internationalized Panels have to provide ICTY with legal assistance, if requested. For example, they have to defer prosecutions, hand over documents, or take testimony from witnesses. More important for the purpose of this chapter is the question whether the internationalized Panels may expect the provision of legal assistance by ICTY. This assistance will essentially concern the production of evidence. As to the transfer of persons for prosecution to the Kosovo Panels, one has to take into account the legal framework of ICTY and ICTR according to which persons cannot be transferred for prosecution to other states than where they were arrested.[47] ICTY

---

had to apply again for membership (see UNSC Res 777 (1992), UNGA Res 47/1 (1992), UNSC Res 1326 (2000), and UNGA Res 55/12 (2000)).

[47] See Rule 11*bis* of the ICTY Rules of Procedure and Evidence; see also *Prosecutor v Ntuyhaga* ICTR-98-40-T, T Ch I (18 March 1999) Decision on the Prosecutor's Motion to Withdraw the Indictment in Klip/Sluiter ALC-II-106, and G Sluiter 'Comment on Declaration on a Point of Law by Judge Laïty Kama, President of the Tribunal, Judge Lennart Aspegren and Judge Navanethem Pillay, 22 April 1999' in André Klip and Göran Sluiter (eds) *Annotated Leading Cases of International Criminal Tribunals vol II The International Criminal Tribunal for Rwanda 1994 –1999* (Intersentia Antwerp 2001) 118–22.

It should be mentioned that with a view to an expeditious completion of the trials, the President of ICTY is currently exploring the possibilities for transferring criminal proceedings in a number of relatively minor cases to national courts. However, it seems that, if this were to occur, the proceedings should be transferred to the courts of the *loci delicti*, being Bosnian courts; see an interview with Claude Jorda, President of ICTY in (2002) 88 *Diplomatie Judiciaire* (August) 24–6.

has no obligation to provide any other criminal jurisdiction with legal assistance.[48] The ICTY Prosecutor, however, has repeatedly declared readiness to assist national authorities in the prosecution of crimes within ICTY's jurisdiction.[49] In particular, the evidence gathered by the ICTY Prosecutor in Kosovo could be of great value for the internationalized Panels.

E. LEGAL ASSISTANCE TO THE CAMBODIAN EXTRAORDINARY CHAMBERS AND THE SIERRA LEONEAN SPECIAL COURT

In this section it will be examined how the Cambodian Extraordinary Chambers and the Special Court for Sierra Leone can obtain the necessary legal assistance. A distinction will be made between the positions and duties of the states most concerned, Cambodia and Sierra Leone, and other states.

1. Cambodia and Sierra Leone

The Cambodian Extraordinary Chambers and the Sierra Leonean Court are the result of negotiations and agreements between the United Nations and these two states.[50] As a result, one may expect both states to cooperate fully with the Chambers and Court operating on their territories. There are, however, distinctions which may explain different cooperative attitudes. It has already been mentioned that the Sierra Leone Court Agreement was concluded at the explicit request of the UN Security Council, which puts greater obligations on Sierra Leone to cooperate, in the interest of international peace and justice. In the Cambodia situation, however, it was the Cambodian government that sought assistance of the United Nations in dealing with the atrocities committed during the rule of the Khmer Rouge.[51] As a result, Cambodia had a stronger position in the negotiation process and could even pull out of the entire project (as it did) without violating any international obligation. Since Cambodia's negotiation position is stronger than that of Sierra Leone, the result could be a weaker legal assistance regime than in the case of Sierra Leone.

Another crucial difference between the Cambodia Extraordinary Chambers and the Sierra Leone Special Court concerns their legal status. As has already been mentioned, the Special Court has separate international legal

---

[48] This lack of reciprocity is a feature of the so-called vertical cooperation relationship; see 377 ff.

[49] cf the statement by the ICTY Prosecutor following the withdrawal of the charges against 14 accused in May 1998: 'I am also prepared to provide assistance to those jurisdictions which pursue, in good faith, charges of serious violations of international humanitarian law against any of these fourteen accused': Press Release CC/PIU/314-E.

[50] In more detail on the drafting history, see Linton (*supra* n 29) 187–99, 231–3.

[51] ibid 187–8.

personality and is not part of the national court system in Sierra Leone; the Extraordinary Chambers, however, are part of the domestic court system. This need not necessarily affect the provision of assistance by Sierra Leone and Cambodia, which is regulated by the Agreements, but may have serious consequences for the provision of assistance by other states, as will be examined below.

The provision of legal assistance has been regulated by the Agreements concluded with the United Nations. In the case of Sierra Leone the Special Agreement has been implemented at the national level through the Special Court Agreement (Ratification) Act 2002.[52] This Act should also be analysed in order to better characterize and understand the legal assistance regime. Furthermore, account should be taken of the Rules of Procedure and Evidence of the Sierra Leone Court, as amended on 7 March 2003, which contain a number of provisions on state cooperation.[53]

The draft Agreement between the United Nations and Cambodia contains a separate article on legal assistance. Article 25, entitled 'Obligation to assist the co-investigating judges, the co-prosecutors and the Extraordinary Chambers', provides as follows:

The Royal Government of Cambodia shall comply without undue delay with any request for assistance by the co-investigating judges, the co-prosecutors and the Extraordinary Chambers or an order issued by any of them, including, but not limited to:

a. identification and location of persons;
b. service of documents;
c. arrest or detention of persons;
d. transfer of an indictee to the Extraordinary Chambers.

The language used in this provision seems to be modelled on the second paragraph of Article 28 of the ICTR Statute and Article 29 of the ICTY Statute.[54] One notices that, contrary to these provisions, Article 25 does not explicitly mention the taking of testimony and the production of evidence as a form of assistance. This should not necessarily be problematic for the functioning of the Extraordinary Chambers, because the forms of assistance mentioned are only illustrative. Nevertheless, explicitly mentioning the taking of testimony and the production of evidence would have been preferable.

---

[52] Special Court Agreement (Ratification) Act 2002 CXXX(II) *Sierra Leone Gazette* Supplement (7 March 2002) (hereinafter 'Ratification Act').
[53] See Rules 8–13.
[54] This paragraph reads as follows: '2. States shall comply without undue delay with any request for assistance or an order issued by a Trial Chamber, including, but not limited to: (a) the identification and location of persons; (b) the taking of testimony and the production of evidence; (c) the service of documents; (d) the arrest or detention of persons; (e) the surrender or the transfer of the accused to the International Tribunal'.

The language of Article 25 and the absence of grounds for refusal in the draft agreement appear to result in the imposition of far-reaching duties on the Cambodian authorities vis-à-vis the Extraordinary Chambers. Whether this will lead in future practice to an effective legal assistance regime remains to be seen. The cooperation relationship as set out in the draft Agreement has not adopted another crucial element of the vertical legal assistance model. There is no compulsory dispute settlement mechanism regarding the extent of the duty to provide assistance, which is vested with the requesting tribunal in a vertical legal assistance relationship.[55]

It is interesting that according to Article 2 of the Cambodian Law on the Extraordinary Chambers, the Chambers shall be established in the existing court structure. This would normally imply that these Chambers can count on the assistance of Cambodian authorities in respect of, for example, the arrest of persons and searches of houses for evidence, in the same way as any other Cambodian court. Article 25 of the draft Agreement, on the other hand, appears to be modelled on cooperation provisions between separate criminal jurisdictions. Does this mean there is no need for such a provision in this particular situation? I believe this is not the case. The provision of assistance to the Extraordinary Chambers, as part of the national court structure, may suffer from certain limitations which are unacceptable in the light of the 'internationalized' status of these Chambers. In this respect one can think of the example of immunities under Cambodian law which may hamper the arrest or taking of testimony of certain categories of persons, such as politicians and military figures. The advantage of Article 25 of the draft Agreement is that it does not take account of these limitations under national law and can serve as the legal basis for more extensive legal assistance than Cambodian authorities are required to provide to 'ordinary' national courts. The combination of Article 25 of the draft Agreement and Article 2 of the Cambodian Law offers the Extraordinary Chambers the 'best of both worlds'. As 'national courts' they can issue orders directly to national authorities, thereby choosing the most effective route to collection of evidence or arrest of persons. Furthermore, they can use their status as 'internationalized court' to ensure effective implementation of these orders.

Unlike the Cambodian Extraordinary Chambers, the Special Court for Sierra Leone is not part of the domestic court system. According to Article 1 of the Agreement between the United Nations and Sierra Leone on the Establishment of a Special Court for Sierra Leone a separate Court is established, which shall function in accordance with its Statute. The independent nature of the Court, not being part of the domestic court system, is furthermore confirmed by the Sierra Leonean Ratification Act, dealing

---

[55] cf Art 29 of the draft Agreement, which provides that disputes shall be settled by negotiation or by any other mutually agreed upon mode of settlement.

with matters such as the legal capacity and immunities of the Court in Sierra Leone. As a result, one would expect that legal assistance is to be provided to a separate criminal jurisdiction and the Special Court cannot issue orders directly to the national authorities of Sierra Leone, as ordinary national courts in Sierra Leone can do. Nevertheless, one sees that in order to ensure the Court's effective operation it has been integrated into the domestic court structure, in the sense that an order of the Special Court will have the same force or effect as if it had been issued by a judge, Magistrate or Justice of the Peace of a Sierra Leone court.[56] This is an interesting difference from the legal assistance regimes of ICTY and ICTR. These tribunals can also issue requests and orders for assistance. However, in that context, there is no legal distinction between them, in that they both create legal obligations for states, which remain free in choosing means and methods for their implementation.[57] In the Ratification Act a legal distinction between orders and requests has been made. A request for assistance is to be made to the Attorney-General of Sierra Leone, who then bears responsibility for its implementation.[58] A request for assistance entails obligations for the state. An order, on the other hand, has direct effect within the Sierra Leonean legal order, and the same legal status as a domestic court order.[59] It thus entails in principle direct obligations for individuals, companies or specific state authorities.

The above legal distinction between requests and orders, as made in the Ratification Act, is highly beneficial to effective assistance to the Special Court. The latter has always two available options to obtain the desired result: the indirect way, by issuing a request for assistance to the Attorney-General, or the direct way, by issuing a direct order to, for example, a local police officer. The latter avenue appears to be most attractive. However, one can also imagine situations of urgency in which the Court decides to exploit both avenues simultaneously.

The exercise of concurrent jurisdiction between the Special Court and the national courts of Sierra Leone is governed by Article 8 of the Special Court's Statute, as further implemented through Rules 9, 10, and 11 of the Court. Article 8 of the Statute contains almost identical language as Article 8 of the ICTR Statute and Article 9 of the ICTY Statute. As a result, the Special Court has primacy over national courts in Sierra Leone. These courts must at the request of the Special Court defer to its competence.

---

[56] See Art 20 of the Ratification Act. See also Rule 8(A) confirming this: 'An order issued by a Judge or Chamber shall have the same force or effect as if issued by a Judge, Magistrate or Justice of the Peace of a Sierra Leone Court.'

[57] One exception is that under strict circumstances orders from ICTY and ICTR can impose direct obligations for individuals; see n 64. For more detail, see Sluiter (*supra* n 7) 75–9, 147–50.

[58] See arts 15 and 16 of the Ratification Act.

[59] See ibid art 20.

The provision of legal assistance is not addressed in the Statute, but has been regulated in the Agreement between the United Nations and Sierra Leone.[60] However, in the Rules of Procedure and Evidence reference is made to the obligations flowing from the Agreement.[61] Article 17 of the Agreement is modelled on Article 28 of the ICTR Statute and Article 29 of the ICTY Statute[62] and reads as follows:

Cooperation with the Special Court
1. The Government shall cooperate with all organs of the Special Court at all stages of the proceedings. It shall, in particular, facilitate access to the Prosecutor to sites, persons and relevant documents required for the investigation.
2. The Government shall comply without undue delay with any request for assistance by the Special Court or an order issued by the Chambers, including, but not limited to:

   (a) Identification and location of persons;
   (b) Service of documents;
   (c) Arrest or detention of persons;
   (d) Transfer of an indictee to the Court.

A crucial difference with respect to Article 28(1) of the ICTR Statute and Article 29(1) of the ICTY Statute is that Article 17(1) explicitly obliges Sierra Leone to facilitate the conduct of onsite investigations by the Prosecutor. This provision was included in the United Nations–Sierra Leone Agreement on the basis of the experience of ICTY and ICTR, which demonstrated that onsite investigations are of vital importance with a view to effective and fair prosecution.[63] However, such a provision appears redundant. Pursuant to Article 17(1) of the Agreement Sierra Leone has to cooperate with the Special Court in the lawful exercise of its powers. The power to conduct onsite investigations has been attributed to the Prosecutor by Article 15(2) of the Statute, which also mentions the duty incumbent on Sierra Leone to assist the Prosecutor, as appropriate.

Article 17 of the Agreement lays the foundation for an effective legal assistance regime, even if it cannot be regarded as truly vertical in nature, because there is no compulsory dispute settlement mechanism regarding cooperation disputes.[64] Be this as it may, it follows from the Rules of the Court that non-compliance with requests will not be accepted. Rule 8(B)

---

[60] Agreement between the United Nations and the Government of Sierra Leone on the Establishment of a Special Court for Sierra Leone (16 January 2002).

[61] See Rule 8(A) and (E).

[62] For an analysis of the extent of the duty to cooperate under these provisions, see Sluiter (*supra* n 7) 145–55.

[63] See ibid 303–4.

[64] See Art 19 of the Agreement:

'Any dispute between the Parties concerning the interpretation or application of this Agreement shall be settled by negotiation, or by any other mutually agreed-upon mode of settlement'.

stipulates that after a judicial finding of non-cooperation the matter may be referred to the President to take appropriate action. The question arises as to what could constitute 'appropriate action'. Ultimately, the use of Article 20 of the Agreement, dealing with settlement of disputes, could be triggered via the Court's President.

The Court's Rules have already been mentioned. They may play an important additional role in underlining and making maximum use of the cooperation obligations imposed on Sierra Leone. Rule 8, for example, confirms the obligation to comply with both requests and orders from the Court. The possibility of amending and inserting new Rules offers the judges the advantages of shaping a considerable part of the cooperation relationship. Although the judges may not act ultra vires the Statute, the experiences with ICTR and ICTY demonstrate that there still is considerable room to adopt rules enhancing effective legal assistance.[65]

As an example of a Rule with great potential in the field of legal assistance one could mention Rule 54 which reads as follows:

At the request of either party or of its own motion, a Judge or a Trial Chamber may issue such orders, summonses, subpoenas, warrants and transfer orders as may be necessary for the purposes of an investigation or for the preparation or conduct of the trial.

Taking account of the ICTY and ICTR context, in which there is an almost identical Rule 54, this Rule could be used as an important legal basis to issue requests or orders for assistance for the benefit of the defendant. Indeed, because the defendant is not an organ of the Court, Sierra Leonean authorities are not bound by the provision of Article 17 of the Agreement in relation to the defendant. However, by relying on Rule 54, the defence can invoke the assistance of a judge or Chamber with a view to the collection of evidence or the conduct of onsite investigations. Sierra Leone is pursuant to Article 17 under an obligation to give effect to orders issued by judges. Furthermore, Rule 54 may also be used to issue orders directly to individuals on the territory of Sierra Leone.[66] Case law of ICTY has established that, exceptionally, ICTY may directly issue orders to individuals, which create binding obligations for them.[67]

---

[65] See Sluiter (*supra* n 7) 344.
[66] I believe that the issuance of orders having effect in other states would amount to unlawful intervention in those states, since they are not parties to the Agreement establishing the Special Court.
[67] See also art 21 of the Ratification Act and Rule 8(A), clearly confirming this possibility. The duties for witnesses to comply with orders to appear issued by judges of ICTY has been established in *Prosecutor v Blaskic* IT-95-14-AR108bis A Ch (29 October 1997) Judgment on the Request of the Republic of Croatia for Review of the Decision of Trial Chamber II of 18 July 1997 in Klip/Sluiter ALC-I-245.

While the combination of Article 17 of the Agreement and the Court's Rules of Procedure and Evidence endows the Special Court with a potentially effective cooperation regime vis-à-vis Sierra Leone, it remains to be seen to what extent the Special Court will exploit it.

In this light, it is to be regretted that the Agreement and Statute do not contain any mechanism to enforce the duty incumbent on Sierra Leone to provide assistance. It has already been mentioned that Article 20 of the Agreement, regarding the settlement of disputes, is rather weak. Given the fact that the Security Council has been instrumental in the establishment of the Special Court, and has welcomed the conclusion of the Agreement,[68] one may have expected the Security Council to continue playing a role in the implementation of the Agreement. There is, however, no possibility of referring violations of the duty to cooperate to the Security Council, neither under the Agreement nor under the Statute. However, mention has already been made of Rule 8(B) which allows the Court's President to take 'appropriate action' in situations of non-cooperation. Nothing seems to prevent the President from submitting situations of non-cooperation to the Security Council, bearing in mind that organ's involvement in and support for the Sierra Leone Court.[69] It will then be up to the Council to decide whether it wishes to respond.

2. Other states

The question arises here also as to how the Extraordinary Chambers and the Special Court can obtain the legal assistance of states other than Cambodia and Sierra Leone, in particular neighbouring states.

It is a fundamental rule of international law that treaties can only impose obligations on their parties.[70] Therefore, other states cannot be obliged to provide assistance on the basis of the bilateral Agreements with Cambodia and Sierra Leone. With respect to the Sierra Leone Court recent Security Council Resolutions might be used as a legal basis for an obligation to provide assistance, in relation to all UN Member States. It has already been mentioned that in Resolution 1470 (2003) the Security Council 'urges all States to cooperate fully with the Court'. Furthermore, in the preamble to Resolution 1478 (2003) the Security Council called 'on all States, in particular the Government of Liberia, to cooperate fully with the Special Court'. The question arises as to what the consequences are of the duty to cooperate for states other than Cambodia and Sierra Leone. The central question is whether 'urges' and 'calling on' can be seen as decisions in the sense of Article

---

[68] See UNSC Res 1400 (2002), operative para 9.

[69] Again see UNSC Res 1470 (2003), operative para 11.

[70] This rule is known by the Latin maxim of *pacta tertiis nec nocent nec prosunt*, and has been codified in Art 34 of the Vienna Convention on the Law of Treaties (1969).

25 of the UN Charter. These interpretative exercises in relation to Security Council Resolutions are always highly problematic; it is difficult to consider language such as 'urges' and 'calling' as decisions in the sense of Article 25.[71] The language is in any event falling short of the unequivocal language used in Resolutions 827 (1993) and 955 (1994) in relation to ICTY and ICTR, which without any doubt qualify as decisions in the sense of Article 25. As a result, a clear duty under the UN Charter for all UN Member States to provide legal assistance to the Sierra Leone Court may not be too easily assumed. This is not to say the aforementioned Resolutions 1470 and 1478 are without any legal effect. The principle of *Organisationstreue*, meaning that states should behave as loyal members, set out in Article 2(2) of the UN Charter, entails that UN Member States should respond 'benevolently' to requests from the Sierra Leone Court, in as much as possible.

Given the above analysis, it could be of help if the internationalized tribunals could make use of the legal assistance agreements that Cambodia and Sierra Leone have concluded with other states. One should, however, not expect too much of this, because both states have hardly concluded agreements in this field.[72] It is nevertheless worth exploring the matter, since certain forms of assistance could be provided in the absence of a treaty. Furthermore, it is not excluded that ad hoc cooperation agreements are concluded with certain states, with a view to assisting the Extraordinary Chambers and the Special Court.

In the Cambodian situation the Extraordinary Chambers could order the Cambodian government to request, for example, the extradition of an accused in a neighbouring state. It could be argued that the duty to transmit the request through existing extradition channels falls within the scope of Article 23 of the draft MOU. It would, however, in my view exceed the scope

---

[71] See in this sense, E Suy 'Article 25' in Jean-Pierre Cot and Allain Pellet (eds) *La Charte des Nations Unies: Commentaire article par article* (Economica Paris 1991) 476.

[72] Cambodia is, to my knowledge, not a party to any multilateral or bilateral legal assistance treaty. As to Sierra Leone, this country is part of the Commonwealth and could therefore make use of Commonwealth Schemes in the field of legal assistance (eg, Scheme Relating to the Rendition of Fugitive Offenders Within the Commonwealth, London, 3 April 1996, also referred to as the Commonwealth Extradition Scheme). This potentially results in legal assistance relationships with a considerable number of states. However, one of the problems of these so-called Schemes is that they do not create binding obligations for the Commonwealth states; they rather represent an agreed set of recommendations for legislative implementation by each government (see David McClean *International Judicial Assistance* (Clarendon Press Oxford 1992) 151). Besides the Commonwealth Schemes, Sierra Leone is a party to two rather old Extradition Treaties with the United States and Liberia (Bilateral Extradition Treaty with the United States, signed on 22 December 1931 and entered into force on 24 June 1935, 47 Stat 2122; the Court of Appeal of Sierra Leone in *Lansana v R* (1971) 70 Int'l Rep 2 found that Sierra Leone had succeeded to the Anglo-Liberian Extradition Treaty of 1894 due to a mutual exchange of letters between the two countries). Finally, one should mention that the legal assistance treaties which have been elaborated in the framework of the Economic Community of West African States, of which Sierra Leone is a member, have not entered into force.

of application of this provision to require the Cambodian authorities to negotiate extradition arrangements where these are not already in place. Whether or not the requested third state is prepared to satisfy the request depends on a number of factors, including the nature of the cooperation relationship, if existent. An advantage of the Cambodian situation is that the rule of speciality, as contained in practically every extradition treaty,[73] does not apply here, because the Extraordinary Chambers are part of the Cambodian court structure. This, however, also entails an important disadvantage. The Extraordinary Chambers, being part of the Cambodian court system, have no international legal personality and cannot enter into (ad hoc) cooperation arrangements with states. It is thus entirely in the hands of the Cambodian government to what extent they are prepared to seek the (ad hoc) provision of assistance by third states.

The Special Court for Sierra Leone is in a far better position in this respect. It has international legal personality. Article 11(d) of the Agreement between Sierra Leone and the United Nations endows it explicitly with the juridical capacity to '[e]nter into agreements with States as may be necessary for the exercise of its functions and for the operation of the Court'. This provision clearly envisages the conclusion of ad hoc cooperation agreements with third states.[74] Whether or not these states are prepared to enter into such agreements and what will be their content is a matter of speculation at this moment. One might expect that the role of the Security Council in the establishment of the Special Court may give it a certain authority when seeking to obtain the assistance of third states. Yet, there is no obligation under international law for any State other than Sierra Leone to provide assistance to the Special Court.[75]

In this respect the question arises as to whether the Special Court may make use of the existing legal assistance treaties between Sierra Leone and other states. The difficulty may be that other states generally only provide assistance in relation to proceedings in Sierra Leonean courts, which do not include the Special Court. It has already been mentioned that re-extradition by a Sierra Leonean national court to the Special Court is in violation of the rule of speciality and furthermore amounts to a disguised extradition, which is considered to be in violation of internationally protected human rights. One could try to solve this problem by considering the Special Court part of the Sierra Leonean legal order, for the purpose of extradition. There is indeed

---

[73] According to this rule, an extradited person cannot be re-extradited to a third state; see, as an example, Art 14 of the UN Model Treaty on Extradition, UNGA Res 45/116 (1990) (14 December 1990).

[74] cf Art 87(5) of the ICC Statute, providing for the possibility of conclusion of similar agreements with states non-parties to the ICC Statute.

[75] The situation could, however, arise that a state could only live up to its *aut dedere aut iudicare* obligation by extraditing an individual to Sierra Leone.

a difference between Sierra Leone re-extraditing an individual to Liberia or to a Special Court which is operating on its territory, applying part of its law and being composed (in part) of its nationals.

In sum, although the Special Court cannot make use of the existing legal assistance relationships between Sierra Leone and other states, it has the power to enter into ad hoc cooperation arrangements with every state in the world. This is a clear advantage over the proposed Extraordinary Chambers. In a practical sense this means that whereas persons suspected by the Extraordinary Chambers may easily evade arrest by choosing states that do not maintain legal assistance relations with Cambodia, persons indicted by the Special Court may always be the object of an ad hoc cooperation arrangement, wherever they may reside.

F. CONCLUSION

I have tried above to address the question how the internationalized tribunals can obtain the necessary assistance and what the duties, if any, of states are in this respect. The foregoing analysis made clear that the outlook is bleak. It has been argued that, given the mandates of the internationalized tribunals and the support and participation, to varying degree, of the United Nations in these endeavours there is reason to adopt legal assistance models that are more than horizontal, but not necessarily vertical. With respect to the states most concerned, rather far-reaching duties to provide assistance have come into existence for the Federal Republic of Yugoslavia, Cambodia, and Sierra Leone. Compared to them, the duties incumbent upon Indonesia are fairly limited.

As far as third states are concerned, one can fairly conclude that they are under no obligation at all to assist the internationalized criminal tribunals *as such*. In the case of internationalized tribunals which owe their establishment to the participation and support of the United Nations this is a rather unsatisfactory situation. In particular, where the internationalized criminal tribunals owe their establishment either directly or indirectly to the UN Security Council, the imposition of a duty to cooperate for UN Member States would, with a view to preserving international peace and security, seem to be a feasible and logical choice.

The central question is whether the legal assistance regimes as analysed above will enable the internationalized criminal tribunals to fulfil their mandates. It is fair to say that the cooperation regimes of the internationalized tribunals are all based on the assumption that accused persons and evidence (witnesses, documents etc) can be located in the region. This explains the focus of the legal assistance regimes on the states most concerned, being neighbouring states or the state where the internationalized tribunal performs its functions. This assumption may be true to some degree. However, it apparently accepts the fact that it is not difficult for indicted persons, especially those with considerable resources, to remain beyond the reach of the internationalized criminal tribunals. One must therefore fear that the latter will not be in a position to fulfil their mandates satisfactorily.

18

Some Tentative Remarks on the Relationship Between Internationalized Criminal Jurisdictions and the International Criminal Court

Markus Benzing* and Morten Bergsmo**

A. INTRODUCTION

The present chapter is designed to identify preliminary issues and possible difficulties in the relationship between the International Criminal Court (ICC) and internationalized criminal jurisdictions, from a viewpoint of policy, law, and practical aspects. Although all of the hybrid jurisdictions presently operating or about to start operation in the near future are concerned with crimes that occurred before the entry into force of the Rome Statute[1] and a conflict between these institutions and the ICC would not seem to be possible, given that its jurisdiction *ratione tempore* does not reach further back than 1 July 2002, such courts may serve as models for future hybrid tribunals.[2] Questions concerning the relationship between the ICC and such possible future courts could arise in connection with (a) an assessment of the efficacy, viability or independence of such jurisdictions; (b) a consideration of how multiple hybrid tribunals could affect the ICC's aspiration to be a permanent, universal institution; (c) possible future cooperation between the ICC and such jurisdictions; and (d) in connection with the complementarity regime of ICC.

* Markus Benzing is a former Consultant in the Office of the Prosecutor, International Criminal Court. He presently works as a Junior Research Fellow for the Max Planck Institute for Comparative Public Law and International Law, Heidelberg.

** Morten Bergsmo, Senior Legal Adviser and Chief of the Legal Advisory Section, Office of the Prosecutor, International Criminal Court. The views expressed in this article are those of the authors and are not necessarily shared by the ICC Office of the Prosecutor.

[1] In Sierra Leone, the hostilities did not completely subside until early 2002, in Kosovo and in East Timor in 1999. In the case of Cambodia, the crimes in question date back to a period between 1975 and 1979.

[2] cf. LA Dickinson 'Transitional Justice in Afghanistan: The Promise of Mixed Tribunals' (2002) 31 *Denver J Int'l Law and Policy* 23.

B. INTERNATIONALIZED COURTS AND THE ICC: COOPERATION OR JURISDICTIONAL CONFLICT? SOME CONSIDERATIONS

1. The limited scope of action of the ICC

The ICC is the first permanent criminal court with jurisdiction over the most serious crimes of concern to the international community as a whole. As stated in the Preamble to the Rome Statute, a primary reason for establishing the ICC was to put an end to impunity for the perpetrators of these crimes and to contribute to their prevention. However, even though the ICC is mandated to achieve these goals, the Preamble expressly acknowledges the obvious fact that the Court will not be in a position to accomplish this objective in isolation: it affirms that the effective investigation and prosecution of such crimes must be ensured by taking measures at the national level and by enhancing international cooperation, 'recalling' that it is the duty of every state to exercise its criminal jurisdiction over those responsible for international crimes.

This acknowledgement of the limited scope of the ICC's activities has fundamental legal and practical reasons. First, the jurisdiction of the Court is limited in multiple ways. As far as the jurisdiction *ratione materiae* is concerned, the Court is limited to adjudicating over the most serious crimes. Its jurisdiction *ratione temporis* only exists with a view to crimes committed after 1 July 2002. Also, as of May 2004 only 94 states have become parties to the Rome Statute, which necessarily restricts its jurisdictional reach (jurisdiction *ratione loci* and *personae*). Moreover, states which could predictably become territorial states (where relevant crimes occur) are less likely to become states parties in the reasonably near future,[3] so that the objective identified by the Preamble to the Rome Statute may become frustrated for lack of jurisdiction of the Court in many instances.

In addition to its limited jurisdiction, the ICC was given a deliberately restrictive admissibility regime. According to the all-important principle of complementarity, the Court will only be able to commence proceedings where relevant states are not investigating or prosecuting the alleged international crimes, or where they purport to do so but in reality are unwilling or unable to genuinely carry out proceedings (article 17 of the Rome Statute).

Apart from these legal thresholds to the operation of the Court, there are considerable practical limitations on the work of the ICC: due to its limited resources, and since it is not per se restricted in its operation to only one conflict region,[4] the Court will not be in a position to judicially process all

---

[3] William W Burke-White 'A Community of Courts: Toward a System of International Criminal Law Enforcement' (2002) 24 *Michigan J Int'l Law* 1 at 8.

[4] As opposed to the two ad hoc tribunals.

conflicts and situations in which crimes under the jurisdiction of the Court have been or are being committed. The reality is such that 'work' (*horribile dictu*) regrettably seems to exist in abundance for both the ICC and national courts in the foreseeable future. The issue at hand is how internationalized courts can fit into the picture, and whether and how these courts can be utilized to help render criminal justice in a timely, efficient, and consistent manner.

The Rome Statute itself provides in its Preamble, as remarked earlier, that the main responsibility for the investigation and prosecution of crimes under the ICC's jurisdiction lies with states. It thus seems that if states avail themselves of the possibility to discharge their duties with the help of the international community, specifically the United Nations with regard to the management of their criminal justice system, and more specifically by cooperating with the United Nations within the framework of internationalized courts, then this is entirely in accordance with the object and purpose of the Rome Statute.

2. Possible advantages of and concerns about internationalized jurisdictions

I. Possible advantages of internationalized jurisdictions

Ad hoc internationalized jurisdictions *strictu sensu*—depending on their organization, procedures and management—generally have the potential to involve and draw upon the expertise of the local legal community in the territorial state(s). They are proximate to the events in question and thus may have reasonably immediate access to relevant potential evidence. The experience of the two ad hoc tribunals has made it clear that parts of the population of the countries in which crimes occurred can easily be made to feel estranged from a tribunal that is perceived to be far away, operating in a language not widely spoken in the country where the crimes occurred, with a panel of judges from foreign countries, and may come to consider it biased or engaged in 'victor's justice'. At times professing such a perception, authorities in territorial states have been reluctant to cooperate fully with for example the ICTY. The ICC, as a permanent international criminal court, could possibly be criticized in a similar way. Even though the Rome Statute allows for the Court to sit at any other place than its normal seat (articles 3(3) and 62), its standard field of operation is likely to be The Hague.

However, two differences should be highlighted. First, due to its jurisdictional regime, the ICC can only exercise its jurisdiction where the person allegedly having committed the crimes is a national of a State Party, or where the crimes have occurred on the territory of a State Party, for crimes committed *after* the coming into force of the Rome Statute. Thus, the competence of the Court would have been established in advance, precluding the argument that an international forum was imposed on a country against its will and consent after the commission of alleged crimes. Furthermore, its permanence and the fact that its jurisdiction is not limited to one conflict or country gives the ICC stronger immunity against the reproach of having been established selectively and arbitrarily for one specific situation.

However, it is never difficult for leaders to create doubts and scepticism. It can easily be imagined that other forms of ad hoc internationalized jurisdictions may be more readily accepted by local communities in the territorial state(s). The concept of establishing ad hoc internationalized jurisdictions *strictu sensu* thus potentially combines legitimacy and credibility vis-à-vis the international community and legitimacy and acceptance by the domestic audience,[5] although it should be noted that such legitimacy will largely depend on a sound balance between international and national 'elements'. Furthermore, the states concerned may be more willing to agree with international involvement in the form of ad hoc internationalized jurisdictions *strictu sensu* than wholly international institutions since they can be perceived as less 'intrusive' and preserve national sovereignty to a greater extent than a completely international criminal tribunal.

Internationalized jurisdictions *strictu sensu* can easily contribute to institution-building in a situation of transition by involving and training local legal experts who stay on after the court's work is done.[6] Such institution-building is more difficult from afar. Its importance is however, readily recognized under the complementarity regime of the Rome Statute.[7] The ICC is able to receive prosecutors, investigators, military lawyers and others to serve as Visiting Professionals in the Office of the Prosecutor and thus share its expertise and, at the same time, foster understanding of human rights standards applicable during the investigative and trial processes.

II. Possible concerns about internationalized jurisdictions

As mentioned, the ICC has been set up as a permanent institution. It will gather experience and accumulate expertise over time, which will lead to greater consistency in its jurisprudence than other internationalized criminal jurisdictions will be able to attain. There is a danger that the governing instruments of other internationalized courts will be diverging from or even be inconsistent with the Rome Statute and/or that the jurisprudence of the

---

[5] Suzannah Linton 'Cambodia, East Timor and Sierra Leone: Experiments in International Justice' (2001) 23 *Criminal Law Forum* 185 at 245; Robert Cryer 'A "Special Court" for Sierra Leone?' (2001) 50 *Int'l and Comp LQ* 435 at 446; Burke-White (*supra* n 3) at 24.

[6] Suzannah Linton 'New Approaches to International Justice in Cambodia and East Timor' (2002) 84 *Int'l Rev of the Red Cross* 93 at 113.

[7] Policy Paper of the Office of the Prosecutor of the International Criminal Court.

courts established thereby may differ substantially.[8] It would be preferable to ensure consistent interpretation and application of international criminal law. The ICC may serve this interest through its activities, in particular by adjudicating and setting international precedents which may be used as guidelines in other jurisdictions.

Furthermore, the procedure before the ICC is designed to guarantee a high standard of fair trial to the accused. It is imperative that other internationalized courts adhere to the same due process guarantees.

Finally, it is assumed that the ICC will be able to operate and plan its work on a firm financial basis, ensuring a high degree of independence. That is essential.[9] Some of the ad hoc internationalized jurisdictions have had problems with their funding. Such problems can affect the entire legitmacy and legacy of a jurisdiction.

C. INTERNATIONALIZED COURTS AND THE COMPLEMENTARITY PRINCIPLE OF THE ROME STATUTE

Apart from the aforementioned policy considerations, the relationship between the ICC and other internationalized courts also raises legal questions. The ICC, as opposed to the ad hoc fully international tribunals, such as the ICTY and ICTR, does not have primacy over national jurisdictions. There does not seem to be an hierarchical structure in the emerging international criminal justice system.

The relationship between the ICC and national jurisdictions is governed by the principle of complementarity which determines that a case is not admissible before the Court if a state fulfils its duty genuinely to investigate and/or prosecute international crimes (article 17 of the Rome Statute). From its express text, article 17 only envisages national rather than internationalized jurisdictions: article 17(1)(a) and (b) speak of investigation and prosecution 'by a State' which has jurisdiction over a case; article 17(2)(a) refers to a 'national decision'; and article 17(3) to a 'national judicial system'. Can an internationalized court be regarded as a 'national court' for the purposes of article 17? Would it be relevant if a majority of judges on the panel were international? Would it matter that the court is funded in part or in whole by the international community or by foreign states? And finally, is it relevant how exactly the internationalized legal entity was created? Would it be

---

[8] Cesare P Romano and Théo Boutruche 'Tribunaux pénaux internationalisés: état des lieux d'une justice "hybride" ' (2003) 107 *Revue générale de droit international public* 107 at 124.

[9] Payam Akhavan, 'Beyond impunity: can international criminal justice prevent future atrocities?' (2001) 95 *AJIL* 7, at 30; Beth K Dougherty, 'Right-sizing international criminal justice: the hybrid experiment at the Special Court for Sierra Leone' (2004) 80 *International Affairs* 311.

correct to equate a hybrid tribunal with a national court for the purpose of article 17 where it was created through the efforts of a representative of the UN Secretary-General, who in turn derives his authority from a UN Security Council resolution under Chapter VII of the UN Charter?

The answer depends on the interpretation of article 17 of the Rome Statute. As already mentioned, the Rome Statute, as encapsulated specifically in the complementarity principle, relies primarily on the states themselves to prosecute international crimes. The underlying reasons may not be limited to a concern to preserve state sovereignty to the extent possible, but may also include a recognition that prosecution of severe crimes, for reasons stated above, is generally best implemented in the territorial state.

One could possibly say that from a narrow textual point of view it is doubtful whether internationalized courts in general can be deemed 'national' under article 17. Even though internationalized courts *per definitionem* have some national elements, 'national' in article 17 could of course be interpreted to mean 'fully national'. The text is however, too ambiguous to make that a viable interpretation. Some national involvement should suffice.

A teleological interpretation of article 17—consistent with article 31(1) of the Vienna Convention of the Law of Treaties—would seem to support the conclusion that internationalized courts generally can be subsumed under the term 'national': one of the primary objectives behind the creation of the ICC is to avoid or put an end to impunity. Article 17 recognizes this in that it enables the ICC to proceed where states are not able or willing to fulfil this objective. Since internationalized jurisdictions *strictu sensu* are designed to assist states in attaining exactly that objective, it is reasonable to regard them as 'national courts' or belonging to a 'national judicial system' for the purposes of article 17. Even though some internationalized jurisdictions, such as the ones in East Timor and Kosovo, were not co-created by the states concerned, but rather are the product of international initiative and derive their authority from the international level, it is reasonable to say in the light of the above rationale that the mere involvement of the state in the *operation*, rather than its setting-up, may be sufficient for deeming it a national court for the purpose of article 17. Tribunals set up by way of an agreement with the United Nations undoubtedly are covered by the norm according to the interpretation given above. This, at first glance, may seem to be problematic where the agreement setting up the court in question specifically provides that it is not to be considered part of the national judiciary and where the court in question has expressly determined that it is an 'international criminal court'.[10] However, this characterization for the purposes of domestic and

---

[10] Special Court Agreement Ratification Act 2002 s 11(2), reprinted in: R Dixon, KAA Khan, and R May *Archbold on International Criminal Courts* (Sweet & Maxwell 2003) 1189 et seq. Special Court for Sierra Leone, Decision on Immunity from Jurisdiction, *Prosecutor v Charles Ghankay Taylor* (Case No SCSL-2003-01-AR72(E)), 31 May 2004, available at www.sc-sl.org.

general international law (in the case cited, the question of immunity for heads of state) does not necessarily influence the result found, given the object and purpose of the complementarity principle.

If one accepts that a state can discharge its duty to investigate and prosecute by resorting to internationalized jurisdictions, the full complementarity regime must be applicable. In other words, the work of the internationalized jurisdiction remains under the scrutiny of the ICC. If it proves to be unable or unwilling genuinely to investigate or prosecute by, for example, shielding the perpetrators from criminal responsibility, the ICC has to be able to step in. A situation like this may be improbable, but it is not entirely impossible, especially in situations where national judges constitute the majority on the panel of an internationalized jurisdiction.[11]

D. THE ROLE OF THE ICC IN 'INTERNATIONALIZING' NATIONAL COURTS AND IN 'SUPERVISING' INTERNATIONALIZED COURTS

1. 'Internationalizing' national courts

'Internationalizing' national courts may mean setting standards for national courts on the international level which they may use as guidance or persuasive authority. Since the ICC does not have any authority to intervene directly in proceedings before national courts as such, the role of the Court will be limited to indirect influence. However, the forms such indirect influence can take are manifold and should not be underestimated.

First, the jurisprudence of the Court in relation to substantive law, including modes of liability, evidentiary and procedural questions, may be taken into consideration and followed by national courts. Such influence can already be seen in the references of national courts to the jurisprudence of the ad hoc tribunals.[12] 'Nationalized' international crimes (that is, international crimes that have been incorporated into national systems, in particular after the adoption of the Rome Statute) thus retain their international character in that they are applied with regard to international jurisprudence. This phenomenon also demonstrates that national and international jurisdictions are interdependent and cross-fertilize each other.[13]

Secondly, influence may be exerted by the ICC through its interpretation of article 17. The Court will contribute to a clarification of the exact scope of the states' duty to investigate and prosecute crimes under the Statute by defining unwillingness and inability, in particular the terms 'for the purpose

---

[11] eg. in Cambodia, cf David Boyle 'Une juridiction hybride chargée de juger les Khmer Rouge' (www.droits-fondamentaux.org/ download/boydcam.pdf).

[12] As an example, cf. the decision of the German Federal Constitutional Court (Bundesverfassungsgericht) of 12 December 2000 (reprinted in *Neue Juristische Wochenschrift* 2001, 1848).

[13] ICTY, for instance, in turn frequently relies on national jurisprudence.

of shielding the person concerned from criminal responsibility' (article 17(2)(a)), 'unjustified delay in the proceedings' (article 17(2)(b)) and 'proceedings [that] were not conducted independently or impartially' (article 17(2)(c)). It will in particular have to determine how far a more or less exact incorporation of the crimes and modes of liability under the Rome Statute into national law is required in order to satisfy the standard of ability genuinely to investigate and prosecute. Equally, it will influence the standards of 'due diligence' in the national prosecution of international crimes.

Thirdly, the establishment and commencement of the operation of the ICC will introduce what could be called the 'embarrassment factor': states will generally seek to avoid the possibility of the Court opening an investigation after the preliminary examination (article 15) or evaluation (article 53(1) and rule 104 of the Rules of Procedure and Evidence) of a situation has been concluded so as not to be seen to be in breach of their duties. The standards set on the international level as regards the investigation and prosecution of international crimes will thus be closely watched and possibly transformed into the national system within the margin of appreciation that the complementarity regime of the Court is likely to give states in their investigative and prosecutorial activities.

2. *'Supervising' internationalized jurisdictions?*

It is questionable whether the ICC can exercise a supervisory role vis-à-vis internationalized jurisdictions *strictu sensu*. However, as already pointed out, the Court will have to examine closely the activities and proceedings of such jurisdictions from the viewpoint of article 17 (unwillingness/inability), to the same extent as with regular national courts.

Along the lines of what has been suggested with regard to the supporting role the ICC may fulfil vis-à-vis national authorities, the Court may well cooperate with internationalized jurisdictions in various ways, including training, exchanging personnel, and generally making its expertise available to these jurisdictions. In this way, the ICC could contribute to what has been called 'a standby network of international lawyers', ready to help out and cooperate with countries in transition,[14] for example by keeping a roster of and training qualified lawyers and by exchange of personnel. The Policy Paper of the Office of the Prosecutor of the ICC envisages cooperation with national prosecution authorities; nothing speaks against an equal treatment of internationalized jurisdictions.

Another question—beyond the scope of this section—is which form this cooperation between the ICC and the respective internationalized jurisdiction

---

[14] Hans-Jörg Strohmeyer 'Collapse and Reconstruction of a Judicial System: The United Nations Missions in Kosovo and East Timor' (2001) 95 *American J Int'l Law* 46 at 61.

should take. It could either be informal or formalized, for instance by way of an agreement concluded with the Court as a whole or different organs.[15]

E. CONCLUDING REMARKS

Considering the number of conflicts in the world today, it is hard to imagine that the ICC will make ad hoc internationalized jurisdictions *strictu sensu* obsolete. As a relatively new type of actor in the investigation and prosecution of international crimes, they still have to prove their effectiveness and practicability; much of their success will depend on whether they are able to bring justice to war-torn countries in a timely manner, with due regard to the rights of the accused and a high-quality standard in their jurisprudence. However, the practical difficulties they could encounter are manifold. Legal hurdles such as that which faced the Special Court for Sierra Leone regarding the indictment of the former Liberian President Charles Taylor are difficult to overcome and may prove to limit the scope of action of such courts significantly.[16]

The limits of the jurisdictional reach of the ICC suggest that there may be a role for internationalized jurisdictions *strictu sensu*, maybe an even greater role in the future than at present.[17] Some would even argue that the very effectiveness of the ICC depends to a large extend on its being part of a larger system of international criminal law enforcement, also comprising internationalized jurisdictions.[18] Even in situations where the ICC does have jurisdiction and decides to act, its limited resources will only allow for the prosecution of the gravest crimes and the high-level perpetrators.[19] As an

---

[15] Article 4(2) of the Rome Statute provides that 'the Court shall also have such legal capacity as may be necessary for the exercise of its functions and the fulfilment of its purposes'. Putting an end to impunity may be considered such a purpose; arguably, the Court thus has the power to enter into agreements with internationalized courts.

[16] The Special Court for Sierra Leone only has primacy over the national courts of Sierra Leone (article 8(2) of the Statute of the Special Court). The treaty establishing the Special Court was concluded between the United Nations and Sierra Leone, and is thus not binding on third parties (cf. article 34 of the Vienna Convention on the Law of Treaties). The clause providing that the official position of any accused, even as Head of State or Government, shall not relieve such person from criminal responsibility or mitigate punishment (article 6(2)) can thus not be applied against non-parties. Consequently, and in the light of the arguments of the International Court of Justice in *Democratic Republic of Congo v Belgium* (Case Concerning the Arrest Warrant of 11 April 2000) (14 February 2002), Liberia brought a case to ICJ seeking a declaration that the issue of the indictment and the arrest warrant against President Charles Taylor failed to respect the immunity from criminal jurisdiction of a Head of State (ICJ Press Release 2003-26 (5 August 2003) (www.icj-cij.org/icjwww/ipresscom/ ipress2003/ipresscom2003-26_lsl_20030805.htm).

[17] Sylvia de Bertodano 'Current Developments in Internationalized Courts' (2003) 1 *J Int'l Criminal Justice* 226 at 244.

[18] Burke-White (*supra* n 3) at 11.

[19] cf. Draft Policy Paper of the Office of the Prosecutor of the International Criminal Court; Micaela Frulli 'The Special Court for Sierra Leone: Some Preliminary Comments' (2000) 11 *European J Int'l L* 857 at 869.

alternative to handing over the prosecution of lower-level perpetrators to the national judicial system as such, a cooperative approach taken by the international community (in the form of internationalized jurisdictions) may be beneficial to putting an end to impunity, especially in situations after an extended period of civil war where the domestic justice system has to be largely reconstructed.[20]

Internationalized jurisdictions may be particularly appropriate in the following situations: (1) the ICC does not have jurisdiction *ratione personae, temporis, materiae* or *loci*; (2) the ICC is entangled in resource-intensive and protracted investigations and prosecutions and consequently may not be able to take on another situation; (3) the ICC is seized of a situation but, with its limited resources, may only be able to deal with the perpetrators of the highest level; (4) for reasons of institution-building, the creation of a 'hybrid' jurisdiction seems beneficial to the country's future development.

In all scenarios, it would be preferable to harmonize to the greatest extent possible the instruments establishing internationalized jurisdictions, in particular in the area of the definition of crimes, with a view to preventing inconsistencies.[21] Moreover, it would seem desirable that these internationalized jurisdictions should take as guidance the jurisprudence of the ICC. A first step towards harmonization, both in standards of conduct and jurisprudence, would be a constructive cooperation between the ICC and internationalized jurisdictions.

---

[20] Bruce Broomhall *International Justice and the International Criminal Court: Between Sovereignty and the Rule of Law* (Oxford University Press 2003) 103–4.

[21] On this aspect, see also Chapter 14 (Swart).

19

Geographical and Jurisdictional Reach of ICC: Gaps in the International Criminal Justice System and a Role for Internationalized Bodies

*Mariacarmen Colitti**

A. INTRODUCTION

On 1 July 2002, after slightly less than four years since its adoption, the Rome Statute of the International Criminal Court entered into force.[1] The establishment of the International Criminal Court (ICC) can be aptly described as a great achievement in the work for prosecution of gross violations of humanitarian law and human rights by individuals. The Nuremberg and Tokyo tribunals, and the establishment of ICTY and ICTR, have been significant milestones of this advance, but they could be seen as only temporary efforts. ICC was created to provide a permanent criminal forum, potentially with universal reach, to try war crimes and gross violations of human rights. On the other hand, the internationalized criminal bodies examined in this book were created in the interregnum between the adoption of the Rome Statute and its entry into force.

With regard to the Rome Statute, to date[2] 91 states have ratified or acceded to it. Of these, 22 are from Africa;[3] 37 are from Europe;[4] 18 from Latin America and the Caribbean;[5] 12 are from Asia and the Pacific;[6] one from the

* Mariacarmen Colitti is the former legal adviser of No Peace Without Justice.

[1] By virtue of Art 126(1), in fact, the Rome Statute of the International Criminal Court 'shall enter into force on the first day of the month after the 60th day following the date of the deposit of the 60th instrument of ratification, acceptance, approval or accession with the Secretary General of the United Nations'.

[2] 31 August 2003.

[3] Senegal, Ghana, Mali, Lesotho, Botswana, Sierra Leone, Gabon, South Africa, Nigeria, Central African Republic, Benin, Mauritius, Democratic Republic of Congo, Niger, Uganda, Namibia, Gambia, Tanzania, Malawi, Djibouti, Zambia, Guinea.

[4] San Marino, Italy, Norway, Iceland, France, Belgium, Luxembourg, Spain, Germany, Austria, Finland, Andorra, Croatia, Denmark, Sweden, Netherlands, Yugoslavia (FRY), Liechtenstein, United Kingdom, Switzerland, Poland, Hungary, Slovenia, Estonia, Portugal, Macedonia, Cyprus, Ireland, Bosnia and Herzegovina, Bulgaria, Romania, Slovakia, Greece, Latvia, Malta, Albania, Lithuania.

[5] Trinidad and Tobago, Belize, Venezuela, Argentina, Dominica, Paraguay, Costa Rica, Antigua and Barbuda, Peru, Ecuador, Panama, Brazil, Bolivia, Uruguay, Honduras, Colombia, Saint Vincent and the Grenadines, Barbados.

[6] Tajikistan, New Zealand, Fiji, Marshall Islands, Nauru, Cambodia, Mongolia, Australia, East Timor, Samoa, Republic of Korea, Afghanistan.

Middle East;[7] and one from North America.[8] This is less than half of the members of the United Nations (ie 191).

We thus have entire regions of the world that are significantly lagging behind in the ICC ratification process.[9] We are also aware of some weaknesses of the Statute, particularly those based on preconditions to the exercise of ICC jurisdiction, which can be, obviously, overcome by universal ratification of the ICC Statute and by full state cooperation with ICC once it becomes operational.

The main fear is that the Court's jurisdiction will not reach every single country of the globe, and this is more significant when we think about the many 'hot' areas in the world, where conflicts arise and gross violations of human rights are constantly perpetrated. In addition there are a number of countries that clearly stated their intention not to become parties to the Rome Statute. It is worth mentioning, in this respect, the cases of United States and Israel. Although on 31 December 2000 they both signed the Statute, at a later stage they declared their clear and firm intention not to ratify the Statute at all.[10]

Out of the list of states where major armed conflicts are taking place, yearly compiled by the Stockholm International Peace Research Institute (SIPRI), in 2003 only the Democratic Republic of Congo,[11] Sierra Leone,[12] Afghanistan,[13] and Colombia[14] were parties to the Rome Statute. Conversely, Algeria, Angola, Burundi, India, and Pakistan (think of Kashmir), Indonesia, Israel, Philippines, Russia (think of Chechnya), Somalia, Sri Lanka, and Sudan were not.[15] To this list one must also add Iraq and Côte d'Ivoire, of course, which at the time of the compilation of the 2002 *Yearbook* of the Stockholm International Peace Research Institute were not considered likely

---

[7] Jordan.   [8] Canada.

[9] See 'The NPWJ's Regional Update on Ratification' at www.npwj.org.

[10] In particular, in a communication submitted on 6 May 2002, the government of the United States informed the Secretary-General of the following: 'This is to inform you, in connection with the Rome Statute of the International Criminal Court adopted on July 17, 1998, that the United States does not intend to become a party to the treaty. Accordingly, the United States has no legal obligations arising from its signature on December 31, 2000. The United States requests that its intention not to become a party, as expressed in this letter, be reflected in the depositary's status lists relating to this treaty'. With regard to Israel, on 28 August 2002, the government sent a similar communication to the UN Secretary-General: 'in connection with the Rome Statute of the International Criminal Court adopted on 17 July 1998, ... Israel does not intend to become a party to the treaty. Accordingly, Israel has no legal obligations arising from its signature on 31 December 2000. Israel requests that its intention not to become a party, as expressed in this letter, be reflected in the depositary's status lists relating to this treaty.'

[11] Ratified on 11 April 2002.

[12] Ratified on 15 September 2000.

[13] Acceded on 10 February 2003.

[14] Ratified on 5 August 2002.

[15] Stockholm International Peace Research Institute (SIPRI) *Yearbook 2002: Armaments, Disarmament and International Security* (Oxford University Press Oxford 2002).

to be torn by conflicts, and countries in a precarious situation, or where significant military activities take place, such as North Korea, Uzbekistan, Kuwait, or Zimbabwe (while Venezuela ratified on 7 June 2000, Tajikistan on 5 May 2000, and Djibouti on 5 November 2002). If the list is also extended to states whose troops are engaged in combat in foreign territory, it soon becomes evident that ICC is still short of the comprehensive international criminal legal regime that it was designed to be.

Once the International Criminal Court becomes operational, will there still be a need for internationalized courts and tribunals to try the most horrendous crimes? A survey of the range of the ICC's jurisdiction is necessary to determine to what extent and in which instances internationalized criminal bodies might help fill the interstices. This is what this chapter intends to do. The conclusions of this book, by Condorelli and Boutrouche, dwell on the issue of the future of internationalized criminal bodies in the shadow of ICC. Markus Benzing and Morten Bergsmo describe the legal issues arising out of the coexistence between ICC and internationalized criminal bodies. Thus, these two aspects of the issue are better left to these co-authors and only a few further references will be made here.

B. INTERSTICES IN THE ROME STATUTE

1. Territorial limits on ICC jurisdiction (Article 12) and built-in correctives

The Rome Statute fixes detailed preconditions to the exercise of jurisdiction. Needless to say, the limits to the ICC jurisdiction was one of the most intensively negotiated items at the Rome conference.[16]

Article 12 of the Statute[17] provides that the Court may exercise jurisdiction when either the state of the territory where the crime is committed (ie the *territorial state*), or the state of nationality of the accused (ie the *national*

---

[16] See Roy S Lee 'The Rome Conference and its Contributions to International Law' in Roy S Lee (ed) *The International Criminal Court: The Making of the Rome Statute; Issues, Negotiations, Results* (Kluwer Law International 1999) 1–39.

[17] Article 12 on 'Preconditions to the Exercise of Jurisdiction' reads:

'1. A State which becomes a Party to this Statute thereby accepts the jurisdiction of the Court with respect to the crimes referred to in article 5.

2. In the case of article 13, paragraph (a) or (c), the Court may exercise its jurisdiction if one or more of the following States are Parties to this Statute or have accepted the jurisdiction of the Court in accordance with paragraph 3: (a) The State on the territory of which the conduct in question occurred or, if the crime was committed on board a vessel or aircraft, the State of registration of that vessel or aircraft; (b) The State of which the person accused of the crime is a national.

3. If the acceptance of a State which is not a Party to this Statute is required under paragraph 2, that State may, by declaration lodged with the Registrar, accept the exercise of jurisdiction by the Court with respect to the crime in question. The accepting State shall cooperate with the Court without any delay or exception in accordance with Part 9'.

state), is party to the Statute. Moreover, paragraph 3 of the same Article, allows also states which are not party to the Rome Statute to give their consent to the Court's jurisdiction by way of an ad hoc declaration filed with the Registrar.[18]

These are preconditions to the exercise of the Court's jurisdiction, and the power of the Prosecutor to start investigations. It is evident that the Rome Statute does not reflect the current move towards universal jurisdiction for genocide, war crimes, and crimes against humanity. It does not either provide that ratification or ad hoc consent to ICC jurisdiction by the state of custody of a suspect or the state of nationality of victims would allow the Court to proceed.

At the last session of the Preparatory Committee of the ICC,[19] just before the convening of the Rome Diplomatic Conference, Germany tabled a proposal whereby the Court could exercise jurisdiction over any suspect, irrespective of whether the territorial state, custodial state, or any other state concerned was a party to the Statute.[20] The German proposal was based on the assumption that there existed universal jurisdiction under international law for the crimes under the jurisdiction of the Court, and thus the Court should be placed in the same favourable position as states to exercise jurisdiction. The proposal was included in the draft Statute submitted to the Diplomatic Conference, but in Rome it enjoyed the support of only about 30 countries.[21]

At the Rome Conference, the delegation from South Korea also submitted a proposal.[22] It incorporated automatic jurisdiction for states parties, and allowed jurisdiction if one of the following states was a party to the Statute: (a) the territorial state; (b) the national state; (c) the custodial state; (d) or the state of nationality of the victim.[23] Conversely, the United States tabled a proposal that required the consent of the territorial state and of the state of nationality of the accused for the Court to exercise its jurisdiction.[24] In the end, the final compromise reached by the Diplomatic Conference was

---

[18] See Manhoush H Arsanjani 'The Rome Statute of the International Criminal Court: Exceptions to the Jurisdiction' in Mauro Politi and Giuseppe Nesi (ed) *The Rome Statute of the International Criminal Court: A Challenge to Impunity* (Ashgate 2001) 49–53.

[19] From 16 March to 3 April 1998.

[20] See an informal Discussion Paper presented by Germany 'The Jurisdiction of the International Criminal Court' UN Doc A/AC249/1998/DP2.

[21] See Hans-Peter Kaul 'The International Criminal Court: Jurisdiction, Trigger Mechanism and Relationship to National Jurisdictions' in Politi and Nesi (ed) (*supra* n 18) 59–62.

[22] See Proposal submitted by the Republic of Korea for Articles 6 [9], * 7 [6], and 8 [7] UN Doc A/CONF.183/C.1/L.6.

[23] See Elizabeth Wilmshurst 'Jurisdiction of the Court' in Lee (ed) (*supra* n 16) 127–41.

[24] See Proposal submitted by the United States UN Doc. A/CONF.183/C.1/L.70; see also David J Scheffer 'The United States and the International Criminal Court' (1999) 93 *Am J Int'l L* 12.

half-way between the South Korean and US proposal, and is now reflected by the text of Article 12 of the Statute.

Despite these strictures, the Statute does offer ways to offset the lack of a universal jurisdictional regime. Apart from the above-mentioned possibility, provided by Article 12.3, for a non-state party to accept the Court's jurisdiction by a declaration lodged with the Registrar, there is Article 13.b.[25] This Article provides that the Court may exercise its jurisdiction with respect to the 'core crimes', if 'a situation in which one or more of such crimes appears to have been committed is referred to the Prosecutor by the Security Council acting under Chapter VII of the Charter of the United Nations'. Article 13.b thus acknowledges the enforcement powers of the Security Council acting under Chapter VII of the UN Charter, whereby the situation is referred to the Prosecutor and such enforcement powers are binding on all Member States of the United Nations.

In other words, if ICC is barred from exercising jurisdiction because neither the territorial state, nor the national state are party to the Rome Statute, the Security Council, acting under Chapter VII of the Charter, could still decide to refer the situation to the Prosecutor.[26] The rationale for this provision is that at the Rome Conference a great majority of delegations supported the power of the Security Council to initiate proceedings before the Court, especially because they thought that this would remove the need for the creation of other ad hoc tribunals in the future, as in the case of former Yugoslavia and Rwanda.[27] For those delegations that objected in Rome that the Council had no legal competence under the UN Charter to refer matters for prosecution by an international tribunal, the answer was already contained in the 1995 decision of the Appeals Chamber of ICTY in the *Tadić* case,[28] which supported the validity of the creation by the Security Council of ICTY according to its powers under Chapter VII of the Charter, in particular under Article 41.[29]

[25] Article 13, on 'Exercise of Jurisdiction', reads:
'The Court may exercise its jurisdiction with respect to a crime referred to in article 5 in accordance with the provisions of this Statute if: (a) A situation in which one or more of such crimes appears to have been committed is referred to the Prosecutor by a State Party in accordance with article 14;
    (b) A situation in which one or more of such crimes appears to have been committed is referred to the Prosecutor by the Security Council acting under Chapter VII of the Charter of the United Nations; or
    (c) The Prosecutor has initiated an investigation in respect of such a crime in accordance with article 15.'
[26] See Nabil Elaraby 'The Role of the Security Council and the Independence of the International Criminal Court' in Politi and Nesi (ed) (*supra* n 18) 43–7.
[27] See Lionel Yee 'The International Criminal Court and the Security Council: Articles 13 (b) and 16' in Lee (ed) (*supra* n 16) 143–52.
[28] See *Prosecutor v Dusko Tadić* IT-94-1-T Opinion and Judgment 'Prijedor' (13 February 1995), amended IT-1-T (1 September 1995), amended IT-94-1-T (14 December 1995), IT-94-1-T Opinion and Judgment (7 May 1997), reported in (1996) 35 ILM 32 paras 28–48, and (1997) 36 ILM 908.
[29] Article 41 of the UN Charter reads: 'The Security Council may decide what measures not involving the use of armed force are to be employed to give effect to its decisions, and it may call

Be that as it may, to decide to refer matters to ICC, the Security Council still needs to vote under Article 27.3 of the Charter,[30] thus giving the five permanent members a veto power. Hence, situations like that in Iraq in the spring of 2003, where neither Iraq (ie the territorial state), nor the United States (the national state) are party of the Rome Statute, could still hardly be submitted to the judicial scrutiny of the Court because the United States would most certainly veto it.[31]

2. *Limits to jurisdiction ratione materiae and temporis*

In sum, limits to the court's jurisdiction *ratione loci* can be counteracted by Article 12.3 and Article 13.b of the Statute.

Then, with regard to jurisdiction *ratione materiae*, Article 5 of the Rome Statute lists only genocide, crimes against humanity, and war crimes, as crimes under the Court's jurisdiction.[32] With regard to the crime of aggression, as an agreement on its definition was not reached at the Rome Conference, the compromise solution was to include paragraph 2 under Article 5 to provide that the definition 'shall be consistent with the relevant provisions of the Charter of the United Nations'. This means that the jurisdiction of the Court over the crime of aggression could be exercised only once a definition has been found and approved.

upon the Members of the United Nations to apply such measures. These may include complete or partial interruption of economic relations and of rail, sea, air, postal, telegraphic, radio, and other means of communication, and the severance of diplomatic relations'.

[30] 'Decisions of the Security Council on all other matters [ie non-procedural] shall be made by an affirmative vote of nine members including the concurring votes of the permanent members'.

[31] Besides, on 7 April 2003, Pierre-Richard Prosper, US Ambassador-at-Large for War Crimes Issues, at a briefing on Geneva Conventions, EPWs and War Crimes, announced that it is the intention of the United States not to try Iraqi suspects of war crimes and gross violations of human rights before international or internationalized criminal courts or tribunals, but before US courts, regular or military. In particular he stated the following: 'For the current abuses, the crimes particularly against US personnel, we believe that we have the sovereign ability and right to prosecute these cases. There is a range of options, ranging from military proceedings to our civilian courts. We are of a view that an international tribunal for the current abuses is not necessary'. For full text, see www.defenselink.mil/news/Apr2003/ t04072003_t407genv.html (site last visited August 2003).

[32] Article 5 of the Statute, on 'Crimes within the Jurisdiction of the Court' reads:
'1. The jurisdiction of the Court shall be limited to the most serious crimes of concern to the international community as a whole. The Court has jurisdiction in accordance with this Statute with respect to the following crimes: (a) The crime of genocide; (b) Crimes against humanity; (c) War crimes; (d) The crime of aggression.
2. The Court shall exercise jurisdiction over the crime of aggression once a provision is adopted in accordance with articles 121 and 123 defining the crime and setting out the conditions under which the Court shall exercise jurisdiction with respect to this crime. Such a provision shall be consistent with the relevant provisions of the Charter of the United Nations'.

The jurisdiction of the ICC is therefore limited to the core crimes, as the majority of delegations that negotiated the Statute believed that this would increase a broad acceptance of the Court and its credibility and moral authority.[33] In addition, at the end of the negotiations, it was decided to exclude from the list of crimes those relating to terrorism and drug trafficking. While no provision seems to be applicable for prosecuting the crime of drug trafficking,[34] it could be argued that the same cannot be stated with regard to the crime of terrorism. Although terrorism as such was not included in the Rome Statute, it is also true that its consequences could be construed as crimes under the jurisdiction of the Court.[35] In particular, acts of terrorism, if 'committed as part of a widespread or systematic attack directed against any civilian population, with knowledge of the attack',[36] could widely be considered as crimes against humanity, as defined under the Rome Statute.

The main reasons drug trafficking and terrorism were not included in the Statute were the concern that the Court would be overburdened with apparently less important cases, and the fact that states could deal with these crimes through international cooperation agreements. However, upon request by concerned states such as Turkey, in the Final Act of the Rome Diplomatic Conference a Resolution was included to recommend that a future Review Conference 'consider the crimes of terrorism and drug crimes with a view to arriving at an acceptable definition and their inclusion in the list of crimes within the jurisdiction of the Court'.[37]

Because ICC jurisdiction is restricted to core crimes, internationalized criminal courts and tribunals could still be established to prosecute crimes other than core crimes. For instance, as it has been described elsewhere in this

---

[33] For an analysis on the criteria for selecting crimes under the jurisdiction of the International Criminal Court, see Herman Von Habel and Darryl Robinson 'Crimes within the Jurisdiction of the Court' in Lee (*supra* n 16) 79–126. See also 'Report of the Ad Hoc Committee on the Establishment of an International Criminal Court' United Nations General Assembly Official Records, 50th Session, Supplement 22 UN Doc A/50/22 (1995) para 54.

[34] It was only a proposal put forward by the delegation of Trinidad and Tobago in 1989 to establish an international court to prosecute crimes of drug trafficking that invigorated the process and finally led to the establishment of the International Criminal Court. During the negotiations in Rome, delegations realized that, because of the significance of the problem of drug trafficking, to include it in the Court's mandate, with the investigations that would be required, would very likely result in the limited resources of the Court promptly being weighed down.

[35] After the 11 September 2001 terrorist attacks in New York, United Nations High Commissioner for Human Rights Mary Robinson stated: 'The targeting with civilian aircraft being commandeered with full gasoline tanks and being deliberately targeted on buildings where there were thousands of people working, with the intent to kill as many as possible, that deliberately planned assault on a large number of civilians, in my view undoubtedly constitutes a crime against humanity'.

[36] See Art 7 of the Statute, on 'Crimes Against Humanity'.

[37] See Resolution E, ANNEX I, Final Act of the United Nations Diplomatic Conference of Plenipotentiaries on the Establishment of an International Criminal Court (17 July 1998) UN Doc A/CONF.183/10.

book, the jurisdiction of the Special Court for Sierra Leone was carefully crafted so as to include certain particular crimes under the laws of Sierra Leone (ie certain offences relating to the abuse of girls, under the Prevention of Cruelty to Children Act 1926; and the wanton destruction of property under the Malicious Damage Act 1861), which were believed not to be addressed by international law.[38] Similarly, the Extraordinary Chambers in the Courts of Cambodia will have the power to bring to trial all suspects 'responsible for crimes against internationally protected persons, pursuant to the Vienna Convention of 1961 on Diplomatic Relations'.[39]

Time is another fundamental factor when analysing the limits to ICC jurisdiction (and thus the room left for internationalized criminal bodies). During the negotiations of the Rome Statute there was general agreement on the principle of non-retroactivity, under Article 24, as this was in line with the principle of legality set out in Article 22 of the Statute about *nullum crimen sine lege*.[40] In the context of Article 24, the Rome Diplomatic Conference addressed also the issue of 'continuous crimes'.[41] In particular, the main problem was how to relate the principle of non-retroactivity to crimes like forced disappearances which were commenced before the entry into force of the Statute and continued thereafter. The issue was never discussed explicitly. The main issue was to decide which verb would accompany the expression 'conduct in question'. The dilemma was whether to use 'committed', 'occurred', 'commenced', or 'completed'. As it seemed impossible to find a verb that was acceptable in all six UN official languages, the final decision was not to use any verb at all. Article 24(1) now reads: 'No person shall be personally responsible under this Statute for conduct prior to the entry into force of the Statute'. The issue would then be for the Court to find a solution to be used where no agreement could be reached.

Article 24 on non-retroactivity is closely related to Article 11 on jurisdiction *ratione temporis*, which states that the Court has jurisdiction only with respect to crimes committed after the entry into force of the Statute.[42] As it was explained, the twentieth century has left a grim legacy of gross violations

---

[38] See Chapter 7 (Smith).

[39] Law on the Establishment of Extraordinary Chambers in the Courts of Cambodia, Art 8.

[40] Article 22, on '*Nullum crimen sine lege*' reads:

'1. A person shall not be criminally responsible under this Statute unless the conduct in question constitutes, at the time it takes place, a crime within the jurisdiction of the Court.

2. The definition of a crime shall be strictly construed and shall not be extended by analogy. In case of ambiguity, the definition shall be interpreted in favour of the person being investigated, prosecuted or convicted.

3. This article shall not affect the characterization of any conduct as criminal under international law independently of this Statute'.

[41] See Per Saland 'International Criminal Law Principles' in Lee (*supra* n 16) 189–97.

[42] Article 11 on 'Jurisdiction *ratione temporis*' reads:

'1. The Court has jurisdiction only with respect to crimes committed after the entry into force of this Statute.

of human rights and war crimes that cry out for judicial punishment, which would otherwise go unpunished. Thus, for instance, the Extraordinary Chambers in the Court of Cambodia are established to try 'those who were most responsible for crimes and serious violations of Cambodian penal law, international humanitarian law and custom, and international conventions recognized by Cambodia, that were committed during the period from 17 April 1975 to 6 January 1979'.[43] The crimes of the Khmer Rouge are obviously beyond the ICC's reach, but should not be left unpunished.

C. CONCLUSION: LIFE IN THE SHADOW OF THE ICC—A CASE FOR SYMBIOSIS?

In conclusion, the legal regime created by the Rome Statute is clearly not all-inclusive. Although territorial limits to jurisdiction could be overcome *de imperio* by the Security Council (of course, provided the permanent members could agree to do so), limits *ratione materiae* and *temporis* are much more arduous obstacles.[44] It is in these crevices that, once ICC has reached widespread acceptance, internationalized criminal bodies could breed.

The answer to the urgent need to end impunity for gross violations of human rights which occurred before 1 July 2001, and then to fill the gaps in the ICC's non-retroactive jurisdiction, will be to choose only between internationalized and ad hoc tribunals. Considering that internationalized (national) tribunals have the potential to bring justice closer to the population concerned, and that national sovereignty is thus preserved, it will be the more likely approach to international justice. In fact, ad hoc tribunals, by being far from the place where the crimes were committed, will not help the country in question to rebuild the rule of law and judicial system. However, internationalized tribunals could benefit both from the ICC Statute and from the experience of the two ad hoc tribunals.

In the future, ICC and internationalized criminal bodies are likely to coexist (more or less peacefully, as Benzing and Bergsmo described),[45] and to bolster each other. The Rome Statute provides an excellent model law (both procedural and substantial), which incorporates the highest standards,

---

2. If a State becomes a Party to this Statute after its entry into force, the Court may exercise its jurisdiction only with respect to crimes committed after the entry into force of this Statute for that State, unless that State has made a declaration under article 12, paragraph 3'.

[43] Draft Agreement between the United Nations and the Royal Government of Cambodia Concerning the Prosecution under Cambodia Law of Crimes Committed during the Period of Democratic Kampuchea, Art 1.

[44] However, the Rome Statute could be amended after the expiry of seven years from the entry into force of the Statute, as provided by Art 121 of the Statute.

[45] See Chapter 18.

for internationalized courts. The architects of the Sierra Leone Special Court and the East Timor Serious Crimes Panels have relied on it.[46] Moreover, internationalized prosecutions, which apply the norms contained in the Rome Statute, could help in interpreting the Statute, disseminating international standards, and bringing the highest levels of legal professionalism to local judges, prosecutors, and lawyers, contributing to the institution-building process.[47]

Finally, should the Court's docket ever become overcrowded, burden-sharing between ICC and internationalized panels in the countries where crimes were committed could be resorted to, to ensure expedited proceedings. Internationalized courts could perhaps focus on low rank suspects of crimes under the jurisdiction of the Court, while ICC targets the high-profile individuals.[48]

[46] See Chapters 7 (Smith), 5 (De Bertodano), 6 (Lyons) and 9 (Schabas).

[47] See Suzannah Linton 'Cambodia, East Timor and Sierra Leone: Experiments in International Justice' in (2001) 12 *Criminal Law Forum* 185.

[48] This is exactly what ICTY and the Office of the High Representative in Bosnia Herzegovina have recently planned to do to help ICTY complete its mission. See www.ohr.int/print/?content_id=29301 (site last visited August 2003).

Internationalized Criminal Courts and Tribunals: Are They Necessary?

Luigi Condorelli* and Théo Boutruche**

A. INTRODUCTION

Facing the development of a new family of judicial bodies means the analysis of the implications for the legal order of such an evolution in negative and positive terms. In this respect, the different chapters of this book have shown the complexity and the importance of the questions raised by the internationalized criminal tribunals. As a consequence, it seems logical to conclude by asking a last question, which is whether this new family of tribunals is necessary or at least useful. Considering the issues highlighted in this volume, it is obvious that this is not simply a theoretical and controversial question. In fact, answering this question will shed some light on the prospects of this new kind of court: is it a model to be reproduced or instead a development of little use in the present international judicial system?

The question whether internationalized criminal courts are necessary or useful is difficult to answer because it encompasses a heterogeneous reality. These tribunals and courts are not one species but in fact different species that we include under one expression. Each is a different reality in itself. Therefore wondering whether they are useful is like asking oneself whether a dog, a fly, a hen, and a snail should be considered useful or not: does it make sense to discuss together creatures which are so different from one another? But it is true that they all still have something in common, which is the fact of being a living creature, needing, for instance, food, warmth, and oxygen.

In order to answer our question, we then need to point out the common features among these creatures that appear so different. This first step toward a systematization of the phenomenon is crucial to understand whether these internationalized tribunals are necessary. However, in order to draw a complete picture of the internationalized criminal tribunals as a tool for the international legal system, we will also have to say something about the particularity of each of them. Finally, the question of the future of the

* Professor at the University of Florence, and Honorary Professor at the University of Geneva.

** PhD candidate at the Graduate Institute of International Studies, Geneva, and Research and Teaching Assistant, International Law and International Organization Department, University of Geneva.

internationalized courts is closely linked to their relationship with the International Criminal Court. Are they complementary or in competition?

B. TOWARDS A DEFINITION OF THE INTERNATIONALIZED CRIMINAL TRIBUNALS

It seems possible to identify three common features of internationalized criminal courts: the exercise of a judicial function, the fact that they are characterized by a truly international element combined with internal elements, and their ad hoc nature.

1. The exercise of a judicial function

The first common feature is self-evident; it is the fact that they all exercise a judicial activity in penal matters. They have to judge criminal issues. Therefore their judges are penal judges. This carries with it a series of consequences. If they are penal judges, then they are judges who within the international context must operate in compliance with a series of international rules, principles, and standards, which govern the judicial function. For example, the judge must apply the principle of legality. There is a body of laws and principles of international law that applies because of the very fact that we are speaking about judges in criminal matters.

2. The internationalized element

The second element that we need to consider is a core question: the internationality or the internationalization of the entities. It implies a mix between internal and international elements, which we can find at many different levels, such as the question of applicable law, both substantive and procedural. There is the integration of an international feature within the domestic structure—for example, international judges sitting beside national judges—through an international act or decision. The degree of this internationalized element can be very different from one tribunal to another. However, since in each situation there is a mix between domestic and international aspects, this is an issue of scale not of nature. The range runs from a domestic system with some international elements, as in Cambodia, to a quasi-international tribunal with some national components, as in Sierra Leone.

This characteristic highlights the general tendency in the international system toward internationalization of judicial functions.[1] The four bodies

---

[1] It is worth noting that in some cases such as Cambodia, the process could also be seen as a 'nationalization' of international judicial functions in the sense that purely international tribunals are too time- and resource-consuming and politically sensitive.

explored in this book are an example of this trend in the sense that there is an international element.

However, this is not enough to capture the very essence of the phenomenon. We need more than just a foreign element in the structure of the court to distinguish between mixed tribunals, such as the nineteenth-century African slave trade mixed tribunals,[2] and the internationalized tribunals considered in this book. If we reflect more in depth on their international nature, we will realize that in substance what characterizes these four instances is the fact that they are linked to the United Nations: their internationalization derives from a more or less close tie with the United Nations. This link with the United Nations is manifested in two ways: first, the aims of these tribunals are those of the United Nations, and secondly the United Nations participates in the creation of the courts.

This point is of great importance in understanding the raison d'être of these tribunals. Because they pursue UN goals, the internationalized tribunals respond to a twofold rationale. On the one hand, they contribute to the fight against impunity. As the international community is increasingly worried about impunity, there is a need to establish a system that will enable us to avoid impunity, when the domestic systems do not work at all or work badly. On the other hand, there is another element that comes under the umbrella of UN rationale, which is the fact that the creation of tribunals contributes to reconstructing a national system that is in decay or has failed, and to the maintenance or the restoration of peace.

3. The 'ad hoc-ism'

The third common feature that characterizes these four entities is what we could call 'ad hoc-ism'. Internationalized tribunals are entities that have been created on an ad hoc basis to respond to special situations. They have a temporary nature. Indeed, they aim to accomplish a certain objective and are bound to disappear once they do so. This 'ad hoc-ism' has two implications. On one hand, it represents a common feature to identify this category of tribunals. On the other hand, it stresses that since each tribunal is of an ad hoc nature, it is moulded onto each singular situation. Therefore each internationalized criminal tribunal is different from the others.

---

[2] In the 19th century, several treaties for the suppression of the African slave trade provided for the establishment of mixed tribunals to adjudicate upon seizures of vessels suspected of slave trading. Great Britain, which was the most proactive country in trying to eradicate the slave trade (and had the naval power to do so) interwove a web of bilateral treaties with several countries engaged in the practice. To ensure enforcement of the abolitionist agreements, mixed courts, composed of an equal number of British and foreign officers, were to decide whether the vessel was actually engaged in slave trading and could therefore be rightfully seized. On this issue, see Henry de Montardy *La traité et le droit international* (1899) 75–98.

When ICTY and the ICTR were created, one of the first criticisms levelled was about the ad hoc nature of these courts, objecting that there was a dangerous selectiveness in the way the international crimes were addressed. This problem led experts and states to consider replacing the ad hoc edifice by a permanent and universal body, ie the International Criminal Court.

A similar question has then to be addressed concerning the internationalized criminal tribunals: what should be the relationship between these ad hoc mechanisms and the permanent International Criminal Court? According to the critics the only justification for the internationalized tribunals to date was the absence of a permanent court. Hence, are these creatures bound to disappear with the Rome Statute or will they continue to have a raison d'être of their own?

We have reasons to question the automatic disappearance of the ad hoc bodies. Indeed, it may well be enriching for the international system to have a coexistence of ad hoc and permanent structures. It is well known that the scope of the ICC's jurisdiction is limited. Even with the Statute of the ICC in force, these tribunals would have a raison d'être because they could address crimes that fall outside the scope of the ICC's jurisdiction.

Nevertheless, once (and if) the different problems limiting the jurisdiction of ICC are solved, will the internationalized tribunals continue to serve a purpose? The three common features identified—the judicial nature of the entity, the phenomenon of internationalization and the ad hoc characteristic—are not enough to allow us to answer this question. We now need to point out the specificities of each organ, and in what way they differ from each other. With this second set of characteristics in mind, we will be able to distinguish what makes them special and to express a reasoned opinion. It is only with the picture thus completed that it will be possible to say in what way the internationalized tribunals fulfil functions that ICC could never achieve.

C. THE DIFFERENCES BETWEEN THE INTERNATIONALIZED CRIMINAL TRIBUNALS

Among the four entities we have examined, two are very similar and follow the same rationale: in short, they are animals of the same genus. That is the case of the Kosovo and the East Timor entities.

1. The Kosovo and the East Timor cases

The Kosovo and East Timor courts are judicial facilities that have been entirely created by the UN temporary administrations responsible for these territories. But what must be underlined here is that these judicial bodies have been set up as part of a global task, ie the performance of basic civilian administrative functions. Indeed, the founding documents adopted by the UN Security Council concerning the administration for Kosovo and East Timor state that the authorities must maintain law and order. In these instances, the United Nations fulfils the state functions within a territory that was not yet a state (East Timor) or where the government is not carrying out its duties (Kosovo). Amongst other things, the UN administration is responsible for providing or administering justice. For East Timor, the Security Council established the UN Transitional Administration in East Timor (UNTAET), 'which will be endowed with overall responsibility for the administration of East Timor and will be empowered to exercise all legislative and executive authority, including the administration of justice'.[3]

In this respect, the internationalization of the judicial function fits into a context where the state has been replaced in all areas of activity by an international administration. Framed this way, internationalization is a response to a series of problems, such as the difficulty of finding competent local judges, as well as judges capable of withstanding pressures. This means that the system in Kosovo and East Timor is one in which the judicial function may concern any issue, even petty crimes such as burglary. That too must be judged by the UN administration. Thus, the jurisdiction of the judicial organs in Kosovo and East Timor, unlike the other internationalized tribunals, covers all type of offences, including grave international crimes.

The prosecution of international crimes that have occurred in Kosovo and in East Timor is a function that is part of the rationale of the UN action. In this respect, if we look at the case of Kosovo, as there is already an international criminal tribunal (ie ICTY), set up by the United Nations, that has jurisdiction over Kosovo until its closure, there is no special mention of the core crimes among the Regulations adopted by the interim administration. Therefore, the judges of the internationalized courts for Kosovo, created by the UN administration, will interplay with a truly international body, ICTY. This means that the relationships between the domestic internationalized judges and the international judges are regulated by Article 9(2) of the ICTY Statute. ICTY will have primacy over the internationalized tribunals for Kosovo.

In the case of East Timor, since no international criminal tribunal such as ICTY has been set up, internationalized Panels have exclusive jurisdiction over serious criminal offences. This exclusive jurisdiction 'shall not preclude the jurisdiction of an international tribunal for East Timor over those offences, once such tribunal is established'.[4] Therefore, here, as in Kosovo, the judges of the internationalized Panels would be considered as domestic judges in relation to a possible international penal tribunal (which, however, has not been created).

---

[3] UNSC Res 1272 (1999) para 1.   [4] cf s 9.4 of UNTAET Reg 2000/11.

With regard to East Timor, it seems important to add a remark about the jurisdiction of the Panels over serious criminal offences. If we look at the rules on this subject matter, we discover that they are taken from the Rome Statute. Since the situation of ICC is totally different from that of the East Timor Panels, it may raise some problems. Indeed, we have a transposition which is not logical, if one thinks that the criminal offences that are dealt with here cannot be all those envisaged by the Rome Statute.

These two cases, therefore, are similar, as stated above.[5] They are two creatures of the same family. Several chapters in this volume have made clear that they do not work properly, that there are enormous difficulties that would require more appropriate means. But these difficulties are problems that do not rule out the usefulness of, or rather the necessity for, the existence of these internationalized entities, especially in those cases where (today as in the future) the United Nations takes on the responsibility of administering a territory.

In contrast, the Cambodia and Sierra Leone tribunals have nothing in common, either with the former two cases or with one another.

2. *The Cambodia case*

The Cambodian government wishes to create a judicial body with international participation, but, at the same time, wants to exercise control over these external judges, whereas the United Nations wishes to retain the control itself. Consequently, the Cambodian tribunal is the least internationalized tribunal. It is a Cambodian domestic criminal tribunal; it has specific international elements, but it is still part of the national judicial system with domestic judges.

Therefore, if a judicial body of this sort was to be created given the existence of ICC, the internationalized judge should be assimilated to a domestic judge, in the sense that he or she would be subjected to the mechanisms envisaged in the Rome Statute with regard to the relationships between the international and internal judge. Another observation on the Cambodian case raises the general issue of the incorporation of international law within the domestic legal order in the context of these internationalized tribunals. The Law on Extraordinary Chambers has been passed by the National Assembly of Cambodia in January 2001. This Act, which was adopted in anticipation of the potential agreement with the United Nations, is unique from the point of view of an international expert. Article VI states that these Chambers 'shall have the power to bring to trial all Suspects who committed or ordered the commission of grave breaches of the Geneva Convention of

---

[5] See 425–7.

August 12, 1949'. As far as we know the 'grave breaches' provision can only apply to international armed conflict. Under the Geneva Convention, this grave breaches provision does not apply to other armed conflicts[6] (as was the case for the Khmer Rouge conflict).

This issue highlights the danger of the mixed nature of these tribunals, where international law might be changed or denatured. Another illustration of the problem is the second part of Article VI. This provision gives as example of a crime 'compelling a prisoner of war ... to serve in the forces of a hostile power', but there are no prisoners of war in non-international armed conflicts according to humanitarian law.

After having described the Cambodia case, we now need to say something about Sierra Leone.

3. The Sierra Leone case

Here we have a creature that is fairly different from the others, because this comes very close to a true international tribunal.[7] If the Extraordinary Chambers for Cambodia were to come into being they would be identified as domestic entities, with international elements in them. As stated above, the provisions of the Rome Statute concerning the relationship between domestic judges and international judges would therefore regulate their relationship with ICC. This is not the case with the Special Court for Sierra Leone, because it is not only a tribunal created by an international treaty, it has also been created and shaped in such a way as to be very similar to an ad hoc international criminal tribunal.

For instance, the Articles defining the jurisdiction of the Special Court for Sierra Leone are the same, word for word, as those of ICTR. Some elements of jurisdiction of a domestic nature have been added, but the core international aspects stem from the Statute of the ICTR. Other elements common to the Sierra Leone Court and ICTR include the rule on concurrent jurisdiction.[8]

It would be useful to mention the question raised by Article XX of the Statute of the Special Court which deals with appellate proceedings. If we look at the third paragraph of Article XX, we will find an indication stating that 'the judges of the Appeals Chamber of the Special Court shall be guided by the decisions of the Appeals Chamber of the International Tribunals for the former Yugoslavia and for Rwanda'. For different political and economic reasons, a truly international tribunal has not been created, nor has

---

[6] See on this issue, *Prosecutor v Tadić* ICTY Appeals Chamber (2 October 1995) Decision on the Defence Motion for Interlocutory Appeal on Jurisdiction para 80.

[7] In this regard, *see Prosecutor v Norman, Kallon and Kamara*, Special Court for Sierra Leone (13 March 2004), Decision on Constitutionality and Lack of Jurisdiction, paras 49–53, and *Prosecutor v Taylor*, Special Court for Sierria Leone (31 May 2004), Decision on Immunity from Jurisdiction, paras 37–42. The Special Court qualities itself as an international tribunal.

[8] Article VII of the Statute of the Special Court for Sierra Leone.

the existing Appeals Chamber of the international tribunals been used. The decision was to set up an internationalized court working, as far as possible, with international tribunals which will apply the standards of the jurisprudence of the Appeals Chamber of ICTY and of ICTR. This solution could also help to avoid problems linked with the proliferation of tribunals, such as the lack of coherence in the jurisprudence.

In this instance, therefore, we are facing an international type of system. This raises some important issues for the work of the Special Court because, as has been pointed out, there is no resolution of the Security Council which would have an effect on all Member States of the United Nations. There is only a bilateral agreement, which binds the United Nations and Sierra Leone. This entails a number of consequences that were underlined by Professor Cassese. He is, for instance, worried that, when the state itself or other states do not cooperate with the tribunal, there would be a total lack of mechanisms aimed at ensuring that the system will function.[9]

We would like to highlight a very important point concerning this issue. It is true that these bodies deal with the prosecution of core international crimes and can find themselves in situations where they are impotent and where nothing can be done. However, we must not forget that these organs act within a global effort to end impunity and to accomplish one of the aims of the Charter of the United Nations. Indeed, the Preamble to the ICC Statute states very clearly that grave international crimes 'threaten the peace', and that the prosecution of such crimes contributes to the maintenance of the international peace and security which is one of the fundamental duties of the United Nations.

Therefore, if prosecution through these organs is hindered, this will constitute a threat to peace. As a result, it would trigger a situation calling on the Security Council to intervene through the measures envisaged under Chapter VII of the UN Charter. Of course we must not be too optimistic about the willingness of the Security Council to intervene. The mechanism of reporting to the Security Council in cases of failure to cooperate has to date only led to a declaration by the Security Council and nothing more in terms of measures to facilitate or impose such cooperation.

This issue is also important for the International Criminal Court. The rules on cooperation between states and the Court declare that if the state fails to comply with a request of the Court, the Court may make a finding to that effect and refer the matter to the Assembly of States Parties or, where the Security Council referred the matter to the Court, to the Security Council.[10] But the fact that the rules do not provide anything else does not mean that the Security Council should not have competence for all those situations that may be a threat against peace. Where the rules are silent, the powers and

---

[9] See Chapter 17 (Sluiter).   [10] Article 87(7) of the Rome Statute.

responsibility of the Security Council in relation to Chapter VII of the Charter still stand.

Finally, the relation of the Special Court for Sierra Leone with ICC should not be problematic, since the Sierra Leone organ deals with acts previous to the entry into force of the Rome Statute. In the future, if there were to be any situation of this sort, then there would be an overlap. But we can say that the tribunal for Sierra Leone has been set up because there was no other alternative, because there would never have been any jurisdiction of the International Criminal Court over the crimes committed in that area and in that war.

D. CONCLUSION

The internationalization of domestic courts is possible, even given the existence of ICC. But, from the standpoint of the rationalization of the system, in cases such as Cambodia and Sierra Leone, creating ad hoc tribunals or internationalized courts would be nonsense. ICC has been designed to create a permanent facility that serves for all the situations of this type that might arise. Hence, if there is an ICC that works and that has jurisdiction over the area and perpetrators of future crimes, we will not need to create other ad hoc or internationalized tribunals.[11]

It is true that justice may not be acknowledged by those in whose name it should be delivered. Justice that comes to regulate a domestic situation from afar may well be felt to be neither appropriate nor efficient. These problems of participation and closeness are of a psychological nature. Therefore, it is necessary that the international judge not be distant, but close to the country, and that it is perceived as such. Such bridges between the victims and the judicial bodies could be built through both the International Criminal Court and internationalized criminal tribunals, by advancing the perception that international justice is not the monopoly of a unique court but also belongs to some tribunals composed of national judges.

In this respect, it is not so much an evaluation of the whole system, but rather a criticism of the Rome Statute, which is at issue here. The Rome Statute may have created a form of justice that will be thought of as being very distant. This criticism is valid, and we need to respond to it. This can be done through the creation of mechanisms which would not replace the Rome Statute, but which would rather complement it. These bodies could adjust

---

[11] We should put in a caveat to this in two extreme cases: where the creation of such tribunals is seen just as a deliberate way to undermine ICC, or where a national criminal jurisdiction would be generally unwilling or unable to render judgment, which would make potentially a large number of cases admissible before ICC. In the latter case, an internationalization of the national jurisdiction might be able to mitigate the problem and avoid a majority of cases being left unadjudicated.

provisions of the Rome Statute so that justice may be administered in such a way that it is not perceived as being dispensed by a far-off body or person issuing extraneous decisions.[12]

In conclusion, it seems that this should lead to an effort one day to revise the Rome Statute so that ICC will be a court that is much closer to those for whom justice is administered.

---

[12] It is worth noting that this drawback can be attenuated because the Statute provides for the possibility of ICC sitting elsewhere (Art 3(3)).

21

Internationalized Courts:
Better Than Nothing . . .

Alain Pellet*

This post-face is an expression of remorse. Circumstances beyond my control have deprived me of the opportunity to participate in the fascinating conference held in Amsterdam in 2002 which has resulted in the present book. The organizers have nevertheless been kind enough to ask me to offer some views on the general topic of the conference. An imprudent proposal, however, for at least two reasons: first, contrary to most of the participants in the conference, I am a 'general international lawyer', not a specialist of criminal (not even international criminal) law; secondly, the present chapter has been written very late in time which means that I have had the good/bad fortune to read Antonio Cassese's Introduction and Luigi Condorelli and Théo Boutruche's general Conclusion: good since they are excellent and stimulating pieces which offer a thoughtful overview of the topic; bad in that I do not see what is left to be said at a general level. Moreover, I would hesitate to disagree with them on a topic they master infinitely better than I do. And yet, I am not sure that I am in 100 per cent agreement with them since, in particular, I am probably less persuaded than they are that internationalized courts are globally to be praised. I will try to explain why.

A. THE REASONS FOR INTERNATIONALIZATION OF NATIONAL COURTS

In some respects, it can be maintained that internationalized or 'hybrid' criminal tribunals combine all the advantages and disadvantages of both national and international criminal courts. However, this would probably not give a true picture.

First, as rightly underlined at length in this book, even though limited to four particular 'animals' the general 'species' of internationalized tribunals is highly heterogeneous; the circumstances of their creation are extremely different; their degree of 'internationalization' is far from uniform; the scope of their jurisdiction is varied; their modes of functioning are hardly comparable.

---

* Professor, University of Paris X-Nanterre, Member and former Chairman, International Law Commission.

Secondly, their common characteristics, mainly their 'ad hocism' and their semi-internationalization, raise specific issues compared with national courts as well as with truly international judicial bodies (in particular the *permanent* International Criminal Court).

It seems to be largely accepted that one of their main advantages over truly international bodies is their 'proximity'—proximity to the place where the crime has been committed, proximity to the evidence, proximity to the population more directly concerned. On the other hand, proximity must not amount to partiality and it can be argued that trials rendered 'on the spot' in a post-trauma context are more open to criticism and to the dangers of revenge than expatriated trials in remote countries where the heat can be more easily taken out of the situation.

Moreover, and more important, it must be kept in mind that only crimes which 'deeply shock the conscience of humanity' can justify an internationalization of their prosecution, which involves a far-reaching blow to the competence of domestic courts on an issue which otherwise would come under 'matters which are essentially within the domestic jurisdiction of States'. However, when such serious crimes are at stake they are 'of concern to the international community as a whole', as stated in the Preamble to the Rome Statute of the ICC, and it is then important that they not be 'confiscated' by any particular state, including the one in which the crime has been committed or of which the victims or the authors are nationals.

B. THE CONDITIONS FOR AN ACCEPTABLE PARTIAL INTERNATIONALIZATION

Mixed tribunals can indeed be a balanced solution, preserving both the special interests of a given country and the common interest of the international community as a whole in the prosecution of international crimes. But several conditions must be met to that end:

(1) the relevant tribunal must concentrate on the prosecution of the most serious crimes which, alone, are of concern to the still poorly integrated international community; in this respect, the Cambodia and Sierra Leone precedents are more convincing than the Kosovo and East Timor cases where the jurisdiction of the internationalized judicial bodies covers the whole range of criminal justice and answers other needs than the uncertain need for truly *international* justice; this is particularly blatant in the case of Kosovo where ICTY may (and probably should) demand that the authors of the most serious crimes be transferred to The Hague;

(2) the decision must, at the end of the day, belong to the judges representing the international community; but for example in the cases of Cambodia or Kosovo foreign judges are a minority, and in several cases, the voting

rules do not guarantee that the international judges can make or block the final decision and, when they can, a deadlock is not excluded;

(3) finally, the applicable law must be in full conformity with *international* criminal law both procedurally and substantively; this is not the case when the 'mixture' of national and international law leans to the former as seems to be the case at least in Cambodia.

It can, of course, be objected that it is the essence of hybrid courts to be half-way between purely national tribunals on the one hand and purely international tribunals on the other hand. But it is precisely on this point that I have doubts: if the very concept of 'concern to the international community as a whole' is to be taken seriously, there is no reason why this concern should be subordinated in any respect to national concerns or interests, whatever they may be.

C. INTERNATIONAL CRIMES DEMAND TRULY INTERNATIONAL JUSTICE

For this same reason, I am among those who think that, in cases of international crimes, national courts are not the appropriate fora to judge the perpetrators. With the exception of war crimes (which should probably be defined more tightly than they are in Article 8 of the ICC Statute to cover international crimes comparable with genocide, aggression, or crimes against humanity), international crimes are few; they are destabilizing for the international community as a whole and this community alone is—or should be— entitled to render international justice as far as they are concerned.

In this respect, the creation of the ICC is progress—but a very imperfect and incomplete one:

(a) it has been created by a treaty whereas, as the criminal tribunal of the international community as a whole, it should have been an emanation of this community as represented by the General Assembly of the United Nations; moreover, the treaty has, up to now, been ratified only by half of the existing states;

(b) States Parties have reserved an important degree of control as regards the jurisdiction and the activities of the Court; and

(c) it is endowed only with 'complementary' jurisdiction, with national courts retaining their primary competence in international criminal matters.

In a way, internationalized criminal courts present the same features. They are stamped with both the recent (limited) progress of worldwide common values and the persistency and resistance of national sovereignties. According to personal disposition, the bottle will be seen as 'half full' or 'half empty'.

But one thing is certain: internationalized criminal courts cloud the issues. They are an expression of the international community's concerns but, at the same time, they are part of the reconstruction enterprise of a new judicial system in countries where the entire administration had been destroyed by civil wars (Kosovo, East Timor) or they facilitate acceptance of accountability to justice of former national rulers (Cambodia and, in some respects, Sierra Leone) in view of a purely national process of reconciliation. They bear witness to the will of the international community to have its own peremptory norms respected and to fight impunity but, at the same time, they will generally answer a national need and, at least to some extent, fulfil national purposes. They are supposed to make the search for evidence and the arrest of authors of crimes easier than when performed by international tribunals, but at the same time they face enormous problems of judicial cooperation, the most illustrative case being the Special Court for Sierra Leone, which is not part of a UN mission (and, as such, cannot call on UN support) nor of the national judiciary, and, as such, cannot issue orders to the national authorities nor benefit from judicial cooperation agreements with other states; similarly, in East Timor, it has become clear that Indonesia is reluctant, to say the least, to cooperate with the Serious Crimes Panels of the District Court of Dili, while it is crystal clear that such cooperation is crucial for the efficient work of the Panels.

However, there is no question that, when crimes against the peace and security of mankind are at stake, mixed criminal tribunals are better than purely national courts. Their 'semi-internationalization' enhances their legitimacy and at least shows that prosecution of such crimes is not a purely national concern. It can also be acknowledged that they are a lesser evil than purely national justice in the absence of a truly international competent tribunal; in this respect, the creation of the ICC and the generalization of the acceptance of its jurisdiction should, hopefully, make the question of the creation of new internationalized tribunals moot.

D. DOUBLE STANDARDS

But there is another connected issue. If you take the (for the time being short) list of the existing internationalized criminal tribunals, it will be apparent that they are functioning either in small, weak, and very poor countries (Cambodia, East Timor, Sierra Leone) or in a 'province' under de facto UN trusteeship following the weakening of the central state (Kosovo). This shows at least two different things.

First, this confirms that those tribunals are created much more with a view to strengthening the local judiciary than to rendering *international* justice and punishing the perpetrators of *international* crimes as such.

Secondly, it shows that they can exist when, and only when, the international community is willing to impose their creation, which appears as an illustration of the double standards applied by the United Nations.

It can hardly be denied that, in the absence of a competent international court, there is a need for internationalized tribunals in a great variety of situations. I have doubts that they would be appropriate in the case of the Palestinian conflict where both sides commit international crimes (even though I am convinced that they are state crimes on the Israeli side and 'private' crimes on the Palestinian side); if a mixed court were created in this context it could only be 'tripartite' and it is not realistically foreseeable to have Israeli and Palestinian judges sitting in the same judicial organ. Nor do I share Antonio Cassese's opinion that there is a case for having Hissène Habré, the former Chadean dictator, judged by a mixed tribunal—or that this should be done for all other deposed dictators; in the future, the ICC can deal with such a situation and, in cases where it has no jurisdiction, national courts will do so.

On the other hand, given the circumstances, mixed criminal courts would appear to be clearly appropriate for judging eg:

(a) terrorists acting on a large scale as so dreadfully illustrated by the attacks of 11 September 2001;

(b) Afghani (and US?) combatants who committed war crimes during the fight against the Taliban in Afghanistan;

(c) the former leaders of Saddam Hussein's regime in Iraq (since the ICC has no jurisdiction—the case is different from that of 'usual' former dictators since the Iraq question itself has been internationalized since 1990);

(d) the members of the armed forces of the 'Coalition' who might have committed war crimes during the recent invasion of Iraq and the Iraqis who have committed terrorist crimes after the invasion.

These probably are the most obvious examples. However, it is striking that, in all four cases, the United States is deeply involved and it is certainly not open to seeking ways of 'internationalizing' prosecutions and trials—even less so since in at least two of them (Afghanistan and the Coalition invasion of Iraq) it would clearly be unthinkable not to allow for the possibility of prosecution of US citizens accused of war crimes, even if, at the end of the day, no prosecution occurs (as happened for NATO leaders before ICTY in respect of the bombing directed against the former Yugoslavia).

E. NATIONALIZING INTERNATIONAL TRIBUNALS?

Now, the question can also be put the other way: instead of internationalizing national courts, is there a case for 'nationalizing' international tribunals?—a result which is not far from that obtained with the Special Court of Sierra Leone which, as rightly noted by Luigi Condorelli and Théo Boutruche, comes close to a truly international criminal tribunal but with an important nuance: it is statutorily, and then symbolically, a national court.

I have in mind in this respect another example given by Antonio Cassese, that of Colombia. There is some doubt whether drug trafficking as such can qualify as a crime against humanity but there is no doubt that it is a crime of international concern. Moreover, Colombian drug traffickers also commit other serious violations of international law in parallel with their traffic and it is clear that national judges rightly fear for their lives when they judge these criminals. It would therefore be appropriate to create an international tribunal having competence to deal with drug trafficking and related crimes. However, it could be valuable to appoint one or two judges from the relevant country to the Bench, even though this does not entirely solve the question of their personal security; and this also raises the question of the place of the hearings.

A subsidiary question in this respect is the way of establishing such a mixed international tribunal. Even though drug trafficking may be seen as destabilizing the international community as a whole and threatening peace and international security, it seems unorthodox to have such a tribunal created by a resolution of the UN Security Council in spite of the recent trend of this body to 'legislate', as was so strikingly the case with Resolution 1373 (2001) in the case of terrorism. A treaty is, of course, possible; however, it would have the same inconveniences as the Rome Statute of the ICC: while the whole international community is concerned by drug trafficking on a large scale, the tribunal would have jurisdiction only vis-à-vis states becoming parties. It would seem more appropriate that the Statute of this new mixed tribunal be adopted by the General Assembly of the United Nations. Indeed, this would not radically change the picture, since the General Assembly in principle cannot adopt decisions binding upon states, which would still have to accept the Statute expressly; but thus created the International Tribunal for Drug Traffic would at least be an emanation of the least imperfect representative of the international community (of states) as a whole. This would also facilitate the links with the Security Council and make less questionable the possibility of it seizing the tribunal than in the case of the ICC.

It also goes without saying that such a new judicial body would be a permanent structure, not an ad hoc creation such as ICTY or ICTR or the existing mixed tribunals. It would thus escape criticisms founded on the accidental creation of the latter.

Such an international mixed criminal tribunal could also be envisaged for the crime of terrorism, even though it can be argued that the ICC could have jurisdiction for those crimes, at least where committed on a large scale.

However, the *travaux préparatoires* of the Rome Statute deny it. Moreover, given the absolute hostility of the United States towards the ICC it might be a better idea to envisage a new body to this end, and the inclusion of 'national judges' in the primarily international tribunal could be reassuring for the United States—not the actual internationally obtuse one, but a future US Administration more open to international community concerns.

Internationalized national tribunals or international tribunals with national judges, what is the difference? Quite big in my mind: in the first case, the international component is, so to speak, secondary, incidental; those tribunals (including their mixed nature) answer primarily national concerns; in the second scenario, the concerns of the international community as a whole become predominant while at the same time, the special interests of one or some given States would be taken into consideration. And when Serbia and Montenegro have been reintegrated into the bosom of 'civilized nations', it could not be a bad idea to partially 'nationalize' the ICTY in order to achieve such a result.

It must however be noted in this respect that the same result is achieved in a way with the plan to transfer some (or many) of the accused to their respective States in order to be tried there. But, here, it is not the Tribunal which is 'nationalized' or 'internationalized' but the whole prosecution process which is shared—and this in turn raises enormous problems as shown by the Rwanda case.

F. UNIVERSAL JURISDICTION

Of course, the creation of international or mixed tribunals is not the only means of indicating the concerns of the international community as a whole. Promoting universal jurisdiction and reinforcing the application of the principle *aut dedere aut judicare*—which is but a consequence of the former—also point at this direction.

This direction certainly is more in line with the structure of the international community and of international law where national courts are the usual means to apply international law.

However, this *dédoublement fonctionnel* (functional division) is not without inconveniences. First, as underlined by Luigi Condorelli and Théo Boutruche, there is a danger that international standards be denatured and, in any case, applied in diverse ways by the various internationalized tribunals; this is even more true for purely national courts where no input from abroad limits the risk of arbitrary or *pro domo* interpretations. Secondly, it is averred that States do not usually take universal jurisdiction seriously; and when they do, like in Belgium or Spain, they interpret it with excessive zeal: States can only act at the international level when they can invoke a title (based in most cases on territory or nationality); absent such a title they have no jurisdiction; for having forgotten this wise and basic principle, Belgium has put itself in a very uncomfortable position.

But there is more. 'Universal' jurisdiction is fundamentally *national* jurisdiction. This shows the limits of the breakthrough of international concerns in criminal matters. Indeed, through universal jurisdiction, all States are made sensitive to the international dimension of the most grave crimes, the perpetration of which endangers the international peace and security. However, it remains part of the 'classical' international law when only States had 'executive powers' in the international sphere. At the dawn of the twenty-first century, when the existence of peremptory norms of international law is no longer challenged (even by France) and the notion of 'State crimes' is generally accepted—without the name: but 'serious violations of peremptory norms' as embodied in the ILC articles on State Responsibility have the same effect—the absence of a generally accepted international criminal court with automatic jurisdiction for judging the authors of grave crimes which 'threaten the peace, security and well-being of the world' is a matter of perplexity and, to tell the truth, of scandal.

In this context, the creation of the ICC was indeed a step forward; but it remains hesitant and partial. And the multiplication of internationalized tribunals is only a stopgap solution—better than nothing; but also an illustration of the present incapacity of the international community to take over its responsibility to protect the common interests of mankind.

Select Bibliography

General works

Ambos, Kai and Othman, Mohamed (eds), *New Approaches in International Criminal Justice: Kosovo, East Timor, Sierra Leone and Cambodia,* (Freiburg: Max Planck Institut für ausländisches und internationales Strafrecht, 2003)

Dickinson, Laura A, 'The promise of hybrid courts', 97 *American Journal of International Law* 295 (2003)

Romano, Cesare, 'Mixed Jurisdictions for East Timor, Kosovo Sierra Leone and Cambodia: The Coming Of Age of Internationalised Criminal Bodies?', 2 *The Global Community: Yearbook of International Law and Jurisprudence* 97 (2002)

Romano, Cesare and Boutrouche, Thèo, 'Tribunaux pénaux internationalisés: état des lieux d'une justice hybride', 107(1) *Revue générale de droit international public* 109 (2003)

Sierra Leone

Adebajo, Adekeye, *1966 Building Peace in West Africa: Liberia, Sierra Leone, and Guinea-Bissau* (Boulder, Colo: Lynne Rienner Publishers, 2002)

Akinrinade, Babafemi, 'International Humanitarian Law and the Conflict in Sierra Leone', 15(2) *Notre Dame Journal of Law, Ethics & Public Policy* 391 (2001)

Alao, Abiodun, 'Sierra Leone: Tracing the Genesis of a Controversy', *The Royal Institute of International Affairs, Briefing Paper No 50* (June 1998)

American Embassy of Freetown, *Sierra Leone* (Washington, DC: US Dept of Commerce, International Trade Administration, February 1988)

Amman, Diane Marie, 'International Law Weekend—West Symposium Issue: Calling Children to Account: The Proposal for a Juvenile Chamber in the Special Court for Sierra Leone', 29 *Pepperdine Law Review* 167 (2001)

Amman, Diane Marie, 'International Law Weekend Proceedings: Message as Medium in Sierra Leone', 7 *ILSA Journal of International & Comparative Law* 237 (Spring 2001)

Amnesty International, *Sierra Leone: A Casualty of Conflict* (New York, NY: Amnesty International Publications, 2000)

Amnesty International, *Sierra Leone: Ending Impunity—An Opportunity Not to Be Missed* (New York, NY: Amnesty International USA Publications, 2000)

Bald, Stephanie, 'Searching for a Lost Childhood: Will the Special Court of Sierra Leone find Justice for Its Children?' 18(2) *American University International Law Review* 537 (2002)

Bankole, Thompson, *The Criminal Law of Sierra Leone* (Lanham: University Press of America, 1999)

Beigbeder, Yves, *Judging Criminal Leaders: The Slow Erosion of Impunity* (The Hague: Kluwer Law International, 2002), 171–214.

Beresford, Stuart, 'The Special Court for Sierra Leone: An Initial Comment', 14 *Leiden Journal of International Law* 365 (2001)

Berger, Lee F, 'State Practice Evidence of the Humanitarian Intervention Doctrine: The ECOWAS Intervention in Sierra Leone', 11(3) *Indiana International & Comparative Law Review* 605 (2001)

Betts, Wendy S, Scott N Carlson and Gregory Gisvold, 'The Post-Conflict Transitional Administration of Kosovo and the Lessons Learned in Efforts to Establish a Judiciary and Rule of Law', 22 *Michigan Journal of International Law* 371 (2000–01)

Binns, Margret and Tony Binns (compilers), *Sierra Leone* (Oxford; Santa Barbara, Calif: Clio Press, 1992)

Campbell, Greg, *Blood Diamonds: Tracing the Deadly Path of the World's Most Precious Stones* (Boulder, Colo: Westview Press, 2002)

Cerone, John, 'The Special Court for Sierra Leone: Establishing a New Approach to International Criminal Justice', 8(2) *ILSA Journal of International & Comparative Law* 379 (Spring 2002)

Cohn, Irene, 'The Protection of Children and the Quest for Truth and Justice in Sierra Leone', 55 *Journal of International Affairs* (Fall 2001)

Conteh-Morgan, Earl and Mac Dixon-Fyle, *Sierra Leone at the End of the Twentieth Century: History, Politics, and Society* (New York: Lang, 1999)

Corriero, Michael A, 'The Involvement and Protection of Children in Truth and Justice-Seeking Processes: The Special Court for Sierra Leone', 18 *New York Law School Journal of Human Rights* 337 (2002)

Cortright, David, George A Lopez and Conroy, Richard W, 'Sierra Leone: The Failure of Regional and International Sanctions,' in: David Cortright and George A Lopez (eds), *The Sanctions Decade: Assessing UN Strategies in the 1990s* (Boulder, Colo: Lynne Rienner Publishers, 2000)

Cryer, Robert, 'A Special Court for Sierra Leone?', 50(2) *International & Comparative Law Quarterly* 435 (April 2001)

Denis, Catherine, 'Le Tribunal spécial pour la Sierra Leone. Quelques observations', 1 *Revue Belge de Droit International* 236 (2001)

De Sanctis, Francesco, 'Il processo di istituzione di una Special Court per i crimini della guerra civile in Sierra Leone', 56(3) *La Comunità Internazionale* 475 (2001)

Fritz, Nicole and Alison Smith, 'Current Apathy for Coming Anarchy: Building the Special Court for Sierra Leone', 25 *Fordham International Law Journal* 391 (2001)

Frulli, Micaela, 'The Special Court for Sierra Leone: Some Preliminary Comments', 11 *European Journal of International Law* 857 (2000)

Gallagher, Karen, 'No Justice, No Peace: The Legalities and Realities of Amnesty in Sierra Leone', 23(1) *Thomas Jefferson Law Review* 149 (Fall 2000)

Garcia, T, 'La mission d'administration intérimaire des Nations Unies au Kosovo', 104 *Revue génerale de droit international public* 61 (2000)

Haines, Avril D, 'Accountability in Sierra Leone: the Role of the Special Court', in: Jane E Stromseth (ed) *Accountability for Atrocities* (Ardsley on Hudson: Transnational Publishers, 2003), 173–235

Hall, Laura R and Nahal Kazemi, 'Recent Development: Prospects for Justice and Reconciliation in Sierra Leone', 44 *Harvard Journal of International Law* 287 (Winter 2003)

Hirsch, John L, *Sierra Leone: Diamonds and the Struggle for Democracy* (Boulders, Colo: Lynne Rienner Publishers, 2001)

Hoffmann, Michael, 'May We Hold Them Responsible? The Prosecution of Child Soldiers by the Special Court for Sierra Leone', 14 *International Children's Rights Monitor* 23 (2001)

Human Rights Watch, *Sierra Leone: Sowing Terror: Atrocities against Civilians in Sierra Leone* (New York, NY: Human Rights Watch, 1998)

Kup, Alexander P, *Sierra Leone: A Concise History* (New York, NY: St Martin's Press, 1975)

Linton, Suzannah, 'Cambodia, East Timor and Sierra Leone: Experiments in International Justice', 12(2) *Criminal Law Forum* 185 (2001)

Lun, Jon and John Caulker, *Moments of Truth in Sierra Leone: Contextualizing the Truth and Reconciliation Commission* (Freetown, Sierra Leone: Article 19; Forum for Conscience, 2000)

Macaluso, Daniel J, 'Absolute and Free Pardon: The Effect of the Amnesty Provision in the Lomé Peace Agreement on the Jurisdiction of the Special Court for Sierra Leone', 27 *Brooklyn Journal of International Law* 347 (2002)

Magliveras, Konstantinos D, 'The Special Court for Sierra Leone: A New Type of Regional Criminal Court for the International Community?', 17 *International Enforcement Law Report* 81 (2001)

Malan, Mark, Rakate Phenyo and Angela McIntyre, *Peacekeeping in Sierra Leone: UNAMSIL Hits the Home Straight* (Pretoria, South Africa: Institute for Security Studies, 2002)

Markees, Curt, 'The Difference in Concept between Civil and Common Law Countries as to Judicial Assistance and Cooperation in Criminal Matters', in: M Cherif Bassiouni and Ved P Nanda (eds), *A Treatise on International Criminal Law, Vol II: Jurisdiction and Cooperation* (Springfield, IL: Thomas 1973)

Matheson, Michael J, 'United Nations Governance of Post-Conflict Societies', 95 *American Journal of International Law* 76 (2001)

McDonald, Avril, 'Sierra Leone's Uneasy Peace: the Amnesties Granted in the Lomé Peace Agreement and the United Nations' Dilemma', 1 *Humanitäres Völkerrecht— Informationsschriften* 11 (2000)

McDonald, Avril, 'Sierra Leone's Shoestring Special Court', *International Review of the Red Cross*, no 845 121 (2002)

Miraldi, Marissa, 'Overcoming Obstacles of Justice: the Special Court of Sierra Leone', 19 *New York Law School Journal of Human Rights* 849 (2003)

Nowrot, Karsten et al, 'The Use of Force to Restore Democracy: International Legal Implications of the ECOWAS Intervention in Sierra Leone', 14(2) *American University International Law Review* 321 (1998)

O'Neill, William, 'Conflict in West Africa: Dealing with Exclusion and Separation', 12 *International Journal of Refugee Law* 171 (Winter 2000)

Pratt, David, 'Sierra Leone: The Forgotten Crisis', *Report to Canada's Minister of Foreign Affairs* (23 April 1999) (available at: http://www.sierra-leone.org/pratt042399.html)

Puy-Denis, Patrick, *La Sierra Leone* (Paris: Karthala, 1998)

Romano, Cesare and André Nollkaemper, 'The Arrest Warrant against the Liberian President Charles Taylor', *ASIL Insights* (June 2003) (available at: http://www.asil. org/insights/insigh110.htm)

Schabas, William, 'The Relationship between Truth Commissions and International Courts: the Case of Sierra Leone' 25 *Human Rights Quarterly* 1035 (2003)

Scharf, Michael P, 'The Special Court of Sierra Leone', *ASIL Insights* (October 2000) (available at: http://www.asil.org/insights/insigh53.htm)

Schocken, Celina, 'The Special Court for Sierra Leone: Overview and Recommendations', 20 *Berkeley Journal of International Law* 436 (2002)

Shawcross, William, *Deliver Us from Evil: Peacekeepers, Warlords, and a World of Endless Conflict* (New York: Simon & Schuster, 2000)

Sieff, Michelle, 'Prosecuting War Crimes in Sierra Leone. War Crimes: Watch Out' *The World Today*, (2001), 18–20.

Tejan-Cole, Abdul, 'Painful Peace: Amnesty under the Lomé Peace Agreement', *Revue Africaine des Droits de l'Homme* 238 (2000)

Tejan-Cole, Abdul, 'The Special Court for Sierra Leone: Conceptual Concerns and Alternatives', *African Human Rights Law Journal* 107 (2001)

Udombana, Nsongurua J, 'Globalization of Justice and the Special Court for Sierra Leone's War Crimes', 17 *Emory International Law Review* 55 (2003)

Webster, Jeanna, 'Sierra Leone: Responding to the Crisis, Planning for the Future: The Role of International Justice in the Quest for National and Global Security', 11(3) *Indiana International & Comparative Law Review* 731 (2001)

East Timor

Ambos, Kai and Steffen Wirth, 'The Current Law of Crimes against Humanity: an Analysis of UNTAET Regulation 15/2000', 13 *Criminal Law Forum* 1 (2002)

Beauvais, Joel C, 'Benevolent Despotism: A Critique of U.N. State-Building in East Timor', 33 *NYU Journal of International Law & Politics* 1101 (2000–01)

Blauvais, Joel C 'Cambodia, East Timor and Sierra Leone: Experiments in International Justice', 12 *Criminal Law Forum* 185 (2001)

Bongiorno, Carla, 'A Culture of Impunity: Applying International Human Rights Law to the United Nations in East Timor', 33 *Columbia Human Rights Law Review* 623 (Summer 2002)

Cardoso, Luis, *The Crossing: A Story of East Timor* (London: Granta Books, 2002)

Coakley, Victoria, 'Towards Justice and Reconciliation in East Timor', 26 *Alternative Law Journal* 229 (October 2001)

Charlesworth, Hilary, 'Mainstreaming Gender in International Peace and Security: The Case of East Timor', 26 *Yale Journal of International Law* 313 (2001)

Charney, Jonathan, 'Self-determination: Chechnya, Kosovo and East Timor', 34 *Vanderbilt Journal of Transnational Law* 273 (2000)

Chesterman, Simon, 'East Timor in Transition: Self-Determination, State-Building and the United Nations', *International Peacekeeping* 9: 1 (2002): 45–76.

Chinkin, Christine, 'East Timor: A Failure of Decolonization', 20 *Australian Yearbook of International Law* 35 (1999)

Chomsky, Noam, *A New Generation Draws the Line: Kosovo, East Timor and the Standards of the West* (London: Verso, 2000)

Chopra, Jarat, 'The UN's Kingdom of East Timor', *Survival* 42: 3 (2000): 27–39.

Clark, Roger, 'Decolonization of East Timor and the United Nations Norms on Self-determination and Aggression', 7 *Yale Studies in World Public Order* 2 (1980–81)

Commission for Reception, Truth and Reconciliation in East Timor, URL: http://www.easttimor-reconciliation.org/

Department of Foreign Affairs and Trade (Australia), *East Timor in Transition 1998–2000: An Australian Policy Challenge* (Canberra: Brown and Wilton, 2000)

Dickinson, Laura A, 'The Dance of Complementarity: Relationships among Domestic, International, and Transnational Accountability Mechanisms in East Timor and Indonesia', in: Stromseth (ed) *Accountability for Atrocities* 319–74

Drew, Catriona, 'The East Timor Story: International Law on Trial', 12 *European Journal of International Law* 651 (September 2001)

Dugard, John, '1966 and All That: The South West Africa Judgment revised in the East Timor Case', 8 *African Journal of International and Comparative Law* 549 (1996)

Dunn, James, 'Crimes against Humanity in East Timor, January to October 1999: Their Nature and Causes', ('The Dunn Report') (2001) (available at http://www.etan.org/news/2001a/dunn1.htm)

Fitzpatrick, Daniel, 'Developing a Legal System in East Timor: Some Issues of UN Mandate and Capacity', 5 *Austrian rev int Eur law* 5 (2000)

Grant, Thomas, 'East Timor, the U.N. System and Enforcing Non-recognition in International Law', 33 *Vanderbilt Journal of Transnational Law* 273 (2000)

Hainsworth, Paul, and Stephen McCloskey (eds), *The East Timor Question: The Struggle for Independence from Indonesia* (London: IB Tauris, 2000)

Hoogh, André JJ de, 'Attribution or Delegation of (Legislative) Power by the Security Council?: The Case of the United Nations Transitional Administration in East Timor (UNTAET)', 7 *International Peacekeeping* (Dordrecht) 1 (2001)

Howard, Jessica, 'Invoking State Responsibility for Aiding the Commission of International Crimes—Australia, the United States and the Question of East Timor', 2 *Melbourne Journal of International Law* 1 (2001)

Jardine, Matthew, 'East Timor: Genocide in Paradise' (Odonian/Common Courage Press, 2nd edn 1999)

Judicial System Monitoring Program, *Thematic Report Number 1: Justice in Practice—Human Rights in Court Administration* (November 2001) (available at: http://www.jsmp.minihub.org/Reports/JSMP1.pdf)

Judicial System Monitoring Program, *The General Prosecutor v Joni Marquez and 9 Others (The Los Palos Case)* (March 2002) (available at: http://www.jsmp.minihub.org/Reports/Los%20Palos%20trial%20report.pdf)

Judicial System Monitoring Program, *Findings and Recommendations: Workshop on Formal and Local Justice Systems in East Timor* (July 2002) (available at: http://www.jsmp.minihub.org/Reports/Tradjusteng.pdf)

Katzenstein, Suzanne, 'Hybrid Tribunals: Searching for Justice in East Timor', 16 *Harvard Human Rights Journal* 245 (2003)

Kondoch, Boris, 'The United Nations Administration of East Timor', 6 *Journal of Conflict and Security Law* 145 (2001)

Krieger, Heike, and Dietrich Rauschning, *East Timor and the International Community: Basic Documents* (Cambridge: Cambridge University Press, 1997)

Linton, Suzannah, 'Cambodia, East Timor and Sierra Leone: Experiments in International Justice', 12 *Criminal Law Forum* 185 (2001)

Linton, Suzannah, 'Prosecuting Atrocities at the District Court of Dili', 2 *Melbourne Journal of International Law* 414 (2001)

Linton, Suzannah, 'Rising from the Ashes: The Creation of A Viable Criminal Justice System In East Timor', 25 *Melbourne University Law Review* 122 (2001)

Linton, Suzannah, 'Making Multilateral Interventions Work: The U.N. and the Creation of Transitional Justice Systems in Kosovo and East Timor', 25 *Fletcher Forum of World Affairs* 107 (2001)

Linton, Suzannah, 'New Approaches to International Justice in Cambodia and East Timor', 845 *International Review of the Red Cross* 93 (2002) (available at: http://www.icrc.org/Web/eng/siteeng0.nsf/iwpList74/7B6428D7E40DD0D3C1256 BA70 03477CE)

Martin, Ian, *Self-Determination in East Timor: The United Nations, the Ballot, and International Intervention* (International Peace Academy Occasional Paper Series) (Boulder, Colo: Lynne Rienner Publishers, 2001)

Martinkus, John, *A Dirty Little War: An Eyewitness Account of East Timor's Descent into Hell, 1997–2000* (Sydney: Random House Australia, 2001)

Mello, Sergio Vieira de, 'United Nations Transnational Authority in East Timor', in: Nassrine Azimi and Chang Li Lin (eds), *The Reform Process of United Nations Peace Operations* (London: Kluwer Law International for UNITAR 2001), 93–9

Mundis, Daryl A, 'New Mechanisms for the Enforcement of International Humanitarian Law', 95 *American Journal of International Law* 934 (2001)

Pinto, Constancio, *East Timor's Unfinished Struggle: Inside the Timorese Resistance* (Boston, MA: South End Press, 1997)

Pritchard, Sarah, 'United Nations Involvement in Post-Conflict Reconstruction Efforts: New and Continuing Challenges in the Case of East Timor', 24 *University of New South Wales Law Journal* 183 (2001)

Pritchard, Sarah, 'Prosecuting Atrocities at the District Court of Dili', 2 *Melbourne Journal of International Law* 414 (2001)

Quarterman, Mark, 'UN Leverage in East Timor: Inducing Indonesian Compliance through International Law', in: Jean Krasno, Bradd C Hayes, and Donald CF Daniel (eds) *Leveraging for Success in United Nations Peace Operations* (Westport, CT: Praeger Publishers, 2003), 141–68

Ramos-Horta, José, *The Unfinished Saga of East Timor* (Lawrenceville, NJ: Red Sea Press, 1987)

Rothert, Mark, 'U.N. Intervention in East Timor', 39 *Columbia Journal of Transnational Law* 257 (2000–01)

Ruffert, Matthias, 'The Administration of Kosovo and East-Timor by the International Community', 50 *The International & Comparative Law Quarterly* 613 (July 2001)

Saul, Ben, 'Was the Conflict in East Timor "Genocide" And Why Does It Matter?' 2 *Melbourne Journal International Law* 477 (2001)

Stahn, Carsten, 'Accommodating Individual Criminal Responsibility and National Reconciliation: The UN Truth Commission for East Timor', 95 *American Journal of International Law* 952 (2001)

Stahn, Carsten, 'The United Nations Transitional Administrations in Kosovo and East Timor: A First Analysis', 5 *Max Planck Yearbook UN law* 105 (2001)

Strohmeyer, Hansjörg, 'Collapse and Reconstruction of A Judicial System: The United Nations Missions in Kosovo And East Timor', 95 *American Journal of International Law* 46 (2001)

Strohmeyer, Hansjörg, 'Making Multilateral Interventions Work: The UN and the Creation of Transitional Justice Systems in Kosovo and East Timor', 25 *Fletcher Forum of World Affairs* 107 (2001)

Strohmeyer, Hansjörg, 'Policing the Peace: Post-Conflict Judicial System Reconstruction in East Timor', 24 *University of New South Wales Law Journal* 171 (2001)

Taudevin, Lansell, and Jefferson Lee (eds), *East Timor: Making Amends? Analysing Australia's Role in Reconstructing East Timor* (Sydney: Oxford University Press, 2000)

Tool, Jennifer, 'False Sense of Security: Lessons Learned from the United Nations Organization and Conduct Mission in East Timor', 16 *American University International Law Review* 199 (2000–01)

Tracol, Xavier, 'Justice pour le Timor oriental', *Revue de Science Criminelle et de Droit Pénal Compare* (no 2) 291 (2001)

United Nations, *The United Nations and East Timor: Self-Determination Through Popular Consultation* (New York: UN Department of Public Information, 2000)

Wilde, Ralph, 'From Bosnia to Kosovo and East Timor: The Changing role of the United Nations in the Administration of Territory', 6 *ILSA Journal of International and Comparative Law* 467 (Spring 2000)

Wilde, Ralph, 'From Danzig to East Timor and Beyond: The Role of International Territorial Administration', 95 *American Journal of International Law* 583 (2001)

Wilde, Ralph, 'Accountability and International Actors in Bosnia and Herzegovina, Kosovo and East Timor', 7 *ILSA Journal of International and Comparative Law* 455 (Spring 2001)

Kosovo

Abrams, Jason, 'The Atrocities in Cambodia and Kosovo: Observations on the Codification of Genocide', 35(2) *New England Law Review* 303 (Winter 2001)

Amnesty International, *Kosovo: The Evidence* (London: Amnesty International, 1998)

Auerswald, Philip E, David P Auerswald and Christian Duttweiler (eds), *The Kosovo Conflict: A Diplomatic History Through Documents* (The Hague; Cambridge Mass: Kluwer Law International, 2000)

Bellamy, Alex J, *Kosovo and International Society* (Houndmills; New York: Palgrave, 2002)

Betts, Wendy S, Scott N Carlson and Gregory Gisvold, 'The Post-Conflict Transitional Administration of Kosovo and the Lessons Learned in Efforts to Establish a Judiciary and Rule of Law', 22 *Michigan Journal of International Law* 371 (2000–01)

Bilder, Richard B, 'Kosovo and the "New Interventionism": Promise or Peril?', 9 *Journal of Transitional Law & Policy* 153 (Fall 2001)

Booth, Ken, *The Kosovo Tragedy: The Human Rights Dimensions* (London; Portland, Oreg: Frank Cass, 2001)

Brand, Marcus G, 'Institution-Building and Human Rights Protection in Kosovo in the Lights of UNMIK Legislation', 70 *Nordic Journal of International Law* 461 (2001)

Brownlie, Ian and C J Apperley, 'Kosovo Crisis Inquiry: Memorandum on the International Law Aspects', 49 *The International & Comparative Law Quarterly* 878 (October 2000)

Bush, George W/United States Congress, Committee on International Relations, *Report on continued contributions in support of peacekeeping efforts in Kosovo: Communication from the President of the United States transmitting a supplemental report, consistent with the War Powers Resolution, to help ensure that the Congress is kept fully informed on continued U.S. contributions in support of peacekeeping efforts in Kosovo* (Washington: US GPO, 2002)

Caplan, Richard, 'International Diplomacy and the Crisis in Kosovo', 74(4) *International Affairs* 745 (1998)

Carlowitz, Leopold von, 'UNMIK Lawmaking between Effective Peace Support and Internal Self-Determination', 41 *Archiv des Völkerrechts* 336 (2003)

Cerone, John, 'Minding the Gap: Outlining KFOR Accountability in Post-conflict Kosovo', 12(3) *European Journal of International Law* 469 (June 2001)

Cerone, John, 'Legal Constraints on the International Community's Responses to Gross Violations of Human Rights and Humanitarian Law in Kosovo, East Timor, & Chechnya', *Human Rights Review*, vol 2, no 4 (September 2001)

Cerone, John, 'Reasonable Measures in Unreasonable Circumstances: A Legal Accountability Framework for Human Rights Violations in Post-Conflict Territories under UN Administration,' in: Nigel White and Dirk Klaasen (eds), *The UN, Human Rights, and Post-Conflict Societies* (forthcoming, October 2003)

Chandler, David, *From Kosovo to Kabul: Human Rights and International Intervention* (London: Pluto press, 2002)

Charney, Jonathan, 'Self-determination: Chechnya, Kosovo, and East Timor', 34(2) *Vanderbilt Journal of International Law* 455 (March 2001)

Chomsky, Noam, *The New Military Humanism* (Monroe, Me: Common Courage Press, 1999)

del Re, Emmanuela C, 'When Our Men Arrive: UNMIK's Post-Conflict Administration of Kosovo', in: Peter Siani-Davies (ed) *International Intervention in the Balkans since 1995* (London: Routledge 2003), 88–104

Dickinson, Laura A, 'The Relationship between Hybrid Courts and International Courts: the case of Kosovo', 37 *New England Law Review* 1059 (2003)

European Action Council for Peace in the Balkans and Public International Law & Policy Group of the Carnegie Endowment for International Peace, *Kosovo: From Crisis to a Permanent Solution* (1 November 1997)

Falk, Richard A, 'Kosovo, World Order, and the Future of International Law', 93 *American Journal of International Law* 847 (October 1999)

Franck, Thomas M, 'Lessons of Kosovo', 93 *American Journal of International Law* 857 (October 1999)

Garcia, T, 'La mission d'administration intérimaire des Nations Unies au Kosovo', 104 *Revue Génerale de Droit International Public* 61 (2000)

Gerber, Paula, 'Rebuilding the Law in Kosovo', 76(1) *Law Institute Journal* 72 (February 2002)

Glennon, Michael, *Limits of Law, Prerogatives of Power: Intervention after Kosovo* (Houndmills; New York: Palgrave, 2001)

Goldstone, Richard, J, 'Wither Kosovo? Wither Democracy', *Global Governance*, vol 8 (2002)

Grant, Thomas, D, 'Extending Decolonization: How the United Nations Might Have Addressed Kosovo', 28 *Georgia Journal of International & Comparative Law* 9 (Fall 1999)

Green, LC, 'The Rule of Law and Human Rights in the Balkans', 37 *The Canadian Yearbook of International Law* 223 (1999)

Henkin, Louis, 'Kosovo and the Law of Humanitarian Intervention', 93 *American Journal of International Law* 824 (October 1999)

Ignatieff, Michael, *Virtual War: Kosovo and Beyond* (New York: Picador, 2001)

Independent International Commission on Kosovo, *The Kosovo Report: Conflict, International Response, Lessons Learned* (Oxford; New York: Oxford University Press, 2000)

Joyner, Daniel H, 'The Kosovo Intervention: Legal Analysis and a More Persuasive Paradigm', 13(3) *European Journal of International Law* 597 (June 2002)

Judah, Tim, *Kosovo: War and Revenge* (Yale, New Haven: Yale University Press, 2000)

Koskenniemi, Martti, ' "The Lady Doth Protest Too Much": Kosovo, and the Turn to Ethics in International Law', 65(2) *The Modern Law Review* 159 (March 2002)

Krieger, Heike, *The Kosovo Conflict and International Law: An Analytical Documentation 1974–1999* (Cambridge: Cambridge University Press, 2001)

Lorenz, FM, 'The Rule of Law in Kosovo: Problems and Prospects', 11 *Criminal Law Forum* 127 (2000)

Lowe, Vaughan, 'International Legal Issues Arising in the Kosovo Crisis', 49 *International & Comparative Law Quarterly* 934 (October 2000)

Malcolm, Noel, *Kosovo: A Short History* (New York: New York University Press, 1998)

Malone, Linda A, 'Seeking Reconciliation of Self-determination, Territorial Integrity, and Humanitarian Intervention', 41 *William and Mary Law Review* 1677 (May 2000)

Marshall, David, 'Reviving the Judicial and Penal System in Kosovo', in: Michael Pugh, Waheguru Pal Singh Sidhu, and David Marshall (eds) *The United Nations and Regional Security: Europe and Beyond* (Boulder, Co: Lynne Rienner, 2003), 155–74

Matheson, Michael J, 'United Nations Governance of Post-Conflict Societies', 95 *American Journal of International Law* 76 (2001)

Mertus, Julie, *Kosovo: How Myths and Truths Started a War* (Berkeley: University of California Press, 1999)

McGregor, Lorna, 'Military and Judicial Intervention: The Way Forward in Human Rights Enforcement?' 12(1) *Indiana International & Comparative Law Review* 107 (2001)

Moorman, William, 'Humanitarian Intervention and International Law in the Case of Kosovo', 36(4) *New England Law Review* 775 (Summer 2002)

Nevin, Jack, 'Kosovo Detention Review Commission', 56(7) *Washington State Bar News* 18 (July 2002)

Nester, Pat, 'CLE in Kosovo', 65(11) *Texas Bar Journal* 992 (December 2002)

O'Neill, William G, *Kosovo: An Unfinished Peace* (Boulder, Colo: Lynne Rienner Publishers, 2002)

Reisman, Michael, 'Kosovo's Antinomies', 93 *American Journal of International Law* 860 (October 1999)

Ruffert, Matthias, 'The Administration of Kosovo and East Timor by the International Community', 50 *The International & Comparative Law Quarterly* 613 (July 2001)

Rupnik, Jacques, 'Dilemmas of the Protectorate', 9 *East European Constitutional Review* 48 (Winter/Spring 2000)

Schabas, William, 'Problems of International Codification—Were the Atrocities in Cambodia and Kosovo Genocide?' 35(2) *New England Law Review* 287 (Winter 2001)

Scharf, Irene, 'Kosovo's War Victims: Civil Compensation or Criminal Justice for Identity Elimination?' 14(3) *Emory International Law Review* 1415 (Fall 2001)

Schnabel, Albrecht and Ramesh Chandra Thakur, *Kosovo and the Challenge of Humanitarian Intervention: Selective Indignation, Collective Action, and International Citizenship* (Tokyo; New York: United Nations University Press, 2000)

Schmidt, Albert, 'Toward the Rule of Law: Kosovo 2000 Elections', 20(3) *QLR* 467 (Winter 2001)

Serwer, Daniel Paul, *Kosovo Decision Time: How and When?* (Washington DC: United States Institute for Peace, 2003)

Shawcross, William, *Deliver Us from Evil: Peacekeepers, Warlords, and a World of Endless Conflict* (New York: Simon & Schuster, 2000)

Sofaer, Abraham, D, 'International Law and Kosovo', 36 *Stanford Journal of International Law* 1 (Winter 2000)

Stahn, Carsten, 'The United Nations Transitional Administrations in Kosovo and East Timor: a First Analysis', 5 *Max Planck Yearbook UN Law* 105 (2001)

Strohmeyer, Hansjörg, 'Collapse and Reconstruction of a Judicial System: The United Nations Missions in Kosovo and East Timor', 95(1) *American Journal of International Law* 46 (January 2001)

Szasz, Paul, 'The Irresistible Force of Self-determination Meets the Impregnable Fortress of Territorial Integrity: A Cautionary Fairy Tale about Clashes in Kosovo and Elsewhere', 28 *Georgia Journal of International and Comparative Law* 1 (Fall 1999)

Tomuschat, Christian, *Kosovo and the International Community: A Legal Assessment* (Hague; New York: Kluwer Law International, 2002)

Villmoare, Edwin, 'Ethnic Crimes and UN Justice in Kosovo: The Trial of Igor Simic', 37 *Texas International Law Journal* 373 (2002)

Wilde, Ralph 'From Bosnia to Kosovo and East Timor: The Changing Role of the United Nations in the Administration of Territory', 6 *ILSA Journal of International & Comparative Law* 467 (Spring 2000)

Wilde, Ralph, 'Accountability and International Actors in Bosnia And Herzegovina, Kosovo and East Timor', 7 *ILSA Journal of International & Comparative Law* 455 (2001)

Wippman, David, 'Kosovo and the Limits of International Law', 25(1) *Fordham International Law Journal* 129 (November 2001)

Zacklin, Ralph, 'Beyond Kosovo: The United Nations and Humanitarian Intervention', 41(4) *Virginia Journal of International Law* 923 (Summer 2001)

Yannis, Alexandros, *Kosovo Under International Administration: An Unfinished Conflict* (Athens: Hellenic Foundation for European and Foreign Policy, 2001)

Yannis, Alexandros, 'The Concept of Suspended Sovereignty in International Law and its Implications in International Politics', 13(5) *European Journal of International Law* 1037 (November, 2002)

Cambodia

Ablin, David A and Marlowe Hood (eds), *The Cambodian Agony* (Armonk, NY: ME Sharpe, 1990)

Abrams, J, 'The Atrocities in Cambodia and Kosovo: Observations on the Codification of Genocide', 35(2) *New England Law Review* 303 (Winter 2001)

Adams, Brad, 'The UN Must Stand Firm on Principles for KR Trial', *Phnom Penh Post*, 17–30 March 2000.

Amnesty International, *1998 Report on Cambodia* (available at: http://www.amnesty.org/ailib/aireport/ar98/asa23.htm)

Amnesty International, *Kingdom of Cambodia: Human Rights at Stake* (New York: Amnesty International, 1998)

Andreopolous, George J, 'The Calculus of Genocide', in: George J Andrepolous (ed), *Genocide: Conceptual and Historical Dimensions* (Philadelphia: University of Pennsylvania Press, 1994), 1–28.

Asia Watch, *Khmer Rouge Abuses along the Thai–Cambodian Border* (New York, NY: The Asia Watch Committee, 1989)

Beauvais, Joel C, 'Cambodia, East Timor and Sierra Leone: Experiments in International Justice', 12 *Criminal Law Forum* 185 (2001)

Becker, Elizabeth, *When the War Was Over: The Voices of Cambodia's Revolution and Its People* (New York: Simon and Schuster, 1986)

Boutros-Ghali, Boutros, *United Nations and Cambodia, 1991–95* (New York, NY: United Nations, Dept of Public Information, 1995)

Boyle, David, 'Quelle justice pour les Khmers rouges?' *Revue Trimestrielle des Droits de l'Homme* 773, 10e année, N° 40 (1999)

Boyle, David, 'One More Step—Adoption of the Khmer Rouge Trial Law', *Judicial Diplomacy*, 5 August 2001, available at: http://www.diplomatiejudiciaire.com

Bunyanunda, Mann, 'The Khmer Rouge on Trial: Wither the Defense?' 74 *Southern California Law Review* 1581 (2000–01)

Buckley, Aaron J, 'The Conflict in Cambodia and Post-Conflict Justice', in: M Cherif Bassiouni (ed) *Post-Conflict Justice* (2002), 635–57

Center for Social Development, *The Khmer Rouge and National Reconciliation—Opinions from the Cambodians* (Phnom Penh: Center for Social Development, April 2001)

Chandler, David P, *Brother Number One: A Political Biography of Pol Pot* (Boulder, Colo: Westview Press, 1992)

Chandler, David P, *Voices from S-21: Terror and History in Pol Pot's Secret Prison* (Berkeley: University of California Press, 1999)

Chandler, David P, 'Will There Be a Trial for the Khmer Rouge?' *Annual Journal of the Carnegie Council on Ethics and International Affairs*, 2000 (vol 14)

Chandler, David P, *A History of Cambodia* (Boulder, Colo: Westview Press, 2000)

Chigas, George, 'The Politics of Defining Justice after the Cambodian Genocide', *Journal of Genocide Research*, vol 2, 2000

Chigas, George, 'The Trial of Khmer Rouge: The Role of the Tuol Sleng and Santebal Archives', *Harvard Asia Quarterly*, 2001

Cortright, David and George A Lopez, 'Cambodia: Isolating the Khmer Rouge', in: David Cortright and George A Lopez (eds), *The Sanctions Decade: Assessing UN Strategies in the 1990s* (Boulder, Colo: Lynne Rienner Publishers, 2000)

Criswell, Dianne M, 'Durable Consent and a Strong Transitional Peacekeeping Plan: the Success of UNTAET in Light of the Lessons Learned in Cambodia', 11(3) *Pacific Rim Law & Policy Journal* 577 (June 2002)

DeNike, Howard J, John Quigley and Kenneth J Robinson (eds), *Genocide in Cambodia: Documents from the Trial of Pol Pot and Ieng Sary* (Philadelphia: University of Pennsylvania Press, 2000)

Donovan, Daniel Kemper, 'Joint UN–Cambodia Efforts to Establish a Khmer Rouge Tribunal', 44 *Harvard International Law Journal* 551 (2003)

Doyle, Michael, Ian Johnstone and Robert C Orr (eds), *Keeping the Peace: Multi-dimensional UN Operations in Cambodia and El Salvador* (New York: Cambridge University Press, 1997)

Ea, Meng-Try, and Sorya Sim, *Victims and Perpetrators? Testimony of Young Khmer Rouge Comrades* (Phnom Penh: Documentation Center of Cambodia, 2001)

Etcheson, Craig, *The Rise and Demise of Democratic Kampuchea* (Boulder, Colo: Westview Press, 1984)

Etcheson, Craig, 'From Theory to Facts in the Cambodian Genocide', *International Network on Holocaust and Genocide*, 12:1–2 (1997), 4–7

Etcheson, Craig, 'Accountability Beckons During a Year of Worries for the Khmer Rouge Leadership', 6 *ILSA Journal of International & Comparative Law* 507 (2000)

Etcheson, Craig, *The Number—Quantifying Crimes Against Humanity in Cambodia* (Phnom Penh: Documentation Center of Cambodia, 2000)

Etcheson, Craig, *Retribution and Reconciliation: Healing What Ails Cambodia. A Project Report to the US Institute of Peace* (Washington, DC: 2002)

Findlay, Trevor, *Cambodia: The Legacy and Lessons of UNTAC* (New York: Oxford University Press, 1994).

Gottesman, Evan R, *Cambodia after the Khmer Rouge: Inside the Politics of Nation Building* (New Haven: Yale University Press, 2003)

Gunn, Geoffrey C, 'Kampuchea: The Case for a Genocide Tribunal?' *ARENA*, vol 81, 1987: 97–108

Hannum Hurst, 'International Law and Cambodian Genocide: The Sounds of Silence', *Human Rights Quarterly*, vol 11, no 1, February 1989: 82–138

Hawk, David, 'The Cambodian Genocide', in: Israel W. Charny (ed), *Genocide: A Critical Bibliographic Review* (New York: NY: Facts on File Publications, 1988), 137–54

Heder, Stephen, 'Hen Sen and Genocide Trials in Cambodia: International Impacts, Impunity and Justice', in Judy Ledgerwood (ed), *Legacies of Pol Pot: Beyond Democratic Kampuchea,* (DeKalb, Northern Illinois: University of Southeast Asia Publications, forthcoming)

Heder, Stephen and Judy Ledgerwood, *Propaganda, Politics and Violence in Cambodia: Democratic Transition under United Nations Peace-Keeping* (Armonk, NY: ME Sharpe, 1996)

Heder, Stephen and Brian D. Tittemore, 'Seven Candidates for the Prosecution: Accountability for the Crimes of the Khmer Rouge', *War Crimes Office of the Washington College of Law, American University and the Coalition for International Justice* (June 2001), available at: http://www.wcl.american.edu/warcrimes/khmer-rouge.pdf

Human Rights Watch, Press Review, 'Core Issues in Khmer Rouge Tribunal Law Unresolved', available at: http://www.hrw.org/press/2000/01/cambo0121.htm

Jackson, Karl (ed), *Cambodia 1975–78: Rendezvous with Death* (Princeton, NJ: Princeton University Press, 1989)

Jarvis, Helen and Nereida Cross, 'Cambodian Genocide Program', available at: http:/www-cgo.sistm.unsw.edu.au/communic.htm

Kiernan, Ben, *How Pol Pot Came to Power: A History of Communism in Kampuchea, 1930–75* (London: Verso, 1986)

Kiernan, Ben, (ed), 'Genocide and Democracy in Cambodia: The Khmer Rouge, the U.N., and the International Community', *Yale Southeast Asia Studies* (New Haven, Conn: Yale University Southeast Asia Studies, 1993)

Kiernan, Ben, 'The Cambodian Genocide', in: George Andrepolous (ed), *Genocide: Conceptual and Historical Dimensions* (Philadelphia: Pennsylvania University Press, 1997), 191–228

Kiernan, Ben, *The Pol Pot Regime: Race, Power and Genocide in Cambodia under the Khmer Rouge, 1975–79* (2nd edn) (New Haven, Conn: Yale University Press, 2002)

Klosterman, Theresa, 'The Feasibility and Propriety of a Truth Commission in Cambodia: Too Little? Too late?' 15 *Arizona Journal of International and Comparative Law* 833 (Fall 1998)

Linton, Suzannah, 'Building a Future Is Hard to Do', *Far Eastern Economic Review* (25 May 2000)

Linton, Suzannah, 'Cambodia, East Timor and Sierra Leone: Experiments in International Justice', 12 *Criminal Law Forum* 185 (2001)

Linton, Suzannah, 'New Approaches to International Justice in Cambodia and East Timor', 845 *International Review of the Red Cross* 93 (2002) (available at: http://www.icrc.org/Web/eng/siteeng0.nsf/iwpList74/7B6428D7E40DD0D3C1256-BA7003477CE)

Magliveras, Konstantinos, 'Difficulties and Status of Efforts to Create an International Criminal Court in Cambodia', 2 *Asia-Pacific Journal of Human Rights and Int Law* 105 (2002).

Marks, Stephen, 'Forgetting "The Policies and Practices of the Past": Impunity in Cambodia', 18 *Fletcher Forum for World Affairs* 17 (Summer–Fall 1994)

Marks, Stephen, 'Elusive Justice for the Victims of the Khmer Rouge', 52 *Journal of International Affairs* 691 (1999)

Martin, Marie Alexandrine, *Cambodia: A Shattered Society* (Berkeley, Calif: University of California Press, 1994)

Metzl, Jamie Fredreric, 'The U.N. Commission on Human Rights and Cambodia, 1975–1980', 3 *Buffalo Journal of International Law* 67 (Summer 1996)

Ponchaud, François, *Cambodge année zéro* (Paris: Editions Julliard, 1977)

Railsback, Kathryn, 'A Genocide Convention Action against the Khmer Rouge: Preventing a Resurgence of the Killing Fields', 5 *Connecticut Journal of International Law* 457 (Spring 1990)

Ramji, Jaya, 'Reclaiming Cambodian History: The Case for a Truth Commission', 24 *Fletcher Forum of World Affairs* 137 (2000)

Ratliff, Suellen, 'UN Representation Disputes: A Case Study of Cambodia and New Accreditation Proposal for the Twenty-first Century', 87 *California Law Review* 1207 (October 1999)

Ratner, Steven, 'The Cambodia Settlement Agreements', 87 *American Journal of International Law* (1993): 1–41

Ratner, Steven, 'The United Nations in Cambodia: A Model for Resolution of Internal Conflicts?' in: Lori F Damrosch (ed), *Enforcing Restraint: Collective Intervention in Internal Conflicts* (New York: Council on Foreign Relations Press, 1993), 241–73

Ratner, Steven, 'The United Nations Group of Experts for Cambodia', 93 *American Journal of International Law* 948 (October 1999)

Ratner, Steven, and Jason S. Abrams, *Accountability for Human Rights Atrocities in International Law: Beyond the Nuremberg Legacy* (Oxford: Oxford University Press, 1997)

UN Group of Experts on Cambodia, Report to the Secretary-General (UN Doc, A/53/850, 16 March 1999)

Ross, James, *Cambodia: The Justice System and Violations of Human Rights* (New York, NY: Lawyers Committee for Human Rights, 1992)

Rumney, PNS, 'The Khmer Rouge on Trial: Law, Genocide and Impunity', 4 *Contemporary Issues in Law* 169 (1999)

Rupp, Richard, 'Cooperation, International Organizations, and Multilateral Interventions in the Post-Cold War Era: Lessons Learned from the Gulf War, the Balkans, Somalia, and Cambodia', 3 *UCLA Journal of International Law and Foreign Affairs* 183 (1998–99)

Schabas, William A, 'Cambodia: Was It Really Genocide?' *Human Rights Quarterly*, Vol 23, 2001: 470–77

Schabas, William A, 'Should Khmer Rouge Leaders Be Prosecuted for Genocide or Crimes against Humanity?' in: *Searching for the Truth*, no 23, 2001

Schabas, William A, 'Problems of International Codification—Were the Atrocities in Cambodia and Kosovo Genocide?' 35(2) *New England Law Review* 287 (Winter 2001)

Stanton, Gregory H, *Blue Scarves and Yellow Stars: Classification and Symbolization in the Cambodian Genocide* (Montreal: Montreal Institute for Genocide Studies, Concordia University, 1989)

Stanton, Gregory H, 'Kampuchean Genocide and the World Court', *Connecticut Journal of International Law* 341 (Spring 1990)

Stanton, Gregory H, 'The Khmer Rouge Genocide and International Law', in: Ben Kiernan (ed), *Genocide and Democracy in Cambodia* (New Haven: Yale University Southeast Asia Studies, 1993), 141–62

Sliwinski, Marek, *Le Génocide Khmer Rouge: un analyse démographique* (Paris: Editions L'Harmattan, 1995)

Taylor, Rachel S, 'Better Late than Never: Cambodia's Joint Tribunal', in: Stromseth (ed) *Accountability for Atrocities*, 237–70

Thayer, Carlyle A, 'The United Nations Transitional Authority in Cambodia: the Restoration of Sovereignty', in: Tom Woodhouse, Robert Bruce and Malcolm Dando (eds), *Peacekeeping and Peacemaking* (1998), 145–65

Thayer, Nate, 'Day of Reckoning', *Far Eastern Economic Review*, vol 160, no 44, 1997, available at: http://www.icij.org/about/nate2.html

Vickery, Michael and Naomi Roht-Arriaza, 'Human rights in Cambodia', in: Naomi Roht-Arriaza (ed), *Impunity and Human Rights in International Law and Practice* (New York: Oxford University Press, 1995), 243–51

Websites

The following is a list of useful websites where legal documents, case law (where applicable) and news about the internationalized judicial bodies treated in this book can be found.

Kosovo

UNMIK: www.unmikonline.org
The official website of the United Nations Mission in Kosovo. Here one can find all legal documents (Security Council Resolutions, UNMIK Regulations, etc), and information on Kosovo's internationalized judiciary.

OSCE Mission in Kosovo: http://www.osce.org/kosovo/
The section of the Organization for Security and Cooperation in Europe website dedicated to the organization's mission in Kosovo. Here one can find OSCE's reports on the Kosovo judiciary and operation of internationalized panels.

East Timor

UNTAET: http://www.un.org/peace/etimor/htm
The official website of the United Nations Transitional Administration in East Timor, which administered the country until East Timor's independence on 20 May 2002. Here one can find all legal documents on the internationalized judiciary in East Timor (Security Council Resolutions, UNMIK Regulations, etc) up to independence.

UNMISET: http://www.un.org/Depts/dpko/missions/unmiset/index.html
The official website of the United Nations Mission of Support in East Timor, which replaced UNTAET upon East Timor's independence. Here one can find all legal documents on the internationalized judiciary in East Timor (Security Council Resolutions, UNMIK Regulations, etc) since independence.

Commission for Reception, Truth and Reconciliation in East Timor: http://www.easttimor-reconciliation.org/
The official website of the Commission for Reception, Truth and Reconciliation in East Timor.

Judicial System Monitoring Programme: http://www.jsmp.minihub.org/
The JSMP is an NGO which keeps track of the activities of East Timor's courts and serious crimes trials, both in East Timor and Indonesia. This is the best one-stop website containing all legal documents, case law, and news. It is constantly updated and well maintained.

Sierra Leone

Special Court for Sierra Leone: http://www.sc-sl.org/
The official website of the Special Court for Sierra Leone. It contains all information regarding the Court's work, documents, case law, indictments, judges' bios, etc.

UNAMSIL: http://www.un.org/Depts/dpko/missions/unamsil/index.html
The official website of the United Nations Mission in Sierra Leone.

Sierra Leone Government: http://www.sierra-leone.org/documents.html
The official website of the government of Sierra Leone. Here, besides news on the country, one can find all basic documents leading to the establishment of the Special Court, as well as information about the Truth and Reconciliation Commission for Sierra Leone (http://www.sierra-leone.org/trc-documents.html).

No Peace Without Justice's SCSL website: http://www.specialcourt.org/
The website of one of the major NGOs which have contributed to the establishment of the SCSL, and assist its work. It contains the background and basic documents, news and analysis of the work of the Court.

Cambodia

Since, at the time of writing, the Special Chambers in the courts of Cambodia have not yet been established, there is not yet a single official website where all documents, and news can be found.

The basic documents leading to the establishment of the Extraordinary Chambers can be found here:

- Articles of Cooperation Between the United Nations and the Royal Government of Cambodia [in/Concerning] the Prosecution under Cambodian Law of Crimes Committed During the Period of Democratic Kampuchea (as published by the *Phnom Penh Post*, Issue 9/22, 27 October–9 November 2000): http://www. yale.edu/cgp/mou_v3.html
- Law On The Establishment Of Extraordinary Chambers In The Courts Of Cambodia For The Prosecution Of Crimes Committed During The Period Of Democratic Kampuchea (10 August 2001, as translated by the Council of Jurists, on 6 September 2001): www.derechos.org/human-rights/seasia/doc/krlaw.html; http://csf.colorado.edu/bcas/main-cas/camb-law.htm
- Report of the UN Secretary-General on Khmer Rouge Trials (UN Doc A/57/769, 31 March 2003): http://www.un.dk/doc/A.57.769.pdf
- Draft Agreement between the United Nations and the Royal Government of Cambodia concerning the Prosecution under Cambodian Law Of Crimes Committed during the Period of the Democratic Kampuchea, as adopted by the UN General Assembly (UN Doc A/57/806, 22 May 2003): http://www.pict-pcti.org/courts/pdf/Cambodia/Cambodia_052203.pdf

Cambodian Genocide Program at Yale University: http://www.yale.edu/cgp/index.html
This website contains a large database of information about the Khmer Rouge years, and also some information about the planned internationalized prosecution and trials.

Jurist (University of Pittsburgh): http://jurist.law.pitt.edu/world/cambodia.htm

This website contains useful information on the Cambodian legal and judicial system at large.

Maps

UN Cartographic Department. Maps of Kosovo, Cambodia, Sierra Leone and East Timor:
http://www.un.org/Depts/Cartographic/map/profile/kosovo.pdf
http://www.un.org/Depts/Cartographic/map/profile/timor.pdf
http://www.un.org/Depts/Cartographic/map/profile/sierrale.pdf
http://www.un.org/Depts/Cartographic/map/profile/cambodia.pdf

Index